POBEDONOSTSEV

HIS LIFE AND THOUGHT

Indiana University International Studies

ROBERT F. BYRNES

POBEDONOSTSEV

His Life and Thought

INDIANA UNIVERSITY PRESS

BLOOMINGTON
LONDON

In Memory

of My Parents, the Finest Ever

Contents

Preface

I PROPOSE IN THIS VOLUME to describe and analyze the life and thought of Constantine P. Pobedonostsev, who was a significant and most interesting political leader in Russia in the last third of the nineteenth century. As a young man, before he abandoned Moscow for St. Petersburg and service in the high bureaucracy in 1865, Pobedonostsev displayed outstanding promise as a scholar on the history of Russian institutions and on Russian civil law. He played an important role in the transformation of Russia's judicial system in 1864, and he was one of those who helped persuade the Russian government to go to war against Turkey in 1877. He is best known, however, for his sixty years of service in the central Russian state bureaucracy. He was a senator for almost forty years, a member of the Council of State for thirty-five years, a member of the Council of Ministers for twenty-five years, the Director General of the Most Holy Synod of the Russian Orthodox Church for twenty-five years, the tutor of the last two tsars, the man most responsible for destroying the efforts of Loris-Melikov and others to close the gap between state and society in 1881, and the principal determinant of Russian domestic policy during the reign of Alexander III. His career therefore provides substantial insight into the administrative shortcomings and failures of the old regime in Russia, a subject which has been slighted by historians.

Pobedonostsev was also an important figure in Russian intellectual life, both for his role in restricting and controlling access to information and education and the expression of ideas and for his position in the history of the Slavophil movement and of panslavism. He was an unoriginal and therefore a representative philosopher; hence he serves particularly well to illustrate or reflect the views and qualities of extreme conservative thought in Russia in the half-century before the revolutions. Finally, he was both a Muscovite Russian nationalist and a Westerner; he spoke several European

languages, read widely and deeply in European and American literature, travelled often to western Europe, proposed the transformation of the Russian economy along lines already affecting western
Europe, and yet was bitterly opposed to the introduction of Western ideas and institutions into his native land. In this aspect of his
life and thought, he therefore symbolizes one of the principal issues
facing Russia in modern times.

   The ideas and actions of Pobedonostsev are of interest and significance to all those who seek to understand what has happened
within Russia during the past century. His view of Russian society
and of the larger world of which his country was and remains a part
has been systematically rejected and denounced by more liberal
Russians and by the Communists. Indeed, few responsible men and
women in any society would support or accept many of his views and
policies. Nevertheless, the problems with which he dealt have not
all disappeared, and the careful reader will be impressed by the
continuity between some official Soviet policies and those recommended by this reactionary statesman. In addition, this analysis of
the life and views of a significant political figure of another time and
of another society should help illuminate the problems which other
underdeveloped countries in particular have to face in the twentieth
century. Finally, I hope that this study will contribute to our understanding of the curious failure of conservatism in modern times.
Pobedonostsev considered himself, and was considered by others, a
conservative. In fact, he was not a conservative by any careful definition of that word, which is heavily laden with multiple meanings.
His failures, and the failures of the society of which he was a leading
representative, should help us to understand that important development of our era.

   This volume has been in process a very long time. One reason for
this concerns the nature of the study and the fact that many of the
principal sources were available only in the Soviet Union. More
important, though, was the nature of the age in which we are living.
Americans in general, and those of us in academic life in particular,
must now respond to new requirements and responsibilities which
no one could have foreseen as recently as ten or twenty years ago.
The enormously changed role of the college and the university in
both national and international affairs; the revolutionary developments within the college and the university with regard to curricula
and spirit, as the Anglo-Saxon frame and atmosphere of earlier

years have been replaced by policies which have enormously widened the boundaries of our interests and programs; the responsibilities placed upon any scholar interested in this century and in Russia
and Eastern Europe—these developments have persuaded me on occasion to put this volume aside for challenges which seemed even
more important.

These other obligations have produced a number of distressing
delays. At the same time, these responsibilities—especially those involved in teaching undergraduate and graduate students and in
working with Soviet educational organizations—have contributed
substantially to my understanding of administrative problems and
practices in Russia and have given me insights I could have acquired
in no other way.

I have profited enormously from the work of others in this country and in the Soviet Union. Indeed, this volume stands as an individual achievement in the sense of its peculiar qualities and shortcomings, but it rests on the collective work of many others. It has
benefited from the generous assistance of librarians in the New York
Public Library and the Library of Congress and in the libraries of
the University of California at Berkeley, Columbia University,
Harvard University, Indiana University, and Rutgers University.
Abroad, I was immensely assisted by the courteous and efficient
staffs of the British Museum, the Bibliothèque Nationale, the Bibliothèque Polonaise in Paris, the Lenin Library, the Social Science
Library in Moscow, the libraries of the Soviet Academy of Sciences
in Moscow and in Leningrad, and the Saltykov-Shchedrin Library
in Leningrad. The Manuscript Division of the Lenin Library was
an especially rich source for this work, and the Central State Historical Archive in Leningrad, the Manuscript Division of the Institute of Russian Literature (Pushkinskii Dom) also in Leningrad,
and the archival collections of the other Soviet libraries were also
of great use.

The translation of Russian terms and the spelling of Russian
names are perpetual problems for Americans. In this study, I have
used the customary spelling of the names of Russians such as Dostoevsky and Count Leo Tolstoy, but have followed the Library of
Congress system of transliteration for others, such as Sergei A.
Rachinskii. However, I have not used feminine endings for names
such as those of Catherine Tiutchev. I have referred consistently to
the Council of Ministers, instead of Committee of Ministers, al-

though that institution was called a Council only when the tsar presided, as he usually did. I have translated the title of Pobedonostsev's most important position, *Ober-Prokuror* of the Most Holy Synod of the Russian Orthodox Church, as Director General. There is no clear English definition of *Ober-Prokuror*, but the functions of that high state official were similar to but greater than those of an executive director. Director General constitutes an accurate title for that important position. Finally, quotations of rubles and dollars throughout the text are based on the rate of exchange that existed during the second half of the nineteenth century, approximately two rubles to one dollar. All dates are old style, or according to the Julian calendar, which in the nineteenth century was twelve days behind the Western, or Gregorian, calendar.

It is a pleasure to thank the editors of the *Review of Politics*, *Indiana Slavic Studies*, the *Russian Review*, the *Journal of Modern History*, and the *Jahrbuch für Geschichte Osteuropa* for permission to reprint in this volume materials which were originally published in different form in those journals. Parts of this manuscript have also appeared in H. Stuart Hughes (editor), *Teachers of History: Essays in Honor of Laurence Bradford Packard* (Ithaca, New York: Cornell University Press, 1954); Ernest J. Simmons (editor), *Continuity and Change in Russian and Soviet Thought* (Cambridge: Harvard University Press, 1955); Ivo J. Lederer (editor), *Russian Foreign Policy: Essays in Historical Perspective* (New Haven: Yale University Press, 1962); and John S. Curtiss (editor), *Essays in Russian and Soviet History* (New York: Columbia University Press, 1963). I am also grateful for permission to reprint from these essays.

This volume was begun when I was a Senior Fellow of the Russian Institute of Columbia University. I take immense pleasure and pride in thanking Professor Geroid T. Robinson and his colleagues for providing me the initial opportunity for the training and research which are at the core of this work. I am especially grateful to the Russian Institute for the understanding it has shown during those periods when I have diverted my time and energy to other issues. No one who has ever worked with Ernest J. Simmons and Philip E. Mosely could fail to appreciate their wisdom and generosity. Above all, no formal expression of appreciation can ever repay Professor Robinson for the immaculate and consuming care with which he reviewed my work in its early stages and for the generosity with which he viewed my delay in completing a volume in which he has always been especially interested.

Nothing I have ever done could have been completed without the constant joyful support of my wife and our children. This is a collective work in many ways, because they have all contributed to it.

Robert F. Byrnes

POBEDONOSTSEV

HIS LIFE AND THOUGHT

I

The Pobedonostsev
Family

CONSTANTINE PETROVICH POBEDONOSTSEV was born on May 21, 1827, on Bread Lane, a quiet old street in the Arbat section of Moscow, within easy walking distance of the university, the Kremlin, and the main centers of life and activity of the capital of old Russia. The comfortable old house in which he was born was in a section then inhabited largely by bureaucrats, merchants, and a small group of professors and writers. It had been the family residence since 1816 and was still the family's property when Pobedonostsev died in 1907. Close to the parish church, Simeon Stolpnik, and surrounded by a number of churches, the home on Bread Lane remained the central focus of his life, just as the church bells with which he became familiar as a youngster continued to symbolize Moscow and Russian civilization for him.

Information concerning his mother is rather scanty. She came from an old service nobility family named Levashov near Kostroma, and she was apparently a woman of inconsequential education, deep religious sentiment, and considerable courage and character. Born in 1780 and married early in the nineteenth century to a man fifteen years her elder, she remained the spiritual center of the family throughout her long life. It is difficult to estimate the influence she had on her youngest son, but she clearly did help impress strong religious feelings upon all of her children. She survived her husband by almost a quarter of a century. During most of that period, her youngest son, who married only a year before her death in 1867, lived with her on Bread Lane. Until the end of his life, forty years

3

later, he tried to come to Moscow from St. Petersburg each September to visit her grave on the anniversary of her death, although he never mentioned the anniversary of the death of his father, who died in the same month in 1843.[1]

Constantine Petrovich Pobedonostsev was remarkably reticent about his father, as he was about all the members of his family. Even so, the information available concerning Professor Peter V. Pobedonostsev is surprisingly abundant when one considers that he was an undistinguished member of the Moscow University faculty and an insignificant bureaucrat in the first third of the nineteenth century. However, Peter V. Pobedonostsev was himself an author, the fugitive journals he edited in the last years of the eighteenth century and the first three decades of the nineteenth century have survived, and some of his colleagues and students have also provided data about him.

Professor Pobedonostsev's father was a Russian Orthodox priest in a small village just northeast of Moscow. We have no knowledge concerning him, except that he did move briefly to Moscow from the countryside before his son was born on September 22, 1771, and that he allowed or encouraged his son to obtain an education. Similarly, we have no data concerning Pobedonostsev's grandmother, except that she was a strong and courageous woman who remained in Moscow in 1812 in an effort to preserve her son's home and modest library, while he and his wife and children fled to Kostroma.

Peter V. Pobedonostsev was educated for the Orthodox priesthood in Zaikonospasskaia Academy on Nikolskii Street near Red Square and the Kremlin in Moscow. After completing his training for the priesthood in 1796, he was allowed to leave that calling to become a teacher. As a student, he had become especially proficient in Latin, which he loved, and in Greek, but his first teaching post, in 1797, involved instruction in French and in rhetoric at the Moscow University gymnasium or high school. In the fall of 1797, he received the equivalent of an M.A. degree in Philosophy and Literature from Moscow University, and in 1805 he transferred to Alexandrovskii Institute, where he taught Russian literature to young ladies of good family until 1831. Just before the French invasion of Russia in 1812, he became an assistant to Professor A. F. Merzliakov at Moscow University, which he considered an enormous advance and opportunity, even though Moscow University was not then a distinguished institution. Indeed, the level of instruction was low by contemporary European standards, and the faculty in 1812 numbered only twenty-five, of whom ten were Germans. In 1814, Peter V. Pobedonostsev joined the faculty of Moscow University as a lecturer in rhetoric and in Russian literature, where he emphasized "purity of speech and strict observation of the rules of grammar." He became an extraordinary, or associate, professor in 1826 and retired in 1835. He died September 30, 1843, in Moscow.[2]

Peter V. Pobedonostsev and his wife had eleven children, at least eight of whom survived into adult life. The demands of this family led the energetic professor to supplement his income from his two teaching positions by work as a translator and editor, censor, and tutor. He was a prolific translator and publicist, from the time of his graduation from the Academy in 1796 until he retired in 1835. He served as a member of the Censor Committee from 1811 until 1827, a function which significantly increased his ability to support his family and which also reflects a clear attitude toward the role of the state in society. Finally, he tutored the sons of wealthy Moscow nobles and merchants, which established profitable relations and even friendships for him and for his children. One of his charges became the celebrated historical novelist, Lazhechnikov, who later introduced one of his sons, Sergei, to publishers and who took a fatherly interest in Constantine Pobedonostsev when he was in the School of Jurisprudence in St. Petersburg after the professor died. This acquaintance proved to be stimulating for Constantine, who was able to repay the novelist in his declining years.

Perhaps even more important, Professor Pobedonostsev's relations with the parents of his students helped obtain opportunities for higher education and for appointments in significant offices or regiments for his energetic sons and daughters. One of his elder daughters, Barbara, was able to attend a select school for young ladies in Moscow, and Constantine became a student in the School of Jurisprudence from 1841 to 1846 because of their father's influence. Similarly, his son Sergei, who was born in 1816, joined the First Cadet Corps and received a splendid appointment in an engineering battalion in Warsaw because of his father's diligence in obtaining assistance for his children from the grandees he came to know. Sergei and his sister Maria were also aided in publishing articles and stories in the 1840's in the Slavophil journal, *Moskvitianin* (The Muscovite), by Professor Pobedonostsev's friendship with the journal's editor, Michael Pogodin, who had been a student of Professor Pobedonostsev and became a colleague and friend.[3]

Professor Pobedonostsev had an especially powerful interest in

Russian literature and a strong conviction that knowledge of it should be increased. Thus, while his translations and editing helped increase Russian knowledge of the Greek and Roman classics and the literature of the eighteenth century Enlightenment, he was also one of the founders of the Society of Lovers of Russian Literature, established at Moscow University in 1811 "to spread abroad information on the rules and forms of good literature and to give to the public selections of Russian prose and poetry, chosen and read first in the Society's meetings." His service as librarian of this organization, which ultimately gave its book collection to the Moscow University Library, reflects his love of books and of learning. He participated in the Society's meetings by preparing reports and selecting readings on Russian patriotism and on important eighteenth-century Russian poets, novelists, and dramatists, and by editing some of the Society's publications. The Society was most active in the decade following the Napoleonic wars. It went into eclipse after the accession of Nicholas I, perhaps because the emperor was somewhat critical of it, and it died in 1836. However, it was revived in 1858 by Khomiakov, Constantine Aksakov, Pogodin, Tiutchev, and other Slavophils, serving them in the 1860's and 1870's as a prominent and effective instrument. Indeed, the Society was a bridge linking Russian patriotism of the early nineteenth century with the Slavophils and with the panslav movement.[4]

Peter V. Pobedonostsev was probably best known among his contemporaries as an editor and translator. As a young man, presumably in the seminary, he acquired the ability to read Old Church Slavonic, Greek, Latin, German, French, and English. His first publication, *Plody melankholii* (Fruits of Melancholy) appeared in Moscow in 1796, when he was only twenty-five years old and in his final year at the Zaikonospasskaia Academy. Within the following thirty-five years, he translated, edited, and published at least ten more anthologies of foreign works, some of them two or three volumes in size. In addition, he served as editor or associate editor of six short-lived bimonthly or weekly journals designed to make available to Muscovites translated selections from foreign literature or poems, tales, and moral exhortations written originally in Russian. Only one of the anthologies was published in a second printing, and the most successful journal survived for only thirty-four months. Indeed, one of the journals, *Detskii vestnik* (Children's Messenger), lasted less than a year in 1813.[5]

Primitive journals and anthologies of the kind which Professor

Pobedonostsev produced and distributed for the citizens of Moscow began to appear in Russia in the last quarter of the eighteenth century and marked an early stage of Russian journalism and of the effort to introduce foreign literature to a wider public than the nobility who had received a foreign education. Translation and publication of this literature did enable the young father, just a few years removed from the stagnant life of a sleepy Russian village, to supplement his income, to utilize his apparent energy and his ability to read several European languages, and to satisfy his compelling ambition to educate others. He worked under heavy handicaps, with little assistance from his academic colleagues, who tired quickly of the labors involved in translating and in finding purchasers. He was not a man of confident learning. His own library was pitifully small. He lacked access to an institutional library until he became a member of the faculty of Moscow University, and even that collection was far smaller than that of a small American college in the twentieth century. He could not afford to subscribe to any foreign journals or newspapers, and he had no friends or colleagues who obtained these publications regularly. His journals and anthologies, like others published at that time and even much later in Moscow and St. Petersburg by eminent publishers and editors, lacked financial backing and indeed were published on a hand-to-mouth basis. Most of those who contributed original pieces in Russian or who translated foreign works for publication were no doubt rewarded by the thrill of seeing their work in print and by complimentary copies. For most of the translations from the classics and from French, German, and English literature, the editor had to rely upon materials he had read while a student or had obtained on an unsystematic basis, upon translations submitted by readers, and upon selected pieces which he found in earlier journals and anthologies. As one progresses chronologically through these tomes, one is increasingly impressed by the gradual deterioration in quality and by the rising percentage of selections made from contemporary French newspapers and popular journals.

These publications are unimportant historically, although they do represent a part of the Russian effort of that period to raise the national cultural level and to absorb some of the new humanistic learning from Europe. Indeed, Professor Pobedonostsev exposed himself to jealous criticism and was ridiculed for the poverty of his selections and the fleeting character of his enterprises. However, these publications provide us substantial knowledge of him, his interests, his ideas, and his qualities. They are especially valuable because they constitute reliable information concerning the atmosphere in which Constantine P. Pobedonostsev was raised, particularly because Constantine had some of the same instincts as a publicist as his father. At several stages of his long and busy life, particularly during the last twenty years, when he had the press of the Holy Synod of the Russian Orthodox Church at his command, Constantine P. Pobedonostsev devoted a great deal of energy and attention to work as a publicist.[6]

The more signal characteristic of Professor Pobedonostsev's work as a publicist was his burning interest in education and in spiritual and moral improvement. Indeed, the translated titles of the journals which he edited or helped to edit reveal his powerful concern in learning and in enlightenment: The New Science of Enjoying Life, True and False Happiness, A Treasury of Useful Entertainment, or Medicine for Doctoring People Subject to Grief and Boredom, Selected Moral Tales Useful for Producing a Feeling of Moral Beauty in the Heart, and Directing the Mind and Heart to Truth and Virtue.

A second characteristic was a deep and genuine interest in the classics and in eighteenth-century European literature, especially that of France. Professor Pobedonostsev taught rhetoric and Russian literature at Moscow University, and his journals did include substantial selections from contemporary Russian writing, but the quality of the Russian writing chosen was not high and the journals consistently emphasized foreign literature. Moreover, quite a high percentage of the Russian work published was not contemporary, but was taken from the works of Lomonosov and his contemporaries or consisted of memoir material or letters concerning great Russian rulers or military heroes.

Pobedonostsev's publications also included numerous snippets from Cicero, Livy, Virgil, Sallust, Plutarch, Seneca, Quintilian, Horace, Pliny, and Homer, in about the same proportion as in an eighteenth-century journal in France or England. Moreover, Pobedonostsev included selections from English authors, particularly Gray, Pope, and Sterne, and from Germans, such as Kleist, Lessing, and Uz.

However, the main source for his selections was the body of French literature, particularly the great essayist Montaigne, the seventeenth-century moralists La Bruyère and La Fontaine, and the leading representatives of the Enlightenment, Diderot, Voltaire, and Rousseau. The Enlightenment was the center of attraction, both before and after the French invasion of 1812. In fact, some critics noted that Professor Pobedonostsev devoted a higher percentage of his journals to the Enlightenment than had earlier such ventures, which had given priority and emphasis to eighteenth-century English prose. It is apparent that the French writings selected emphasized more the sentiment of the eighteenth century than its philosophy or politics. Reading these anthologies today, in an age of intense nationalism and of national and ideological conflict, provides a measure of some of the changes which have occurred since the early years of the nineteenth century, when French literature was circulated in Russia at a time of bitter conflict with France.

While this deeply religious and conservative teacher and member of the Censor Committee was printing extracts from the writings of some of those who helped prepare for the French Revolution but which he obviously hoped would improve morality and spread learning in Russia, he also emphasized fervent patriotism, respect for Russia's rulers and leaders, and absolutely unquestioning acceptance of the status quo. Professor Pobedonostsev respected and even venerated Peter the Great, Catherine the Great, Alexander I, and Nicholas I. Indeed, there is no evidence in all of his public and private materials that he ever questioned the world in which he lived. His acceptance of the institutions by which he was ruled and his faith in Russia have the unthinking character often ascribed, probably incorrectly, to medieval peasants, although they also remind one of the rudderless robot who is the ideal servant of today's totalitarian state.

Peter V. Pobedonostsev's patriotism bears a pre-nationalistic flavor. He had a great admiration for Peter the Great and his successors as Russian rulers, and he lauded Russian national customs and cultural achievements. However, he was just as impressed by foreign leaders and institutions. There is no evidence in his publications of animosity toward other peoples, either groups living within the empire toward whom many Russians traditionally have expressed suspicion or animosity, such as the Poles and Jews, or toward foreigners, such as the Germans or French. The Pobedonostsev family always participated in the ceremonies commemorating 1812 in the Kremlin, but the invasion did not lead Professor Pobedonostsev to make any changes in his literary values, even though his library was burned in the Moscow fire and he and his family had to flee from the city. In fact, he seemed unaware of the existence of national or religious minorities in Russia, which no doubt reflects the small, even parochial, Russian world in which he lived.[7]

His children represented a different generation, both in their awareness of the different groups of peoples who populated the empire and in their attitudes toward some of these peoples. Sergei, one of his older sons, lived briefly in Warsaw, knew Polish, was well informed about Polish literature and the Polish theater, and had a great affection for the Poles, but he was strongly antisemitic. His youngest son, as this essay will demonstrate, had a deep dislike for both the Poles and the Jews and was suspicious of the Baltic Germans, the Ukrainians, and other important minority groups, especially those who lived on the frontiers of the empire.[8]

Expanding the analysis of Professor Pobedonostsev from the journals he edited to his own writings, his teaching at Moscow University, and the other recorded data we possess confirms these conclusions and provides additional insight into his qualities and beliefs and into the atmosphere in which his children were raised. One of his principal characteristics was a belief in progress. He assumed that the community in which he lived and the outer European world about which he read were almost inevitably going to improve materially, but above all morally, as knowledge became more widespread and as more men and women became acquainted with the highest human ideals and the finest expressions of those great goals. This faith in steady cultural improvement was imprecise. Indeed, Professor Pobedonostsev never referred to serfdom or suggested the desirability of reducing its burdens or of abolishing it. Although he was an educator and publicist with a powerful interest in raising the cultural level of his community, he did not write about the expansion of public or private education, the role of Moscow University in Russian intellectual life, or the function of the Russian Orthodox Church. He simply did not think in this way. Indeed, he was fundamentally an unthinking and uncritical man who concentrated on the concrete problem directly before him.

Nevertheless, Professor Pobedonostsev's energies were devoted almost entirely to what he considered the intellectual and moral advancement of the peoples among whom he lived—the only ones of whom he thought—and his judgments of institutions and persons reflected this concern. One indication of this was his selfless generosity toward his students. Another was his labor on behalf of the Society of Lovers of Russian Literature. The journals and anthologies he translated and published constitute even more convincing demonstrations; they are educational enterprises, filled with moralizing tales, studded with edifying quotations from the classics and the great writers of the énlightened century, and directed in general toward the good and the beautiful, usually with a strongly sentimental touch.

Peter V. Pobedonostsev's interest in the edification of his students and readers is most noteworthy in his essays on Russian writers and in his comments concerning Russian rulers. Writing that "living and acting for the benefit of our contemporaries and descendants is the most sacred of all laws," he praised Peter the Great, Catherine the Great, and Alexander I, not for their military victories or their additions to state power and territory, but for the leadership they provided toward spreading science, perfecting the Russian language, promoting learning, encouraging love of "the true and the good," and developing the civic virtues.[9]

Professor Pobedonostsev's accolades for Russian writers also reflect his ambition to elevate learning and good taste in Russia. He praised Lomonosov and Derzhavin as "the Demosthenes and Cicero, the Pindar and Horace of Russia" because of their contributions to advancing knowledge and improving the Russian language. In an essay devoted to his contemporary, Peter Alekseevich Plavilshchikov, a celebrated actor and dramatist, he lauded his patriotism, his devotion to instruction, and his generosity, frankness, and high spiritual qualities. He celebrated "the Russian Homer, . . . the unforgettable Kheraskov," for the devotion with which he learned foreign languages and practiced his craft, and for the "pure morality" of his writings.[10]

Professor Pobedonostsev was by no means an outstanding scholar or publicist, although his pride in his achievement in rising from lowly origins is clearly justified. His journals were not of high quality, his own writing was sentimental and uncritical, and even his own student, Pogodin, triumphed over him in their race for a coveted professorship in Moscow University. Moreover, while he was able to translate five languages, there is some evidence he could speak none of them. He never travelled abroad; indeed, it appears that he did not visit St. Petersburg, Kiev, or Warsaw. His world was purely Muscovite, in fact limited to the city of Moscow, and his knowledge of the rest of Russia was extremely limited.

Moreover, his was a world in which one learned only from reading and the theater. The emphasis throughout his work on reading and on learning via the printed page was one of the characteristics he passed to his son. His range of interests as an omnivorous reader was extraordinary, particularly for that period, from the classics and the patristic writings through Orthodox theology to the literature of France, Germany, England, and Russia. However, his intellectual horizons were restricted by his unquestioning endorsement of what he saw and read and by the absence of any concern with or understanding of general or abstract ideas. His articles are a curious combination of factual data and sentimentalism, with the qualities of an after-dinner speech honoring a distinguished friend. Moreover, while the leading representatives of the Enlightenment constituted one of the staples of his journals and anthologies, the selections are insignificant and anecdotal, such as personal letters from Voltaire to Catherine, descriptions of incidents involving the great men and women of that era, and biographical data. Even the most careful reader of these collections would have learned nothing from them concerning Rousseau's political philosophy, Diderot's attitude toward religion, or Voltaire's views of the Catholic Church. In addition, Professor Pobedonostsev was completely unaffected by the wave of German philosophy which swept over educated Russia after the Napoleonic wars, just as his two most eminent sons were unaffected by the controversy in the 1840's between the Westerners and the Slavophils concerning the nature of Russia and its historical destiny.

Peter V. Pobedonostsev's personal qualities naturally contributed to creating the values and the atmosphere of the household he directed on Bread Lane in Moscow. First of all, he was patriarchal in his relations with his wife, his children, and his students. His children have left remarkably little direct information concerning their life at home, but some of his students who later became eminent have written most valuable comments about their instructor. Belinsky, for example, could not endure his lectures, which he thought dull and florid, and he was both discourteous and a prankster in Pobedonostsev's class. Constantine Aksakov was annoyed by his old-fashioned ways and archaic language, and Goncharov considered him "the patriarch of the faculty" and "the man of the old century." During his last years at the university in particular, Professor Pobedonostsev was the target for student tricks and often the butt of their jokes.[11]

The students were especially annoyed by Professor Pobedonostsev's obsession with grammatical rules, by his reverence for Lomonosov, and by his dull lectures and poetry readings. Some asserted that he was using the same notes when he retired in 1835 which he had read when he began to teach at Moscow University in 1814. Years later, the father of the eminent jurist, Anatole F. Koni, entertained his children with tales of his student life in Moscow, regaling his listeners with the gestures of Professor Pobedonostsev as he recited the opening lines of a poem, "From behind the columns a clear moon drank, looking down into the water."[12]

Professor Pobedonostsev was quite likely just as grim and determined a supporter of hard work and the search for truth and beauty at home as in the lecture hall. In fact, in his faithful commitment to precise rules and to the observance of established little habits, he must have been the very model of the neat, diligent, and earnest plodder. His record is so impressive in quantity that he cannot have been idle or relaxed. Moreover, it is difficult to believe that he would have encouraged or even tolerated inaction or diversion. His own performance and the known habits of his children suggest that the Pobedonostsev household had the characteristics generally associated with the Puritan and Victorian eras in England: austerity, prudishness, grimness, and fastidiousness. His devotion to his work was such that in March, 1813, while Moscow was in ruin and in chaos, he worried about his possible failure to meet a publication deadline.[13]

Constantine P. Pobedonostsev, in his philosophy, placed heavy emphasis upon the family as a peculiarly significant social institution in all stable societies. In middle age, as a specialist on Russian civil law, he necessarily devoted much attention to the family and to the legal issues and principles surrounding it. Thus, the second volume of his *Kurs grazhdanskago prava* (Course on Civil Law) concentrates almost entirely upon the family and problems related to it. Constantine P. Pobedonostsev also translated the principal works of two of the outstanding western European advocates of the family as the central social institution, the Frenchman Frederick Le Play and the German Heinrich Thiersch. In the early 1890's, he wrote an essay describing the family farm, or homestead, as the solution to Russia's political and economic problems, and in the last decade of his life, the family more and more appeared to him as the institution which could save Russia. Thus, he wrote that the child from birth was weak and evil, that the parental power was "the only power established by God in the Decalogue," and that God "in entrusting the child to his parents gave to them the choice of raising either a dutiful or a parasitic and destructive child." He saw the family as "the foundation of the State," "the eternal element of prosperous societies, and the primary instrument for educating and controlling man."[14]

Constantine P. Pobedonostsev's reliance upon the family as the institution which assured stability in a society was clearly central, and it is evident that his parents and the life of their family exerted a profound influence upon his thought during his formative years. Some of the interests, habits, qualities, and values of Peter V. Pobedonostsev appear later among all of his children, particularly the two sons of whom we have the most complete knowledge. In the mountain of data available on the large and literate Pobedonostsev family, there is no evidence of any affection or warmth. The hundreds and even thousands of letters of Constantine P. Pobedonostsev which have survived make almost no reference to his father, even though—perhaps because—Professor Pobedonostsev educated his youngest son at home until he was fourteen years old, when he was sent to the School of Jurisprudence in St. Petersburg. Even the diary which the young lad kept while in school in St. Petersburg has no reference to any member of his family. In all the materials available concerning the life and thought of Constantine P. Pobedonostsev, we learn of his mother only from one or two minor comments in a spiritual diary he kept in the late 1850's and the early 1860's, which was published in 1894, and in a letter to his close friend, Anna Tiutchev, the wife of Ivan Aksakov, in September, 1867, telling of her death. Moreover, the voluminous Pobedonostsev papers provide a total of only five references to Constantine P. Pobedonostsev's sisters, although two or three lived to be more than seventy years of age. Thus, Pobedonostsev much resembles Marshal Pétain, who was also heavily influenced by Le Play, who came from a large family which he never mentioned later in life, who married relatively late in life and had no children, and who placed the family at the center of his political and social philosophy.[15]

Family friends are just as absent. Sergei and Constantine P. Pobedonostsev both retained a slight connection with the historical novelist Lazhechnikov, who had been a student of Professor Pobedonostsev and whose father had helped finance one of the professor's journals. Both men on occasion visited or corresponded with Professor Michael Pogodin, the panslav historian who had been a student and later a colleague of Professor Pobedonostsev at Moscow University and who lived near Bread Lane. However, these relationships were by no means close or lasting, and the Pobedonostsev household appears to have isolated itself from any neighbors or close friends.[16]

Thus, one must conclude that Constantine P. Pobedonostsev was a lonely boy in a severe and gloomy home, quite unlike the relaxed and open mansions of the landed nobility of Russian history and of the Russian novel. Indeed, in Constantine P. Pobedonostsev's writing the home on Bread Lane itself receives less attention than does his old parish church, Simeon Stolpnik. The impersonal, generally friendless life which he led is surely related to the kind of home in which he was raised and educated.

Peter V. Pobedonostsev had eleven children, of whom Constantine was the youngest son. We have information concerning seven of the other ten children and can assume that some of the other three died in infancy or while young. Concerning Nicholas Pobedonostsev, we know only that he was alive in Moscow in 1847. The other six of whom we have any knowledge were all interested in writing and publishing, an extraordinary record even for the children of a university professor who translated and edited extensively. One son, Alexander, was a student of Russian literature at Moscow University, became a member of the Society of Lovers of Russian Literature in March, 1829, presented a paper on Quintilian at that time, and died in June, 1890. Constantine Pobedonostsev's only mention of either of these brothers is in an 1856 letter referring to the desperate illness of one of them.[17]

Four daughters demonstrated some interest in writing and publishing. Catherine, probably the oldest, who taught at the Ekaterinskii Institute, published an article on the Tartar conquest of Russia in the *Russkii vestnik* (Russian Herald) in 1819, eight years before her distinguished brother was born. She apparently died in Moscow in December, 1863, leaving two daughters, one of whom became insane in 1878. Another daughter, Olga, a blind spinster still alive in Moscow in 1890, but not living in the family home, published a letter from Lazhechnikov to her father in *Russkaia starina* (Russian Antiquity) in 1891.

A third daughter, Maria, contributed in the 1840's to Pogodin's Slavophil journal, *Moskvitianin,* and at the same time to the rival Westerner publication, *Otechestvennyia zapiski* (Notes of the Fatherland). She served as a French translator for *Moskvitianin,* her principal contribution being the translation of Rudolf Tepfer's romantic and sentimental novel, *Presbytère,* published in the journal in 1852 and perhaps also as a book later in the same year. A fourth daughter, Barbara, was born in Moscow in 1810, was graduated from a girls' school in 1828, contributed translations from French and English and at least one original article to the *Damskii zhurnal* (The Ladies' Magazine) between 1830 and 1833, and was still alive and unmarried in 1880. Pobedonostsev in letters to his closest friend, Catherine Tiutchev, referred in 1878 and in 1881 to a sister in Tambov province; this was either Maria or another sister of whom this is our only information. From careful examination of all available evidence, it seems Pobedonostsev, his brothers, and his sisters together produced a total of only three children.

The most distinguished of Peter V. Pobedonostsev's sons, except for Constantine, was Sergei, who was born in Moscow on November 8, 1816, and who before his death in 1850 had achieved some repute as a government official, particularly in Kazan, Novgorod, and St. Petersburg.[18] Sergei received his primary education at home from his father, who then obtained an appointment for him in the First Cadet Corps. After serving in Moscow and in an engineering battalion in Poland, he retired from the army in 1842 and worked briefly in the special commission for Kazan under Governor Sergei P. Shipov, an old friend of his father's under whom he had served in Warsaw in the army. He was transferred briefly to Novgorod and then to the Ministry of State Property in St. Petersburg. He retired in 1848 and died a bachelor in Moscow two years later, after suffering from poor health for several years. He read German, French, Italian, English, Czech, and Polish, and he could speak Polish and French. In the 1840's, he was probably the most important Russian specialist on Polish literature. He translated a number of Polish novels, tales, and plays into Russian, published critical articles in the Russian press on Polish literature, especially drama, was a correspondent for several Polish newspapers, and translated one of Lazhechnikov's novels into Polish. He had a strong interest in Russian history, hoping at one time to write a history of Russia's military campaigns, and he was also an important supplier of ancient manuscripts and weapons to Pogodin and his Slavophil friends in Moscow.[19]

Sergei, like his father and his brother Constantine, was an energetic author, translator, and editor. He contributed consistently to the leading journals on both sides of the controversy between the Slavophils and the Westerners in the 1840's, concerning whether Russia was a unique and superior society which should guard and maintain its special characteristics or whether western Europe was the norm of all societies and Russia should adopt Western ideas and institutions as rapidly as possible. Thus, between 1843 and 1848 he published six articles or stories in *Otechestvennyia zapiski*, which was edited and published between 1839 and 1858 by A. A. Kraevskii, who made it a popular and successful center for the views of the Westerners. All of Belinsky's writings between 1839 and 1846 appeared in this journal. Herzen, Nekrasov, Granovskii, Dostoevsky, and Saltykov-Shchedrin were among the other prominent contributors. In the 1840's in particular, *Otechestvennyia zapiski* was known as an organ of Utopian socialism, printing translations from the works of Thomas More, Cabet, Louis Blanc, and the Saint-Simon socialists, as well as from Hegel and Feuerbach.

Sergei also was close to Pogodin and to the Slavophil circle. Thus, in 1842 and 1843 he contributed eight articles or stories to *Moskvitianin*, which Pogodin edited from 1841 until 1856 and which reflected the views of the Slavophils. *Moskvitianin* was also an unofficial or informal representative of the point of view of the Minister of Education, Uvarov, whose formula of Orthodoxy, Autocracy, and Nationality it defended. As if to prove his impartiality, Sergei also contributed to other journals, including *Biblioteka dlia chteniia* (A Reading Library), which had inferior contributors and no apparent political or philosophic position, and the *Repertuar i Panteon russkago i vsekh inostrannykh teatrov* (Repertoire and Pantheon of Russian and of All Foreign Theaters), formed in 1842 by the merger of two other theater journals, which avoided politics and which published Russian plays and critiques of the European theater for a very limited circle in St. Petersburg and Moscow.[20]

Sergei P. Pobedonostsev's writings are of three types or varieties: translations of and articles about Polish literature, particularly the theater; sentimental novels and short stories; and articles concerning the French theater and Paris, which he visited in 1847. The publications concerning Polish letters are remarkable for the thorough knowledge they reflect and their spirit of friendly objectivity. Moreover, several of Sergei's novels have Polish settings and characters, and the Poles and Poland are always treated with respect and even affection. Thus, Constantine P. Pobedonostsev's contempt for the Poles was not acquired from his brother Sergei or from his father, who never alluded to the Poles or Poland.[21]

Sergei's interest and enthusiasm for things Polish once led him to commit several egregious errors for which Herzen roundly criticized him. In 1843, on the three hundredth anniversary of the

donostsev family in the first half of the nineteenth century as well as to the great emperor and to others in less developed countries attracted later by the immense achievements of the West:

> He did not explore the springs and motives of this Western achievement; he did not seek to understand the workings of financial, political, or administrative institutions; and he had little or no conception of the slow and varied stages by which England or Holland had grown to be what they were. What never left his mind was the forest of masts on the watersides of Amsterdam and London, symbols of enriching trade reaching out to the Indies and all parts of the world; the clusters of busy towns, the creation of that industrial middle class, rich in invention, industry, and initiative, which his own country so much lacked.[26]

Moreover, the Pobedonostsev family was one in which every member had a deep respect for the immortality conferred by the printed word. Just one generation removed from village life, the Pobedonostsevs clearly lacked the depth of learning, position, and sense of assurance of families such as the Adamses or the Trevelyans, but knowledge was admired and imitated, and continuous study, writing, and publishing were considered important achievements to which an educated man naturally devoted much of his life. Indeed, Professor Pobedonostsev assumed, as did his sons and daughters and most literate men and women of his generation, that Russia would continue to progress and that those who wrote and taught had an especially important role and responsibility in advancing the cultural level.

I I

The Young Scholar

PROFESSOR POBEDONOSTSEV educated all of his eleven children at home, but it was Constantine who drew his father's closest attention, in part because he was the youngest son and in part because Professor Pobedonostsev retired from Moscow University in 1835, when he was sixty-four years old and the boy only seven. The future Russian statesman was educated entirely by his father until he went to St. Petersburg to attend the School of Jurisprudence in 1841, two years before Professor Pobedonostsev died. It is clear that Constantine P. Pobedonostsev never escaped the stamp his father impressed upon him. Even his literary style, which is clear, marked by eighteenth century words and expressions, and remarkably rich in vocabulary, resembles that of Kheraskov and Lomonosov, whose works his father often read in class to Belinsky and other bored students and at home to his bright young son.

As a teacher, Professor Pobedonostsev emphasized rigorous work, the mastery of fundamental rules and of good habits, memorization, and imitation of the masters. He believed that "nature does not produce results quickly," and that wide reading of the most significant works was essential because "reading cultivates all of the talents of the spirit." It is evident from his essays on education, his career as a teacher and professor, and the later writings of his son that the boy's childhood was devoted almost entirely to study. Constantine learned how to read Old Church Slavonic, French, Latin, and German at home from his father. He became a student of the Bible, which the professor was certain contained both the highest truths and a key to accuracy of expression. While still a youngster, he

studied the Russian Orthodox Church fathers, who Professor Pobedonostsev thought would bring deep human feeling, wisdom, and
morality to anyone who studied them attentively. He also devoted
intensive effort to the Greek and Roman classics, which his father
thought would awaken his interest in nature and in government,
develop a critical mind, strengthen his appreciation of beauty and
his sense of taste, and add strength and variety to his written and
spoken language. Finally, of course, he studied Russian history
and literature, especially Professor Pobedonostsev's favorites and
Karamzin.[1]

In these early years, Constantine Pobedonostsev therefore acquired a deep knowledge of and love for the Bible and for Russian
and Western religious writings, the Latin classics, and the history
and literature of Russia. He developed an interest in western European literature which he retained throughout his life. In addition,
he learned early in life to work, and he was trained to remember
what he had read. As a consequence, his published works, particularly those which appeared before 1880, are distinguished by truly
remarkable learning. Everyone who became acquainted with him,
from his closest colleagues to foreign visitors such as Marquis Hiro-
bumi Ito, Japanese statesman, Bishop Mandell Creighton of Peterborough, later of London, and Senator Albert Beveridge, was aston-
ished at his capacity and love for intellectual work and at the depth
and range of his knowledge.[2]

When Constantine was thirteen years old, his father obtained
admission for him to the School of Jurisprudence in St. Petersburg,
from which he graduated in 1846 after five years of study. This
institute, which became the Imperial School of Jurisprudence in
1885, had been founded in December, 1835, by Prince Peter G.
Oldenburg, a nephew of Nicholas I, who had been horrified by the
poor quality of the Senators and of the Senate staff after he had been
made a Senator and who had been permitted to establish a new institution "to educate and prepare young noblemen for legal work in
the civil services." Most of the students came from aristocratic
families (there were four Obolenskiis in the Institute while Constantine was a student), so admission represented a signal achievement for Professor Pobedonostsev and a great opportunity for his
bright and well-trained son, who was first in his class at the end of
three years and who graduated second in his class of twenty-five.[3]

The Oldenburg School was designed to create a flow of educated
and honorable jurists for work in the various departments of the

Senate, so the curriculum naturally emphasized the study of Russian law. However, Oldenburg and his small faculty, some of whom were German, hoped to produce a group of young men who were well informed also concerning Roman, French, and German law. Moreover, the curriculum included theology, canon law, Russian history, and foreign languages. In his five years in the school, Pobedonostsev completed twenty-five of the thirty-six courses offered, and received training, some of it of dubious quality, in legal institutions and philosophy. In addition, he improved his competence in Latin, German, and French and began the study of Greek and English. He excelled in the languages he had studied with his father, made a hobby of singing Latin songs, and was often called upon to recite in French or German when Prince Oldenburg, the Minister of Education, Count Sergei S. Uvarov, or some other dignitary visited classes.

Pobedonostsev's principal characteristic as a student was his devotion to his studies. He completed his assignments on time, studied intensively for his examinations, and read so much that he had to wear glasses after his first year. At the same time, however, he enjoyed the cultural activities which the school arranged in St. Petersburg, particularly the opera and the theater, and he found time to read Paul de Kock, the contemporary light French dramatist and novelist, Gogol's *Dead Souls*, and *Otechestvennyia zapiski*. He had some popularity with his classmates, although the diary which he kept in the last four years of his student days (and of which he published substantial extracts in a private edition in 1885) reveals that he had only a recluse's interest in the parties and escapades of his fellows, and that he did not participate in them. Indeed, he never liked parties or friendly celebrations. His most pleasant experiences were taking long lonely walks in St. Petersburg and, on occasion, rising at five o'clock in the morning to attend an early Mass at the Alexander Nevsky monastery, which he compared favorably to the Monastery of the Holy Trinity at Sergiev Posad (now Zagorsk).[4]

It is, of course, difficult to measure the impact of any educational experience, even when quantities of data are available. In some ways, the School of Jurisprudence had remarkably little effect upon Pobedonostsev. His study habits, his love of reading, and his interests, for example, had been established under his father and were not changed by the school. There is no evidence in his writings or in his later activities in St. Petersburg that he had any particular admiration or friendship for his instructors or that his political and social views were sharply influenced. Similarly, he did not retain close ties or friendships with any of his classmates, although most of them worked in the Senate, as did he, following graduation. Even St. Petersburg itself had little influence upon him; his great dislike of Peter's capital had its origins not in these school years but in the 1860's.

Nevertheless, attending the School of Jurisprudence did constitute a critical turning point in Pobedonostsev's life. First of all, it nourished and strengthened his interest in western Europe, in its scholarship and learning in particular. He emerged from the school with excellent command of Latin, French, and German, with good reading knowledge of Western judicial institutions, law, and literature, and with a fixed assumption, which his father had first instilled in him, that an educated Russian must devote especial attention to western Europe and its achievements. Thus, the fundamental tension which affected Pobedonostsev's official and intellectual life, the strife between the magnetic fascination European ideas exerted upon him and his growing admiration for Russian traditions and institutions, was reinforced.

Pobedonostsev first attained eminence as an historian of Russian judicial institutions and as a specialist on Russian civil law, in both of which he had received training in the School of Jurisprudence, and later in the official career for which that institution had helped prepare him. Thus, the particular direction his career in state service took was determined by the school, most of whose graduates were employed immediately by the Senate.

Established in 1711 by Peter the Great as "the highest governing authority," the Senate had its functions and responsibilities changed several times during the history of the empire. In April, 1866, two years before Pobedonostsev became a Senator, two cassation departments were created as courts of last resort in the new judicial system, one for civil cases and the second for criminal cases. By 1888, seven of the previous twelve departments had been abolished, and the two cassation departments not only predominated in the Senate but strengthened the belief which had been prominent throughout the nineteenth century that the Senate was "the guardian of the law" and a kind of Supreme Court, although its authority was greater concerning judicial procedures than concerning the essence of legal cases brought to it.

However, in May, 1846, when Minister of Justice Panin assigned the new law school graduate to the eighth department of the Senate in Moscow, the institution's responsibilities and reputation were not clearly defined. At that time, the Senate was considered the supreme tribunal or court of last resort for judicial matters and for appeals against administrative acts of the government, but its authority was not clear, nor its administration effective, nor the channels to it carefully defined. Six of its ten departments were in St. Petersburg, two (the seventh and eighth) in Moscow, and the ninth and tenth (with responsibility for the most western parts of the empire) in Warsaw. In 1847, the department of heraldry was established to resolve questions concerning the status of members of the nobility and of other classes, and another department was created to handle the growing number of disputes over boundaries and surveys. The first department in theory decided questions concerning the legality of administrative actions and had a vague disciplinary power over state functionaries. The other departments were review courts in civil cases, with each department having responsibility for a particular part of the empire. Thus, the eighth department, to which Pobedonostsev was originally assigned, included the governments or provinces of Penza, Riazan, Orlov, Saratov, Simbirsk, Tambov, Tula, and Kharkov, as well as the government of Tavrida, Ekaterinoslav, and Kherson in southern Russia. Cases were referred to this department from areas south and east of Moscow, along the Volga river, and from areas acquired within the previous century which were inhabited at that time largely by non-Russians and where trade centers such as Kerch, Taganrog, and Odessa provided interesting commercial cases, often involving foreigners as well as Russians.[5]

Pobedonostsev's rise in government service was impressive, reflecting his excellent mind, the training he had received, his regular habits, his love of work, and the opportunities provided in the Senate for his generation of Law School graduates. His success in the years after 1846 was considerably greater than that of the sixteen classmates and other recent graduates of the school assigned to Moscow with him. His initial salary was twenty rubles (about ten dollars) a month, but within two years he had received a promotion to assistant secretary of his department at twenty-three rubles a month. In 1853, he was made secretary of the seventh department. Four years later, he became secretary of the two Moscow departments when they were in joint session, at a salary of six hundred rubles a year. In 1859, he was appointed Lecturer in Russian Civil

Law at Moscow University. Two years later, he was named a tutor in Russian history and law for the heir to the throne and at the same time named a state counsellor, awarded the Order of Anne, second class, and transferred temporarily to St. Petersburg, where he was made executive secretary of the first department of the Senate, at a salary of a thousand rubles a year. In the fall of 1863, just after he had accompanied the heir on a trip through much of European Russia, he was named executive secretary of the eighth department in his beloved Moscow. This rapid series of promotions, and congratulations from Alexander II himself for his most recent advance, are a measure of his rapid progress to prominence.[6]

Pobedonostsev's service in the Senate was of extraordinary importance for the direction of his career. He was particularly fortunate in that during his first fifteen years in the bureaucracy, his superiors were two able and friendly men, eager to make the Senate efficient and modern, quick to recognize the ability and the dedication of their new apprentice, and delighted to share with him their knowledge of Russian judicial institutions and their understanding of Russian political ways. As Pobedonostsev's memoirs indicate, the pre-reform Senate was a relaxed and comfortable institution in which a young man eager to learn and willing to listen could acquire an immense amount of information and understanding. The Senators themselves were often not competent; they considered their positions sinecures and relied heavily upon the heads of the departments for advice. The department heads were dependent to a considerable degree upon the chancery clerks, the men whom Oldenburg and Panin wished to replace, because over the years they had acquired the detailed knowledge of practice and tradition and fact upon which any judicial system, particularly a creaking and conservative one, must rest. The bright new law school graduate, voraciously eager to learn, especially interested in details, and accustomed to listening to old men, began to acquire from the chancery clerks an enormous store of information about Russian law and institutions and about the way in which the empire was in fact administered.

V. P. Zubkov, the head of the eighth department of the Senate, and his deputy, Sergei N. Urusov, also contributed to the education of young Pobedonostsev in judicial and political matters. Zubkov was a learned and experienced administrator who had entered government service in 1814 and who became head of the eighth department in 1840. Well educated, a student of both Russian and Euro-

pean history and institutions, fluent in French and German, eager
to reform judicial procedures in Moscow, and a relaxed and comfortable host for the young men in his office, Zubkov introduced
Pobedonostsev to a new level of interest and understanding. Urusov,
who came from a more urban and higher level of society than Zubkov, was the ideal aid, because he shared Zubkov's qualities and
interests and was especially eager to replace the power of the old
chancery clerks with the bright young men of Pobedonostsev's generation. These men, and, somewhat later, Prince Vladimir F. Odoevskii, who as a Senator had a special responsibility for the eighth department, helped give Pobedonostsev opportunities in his work,
confidence in himself, and social assurance and relations which were
crucial in the unfolding of his career and in the development of his
political philosophy. In fact, Pobedonostsev's years in the Senate in
Moscow were so pleasant and fruitful that he later declared that
"the Senate is the first state institution in Russia, that its authority
stands higher than that of any other institution among the people
(*narod*), that it is the equivalent of a constitution, that all classes
have confidence in it, and that all without hesitation accept its
decisions."[7]

Pobedonostsev's outstanding contribution in the Senate office,
his publications after 1858, and the advice and assistance of his
superiors ultimately brought him to the attention of scholars, the
most important salons, and leading court officials. But until the
early 1860's, Pobedonostsev remained a lonely young man on Bread
Lane, where he lived with his widowed mother and his spinster
sisters. His life was consumed entirely by his labors in the Senate,
to which he walked every day, by wide reading among a range of
European authors from Milton and Macaulay to Le Play and Heinrich Thiersch, by deep immersion in the works of Russian poets,
especially A. A. Fet and Apollon N. Maikov, by intensive religious
devotion, and by long hours of research and writing. Much of the
impressive learning which so dazzled his Russian contemporaries
and foreign acquaintances was acquired during these busy and
lonely years. His interest in reforming Russian administration and
the Russian judicial system grew from his experience in the Senate.
In addition, the Senate was the principal source of his waning interest in change, as he became disillusioned about the bureaucracy,
aware of the difficulties in the way of reform, and alert to the hazards of tampering with ancient institutions and ideas.[8]

The life of a bureaucrat in an institution as elevated as the

Senate was not a demanding one, and it was customary then, in
Russia and in other countries as well, for those state employees
interested in research to combine their private studies with their
official duties. Pobedonostsev was led by his education into a strong
interest in the history of Russian judicial institutions and of serfdom. It was therefore easy for him to collect materials on these and
other subjects while engaged in Senate functions. The flood of historical essays which he published in the years after 1858 was based
on materials he accumulated and analyzed in his Senate office. Of
course, having been brought up to waste no time and lacking other
interests and ambitions, he also devoted most of his time away from
his official duties to research and writing. He often indicated later
that the two decades after 1846 were his happiest years, and it is
evident that he truly enjoyed the lonely but blissful life of the
dedicated scholar. In fact, the working habits he had developed and
which he enforced during these years were so strongly imbedded
that he continued to devote every free minute of his time until he
died to reading and writing. Catherine Tiutchev in the 1860's found
it almost impossible to persuade him to spare an evening to visit
the Tiutchev or Aksakov families. Similarly, in the 1890's, a de-
mented seminary student waited six hours outside Pobedonostsev's
study for the old man to rise from his desk so that he might attempt
to shoot at him with some hope of success. After his forced retirement in 1905, when he was seventy-eight years old, he concentrated
upon a new Russian translation of the New Testament, which he
completed just before his death in March, 1907. In the 1850's,
Pobedonostsev's primary goal was to publish a history of Russian
judicial procedure since the middle of the seventeenth century,
with particular emphasis upon the influence which the notaries and
clerks of the courts had had in shaping the judicial system. It is revealing that he did not abandon this aim until the 1880's.[9]

Pobedonostsev was a prolific author, editor, and translator from
1858, when his first publication appeared, until his death in 1907.
However, his most fruitful decade was that following 1858, which
was marked by a kind of thaw in Russia somewhat similar to that
following Stalin's death a century later. During this period, the
young amateur scholar published thirty-two books and articles,
varying in length from only two to more than four hundred pages
and reflecting a wide range of interests in the field of history. Two
of these were translations, one of a Roman poet, and the second of

a full-length book, Henrich Thiersch's *Uber christliches Familien-leben*, published originally in Frankfurt-am-Main in 1854 and translated into several European languages soon after it appeared. One of his most interesting essays was a long review article on Near Eastern travel literature and recent archeological work in the Holy Land, while a second short article reviewed a recent English book on Madagascar. Another article published materials Pobedonostsev had discovered on the establishment and early years of the Russian Academy of Sciences, and a fourth essay analyzed several books and articles on Russia and Russian history which had recently appeared in England, France, and Germany. His longest book published during these years was a detailed account which he and Professor Ivan K. Babst produced of the trip he and a number of others had made through European Russia in the summer of 1863 with the heir to the throne, which appeared originally in the newspaper, *Moskovskii vestnik* (Moscow Herald).[10]

Pobedonostsev's first published work, and among his most important, was a long article on the history of serfdom in Russia which appeared in *Russkii vestnik* (Russian Herald) in the summer of 1858 and which was supplemented by a second article in the same journal in 1861. Within twelve months after this first long article, nine other articles appeared, the product of concentrated research during the period since 1846 and of the relaxations of controls which marked the first years of the reign of Alexander II. The most interesting of these was a long and bitter attack on the administration of Minister of Justice Panin, which was published anonymously in London in Herzen's *Golosa iz Rossii* (Voices from Russia) and which is an index of his views at that time and of his willingness to attack his superior in the radical press, even under a pseudonym.[11]

However, Pobedonostsev's main contributions in 1859 and in the years immediately after were in two other areas, the need for reform of the Russian judicial system and the history of Russian civil law. Thus, the Pobedonostsev study which attracted the most attention was "On Reforms in Civil Law Procedure," which he submitted to the School of Law of Moscow University in 1859 as his thesis for his Master's degree and which was published that summer. This was a critique of the established system and an analysis of the principles upon which Pobedonostsev believed new institutions should be based. It was followed by a series of individual case studies which demonstrated that some judicial decisions had been delayed from

thirty to forty years by red tape and by political pressures; that innocent people had been tortured and sentenced; and that the wealthy
and powerful when guilty usually went unpunished.[12]

Pobedonostsev's principal interest as a scholar gradually moved
from studies which were critical of some of Russia's central institutions and which provided ideas for reformers to the study of Russian
civil law, especially wills, mortgage law, property rights, and various
forms of landholding. Most of these early essays were incorporated
in substance into the first volume of his massive three-volume *Kurs
grazhdanskago prava* (Course on Civil Law), the first edition of
which appeared between 1868 and 1880 and which won him high
repute as a legal scholar, particularly as a specialist on wills and on
inheritance law. The first volume of this work dealt with patri-
monial law; histories of various kinds of landholding in Russia and
of Russian property law occupied about half of this volume. The
second volume, which appeared in 1871, dealt with domestic relations, wills, and inheritance rights; about one quarter of this volume consisted of historical material. The third volume, which was
published in 1880, analyzed contracts and obligations and had very
little historical data. The amount of historical material used in each
of these three volumes was clearly influenced by the subject studied,
but it is significant that as Pobedonostsev advanced, first to become
a Senator in 1868 and then to become a member of the Council of
State in 1872, each successive volume of this massive study and of
the successive editions had less historical material. Indeed, the
third volume relied very heavily on data derived from law cases
which Pobedonostsev reviewed as a member of the Senate.[13]

Pobedonostsev's considerable achievements as a scholar in an age
of great intellectual excitement and ferment had the paradoxical
consequence of setting in motion a series of events which led him
in 1865 to abandon both his scholarship and Moscow for St. Petersburg, an important role in the court, and ultimately a position of
great authority at the center of government. This route began with
a lectureship in civil law at Moscow University, where his circle of
acquaintances began to widen, drawing him on occasion into some
of the more interesting salons. More important, he was so effective
as an instructor that in 1861 he was asked to serve as a tutor to the
heir to the throne, which helped break down his self-imposed isolation, weaken his commitment and dedication to scholarship, and
widen further the circle in which he lived. Finally, when he accepted an invitation to move to St. Petersburg to tutor the new heir

Photograph of young Pobedonostsev, taken about 1861. (From Russia, Gosudarstvennaia kantseliariia, *Gosudarstvennaia kantseliariia 1810–1910* [St. Petersburg, 1910].)

to the throne and to be the executive secretary of the first department of the Senate, he abandoned his beloved Moscow, the Law School, and historical and juridical research for a life high in the central bureaucracy and the court.

Pobedonostsev's master's thesis, on reform in civil law procedure, was considered so excellent that he was asked to serve as a lecturer in Moscow University. There this "well-known jurist" taught eight hours each week for six years, except for 1861–62, while at the same time continuing his work in the Senate, maintaining his research and writing, and playing a significant role in the preparation of the 1864 reform of the Russian judicial system. There is considerable evidence that he was a particularly good teacher and that both his colleagues and his students intensely regretted his resignation in 1865. His years of quiet research had provided him an enormous fund of information from a wide variety of sources, especially the Full Collection of Russian Laws, the records of the Senate, various state and private archives, and the burgeoning field of Russian law, which began to thrive after the middle of the century. He was stimulated enormously by contacts with other scholars, particularly Boris N. Chicherin, who taught state law at Moscow University from 1861 until he resigned in 1866; Ivan K. Babst, who taught political economy, shared Pobedonostsev's interest in German scholarship, and with him was a tutor to the heir; and Fedor I. Buslaev, a specialist in Russian literature and art who was also a tutor to the heir.[14]

Vasilii Kliuchevsky, the great Russian historian, who was a student in Moscow University at this time, found especial pleasure in Pobedonostsev's lectures because of the remarkable clarity with which they were organized and with which they explained accurately even the most complicated affairs. Anatole F. Koni, later a distinguished scholar in the field of Russian law, described Pobedonostsev's course on civil law procedure as "clear, compact, accurate, and instructive," qualities which one does indeed find in the set of lectures he gave at Moscow University from January 15 through March 25, 1863, which survived in a version lithographed by an unknown student. Pobedonostsev was especially helpful in identifying the areas of Russian law about which little was known and to which young scholars might most usefully devote their energy. His students considered the variety of instructional techniques he used most helpful. He devoted great attention to the facts of Russian law and procedure as they were revealed by the oceans of available material through which he had waded and from which he had selected relevant illustrations. At the same time, he urged his classes to devote especial attention to the classics in the field of civil law, especially to Friedrich Carl von Savigny, the German scholar whose works he admired and whose historical approach to the development of law influenced him powerfully. Finally, he emphasized that practice and practical knowledge were central to full understanding of the law. His classes thought especially valuable his detailed descriptions of the operation of the courts and of the Senate in Russia, the effective picture he provided of the routes cases followed, or were supposed to follow, and his suggestions for reform. In these years, he was the only Moscow University professor who took his students to the courts and to the Senate so that they could see in action the principles and practices they were studying in class. Indeed, he even arranged that some of his students work part-time in the Senate, which was considered a revolutionary step at that time.

Pobedonostsev's lectures on Russian civil law so impressed his colleagues on the law faculty that Count Sergei G. Stroganov, the curator of the Moscow Educational District, who was also responsible for educating the sons of Alexander II, invited Pobedonostsev to instruct the heir to the throne, Grand Duke Nicholas Alexandrovich, in Russian civil law and institutions. Pobedonostsev interpreted this as an imperial command and accepted, moving from Moscow to St. Petersburg during the academic year 1861–62 to perform this function and also to serve on the committee preparing the reform of the Russian judicial system. Alexander II had a deep appreciation for the tutoring in Russian law he had received from Speransky and a powerful desire that his son understand both the old and the new judicial systems, so he insisted that his heir's education emphasize law. Professor Boris Chicherin therefore served as a tutor the following year, concentrating on Russian state law. Grand Duke Nicholas Alexandrovich had other tutors in other fields of law and also occasionally attended lectures on law in the universities in both Moscow and St. Petersburg.

However, Pobedonostsev was apparently the most impressive and effective instructor, because in the summer of 1863 he was invited to accompany the heir on a three-month trip through European Russia, explaining Russian institutions, while his colleagues, Professor Ivan Babst and painter A. P. Bogoliubov, commented on the Russian economy and the arts, respectively. This trip was of enormous

importance for Pobedonostsev. With Babst he published a long
series of travel letters in *Moskovskii vestnik* from June through
October of that year and a book the following year. Prior to 1863,
Pobedonostsev had seen very little of Russia. He had naturally
traveled to and from St. Petersburg while in law school, he had
gone on brief pilgrimages to the Monastery of the Holy Trinity in
Sergiev Posad northeast of Moscow, and he had traveled as a boy
with his father to the estate of the historical novelist Lazhechnikov
on the Volga. The tour in 1863 was conducted in highly artificial
circumstances because it was designed to instruct the grand duke
and at the same time to show him to the dignitaries and the people
of the provincial cities. However, Pobedonostsev learned a great
deal about the economy and the peoples of Russia. Indeed, his view
of Russia and his philosophy of history in particular were quite
profoundly shifted by this journey.[15]

Pobedonostsev's responsibilities as a tutor to the heir also introduced him to the court and to the powerful and ambitious men and
women who surrounded the tsar and his family. He naturally reported frequently to Count Stroganov, one of the few notables to
oppose the emancipation of the serfs openly, a fervent opponent of
the reforms of Alexander II, and a close friend of Pobedonostsev's
until Stroganov died shortly after the 1881 crisis. At this time,
Pobedonostsev also became acquainted with Prince Vladimir P.
Meshcherskii, a powerful courtier who was a confidant of the last
three Romanovs and who introduced him to a number of leading
conservatives, most notably Dostoevsky, of whom Pobedonostsev
became a close friend.

Pobedonostsev's friendship with Anna Tiutchev, daughter of the
famous poet and later wife of Ivan Aksakov, and an intelligent and
ambitious Slavophil, and with her sister Catherine, an immensely
intelligent woman who became Pobedonostsev's closest friend and
correspondent, began in 1863, when the Tiutchev daughters were
ladies-in-waiting and he was a tutor. The Tiutchevs introduced him
into the important salons in St. Petersburg, first that of the Grand
Duchess Helen, widow of the Grand Duke Michael Pavlovich,
brother of Nicholas I, who was influential in the emancipation of
the serfs in 1861 and in the liberal tone of the first decade of the
reign of Alexander II, and later into more conservative circles, such
as that of Countess Bludov, who helped lead the reaction against
the reforms of Alexander II.[16]

The principal consequence of Pobedonostsev's service as a tutor, however, was his appointment as a tutor for the new heir to the throne, Alexander Alexandrovich, after Nicholas died in Nice in April, 1865. The period which Pobedonostsev had spent in St. Petersburg in 1861–62 had been a constant torment; at that time he developed the aversion to St. Petersburg which he retained throughout the remainder of his life. Convinced after this experience that it was impossible for him to complete any effective work in the new capital, he told Anna Tiutchev in February, 1865, that leaving Moscow for St. Petersburg was "like throwing myself into the grave." He had refused a splendid appointment as Director of Religious Education in the Holy Synod of the Russian Orthodox Church. However, heart-broken by the death of Nicholas Alexandrovich, whom he had come to admire and to love and for whose death he privately blamed Nicholas' tutors, Pobedonostsev quickly accepted appointments as tutor of the new heir and executive secretary of the first department of the Senate when these posts were offered to him in August, 1865. This decision was of capital importance for him and perhaps for Russia, for it removed him from the library, the study, and the classroom and placed him in a position in which he was to develop a most inflexible political and social philosophy and to exert profound influence upon the course of Russian history.[17]

Pobedonostsev's interest in research and writing remained high, but his ability to devote time and energy to scholarship began to decline rapidly when he moved to St. Petersburg, married in 1866, and began to acquire influence, first, as an imperial tutor and later as a Senator, member of the State Council, Director General (*Ober-Prokuror*)* of the Holy Synod of the Russian Orthodox Church, and closest adviser to the tsar. Pobedonostsev never took a prominent part in St. Petersburg social life. Indeed, he resented the time which social affairs and official functions consumed. He remained a voracious and unsparing reader, devoting to this so much of the time left free from official duties that his wife must often have felt completely abandoned. Moreover, while he was not able to maintain the publication pace he set between 1858 and 1865, he continued to produce scholarly and other works at a remarkable rate.

As the bibliographical essay at the end of this volume indicates, Pobedonostsev was almost incredibly prolific as an author and publicist. Many of his publications in the last forty years of his life con-

---

* It is difficult to translate *Ober-Prokuror* into English. The functions of the *Ober-Prokuror* of the Synod were those of an executive director or director general.

sisted of speeches, official reports, and polemical literature on one subject or another, from attacks on Leo Tolstoy, drinking, various Russian sects, and liberalism to a flood of articles on education, an essay contributed to a famine relief fund in 1873, and the translation of the New Testament. Even if we omit all of his translations, some of which are of great importance, and some other writings as well, Pobedonostsev's continued interest in scholarship and in publication is clear.

The volume for which Pobedonostsev is best known, of course, is the collection of essays describing his political and social philosophy, *Moskovskii sbornik* (Moscow Collection), which he published in May, 1896, on the fiftieth anniversary of his entry into government service. Five editions of this tome were published between 1896 and 1901, three translations were produced in German, and English, French, and Spanish translations also were made.

However, Pobedonostsev's most important work as a scholar was his three-volume *Kurs grazhdanskago prava*. The bulk of the research for this massive study was clearly completed during the twenty years in Moscow after 1846, but he continued to collect material and to incorporate information he acquired as a Senator after 1868. The basic structure of the three volumes was almost unchanged between the time when he prepared his original outline early in the 1860's and the appearance of the final edition in 1896. Thus, while the fourth and last edition of the first volume contains ninety more pages than the first edition twenty-eight years earlier, the changes are all trifling, consisting usually of short footnotes or illustrations. The fourth edition of the second volume was only thirty-four pages longer than the second edition in 1875 (the first edition is not available), and the third and last edition of the third volume was only thirteen pages longer than the first edition sixteen years earlier. Even the bibliography in the final edition included few titles published in the previous quarter of a century.

In fact, the history and development of the *Kurs grazhdanskago prava* is quite similar to that of Pobedonostsev's political and social philosophy. As this volume will demonstrate, the structure and main principles of Pobedonostsev's thought were well established by 1865 or 1870. The only changes he made during the last forty years of his life were minor additions and illustrations, similar to the slight revisions and increments he introduced into the main body of his principal scholarly work.[18]

The *Kurs grazhdanskago prava*, designed for teachers of law, for jurists who needed to understand the new judicial system as well as the roots of Russian legal practice in earlier codes, and for administrators who had to deal with the problems it discussed, constituted a massive handbook or guide through the complexities of the Russian judicial system. Eschewing theory and emphasizing clear knowledge and actual practices, these volumes and his other publications in the field of civil law were of enormous utility. In an age in which Russian scholars produced a large number of excellent studies of Russian law, Pobedonostsev's three volumes were extremely successful, even though the last full edition contained more than 2200 pages and cost nine rubles (approximately $4.50), a very high price at that time. Thus the 1896 edition was the fourth for the first and second volumes and the third for the third volume. The size of the printings for each volume varied from 2400 copies to 3000 copies, so it is clear, for example, that approximately 10,000 copies of the first volume alone were published and sold.[19]

Kurs grazhdanskago prava was supplemented in 1872 by *Sudebnoe rukovodstvo* (Guide to Court Procedure), a 553-page collection of principles, rules, and examples of court procedure which Pobedonostsev had compiled over the quiet years of study and of labor in the Senate. This volume was designed to assist both lawyers and judges confused by the new judicial institutions. Although it was not well organized, it did help shape trial law procedure and for a few years was a valuable book for the legal profession.

By 1885 or so, Pobedonostsev must have concluded that he was never to return to his scholarly labors, because he began to publish materials he had collected for his proposed history of the Russian judicial system, particularly of the role chancery clerks had played. He obviously hoped that the materials he had collected from various unpublished sources would thereby be put to some good use, and he was also satisfying the family urge to publish. In 1890 and 1895, he published the notes which he and his research assistants had compiled during the 1850's from the Full Collection of Russian Laws and from various archives, especially those of the Senate, with the intention of stimulating study of these hidden materials and of promoting legal scholarship.[20]

He also published in these years other historical materials he had collected earlier, such as some of the correspondence of his predecessor as Director General of the Synod, Count Dmitrii A. Tolstoy, letters illuminating the reign of Nicholas I, and data about his brother Sergei. Moreover, after he became a member of the Imperial Russian Historical Society, he was an active supporter of a program for publishing historical materials.[21]

When he became Director General of the Synod, Pobedonostsev devoted great attention to the Synod's Press. By 1884 or 1885, he had reorganized and modernized the Synod's publishing operation so that this Press became one of the largest and most efficient in Russia. He used this publishing office mainly to print and distribute enormous quantities of literature for the Orthodox Church and its new parish schools. However, he also used it to publish historical works. For example, under his direction the Synod's Press in the 1880's and 1890's reprinted the works of Andrei N. Muraviev, who before his death in 1874 had written a large number of books about the history of the Russian Orthodox Church. In addition, it was the Holy Synod Press which first published Kliuchevsky's famous *Kurs russkoi istorii* (Course on Russian History). Pobedonostsev, whose favorite historians had been Carlyle and Froude, became an enthusiastic admirer of Kliuchevsky. One of the principal pleasures of the last three years of his life was reading Kliuchevsky, and he fervently hoped that the Holy Synod Press would complete publication of Kliuchevsky's volumes before he died so that he might read them all.[22]

As an historian, or at least as a former historian, Pobedonostsev was aware of the importance source materials possessed for scholars. He assumed that future historians would be interested in his activities and ideas, and he apparently believed that they would treat him fairly. His principal contribution as an historian in the last twenty years of his life was editing and publishing materials left him by his friends and letters and other documents of his own. For example, in 1893 he published the very lively and valuable correspondence of Baroness Edith Raden with the celebrated Slavophil historian of Russia's Baltic provinces, Iurii Samarin. He also helped Samarin's son publish a complete edition of his father's works, which involved persuading the censors not to interfere.[23]

Pobedonostsev was particularly helpful and generous in releasing correspondence he had received for publication. Thus, all of the letters Nicholas Ilminskii wrote to him from his Kazan school for non-Russians between 1882 and 1891 were published in 1895. He also released letters he had received from many leading churchmen and scholars so that complete editions of their correspondence could be printed.[24]

Above all, Pobedonostsev published quantities of documents

which cast illumination upon his own life. For example, in 1885 he published in a limited edition the diary which he had kept while a student at the School of Jurisprudence, and he produced a second edition of one hundred copies in 1901. He obviously intended that this diary ultimately be made available for scholars, since he gave a copy of it to Peter Bartenev, editor of the *Russkii arkhiv* (Russian Archive), to whom he gave much other material for publication. Bartenev published part of this extremely interesting and valuable diary in his journal immediately after Pobedonostsev's death in 1907.[25]

In 1894, Pobedonostsev published the extraordinarily sensitive religious poetry and meditations which he had written in Moscow between 1856 and 1864. In the 1890's, he reprinted two translations he had issued in the 1860's, but which were out of print. In addition, he published a series of biographical essays concerning some of his closest friends during the period before 1880. Most of these he collected into a volume in 1896; they are all precious sources concerning Pobedonostsev's life and times.[26]

Finally, in his last years he began to organize the letters and documents he had accumulated. He scattered a great many of the letters which he had not already given to others for publication through various historical journals in a flood too large to enumerate here. He neatly bound into bundles the letters which he had received from Alexander III, Nicholas II, and members of the Imperial family. He also carefully arranged the other letters which he decided should not be published during his lifetime. In his will, he provided that these materials should be placed in the Rumiantsev Museum (now part of the Lenin Library) for publication ten years after his death. Many of these letters and documents have been published. A great many still remain unpublished, but are now available for study in the Manuscript Division of the Lenin Library.[27]

The training which Pobedonostsev had received at home from his father had helped prepare him for the scholarly activities that later claimed his attention. His intellectual activities and interests indicated that by character and temperament he was destined to be a scholar. When he made his decision to abandon scholarship and Moscow for service in the high bureaucracy in St. Petersburg, and often later in life, he complained that only the tsar's command and his belief in God's will persuaded him to accept this great transfer. From the very beginning, he lamented his absence from Moscow and his abandoned interests. Some of his friends, notably the liberal jurist, Boris N. Chicherin, saw this as the decisive turning point of his career. Chicherin, for example, became a friend and colleague of Pobedonostsev at Moscow University in the early 1860's and remained in warm relations until after the 1881 crisis. When they first met, he thought Pobedonostsev modest, generous, and pious. He isolated himself from society, lived almost a monkish life, lacked political judgment, and was clearly "a man of the study." Yet, according to Chicherin, he was completely transformed by his move and gradually became a dishonest, cynical manager of men.[28]

As a scholar, Pobedonostsev was distinguished by his wide range of interests and his immense and carefully acquired knowledge. He was a firm believer in long, hard work in primary source material and in mastery of the scholarly secondary works. He insisted that books should be studied, not read, and that "just reading," especially reading books devoted to theory, was "dangerous and deceiving." He urged his students to acquire every tool of scholarship and to be fully prepared before they considered teaching or writing. Reasoning that strength and knowledge can be bought only at hard labor, he declared that "he who wants to argue, to issue glittering phrases, and to express general ideas . . . risks following the wrong road." He had a special admiration and envy of the English and of English scholars in the fields of history and of law because of the enormous collections of historical and legal materials available in England, particularly for the period after the fourteenth century. He considered the great wealth of archival collections responsible in some degree for the care and moderation characteristic of English scholarship.

Pobedonostsev was convinced that the path "for the lover of true knowledge" in the field of Russian law lay first through the forty-nine-volume Full Collection of Russian Laws for the period from 1649 to 1825, as well as the volumes for the period since the death of Alexander I. "Whoever wishes to study Russian law seriously must begin with this, . . . must force his way through the Full Collection, . . . beginning with the very first volume" and taking full notes. "I assure you that such a study of the law will at first require some strength, but that it will gradually become interesting and for some even absorbing reading. With each volume, the student will more deeply appreciate the power and strength of this remarkable work, this healthy and sensible knowledge, that very learning which is absolutely necessary for a Russian jurist." Indeed, the student from this process will also attain mastery of the "pure and clear language" in which Russian laws were written. "In short, the study of the Full Collection of the Laws in my opinion constitutes a necessity for the Russian jurist. It is impossible to provide a better school for him than this school of dead but eloquent memorials."[29]

Pobedonostsev's historical works and his civil law studies were distinguished by the vast amount of data which he had accumulated from the Full Collection of Russian Laws, the archives of the Senate and of the Ministry of Justice, other state and private archives, and other previously published collections of materials and studies of Russian institutions. Moreover, Pobedonostsev excelled in the clarity and simplicity with which he presented the data he had amassed.[30]

His historical studies are cautious and limited in scope, for he believed that providing an "exact and conscientious account of the facts" was a very considerable achievement for an historian. In his monograph on serfdom, he emphasized that a full and clear history of serfdom could be written only after serfdom had been abolished, more materials were available, and scholars were able to analyze more objectively its institutional and intellectual foundations. He was enormously impressed by the way in which the common law had "grown" in England and suspected that much of Russian law had developed in the same slow, organic way. He based his own work solely on ukases, judicial practice, and other written evidence. He refused even to suggest generalizations or conclusions for which there was not clear written evidence. This reluctance to reach a conclusion, or to make a judgment, even on the basis of immense data, is demonstrated most clearly in his *Kurs grazhdanskago prava*. Pobedonostsev proclaimed that these volumes were to provide a comparative study of various systems of civil law. Accordingly, he began each section by describing the history of the particular institution or practice as it had developed in Roman Law and in the law of England, France, Germany, and Russia. However, only very rarely did he make any comparisons or comments on the similarities and contrasts, and he left the reader to make his own judgments from the information which he had presented.[31]

Pobedonostsev's work as a scholar was marked especially by his lack of interest in, or even antagonism toward, the creation of any philosophy or theory concerning the development of Russian law. This was especially remarkable because of the powerful interest in

Russia then in the general theory of law. The study of law in Russia
had begun under the influence of the natural law approach of
Pufendorff and Gross, and Dilthey had even lectured at the university in Moscow. Later, the historical school of Savigny exerted
great influence; indeed, Pobedonostsev himself considered Savigny
the preeminent jurist of the world in the nineteenth century. Moreover, at the time when Pobedonostsev was completing his most
mature works, the influence of Hegel and of Comte was very great
among leading Russian jurists, such as Chicherin and Korkunov.
However, Pobedonostsev distrusted theory and preferred to concentrate on cases. One critic called him "a slave of the Full Collection
of Laws." Others noted that he was so obsessed by accumulated evidence that he did not realize that he worked in a series of deep
grooves and was in fact only a compiler of procedures which everyone, including him, knew needed reform. The *Kurs grazhdanskago
prava* thus became a guide through a labyrinth of ukases and decisions, through a museum of Russian law. Pobedonostsev believed
that Russian civil law had no creative organization or working
principles and that it was not the responsibility of the scholar to
identify or repair that shortcoming. Indeed, he was convinced that
any theoretic inner unity of Russian civil law must grow only from
the forest of laws in which he and other scholars were working.[32]

Pobedonostsev was particularly competent in writing review
articles, which often required little imagination but which did enable him to use his immense fund of well-organized knowledge in
a variety of areas and from a number of languages, his patience, and
his skill in analyzing the use of sources and secondary works.
Chicherin noted that Pobedonostsev was especially effective as a
negative critic. He even said that Pobedonostsev's favorite word was
"but." Pobedonostsev's review articles were clear and precise, particularly when he dealt with careless histories or with collections of
materials which were incomplete or inaccurate. On occasion they
produced devastating effects. For example, his review of Michael M.
Mikhailov's *Russkoe grazhdanskoe sudoproizvodstvo v istoricheskom razvitii* (Russian Civil Judicial Procedure in Its Historical Development) destroyed the reputation of that young scholar. In this
long review, he gave a page-by-page list of errors of fact, and carefully listed the errors Mikhailov had made in transcribing decrees.
Pobedonostsev's insistence as a young scholar on meticulous accuracy is especially worthy of note because of the intellectual dishonesty he often displayed later in life, when he frequently distorted

the meaning of the books and articles he translated by omitting pages, paragraphs, sentences, and phrases, without any indication of this fact. He was also frequently guilty of plagiarism.[33]

Even as a young man and as a supporter of judicial reforms in Russia, Pobedonostsev was dry and impersonal. His style was always clear and simple, although his vocabulary was remarkably rich and accurate. All of his research and writing were neat and orderly. His essays concerning celebrated court cases were factual and arid, although they could easily have been made effective emotional pleas for reform. His essays on serfdom are just as impersonal and cold, and they reflect no strongly felt feelings or convictions. Indeed, they are even more reserved than his studies of the judicial system. Even his travel writings contain excellent descriptions of landscapes and of buildings, especially churches, but rarely refer to or describe men and women. His historical studies are remarkable for lack of affection for Russia's past. He insisted that "the aim of historical research, and of legal research . . . is first of all the impartial search for the truth" and not the support of any political or moral position. He often repeated that the historian must always remember that customs and beliefs of historical ages differ and that he errs grievously who criticizes the acts or beliefs of one age according to the views of another.[34]

Thus, Pobedonostsev's publications during the years when his primary concern was research and writing indicate that he possessed the interests and qualities required of a conscientious and objective historian. Although he lacked the large view, the interest in general conclusions, and the concern with the philosophy of history which usually identify the great historian, his talents as an historian and his vast general learning made his historical studies valuable contributions to the study of Russia's past and reveal that he would almost certainly have enjoyed an outstanding career as a scholar. As this study will later demonstrate, however, Pobedonostsev as a bureaucrat, determined to safeguard the state and system he venerated, abandoned the qualities which had distinguished his work as a scholar and developed qualities, particularly intellectual dishonesty, which disgraced him and the system he sought to defend.

III

The Liberal Reformer

POBEDONOSTSEV was known by his contemporaries and is considered by historians of all persuasions as the extreme conservative, the arch reactionary principally responsible for the repressive policies of Alexander III and of the first decade of the reign of Nicholas II. This view is fundamentally accurate, although his power and influence have been heavily exaggerated, both by his contemporaries and by scholars. Pobedonostsev was a conservative throughout his life, by philosophy, temperament, and practice, and his views simply became more dogmatic and rigid as he grew older. Throughout his life, he accepted the fundamentals of the Russian system of government and of the society in which he lived and worked almost as unthinkingly as his father had before him. He was forever a faithful believer in Orthodox Christianity and in the supremely privileged position of the Russian Orthodox Church in the Russian state. He especially exalted the family as the fundamental base of a stable society. Finally, the European state system of which Russia was a part was also an established, permanent element of his world, one which he did not question.

Like many other modern politicians and political philosophers who have emerged as extremist defenders of the *status quo*, however, Pobedonostsev as a young man not only clearly and consistently advocated radical reforms, but also played an important role in putting these proposals into effect in the reorganization of the Russian judicial system introduced in November, 1864. Pobedonostsev mentioned his activities as a reformer in a letter about his career which he wrote in 1892 to the Académie des Sciences Morales et

44

Politiques in Paris, four years after he had been elected a member of that august body, but he generally tried to conceal his achievements as a reformer from his associates and from the historical record. Thus, in a letter he wrote to Alexander III in 1881, he denounced those responsible for the 1864 reform as "ignorant men" who had created a system incompatible with autocracy and with any form of government. Even more remarkable, in a letter to Alexander Shakhov on March 10, 1884, he said he had protested against extensive borrowing from the French code in the committee meetings to establish the basic principles for the new judicial system and had left St. Petersburg for Moscow in disgust in 1862 when he was unsuccessful. Finally, in an account of his life and service which he wrote for Nicholas II on March 21, 1901, he declared that he was "called to work" on the judicial reform committee, refused "to set out on an unknown sea," but found service impossible to avoid. Thus, he clearly sought to give the impression that he had been drafted into the program for judicial reform and that he had been a most reluctant and ineffective participant.[1]

Despite the conservatism and patriotism of Pobedonostsev's upbringing, the critical attitude he developed toward the administration of the Ministry of Justice and toward the judicial system originated in the training he had received from his father. Professor Pobedonostsev, while an uncritical supporter of the autocracy and of everything Russian, introduced his son to some knowledge of Europe, created in him the assumption that an educated man had both a right and a responsibility to speak and to read other languages than Russian and to be informed concerning other cultures, and thereby established the basis upon which a critical attitude toward things Russian could be created.

The diary Pobedonostsev kept in the School of Jurisprudence between 1842 and 1846 and which he published in limited editions in 1885 and in 1901, when he was a vigorous defender of the established system, provides clear evidence of the friction which developed between the lad, accustomed to some intellectual freedom at home, and the tightly controlled school designed to train new bureaucrats for the government of Nicholas I. The young prizewinner, who considered his teachers inferior to his father and to the men he had known in Moscow, thought the school officials ridiculously petty when they confiscated some of his favorite foreign books, particularly the stories and plays of Paul de Kock. Although he did not smoke, drink, or play cards, he was critical when all cigars, cigarettes, tobacco, and cards were confiscated from the other students. He was furious and insulted when the director of the school went through all of the rooms and removed many books, including Gogol's *Dead Souls*. However, his irritation was greatest when an inspector criticized him for owning a book of Lermontov poems, which he was allowed to retain only if he removed it from the dormitory. He was especially scornful of the inspector's admission that "Lermontov was of course a poet, but he died a bad death."

The young Pobedonostsev protested both privately and publicly against administrative actions which he considered unjust or ridiculous. In December, 1842, when seven members of the first class were expelled for pranks, he confined his criticism of the excessive severity of the punishment to his diary and to his friends. However, when friction developed between some of the students and one of the soldiers on guard at the school, he took the lead in protesting, wrote a letter to the director, and emerged triumphant. He later protested to the director about the food and about the director's decision to restrict the entire class for two months for the actions of only two or three members.[2]

Relatively little information has survived concerning the actions and ideas of Pobedonostsev between 1846, when he graduated from the School of Jurisprudence and returned to Moscow to a position in the Senate, and the late 1850's, when he began to publish extensively and when his letters, various memoirs, and official records provide significant amounts of data. However, he was a voracious reader with catholic tastes, and it is clear that his reading reflected his attitudes and at the same time affected his beliefs. During these years he was attracted by the Whig interpretation of English history, reading the essays of Macaulay as well as his *History of England*. In reminiscences which he published late in life, he recalled his great interest in the revolutions of 1848 and the feverish eagerness with which he met with friends to read and even to copy the latest French newspapers, and to discuss the spread of the revolution beyond Paris. He even recalled reading Louis Blanc, Proudhon, Fourier, and Lamartine's volumes on the Girondins in those exciting days.[3]

However, neither the revolutions of 1848 nor the Crimean War deflected him from his major concerns, his work in the Senate and his research on Russian history and Russian law. Indeed, his labors in the bureaucracy and in the archives fed the critical sense and the human sympathies which his sympathy for 1848 had revealed. His immense dissatisfaction concerning the inequity and inefficiency of the administration of justice as he saw it and as he read about it came to flower just at the time Alexander II relaxed the firm controls Nicholas I had maintained and as he allowed a thaw to sweep over the capital cities of Russia. During this period of relaxation of control, when new newspapers and journals flourished and when intellectuals were encouraged briefly to suggest means of achieving a more noble Russia, a decade which Trotsky later called "the Russian Enlightenment," the young Pobedonostsev joined the critics of the Old Regime and advocated important changes of fundamental institutions and of administrative procedures.

The twenty-eight articles which Pobedonostsev published in the decade after 1857 appeared in eight different journals, but the largest number and the most important were printed in *Russkii vestnik* (Russian Herald), which was edited from 1856 until 1862 by Michael Katkov, and in the *Arkhiv istoricheskikh i prakticheskikh svedenii otnosiashchikhsiia do Rossii* (Archive of Historical and Practical Information Concerning Russia), which was edited and published by Nicholas Kalachov. Both Katkov and Kalachov became close friends of Pobedonostsev and both played important roles in Russian history for thirty years, Katkov as a fervent nationalistic journalist and Kalachov as a scholar, editor, archivist, and Senator.

There is no evidence that Pobedonostsev and Katkov were acquainted before 1862, although Katkov published Pobedonostsev's first article, his 125-page "Zametki dlia istorii krepostnago prava v Rossii" (Notes on the History of Serfdom in Russia), in the summer of 1858. Pobedonostsev was not listed by Katkov as one of the proposed contributors to the new journal when he sought permission for publication in 1855, and the first letter or evidence of any personal relationship between the two men dates from 1862. Nevertheless, over a period of five years, the Katkov journal published eight articles by Pobedonostsev, almost all of considerable length and some of importance in the intellectual history of the period. For example, *Russkii vestnik* in June and July, 1859, published Pobedonostsev's Master's thesis at Moscow University, his stirring attack on the judicial system, "O reformakh v grazhdanskom sudo-proizvodstve" (On Reforms in Civil Law Procedure). The same journal in December, 1860, published a case study describing the remarkable delays and inefficiency shown by the Russian courts in a particularly brutal murder case, and in 1861 it published his final essay on serfdom, "Utverzhdenie krepostnago prava v Rossii v XVIII stoletii" (The Consolidation of Serfdom in Russia in the Eighteenth Century).[4]

Katkov is best known, of course, for the nationalistic and often irresponsible journalism that he published from the middle of the 1860's until his death in 1887. However, the Katkov of the first decade of the reign of Alexander II, of the thaw which lasted until the Polish rebellion in 1863 in particular, was quite a different person and worked effectively for reform. Born in Moscow, nine years before Pobedonostsev, to the family of a minor noble and bureaucrat, Katkov graduated from Moscow University in 1839. In 1840, he was a collaborator of Belinsky on the Westerner journal, *Otechestvennyia zapiski* (Notes of the Fatherland). He was not only quite critical then, and later, of the Slavophils, but he was also deeply influenced by study in Berlin and by his analysis of Hegel, about whom at that time he planned to write a book. However, he returned to Moscow, obtained a doctorate from Moscow University in 1845, and was a member of the philosophy faculty of the university from 1845 until 1850, when Nicholas I discouraged all instruction in philosophy. He then edited an important newspaper, *Moskovskiia Vedomosti* (Moscow News) until 1856, when he founded *Russkii vestnik*, which quickly attained national significance, with a circulation of 5700 in 1861.[5]

Katkov and Pobedonostsev shared ideas and attitudes during these crucial years. Both, for example, were in favor of emancipation of the serfs, although neither was particularly active in the public campaign against serfdom nor did either participate in the work of any of the committees which helped prepare the enormous change. Both were earnest advocates of drastic revision of the judicial system. Katkov's journal published a number of critiques of established procedures as well as reform proposals, while Pobedonostsev not only provided some of the most trenchant attacks on the old system and suggested some of the fundamental bases of the new reform but also participated actively for five years in preparing the November, 1864, decree. Katkov remained a defender of the new courts for some years after they had been established, when many other proponents of that change had become disillusioned and when Katkov himself had become a violent opponent of most of the other changes introduced.[6]

Katkov and Pobedonostsev were probably also drawn together by their common admiration for England, especially pre-reform

England, and by their hopes that Russia would develop institutions and social attitudes similar to those of England. Pobedonostsev, who had not travelled outside Russia until he was forty-one years old, spent three summers in England within five years. He was especially fond of English literature, particularly the poets Shelley, Browning, and Swinburne and the historians Macaulay, Carlyle, and Froude. He was always eager to become acquainted with Englishmen in Russia, from observers such as MacKenzie Wallace to visitors such as Bishop Mandell Creighton. Above all, he admired English institutions, English national unity, and the blend of conservatism and change which the English managed to achieve.

Katkov was perhaps even more an Anglophile than Pobedonostsev. He learned to read and speak English while young, travelled to England, translated some of Shakespeare into Russian, and had an obvious and deep admiration for English style, institutions, and customs. He was especially impressed by the respect shown by the English for their political and social institutions, by the power of prescription, by land reform and the modernization of agriculture, and by the extreme skill with which the English combined political stability, social mobility, and a kind of rugged individualism in economic development.[7]

The other main publisher of Pobedonostsev's research efforts, Nicholas Kalachov, was quite a different kind of person from Katkov, and the relationship Pobedonostsev established with him was dissimilar also. Kalachov was born in 1818 on the same lane in Moscow as Pobedonostsev, and apparently the two were acquainted from their early years. As a youth, Kalachov was especially interested in Russian literature, but he yielded to parental pressure and studied law at Moscow University, from which he graduated in 1840 and from which he received a Master's degree in law in 1846. Through friendship with the Minister of Education, Uvarov, his father obtained him a position in the Ministry's Archeological Commission, where the young Kalachov used the opportunity to increase his knowledge of Russian history and law, as Pobedonostsev did in the Senate. The learning he acquired and his publications led to his appointment as Professor of Russian Law at Moscow University in 1848. However, his main interests were in archives and in archeology. After serving as librarian of the archives of the Ministry of Foreign Affairs for a number of years, he was named Director of Archives in the Ministry of Justice in 1865. His services as an archivist were most important, for he not only collected and organized significant materials, but also was a member of the Archeological Commission after 1851, founded the Archeological Institute in 1877, and established a commission for provincial archives in 1884.[8]

Kalachov played an important role in the life of Pobedonostsev, who considered him a splendid representative of the best type of old Muscovite. As an older friend and neighbor, Kalachov helped his young colleague by identifying important collections of interesting materials. He almost certainly strengthened Pobedonostsev's views concerning Russian history and traditions and his interest in affairs Russian, compared to Western ideas and institutions. In their reviews of old chronicles and in their leisurely visits to old monasteries and cemeteries, the two men rediscovered the attractions of Russian history and their affection for the Russian land and people. It is quite likely that the pious and learned scholar and archivist, the unsung hero who devoted his life to the service of others, more than balanced the impact upon Pobedonostsev of the polemicist Katkov.

Kalachov had a powerful influence upon many young scholars. He not only helped them to find materials and thereby affected the main outlines of their work, but he also encouraged them and prodded them to publish. Convinced by 1848 or 1850 that the educated public should know more about the basic institutions and traditions which had shaped Russian life, and that the shortcomings of Russian institutions should be laid bare if effective changes were to be made, Kalachov in 1850 began a series of publications which helped to achieve these goals. Thus, in the 1850's he published a three-volume series of documents on Russian history and legal institutions. As the thaw progressed and as it became clear that great changes were to be made, in 1859 he launched a journal designed to publish the principal historical facts he thought important concerning serfdom and the judicial system; the twelve volumes he published over the next five years not only provided Pobedonostsev and other young scholars an opportunity to publish the products of their research, but also contributed to the drive for reforms, for many of the articles revealed gross shortcomings and suggested improvements. Finally, in 1867 Kalachov began publication of a journal, *Iuridicheskii vestnik* (Juridical Herald), to assist judges, lawyers, and administrators to keep abreast of the changes introduced by the reform of 1864.[9]

Kalachov's contribution to the abolition of serfdom and to the judicial reform of 1864 reflects the intellectual climate in which the young Pobedonostsev was working. First of all, the journals Kalachov edited were designed to "acquaint the public both with the ancient life of our nation and with those current developments which may reveal to the state and to various individuals some of the means available for resolving our present problems." Thus, the journal published an extended series of articles on serfdom as well as a number by men deeply engaged in the judicial reform, such as Sergei I. Zarudnyi. The moderate and limited aims of Kalachov and his contributors were demonstrated by the attention he paid to Count Michael Speransky; the first article Kalachov published in the principal journal he edited was devoted to the man who had tried to make the Russian administrative machinery efficient in the first decade of the nineteenth century, and two other essays on Speransky appeared within that same year.

Kalachov himself served on the editorial committee which helped prepare the final drafts of the decrees which emancipated the serfs and established the new judicial system. His service on the first committee was particularly crucial, for he helped define the rights and responsibilities of the peasants and the landlords after emancipation. Moreover, it is clear from his own essays that he had considerable knowledge of the conditions in which the workers lived and labored, derived largely from visits to factories and workers' dormitories, and that he believed that the reform movement should also seek to assist the worker.[10]

Pobedonostsev's main concern in the wave of changes which swept over Russia after 1856 was in the administration of justice, about which he wrote scathing attacks and made proposals for reform. His writings on the history of serfdom and his other publications during this period reveal that he was aware of some of the shortcomings afflicting Russian government and society, but that he believed improvements inevitably had to develop slowly and that governments had limited powers in effecting changes in institutions and in people because of the nature of man and of his institutions. Thus, in his preface to his translation in 1861 of Heinrich Thiersch's *Uber christliches Familienleben*, he gave vague and general approval to the current efforts to reform the social order. However, he declared that careful study of the principles on which the social order should be established must precede change and that man himself must not be neglected in the reconstruction programs. Thiersch himself had a deep concern for the welfare of the working class, whose plight he began to recognize, and was not opposed to constitutional government, but both he and his translator were conservatives.[11]

Pobedonostsev's position concerning serfdom reveals also that he was by no means a crusader. There is no evidence that he had any personal knowledge of life on the Russian land, as he did have information concerning the operation of the bureaucracy. Moreover, he did not denounce serfdom as he did judicial abuses, and he did not identify the basic principles which should guide reformers, as he did for the 1864 change. Indeed, his first long article was basically a description of serfdom and of the various kinds of relations between landowners and serfs in the seventeenth century, while the second half of his study was devoted to the changes which had occurred in the eighteenth century. The main thesis was that neither one man nor one particular document was responsible for the establishment of serfdom, "which was formed little by little." Indeed, he argued that Peter the Great, for example, had had little impact on the institution. Peter used it as an instrument of rule, and he tried to eliminate the most flagrant abuses, particularly when changes would not affect the power of the state. Just as Peter had the good sense to realize that serfdom "reflected the inner law of history and of political necessity" in the conditions which prevailed then, so "that same law of historical and political necessity under which serfdom was formed has led to its change." In other words, Pobedonostsev believed that the economic and intellectual changes which had struck Russia since the last quarter of the eighteenth century indicated serfdom should be abolished.[12]

Pobedonostsev's discussions of Count V. N. Panin's administration of the Ministry of Justice, his studies of the judicial system, and his proposals for court reform reveal both more detailed knowledge and far more personal interest than his papers on serfdom. The bitter attack on Count Panin was published anonymously in London in Herzen's *Golosa iz Rossii* (Voices from Russia), and is a most remarkable document in every way. The manuscript must have been written in 1857 or 1858 because the January, 1859, issue of the journal announced its forthcoming appearance. It was probably taken to London by one of Pobedonostsev's friends, Chicherin, Iurii Samarin, Professor Ivan K. Babst (who also submitted an article to Herzen), Constantine Aksakov, or, most likely, Ivan Aksakov, who visited Herzen in 1857. Herzen's influence in Russia at that time was considerable (he published half as many copies of *Kolokol* [The Bell] then as Katkov did of *Russkii vestnik*), and Pobedonostsev's brilliant and direct assault on the Minister of Justice must have had a significant impact upon those seeking to reorganize the central administration. Panin was furious, but apparently neither he nor anyone else in high court circles discovered the identity of the author, although the details provided would indicate that the man responsible almost certainly was a member of the small Senate staff in Moscow.[13]

Panin, who earlier had been considered a liberal, was not highly regarded by his contemporaries. Indeed, Alexander II told Grand Duchess Helen Pavlovna that "Panin's convictions are limited to the exact execution of his orders." However, Pobedonostsev's critique was as much of the system as of the man. The first quarter of the long essay was an attack upon the central administration of Russia, and Panin was described as a representative of the rule of Nicholas I who had retained influence and power in the new reign. Pobedo-nostsev admitted that the history of Russia had been marked by in-competent administration, but said that there had been some im-provement from the seventeenth century until the second quarter of the nineteenth century. Then, however, the reign of Nicholas I abandoned the principles of earlier monarchs, ended Russian prog-ress, isolated the government from the people (*narod*), crippled education, and adopted a system of "unconditional and irrespon-sible power." Nicholas "openly sought to convert the concept of patriotism into that of service to the government" and created a state bureaucracy of servile men. Unfortunately, according to Pobedonostsev, Alexander II, though a man of good will, was sur-rounded by the same men who had advised Nicholas I. The result was "organized anarchy." The ministerial system had deteriorated to the seventeenth century level, with no clear definition of author-ity or responsibility, and continued disasters, such as the Crimean War, lay ahead.

Panin was the perfect example of the system, "devoid of any in-telligence, humanity, or sense of justice." Ignorant, incompetent, vicious, authoritarian, isolated from the people of Russia and even from those who worked in the Ministry, and surrounded by syco-phants, Panin of all people was Minister of Justice. Pobedonostsev admitted Panin was not corrupt—"he had no need to be"—but he declared that he tolerated corruption in the very center of the judi-cial system. He delayed the administration enormously by his fool-ish demands for written reports and the forms and ridiculous regu-lations he issued. He drove able and independent men from the service and after 1848 had refused to appoint any well-educated young men. Above all, he was weakening and destroying the Senate,

one of the principal and most beloved parts of the state. On one
two-month visit to Moscow, he did not even meet the heads of the
Senate departments until the day before he was to return to St.
Petersburg. Finally, he used the censorship to prevent criticism and
to silence suggestions for reform.

The bulk of the article on the Ministry of Justice and on Panin
was a scathing indictment, but Pobedonostsev also introduced a
modest proposal for reform. Arguing that the institutions available
were perfectly satisfactory and that the main problems reflected
incompetence and a kind of deliberate anarchy, he proposed that
Panin be replaced, that the Senate be refurbished, and that each
member of the bureaucracy be made clearly responsible for his own
work. Above all, he suggested the creation of an organ in government separate from the rest of the administration, staffed by independent and able individuals, with the authority to see that the laws
were observed and to punish any member of the bureaucracy responsible for violating the law. "Thus teaches the science of statecraft, on the basis of centuries' experience; so judged the wise legis-
lators of Russia, Peter and Catherine." Such a "high college," in a
position of "material and moral independence and to which every
single person in the Empire except the Tsar was subject" would
restore law and establish the conditions in which economic and
moral strength would revive. In fact, Pobedonostsev suggested that
the Senate, cleansed and exalted, could undertake this central task,
using existing institutions and laws.[14]

Pobedonostsev probably realized that his proposed Inspectorate
General, an institution which resembles supervisory or review agencies which have appeared in Russian history both before and since,
was not practical at that time. Moreover, he surely knew that criticisms published abroad might have considerable influence within
Russia, but that suggestions of reforms or new institutions made in
the Herzen journal could hardly be adopted.

His special interest, of course, was the judicial system. He published at least eighteen articles within a decade, in which he commented in detail on particular aspects of Russian civil law, made
intensive and extensive criticisms of the judicial system, and suggested principles on which reform should be based as well as specific
proposals for change. His long study of the position the bar should
have and his Moscow University Master's thesis reveal that his ideas
concerning radical change in the judicial system were clearly estab-

lished by this time and that his contribution to the judicial reform of 1864 was very significant.

By the middle of the nineteenth century, the judicial system in Russia was under almost as heavy popular attack as was serfdom. Most Russians at all levels of society were aware of the courts' glaring deficiencies and vices. Even Nicholas I was concerned, particularly when he learned in 1842 that 3,300,000 undecided cases were before the courts in that year, compared to 2 million in 1825. He had therefore ordered Count Dmitrii N. Bludov to undertake a study of the courts, to complete new codes for civil and criminal law procedure, and to make proposals for improvement. In fact, Bludov and his colleagues before the end of the reign had reached many of the conclusions concerning the shortcomings of the judicial system and the principles of the reforms needed which were incorporated in the 1864 change.

In 1858, the new tsar sent Zarudnyi, educated as a mathematician but a self-trained lawyer who had worked in the Ministry of Justice and who was a key member of Bludov's committee, to Europe to observe judicial institutions. This kind of review sponsored by the tsars themselves occurred at the same time that officials and scholars such as Pobedonostsev were independently completing their research and taking advantage of the thaw to publish recommendations. Many of those who participated in this campaign had studied in Germany, often with Savigny, the great founder of the historical school of law, or with Russian professors strongly influenced by Savigny or by other Western scholars. Thus, the movement for reform had a number of sources: high government interest and support, the work of jurists familiar with the machinery then in operation, and European influence purveyed in one of several ways. Moreover, the great effort to abolish serfdom inevitably put other institutions under searching analysis. Finally, of course, emancipation so clearly affected the judicial system in the countryside that revision of the entire philosophy and structure of the courts was necessary after 1861.[15]

In the research he published late in the 1850's, Pobedonostsev asserted that a radical reorganization of the Russian judicial system was clearly necessary. He argued that no society could survive unless it were dedicated to truth and to justice. He recognized that these goals, by their nature and because of the nature of man, could never be attained, but he was also certain that the aims themselves and a consistent effort to reach them were indispensable. Courts dedicated to law and justice were especially important in any state because justice was the true goal of the state and the courts were the public conscience. It is interesting to note that Pobedonostsev then quoted Peter the Great and cited his efforts in proof of his contention.

Some, dismayed by the slowness, venality, and injustice of Russian legal procedures, were led to believe that courts were not vital, that trials were unnatural and a stimulant to crime and disorder, and that some kind of patriarchal mediation system would be infinitely preferable. Pobedonostsev demolished this view in a systematic way, urging that every society, even primitive societies, had a judicial system and courts, and that law became both more vital and more complicated as society became more advanced. Russians must therefore come to understand thoroughly Russian law and the operation of the legal system and, second, study closely superior foreign judicial systems. "All law must conform to the basic needs of a given society" and flow from particular historical conditions. Judicial regulations and forms are just as difficult to borrow and use as languages, and any adoption of foreign institutions must be gradual and free to be effective. Indeed, Pobedonostsev suggested that Russia needed a Supreme Court whose high authority was recognized, supported by a research institute to make certain that its decisions reflected an accurate understanding of the law.[16]

He believed that the Russian judicial system was marred by serious faults which must be removed if the state and people were to make material and moral progress. The evidence he cited from the previous century and a half was impressive and was presented in such a way as to combine a rational and an emotional appeal. Thus, he concentrated on bureaucratic red tape, the use of torture, the assessment of barbaric penalties, and cases in which obviously innocent people had been judged guilty and punished, as well as cases in which powerful men, even when clearly guilty, went unpunished. For example, he provided details on one assault case which had been stalled in court for thirty-four years, when the family of the plaintiff, five years after his death, finally abandoned their charge. The cases of torture which he described in detail were all the more impressive because he demonstrated, first, that the state had used torture to cause terror and as a substitute for legal workmanship and, second, that torture was often used to obtain confessions when the charges were particularly ridiculous and the defendants obviously innocent.

Use of the knout, cutting the nostrils, and similar penalties he thought beyond discussion in civilized society.

The reasons for these disgraceful actions and judicial failures were clear, according to the young scholar. The basic weakness was the role played in the courts by the chancery clerks, who prevented the creation and development of a bar, undermined and usurped the position of the judge by making him dependent on them for the facts of cases and for interpretations of the law, and established a complicated system in which papers superseded and crowded out oral discussion, thus making complication, red tape, delay, and corruption inevitable. These ignorant, untutored, small-minded men had successfully separated the science of law from juristic practice. The law in their hands had become a meaningless ritual.

Proceeding from this analysis of the court system, Pobedonostsev suggested that the state, its leaders, and all Russians must first recognize that understanding and respect for law and justice must stand at the center of society because the rule of law is the essence of the good society. Under law, and with respect for civil rights, confidence and energy would return to the state and make possible economic and spiritual progress.

Four major changes were necessary to ensure effective judicial procedures. First, Russia needed a large number of highly skilled and trained lawyers, willing to undertake any case and eager to find and to defend the truth. Lawyers, and an organized bar, would ensure the vigorous search for truth and justice which any judicial system requires. Competing against each other, lawyers would stimulate the entire structure of the judiciary and educate the judges. Indeed, he called the bar "a garden" for the judiciary, suggesting that the kind of learned, humane, and wise judges Russia needed would be provided by the eager lawyers who compete before the judges.

> Only with the help of lawyers can you have pleading in court of such plenitude and liveliness as to enable the judge to consider the case from all sides, to penetrate into its essence and form a definite opinion. . . . When the vivid speech of the lawyers is heard in court . . . when the court and all the participants are not confined behind closed doors, when the public is present and taking a lively part in all events in court, the procedure will take the shape of a real, vivid, and rational contest. Then no judge will be able to remain indifferent and

inattentive. Only under such conditions, i.e., with the participation of the lawyer in public session, will the court become
the best school of education for judges and lawyers. . . . The
struggle of the poor against the rich, of the weak against the
strong, of the dependent against the one on whom he depends, is difficult and dangerous everywhere and at all times.
In some cases, a struggle is impossible without a lawyer. If a
lawyer is in a position independent of the government and
court, as he ought to be; if he relies on the moral force of the
case which he defends, and, at the same time, upon the moral
force of a whole corporation to which he belongs and also upon
the consciousness of the public present at the struggle; then
the lawyer—and, let us add, the lawyer alone—is able to enter
the fight against the personal interest of material force and to
oppose to it the weapon of spiritual force. . . . The lawyer's
guild . . . can reach its goal only if it is a closed guild placed
beside the judiciary and independent of it. . . . As soon as the
guild is organized, it will become necessary to grant to it permission for free and independent activity.[17]

Second, the entire legal system must be completely separated
from the government and the administration. Pobedonostsev demonstrated in principle and by the use of illustrations that the failure
to separate police or administrative functions from judicial functions had been disastrous throughout Russian history. Judges were
to be free from administrative pressure, independent of the government, and granted tenure.

Third, all judicial procedures should rely more on oral than on
written material. Perhaps the basic facts involved in any trial should
be in writing, but all arguments before the judge or jury should be
oral, reducing red tape and delay and providing lawyers skilled in
their craft and in presenting evidence an opportunity to compete in
a vigorous way before a judge, attentive to all materials and proposals made because of devotion to law and because the lawyer's
own competence and integrity were being tested before ambitious
advocates.

Finally, all trials must be open to the public. He recognized that
ordinarily few people would be interested in observing the working
of the courts, but asserted that the right to attend a trial was a
critical one and that justice could not be reached in the dark. In
fact, secrecy and seclusion bore a heavy responsibility for the flaws
and failures of the judicial system.[18]

Many of the changes Pobedonostsev advocated in the late 1850's were put into effect in the great judicial reform of 1864. He was inventive and forthright in his advocacy of the main principles on which the new system was to rest: irremovable judges, public sessions, oral procedures, and a well-trained, independent bar of lawyers who had a social obligation to undertake the defense of anyone charged with violating the law. He was not an ardent advocate of some elements of the 1864 reform, elected justices of the peace, jury trials in criminal cases, and equality of all classes before the courts, and he was not an enthusiastic or consistent supporter of the jury system. However, he was neither for nor against elected justices of the peace in the years before the government itself established committees to prepare the reform, probably because the proposal had not been made or had not occurred to him. Equality before the courts, similarly, was not an issue which he discussed, perhaps because he simply assumed it. Moreover, of course, the 1864 reform, for all the progress it made, did not provide for full equality before the law.[19]

Pobedonostsev was more than a proponent of radical reform of the Russian judicial system. He was also a virulent critic of Panin and all others who defended the established system. Thus, he denounced those who resisted change as "legal Old Believers" who did not see "history as a movement forward from dead ritualism to the soul of life." He ridiculed those who thought that the progress of history must stop in the seventeenth century. The lectures which he gave in the law school of Moscow University between January 15 and March 25, 1863, and the notes of his students reveal that Pobedonostsev carried his campaign against the old system and for radical reform directly into his classes. The lectures provided a simple, clear, and critical description of the principles which underlay the legal systems of western Europe and of those which should be fundamental in Russia. Anatole Koni, one of the great Russian judges in the last quarter of the nineteenth century, later described his "clear, compact, accurate, and instructive course" in 1863 and 1864. Pobedonostsev spoke "with lively sympathy" of the public trial with competing lawyers, of the new courts of review, of the justices of the peace, of the oral courts, and, above all, of the fact that courts were to operate in the open. "That which is hidden from the light and is conducted in secret is surely a falsehood," he told his class. "If justice reflects the truth, corrects and exposes falsehood, and observes the law, then it cannot fear light, and all its actions must be completed openly, because the exposure of injustice in the dark is not exposure, and the declaration of the truth under the cover of an official secret is not a declaration. When justice selects secret paths for itself and carefully conceals its actions from the public view, then it itself demonstrates that there is crookedness in its paths which it is dangerous to reveal to all."[20]

Pobedonostsev's writings and lectures on behalf of judicial reform in the exciting years after 1858 naturally attracted the attention of the tsar and of those responsible for the reorganization of the judicial system. Moreover, his other actions as an intellectual and as a professor indicated that he was among those who advocated a generous degree of change in Russia. In 1861, he was a contributor to the short-lived St. Petersburg weekly, *Vek* (Century), to which a number of radicals, such as Nekrasov and Lavrov, and a number of men prominent in the literary scene, such as Goncharov, Turgenev, and Ostrovsky also contributed. In the same year, he was one of those who signed a letter published in Katkov's newspaper, *Moskovskiia Vedomosti*, which defended a member of the Moscow University faculty, an Orthodox priest named Father N. A. Sergievskii, who in a sermon on April 12, 1861, had argued that Christian faith and philosophy were not opposed to reform or to freedom. In the fall of 1861, he agreed to give a series of public lectures in a campaign to collect funds for University students who had been arrested for disorders, withdrawing only when he learned that Chernyshevsky was to be one of the participants. However, he withdrew not because of Chernyshevsky's political or social views, but because he considered Chernyshevsky a charlatan. Later, when one of his students, Alexander K. Malikov, was imprisoned for his political views, Pobedonostsev helped to obtain his release and corresponded with him. Finally, his advocacy of change expanded also into the economic and social fields. In letters which he and Professor Ivan K. Babst published in Katkov's paper in 1863 and published in book form in 1864, he advocated higher wages and old-age pensions for industrial workers.[21]

Curiously, the judicial reform of 1864, which gave Russia a judicial system then considered the most equitable and efficient in the world, on paper, has not attracted systematic study on the part of Russians or of foreigners for more than sixty years, even though this is one of the landmarks of Russian history in the nineteenth century and although enormous quantities of materials are available. Consequently, while Pobedonostsev obviously played a very important role in this change, it is not yet possible to define his contribution exactly.

Some of the groundwork for the reform of the judicial system was laid during the reign of Nicholas I, when Count D. N. Bludov, head of the second division of His Majesty's Own Chancery, in 1839 began a review of the courts and, late in the reign, drafted both a civil and a criminal code. Under the new reign, however, Bludov became more liberal than he had been under Nicholas I, and his committee prepared new draft codes which incorporated suggestions received from provincial committees that class distinctions within and among courts be abolished, that the judiciary be made independent, and that the courts conduct their affairs openly. However, Bludov, who was seventy-five years old in 1860, was gradually superseded in this work by younger and livelier men placed on his committee by Alexander II. V. P. Butkov assumed the real leadership, although Bludov remained chairman of the committee until he died in 1862. Moreover, Zarudnyi, another energetic younger jurist, became the principal driving force after he joined Bludov in 1857 and was sent to Europe in 1858 to study judicial institutions. It was Zarudnyi who distributed draft proposals to jurists such as Pobedonostsev as early as 1859. It was principally he who identified the liberal jurists and who invited them to work with the various committees in drafting the principles on which the reform was to be based and to help with the final reform.[22]

The emancipation of the serfs gave great impetus to the judicial reform. When the tsar returned to St. Petersburg from vacation in the fall of 1861, full of enthusiasm because of the great change launched, he asked Bludov and his committee for a progress report and, later, for a detailed proposal concerning the next steps to be taken. On October 23, 1861, he agreed that Butkov and a committee of ten jurists attached to the State Chancery should prepare a report describing the main principles on which the new judicial system should be based. These principles, prepared by January 22, 1862, were reviewed by the various departments of the Council of State and by its General Assembly from April until July, and by the Senate in August and September. Approved unanimously by the Senate, they were accepted by the tsar, who had them published and asked for comments from government officials, law professors, and jurists.

In September, 1862, Alexander II named a special committee of thirty-seven men, attached to the State Chancery, to design new judicial procedures and to draft new civil and criminal codes of procedure. This committee was headed by Butkov, with Zarudnyi his deputy. It consisted of the Chancery of the Council of State, seven men selected from the second division of His Majesty's Own Chancery and from the Ministry of Justice, and other jurists named by the tsar from universities and from other state institutions, such as the Senate. This learned group completed its grueling technical work in eleven months, between November 30, 1862, and October 24, 1863. The group on the civil code, of which Pobedonostsev was one of thirteen members, had ninety-one meetings. Each member of this and of the other subcommittees also attended sessions of the full committee, contributed drafts and comments on proposals made in these committees, and produced new versions of critical sections after the long discussions.

The Butkov committee submitted its final report in the fall of 1863 to the second division of His Majesty's Own Chancery, the Ministry of Justice, the Council of State, and the Senate for discussion. The deliberations of these bodies were reviewed finally by the Council of State, which recommended the new system in all its detail to the tsar on October 2, 1864. The tsar then announced the reform in a ukase on November 20, 1864.

In other words, the judicial reform of 1864 was the result of a long and harrowing process involving a great many government institutions and officials. The draft submitted by the Butkov committee in the fall of 1863 reflected the work of thirty-seven eminent jurists and statesmen; in fact, it was accompanied by more than 1,750 pages of explanation from these participants. The tsar himself and the various state institutions invited comments from other jurists and officials. The Minister of Justice, D. N. Zamiatin, alone provided five hundred pages of comment on the draft Butkov's committee submitted.[23]

Pobedonostsev was drawn into this great process because his articles in *Russkii vestnik* and in Kalachov's journal attracted the attention of Zarudnyi, who in 1859 began to send draft reform proposals to him for comment. Zarudnyi was especially impressed by his critique in December, 1859, of a proposal for new civil law procedures which had been prepared in the Council of State. In this critique, Pobedonostsev was eloquent in his denunciation of the chancery courts, in which the clerk was so powerful, and in his advocacy of oral courts. By early 1861, Pobedonostsev and Zarudnyi were together studying the civil codes used in Hannover and in Italy. In the fall of 1861, Zarudnyi in St. Petersburg and Pobedonostsev in Moscow were in frequent communication. When Zarudnyi proposed his name to the tsar as a member of the small committee in the State Chancery to identify the basic principles on which the reform should be based, Pobedonostsev was delighted. The announcement of his appointment was made on November 3, 1861; Pobedonostsev moved to St. Petersburg five days later "for temporary work on the reform of judicial institutions." He wrote forty years later that he refused to "set out on an unknown sea," but it is clear he was an avid and excited participant. In fact, some government leaders then thought him a leader of the radicals, carrying too far the work "sensible conservatives" such as Bludov had launched. In the early 1860's, he was particularly envious of foreign judicial systems, especially that of England, where the courts were open to public view, skilled lawyers represented the two sides in a civil case, and judges were competent and respected. He hoped then that Russia would develop a system equal to others and would use all of its energies toward that goal, "when the business of reforming the entire structure of our administrative system and of our judicial system is in progress."[24]

The written records concerning the preparation of the 1864 reform are voluminous, but it is often impossible to determine precisely the significance of Pobedonostsev's role, largely because so many changes were made during and after meetings in which a large number of men participated and concerning which there is often no accurate record. However, a number of his proposals have survived, and other evidence also indicates that Pobedonostsev participated in an important way in every stage of the reform. Thus, he was in close correspondence with Zarudnyi and reviewed preliminary proposals for more than two years before Alexander II named the committee to determine the fundamental principles on which the new system should be based. He was a member of this critical ten-man committee, writing memoranda for it within a month of his joining it, and he moved to St. Petersburg to share in its work and then to discuss it with various departments of the Council of State and with the general meeting of the Council. After the tsar had approved and published the basic principles, he placed Pobedonostsev on the large committee to draft the final program and on the subcommittee which drafted the new code of civil law procedure. Pobedonostsev participated in the last twelve months of discussion of this draft with the various state agencies listed above, in his capacity as a member of the committee named by the tsar and also as the executive secretary of the eighth department of the Senate, which reviewed the proposals throughout the first nine months of 1864. The committee notebooks which have survived indicate that he participated in all of the meetings of the subcommittee which drafted the new code of procedures and that he prepared many draft proposals and was active in the discussions. He must naturally have played an important role within the Senate when its various departments studied the digest. However, he did not attend many of the sessions in the spring and summer of 1863 in which the full committee discussed the proposals by itself or with officials from the Council of State, the Ministry of Justice, or other government institutions. He was prevented from attending the spring meetings by his classes in law at Moscow University and by his work in the eighth department of the Senate. The summer and early fall he spent on a tour of European Russia with the heir to the throne, which he almost certainly considered a command appointment.

The importance of his work is reflected in his appointment as tutor in law to the future Alexander III and as head of the first department of the Senate in 1865. He became a member of the Council of State in 1868 (only six other participants in the reform of 1864 were so recognized) and a Senator in 1872. Moreover, after the new judicial system was announced, he was awarded two thousand rubles per year for the rest of his life for his work. His annual salary then was two thousand rubles, and no participant in the reform except Butkov and Zarudnyi received a higher award.[25]

Pobedonostsev was especially interested in the new civil law procedures and in those parts of the reform which affected civil law. He devoted a great deal of time and energy to details which do not have great historical significance, such as whether law students or illiterates could serve as lawyers in civil cases, the responsibilities and rights of a lawyer when his client died, the allocation of court costs, and the arrangements under which an inquest could and should be conducted. Some of the sixty-one draft articles he prepared on issues such as these were accepted without change, or with little revision. Others were discussed at length in the committees and then by the various state organizations.

In general, he supported the major changes, including the introduction of ideas and institutions which had proved effective in other countries, but he urged always that the new principles and institutions reflect "the economy of our life" and not be introduced simply because they had worked in other countries, where the customs and traditions were quite different. In addition, he consistently argued that a perfect judicial system was impossible of attainment, that the committees should seek only the best possible, and that compromise agreements should be accepted by all until experience showed which was the best procedure.[26]

For most of those engaged deeply in the judicial reform, separation of the courts from administrative influence or control was the keystone of any improved system. From the very beginning of the drafting process, Pobedonostsev supported the establishment of a judicial system independent of the state administration, stating that administrative rule and dispensing justice were very different activities, that any judicial system required specially trained staff, and that blending political rule and justice could only cause confusion and harm. He wrote in 1861 that the judge at the provincial level should have "a position fully independent of that of the governor. He should stand beside the governor, not under him, and neither should interfere in the other's activity." Pobedonostsev therefore argued that judicial power in the Empire "belongs exclusively to the positions and people invested with that power. . . . In everything concerned with the administration, execution, and decisions of legal issue, no state position or person should interfere or give orders or instructions."[27]

Apparently, the only officials of any significance who opposed the separation of judicial and executive powers were Prince Oldenburg, the founder and director of the School of Jurisprudence from which Pobedonostsev had graduated in 1846, and Pobedonostsev's old superior, Count Panin. However, when those preparing the new judicial system descended from the great abstract heights of judicial independence to concrete problems, the resolution of Pobedonostsev and others like him wavered. For example, Zarudnyi, Pobedonostsev, and most of the other participants in this work supported the principle of irremovability of judges only after considerable analysis and hesitation. Thus, in December, 1861, Pobedonostsev suggested that Russia might not possess sufficient trained and honorable people for the institutions they envisaged.

> We lack the judicial estate, with its professional spirit and its inner discipline of honor and public service, and we have an inadequate number of people to meet the demands. We can

only conjecture, we cannot be certain now concerning the ability and worth of the people who should fulfill the demands. Finally, the almost universal custom of accepting tokens of gratitude from petitioners is divided from bribery only by an equivocal line, so that it is rarely possible to distinguish where custom ends and abuse begins. We lack judges. There is no reason to hope that the introduction of new regulations will make rare either misuse or laziness and simple inefficiency in our judicial system. In such circumstances, to establish the irremovability of judges would simply remove from the government's hands its means of correcting errors in the appointment of judges, errors which are sometimes unavoidable, and to substitute a new and superior judge for a worthless one, and to end or lessen bribery.[28]

Pobedonostsev thus recognized, as did many of his colleagues, that Russia almost certainly lacked "the storehouse of legal custom and doctrine" and the necessary class or estate which would "give durability to knowledge, foundation to thought, and order to discussion" and would form statesmen and scholars from those newly entering the profession. However, after reviewing this serious issue, he asserted that "even the best and most perfect institutions" would not by themselves bring the goals they sought because of the handicaps of "an insufficiency of people and carelessness and poor luck in the selection of those we have." The legislator, he continued, cannot stop with this observation, or he will never reform fundamental institutions. The effectiveness of institutions depends on those who work with them, but institutions also form people. In other words, he ultimately and reluctantly supported the irremovability of judges and of elected justices of the peace. However, his position and that of many of his colleagues was so troubled and indecisive that the Ministry of Justice decided to introduce the new courts only gradually. Elected justices of the peace, for example, first appeared in Moscow and St. Petersburg only in 1866 and were then introduced very slowly in European Russia.[29]

One of the thorniest and most delicate problems facing those engaged in preparing the reforms involved the procedure for civil suits against government officials. Many Russian statesmen and bureaucrats thought that neither the state itself nor its agents could be brought into court by a suit of a private citizen. Others agreed that some state actions had to be above the authority and judgment of the courts, but asserted also that the courts were the guardians of civil rights and that the executive and its officials should submit to the authority of the court in all instances affecting the rights of private citizens.

In this swirling, confused, and prolonged controversy, Pobedonostsev saw all sides of the issue, because he was both a bureaucrat and a juridical reformer. His draft articles and comments in the discussions were therefore quite carefully balanced, as were his university lectures on this subject. However, he did not join the group which insisted that the courts should define the law of the land and that the courts alone should determine which instances were a part of their jurisdiction and which were not. Indeed, it was his masterly fifteen-page memorandum in 1864 which led to the compromise agreement which preserved the principle the reformers thought vital and yet won the support of those who feared that any new definition of authority would weaken the power of the state and hamper the work of responsible officials. Pobedonostsev argued in this important paper that Russia required a strong, centralized government because conditions were different from those of countries in western Europe and that administration would be impossible and the economy would decline if every office and official were responsible to a court. He agreed that a private individual must be able to obtain redress from the improper actions of a state official, but asserted that the state's interests had priority. His compromise proposal, which was adopted, suggested that a committee composed of an equal number of representatives of the state administration and of the courts, but chaired by a member of the judiciary, should determine which disputes were subject to judicial decision.[30]

The new institution that most attracted popular attention after 1864 was the jury, which was introduced into the Russian judicial system at that time. Some of Pobedonostsev's colleagues balked at establishment of the jury, even though the requirements for service were set rather high. However, even Count Panin supported the jury system in the discussions in the Council of State, arguing that this constituted the best way to attain independent courts, if this was the government's goal. Pobedonostsev accepted the jury because he believed that the institution would operate effectively and that it would "shape" the people who used it, as they "shaped" the institutions they developed.[31]

Pobedonostsev's principal target before 1864 was the pre-reform chancery court, and the most deeply felt and effective paper that he wrote for the reform committees was a thirty-one page memorandum he prepared for the committee on basic principles in December, 1861. Here he admitted that Russia lacked legal authorities and "storehouses of legal doctrines and customs," but was savagely critical of the half-educated chancery clerks responsible for the "soulless, heartless formalism" of Russian judicial procedures, "the secret and inquisitorial proceedings with their doctrine of formal evidence," and the prolonged delays, injustice, and cruelty the system produced. His solution was simple: to limit the significance of written briefs, especially in simple cases, increase the importance of oral evidence produced under oath, and emphasize a verbal contest or oral competition between the plaintiff and the correspondent, or between their lawyers, before the judge, who could thereby see the issues clearly and render quick and just decisions. He was unsuccessful in his effort to insert a clear statement reflecting his views into the 1862 definition of the basic principles upon which the reform should be based, but the final code not only elevated the significance of oral debate before the court but also simplified the forms and emphasized the role skilled lawyers were to play, which he thought essential for the efficient administration of justice. By the time these proposals were in the final stages of review in 1864, Pobedonostsev had modified them so that the amount of written material involved varied according to the complexity of the case. Indeed, the majority of the committee in 1864 ultimately approved a greater emphasis on oral proceedings than did Pobedonostsev himself.[32]

Just as the chancery clerk and the old court were Pobedonostsev's favorite targets, so the Ruling Senate was his central institution. In the long effort to reform the judicial system, he resisted the effort to make the Senate a cassation court or kind of court-of-last-resort for all civil and criminal cases. Arguing that the *narod* (people) had become accustomed to the title of Ruling Senate and that the idea of a superior court of appeal was a Western one which had no roots in Russian tradition and was the cause of deep quarrels even in the West, he asserted instead that Russia should make the Senate the institution responsible for regularity of procedure and uniform interpretation of the law. Moreover, he insisted that the chairman of the Senate should have direct access to the tsar in order to ensure that the Senate would have full power in its functions. In fact, as clearly as one can determine from his imprecise language, the Senate was to be an instrument of the state, working closely with the Ministry of Justice. The Ministry was to be responsible for the maintenance of the law, and the Senate was to ensure that the courts be consistent and accurate in their judgments. Indeed, in order to enable the Senate to concentrate its efforts upon what Pobedonostsev considered its most significant functions, he suggested that some of its judicial review and inspection functions be transferred to the new district courts.[33]

Even during the years when he was a most exuberant and vigorous proponent of a new judicial system, Pobedonostsev on occasion was troubled by doubts concerning Russia's readiness to master and assimilate the splendid system he and his colleagues were preparing. These doubts were greatest when he considered the size of Russia, the severe shortage of well-trained lawyers and judges, and the varieties of peoples and traditions with which the judicial system had to deal, or when he was on one of his rare excursions outside his study and conference rooms in the capital cities. He wrote to a friend in June, 1862, just after he had returned from six months in St. Petersburg, that he felt like a Jew returning from Babylonian captivity. While travelling through the Don country with the heir apparent in the late summer of 1863, he was impressed by the ways in which the economic and social structure and the traditions and attitudes of Cossack society differed from those elsewhere in Russia. He reflected that it was certainly impossible to apply the same changes in the Don area as in the sections with which he had been more familiar. By the fall of 1864, when his work had been completed, he began to rail at the popularity of abstractions, at the personal ambition he saw everywhere, and at the evidence of "decomposition and weakness and untruth." On December 14, 1864, less than a month after the reform had been announced, he wrote Anna Tiutchev that he was sick and tired of reform, that he had lost faith in reform programs, and that he hoped somewhere to find some firm ground on which to stand with some confidence.[34]

His early disillusion became more profound after a decade, and he later became a virulent critic of the new court system. However, there is substantial evidence that he remained a resolute defender of the reformed courts for a number of years and that he sought to assist the hundreds of judges trying to improve the administration of justice. There is no evidence that he criticized the new judicial system between 1865 and 1872. In an article published in 1866, he asserted that there was little partiality or deliberate injustice in the new courts and that explainable ignorance and confusion in the new system were responsible for delay and absurd decisions. He was hopeful then that the new courts would be able to master the labyrinth bequeathed them. In the winter of 1871–72, in the Council of State, he opposed the efforts of Minister of Justice Palen to tinker with the judicial review procedure established in 1864. In the third volume of his *Kurs grazhdanskago prava,* he lamented the lack of confidence the higher courts had demonstrated in the new justices, especially in the elected justices of the peace, and reiterated his belief that the courts should rely more on oral evidence and discussion than on written material, which had been responsible for many of the faults of the old system.[35]

More important, in 1872, when Pobedonostsev was both a Senator and a member of the Council of State, he published *Sudebnoe rukovodstvo* (Guide to Court Procedure) as a handbook for judges, especially justices of the peace, who were bewildered and confused by the new requisitions. Noting the absence of a general explanation of the theory of Russian civil law and of the connection between general concepts and practice, he declared that these shortcomings had contributed to the conflicts and contradictions which were confusing even the most seasoned judges. He asserted that the difficulties Russia's jurists were undergoing were not remarkable, because the new judges were inevitably inexperienced and unprepared and Russia simply lacked the knowledge and wisdom concerning civil law procedure which only experience could provide. He therefore published five thousand copies of a 575-page guide to provide the new jurists information on the principles of civil law procedure, or "a short and clear account of the general rules" concerning the main problems. Of the 1,540 theses which Pobedonostsev discussed or for which he gave "sample" decisions, he had participated in the Senate discussions of about four hundred.

Sudebnoe rukovodstvo was criticized by some reviewers because it contained too many examples and confused the simple jurist seeking assistance rather than aiding him. Others noted that the volume may even have been harmful because it lacked any apparent system of selection and because Pobedonostsev sometimes was not aware of important Senate decisions which deeply affected or even reversed his theses. Yet, although he did not publish supplements to the book, or a revised edition, as he promised, his guide was clearly of considerable assistance to those who wanted to make the new judicial system effective.[36]

The suspicion and hostility toward the 1864 court reform which Pobedonostsev had harbored must have grown gradually until it burst forth in two bitter anonymous articles which he wrote in 1873 for a weekly, *Grazhdanin* (The Citizen), which Prince Mesh-cherskii founded and published and which Dostoevsky edited at that time. One of his articles was a direct attack upon the jury system. In 1859, he had written that the English and the Scandinavians had succeeded in changing the system of formal proof and in eliminating torture from the judicial process because of the jury and that this institution would also help remove the use of torture from Russia. However, in 1873 he argued that the jury was effective only in England, where it had well-established popular national roots and where it had long been used to decide issues other than political ones. It was based on custom, not law, and it was not effective, and could not be effective, in countries such as Italy and Russia, where the traditions simply differed from those in England.[37]

After 1873, he was a consistent and bitter critic of the jury in Russia. He ignored those studies which demonstrated that jury courts had been even more repressive than those without juries and that the jury as a whole had had "an ennobling influence on the people's sense of equity." In 1876 and 1878, he urged that cases involving violent attacks on government officials be transferred to special courts staffed by officials of the Ministry of Justice who were strong, reliable, devout defenders of the state and who could "distinguish clearly between truth and untruth." He helped raise the requirements for jury duty in 1877 and to remove some kinds of cases from jury courts in 1889. In his principal statement of his political philosophy late in life, he took malicious pleasure in quoting the celebrated conservative English scholar, Sir Henry Maine, in his final outburst against this judicial institution.[38]

Pobedonostsev also used his anonymous platform in Dostoevsky's *Grazhdanin* to attack Russian law professors and Russian jurists in general. His old friend and his colleague, Kalachov, now also a member of the Senate, and a number of law professors at Moscow University planned a congress of jurists on the model of congresses held in Austria and Germany since 1860, which more than 220 professors and other jurists attended in Moscow in 1875. Meanwhile, Pobedonostsev loosed a vicious attack on the Moscow law faculty, naming individuals and identifying what he considered their shortcomings. He went on to denounce the products of the law schools as shallow charlatans who had studied law only to obtain comfortable positions created by the 1864 legislation. Although unsuccessful in preventing the 1875 congress of jurists by these attacks, Pobedonostsev did persuade Alexander II and the Minister of Justice to refuse permission for a later meeting.[39]

In 1873, he astounded even his associates in the Council of State with his attack on the final stages of the reform of the army which Count Dmitrii A. Miliutin was just then bringing to a conclusion. In a long and spirited speech, he unsuccessfully attacked Miliutin's proposal that officers be chosen by ability and urged instead that only members of the gentry class be eligible to serve as officers. His defeat on this issue was so crushing that he reversed his position before the final vote.[40]

The Balkan crisis and war in 1877–78 and the celebrated public trial of Vera Zasulich helped to turn Pobedonostsev against every aspect of the reform of 1864. Indeed, he was opposed to any trials for the revolutionaries and said he would "stand this flock of stray sheep against the wall." His correspondence during the last years of the reign of Alexander II and the first years of the reign of Alexander III is filled with denunciations of the Russian judicial system as one of the prime causes of the political and moral crisis.[41]

This full revulsion and the development of a political philosophy which reflected this change and Pobedonostsev's turn toward repression will be described later. The process of the change between 1859 and 1874 is still impossible to decipher. It is significant that the available materials contain no reference to the Polish revolt in 1863, which many believe was a turning point in Russian political development similar to the revolution of 1848 in Prussia and Austria. None of his publications or private letters refers to the nihilists or to the radical and revolutionary movement of the 1860's, although he must have known and opposed them. Moreover, until he wrote another anonymous article in *Grazhdanin* in 1873, he did not refer to the zemstvos or the municipal dumas, the local self-government institutions established during the great reform wave.

In other words, the principal developments of the 1860's must have influenced Pobedonostsev considerably, but we have no direct evidence and the effect of the entire period must have been cumulative. However, he was probably influenced just as much, or even more, by other factors. For example, his interest in change was clearly restricted to his own field of special and technical interest, the judicial system. He was not a reformer; in fact, he was always quite conservative. He simply wanted a more efficient and equitable system of law. Moreover, it is quite likely that the process through which Pobedonostsev and others labored to bring forth the 1864 legislation had the impact which long campaigns for radical change often have upon those involved. Thus, his zeal to attain a clearly defined change may have been exhausted by the struggle, particularly when the program had to be squeezed through one of the most inefficient and obdurate of contemporary bureaucracies. It is interesting to note that his scorn for bureaucrats developed at the same time he became opposed to all change, and that he returned in disgust to the placid and quiet life from which his reform activities had yanked him. Finally, of course, he was never an independent or original thinker, and the development through which he proceeded during these years may simply reflect the process through which the society he knew advanced.[42]

IV

The Petersburg Tutor

POBEDONOSTSEV'S entrée into high positions and into the centers of Moscow and St. Petersburg intellectual and social life was based on the artitcles he wrote in the late 1850's concerning the history of serfdom and the need for judicial reform. These and the quality of his work on the old judicial system led to his appointment as a lecturer at Moscow University, where the clarity and vigor of his lectures persuaded Count Stroganov to recommend his appointment in 1861 as special tutor for the heir to the throne, Grand Duke Nicholas Alexandrovich. Four months after the death of Nicholas in April, 1865, just before Pobedonostsev married, he was asked to become the tutor of the new heir, Alexander Alexandrovich, who became Alexander III in 1881. He accepted this appointment and moved to St. Petersburg in the fall of 1865, because he interpreted it as an imperial command and because he believed his future bride would prefer St. Petersburg and the increased salary and opportunity he would have.[1]

Pobedonostsev came to know the future Alexander III briefly in 1861 when he taught Russian civil law to Nicholas Alexandrovich, but he paid little attention to him then. His initial impression of Alexander was not especially favorable, and his correspondence with Catherine Tiutchev, which was naturally quite discreet, contains some remarkably unflattering comments about Alexander and his wife, the Danish fiancée of his late brother, whom Alexander married on October 20, 1866. Beginning in December, 1866, Pobedonostsev met three times a week with Alexander, four times with the future empress, and twice a week with one of Alexander's younger brothers, Vladimir. At first he considered Alexander a simple soul who was lazy and who used all of his energy trying to escape assignments. In December, 1868, he exclaimed that the future heir and his wife lived "like children in a wilderness, like sheep." Catherine Tiutchev wrote in 1875 that she pitied him for wasting time bending his mind "to an almost childish level, without even the hope of creating a man." Even after his pupil became tsar, Pobedonostsev often despaired of his understanding affairs of state and lamented his blind optimism.

The future empress also annoyed Pobedonostsev. She was homesick for Denmark, learned about Russia very slowly, seemed little interested in learning to speak Russian well, was often bored with her studies, and appeared empty-headed and dull. Moreover, Pobedonostsev did not enjoy reading to her in Russian, trying to persuade the young couple to speak Russian with each other, or assuming responsibility for their education in all fields of knowledge.

However, as the years passed and as he began to feel more comfortable with his pupils, he began to have hope. He thought that the happy marriage had made Alexander brighter, more cheerful, and more responsible, and that he had a "Russian heart." The future empress made considerable progress in understanding her new country and its history, and Pobedonostsev began to enjoy breakfast with the couple and their small children, whom he considered a kind of ideal family. Moreover, his relations with Alexander's younger brothers, Vladimir, Paul, and Sergei, were excellent, and Pobedonostsev began to feel at home in the various palaces to which his duties took him. The trips with the new heir through European Russia in the summers of 1866 and 1869 were both quite successful, and the Pobedonostsevs were invited in the summer of 1869 to travel to Denmark with the future ruler.[2]

Throughout the life of his charge, Pobedonostsev remained bothered by some of his personal habits, particularly his heavy drinking, and by what Pobedonostsev considered his lack of will and resolution. However, Pobedonostsev gradually acquired practical mastery over the mind of Alexander III. He benefited considerably from the authority he possessed as the scholarly professor, particularly since his pupil was not gifted intellectually, had not been prepared to be the heir until his older brother died suddenly, and tended to revere men who were well informed and who spoke with assurance and authority.

In any case, Pobedonostsev used his tutorial position to shape the views of his student. Alexander apparently was a young man of deep Orthodox faith before he came into contact with Pobedonostsev, but Pobedonostsev was immensely active in strengthening that faith and in emphasizing the ties between Orthodoxy and Russian national history. He persuaded Alexander to visit famous and beautiful monasteries and churches in northern Russia. He helped arrange summer tours to increase the heir's knowledge of Russian economic resources and of the wealth of Russian historical and cultural tradition. He suggested that he and his wife read the historical novels of Zagoskin and Lazhechnikov; he had Professor Sergei M. Soloviev, then the most distinguished Russian historian, meet with him for a series of talks and discussion about the main forces in Russian history; and he arranged lectures and panel meetings with other Moscow and St. Petersburg scholars. After two or three years, Pobedonostsev began to send him books dealing with current problems, such as those by Samarin on the Baltic Germans, Schuyler on Central Asia, and Pogodin or Popov on the Balkan Slavs. He introduced the heir to Ivan Aksakov's journal *Moskva* (Moscow), sent him the literature published by the panslav society, had him subscribe to Dostoevsky's *Grazhdanin* (The Citizen), and had Dostoevsky read him selections from his novels. By 1873 or so, Alexander was not only heavily influenced by Pobedonostsev's selections on Russian history and culture and on current issues, but began to turn to him for advice. The Balkan crisis and the Russo-Turkish War in 1877–78 brought them very close together; they talked and corresponded frequently about the issues and campaigns, and were in complete agreement. After the war, the creation of the Volunteer Fleet cemented their relationship because the heir was the honorary chairman of the Fleet and Pobedonostsev was vice-chairman and actual manager.

Consequently, by the late 1870's Pobedonostsev had indeed become the "grey eminence" for the future Alexander III, even criticizing the tsar and government ministers in his letters to his pupil. Their relationship was close and reflected basic agreement on everything affecting the Russian state. Except for one short period late in the summer of 1879, when a cool spell developed because of the Grand Duke's heavy drinking, they cooperated splendidly. Most important, Alexander III remained the student and disciple of Pobedonostsev in matters of public policy.[3]

Pobedonostsev's position in the court between 1866 and 1880 was based on his role as a tutor in the royal family, but he did have

other positions in the high bureaucracy. When he went to St. Petersburg in the fall of 1865, he was named a consultant to the Ministry
of Justice, but there is no evidence that he actually worked in the
Ministry. However, on February 19, 1868, the seventh anniversary
of the emancipation of the serfs, Alexander II named him a Senator,
an appointment which ended his worries about his career in the
bureaucracy. He was at first placed in the second department, but
in November, 1868, was shifted to the department which reviewed
civil court cases, where he developed a special interest in wills. It is
evident from his correspondence that he devoted enormous time to
the Senate, generally working from twelve until seven each day
except Saturday and Sunday, and that he found his colleagues of
very low quality, lazy, and inefficient.

On January 1, 1872, Pobedonostsev was made a member of the
Council of State, a promotion which he thought would make his
work easier, although he remained a Senator and continued his
tutoring duties as well. The Council of State was an advisory body
to the Emperor concerning projected laws. Most of the important
legislation or decrees of the nineteenth century were given their
final review and final drafting in the Council. The Council at this
time was also responsible for the administration of some important
non-Russian areas, such as the Baltic provinces, Georgia, and Kamchatka, and one of its departments kept under review the ministries which dealt with economic and financial affairs. Pobedonostsev's main responsibility was in the second department, which
dealt with civil and ecclesiastical affairs and which in 1872 was
headed by his old friend and teacher, Prince Oldenburg. Pobedonostsev's work in this division of the Council of State almost certainly contributed to his appointment as Director General of the
Holy Synod of the Russian Orthodox Church in April, 1880.

For the rest of his life he remained a member of both the Senate
and the Council of State. He was most conscientious, faithfully
attending the sessions of his own department and of the full Council
of State as well. The special committees to which he was appointed
no doubt reflect his own particular interests. After 1875 he was a
member of the special committee named to review the work of the
Ministry of Education; from 1876 through 1880, he served on a
committee on prisons; and in 1877, he joined a committee to review
the situation in the Baltic provinces, where Samarin had taught him
that the power of the German Protestants must be reduced.

Pobedonostsev's service in the highest levels of the bureaucracy naturally gave him some influence on Russian domestic policy, particularly in those fields in which he had considerable knowledge and strong points of view. At the same time, and perhaps more important, he came to have a clear understanding of the processes of the autocracy. His letters throughout the 1870's are filled with complaints about the quality of his colleagues and of the Russian administration in general, the incredible inefficiency and waste of time within the Senate and the Council of State, and the need for more vigorous leadership and more efficient management. In fact, the substance of his later views about autocratic government and the need to surround the tsar with a small elite group of highly competent, well-trained advisors almost certainly reflects his experiences in the St. Petersburg bureaucracy, from 1866 until 1880 in particular.[4]

Pobedonostsev developed a powerful dislike for St. Petersburg when he lived there for several months in 1861–62 to serve on the committee appointed to define the basic principles for the judicial reform. The months he spent there in 1863–64 on the judicial reform committee and the forty-two years he lived there after the fall of 1865 only increased his discontent and restlessness in Peter's capital. He retained his house on Bread Lane in Moscow and never purchased a home in St. Petersburg. He always felt in exile away from Moscow. Indeed, after he had lived in St. Petersburg for more than fifteen years, he wrote Catherine Tiutchev that it still seemed a foreign city and that he felt as though he were living in a brothel.[5]

The judicial reform campaign to which he devoted so much time and energy between 1859 and 1864 and his work with Kalachov, Zubkov, Zarudnyi, and the other members of the judicial committees brought him into stimulating contact with some of the most lively and learned people in Russia. Moreover, his scholarly work and his reputation as one of the liberals or reformers drew him to the attention of some of the leading salons in Moscow and in St. Petersburg at a time of relaxation when even official circles buzzed with fascinating projects and there was a kind of competition for the most articulate men of the day. Thus, Pobedonostsev was drawn into the circle of Prince Vladimir Odoevskii, in Moscow, when that celebrated critic and philanthropist moved from St. Petersburg to Moscow in the winter of 1862–63, and later into that of Grand Duchess Helen Pavlovna, when Pobedonostsev went to St. Petersburg in 1865. The men and women he met in these groups helped

to sustain his liberalism into the early 1870's, when his native conservatism, the peculiar view he had of court and official life, and his
reaction to Russian policies after the great reforms moved him into
a ruthlessly reactionary position.

Prince Odoevskii, who was especially close to Pobedonostsev during the last two or three years of the latter's residence in Moscow,
resembled some of the other Muscovites who contributed most to
his education and training. Born in 1803, Odoevskii was educated
in Moscow boarding schools and at Moscow University, where he
studied in a faculty of which Pobedonostsev's father was a member.
By the late 1820's, he had acquired a reputation as an original and
independent literary critic and as a man of burning social conscience. Indeed, his learning was so considerable, the range of subjects about which he wrote with wit and wisdom so great, and his
position in the main salons late in the 1830's so commanding that
even critics such as Belinsky considered him a great writer. At that
time, Odoevskii was a brilliant defender of the political and social
system, praised the landed aristocracy and saw no need to abolish
serfdom, declared that social inequality reflected only the nature of
man, and believed that progress could best be achieved if the bureaucracy were better educated and more virtuous. He wrote in
1835 that "government service is the only way Russians can serve
their country." He was a man of considerable human sympathy,
however, and he was the founder of a society for aiding the poor
which flourished for more than twenty years.[6]

Odoevskii's literary reputation began to decline in the 1840's,
when his creative energies and production failed to satisfy the high
expectations he had created. Perhaps because his estates ceased to
be profitable at the same time, in 1846 he became Assistant Director
of the St. Petersburg Public Library (now the Saltykov-Shchedrin
Library), a position he retained until he was named a Senator in
1862 and returned to Moscow. During the 1850's, he became a convinced partisan of the movement to abolish serfdom, and in the
1860's he was an enthusiastic advocate of the other changes which
followed emancipation. He was a particular advocate of increased
freedom of thought and expression, expanded education, civil
rights, and prison reform. However, while he saw the need for
radical reform of the social structure and of the courts and local
government, he did not believe constitutional monarchy was possible in Russia because of the "insufficient development of the Rus-

sian people." Indeed, he thought Russia would not be ready for an elected parliament for a century, and he considered that educating the landowning nobility was the country's central problem.

Enthusiastic, full of good cheer, a profound believer in education and in progress, convinced that the day on which the serfs had been emancipated was the happiest day of his life and that Alexander II was "the greatest of Russian tsars," Odoevskii brought a fresh new spirit and tone to Pobedonostsev's life. He was given special responsibility in the Senate for working in the eighth department, in which Pobedonostsev then held a high position. A hard worker who arrived at his office every morning before any of the clerks, Odoevskii brought his lunch with him and reminisced with Pobedonostsev as they relaxed in his quiet office. Odoevskii worked closely with Pobedonostsev for his first six months as a Senator, trying to master the main principles and procedures. In addition, he invited Pobedonostsev to his handsome old home on Smolensk boulevard, where Pobedonostsev met prominent and young artists and writers whom Odoevskii thought lively and interesting. Urbane, a polished and charming conversationalist whose mind and tongue ran nimbly over all the important events and people of the previous forty years, Odoevskii dazzled and delighted the young bureaucrat and scholar. In an essay he wrote about Odoevskii when he died in 1869 and in a letter he wrote about him thirty-five years later, Pobedonostsev spoke with most unusual affection about "the last of the good old days" and of the warmth, sympathy, and generous high hopes which Odoevskii radiated. When Pobedonostsev left Moscow for St. Petersburg, he cut off the influence toward a relaxed, humane, and optimistic view of life which Odoevskii had provided.[7]

Until her death in January, 1873, the Grand Duchess Helen Pavlovna and her salon helped make St. Petersburg somewhat resemble Moscow for the young jurist and scholar and kept his political views respectably close to the center. The Grand Duchess represented a liberalizing and humanizing force like that of Prince Odoevskii. Indeed, her death probably contributed seriously to the conservatism which burgeoned in Pobedonostsev during the years after 1864 and which became a rigid and relentless philosophy before 1880.

The Grand Duchess was born in Stuttgart in 1803 and educated largely in Paris. In December, 1823, she married a younger brother of Nicholas I, the Grand Duke Michael Pavlovich, who left her a widow in 1849. Even during the icy reign of Nicholas I, she drew around her interesting and exciting men and women. Blessed with enormous energy and greatly interested in assisting others, she helped establish schools and hospitals, created a program for helping the wounded during the Crimean War, and sponsored young writers and artists. Anton Rubinstein wrote that he never met her equal. Pobedonostsev was impressed by her sense of dignity, the grace and style she sought to impress upon Russian society, the confidence she patiently encouraged in talented young men and women, and the sensible and reasonable approach she displayed toward developing improved social institutions for Russia.

Grand Duchess Helen's greatest forte was identifying promising young men and in creating an atmosphere in her home which contributed to the flowering of their abilities. After the death of her husband and during the thaw of the first decade of the reign of Alexander II, she acquired enormous influence in the higher levels of Russian political and intellectual life. She was one of the earliest and most effective advocates of emancipation and also labored successfully for the other reforms, especially of the courts and of local government. Thus, she identified Nicholas Miliutin, one of the architects of emancipation, as early as 1846, helped give him the social graces and connections in high circles which he needed, prodded her nephew, Alexander II, to make use of Miliutin and others like him, and used her influence during the years from 1856 through 1861 to help break the various log jams which threatened on occasion to prevent or delay or cripple this great achievement. She and Miliutin freed her serfs in 1856 in a move designed to serve as a model for others who were interested but paralyzed by the complex problems involved.

Pobedonostsev came to the attention of Grand Duchess Helen when his articles on the court system were published, and he was drawn into her lively reformist circle when he went to St. Petersburg in 1861. There he encountered the men whom the Grand Duchess thought the most exciting and able in Russia. Fluent in several languages and interested in European culture, she also introduced him to interesting and important foreign visitors, who added an international touch to her soirées. Mikhailovsky Palace therefore became one of the few places in St. Petersburg for which Pobedonostsev had any affection. The musical soirées and the charity teas became of less political importance after 1863, when Miliutin's position declined somewhat and the Polish uprising dampened the enthusiasm of many for further changes. The Grand Duchess in the last ten years of her life therefore accented charities and the arts in her gatherings, which remained among the most international and stimulating in St. Petersburg.[8]

Grand Duchess Helen not only introduced the shy and reserved Pobedonostsev to some of the great names of Russian political and social life and to interesting foreign visitors, but she also gave him some insight into the ways of the world. Moreover, when Pobedonostsev brought his very young, provincial bride to the capital city in 1866, the great lady adopted the youngster, introduced her to St. Petersburg, and made her home a place of enlightenment and refuge. When the Grand Duchess died, at the age of 70, she was the closest friend in St. Petersburg of both Pobedonostsev, who was then forty-five, and of his wife, who was only twenty-five.[9]

Grand Duchess Helen's closest friend and associate was another widow of wide culture and humane views, great energy, intellectual ability, and forcefulness, Baroness Edith Raden, whom Pobedonostsev met in St. Petersburg in the winter of 1861–62 and who remained a close and humanistic friend until her death in September, 1885. Born in Kurland in a Baltic German family, Baroness Raden served at the court of Alexander II as a lady-in-waiting and was particularly close to the empress. She travelled extensively in western Europe with Grand Duchess Helen Pavlovna after the Crimean War, and she helped to arrange her soirées and other parties. Well educated, fluent in French as well as in German, vigorous and orderly in everything she undertook, she joined the Grand Duchess in efforts to promote reform in Russia and to bring together important and fascinating people.

Pobedonostsev was impressed by Baroness Raden's intellectual ability, energy, and self-assurance. He paid tribute to her remaining faithful to Lutheranism without adopting "the fanaticism so common among Germans." He exulted when she overcame the temptation to join the Catholic Church when a spiritual crisis and a visit to Rome tempted her. He rejoiced when she developed a great fondness for Orthodox Church services and for Russian history and tradition. He was similarly impressed by her remarkable charitable activities.

After 1866, Baroness Raden brought Pobedonostsev and his wife into her cultured circle. She helped to widen his intellectual horizons and to shake briefly his profound belief that only convinced members of the Russian Orthodox Church could be truly patriotic. Pobedonostsev listened to the long discussions which she had with Iurii Samarin, a burning nationalist, critical of the position and

role of the Baltic Germans, and to her vigorous defense of the virtues of the German aristocracy, their provincialism, love of work,
and conservatism. After she died in 1885, Pobedonostsev helped
Samarin's son publish their long correspondence on this issue, as
well as all of Samarin's other works. It is interesting that Pobedonostsev did not attack the Baltic Germans for their power at court
or their authority in the Baltic area until after Baroness Raden
died.[10]

Pobedonostsev helped to introduce Baroness Raden to old Muscovite religious and cultural traditions, particularly when she lived
for some time in Kostroma, one of his favorite old Russian cities
and one which had a convent which he thought particularly handsome and excellent. She, in return, brought Pobedonostsev into
contact both with numerous Western cultural influences and with
the waning Slavophil centers at the court, in particular with Samarin, who led a resolute campaign to reduce the privileges of the
Baltic Germans until he died in 1876—in Germany—and to unify
Russia under the direct rule of Russians. Samarin was a member of
the circle of Grand Duchess Helen in the 1850's and was an earnest
advocate of emancipation as early as 1856. Moreover, although he
had become conservative by 1870 and was strongly antisemitic,
throughout his life he supported "freedom of conscience, absolute
and for everyone without restriction." He defended the cultured
and civilized Slavophil doctrines of Khomiakov against more repressive programs, and he did not join the panslav movement in
the 1870's. Thus, Samarin in general reflected the culture and ur-
banity of the Grand Duchess and Baroness Raden and therefore
influenced Pobedonostsev as they did.[11]

There is no evidence that Pobedonostsev or any of his family
took part in the famous controversy between the Slavophils and the
Westerners in the early 1840's concerning the nature of Russia and
its future. His father died in 1843 as an old man. He had not engaged
in controversies of any kind, particularly over philosophy or the
philosophy of history, and it is quite unlikely that he was even interested in the quarrel. His brother Sergei was in his most active
period, but he wrote for both Westerner and Slavophil journals
and showed no partiality in or even knowledge of the dispute. Constantine himself was a youngster in the School of Jurisprudence in
St. Petersburg while the battle raged in Moscow, but he must naturally have been aware of the issues, even though he may not have
understood them fully or taken even a modest position. When he

had completed his schooling and had begun his work in the Senate, the formal discussion was ended. Moreover, he was never especially interested in abstract ideas; he thought all such discussions wasteful and even harmful. In any case, there is no evidence concerning his stand in this controversy, and it is almost certain that he concentrated entirely upon his own work and ignored the dispute. Samarin, who revered Khomiakov and who had long discussions with Baroness Raden in the apartments of Grand Duchess Helen about the nature of Russia, was therefore of especial importance because he introduced Pobedonostsev directly to the Slavophil doctrine and to the Slavophils active in Moscow and St. Petersburg in the twenty years after the Crimean War.

Pobedonostsev's service as a tutor to the tsar's children opened other avenues into the Slavophil circle. At the end of the tour through European Russia in the summer of 1863 with Grand Duke Nicholas Alexandrovich, he vacationed briefly in the Crimea with the imperial family. There he became acquainted with one of the ladies-in-waiting, Anna Tiutchev, a daughter of the celebrated Slavophil poet, who was tutoring the Grand Duchess Maria Alexandrovna and the Grand Duke Sergei. This friendship led to Pobedonostsev's acquaintance with the great poet. Moreover, Anna Tiutchev in January, 1866, married Ivan Aksakov, the irrepressible and often irresponsible tribune of the panslav movement with whom Pobedonostsev was in frequent, sometimes cautious, contact until Aksakov died in January, 1886.[12]

At the time Pobedonostsev became acquainted with Fedor Tiutchev, the romantic poet had become a deep conservative. Yet he had approved the reforms instituted by Alexander II, although he had not advocated any of them. Moreover, despite being chairman of the committee responsible for censoring foreign literature and a member of the committee which kept the Russian press under review, he believed the restrictions too tight, even during the thaw after 1856, and urged that writers and journalists be given more freedom. A man who spent a large part of his life abroad, partly as a diplomat, Tiutchev spoke French and German and was as familiar with the works of Lamartine, Heine, and Goethe as he was with those of Pushkin. Nevertheless, after the Crimean War in particular, he was violently anti-Western, often denouncing the West, especially the Papacy, and speaking of "the eternal antagonism of East and West"—in fluent French. He was also a vigorous panslav. He attended the celebrated Moscow congress of panslavs in 1867, and he saw this movement, led by the Russians, as an important weapon for revenge over those who had triumphed in the Crimean War.

Pobedonostsev was a great admirer of Tiutchev, his poetry, and his profound Russian nationalism. Indeed, one of Tiutchev's poems attacking Lutheranism so excited Pobedonostsev that he could barely sleep after reading it. He enjoyed evenings at the Tiutchevs' or parties which the poet attended. He even helped Tiutchev's youngest son obtain a position in the Senate in Moscow when he graduated from the School of Jurisprudence in 1867, the kind of favor he ordinarily refused to seek for anyone, even close relatives.[13]

Tiutchev's son-in-law, Ivan Aksakov, was born just four years earlier than Pobedonostsev and completed four years of schooling in the School of Jurisprudence in St. Petersburg in 1842. Aksakov then worked in the Senate in Moscow. It seems most likely that Pobedonostsev and Aksakov would have met, but there is no evidence that they were acquainted before Anna Tiutchev and Aksakov were married in January, 1866. The Aksakovs lived for the next twenty years in Moscow, and the correspondence between Anna Aksakov and Pobedonostsev was often strained and sometimes broken because of some of Aksakov's policies as a newspaper publisher and editor. Pobedonostsev wrote, "There are few men as pure and honest and with such a burning love for Russia and for everything Russian" as Aksakov. Even when he was bitterly annoyed with Aksakov for his attacks on the government's policy in the Russo-Turkish War in 1877–78 and at the Congress of Berlin, Pobedonostsev admitted it was impossible not to love and respect Aksakov, and to appreciate his patriotism and his love for the Russian people. However, he thought him a child in political and administrative affairs, and noted that Aksakov "goes in a straight line" and did not know that "curves rule" in human affairs. Above all, he thought him irresponsible in his continued defense of the judicial reform of 1864, his struggle for more freedom for the press, and his efforts for religious freedom for the Old Believers. However, in spite of the frequent friction between Aksakov and Pobedonostsev, Anna Aksakov kept open the line of communication, providing Pobedonostsev another important link with the Moscow Slavophils and panslavs and with those members of the court who shared Aksakov's vigorous, nationalistic views.[14]

Of all Pobedonostsev's friends, Catherine Tiutchev was clearly the closest and exerted the most influence. Pobedonostsev became acquainted with Catherine through her sister Anna, and the two exchanged a total of more than five hundred letters between 1866 and Catherine's death in Moscow on March 11, 1882. They were brought together originally by their roles at court and by their interest in court politics. Catherine served as a lady-in-waiting for the Empress between 1859 and 1862, when her poor health (tuberculosis) forced her to retire and to divide her life between Moscow and a country estate at Varvarino.

The interests which Pobedonostsev and Catherine Tiutchev shared were fortified by their common affection for the Russian Orthodox faith and for Moscow. She kept him in contact with his native city and served as a confidante to whom alone he could entrust his views concerning policies, conflicts within the court and the high bureaucracy, and even the faults of the emperor, the heir to the throne, and other members of the imperial family. Pobedonostsev was often so candid in his letters to Catherine Tiutchev that he worried that they be read in the post, so he had them delivered by hand by friends who were going to Moscow. A week after she died, he obtained all of his correspondence with Catherine from her sister Anna, retaining it until he died in 1907. This voluminous correspondence not only serves as a splendid source concerning fifteen years of Russian history, but provided him a test of his attitudes and views against the shrewd and critical mind of an uncommonly perceptive woman who knew well the atmosphere and the people of which he wrote.

Catherine Tiutchev was indeed a remarkable woman. Educated in part in Europe, fluent in English, French, and German, and of independent judgment, she served as a stimulating intellectual correspondent, criticizing books and artitcles he had written, reading Emerson or Le Play at his suggestion, and in turn persuading him to read some of the volumes which most excited her, from eighteenth century memoirs of Russian, Prussian, Austrian, or French statesmen to Bossuet, de Maistre, Stein, Froude, Carlyle, and Palmerston. She was also frank in her criticism when he advocated policies restricting the rights of Old Believers or throttling the Russian press. Indeed, her death, and that of Baroness Raden in 1885, removed important humanistic influences from Pobedonostsev, who had already become thoroughly repressive in his policies.[15]

Most of the women Pobedonostsev met socially in Moscow and St. Petersburg were married and considerably older than he. However, when he married on January 9, 1866, at the age of thirty-eight, he selected a young girl of eighteen, the daughter of a landowner near Mogilev in Smolensk province who was a niece of one of his classmates in the School of Jurisprudence and a member of a family known well by Baroness Raden. Pobedonostsev's marriage to Catherine Alexandrovna Engelhardt was a very important step in his life. His engagement, July 14, 1865, came as a complete surprise to Anna Aksakov and his other friends. Indeed, the letter in which Pobedonostsev announced his betrothal is extraordinarily revealing:

I have always loved children, loved to become acquainted with them, loved to join them in their childish games. Ten years ago, God sent me a dear child, my Katia, a seven-year-old girl, niece of my classmate Engelhardt, when I visited him in· the country. I came to know her as any child, recognized her deep soul, and became attached to her with all my heart. I sought to awaken her to the good and the true. I talked with her about God, I prayed with her. I read to her and taught her, I sat with her for hours and days, and she grew up and developed before my eyes. The more I looked into her soul, the more deeply I devoted myself to her and confided my soul to her. She loved me deeply and tenderly with all her childish soul, and my first happiness was looking into her soul, standing over it, guarding it, bringing joy to it.

The years passed, my Katia grew up, and fear fell upon me: what will happen when my child grows up before my very eyes into a young lady? She grew up and there was a time when it seemed my Katia had left me and had got out of my hands. That was a difficult time, that time when I lived in Petersburg and in Tsarskoe Selo.

It seemed to me that my Katia was lost for me, but now I see that God at that time was testing me and punishing me. He punished me, but he did not put me to death. I do not know how—I know that I did not do it but that God did—my Katia again returned to me. But then last year all dissolved in misunderstanding; we entered into new relations in shyness and timidity. Our relations were only pale shadows of our earlier ones, and I began to think that all was ended and began to close all the doors around myself and to abandon all hope. However, I felt that I was necessary for her, that her heart fully believed in me alone, that she trusted in and relied upon me alone— but whether or not she loved me, that I did not know and could not find out.

I arrived here July 4 and spent a whole week troubled. We

both felt that we could not even talk freely and easily about anything so long as we could not clear up this misunderstanding, but neither of us could say a word about it. The position was becoming impossible, and I in fear decided to tell all to my Katia. Then there was a whole day of fear and agitation. Finally, I heard the word my soul had waited for, and my happiness appeared before all. Oh, to what a wide-open place God has brought me from sorrow and darkness.[16]

The Engelhardts were a Baltic German family who had moved into the Mogilev-Smolensk area, where Mrs. Pobedonostsev had a number of relatives who were landowners. Close relatives also resided in Warsaw, and an uncle of Mrs. Pobedonostsev, Baron von Engelhardt, was a celebrated astronomer in Dresden at that time. These family connections, her knowledge of Western languages, and her interest in Western culture increased Pobedonostsev's interest in Europe, which was already strong. Thus, although he had not been able to travel abroad before his marriage, he visited Europe more than twenty times before the turn of the century, accompanied in every case by his wife.[17]

Catherine Engelhardt was in some ways an ideal companion for Pobedonostsev, but her age, shyness, health, and the problems her family created certainly had a powerful influence in making him a lonely, gloomy, and ferociously antisocial statesman. No photographs of her have survived, even though she lived until 1932. Moreover, none of her friends or acquaintances has left descriptions of her. Even foreign visitors, such as the archbishop of York, who visited her school and commented upon her excellent English and French and upon her wide knowledge, provide us no information concerning her physical appearance. She was a woman of deep religious faith who enjoyed Orthodox religious services and who looked forward to spending Passion week in a monastery, usually the Sergiev monastery, between St. Petersburg and Peterhof. She possessed a clear and retentive mind, loved to read both Russian and Western literature, and appreciated travel and life abroad. When he was ill, she often read him French novels or English history. She had a particular fondness for Pushkin, and in 1888, Pobedonostsev had published a handsome limited edition of Pushkin poems which she had selected, *Severnye tsvety* (Northern Flowers), which he presented to Russian and foreign friends. In 1897, the Holy Synod printing office published her translation of a popular sentimental English novel, *The Mighty Atom*, by Minnie Mackay, under the pseudonym of Marie Corelli, who was a kind of Fannie Hurst in late Victorian England. *The Mighty Atom* was a most effective attack upon what the French call "lay schools," or schools in which there was no religious education, and Mrs. Pobedonostsev's translation reached a fifth edition in 1911. She probably also assisted her husband in the numerous translations he made from English, of which her command was conspicuously better than his.[18]

There is no record of any discontent or dissatisfaction on Pobedonostsev's part with his wife, except for the great disappointment, expressed often in the first years of their marriage, that they had no children. However, just as his solitary and quiet life of work in his office and in his study must have made life dreary for his young bride, so her inability to meet effectively even the minimal social obligations St. Petersburg imposed must have annoyed and hampered him. While the young and provincial Mrs. Pobedonostsev was perfectly at ease in small groups, especially with Pobedonostsev's elderly friends, she was unable to conduct a satisfactory conversation in large gatherings. Basically, therefore, Mrs. Pobedonostsev's social life in the 1870's was restricted to the circle of two *grandes dames*, both almost fifty years older than she. Indeed, she had been married fifteen years before she met her husband's closest friend and correspondent, Catherine Tiutchev. By 1890, perhaps even before that, she had abandoned society altogether, except for brief appearances at those formal palace functions which they found it impossible to escape. As a young man in a family which much enjoyed the theater, Pobedonostsev had frequently attended the opera and the theater, but he saw only one play during the last thirty years of his life, although he continued to read the works of Shakespeare, Ibsen, and other great dramatists.[19]

In 1880, Mrs. Pobedonostsev was drawn into two charitable activities which absorbed a considerable amount of her time and energy thereafter. When her husband helped establish and then directed for several years the Volunteer Fleet (used in time of peace to ferry troops and convicts to the Russian Far East and to engage in trade with China and designed to provide a reserve of cruisers for naval war), she became interested in the island of Sakhalin and the welfare of the convicts, their families, and others who lived there. Consequently, in 1880 she began annual campaigns to collect funds, food, clothing, and books for Sakhalin. The Grand Duchess Catherine Mikhailovna also persuaded her to establish a school for girls interested in teaching in rural areas, and St. Vladimir's occupied a great deal of her time after 1880. The school had approximately one hundred students. It emphasized religious instruction, and Mrs. Pobedonostsev sought to prepare young ladies who would marry priests and help them establish parish schools.[20]

Mrs. Pobedonostsev influenced Pobedonostsev's working habits and isolation in other ways as well. Perhaps because of the St. Petersburg climate, perhaps because she was frail, she was constantly ill. Pobedonostsev's correspondence with Catherine Tiutchev and even with some of the Orthodox church hierarchy is studded with references to her continued poor health. She was seriously ill only through the winter of 1875–76, and she died in 1932, twenty-five years after her husband, but her constant poor health strengthened his tendency to live a solitary existence and to attend social functions and court affairs only when absolutely necessary.

Pobedonostsev's elderly mother-in-law lived with the newly married couple until she died after a prolonged illness in May, 1874. Three years later, Mrs. Pobedonostsev's eighty-four-year-old aunt succumbed after living with them for more than a decade. Pobedonostsev's wife not only served as nurse for these two old ladies during their last painful months, but also assumed responsibility for raising her younger brother and sister in their home. Vladimir, who was born about the time the Pobedonostsevs were married, was a very heavy burden because he too was afflicted with poor health and may have been mentally retarded. The Pobedonostsev correspondence of the 1870's is full of references to the labor he caused Mrs. Pobedonostsev, who had to care for him and tutor him.

Sonia Engelhardt, Mrs. Pobedonostsev's headstrong and melancholy younger sister, caused even more trouble. He was never able to control this young lady, who defied him in her reading habits, in her diet of chocolates, and in her tantrums. In the spring of 1877, against his wishes, she volunteered to serve as a nurse with the Russian forces in the Balkans. There, exhausted by overwork, she acquired typhus. Her health was so damaged that Mrs. Pobedonostsev had to leave her husband to take care of her. Moreover, while serving in a field hospital in Bulgaria, Sonia fell in love with a member of General Skobelev's staff, Colonel A. A. Bogoliubov, who was so badly wounded during the war that he was not able to come to St. Petersburg for more than two years. Pobedonostsev had then to agree most reluctantly to their marriage, although the colonel was badly crippled and had no position or promise of one.

Several months after Sonia's marriage, Bogoliubov was appointed

to the customs office in Baku. However, he had hardly been there a
year when he died of typhus. Mrs. Pobedonostsev, who had made all
of the arrangements for the marriage, then had to assume responsibility for the funeral. Sonia lived with the Pobedonostsevs for the
next fifteen years, constituting a heavy drain because of her fits of
despondency, her poor health, and her general helplessness.[21]

Two other trials and tragedies harassed the Pobedonostsevs early
in the 1880's, tended to isolate them from the social world, and
strengthened their intense dislike for public opinion. It is quite
likely that there was little real warmth or affection between the
Pobedonostsevs by 1880 or so, and the young wife—thirty-five years
old in 1882, when her husband was fifty-five—may on occasion have
resented the cheerless and ascetic life they led. In any case, in the
fall and winter of 1882, malicious rumors were common in St.
Petersburg that the Pobedonostsev marriage was collapsing and
that Mrs. Pobedonostsev was going to divorce him and marry
Nicholas Baranov, a fiery and irresponsible captain who had been
cashiered from the navy in December, 1879, but who served before
and after that as Pobedonostsev's deputy director of the Volunteer
Fleet. The rumors almost certainly had no foundation, except perhaps a certain restlessness and lack of deep happiness on the part
of Mrs. Pobedonostsev. However, the gossip did circulate. Pobedonostsev, a man of great propriety and then the lay head of the
Synod of the Orthodox Church, must have been profoundly upset.
His withering scorn for society, for idle minds and gossip, and for
the outside world in general was enormously increased.[22]

The second scandal involved Mrs. Pobedonostsev's father, Alexander Alexandrovich Engelhardt, and was even more important
because it was discussed in the Ministry of Finance for two years
and flurries of comment appeared in the press. In April, 1883, Pobedonostsev made his only personal plea to the tsar for a special favor
in order to keep the case of "the senile old man" from the courts
and to close the issue by administrative order. This petition was
quietly honored during the celebrations surrounding the coronation of Alexander III the next month. However, the scars left by this
affair on Pobedonostsev were deep and affected his attitude toward
his associates and the press from that time forward.

Engelhardt was raised in a wealthy, luxury-loving, relaxed landowning family, but the family and clan fortunes had all evaporated
by the time Pobedonostsev married his daughter. Sometime in the
late 1860's or early 1870's, Pobedonostsev obtained a position for

his father-in-law in the customs office in Taganrog. In May and June, 1881, he and thirty-four other officials were accused of embezzlement of state funds over a long period of time. Many of those whom Pobedonostsev had angered late in April of that year for the way in which he had upset the plans of General Loris-Melikov and most other government leaders for some slight modification of the autocratic government, referred to generally as the "Loris-Melikov constitution," must have rejoiced at these charges. Pobedonostsev was deeply hurt, and was bewildered when even his landlady accepted the truth of the charges and when most of his associates treated him as the relative of a known thief.

The Pobedonostsevs suffered several harrowing periods, especially in the summer of 1881, when a zealous official in the Ministry of Finance made the charges public, and in March, 1882, when the Ministry of Finance debated whether or not to bring the men to trial. Boris Chicherin, who had been a friend of Pobedonostsev's since they were colleagues on the law faculty of Moscow University, broke with Pobedonostsev at this time because of his policy on the Loris-Melikov plan and because the government official who posed as the most righteous of all intervened to protect a relative. Chicherin also asserted that his ruthlessness toward the bureaucracy and toward the press increased enormously at that time.[23]

V

Dostoevsky

FEDOR M. DOSTOEVSKY and Pobedonostsev were close acquaintances from late 1871 until January, 1881, when Dostoevsky died,
not long before the assassination of Alexander II elevated Pobedonostsev to great prominence as the "grey eminence" of Alexander
III. This relationship and the influence each of these men exercised
has led many scholars to make careless comparisons of their ideas
and, in particular, to compare the Dostoevsky of the 1870's with the
Pobedonostsev of the 1890's. Moreover, scholars have also been
fascinated concerning the influence these men may have exerted
upon each other, particularly because of the great role Pobedonostsev played in Russian history between 1880 and 1905 and because
of claims he made after Dostoevsky's death concerning his responsibility for some of Dostoevsky's achievements, especially his last
novel, *The Brothers Karamazov*. Thus, within two days after Dostoevsky's death, Pobedonostsev wrote to Ivan Aksakov that Dostoevsky frequently spent his Saturday evenings with him, that the
novelist "conceived his Zosima according to my instructions," and
that they had been in complete agreement since they had worked
together on the journal, *Grazhdanin* (The Citizen) in 1873. Late
in his life, Pobedonostsev twice wrote in letters to Dostoevsky's
widow that Dostoevsky had discussed the novel with him as he
wrote it. Finally, just after he had finished *The Brothers Karamazov*
and returned to *The Diary of a Writer*, Dostoevsky himself wrote to
Pobedonostsev, "Then I shall again run to you, as I came to you in
other days, for instructions, which I am sure you will not refuse
me."[1]

These claims and data have led some scholars, especially several Soviet scholars in the periods when Dostoevsky has not been viewed sympathetically by the Soviet authorities, to assert that Dostoevsky had been powerfully influenced by the man who after 1881 served as the symbol for reaction in Russia. Leonid Grossman, who has published careful and valuable collections and analyses of Dostoevsky materials, even asserted in 1934 that Pobedonostsev "directed Dostoevsky's work" and that Dostoevsky would have exerted a powerful influence through Pobedonostsev on Russian state policy in the 1880's, if he had lived.[2]

Scholars interested in Dostoevsky or in Pobedonostsev, or in both, have not been able to determine the degree to which they influenced each other, or indeed to describe with confidence the entire relationship between them during the 1870's, in spite of the masses of material they both published and in spite of the quantities of letters and other documents which have been made public. However, now that the Soviet government has allowed foreign scholars to study the immense mass of unpublished Pobedonostsev material and to review published material not available outside the Soviet Union, such as *Grazhdanin*, edited by Dostoevsky in 1873–74, to which Pobedonostsev contributed twenty-two articles, it is possible to assess the relationship with some accuracy.[3]

Some questions still remain unsolved, but may approach solution when Dostoevsky materials not now available are published. Others, in particular that concerning any influence Pobedonostsev may have exerted upon Dostoevsky in the last year of Dostoevsky's life, are probably beyond satisfactory solution, because of the virtual impossibility of determining to what degree one man has influenced another, particularly in the field of literature. After careful analysis of all the evidence, I have concluded that the ideas or philosophies of the two men were in many ways similar, but that there were also basic differences. The two men were close acquaintances for almost ten years, but they were profoundly different in personality and interests. Each had a different definition or concept of the West, which powerfully affected all of his thinking. In addition, both men had defined their fundamental philosophical positions before they met, and their general agreement during the months they each wrote for *Grazhdanin* demonstrates that neither influenced the other appreciably. Finally, while Dostoevsky's last novel "contains many echoes of Dostoevsky's conversations with Pobedonostsev," Dostoevsky's basic ideas were "apparent in Dostoevsky's work earlier," and *The Brothers Karamazov* is the product solely of Dostoevsky's genius.[4]

Dostoevsky and Pobedonostsev met sometime late in 1871 at the home of Prince Vladimir Meshcherskii, a prominent courtier and author. Meshcherskii had played with the children of Alexander II when they were youngsters and apparently became acquainted with Pobedonostsev in 1863, when Pobedonostsev was a tutor of the heir to the throne and was assisting in preparing the judicial reform of 1864. In 1866, Meshcherskii accompanied the young man who was to become Alexander III and his tutors on a two-week trip, including Tver, Kostroma, and Kazan, and apparently he and Pobedonostsev were close acquaintances by the winter of 1871–72, when Meshcherskii began to think seriously of undertaking publication of a new weekly, *Grazhdanin*. Dostoevsky and Pobedonostsev were among the "godfathers" of the journal, and they apparently met at the Meshcherskii home to discuss the future of the journal. The first issue appeared in January, 1872, and in December of that year, Pobedonostsev was among the group which decided that Dostoevsky should replace G. K. Gradovskii as editor. The great novelist accepted the post on December 15, for a salary of 3,000 rubles per year (approximately $1,500) and additional payment for each line he contributed. The third section of His Majesty's Own Chancery approved the appointment three days later, and the change was announced in the January 25, 1873, issue. Apparently, one of the conditions Dostoevsky named was the active participation of the "godfathers" through extensive contributions to the journal, a condition which Pobedonostsev and the others readily accepted.[5]

In 1871, at fifty years of age, Dostoevsky was already recognized as one of the giants of Russian literature, with *Notes from the Underground, Crime and Punishment, The Idiot,* and other distinguished novels among his most significant achievements. He was also in the midst of writing *The Possessed,* which was published serially in Katkov's *Russkii vestnik* (Russian Herald) between January, 1871, and December, 1872. Moreover, by late 1871 he was clearly one of the most authoritative reactionary and anti-Western voices in Russia. At the same time, he was debt-ridden, and he lacked connections with important political and intellectual circles. In particular, he lacked—and sought—an entrée to the court, which Prince Meshcherskii and Pobedonostsev could provide.

Pobedonostsev in 1871 was forty-four years old. He was recognized as a rising man, particularly because of his close association with the heir to the throne, and he was also considered a scholar of some distinction. Apparently the distinguished conservative novelist, fresh from an unhappy experience in western Europe, and the bureaucrat impressed each other. In any case, by 1873 they were intellectual companions. Pobedonostsev was one of those to whom Dostoevsky read the Stavrogin confession in 1872 and who advised him not to publish it. During 1873, he contributed twenty-two articles to *Grazhdanin*, a mark of his special friendship for the great novelist, because he rarely wrote for journals such as the one Dostoevsky was then editing.[6]

The mass of material now available indicates that Dostoevsky and Pobedonostsev were close friends between 1873 and January, 1881, when Dostoevsky died, although there is some evidence of a quarrel in December, 1873, and there are no letters between the two men from that month until January, 1876. They frequently met Saturday evenings in Pobedonostsev's apartment for three or four hours of talk. Dostoevsky had a portrait of Pobedonostsev in his home, and his library contained copies of most of Pobedonostsev's books. Apparently he was especially impressed by Pobedonostsev's 1869 translation of Thomas à Kempis, and his admiration of Pobedonostsev as an intellect and a scholar was very high; when Pobedonostsev's *Istoricheskiia izsledovaniia i stat'i* (Historical Studies and Essays) was published in 1876, he wrote, "This [book] must be particularly serious, beautiful, and scholarly. I expect something very significant in this book, because he has an enormous mind." They exchanged cards on birthdays, introduced each other to distinguished friends, visited each other when ill, recommended Russian and foreign books and newspaper articles to each other, and provided materials for each other's work. When Dostoevsky died, Pobedonostsev arranged for a state funeral and for burial in the Alexander Nevsky monastery, ensured that Dostoevsky's widow receive a pension of 2,000 rubles a year, and served as executor of Dostoevsky's will and guardian of his children.[7]

Pobedonostsev also assisted Dostoevsky's widow from 1881 until he died in 1907. He advised her on business policies with publishers and on arrangements with relatives; he gave her financial advice; he sent her documents and clippings for her collection of materials concerning her husband; he gave advice when others wished to make use of this collection; and he kept important papers for her in the Holy Synod safe. The wives became close friends. Mrs. Dostoevsky had often accompanied the novelist on his Saturday evening visits, and there is some evidence the wives remained friends until Mrs. Dostoevsky died in 1918.[8]

For Pobedonostsev, friendship with Dostoevsky must have been a most stimulating and challenging experience, if only because in 1865 he had abandoned his beloved Moscow and his scholarly career for life in the high bureaucracy and court of St. Petersburg in an atmosphere which he never came to like. The number of his acquaintances and friends among Russian intellectuals was not great, because of his reserved nature, his official position, and the wide gap between his views and those of most writers and artists on the most critical issues facing Russia. He enjoyed talking with the distinguished historian, Sergei Soloviev, when he was in Moscow, and he was fascinated by the lectures of Vladimir Soloviev on the philosophy of religion in the winter of 1878. Indeed, he often wrote that his favorite evening was one spent with two or three able and lively writers. Such discussions refreshed him, revived memories of earlier literary circles, and illuminated the most basic issues Russia faced.

Even so, Pobedonostsev knew few Russian intellectuals. The poets Maikov and Polonskii were among his associates, and he had a slight acquaintance with Goncharov, but the other leaders of his generation were unknown to him. In spite of his long concern over the ideas and influence of Leo Tolstoy, he apparently never met the great writer. In fact, he read *War and Peace* for the first time in Salzburg in September, 1875. Pobedonostsev must therefore have welcomed and especially enjoyed close association with one of Russia's most distinguished novelists, particularly when their views on many issues were similar.[9]

For Dostoevsky, friendship with Pobedonostsev brought a number of advantages, of which the most obvious, but perhaps the least important, was introduction into high bureaucratic and court circles. Dostoevsky's history was considerably different from that of Pobedonostsev, and the novelist welcomed access to the kind of society which often annoyed Pobedonostsev. Dostoevsky was born into the lower middle class, his father had been an unsuccessful army doctor, and his early life had been marked by poverty, misfortune, and poor health. *Poor Folk* in 1846 made Dostoevsky a literary celebrity almost overnight, but he was arrested in 1849 because he was a member of the Petrashevtsy Circle, and he spent ten years in Siberia, after his sentence of execution had been halted at the last minute. He lived much of the period between 1862 and 1871 in western Europe, particularly in Germany, and he was not well known to Russian leaders and intellectuals, in spite of his achievements.

In this situation, because of his influence and because of his acquaintance with some of the most interesting and competent bureaucrats and intellectuals in St. Petersburg, Pobedonostsev was able to provide some protection for Dostoevsky as an editor, to attract subscribers, and to introduce him into the principal social circles. Prince Meshcherskii remarked in his *Memoirs* that Pobedonostsev had been made a consultant or "godfather" to *Grazhdanin* in order to provide advice and assistance with the censors; apparently, Pobedonostsev by writing for *Grazhdanin* in 1873, even though anonymously, by advising Dostoevsky on editorial problems, and by interceding with government officials at critical times did help shield the new journal from the censor. Even so, the October 10, 1873, issue was barred from sale because of comments concerning education and the zemstvos; trouble was barely avoided in January, 1874, over comments concerning Grand Duchess Maria Alexandrovna; and a warning was issued after the March 11, 1874, issue commented on the Baltic-German problem.[10]

Grazhdanin had only one thousand subscribers when it was launched early in 1872, and Pobedonostsev devoted much effort to persuading important friends, especially among the clergy, to subscribe, and to persuading some intellectuals to write for it. When Meshcherskii applied to the heir, Grand Duke Alexander Alexandrovich, for a subsidy for *Grazhdanin*, Alexander turned immediately to Pobedonostsev for advice, as Meshcherskii must have assumed he would. Apparently Alexander decided in 1873 not to provide a subvention for the journal, but Witte noted in 1892 and 1893 that Meshcherskii was then receiving 80,000 rubles a year for *Grazhdanin*, at a time when the ruble was valued at approximately fifty cents and long before the waves of inflation which have swept the world in the twentieth century.[11]

Pobedonostsev wrote a number of letters to the future tsar recommending Dostoevsky's articles very strongly. He sought also to have other members of the imperial family subscribe to and read *Grazhdanin*, and, later, *The Diary of a Writer*, which Dostoevsky published as a monthly in 1876 and 1877, with other issues in August, 1880, and January, 1881.

Pobedonostsev was especially effective in putting Dostoevsky's novels and other writings into the hands of the tsar and the members of the imperial family. He forwarded copies of Dostoevsky's latest books to various grand dukes, and he arranged in December, 1880, for Dostoevsky to meet the heir and his wife and to present them an autographed copy of *The Brothers Karamazov*. Indeed, the Grand Duchess Maria Fedorovna attended a reading of a part of *The Brothers Karamazov*. In addition, Pobedonostsev introduced the great novelist into the important salons, particularly after 1876. Through Admiral Arseniev, Pobedonostsev had Dostoevsky introduced to the tsar's youngest sons, the Grand Dukes Sergei and Paul. He also persuaded the tsar's brother, Grand Duke Constantine, to invite Dostoevsky to serve as a tutor in contemporary history and literature for his two sons, Constantine and Dmitrii. The Grand Duke Dmitrii attended Dostoevsky's funeral, while Sergei, Paul, and Constantine, who were abroad, sent telegrams of condolence to the widow.[12]   *130443*

Pobedonostsev also provided Dostoevsky with information which was incorporated, directly or indirectly, into his work. He frequently sent Dostoevsky newspaper clippings which illustrated principles on which they were in general agreement. He forwarded clippings on Russian education, the intelligentsia, anarchists, anticlericalism, the decline of Protestantism and Catholicism in western Europe, Turgenev, relations between Germans and Slavs, and Russian qualities. He probably suggested Dostoevsky visit Father Amvrosii, a monk in Optina monastery, whom Dostoevsky did visit in 1878 and who served as a kind of model for Zosima in *The Brothers Karamazov*. In February, 1879, he gave Dostoevsky a book on the funeral of monks for use in the description of the Zosima funeral, which was published in *Russkii vestnik* in September of that year. In August, 1880, he forwarded an article attacking Russian courts to supplement annotated material he had sent earlier from his three-volume *Kurs grazhdanskago prava* (Course on Civil Law). Perhaps the most explicit illustration is the data he forwarded to Dostoevsky in June, 1876, concerning the tragic suicide of Herzen's daughter: this information was published by Dostoevsky in the October, 1876, issue of *The Diary of a Writer*.[13]

Pobedonostsev also served Dostoevsky as a critic, a function for which he was well prepared by the nature of their friendship, by his wide knowledge of Russian and Western literature, and by his acute critical sense. Dostoevsky had a very high regard for Pobedonostsev's critical acumen. Indeed, on several occasions he wrote that Pobedonostsev was "a person whose opinion I value very highly."

Dostoevsky and Pobedonostsev worked very closely together when the novelist was editor of *Grazhdanin*, from January, 1873, until April, 1874, and Pobedonostsev was a constant critic of the columns Dostoevsky wrote in *The Diary of a Writer*. He persuaded Dostoevsky not to incorporate materials and opinions he thought might damage their cause; thus, in 1876, he persuaded the novelist not to describe his experiences in a séance with a renowned medium. He commented in letters, and presumably even more in their extended conversations, concerning the style and the substance of the columns, and his interest and encouragement had some influence in Dostoevsky's decision to continue to write these essays. It is apparent that Dostoevsky's famous memorial address for Pushkin in June, 1880, reflected much discussion with Pobedonostsev concerning the general theme of the lecture and the reaction it would create, although it is also clear that Pobedonostsev had not read the speech before it was given. Referring to his draft of the speech, Dostoevsky wrote that he and Pobedonostsev were of the same spirit and were in complete agreement.[14]

However, there is no evidence to indicate that Dostoevsky was influenced significantly by Pobedonostsev in writing his last and probably best novel, *The Brothers Karamazov*. Dostoevsky started writing the novel in 1878, and it began to appear serially in January, 1879; however, the first reference to it in the Dostoevsky- Pobedonostsev correspondence, or in any of the Pobedonostsev material, is a letter Dostoevsky wrote on May 19, 1879, to Pobedonostsev. Pobedonostsev wrote detailed, perceptive, and appreciative critical comments on the Grand Inquisitor sketch and on Ivan Karamazov's denial of God, particularly the powerful section on the sufferings inflicted upon children. He also pointed out to Dostoevsky that the novel needed a counterpart to the Ivan Karamazov denial of God, and he did provide material for the Zosima funeral section. However, while Dostoevsky sometimes talked about the novel to "cure his spirit," there is no evidence in these letters that the two men had discussed these parts of the novel before they were written or while they were being composed. Indeed, Pobedonostsev's comments always reveal that he had not seen the material before publication, as he did see or hear part of *The Possessed* in 1872. Moreover, it is almost certain that Dostoevsky had the Russian monk section in mind as early as 1878, when he visited Father Amvrosii in his monastery. Thus, while the two men were in general agreement, and while the writings of Dostoevsky may reflect in some ways his correspondence and conversations with Pobedonostsev, it is also clear that Pobedonostsev was not a political-spiritual advisor for this great novel. In particular, there is no foundation for the charge made in 1955 by a Soviet scholar, Vladimir Ermilov, that Dostoevsky in writing his last novel was "toadying to the oily-unctuous advice of the chief lackey of the tsar" and that the "fading" of Dostoevsky's talent was due to the influence of Pobedonostsev, particularly through their evening discussions.[15]

Pobedonostsev's most obvious contributions to Dostoevsky's work and welfare were the twenty-two articles he contributed to *Grazhdanin* in 1873. These articles are of particular value for the analysis of the relationship between the two men, because they are the clearest kind of evidence concerning cooperation between them and concerning the similarities in their ideas. They are of especial use to the student of Pobedonostsev because they constitute one of the main sources concerning his ideas between 1865 and 1876, when his correspondence with the future Alexander III and with his associates became especially rich. The significance of these articles is demonstrated by the fact that Pobedonostsev only very rarely wrote for popular journals such as *Grazhdanin*; the essays he wrote for Dostoevsky were the product of special friendship and cooperation. Dostoevsky on three occasions sought to call especial attention to articles Pobedonostsev had contributed. Moreover, the two men made great efforts to ensure the anonymity of these publications, a very important issue for Pobedonostsev. Dostoevsky told no one the name of the author and gave the draft articles to a different clerk in his office each time for copying before the material was taken to the printer; Pobedonostsev used a variety of pseudonyms and was not asked to do proofreading.[16]

Of the twenty-two essays Pobedonostsev wrote for *Grazhdanin* in 1873, thirteen dealt with religious problems, or more accurately, with the significance of religious life and with the position of organized religion in the nineteenth century; seven of these described religious life and traditions in England, of the evangelical sects in particular; three, the *Kulturkampf* in Germany; one, anticlericalism in France; one, the prospects for Christian unity; and one, Darwinism and other systems of thought "subversive of Christianity." Pobedonostsev's concern with the position of religion in the contemporary world and with the problems raised by political and intellectual developments in western Europe was one shared by Dostoevsky, as demonstrated by the publication of these articles and by the central issues which Dostoevsky considered in his greatest novels.

Pobedonostsev not only had a powerful interest in religious life and in antireligious developments in western Europe, but he also described them in such a way as to demonstrate to Russians that Orthodoxy represented the only true way for them if not for all Christians. Strangely enough, he had particular respect for the English evangelical sects. Indeed, his essays on them in *Grazhdanin* glorify genuine religious feeling and emotion in precisely the same way the Dostoevsky novels do. There is a great parallel between the point of view reflected in the pages about Zosima in *The Brothers Karamazov* and these essays. Moreover, Pobedonostsev's comments in all of these essays, and indeed in most of his writing, concerning Roman Catholicism are identical with those of Dostoevsky, as represented, for example, in the famous section concerning the Grand Inquisitor, although Pobedonostsev did not see the connection between Catholicism and socialism which Dostoevsky believed existed.[17]

Dostoevsky and Pobedonostsev also agreed in their analysis of Bismarck's *Kulturkampf* and its significance. Pobedonostsev devoted three essays in 1873 to this subject, which he defined as "one of the most interesting and important political events of our time." Dostoevsky, in calling attention to one of these articles, noted that "it touches upon the main, fundamental point upon which the political future of Europe in our time will be decided."[18]

In addition, Pobedonostsev's 1873 essays on European political thought, especially his three long review articles on Sir James F. Stephens' *Liberty, Equality, Fraternity* and on John Stuart Mill, reflect complete agreement with the views of Dostoevsky in *The Possessed*, which was published serially in 1871 and 1872, and with the point of view Dostoevsky revealed in his own articles in *Grazhdanin* in 1873. Both men were highly critical of democratic government, of the political theory upon which it was based, and of the concept of the nature of man which it reflected.[19]

Their agreement concerning the dangers to Russia's system developing within the West were also reflected in their articles on Spain. Their analyses of the reasons for the decline of Spain were substantially identical, and they both saw Spain as the main center for anarchist ideas and for the Third International. Finally, their identity of views was revealed in their description and analysis of political developments in France, which fascinated and alarmed them both. Dostoevsky and Pobedonostsev were equally impressed by the effort to build Sacré Coeur on Montmartre and by the pilgrimages to Lourdes and other shrines; both saw lessons for Russia in the history of France since the Revolution, in the divisions among the monarchists, and in the failure of Chambord to assume his position as Henry V. Pobedonostsev wrote that the French situation taught that "the first and most fundamental benefit for the people [*narod*] is the stability of the ruling dynasty and, together with that, clarity and firmness on the part of the legal government. . . . This must be a fact, not just an idea," and must be "beyond quarrel, clear as the sun in heaven." While not quite so clear and forthright, Dostoevsky at the same time in his articles on France emphasized the virtues of autocracy, and ascribed the troubles and confusion from which France was then suffering to the overthrow of the monarchical system.[20]

Dostoevsky and Pobedonostsev apparently were in general agreement about the judicial system created by the great reform of 1864, particularly on trial by jury. Pobedonostsev had been a prominent participant in the reform campaign. However, by the time they become close acquaintances, both were severe critics of the court system. This is shown by their articles in *Grazhdanin*, by their letters, and by the critique of the courts in Dostoevsky's novels. Thus, *Grazhdanin* in 1873 published three Pobedonostsev articles on the courts and on the zemstvo institutions. One of these was a direct attack upon the jury trial system in Russia, which Pobedonostsev charged worked effectively only in England, where it had a long and popular tradition. A second article was a bitter attack upon a congress of jurists planned at Moscow University. Pobedonostsev urged Dostoevsky to make a particular effort to ensure the anonymity of this article, because he criticized his former colleagues and his close friend of reform days and fellow Senator, Kalachov, who helped organize the meetings and gave the opening and concluding addresses.[21]

Dostoevsky was just as critical in his *Grazhdanin* articles, although he did not emphasize that trial by jury and public trial should be abolished. He indicated he thought most Russian lawyers were unscrupulous and dishonest, he ridiculed distinguished lawyers such as Spasovich, for particular defense pleas, and he attacked the courts for their leniency. Both became more critical of the court system as the 1870's wore on. There is some evidence that the trial of Dmitrii Karamazov reflects the discussions of Dostoevsky and Pobedonostsev, materials concerning Russian law and the judicial system Pobedonostsev sent to Dostoevsky, and the general atmosphere of the government-sponsored critique of the courts, particularly for the decision concerning Vera Zasulich, whose trial Dostoevsky attended.[22]

Dostoevsky and Pobedonostsev were also in agreement concerning national minorities in Russia, particularly the Jews and the Poles. Antisemitism was powerful and popular in many strata of Russian society at this time. Many government officials, intellectuals, and other leaders in society were strongly antisemitic; Dostoevsky and Pobedonostsev in their corrosive comments on the Jews were quite typical. Their charges were the common ones: cosmopolitanism, materialism, financial power and corruption, responsibility for liberalism and socialism, influence over the press and publishing, and the creation of anti-Russian feeling in other countries. Pobedonostsev used the term "Jewish [evreiskii] organ" as a synonym for liberal or progressive, while Dostoevsky was dismayed to find that half the people in German resorts were Yids (zhidi). Dostoevsky's articles in Grazhdanin, his last novels, and The Diary of a Writer are studded with antisemitic comments and characters in the general tradition.[23]

Poles were an especial target for Pobedonostsev, because of his belief that all inhabitants of the Russian Empire should be Orthodox Christians and because of his conviction that the Catholic Poles, agents of both the Vatican and Austria-Hungary, were a threat to this internal unity. Dostoevsky was just as nationalistic, but even more aggressive. He believed that Christianity had been perverted by Rome. Catholicism, in his view, was one of the principal enemies of Russia and of Orthodoxy, and The Brothers Karamazov and The Diary of a Writer in particular are marked with anti-Catholic and anti-Polish sentiment. Some of Dostoevsky's most unpleasant characters are Poles.

Dostoevsky and Pobedonostsev were also ardent panslavs, particularly in the exciting year 1877, when Russia and Turkey went to war. Dostoevsky, who was vice-president of the panslav organization just before his death, was convinced that European civilization was in decline and that the future belonged to Russia. He had great faith in the Russian people and thought that the Russian state and people had a mission to free the Balkan Slavs. Thus, *The Diary of a Writer* in 1877 was a long glorification and justification of war against Turkey, and Dostoevsky "firmly pronounced that Russia fought the Turks in order to preserve the life and liberty of the oppressed Southern Slavs. . . . His country was fighting not only for the unity of its Slav brothers, but for a spiritual alliance of all those who believed that Russia, at the head of a united Slavdom, would bring by its self-sacrifice a message of universal service to mankind." When the Congress of Berlin reduced the gains of Russia and its allies and in particular established another barrier to Russian control over Constantinople and the straits, Dostoevsky urged expansion in the Far East and a regrouping of Russian strength in preparation for a later drive into the Balkans and toward Constantinople.[24]

As the next chapter will demonstrate in some detail, Pobedonostsev was an enthusiastic panslav for a brief time from the early summer of 1876 into the early fall of 1877, and even before that he had sought to educate the heir to the throne concerning the Balkan Slavs and their relationship with Russia and with Orthodoxy. Both he and the heir were strong supporters of war with Turkey, until Russian losses grew great, particularly at Plevna, and until both realized that the panslav movement, as a popular force, might easily get out of government control and even turn against the government. Moreover, they discovered, "As Russians, we can always find allies in Europe; as Slavs, we can find only enemies."[25]

Consequently, even with regard to panslavism, Pobedonostsev differed from Dostoevsky in two significant ways. First, Pobedonostsev had a static view of the world and of relations among societies and peoples; consequently, except for the brief period when he was carried away by war fever, he did not accept the thesis that Russia had a mission to free the Slavs or to carry her peculiar form of civilization beyond the borders of the empire. Second, he did not support Dostoevsky when the latter advocated expansion into Asia and a rebuilding process, in preparation for another drive into the Balkans.

These differences are only two of many which separate Dostoevsky and Pobedonostsev. Some of the differences or disagreements are only minor or temporary, such as Dostoevsky's affection for the *zemskii sobor* (territorial assembly), which Pobedonostsev abhorred, or Dostoevsky's lack of enthusiasm for persecuting the Stundists. Others were more basic.

To begin with, Dostoevsky and Pobedonostsev were quite different in personality and interest. Dostoevsky, who had suffered for almost a decade in Siberia and who did not attain the status or security he wished, was a vital, original genius, one of the world's great novelists. He was a man of powerful passions, who gambled recklessly until the late 1860's, and who demonstrated a fierce interest in the sensual side of life. Moreover, he was torn by his instincts, some of which were strongly conservative, and others of which were powerfully revolutionary; he is almost a caricature of one of his own "doubles" in his ambivalence. Finally, his attitude toward the Russian Orthodox Church, or, more specifically, his own personal religious beliefs, are subject to question and dispute. Many scholars are convinced that Dostoevsky was in fact not a believing Christian, though he had a driving concern about religion and though on occasion he may have tried desperately to accept Christianity.

Pobedonostsev was quite a different type of person, almost the impersonal bureaucrat incarnate. Cold, sober, simple, neat, almost miserly, Pobedonostsev was the very model of the proper gentleman. Unmarked by any passions—even his hatreds were cold and harsh—he was a man of balance, a self-controlled but unoriginal scholar who loved the ivory tower and whose principal pleasures were long evenings with books. His travel writings contain excellent descriptions of landscapes and of buildings, especially churches, but very rarely mention people. Moreover, he had a positive dislike and distaste for any kind of enthusiasm or liveliness, and he lacked a sense of humor. He was a believer in painful, slow growth, and he was suspicious generally of grandeur, eloquence, and striking ability. Finally, while there was a strong note of cynicism hidden deep in his make-up, growing deeper as he grew older, he was profoundly religious, and his life was marked by a deep personal belief in God and by considerable private charities.

Early in life, both Dostoevsky and Pobedonostsev had been radical reformers. However, Pobedonostsev after the mid-1860's was a consistent conservative, even a reactionary. On the other hand, Dostoevsky, after his conversion, wanted desperately to be a conservative, but had a profound, innate understanding of and interest in the forces behind revolution. While Dostoevsky's knowledge of the intelligentsia in particular may have been inaccurate and warped, his novels are studies of the conflict between conservatism and revolution among them.

Pobedonostsev had grown up in a Slavophil circle in Moscow and wished to be considered in the Slavophil tradition. His most important book, published in 1896 on the fiftieth anniversary of his entry into government service, was given the title of a famous Slavophil publication of 1846, *Moskovskii sbornik* (Moscow Collection). However, in many ways Pobedonostsev represents the dusty death of Slavophilism, for he lacked the spontaneity, the youthful vigor, the lively affection for Russia's past, and the romanticized knowledge of Russia's institutions which the Slavophils had. He was spiritually a descendant of Nicholas I and Uvarov, and his motto or slogan should have been Orthodoxy, Autocracy, and Nationality. He believed that the Church should be a part of the state and that all inhabitants of the empire should belong to the Orthodox Church. He emphasized the autocracy, and he sought to strengthen the absolute power of a patriarchic, functional monarchy. This is revealed most clearly in the mass of his writings concerning the nature of man and his attacks on the tendency of Western thought to "exalt" individualism. With regard to the nationalities, Pobedonostsev again believed in Russification, with his particular enemies, in order, the Jews, the Poles, and the Baltic Germans. Under this triple arch, he installed the family as the most significant conservative institution in a society where status was frozen and where each should know and accept his own place.

It is as difficult to outline Dostoevsky's political and social ideas briefly as it is those of Pobedonostsev. While similarities exist, the contrasts are striking. To begin with, Dostoevsky was not a consistent or instinctive conservative. The Slavophil mark upon him was weak. While he might not have criticized Orthodoxy, Autocracy, and Nationality as a slogan, he would not have categorized his thinking under those headings. He glorified the Orthodox Church, or more accurately, Orthodoxy, on occasion, but it is evident that he thought survival and salvation came through personal suffering, not through the Church. He accepted autocracy, and he was as bitterly opposed to Western concepts of constitutional and democratic government as Pobedonostsev. However, perhaps because he had suffered much under the autocracy and perhaps because of the nature of his interests and abilities, he placed more emphasis upon harmony and submission, as a general principle, than upon acceptance of a form of government or a political system. Moreover, the so-called liberals were not the enemy for him that they were for Pobedonostsev. Dostoevsky, after all, had a belief in the natural goodness of man and in the power of love which Pobedonostsev could never have accepted. In addition, Dostoevsky thought that the socialists and the revolutionaries were the enemy; Pobedonostsev barely recognized the socialists, and the liberals and rationalists were his favorite targets.

This difference derives in large part from the different view of the West each held. Dostoevsky was profoundly affected by his years of residence in the West, especially among the Germans. He was powerfully influenced by the slums, the selfishness, and the money-grubbing he saw and from which to some degree he suffered. On the other hand, while Pobedonostsev spent many summers in Salzburg and Wiesbaden and while he visited England several times and other parts of western Europe on occasion, the West to him consisted of publications and ideas. Pobedonostsev enjoyed what he saw of the West, and he had an especial affection for life in England, but he was convinced that the greatest menace to Russian stability and survival came from Western ideas, particularly those deriving from the French Revolution and those which exalted individualism and constitutional government. Dostoevsky and Pobedonostsev were both bitterly hostile to Catholicism, to the Jews as dissolvents of Russian qualities, and to the Poles as bearers of various kinds of Western infections, but each of them had a different West in mind when he sought to shield Russia from its influences.

V I

Panslavism
and the Balkan Crisis

Pobedonostsev returned to Moscow from St. Petersburg in 1846
to begin his career as a bureaucrat at a time when the celebrated
controversy raged among a handful of intellectuals over the nature
and destiny of Russia. He did not participate in this battle of books,
or of journals, between the Slavophils and the Westerners, in part
because of his youth and in part because he never joined a group or
school or took part in a public discussion of this kind. The other
members of his family also lacked sufficient conviction or interest to
take a stand on either side of this issue. His brother Sergei, for example, published articles and stories in both Slavophil and Westerner journals. Sergei met the leading Slavophil philosopher, Alexei
Khomiakov, by chance on the platform of the North Station in Paris
in 1847, but this introduction did not lead to closer acquaintance-
ship or friendship, in part because of the social gap which separated
the Pobedonostsevs from the leading Slavophils.[1]

Generally, the Slavophils were highly cultured and civilized members of the rural gentry class, intellectuals of some ability, and
leisurely and amateurish in their approach to life and to philosophy.
They were strongly religious, tended to stress religion rather than
rationalism, and were uninterested in politics or political philosophy in the Western sense, largely of course because of the absence
of this tradition in Russia and because the reign of Nicholas I was
forbidding and oppressive. Widely travelled and heavily influenced by Western philosophy, especially by the French and German
romantics of the previous two decades, the loose Slavophil group was

109

highly personal, friendly, and soaked in a quietistic and romantic spirit of good will and brotherly love.

Fundamentally, the Slavophils, particularly their most articulate leaders, such as Khomiakov, Constantine and Ivan Aksakov, Ivan Kireevsky, Iurii Samarin, and Alexander Koshelev, were moderate conservatives in search of a Utopian Christian peasant kingdom. Their rivals, the Westerners, believed that European civilization was clearly superior to any other, that Russia was or should be a part of Europe, and that the future of Russia lay in adapting itself to the main lines of European culture as quickly as possible. The Slavophils, on the other hand, had an especial affection for the peasant and for the *narod* (or *Volk*), the mass in which folk tradition and wisdom resided and which possessed a peaceful, collective insight and harmony which the individualistic, anarchic, money-grubbing West could never envisage. They also thought that Russia was different, indeed unique and superior, largely because it possessed a pure Christianity embodied in the Russian Orthodox Church and sheltered in an harmonious Muscovite state. The fresh, vigorous, unspoiled Russians not only had avoided or escaped the institutions and philosophies which had debilitated western Europe, but they had also created healthy and fruitful institutions of their own, such as the patriarchal family, the commune or village community, and the artel or rural cooperative, all of which promised much for other peoples in the future.

The Slavophils sought to separate society from the state. They supported the autocracy loyally, and they advocated no changes in the Russian political structure. At the same time, partly because they were rural gentry and partly because of the main lines of their thought, they were strongly critical of the bureaucracy, which they considered a barrier between the tsar and the people, an artificial and legal means of conducting government affairs, and a German innovation introduced by Peter the Great and destructive of the living, vital, harmonious springs of the Muscovite system.[2]

Pobedonostsev's political and social philosophy was not firmly established until 1865 or 1870, and even after these dates some emphases changed significantly as Russian history unfolded. As a conservative and traditionalist Muscovite with a strong commitment to Russian Orthodoxy, he accepted throughout his life many of the beliefs fundamental to the Slavophils. Thus, he had a special reverence for Orthodoxy and a growing conviction that Orthodoxy was the distinguishing characteristic of Russian civilization, superior in

every way to Western Christianity and, ultimately, the faith necessary for all those who lived within the Russian empire. He considered the family the basic unit of any stable society and thought the
patriarchal family system, with the tsar at the head, essential for
Russian life. Finally, especially after 1875, he came to believe that
the *narod* existed as a collective entity and that this unified mass
embodied a wisdom and political vision which could be clearly identified and which invariably supported autocracy and conservatism.

While the main outlines of his philosophy as it developed resembled the vague Slavophil doctrine of the 1840's, there were also
substantial differences which prevent us from identifying him as a
Slavophil. First, he emphasized and elevated autocratic rule far
higher than did Khomiakov and his generation. Moreover, he saw
no distinction between the state and society. Indeed, after the 1870's
in particular, he assigned the autocratic state functions of control
which the Slavophils clearly would have denied and even resisted.
His vision of the Russian Orthodox Church was also quite different
from that of the Slavophils: they saw it as a free, popular, independent institution exuding a spirit of harmony and guided by the collective wisdom of the Orthodox community, while he came to define it as an instrument of the state designed to convert all inhabitants of the empire, Russian and non-Russian alike, to reverent submission to autocracy. Pobedonostsev had no faith in the concept of
sobornost' or community, which he would have described as a splendid Christian ideal which had no reality and no possible practical
significance in the hard life of the nineteenth century. While he
wrote a great deal about the *narod* and often professed to be its true
interpreter, or at least to know those who could in fact identify the
people's will, he lacked the special veneration for the people which
marked the Slavophils. In particular, he knew nothing about Russian rural life, had no reverence for the peasant or for rural institutions, such as the commune or artel, and was indeed an urban
Slavophil, with a knowledge and point of view quite different from
that of the romantic, leisurely, amateur gentry of the 1840's.

As the history of Russia and of Europe unfolded in the nineteenth
century, the course of Russian intellectual history changed significantly. Indeed, the changes were so great that both the intellectual
temper and the ideas of the 1870's were sharply different from those
of the 1840's. There were, of course, a number of streams or schools
of thought, which scholars have carefully identified and labelled.
Pobedonostsev had no connection with many of these groups and

their ideas, particularly with the various radical and revolutionary philosophies. In fact, he was so resolutely hostile to these ideas that he made no effort to understand them and hoped that they would be uprooted and destroyed.

Panslavism was one of the most striking and significant of the schools of thought which appeared in Russia in the two or three decades after the Crimean War. The doctrine of the panslavs was so forceful, the vigor with which it was presented so shocking, and their leaders often of such political importance that Russians and foreigners alike tended to exaggerate the significance of the movement. In fact, panslavism sent a wave of alarm throughout western Europe, which saw it as an irresponsibly aggressive doctrine and movement with powerful influence in the highest reaches of the Russian government. Many Western statesmen feared that the panslavs might launch a disruptive drive into the Balkans, thereby threatening the European state system and bringing the states of Europe and Turkey to the brink of a world war.

It is as difficult to define panslavism as it is Slavophilism, in part because it was "an attitude of mind and feeling" and in part because each man in a sense carried his own version of the doctrine. Moreover, the movement as a whole was so harsh and noisy that contemporary observers and scholars have found formidable the task of separating the sound and the fury from the substance. In the twentieth century, scholars and observers alike have encountered the same obstacle in trying to evaluate the significance of the *Action Française*, a doctrine and movement which had some parallels in intellectual temper and forcefulness with the panslav movement in Russia in the 1870's.

The main development in the history of nationalism in Russia between 1850 and 1880 was the gradual transformation of Slavophilism into panslavism, just as a principal change between 1880 and the outbreak of the First World War was the evolution of panslavism into a great Russian nationalism, or pan-Russianism, one of the most profound currents of the last century of Russian history. These transformations were in some ways similar to that which German nationalism underwent in the nineteenth and twentieth centuries, but Orthodoxy and the existence of other Slavic peoples under the rule of foreigners exerted an important influence upon Russian nationalism which German national doctrine lacked until the appearance of Hitler.

Slavophilism developed in Russia during an extremely tight-fisted and repressive reign, one in which there was little freedom of expression or organization and one which gave Russia the reputation of a reactionary police state. The thaw which Alexander II introduced in 1856, the abolition of serfdom and the other basic reforms which followed, and the economic and social changes which began to burgeon in the second half of the nineteenth century launched the transformation of Russia after a silent, frozen period of thirty years. The new Russia was naturally more attractive than that of Nicholas I to Slavs under Ottoman and German rule, particularly when these peoples sought outside support in their efforts to obtain their freedom and to set up independent national states. Even so, the tsarist Russia of Alexander II was gravely handicapped in any effort to attract the support of Slavs and others under foreign rule in the Balkans, as the Russian panslavs discovered in the 1870's. Many of the southern Slavs were not Orthodox and often were firmly hostile to Orthodoxy. Their leaders simply wanted independence from Ottoman, Magyar, or German rule, if possible with Russian support but not with the goal of becoming a part of a Russian-controlled or Russian-protected Slavic federation. Most of the other Slavs, particularly the Czechs, the Croats, and the Slovenes, looked West more than East, were opposed to autocratic government, and wanted to establish liberal, constitutional governments in their own lands. They not only rejected the Russian political model, but they also considered Russia culturally underdeveloped or backward, particularly in comparison with the French and English models they usually preferred. Finally, of course, in any discussions which considered Slavic problems, the position of the millions of Poles under oppressive Russian rule intervened to smash the vision of a Slavic community living in harmony.

Russian panslavism in the 1860's and 1870's was much affected by the changes occurring then within Russia, just as its power among other Slavs was increased by these same reforms. However, even more powerful external forces helped to shape this doctrine and to give it the aggressive, anti-Western character which so alarmed many Europeans. Thus, panslavism was in part a reaction to the bitter defeat Russia suffered in the Crimean War and to the reversal, almost revolution, in Russia's policies toward Europe which resulted from that disaster. Nicholas I had constructed his foreign policy toward Europe on the assumption that the established system must be maintained at all costs. Among other requirements, this meant that Russia must support Austria and therefore assist in maintaining the Austrian empire against Magyars and Poles and Croats as well as against other kinds of revolutionaries. When the Russians learned that their reward for this policy was the "malevolent neutrality" of Austria during the Crimean War, one of the props for the old conservative foreign policy disappeared, to be replaced in some minds by the desire to harass the Ottoman and Austrian empires through exciting their subject Slav populations to revolt. This aggressive policy of intervention, a sharp reversal from the policy of Nicholas, was strengthened also by the national need for action and for recognition to overcome the effects of the Peace of Paris in 1856.

One must remember, too, that panslavism appeared in Russia during the years when Napoleon III dreamed aloud of reorganizing Europe along national lines and when Bismarck and Cavour were using guile and force to unite Germany and Italy and to revise the entire map of Europe. These impressive achievements, launched and completed by leaders of states as relatively insignificant as Prussia and Piedmont, naturally stimulated some Russians into assuming that imaginative use of the resources of the Russian empire and of those Slavs under foreign rule might bring enormous advantages to Russia, perhaps even greater benefits than Bismarck and Cavour had obtained. The defeat Prussia administered to Austria, the creation of a powerful unified Germany on Russia's western border, and the great likelihood that Bismarck's Germany would assume real authority over the Balkan Slavs and the Balkan future, allied with and in the name of Austria, of course, alerted Russians both to the massive new threat and to the means by which it had been achieved. It also awakened them to the vulnerability of Russia's western borderlands to campaigns making skillful use of the disaffected peoples living there.

Panslavism reflects the Russian and European conditions in which it grew. It was therefore less genial, leisurely, and amateurish than was Slavophilism. It placed less emphasis on Orthodoxy and more on power politics, less on internal harmony and the moral order and more on foreign policy, less on purifying and improving Russia and more on assisting the southern Slavs, to the disadvantage of the Turks, the Magyars, and the Germans and to the advantage of the Slavs, including the Russians. Consequently, panslavism was harsh, strident, and aggressive both in tone and in policy.

The substance of Russian panslavism is quite simple. The Russian panslavs believed that the Slavs constituted a definable family with ethnic, psychological, and religious qualities necessary for establishing a superior society, if not a civilization. In this family, the Russians were the responsible big brother, free, powerful, and eager now to assist the other members to win their freedom from foreign rule and then to band together in some sort of Slavic federation, under vaguely defined Russian protection or control. The process of freeing the Balkans from Ottoman, Magyar, and German domination would have the added advantage of providing Constantinople as a reward or prize for Russia.[3]

Although the panslav movement in Russia was small, it was influential. This was true in part because many of its members were important figures in the army, the court, the diplomatic service, the Church, the government, and the wealthy Moscow merchant body, and in part because panslavism enrolled some of Russia's most distinguished journalists and intellectuals in a noisy and effective public relations campaign. Thus, both Russians and foreigners were impressed by the active participation of glamorous and daring generals, such as Chernaiev, Fadeev, and Skobelev, all of whom had played dramatic roles in Russian expansion through central Asia and the Caucasus; by the support provided by the empress, the wife of the future emperor, and women such as Countess Bludov, whose salon in the 1870's assumed the significance which that of Grand Duchess Helen Pavlovna had occupied earlier; by the dramatic and daring diplomacy of Ignatiev; by the blessings of Metropolitan Filaret of Moscow and of other high Church leaders; and by the large gifts made by Moscow merchants, such as Timofei Morozov and A. K. Trapeznikov. Ivan Aksakov, Michael Katkov, and the great Dostoevsky were the thundering scribes of the movement, using their newspapers and journals in a savage press campaign to excite the people of the two capitals to rush to the aid of their fellow Slavs.

The strengths of the panslavs were impressive, but the movement was also shallow and unsound. In addition to the disadvantages the orthodox, autocratic Russian government had to endure in dealing with the southern and western Slavs, the movement was hampered from the very beginning by other serious flaws. First of all, even the leaders were astonishingly ignorant concerning the other Slavs, often not knowing the basic facts concerning their principal beliefs, traditions, and ambitions. Very few had ever travelled in the Balkans, and Pobedonostsev was one of only a handful who could speak another Slavic language. Moreover, the Russian government and

Russian people were even less well informed and were, as well, un-
concerned and even disinterested in the Balkans. The base of panslavism in Russia was shockingly fragile.

Finally, of course, the strength of panslavism was not significant
even where it appeared to be. While Chernaiev, Fadeev, and Skobelev were dashing and successful generals in battle against Central
Asians or Caucasian tribesmen, they had the same lack of political
sense which their contemporaries Boulanger and Gordon displayed.
Moreover, Count Dmitrii Miliutin, Minister of War, and those
who decided military policy, were not among the panslavs. Similarly, Alexander II did not share the enthusiasms of his wife and
sister-in-law, and Gorchakov, who was Minister of Foreign Affairs,
was not in agreement with his stormy petrel, Ignatiev. The responsible authorities in the Russian Orthodox Church after Filaret died
in November, 1867, were well aware that their energies and funds
were demanded by their own people, while the Moscow merchants,
like all fund-givers, quickly reached the limit of their generosity,
even under skillful prodding from panslav courtiers. Finally, the
eminent journalists all encountered difficulties with the censor over
their fiery articles, even though they were protected to some degree
by men such as Pobedonostsev. Aksakov, for example, had a number
of issues of his newspapers confiscated, the Moscow police even
entered homes in an effort to collect all published copies of one
speech he had given, and he was exiled from Moscow and his newspaper closed in June, 1878, for a critique of the government after
the Congress of Berlin which had exceeded the boundaries of accepted toleration.[4]

Panslavism appeared formally in Russia when a number of Muscovites in 1858 established the Slavonic Benevolent Committee to
aid the south Slavs to develop educational and religious institutions
and to bring young Slavs to Russia for higher education. The Committee (later Society) had the approval of Alexander II, and it soon
had somewhat more than three hundred members. A similar organization was established in St. Petersburg in 1868, and Kiev and
Odessa founded branches the following year. The Muscovites concentrated their efforts on Bulgaria, and the St. Petersburg branch
on the Czechs. The organization in St. Petersburg began with one
hundred forty members and had increased to seven hundred by
1872. Its principal achievement before 1875 was financial assistance
for construction of an Orthodox church in Prague which was consecrated in 1874. During the Balkan crisis, the panslavs collected

considerable sums of money. For example, the St. Petersburg branch collected more than 800,000 rubles (approximately $400,000) between September, 1875, and October, 1876. Ivan Aksakov reported in November, 1876, that the Moscow committee had collected 3 million rubles and material worth about 500,000 rubles during the same period.

The Moscow Slavonic Benevolent Society's main undertaking during the first decade was the Slavonic Ethnographic Exhibition it organized in May and June, 1867, which became a Slav congress attended by eighty-one representatives from the other Slav groups. The foreign participants saw a little of Russia, met Aksakov, Pogodin, and other leading Russians interested in the Slavic world, were introduced at receptions to the tsar and to Gorchakov, and discussed political, religious, and cultural problems with each other and with their Russian hosts. A third of the guests were Czechs, and almost another third were Serbs and Croats. Two-thirds of the non-Russian Slavs were not members of the Orthodox Church. German frequently had to be the language used, because few Russians knew other Slavic languages and few of the other Slavs knew Russian. The Muscovites were considered heavy-handed, the absence of the Poles was noted by the guests, there was some friction over inefficient organization, and the conference disclosed basic disagreements over political and religious issues. Yet even though planned later meetings were not held, the Russian hosts considered the conference a success. Panslavism among the other Slavs did increase after 1867, contacts between leaders were established, and a base was laid for the excitement of the years of the Balkan crisis.[5]

Panslavism in Russia was largely the work of men like Danilevsky, Fadeev, and Ignatiev, who reached middle age during the 1870's and who were reacting to developments within and beyond Russia after the Crimean War. B. H. Sumner noted that Professor Nicholas Danilevsky's *Rossiia i Evropa* (Russia and Europe) was called "the Bible of panslavism." This book did indeed have considerable influence. Published first in 1869 in a journal, produced as a book in 1871, reprinted in five Russian editions within twenty-five years, and translated into the principal European languages, this volume gave panslavism a useful pseudo-scientific stamp. A botanist-agricultural economist who was fifty years old in 1872, Danilevsky developed a cyclical philosophy of history, much like that later elaborated by Spengler. He declared that there are recognizably different societies or civilizations and that these civilizations are each like plants which grow, flower, decay, and die. He provided his readers an anti-European review of the nineteenth century, declared that Europe was characterized by individualism and violence, announced that the decline of Europe had begun, and foresaw the rise and triumph of a distinct and superior Slavic civilization. Indeed, he interpreted the conflict between Russia and Europe as the result of the European effort to "Europeanize" Slavic culture, a campaign which Philip of Macedon had launched and of which the Crimean War was only the latest episode. A Slavic federation, minus the Poles but including Constantinople, would ensure the peaceful, historic development of all the Slavs, under Russian leadership and with Russian the necessary common language.[6]

Danilevsky justified Russian expansion and militarism, gave the panslavs a sense of grandeur and of confidence in their inevitable triumph, and provided an apparently lofty metaphysics. General Rostislav Fadeev, on the other hand, in a very brief book published originally in 1869, established a political and military program for the movement. Fadeev, who was quietly dropped from the army by Miliutin in 1867 for his attacks upon the army reforms, had no knowledge of or interest in the main ideas of the panslavs, knew nothing of the other Slavs, and was indeed the very model of the empty-headed soldier. However, his book, which was translated and widely read in western Europe, had the power of a hammerblow in its simplicity. Fadeev argued that "the way to Constantinople lies through Vienna" and that Russia must proceed to liberate the Slavs under Austrian and Ottoman rule by force or retreat to the Dnieper river. After liberation, a Slavic federation, with Russia in control of defense and foreign policy and perhaps with Russian grand dukes on the new Slav thrones, would ensure a Slavic empire from the Pacific to the Adriatic.[7]

A third panslav musketeer was Count Nicholas Ignatiev, who was the foreign minister of the movement and who led the panslavs and the Russian government to the very brink of incredible diplomatic triumph early in 1878, only to see Bismarck and Disraeli snatch the victory from the Russian grasp. He reflects both the strengths and the weaknesses of panslavism. Born in St. Petersburg and forever lacking the attitude toward Moscow, the Orthodox Church, and the *narod* which the earlier Slavophils had had, Ignatiev was a remarkably effective diplomat and agent, often acting independently of the foreign minister and often in contradiction to the policies of the government. He achieved astounding success while only twenty-eight when he negotiated the Treaty of Peking in 1860. This treaty ended border conflicts with China and acquired the Maritime Province and the Amur river boundary for Russia.

Ignatiev's major interest, however, was in the Balkans and in acquiring Constantinople and the straits for Russia. He had visited Vienna in 1857 and had met some of the Czech and Ruthenian leaders, and he devoted the last forty-eight years of his life to promoting a panslav program. Until early 1877, he had splendid positions from which to campaign. From 1861 until 1864, he was director of the Division of Asian Affairs in the Ministry of Foreign Affairs, a section which included European Turkey in its responsibilities, and from 1864 until early 1877 he represented Russia in Constantinople, acting with an authority that is unimaginable for an ambassador today. As minister and then ambassador to the Turks, Ignatiev abused his position by intriguing with the Slavic minorities under Ottoman rule, encouraging various schemes to increase their power, and suggesting that the mighty Russian empire would rush to their assistance if they should rise against their oppressors. Ignatiev boldly fanned the flames of Balkan nationalism in the 1870's, encouraged the revolts and then the wars of 1875 and 1876, hastened Russian entry into the Balkan wars, and drove Russia to the great triumph of the Treaty of San Stefano in the spring of 1878, a victory which was erased by the Congress of Berlin in the summer of that year.[8]

The differences between Pobedonostsev's ideas and the main lines of panslav thought were considerably greater than those which had divided him earlier from the Slavophils. Moreover, the tone and temper of panslavism were quite alien to him, a reserved and quiet person strongly opposed to war and not impressed by large abstract ideas or by noisy campaigns. He never became a member of the panslav organization, although he did accept an honorary membership in 1885, when the movement had lost most of its energy and force. Nevertheless, he did serve as a panslav briefly during the Balkan crisis in 1875–78. The influence on him of this period and of the panslav failure was enormous. Indeed, these years and his flirtation with an aggressive nationalist movement were almost certainly the turning points in his life and thought.

Pobedonostsev's basic concern was the political and spiritual welfare of Russia. Throughout his life, he placed Russia and things Russian first in his thoughts and in his policies. Basically, he was an isolationist, believing that Russia was and should be separated from other states and societies, resisting influences from foreign societies, and not seeking to expand Russian influence there. At the same time, of course, he had been raised and educated as a European, with a deep knowledge of several European languages and of European culture. For him, however, most Slavs, except for the Czechs, were on the periphery of Europe and did not attract interest. Prague was the only Slavic city outside the Russian empire which he is known to have visited. Even when he contributed twenty-two articles to Dostoevsky's *Grazhdanin* (The Citizen), mostly on Europe, none touched a Slavic people, although two or three did concern Spain, which Pobedonostsev never visited and the language of which he could not read. He knew little about the other Slavs, and what little he did know antagonized him. Thus, in July, 1876, when he was already showing signs of becoming a "war hawk," he wrote: "It is impossible not to sympathize with Serbia, but it is bitter to think that this same Serbia in its political and social life reflects the basic forms of Western civilization: they have a parliament, courts, hotels on Western standards . . . and have created a party of progressive youth, striving in Western ways for freedom of every kind. I fear that Serbia will in time become for the western Slavs what Poland became for the eastern."[9]

After Pobedonostsev moved to St. Petersburg and became deeply involved in the education of the future Alexander III, he became interested in learning about the Slavs and in instructing his important student, who confessed in 1867 that he knew "almost nothing" about the Slavs. Pobedonostsev therefore sent Grand Duke Alexander Alexandrovich copies of the works of panslav historians, such as Michael Pogodin of Moscow University, one of the founders of the Moscow Slavonic Benevolent Committee, and Nil Popov, of Moscow University, who in 1869 published a two-volume book, *Rossiia i Serbiia* (Russia and Serbia). Samarin and Fadeev were other authors whom he recommended to his pupil. He also arranged that other panslavs read lectures at the court on the Slavs, and he introduced visiting Orthodox priests from Galicia and the Balkans to the future tsar. In March, 1875, he arranged a twenty-minute appointment for Adolf Dobrianskii, a leader of the Orthodox against the Magyars in Carpathian Ruthenia and a man who was subsidized by the Russian government through the Holy Synod of the Russian Orthodox Church. In the same year, he presented to the heir the publications of the Moscow Slavonic Benevolent Society, praising the organization's work and recommending particular articles and maps for study.[10]

Pobedonostsev developed a special interest in the Czechs, perhaps because he had learned to read Czech as a young man but also because he visited Prague from Salzburg in July, 1874, to attend the consecration of an Orthodox church. He loved Salzburg, but was disappointed that it lacked an Orthodox church, so the Prague church, with a Russian priest, an excellent choir, and bells which sounded like those of Moscow brought joy to his heart. The Pobedonostsevs were delighted by their first four days in Prague, and he compared Hradcany castle to the Kremlin. The ceremonies were conducted in excellent taste and were attended reverently by throngs of Czechs. A tea and a musicale which some Czechs arranged were very pleasant occasions and provided him an opportunity to meet and to have long talks with several Czech leaders, particularly Palacký, Rieger, and Brauner. Pobedonostsev returned to Prague again in 1875 and 1876; in the latter year he served as godfather for two Czechs who joined the Russian Orthodox Church.[11]

Pobedonostsev assured both his Czech friends and the Grand Duke Alexander Alexandrovich that he was not a member of the panslav organization, that he was visiting Prague on vacation, and that he had no official connection or role. However, he did meet and evaluate the Czech leaders and collect information about their views which he passed on to the tsar and to Russian diplomats. Thus, he talked with Palacký, whose conservative approach to political theory he appreciated, on each of his visits before Palacký's death, and he visited Brauner several times whenever he was in Prague. Brauner wrote to him in the fall of 1877, providing him an estimate of the impact among the Czechs of an agreement ending the Balkan crisis which would increase the number of south Slavs under Austrian rule. Brauner thought Pobedonostsev a sound scholar and a shrewd politician, a great Slav leader, and a dreadful reactionary, but he did provide him information and introduce him to other Czechs and to members of the Orthodox Church whom Pobedonostsev used later in his subversive campaigns against the Austrians. Pobedonostsev showed Brauner's letters to other officials and to the heir, and he also had some of them published anonymously in the panslav press.

Pobedonostsev published other materials in the Russian press which Brauner and Rieger forwarded to him through Russian

women who had married Czechs or Austrians and even through
Czech journalists. Rieger and Brauner also assisted young Czechs
going to Russia for higher education, often recommending them to
Pobedonostsev for assistance. In 1878, Fedor Kovařík was helped by
Rieger and a friend to get to St. Petersburg, where Pobedonostsev
obtained a loan for him, procured both a waiver and a scholarship
for university study, and later assisted him in getting positions in
the Ministry of Communications and as a teacher in a gymnasium
in Poltava.[12]

One of Pobedonostsev's Czech acquaintances, probably Brauner,
also put into Pobedonostsev's hands a copy of the popular memoirs
of Wenceslas Wratislaw, Baron von Mitrowitz, a Czech who was a
member of the mission headed by Frederick von Kregwitz which
Emperor Rudolph III sent to the sultan in 1591. *The Adventures
of Baron Wratislaw in Constantinople and as a Captive of the Turks
while with the Austrian Mission in 1591* was written in Czech in
1599. Pobedonostsev translated it into Russian in the summer of
1877 on behalf of the Russian Red Cross, with all the proceeds from
the sale of the ten thousand copies printed devoted to the care of
soldiers wounded fighting the Turks. The volume, which is still a
fascinating memoir, describes in graphic detail the corruption,
brutality, and barbarism of the Turks, with especial emphasis upon
the treatment of Christian slaves and upon the condition of the
prisons. Pobedonostsev's footnotes and comments added anti-Ger-
man and anti-Catholic touches to this propagandistic venture. Thus,
he identified the Janissaries as "blindly and unconditionally devoted to the will of the rulers," a group who "could be compared to
the Jesuits." He had a second edition of this book published in 1904
to assist those wounded in the Russo-Japanese war.[13]

The rise of a popular clamor for war has often been compared to
a fever, and the transformations through which Pobedonostsev proceeded in 1876 and 1877 certainly resemble a strange attack and a
gradual return to normalcy. His interest in the Balkan Slavs was
minimal until 1875, and even the outbreak of the revolts in Bosnia
and Herzegovina failed to move him. However, the victories of the
Turks over those in revolt, the massacres in Bulgaria, the Turk
victories over the Serbs, Montenegrins, and Russian volunteers, and
the general wave of Russian nationalism engulfed him and converted him by late summer, 1876, into a war hawk. He wrote in
May, 1876, how delighted he had been to learn that Russia was far
more significant as a world language than French or German,

equalled English and Spanish already in the geographical extent of the area in which it was used, and was clearly the world language of the future. At the same time, he was in terror of war, "with all of its afflictions, especially with all the disorders and weaknesses which already mark our administration and our society." By June, 1876, while on vacation in Marienbad, he rushed for a newspaper twice a day. He pitied the Serbs, although he considered them Western, but damned the West for inciting the Serbs while at the same time demonstrating a vile hatred for all Slavs.

In July, 1876, Pobedonostsev wrote to the heir that he hoped and believed to be untrue rumors he had heard that the heir had offered the Serbs a large cash subsidy. "The business of liberation is sacred, but patience is golden." In September, however, he urged the heir to use his influence for the release of three hundred thousand "old" weapons for the Serbs. Early in October, he noted the rapid rise in popular feeling, especially in Moscow, and emphasized that the government must immediately seize the leadership of this wave of nationalism and direct it against a foreign enemy or face the likelihood that the movement would turn against the state, first in distrust and then in enmity. "Our people are ready to create miracles of valor if they are given leadership," but failure in policy will create a gap between state and people "larger than any in our history."

His letters to the future Alexander III in the fall of 1876 hammered on the need for leadership, on the cunning, hypocrisy, and ambition of the English, and, finally, on the inevitability of war. Indeed, on October 18, he wrote that without war it would be impossible to untangle the knot Russian diplomacy and irresolution had produced. The heir replied five days later that they were in complete agreement, that Gorchakov and Miliutin were old and wanted to avoid war, and that Ignatiev was a splendid exciting influence. However, "diplomacy has so confused the situation that it is impossible to declare war on Turkey without a clear reason." The heir and his tutor were both disappointed when the Turks accepted a forty-eight-hour ultimatum.

In February, 1877, Pobedonostsev began to worry lest Alexander II, in his eagerness to avoid war, reach an agreement recognizing the Austrian right to rule over additional Balkan territory inhabited by Slavs. "To surrender the Orthodox Slavs to Austria means to surrender them and ourselves to a cunning, selfish, and Jesuitical enemy, with no honor or profit to us." He informed the heir that

Nicholas I had spurned an Austrian offer of its services during the Crimean War because "he was a knight of duty, and he personally and nationally understood deep in his heart where lay the center of gravity of Russian national interest." When war was declared in April, he wrote, "Something sacred has been accomplished." At the same time, however, he admitted that he was uneasy and that he could not forget that the reign had also begun in war.[14]

The Pobedonostsev correspondence with Grand Duke Alexander Alexandrovich and with Catherine Tiutchev is a barometer of his growing bellicosity and of the influence he exerted upon the heir and the court. He did not play a direct role in any of the major policy decisions which ultimately led to war between Russia and Turkey. However, he did help to create a warlike spirit in the court and in the Russian reading public and to support the war effort vigorously once fighting had broken out. He advised the leaders of the Slavonic Benevolent Society about men who might contribute funds and administrators whom the panslavs might employ to ensure effective use of the money and supplies they collected.

He also helped the more eager war hawks, such as Katkov, Ivan Aksakov, and Dostoevsky, to place their publications before Grand Duke Alexander Alexandrovich, and he defended them at court when they were accused of excesses. Ivan Aksakov was in difficulty several times before he was exiled from Moscow, and *Grazhdanin* was closed for printing his attack on the Russian government after the Congress of Berlin. However, Pobedonostsev always defended Aksakov's basic position, extremely nationalistic and aggressive though it was, and assured the heir that his intentions were pure and his sentiments Russian, even though his language on occasion may have been careless and harmful. He devoted a great deal of time and energy to helping the Russian Red Cross, persuaded Catherine Tiutchev to assume important Red Cross responsibilities in Moscow, and rejoiced when his wife transformed their apartment into a "bandage factory." At the request of the empress, he prepared a prayer book for soldiers, although he became terribly annoyed when some of her closest friends began a long discussion over whether the book should be in Russian, or in Old Church Slavonic, which Pobedonostsev preferred and which he was certain all literate soldiers could read.[15]

However, his main contribution during the Balkan crisis was his work as a propagandist, both through important translations he made and through articles he published in *Grazhdanin*, now edited by V. F. Putsykovich, and in Katkov's *Moskovskiia Vedomosti* (Moscow News). Some of the translations, such as that of *The Adventures of Baron Wratislaw in Constantinople,* not only served to excite military spirit but also provided profits for the Slavonic Benevolent Society or the Red Cross. The most famous of these translations was that of Gladstone's stirring pamphlet, *The Bulgarian Horrors and the Question of the East,* which was published in London on September 6, 1876, and of which 200,000 copies were sold that fall in England. This was an emotional and moral attack upon the Turks and upon the British government for its policy toward the Turks. After describing briefly the background of the conflict, Turk and British policies, and the massacres, Gladstone urged that the anarchy and butchery in Bulgaria be halted and that the Turk administration then be withdrawn from Bosnia-Herzegovina and from Bulgaria.[16]

L. K. Alexander, a Scottish Liberal, obtained Gladstone's permission to take his famous brochure to Russia, where a translation might "redeem British honor" and contribute to ending the crisis. He was introduced to Pobedonostsev by the Greek ambassador in St. Petersburg, and Pobedonostsev then arranged the translation, which he did in collaboration with Professor K. N. Bestuzhev-Riumin of Moscow University. Gladstone and Alexander had hoped and assumed that the proceeds of the sale of a Russion translation would be given to the Balkan Slavs, but the profits went to the Russian panslav organization. Ten thousand copies were sold within two months after the pamphlet appeared.[17]

Pobedonostsev and the panslavs were so impressed by the impact of Gladstone's classic that he translated another article written by the British Liberal on the virtues of Montenegro and the Montenegrins, whom Gladstone called "Christendom's most extraordinary people," an article probably called to his attention by Alexander after it had appeared in the May, 1877, issue of the *Nineteenth Century.* Pobedonostsev also wrote a long article in *Grazhdanin* in January, 1877, reviewing a number of recent English books on the Ottoman Empire and on the Balkans and describing the support Gladstone was collecting in England. Later in that same year, he reviewed for *Grazhdanin* a book which brought together a series of articles published originally in English in W. T. Stead's *Northern Echo* and which had in fact been written by Pobedonostsev's close friend, Olga Novikov, whom Disraeli labelled "the MP for Russia in England." Pobedonostsev also assisted in the translation of another English assault on the Turks, Sir Tollemache Sinclair's *A Defense of Russia and the Christians of Turkey*, omitting, however, Sinclair's chapter urging reconstruction of the Byzantine empire. Sinclair was quite antisemitic and exceeded even Aksakov in the fervor of his panslavism: "I firmly believe that the Russian Panslavists, as a body, are infinitely superior, both in intelligence, patriotism, energy, influence, and character, to the great bulk of their countrymen. . . . As far as I can judge, one Panslavist is at least equal to ten average Russians, especially the somniferous Rip Van Winkle Conservative party, who are opposed to all free development of Russian institutions."[18]

Pobedonostsev had a deep appreciation of the importance of the view of Russia held by leading foreigners. He was especially sensitive about England, perhaps because he realized that England stood as a block to Russian foreign policy goals, perhaps because he was so familiar with English literature and politics and enjoyed life in England so much. In any case, he was always especially interested to meet English visitors and to talk about Russia with them. One of his closest English acquaintances during these years was Sir Donald MacKenzie Wallace, who published the first edition of his masterly account of Russia in 1877. During the Balkan crisis, Pobedonostsev used his talks and other connections with MacKenzie Wallace and others to affect the views of the English. Thus, he remained in contact with Alexander, who had brought Gladstone's pamphlet to St. Petersburg, and he forwarded him information on Russia, particularly with regard to Poland, to place in the English Liberal press.[19]

More important, he utilized the close relations which Olga Novikov had developed with Gladstone and other Liberal leaders, such as Sir Henry Campbell-Bannerman, Sir Robert Morier, Lord Napier, and Charles Villiers, and with conservative journalists and intellectuals, such as W. T. Stead, Carlyle, Froude, Freeman, and Kinglake. Pobedonostsev could barely endure Olga Novikov, whom he thought excessively unstable and voluble, but he corresponded with her for more than thirty years and he used her social position in London to advance panslav policy.

Mrs. Novikov had been raised in an Orthodox Muscovite family, strongly Slavophil and Anglophil as well. Both her parents spoke English, and she spent a good part of her life in England after her first visit there in 1868, when she was twenty-eight. She met Gladstone in January, 1873, and became a friend of Carlyle in 1876.

Her salon at Claridge's attracted many Englishmen interested in relations between Russia and England, and Mrs. Novikov became a kind of intermediary or informal ambassador, distributing translations of Aksakov and other Slavophils, introducing visiting Russians to distinguished Englishmen, providing introductions for Englishmen going to Russia, writing essays and translating important Russian articles for English newspapers and journals, and serving as a conduit for some leaders of British opinion to Pobedonostsev and her other friends in St. Petersburg and Moscow. Some of her correspondence with Gladstone during this Balkan crisis was forwarded to Pobedonostsev, who gave it to foreign minister Gorchakov for the tsar. She also forwarded essays and articles which argued that England was not opposed to panslavism, which Pobedonostsev arranged to have translated and published, generally in *Grazhdanin* or *Moskovskiia Vedomosti*. Again, during the 1876–78 crisis and during Gladstone's famous Midlothian campaign, she gave Gladstone material about Russia and the Balkan Slavs which Pobedonostsev and others forwarded to her. The Russian Ministry of Foreign Affairs and the embassy in London were both angered by her private diplomacy, and she herself was received more sympathetically in London than in Moscow, but she did exercise considerable influence in a kind of action more common in the twentieth than in the nineteenth century.[20]

On occasion in 1877 and early 1878, Pobedonostsev became so belligerent against the Turks and so aroused by the possibility of war with England that he suggested very radical steps. At one point, for example, he urged that Russia study the strategy of the South during the American Civil War, with particular attention to breaking the blockade, because he wished to prepare for a long struggle with the British fleet. He was much excited by the possibility of developing and producing a submarine which could destroy British sea power. Once he excitedly encouraged the heir to grant a subsidy to the great chemist, Mendeleev, so that he could develop a new bomb. In fact, Pobedonostsev had high hopes that Mendeleev would invent an aerial bomb, and he looked forward to having these devices dropped on London.[21]

However, even when he was most eager to have war used as an instrument for freeing the southern Slavs, Pobedonostsev was generally worried and pessimistic. As the war progressed into the summer and fall of 1877 and as losses accumulated before Plevna, he became deeply upset. The Crimean War had not touched or affected him in any way, and Russian campaigns in Poland, the Caucasus, and Central Asia apparently were so remote that the war against the Turks in 1877 was his first real exposure to the results of military action. The work he and his wife did for the Red Cross, letters from his sister-in-law from a hospital near the front, and the British newspapers he avidly read filled him with horror, and he began to have nightmares crowded with wounded Russian soldiers. As Olga Novikov wrote, "Our military promenade has transformed itself into a gigantic burial procession."

He was shocked and frightened by the incredible waste, blundering, inefficiency, and weakness which became evident in the Russian army and in the supply and hospital services. The absence of preparation and the incompetent leadership in the capital, in the supply lines, and at the front appalled him. He was dismayed by the intrigues which undermined the military effort and destroyed the golden glow the liberation campaign had first provided. He noted that many in St. Petersburg were calling it "Moscow's war" or "the Grand Dukes' war," and he was alarmed by criticism of the Slavonic Benevolent Society and its leaders for stampeding Russia into an unwanted and unnecessary conflict. He began to wonder whether "our happy-go-lucky administration, completely lacking in sense and calculation, indifferent and careless in the choice of its leaders," could survive.

He was most worried, however, by the criticisms he heard of various members of the imperial family for their intrigues and the failure of campaigns they led. By September, 1877, he was convinced that the autocracy itself was in peril and that the danger was increased because the tsar was unaware of it and was at the front, while the heir to the throne was isolated by family squabbles. He even feared in the summer of 1878 that another "Time of Troubles" was approaching for Russia. In April, 1879, Pobedonostsev urged the heir to avoid concerts and all crowds. At a time when Marx was predicting revolution in Russia, Pobedonostsev foresaw the same possibility. The conclusions he reached because of this crisis shaped his political philosophy and deeply affected developments within Russia for the next quarter of a century. He wrote to Catherine Tiutchev and to the heir that Russia had relied too much on justice, on words, and on arrangements with friends and allies. "We can count now only on our own strength. . . . Our government has lacked intelligence and unity of will." Russia must awaken to the fundamental principles of autocratic rule, or die. Every morning, his first thought was the question, "What happened during the night?" The reign of fear had begun.[22]

The Balkan crisis also cured Pobedonostsev immediately and permanently of his infatuation with the stormy and aggressive doctrine of panslavism. During and after the war itself, he was disappointed by the lack of military virtue displayed by the Bulgarians, by the failures, even though glorious failures, of the Serbs and Montenegrins, and by the inaction of the other Slavs. More important, he began to realize the dangers inherent for the autocratic system in such popular movements as panslavism, particularly when men such as Ivan Aksakov, whom no one could control, assumed the leadership. Even in the exciting fall of 1876, the heir and he agreed that the government should control the panslav committees, for such popular manifestations "left to themselves could lead to regrettable results." He wrote in October, 1876, that the government would have to seize the popular movement and control it, lest it grow and ultimately turn against the state in distrust and then in enmity. The popular reaction to the war blunders, of course, only confirmed this view.

When Ivan Aksakov on June 22, 1878, made his celebrated attack on the Western powers and on Russian governing circles because of the Congress of Berlin, Pobedonostsev sent a copy of the speech to the heir and said the speech was strongly written but just. He told the future tsar that the Russian people would consider the Congress a disgrace for Russia, regardless of what the diplomats said, and that the nationalist feeling which the war enthusiasm had stimulated was going to be difficult to quell, since it had been allied with other discontentments.

Henceforth, he almost never wavered in his insistence upon complete government control, the preeminence of stability and equilibrium in domestic affairs, and peace in international relations. He realized that panslavism represented a doubly revolutionary idea. Thus, a panslav Russia automatically found the European powers aligned against her. On the other hand, a panslav movement at home created and stimulated popular pressures which might ultimately be turned against the state itself. In other words, from that time forward he turned inside, not outside. Power was to be used to bind society and to control the state.[23]

The Balkan crisis in the 1870's constituted an important stage in the history of Russian nationalism. Pobedonostsev, for example, not only recovered from panslavism, but also developed a strong, vigor-

ous pan-Russianism, with a heavy emphasis upon Russian Orthodoxy as the distinguishing characteristic of Russian civilization.
This turn in thought is responsible for his policies in the Holy
Synod of the Russian Orthodox Church and for his advice to the tsar
on education, control of the press and of the arts, and social policy.
The most striking illustration of the new emphasis is the policy
which he designed for the western border areas, where the Finns,
the Baltic peoples, the Poles, and the Jews felt the heavy hand of
Russian nationalism after 1880.

Pobedonostsev simultaneously turned his back upon international politics, in which his interest had never been great but which
had attracted his feverish attention in 1877 and 1878. Thus, there
is no information in any of the materials available of his views concerning the American Civil War, the unification of Italy, Bismarck's
wars to unify Germany, or any of the other events in world politics
which so excited his contemporaries. At the same time, however, he
paid close attention to the principal new philosophies appearing in
Europe, to the *Kulturkampf* in Germany, and to anticlerical Republicanism in France. After the Balkan crisis, throughout which
he had followed international politics closely, he retained his earlier
interest in European cultural development and in the political and
social issues which concerned Europeans most, but he turned away
entirely from international affairs and foreign policy.

Pobedonostsev saw the Russian state as a repressive power and
viewed Russia as a single community which must become and remain a "community of believers." Although his ideas concerning
both the necessary unity of society and the role of autocracy were
similar to those of men such as Barrès in France and Treitschke in
Germany, and to those of Communist leaders later, he lacked completely the conception they had of the dynamic role for the state.
Thus, he became as conservative in his approach to foreign policy
as he was to political and social change. He did not see Russia as a
member of a highly competitive power system. He was a close
acquaintance in the 1880's of the German ambassador, General
Hans von Schweinitz, and the American minister and the French
ambassador were frequent visitors to his apartment in later years.
However, there is no evidence in any of his writings or in the
memoirs of these men, in the volumes published after the First
World War which made available the documents of the various
powers, or in the scholarly studies of international relations in the
years between 1870 and 1914, that he had any interest in or influ-

ence upon Russia's participation in the alliance system. As a matter of fact, according to von Schweinitz, Pobedonostsev resented and resisted Russia's joining the Three Emperors' League, which he thought an Austrian-German trick to delude the Russians.[24]

After 1878, Pobedonostsev remained aloof from discussion or definition of Russian foreign policy, even in times of great tension, such as the years before the outbreak of war with Japan. In fact, his indifference to international politics and to some of the delicate problems facing Russia are responsible for some of the blunders which he committed when promoting the expansion of Orthodoxy beyond Russia's borders. His voluminous correspondence with the last two tsars reveals that his occasional interventions into foreign affairs were limited and discreet. He occasionally forwarded letters from Russians who wished posts as ambassadors. In 1886 and 1887, he supported, without great force and unsuccessfully, the appeals of two Russian financiers, N. A. Novosel'skii and A. S. Poliakov, for government approval and support of their projects for buying the railroad from Ruschuk to Varna in Bulgaria and for building a railroad in Persia. In both instances, he urged government support in order to deny these facilities or opportunities to the British. He was very worried at that time that the new ruler of Bulgaria might be a German Catholic prince and that "Berlin Jews" or Britain might obtain control of Persia.[25]

Whenever Pobedonostsev did act to affect Russian foreign policy, he emphasized a passive and defensive approach. In the fall and winter of 1896, when the Armenian massacres led many Russian officials to fear that the British fleet might seize the straits connecting the Mediterranean and the Black Sea, Alexander I. Nelidov, the Russian ambassador in Constantinople, proposed that the Russian Black Sea fleet be prepared to seize the upper part of the Bosporus, enter the Dardanelles with the British and French fleets, and then negotiate the future of the straits. Witte unsuccessfully opposed this suggestion at a crown council on December 5, arguing that such an action raised the likelihood of war at a time when both Russia and her ally, France, were unprepared. Pobedonostsev later supported Witte, as did the French, so that the Nelidov plan was abandoned in January, 1897. Similarly, in 1899, Pobedonostsev was one of the Russian officials most responsible for persuading the tsar to launch the Hague conference on disarmament, a subject in which he was intensely interested. He was also opposed to the aggressive actions which led Russia to war against Japan in 1904.[26]

The Balkan crisis led to another development which had a profound effect upon Pobedonostsev's life and thought, the creation of the Volunteer Fleet in the spring of 1878, between the Treaty of San Stefano and the Congress of Berlin. This effort to create a Russian merchant fleet which could be converted to a cruiser squadron to prey on British commerce during war was the hasty work of a group of Russian patriots, largely Moscow merchants and officials at first, to fashion some weapon for use against the English navy, which was again at the point of frustrating Russian national ambitions. The idea of collecting funds to buy and maintain ships purchased generally in England for potential use against England came easily to men who had been generous in collecting similar funds to help the Balkan Slavs. The land-bound merchants and officials hoped that the merchant ships would not only provide a reserve nucleus for any naval conflict, but would also serve as a school for Russian sailors and officers and as a merchant fleet carrying Russian goods and the Russian flag into ports around the world dominated by her opponents. Once funds had been collected, several ships purchased, and the fleet launched, Pobedonostsev and other supporters saw it as a means of binding the Russian empire together through trade between the Black Sea and Vladivostok and through helping to establish settlements and markets on Russia's Pacific coast.

Pobedonostsev involuntarily became one of the founders of the Volunteer Fleet when a group of patriots from Moscow asked him to persuade the heir to the throne to grant them permission to solicit funds for the enterprise and even to serve as honorary chairman. The group included such important men—Prince V. A. Dolgorukov, the governor general of Moscow, Count Stroganov, former curator of the Moscow Educational District and Pobedonostsev's old patron, Senator Nicholas Kalachov, Count Komarovsky, two of the Samarins, Ivan Aksakov, Bishop Amvrosii of Moscow, Professor Babst of Moscow University, and wealthy merchants such as I. E. Ginzburg and Timofei Morozov—that Pobedonostsev acceded to their request. He was almost certainly impressed by their plans for contributing funds, and he had learned from experience with the panslav organization that the government ought to assert direction early if it hoped to keep lively organizations under control. He therefore became one of the seventy-six founders; the heir accepted the chairmanship, Pobedonostsev was the vice-chairman and executive director, and the Fleet was launched.

Pobedonostsev from the very beginning was skeptical concerning the soundness of the scheme, and his anxiety grew as the organization did. However, he drew up the original constitution, which resembled that of a religious order, drafted its appeal for contributions, and protected the heir from those contributors who wanted him to become directly involved in an enterprise which was patriotic but also commercial. He supervised the difficult reorganization of the Volunteer Fleet Committee into a formal society in May, 1879, after the initial blush of enthusiasm had worn off and many of the early participants had lost interest, when the hard work of maintaining the ships in operation had to be faced. During the five years the organization was ostensibly independent and private, he served as its vice-chairman and principal officer.[27]

Interest in contributing toward a weapon which might be used against England was high in the spring and summer of 1878. Indeed, the Moscow group, which had been informally organized early in March and which obtained permission to solicit funds only late that month, collected 2 million rubles (about a million dollars) by the end of June. By December, 1879, a total of more than 4 million rubles had been collected, more than half of this in Moscow and about one-third in St. Petersburg, where Anichkov Palace, the residence of the heir to the throne, was the collection center. However, enthusiasm quickly flagged. A total of only 120,000 rubles was contributed in 1880 and 1881, and less than 30,000 rubles in the next twenty years.[28]

As the director of the Volunteer Fleet, Pobedonostsev was handicapped by the supreme lack of concern most of its founders showed after the first few months. He therefore found himself charged with responsibility for managing a corporation which had acquired six sea-going vessels in western Europe, four within six weeks of its formal organization, and which had an original capital of about $2 million, but for whose operations no one had made preparations. He felt incompetent to manage a merchant fleet, particularly in a country where so few had had experience in international trade, and was oppressed by the "blind ignorance" of those with whom he worked. However, Russia's "patriotic aim" consumed all of his time. After a year, he wrote that he had ceased to read books and was now reading people, "quite another kind of literature."[29]

He could not abandon his responsibility, however, because the name of the heir was attached to it, and the Grand Duke wanted him to direct it. He had to rely on volunteer assistance in the harried office for the first five months, and he did not have a clear view of the Fleet's accounts until January, 1879. His life was full of practical managerial problems which he had never encountered before: purchasing, fitting, repairing, and even naming ships, finding office space and secretary-clerks, identifying commanders of ships and helping to locate crews, mastering the customs and rules of international trade, warding off entrepreneurs with unsound schemes, negotiating railroad rates, and persuading the heir to the throne to give awards to pleasant and distinguished men who interfered in the organization but who needed some recognition for the interest they had shown.

The main problem, however, was to find useful and profitable work for the ships purchased so that they could be used to train officers and crews, and could be quickly outfitted for military action if another crisis should arise. None of the eager founders of the Volunteer Fleet had devoted any thought to its use. Indeed, Pobedonostsev's first meeting with the Moscow merchant sponsors to discuss using the fleet to import tea from China and to carry goods from European Russia to the Far East occurred in April, 1879, a year after the enterprise was launched. Pobedonostsev had early been appalled that none of the founders had considered the capital needs of a merchant marine, the need for economic ties with other areas of the world if the fleet were to fulfill its logical function, or the specialized knowledge and skills necessary for any group which wished to engage in international trade. He also discovered, to his horror, that the Moscow merchants really had no interest in international trade, or even in developing markets for their products in the Russian Far East.

However, the several ships of the Volunteer Fleet were put to effective use. In its first six years, the organization carried 1,400,000 poods (a pood is the equivalent of 36.113 pounds) of tea from China to Odessa and other Black Sea ports, approximately 400,000 poods of other imports, and about 1,500,000 poods of export cargo. Over the same period, it also transported twenty-one thousand passengers from Odessa to Vladivostok. The cargoes which most excited Pobedonostsev, however, were shiploads of convicts carried from Odessa to Sakhalin. He devoted enormous effort to negotiating arrangements for the first trip, from June to August, 1879, with the Ministry of the Interior and the Naval Ministry. He found an Orthodox priest to accompany the convicts, collected books for a library, and rejoiced to learn that the convicts attended religious services and organized a splendid choir on their journey.[30]

Curiously, those in autocratic Russia most surprised by the program were high officials of the Ministry of the Navy. Indeed, these men were both stunned and annoyed by this invasion of a field in which they had been lethargic. Pobedonostsev explained to the Ministry officials, especially to the director and to the Grand Dukes Constantine Nikolaevich and Alexander Alexandrovich, that the Fleet had been established to help train Russians and to create a convertible reserve group of ships, that all of the contributors were patriotic Russians, and that the new organization would cooperate with the Navy in every way. His appeals, and his noting that the heir to the throne was most interested in the Volunteer Fleet, were not effective. The conflict was heightened when he obtained a contract with the War Ministry for transporting troops from the Caucasus and Bulgaria to Odessa, rankling Grand Duke Constantine Nikolaevich, who believed that either the Navy or the Black Sea Navigation Company, which he had founded after the Crimean War, should have undertaken the work. By March, 1880, the quarrel had become so bitter and pervasive that Pobedonostsev wrote to the heir, attacking his rivals in the Naval Ministry for advocating that Russia build battleships while the English, alarmed by the Volunteer Fleet, were investing heavily in the construction of new cruisers.

Pobedonostsev lost his struggle to preserve the Volunteer Fleet. In a decree issued on March 14, 1883, of which he learned only after it had been published, the young merchant navy was absorbed into the Russian Navy, although the ships and the basic concept did retain some kind of identity. He protested bitterly, predicted "monstrous consequences," and denounced those in the Navy responsible. His warnings were correct, because the training and cruiser reserve goals for which the Fleet had been founded were neglected. In the Russo-Japanese War in 1904–1905, only three of the Fleet's ships played any role, and their contribution was minor. *Jane's Fighting Ships*, in 1899, declared that the Volunteer Fleet was "no more a war force than the Cunard Line." This authoritative survey pointed out that the ships were old and slow, that they had been built in England, and that Russia had no bases between Odessa and Vladivostok. Five years later, the same source announced, "There is no Russian 'bogey' that is quite so really harmless as the Volunteer Fleet."[31]

The conflict between the Volunteer Fleet and the Russian Navy was embittered significantly by the man whom Pobedonostsev chose as his principal assistant, Naval Captain Nicholas M. Baranov, who had much of the flamboyance and color of his contemporaries, Gordon, Boulanger, Chernaiev, and Skobelev, and who played a brief role in Russian history. Pobedonostsev's judgment of men was generally unsound. He was especially subject to err concerning brash and energetic men, such as the forty-two-year-old Baranov. When Pobedonostsev first met him and accepted him as his principal assistant and technical adviser, he was both impressed and puzzled. He noted that there were "two Baranovs"; while on occasion he was alive with vigor and seemed in perpetual motion, the next week he would collapse in nervous fatigue. Although Pobedonostsev thought him bombastic and sly, he was overwhelmed by Baranov's forceful energy and by his large, if not wild, ideas. Pobedonostsev wrote the future Alexander III in February, 1879, that Baranov, with all his virtues and shortcomings, "which recall to us the French character, is unquestionably Russian." He was so dazzled by a report in which Baranov outlined how Russia could destroy British sea power that he sent it to Count Dmitrii Miliutin, the Minister of War, and to the heir. Pobedonostsev, by the spring of 1879, was wondering why Baranov had not achieved greater eminence, and Catherine Tiutchev, who had originally not been impressed, was then calling him "a man of steel." Pobedonostsev recommended him at that time as the strong man who would resolve the problems facing Russia which Gurko and other weaker men seemed unable to settle.[32]

Baranov was apparently of enormous assistance in establishing and operating the Volunteer Fleet. As an experienced captain in the Russian Navy, he possessed a great deal of technical information and data concerning ports and trade. He purchased ships for the Fleet in western Europe, supervised the construction of one steamer in Marseilles, and did most of the travelling which Pobedonostsev was reluctant to undertake. He came to see Pobedonostsev every day at four o'clock and often interrupted his reading or other work in the evenings as well. On one or two occasions, he even came to a monastery to talk with Pobedonostsev, who began to divide his days into two parts, "before and after Baranov."

Captain Baranov served the Volunteer Fleet while on leave from the Russian Navy. He was annoyed when he occasionally was not given the privileges he expected from the Navy on some of his travels, but his complaints increased the difficulties. More important, he was very critical of a battleship design favored by Admiral Popov and by the Grand Duke Constantine Nikolaevich, who considered Baranov an irresponsible and noisy ignoramus. In the fall of 1879, Baranov sued a journalist for slander and asked to be retired. His superiors in the Navy then charged him with preparing woefully inaccurate reports of his activities during the Russo-Turkish war in 1877–78. Baranov was tried and dismissed from the service on December 19, 1879, in a trial which Pobedonostsev attended and which he thought was a triumph for Baranov and a disaster for the Navy. Baranov used Katkov's paper, *Moskovskiia Vedomosti*, to attack the Naval Ministry, both before and after his court martial. He was not restricted or reprimanded for this by Pobedonostsev. Indeed, the director of the Volunteer Fleet took pleasure in introducing the controversial officer to his friends in court and to the members of Countess Bludov's salon.[33]

Baranov brought a bitter personal element into the quarrel brewing between Pobedonostsev and the Grand Duke Constantine Nikolaevich and others in the court whom Pobedonostsev thought were "liberal." The disagreements over ship design, Russian strategy, the Volunteer Fleet, and Baranov himself sharpened the issues for Pobedonostsev and probably for the Grand Duke as well and therefore helped make 1881 a particularly crucial year for Russia.

None of the dreams of the founders of the Volunteer Fleet was ever achieved. However, the five years which Pobedonostsev devoted to this organization are of considerable significance. They brought him into contact with large numbers of merchants whom he would otherwise not have met, and they gave him considerable insight into their views concerning political and economic issues. He also came to meet a wide range of other nationalists through the Volunteer Fleet, men for whom he purportedly spoke when he advised the tsars later on the wishes of the *narod*. In addition, his services as administrator of this merchant fleet provided him a liberal education concerning the Russian government, supplementing what he had learned as a reformer in the 1860's and as an official in the Senate, as a Senator, and as a member of the Council of State. Being head of the Volunteer Fleet, he obtained first-hand knowledge concerning the inefficiency, red tape, intrigues, and corruption which hampered able and ambitious men. The "viper's wisdom" he acquired during these years affected his view of government from that time forward.[34]

However, the principal significance of the Balkan crisis and of the Volunteer Fleet was the relationship they established between the heir to the throne and Pobedonostsev. Before the crisis, Pobedonostsev was just a tutor to the heir and his wife, one who had retained a close connection but who was basically a former teacher in an important position as a Senator. The Balkan crisis, with its enthusiastic wave of emotional panslavism, the war against the Turks, the triumphs and failures of the peace treaties of 1878, and the fright produced by the discovery that the autocracy was threatened by disunity at the center and by obvious dissatisfaction at several levels in Russian society had brought Grand Duke Alexander Alexandrovich and Pobedonostsev close together; the Volunteer Fleet sealed the alliance and made it effective. The Grand Duke was the chairman of the Fleet and took a personal interest in its affairs, particularly during the first two years, while Pobedonostsev as vice-chairman managed the complex operations, kept his superior fully informed of the main problems and decisions, and served as the ideal executive associate. The Grand Duke and Pobedonostsev were in constant contact and complete agreement concerning the merchant marine. Thus, between June 2, 1878, and May 28, 1879, Pobedonostsev wrote forty-seven letters, most of them quite long, to the heir about the Volunteer Fleet. They conferred frequently, inspected the Fleet's ships, attended meetings and banquets, and toured Russian ports. In short, the Volunteer Fleet allied them in an important enterprise. The heir came to rely upon and trust Pobedonostsev and to consider him both his necessary right-hand man and his confidential advisor. Pobedonostsev's position in Russian politics derives largely from the alliance which was formed during these years, when in the heat of the crisis he forged the core of his political philosophy and impressed it upon the feeble brain of the next tsar. From this base, Pobedonostsev ascended quietly into a position of enormous power when the grand duke became Alexander III.[35]

VII

1881

THE LAST YEARS of the reign of Alexander II were marked by discontent and muted troubles. The enthusiasm which the reforms had stimulated had long since evaporated. Both the reformers themselves and those who had resisted or were reluctant concerning the great changes were disillusioned. Moreover, the Russo-Turkish War and the unsatisfactory arrangements which Russia had had to accept at the Congress of Berlin in the summer of 1878 inflamed many, including some nationalists who saw in this defeat proof that the earlier changes had been errors. More important than this general dissatisfaction were the dismay of the disgruntled landed gentry, who could now measure visibly the economic and social impact which emancipation of the serfs had had, and the rising revolutionary movement, which frightened all government leaders.

In this crisis, Alexander II turned to General Count Loris-Melikov, an Armenian who had had a good record in the Caucasus against the Turks and who had been outstanding afterward as Governor General of Kharkov. The tsar brought Loris-Melikov to St. Petersburg early in February, 1880, and named him chairman of a special committee ordered to inquire into the causes of political disaffection and to propose solutions. Later that year, in August, Loris-Melikov was appointed Minister of the Interior. Through the period from February, 1880, until March 1, 1881, he was the man closest to Alexander II, who considered him his first minister and the leader of the government.

Pobedonostsev did not meet Loris-Melikov until the general came to St. Petersburg in February, 1880. During the Russo-Turkish war, he had been favorably impressed by what he had read and heard about the general's efficiency and military successes and by the skill and resolution he had shown in preventing intrigue and scandal on the Caucasus front. He had applauded his appointment to Kharkov in April, 1879, declaring then that Loris-Melikov was not "one of the sweet liberal generals." He was delighted to learn in February, 1880, that he was considered "able, adept, intelligent, and crafty." The new appointment particularly pleased him because Loris-Melikov had the inestimable advantage of being a "new broom" and providing some hope that Russia would emerge from its troubles. Pobedonostsev was eager to support any forceful Russian leader because he believed that the "court gang" would try to prevent a clear and active policy and because he believed any new leader would have to clean out the Council of Ministers before he could hope to make substantial progress. Pobedonostsev even wrote enthusiastically about Loris-Melikov's appointment as Minister of the Interior, even though he replaced Lev S. Makov, whom Pobedonostsev had long known and whom he thought an excellent official.

Loris-Melikov initially not only benefited from Pobedonostsev's favorable attitude but even strengthened it. Pobedonostsev was pleased by the important assignments Loris-Melikov gave to his protégé, Captain Baranov. He was flattered with the solicitude with which he discussed the political situation with Pobedonostsev himself. As early as March 1, 1880, Loris-Melikov inquired concerning his willingness to accept a major appointment in the new effort to return Russia to some kind of stability. Pobedonostsev was obviously and naturally flattered because he had no important responsibilities at that time. Moreover, his relations then with the Grand Duke Alexander Alexandrovich were not notably warm. Pobedonostsev referred to the heir as "the boss of Anichkov Palace" and noted that a certain coolness or "strengthening of indifference" had developed between them.[1]

Loris-Melikov's proposal that Pobedonostsev be made Director General of the Most Holy Synod of the Russian Orthodox Church, the position which gave him the base from which he influenced Russian policy for the next quarter-century, clearly represented an effort to rally conservative support to him and his proposals. In 1880, Loris-Melikov was engaged in a desperate effort to restrain the revolutionary movement and at the same time to win greater support for the government from among the educated classes by introducing a system of advisory councils to the government. Opposition to the so-called Loris-Melikov constitution was powerful and well organized, and the Armenian general sought support and assistance wherever he could find it. Indeed, he remarked to an associate that he had very little support in the higher levels of government, that Alexander II alone was behind him, and that "a child playing with a revolver" could destroy all of his plans.

Inexperienced in St. Petersburg politics, Loris-Melikov almost certainly assumed that the appointment of Pobedonostsev as Director General of the Synod would dampen conservative religious opposition to his policies and bring behind him a large part of the nationalistic, conservative group deeply worried by the apparent drift of affairs. He no doubt also believed that the Director General of the Synod was not important politically, or at least lacked the power to do anything but strengthen the government. He probably knew, or learned during this period, that Pobedonostsev was engaged in a kind of feud with Grand Duke Constantine Nikolaevich and other liberals, but no doubt assumed that he could cleverly bring both of these groups behind him. Moreover, Pobedonostsev was not a minister at the time and had also indicated freely that Russia needed a strong man at the helm, preferably a new man who had not been contaminated by life in St. Petersburg. He was known to have a powerful influence upon the empress, the heir to the throne, and his wife, and this influence could naturally be used to buttress the support the tsar provided. Loris-Melikov no doubt also believed that he was handicapped in being an Armenian and assumed that the support of such a respected conservative nationalist would reduce opposition based on that ground.

Finally, one of the principal opponents of Loris-Melikov in the Council of Ministers was Count Dmitrii A. Tolstoy, who had been Director General of the Synod since 1865 and Minister of Education as well since April, 1866. In these positions, Tolstoy had led the campaign within the government to restrict and undo the great reforms decreed in the first half of the 1860's. He had been especially open in his resistance to the establishment of primary schools by the zemstvos, the local government organizations allowed and given limited responsibilities in 1864, and his attitude toward the education of women and the curricula and control of universities was a strongly repressive one. Even Pobedonostsev had resisted some of his educational proposals in the Council of State.

Loris-Melikov apparently thought that his policies would have brighter prospects if Tolstoy were removed from his two powerful positions and replaced. He no doubt was aware that many Orthodox leaders, including Pobedonostsev, were deeply dissatisfied with Tolstoy's performance at the Synod. Some members of the hierarchy noted that Tolstoy attended church services only on official occasions, and rumors abounded that he was not even a Christian. Many were dismayed by Tolstoy's lack of vigor and noted that the number of clergy had declined while he was Director General and that some churches had had to be closed for that reason.

Pobedonostsev, on the other hand, was known to be a deeply religious person with very wide contacts throughout the Russian Orthodox Church. He had shown a special interest in church affairs in his work in the Council of State, and his correspondence reveals that he had come to know many members of the hierarchy and many important priests during the 1870's. He was favorably known also to many churchmen throughout European Russia because of his frequent visits to monasteries and celebrated churches. Most churchmen visited him when they were in St. Petersburg, and his knowledge of church problems and affairs may even then have been greater than that of Tolstoy. In fact, he was regarded as a kind of special assistant to the heir for church affairs, and there were rumors late in 1878 that he was going to replace Tolstoy. Loris-Melikov clearly thought, correctly, that appointing Pobedonostsev as Director General of the Synod would please the hierarchy and most churchmen and in this way would increase the support his program would receive, or at least diminish the opposition.[2]

Loris-Melikov found Alexander II most reluctant to accept his suggestion concerning Pobedonostsev, whom the tsar had known for twenty years and had appointed tutor of the heir to the throne in 1865. Apparently, Pobedonostsev's splendid position in the eyes of the tsar had simply melted as Pobedonostsev's views changed and as the tsar came to know him well. He was named a Senator on February 19, 1868, but in October he wrote to Anna Aksakov that the tsar was now suspicious of him, although nothing was ever said and he had no concrete evidence. He wondered then how his Senate appointment had ever been made, and remarked that his position in the court would have been impossible and he would not have been appointed if the decision had been delayed six months. The tensions probably arose over Pobedonostsev's proposed regimen for his students, which Alexander II thought too strict and demanding, over Pobedonostsev's sanctimoniousness, and over his suggestions that the members of the imperial family should participate more actively in religious services and in ceremonies of national importance. Pobedonostsev, for example, was appalled that the Emperor did not go to Moscow in November, 1867, to attend the funeral of the Metropolitan Filaret, the Church leader for whom he had had the very highest admiration. Pobedonostsev urged that the Grand Duke Alexander Alexandrovich attend to represent the family, but Alexander II then assigned Grand Duke Vladimir and forbade Alexander to go.[3]

Pobedonostsev's growing conservatism, the conduct of Russian diplomacy and of the Russian military effort in the Balkan crisis of 1876–78, and Alexander II's open unfaithfulness, which began in 1867 and was climaxed by his marriage to Princess Catherine Dolgorukii less than two months after the death of the empress, led to Pobedonostsev's bitter criticism of the tsar, first to Catherine Tiutchev, his closest friend, and then to the heir to the throne himself. Consequently, during the last years of his reign, Alexander II faced a hostile son and a critical faction within his court and bureaucracy. Moreover, Pobedonostsev suggested to his protégé that the flabbiness and immorality of Alexander's private life were vitally related to the state's weakness and to the disasters of 1877 and 1878. Russia, he said, needed a spiritual revolution and regeneration as well as a new tsar. Thus, Pobedonostsev's letters to Alexander Alexandrovich during the dark days of the fall of 1877 were full of criticism of Alexander II for his decisions, for his absence from St. Petersburg, for his inability to identify competent generals and able administrators, and for Russian failures in general. When the war and the peace negotiations were over, Pobedonostsev returned to the charge, condemning the emperor for his irresolution and his poor choices. The future tsar replied that he recognized the weaknesses of his father and "the absence of intelligence, strength, and will."

The correspondence with Catherine Tiutchev is even more remarkable, revealing the width of the gap which separated Pobedonostsev from the tsar and the way in which this development strengthened Pobedonostsev's ties with the future tsar. Thus, on September 27, 1877, he wrote that Alexander II feared and drove away able men, selected incompetents deliberately, and then cried on one hand and rewarded those who failed on the other. In December, 1879, after predicting "the abomination of desolation," he wrote that Alexander II was "a pitiful and unfortunate man for whom there is no way out. God has struck him. He has no strength to direct his own actions, even though he thinks he is alive and active and powerful. His will is clearly exhausted; he does not *want* to hear, to see, or to act. He wants only the pleasures of the belly." A few months later, after he had served on a special committee to celebrate the twenty-fifth anniversary of Alexander's service as tsar, he wrote: "Both these twenty-five years and this man have been fateful for Russia. He has been the man of destiny for unfortunate Russia. God be with him. God will judge whether or not he has been guilty of wasting and dishonoring the power in his hands, the power and authority given to him by God."

Pobedonostsev suffered the final indignity when Alexander II invited him to a small private dinner in January, 1881, to meet his new princess, who completed her destruction in his eyes by remarking at their introduction that she had always thought Pobedonostsev a general. Pobedonostsev thought her unpleasant, unattractive, uneducated, vulgar, "in short a wench."[4]

Alexander II no doubt did not possess full knowledge of Pobedonostsev's views concerning his morals, his policies, and the impact his reign was having, but the coolness between the two men was not concealed. It appears that in the decade or fifteen years before 1880, Pobedonostsev never conferred privately with Alexander II, nor was asked by the tsar for advice. The tsar certainly understood Pobedonostsev's position sufficiently to resist Loris-Melikov's proposal that he be made Director General of the Synod. He agreed that Pobedonostsev was learned and talented, but he did not want to name "a desperate fanatic" and "a Pharisee" to such a sensitive post. Count Peter A. Valuev, chairman of the Council of Ministers, despised Pobedonostsev as an "impossible man," one "of the class of those who imagine that the miracle of the Pentecost is repeated constantly for their benefit." However, Valuev finally not only supported Loris-Melikov's proposal, but helped persuade Alexander II to remove Tolstoy from his two posts and to replace him with Pobedonostsev as Director General of the Synod and with Andrei A. Saburov as Minister of Education. Apparently, the tsar was particularly impressed by the argument that "no one would be more agreeable to the clergy or would have their interests more at heart." He therefore yielded on April 19, 1880. The appointment was announced officially in the newspapers on April 25. Pobedonostsev was in raptures over the appointment, which he much preferred to one as Minister of Education. Loris-Melikov and Valuev considered the move a great political triumph because they had removed a political opponent and, presumably, obtained strong support from a conservative quarter at the same time.

The *Ober-Prokuror* or Director General of the Synod of the Russian Orthodox Church was an important personage because the Orthodox Church was the state church and because the head of the principal administrative body therefore could have considerable influence on many aspects of government policy, particularly those affecting education, access to information, social legislation, and civil rights. The Director General of the Holy Synod, the ruling body of the church set up by Peter the Great in 1721, sat as the representative of the autocratic tsar and the channel for imperial commands to the church. The other members of the Synod consisted of the three metropolitans, who were ex officio members of the board, and several members of the hierarchy who were appointed by the tsar, ordinarily on the Director General's nomination, for fixed periods of office. The power and authority of the Director General naturally reflected his own character and strength to some degree, but he was in fact the administrative head of the Church and he could exercise absolute authority over the servant church if he wished.

By June, 1880, Pobedonostsev had moved to his large and handsome official residence, a building at the corner of Nevsky Prospect and Liteiny which had once belonged to the Naryshkins. At first he found the mansion too luxurious, and he disliked its busy location, but he soon came to appreciate its spaciousness. In fact, he wrote Catherine Tiutchev that the rooms were so numerous and large that he could shut off the rest of the world and imagine that he was living in the country. He came to enjoy his magnificent establishment so much that he apparently delayed his retirement so that he could retain his privileges.

Pobedonostsev began his new work with great enthusiasm and vigor. However, he soon discovered that the Director General of the Synod did not participate in the official meetings which were at that time crucial for the work of the Church and for resolving Russia's political problems, the sessions of the Council of Ministers, a kind of advisory cabinet of the heads of the principal ministries which met with the tsar to discuss the main issues of the day. Pobedonostsev petitioned the tsar and the committee to raise the Director General to ministerial status. Loris-Melikov was apparently surprised by this request, because he had thought Pobedonostsev would restrict his interests to the administration of the Church. However, after a considerable amount of discussion, Loris-Melikov and Valuev agreed and the tsar accepted on October 20, 1880. The ukase naming him to the Council of Ministers was issued on November 2, and he attended his first session the next day.[5]

Pobedonostsev's appointment as Director General of the Synod and his admission to the Council of Ministers were enormously important moves at that time of crisis. His influence before these changes was considerable but nevertheless limited, because it was applied through the heir to the throne, the empress, and the empress-to-be, none of whom had any direct power. His promotion gave him both authority of his own and direct access to the tsar. More important, nomination to the Council of Ministers made him a member of the most important advisory and administrative group, precisely at the time when Alexander II was reviewing with his ministers a proposal for reducing the tension which afflicted the country.

The last four years of the reign of Alexander II were years of growing fear and indignation for Pobedonostsev, as they were for many Russian leaders. Alexander II and his ministers were deeply aware of the discontent and of the revolutionary agitation, but they were divided concerning the most promising policies. One group advocated firm government action against the press, the university students, and all others who were critical of the government and who sought liberalizing changes. Another group argued that a substantial effort must be made to win the support of the leaders of opinion by relaxing press controls and providing trusted public leaders some opportunity to affect government policy through discussion. Thus, in 1879 and January, 1880, Valuev analyzed the growth of anti-government sentiment among the young intelligentsia and suggested that the police be given considerable flexibility in using their power against the press and against public meetings. At the same time, he renewed a proposal made originally in 1863 that the Council of State be enlarged by adding two members elected by the zemstvos and the marshals of the nobility for each province where the zemstvos existed. This proposal to bring some popular support to the government was not adopted. When Pobedonostsev heard of it, he exploded with rage to the Grand Duke Alexander, calling Valuev a "master of phrases" who received his views from the *London Times* and who dreamed of calling "preservative elements from society into participation in government activity." He denounced Valuev and his colleagues as eunuchs who talked constantly and had no sense of purpose, policy, or unity.[6]

Loris-Melikov either was not aware of Pobedonostsev's views when he urged his appointment as Director General of the Holy Synod or thought that the promotion would silence him or reduce his interest in such questions. He soon discovered that Pobedonostsev was an open and determined adversary of any effort to restore stability by giving elected and appointed representatives the opportunity to participate in the discussion of proposed changes with administrative groups. They quarreled first over Loris-Melikov's proposals for relaxing controls over the press, which Pobedonostsev believed should be further tightened. Then, shortly after Loris-Melikov was named Minister of the Interior in August, Pobedonostsev learned that the tsar's principal advisor was considering the proposals Valuev had advanced and had considerably expanded them. Consequently, in the meetings of the Council of Ministers which Pobedonostsev attended between early November, 1880, and late January, 1881, he openly attacked the program of Loris-Melikov and Valuev. He found some support in a meeting on December 24 at Miliutin's home at which relaxation of controls over student meetings was proposed and endorsed, because four others, including A. A. Abaza, Minister of Finance, and A. A. Saburov, Minister of Education, also opposed the change. However, late in January when the group discussed the press and decided to have the courts review any government complaints against the press, he wrote Catherine Tiutchev that he was alone in opposition. Pobedonostsev simply could not understand his colleagues and thought they were insane even to consider surrendering principles and government power to "ugly and selfish groups seeking influence and power under the disguise of broad general principles."

Loris-Melikov apparently tried in a number of private conversations at his home and elsewhere to explain the rationale of his policy, but Pobedonostsev refused to change his views. Moreover, he launched bitter tirades against Loris-Melikov, who thanked him for his frankness and called him "the original honest man" in Russia. Pobedonostsev reported to Catherine Tiutchev: "From that point of view, I am 'the original honest man,' with whom it is impossible to reach agreement. I tell him, 'remember, I am in the position of a believer who cannot agree with idolators. You are all idolaters, you worship the idols of freedom, and they are all idols, idols. . . .' But he only smiles."

Loris-Melikov's tactics in this situation were quite simple. He made a special effort to maintain friendly personal relations with Pobedonostsev and sought him out after meetings for a brief friendly chat. He made certain that Alexander II did not talk with Pobedonostsev. He also devoted intensive efforts to charming the tsar and those closest to him. In particular, he sought to convert the heir to the throne, explaining his plans in some detail and also seeking to win the grand duke's favor by improving relations between him and the tsar. Finally, and perhaps most important of all, he arranged that Pobedonostsev not be invited to the three critical meetings the tsar held with some of the ministers, which met to discuss his proposal in February. At the last meeting, which was attended by the heir, Valuev, who was chairman of the Council of Ministers, the Grand Duke Constantine Nikolaevich, Loris-Melikov, Minister of Finance Abaza, and Count D. M. Sol'skii, the comptroller, the project was approved and it was agreed that the tsar would meet with the full Council of Ministers on Sunday, March 1, for one last review before it was to be issued a few days later.[7]

Alexander II was assassinated early in the afternoon of March 1, and the Grand Duke Alexander Alexandrovich immediately succeeded to the throne. The horror of the tsar's death and the character and views of the new tsar completely revised the political spectrum in St. Petersburg and gave Pobedonostsev another opportunity to destroy the program of Loris-Melikov, which he succeeded in accomplishing within two months.

Pobedonostsev charged that Loris-Melikov wanted to provide Russia in 1881 with a constitution; his charge then and later was that he had helped save the autocracy and had kept an alien and harmful institution from poisoning the wells of Russian life. Actually, Loris-Melikov was a supporter of autocracy and was not interested in installing constitutional government in Russia. He did on one occasion say that he wished to make use of "the constitutional forms of the West," but this was only a dangerous slip in terminology. Both in his official proposal and in the discussions of it before and after the assassination of Alexander II, Loris-Melikov forcefully declared that he was opposed to introducing Western institutions, that his proposals had "nothing in common with Western constitutional forms," and that a *zemskii sobor* (territorial assembly) was equally far from his mind. He was convinced, however, that the government had to obtain the support of able, well-informed, and reliable men to help resolve the problems affecting the bulk of the population and to narrow the gap between the state and the people, especially the recognized leaders, or those whom the French term the *notables*.

Briefly, Loris-Melikov thought the situation in Russia in 1880 and 1881 something like that following the Crimean War, when dissatisfaction because of the defeat, the long-pent-up attack against serfdom, and the thaw permitted by Alexander II had helped create the climate in which the emancipation of the serfs and the other great reforms were carried out. He first planned to have the autocracy retain full power and authority, and he was clearly determined to crush any effort to weaken or overthrow the government. In 1880, he also reorganized the police to reduce conflict of authority and overlapping, relaxed central controls over the universities and the press, abolished the salt tax, and drafted several proposals to establish some unity of government policy and, above all, "to complete the great reforms" with the advice of informed and reliable elected representatives.

On January 28, 1881, the Minister of the Interior proposed that the tsar establish two temporary committees somewhat like the committee he had named in 1858 to edit the details of emancipation. The chairman of each committee was to be a high state official and was to be named by the tsar. Both committees were to include elected representatives from the zemstvos, the local government institutions, and the dumas or legislatures of the principal cities. The committee established to review administrative and economic issues was to study reform of provincial zemstvo and city government; those peasant obligations to the landlords which still remained; redemption payments; and means of improving cattle-raising and agricultural production in general. The second committee was to analyze the passport system and taxes. Both committees were to draft proposals within two months; these were then to go to a special committee which was to include the chairman and some representatives from each of the two committees, several representatives elected by the zemstvos and by the city dumas, and officials from several St. Petersburg offices or departments. After revision by this committee, the proposals were to be reviewed by the Council of State, which would be joined by ten or fifteen appointed representatives of special experience and skill from zemstvo and city government institutions.[8]

Pobedonostsev believed that this proposal would undermine and destroy autocracy in Russia. He declared that Loris-Melikov had set out to "loosen" the bonds which held the state together, and he was particularly upset that he had not been invited to attend the three February meetings, one at the Winter Palace and the others at the Anichkov Palace, to discuss the proposal. He wrote to Catherine Tiutchev two days after the assassination of Alexander II that the heir had told him that he had not opposed the Loris-Melikov scheme at these meetings, but that he had urged Loris-Melikov to give Pobedonostsev a copy for study. At that time, Pobedonostsev believed that public announcement of "some kind of consultative assembly" would soon be made by the new tsar and that Russia would take a fatally long step toward constitutional government.[9]

Pobedonostsev was shocked and horrified by the assassination of Alexander II, but he showed little grief. Instead, he quickly turned his back upon the past and concentrated intensively upon the new tsar and policies for the new regime. His aims were very simple: to strengthen the will of Alexander III, whom he believed to be a man of irresolution and who had acquired power in a critical time without warning or serious preparation, and to persuade the new tsar to reaffirm autocratic power in ringing terms, to oust Loris-Melikov and his supporters from the highest level of the government, and to destroy root and branch the Loris-Melikov proposals. In his many private conversations with Alexander III, in the fourteen letters he wrote to him during the critical sixty days, and in the meetings of the tsar's advisors, he reiterated his belief in the need to act quickly and decisively in reestablishing authority and destroying once and for all the plans of those who hoped to modify Russia's form of government. "Don't follow the liberal sirens. This will lead to ruin, the ruin of Russia and of you as well . . . There is only one way, and it is the true, straight path. Stand on your own feet and without wasting a minute begin the struggle, the most sacred which Russia has ever faced. All the *narod* await your immediate decision on this."[10]

Pobedonostsev hammered at Alexander III to make his will clear and to reaffirm his autocratic power. At the same time, he began a successful campaign to surround the new emperor with men whom he trusted and who were hostile to the program of Loris-Melikov. His first move in this program was the appointment of his "man of steel," Captain Baranov, as governor of St. Petersburg. Baranov had left his position with the Volunteer Fleet sometime in the spring of 1880, about the same time Pobedonostsev was named Director General of the Synod, to become a kind of special assistant to Loris-Melikov. In the spring and summer of 1880, Baranov undertook missions to Geneva and to Paris to investigate the activities of Russian exiles, but in August he was named governor of Kovno, an important post but one which naturally removed him from the capital. Pobedonostsev's role in these changes is difficult to define, but it seems likely that he recommended Baranov to Loris-Melikov as a man who could crush the revolutionary movement, but that Loris-Melikov quickly discovered he was mercurial and irresponsible. Pobedonostsev considered the transfer to Kovno a plot directed against him and the forces of order by the Grand Duke Constantine Nikolaevich and other "liberals" who had had earlier conflicts with Baranov. He therefore tried, unsuccessfully, to persuade Loris-Melikov and Alexander II to make Baranov governor of St. Petersburg with sufficient authority to crush the revolutionary movement.

On the very day Alexander II was assassinated, Pobedonostsev sent a telegram to Baranov, urging him to come to St. Petersburg, a step Baranov refused to take without an order from the tsar or Loris-Melikov. However, the Minister of the Interior on March 2 ordered Baranov to St. Petersburg, and on March 8 the tsar named him to this critical position. As events unfolded in March and April, 1881, it turned out that Baranov did not play a decisive role in the critical decisions. Indeed, he was a failure. However, Pobedonostsev's promptness in urging this appointment prevented the nomination of someone who might have been favorable to the Loris-Melikov position and who might have exerted some positive influence during those tense days.[11]

The other appointments at the ministerial level made during these two months were also approved and recommended by Loris-Melikov, but they were designed by Pobedonostsev to weaken the position of his opponent and to lead to his resignation. Thus, on March 6 Pobedonostsev wrote a long letter to Alexander III recommending that he replace Loris-Melikov as Minister of Interior with Count Nicholas Ignatiev, the panslav leader whom de Vogüé called "a Gascon of the North" and who had served as ambassador in Constantinople so brilliantly. Pobedonostsev lauded Ignatiev as a resolute man of action, "who still possesses Russian instincts and a Russian soul, and whose name carries great renown among the healthy part of the Russian population, among the simple people." Ignatiev was brought into the government by the tsar, with Loris-Melikov's approval, early in April. Exactly a month later, he succeeded Loris-Melikov as Minister of the Interior, a great triumph for Pobedonostsev.

A second ministerial change which Pobedonostsev arranged led to the resignation of Saburov as Minister of Education and his replacement by Baron A. P. Nikolai, whom Pobedonostsev had come to know when they both served on a Committee on Education in the Senate. Pobedonostsev's closest confidante, Catherine Tiutchev, had urged that this appointment be given to the panslav journalist, Michael Katkov, who deeply desired the post. Moreover, Nikolai himself resisted the appointment in his talks with Pobedonostsev and in a forceful memorandum to the tsar, in which he pointed out that he was old, a Lutheran, well informed only on the Caucasus, a representative of the bygone age of Nicholas I, and uninformed concerning Russian education and those engaged in its administration. However, Pobedonostsev overrode both the reluctance of Nikolai and the objections of his own friends in persuading Loris-Melikov to appoint a man "educated in the old school and in healthy pedagogical principles."[12]

The Nikolai appointment turned out to be a mistake, just as did that of Captain Baranov, for Nikolai early in 1882 proposed that an advisory council from the zemstvos and city dumas advise the Ministry. He also opposed an illegal act of the tsar in prolonging the tenure of a Moscow University professor who had reached retirement age and whose appointment was fervently opposed by a large majority of the faculty. However, during the year he served as Minister of Education, Nikolai did carry out Pobedonostsev's wishes with regard to tightening control over university students, restricting opportunities in higher education for women, and beginning preparations for the reorganization of higher education and for state support for the primary schools operated by the Orthodox Church, called parish schools.

Pobedonostsev's successes were matched, however, by failures which appeared to be just as significant. Thus, he continually urged the tsar to leave St. Petersburg for Moscow, where he would be surrounded by faithful adherents and old traditions, while a thorough cleansing of the capital could be carried out by the police under Baranov. This advice was rejected for that of Loris-Melikov, and the tsar retired to his palace at Gatchina, where he lived under heavy guard for almost two years. Pobedonostsev's continued declarations that this form of isolation from the populace at such a time was destructive were regularly disregarded by the tsar. A second minor failure which might have become important was Alexander III's decision that one of the Cossack guards who had been

killed on March 1 be given an Old Believer funeral. This was made
at the request of Loris-Melikov against the bitter protests of Pobedonostsev, who thought this elementary decency would strengthen
the Old Believers and weaken Orthodoxy.[13]

Pobedonostsev's great advantages, of course, were his close knowledge of the new tsar, his guaranteed access to him on any occasion,
and the remarkable skill with which he played on his former student's uncertainties and fears. When Alexander III assumed the
throne, Pobedonostsev worried because "the juggler Loris-Melikov
enmeshes him now, because he has the key in his hands and guards
his security." In this situation, Pobedonostsev visited the new tsar
on the evening of his father's death, but then remained away until
the tsar asked for him. In fact, throughout 1881, when Pobedonostsev's relations with Alexander III were probably closer than ever
before, he saw the tsar at most only two or three times a week. Ordinarily, when he wished to discuss something he considered important, he wrote a note to the tsar, who then invited him to come to
Gatchina the following day at one. Pobedonostsev arrived in the
middle of the morning and chatted with the empress and Baroness
Edith Raden while waiting. "I arrive, we sit down together, I tell
him everything, he agrees with all, he understands all, and I can
hardly bear not to look upon him but with tears of love and com-
passion." Quite often, nothing happened after these meetings, because the tsar failed to act on his decisions. At times, however, Pobedonostsev won power to act for the tsar. In the most important
instance, the manifesto of April 29 which destroyed Loris-Melikov's
program, Pobedonostsev forwarded a draft paper to the tsar on
April 26. When they discussed the proposal the next day, the tsar
quickly agreed to promulgate the manifesto without even consulting Loris-Melikov or the other ministers.

In his first two letters, on March 1 and March 3, Pobedonostsev
emphasized that Alexander III's elevation was a reflection of God's
will which no one could change, and that it was Alexander's responsibility to God and to the *narod* to accept the burden and,
above all, to assert his authority, to define clearly his autocratic
power, and to shake himself free from all entangling politicians.
After recommending the removal of Loris-Melikov and Saburov,
Pobedonostsev emphasized that he sought nothing for himself. "God
has so placed me that I can speak easily with you, but, believe me,
I would be happy if I had never left Moscow and my little house
on a pleasant little lane."

Pobedonostsev cited two voices in support of his position, that of Count Sergei G. Stroganov and that of the *narod*. For Pobedonostsev Stroganov represented traditional Russia, devoted to the autocracy and to the old ways. He had been close to the new tsar for more than twenty years, and he also represented the link between Alexander III and Pobedonostsev, since he had suggested Pobedonostsev as a tutor for the heir two decades earlier. "Call old S. G. Stroganov to come to talk with you. He is a man of truth, an old servant of your ancestors, and a participant in great historical events. He is on the edge of the grave, but his head is clear and his heart is Russian. There is no other man in Russia from whom it would be more beneficial for you to obtain advice in this terrible time."

Alexander III was impressed by Pobedonostsev's appeal, and invited Stroganov to the first meeting of the Council of Ministers over which he presided, on Sunday, March 8. Stroganov, who had opposed the abolition of serfdom in 1861, began the discussion with a bitter attack on Loris-Melikov and his proposals, preparing the way for Pobedonostsev's assault later in the meeting. The aged count declared that the new proposal would remove power from the hands of the absolute sovereign and give it to various politicians, who thought not of the common welfare but of their personal advantage. Moreover, this action would lead directly to a constitution, which almost no one in Russia wanted.[14]

Count Stroganov did not attend any of the later meetings of the ministers, although he did visit Pobedonostsev several times within the next two months and he may have written to the tsar also. Pobedonostsev's appeals to the *narod*, however, were constant, and he presented himself to the emperor as the voice from the land. "I am a Russian living among Russians, and I know the Russian heart and what it wants." It was the *narod* which understood the will of God and which wanted "a firm hand and a firm will" over Russia. In the first meeting of the Council of Ministers, Miliutin, Minister of War, made the mistake of referring to the *narod* as "an ignorant mass," and Pobedonostsev thereafter contrasted for the tsar the vices of St. Petersburg and the virtues of the people:

> Petersburg impressions are extremely painful and unpleasant. To live in such a troubled time and to see at every step people with no activity, with no clear thought or firm decision, occupied with the petty interests of their "I," submerged in intrigues to advance their own petty ambitions, their greed for

money, their pleasures and idle chatter—all this simply tears one's soul.

Good impressions derive only from within Russia, from everywhere in the country, from the isolated places. There the spring is still salubrious and breathes freshness; from there and not from here is our salvation. There live people with Russian souls, doing good work in faith and in hope.[15]

Pobedonostsev's first opportunity to defend his position in a government meeting came in the Winter Palace on March 8, a week after the death of Alexander II. Loris-Melikov, Miliutin, and most other ministers believed that this meeting would endorse publication of the Loris-Melikov program and the launching of studies by committees including elected representatives from the zemstvos and city government institutions. However, elder statesman Stroganov opened with his violent attack. Makov, Loris-Melikov's predecessor as Minister of the Interior and in 1881 Minister of Communications, supported this position, which was attacked with some vigor by the majority of the ministers. Pobedonostsev then launched his attack in a speech probably as significant as any made in Russia in the nineteenth century. In this harangue, he exalted autocracy, praised the mystical union which existed between the *narod* and the tsar, and declared it was shameful even to discuss such a proposal at a time of national tragedy. "Constitutions as they exist are weapons of all untruth and the source of all intrigue." The reforms introduced by Alexander II were attacked. "And then the new judicial institutions were opened with new talkfests, talkfests of lawyers, thanks to whom the most terrible crimes, murders, and other such evil acts went unpunished." Freedom of the press, the zemstvos, city government—everything but the emancipation of the serfs was denounced. Moreover, instead of acting, Russia now had new proposals based on Western ideas at a time when the ministers needed to recognize that they must all share responsibility for the murder of Alexander II.

Pobedonostsev's colleagues were aghast. Miliutin declared Pobedonostsev's talk "a negation of all which is at the foundations of European civilization." Abaza cried that if everything Pobedonostsev said were true, the tsar should discharge all of his ministers. Grand Duke Constantine Nikolaevich noted that it was clear what Pobedonostsev opposed but that he had made no positive proposals. However, the tsar at the end decided that so many complications had been introduced that no decision could be reached. He asked Stroganov to head another committee of review, but the old man declined because of age. Although a clear majority—nine to four, with three abstaining—favored the Loris-Melikov proposals, the meeting disbanded in some uncertainty, a clear triumph for Pobedonostsev, who had delayed the decision and the announcement of the new program and had confused Loris-Melikov and his supporters. A second triumph on that same day was the appointment of Baranov as governor of St. Petersburg. The tide had turned in Pobedonostsev's favor, although no one at the time realized it.[16]

Loris-Melikov, Miliutin, Abaza, and their supporters committed a number of significant errors in the weeks before and after the death of Alexander II, probably due in large part to Loris-Melikov's inexperience in political life. His principal mistakes were underestimating the pertinacity of Pobedonostsev's opposition and his assumption that the policies he adopted toward Pobedonostsev would isolate the latter from power or direct his interests into other areas, particularly the administration of the Church. He allowed Pobedonostsev to bypass him in obtaining the removal of a supporter of Loris-Melikov, Saburov, and in adding two opponents, Ignatiev and Nikolai, to the Council of Ministers. He also was unpardonably tardy in seeking the new tsar's approval of his proposal and of having it promulgated. Indeed, while he submitted a memorandum on reform to the tsar on April 12, he did not submit a draft manifesto to Alexander III, thus leaving a vacuum which Pobedonostsev skillfully filled. Valuev did not call a meeting of the Committee of Ministers to discuss the Loris-Melikov proposal or related problems from March 8 until April 21. Moreover, Loris-Melikov did not present Pobedonostsev a copy of the proposal at any time, although the heir to the throne had suggested that he do so on February 17, when he himself had approved it, and although the heir and Pobedonostsev had both mentioned this to Loris-Melikov in the following weeks and the Minister of the Interior had assured Pobedonostsev he would present him a copy. Loris-Melikov no doubt assumed that Pobedonostsev's opposition would increase if he read the paper. However, Loris-Melikov himself read it to the March 8 meeting and Pobedonostsev was sufficiently informed from this and from other sources to prepare his celebrated attack.

Loris-Melikov's negligence only increased Pobedonostsev's suspicion and his determination to triumph. While Loris-Melikov waited, Pobedonostsev continued his campaign of educating Alexander III through his letters and through their meetings. He also forwarded to the tsar letters he had received from various parts of the country reflecting his point of view. Through his relations with the empress, Baroness Edith Raden, and other ladies-in-waiting and through his correspondence, he also received information about the tsar's position and about the efforts of his opponents to effect changes. Moreover, his immensely detailed correspondence with Catherine Tiutchev in Moscow gave him an avenue for providing information to Ivan Aksakov and Michael Katkov, who attacked Loris-Melikov and his proposals in their press.[17]

Loris-Melikov finally decided to try to break the deadlock by inviting Pobedonostsev to his home for a talk on the evening of April 14. The two brief reports on this conversation which we have from letters from Pobedonostsev to the tsar and to Catherine Tiutchev and the second-hand account Miliutin provides in his diary are our only sources for this confrontation. Pobedonostsev told Catherine Tiutchev that neither had shifted his position, but that they had agreed that the Minister of the Interior in his meeting with the tsar the next day should request that a meeting of the Council of Ministers be called the following day. Pobedonostsev's letter to the tsar explained that he was delighted that they had talked and that Loris-Melikov would urge a meeting "to define the principles on which the new government must be directed." Miliutin's account declared that Pobedonostsev sought the appointment and that he assured Loris-Melikov that his March 8 diatribe had been misinterpreted.

It seems likely that Loris-Melikov explained that he had no intention of weakening the autocracy, that he was eager to smash the revolutionary movement and its foundations, and that his proposal for creating advisory committees which would include both elected and appointed representatives from the zemstvos and from the city governments was designed only to rally conservative leaders to the government and to help bind society and the government together. Pobedonostsev in return no doubt explained that he was concerned only with the preservation of the autocracy and of order, that he had not had the opportunity to study the Minister of the Interior's proposal, and that his scathing analysis of the previous twenty-five years of Russian history reflected his emotions only a week after the barbarous assassination of Alexander II.[18]

In any case, the April 21 meeting of the Council of Ministers was quite different from that of March 8. Miliutin's diary and Pobedonostsev's two detailed accounts of the session, one written two days

later to the tsar and the other written to Catherine Tiutchev in the
Gatchina railroad station on April 27 after he had drafted the
April 29 manifesto, are in agreement concerning the substance of
the discussion, and their accounts are supported by the secondhand
summary available in the diary of Egor A. Peretts. When the tsar
invited each minister to comment on the policy problems they faced,
Loris-Melikov, Miliutin, Minister of Finance Abaza, Ignatiev, Nikolai, Minister of Justice Nabokov, and Grand Duke Vladimir Alexandrovich all saw the need for closer unity of society and government and for "further improvement of the state structure" as the
most pressing problems. All agreed also in supporting the Loris-
Melikov program.

Then, to everyone's surprise, Pobedonostsev reversed his position
and announced that he shared their opinions on the need for improvement in structure and administration. He blamed Russia's
misfortunes on a profound moral decline, reflected in the pursuit
of easy profit, corruption in the bureaucracy, the absence of high
moral practice at every level of society, the passion for excessive
drink among the peasantry, and the general lack of respect for
authority. In the discussion which followed, Pobedonostsev considered that Abaza was rude and insulting in his queries, but that the
others were polite and friendly. At the conclusion of the meeting,
Alexander asked the ministers to meet once more by themselves to
reach a consensus. Loris-Melikov and his supporters were jubilant.
Abaza and Miliutin had refused to talk with Pobedonostsev from
the March 8 meeting until after the April 21 session. On the train
from St. Petersburg to Gatchina, Pobedonostsev had sat alone while
the others chatted gaily. On the return trip, they all acted "like
schoolboys on vacation," and Pobedonostsev was treated as one of
the group. It appeared that he had been conquered and that the
meeting of the ministers set for April 28 would mark his surrender.[19]

Pobedonostsev may have modified his stand at the April 21 meeting because he believed agreement could be reached with his colleagues. He may also have refrained from another tirade because he
was absolutely alone in his opposition, without Count Stroganov to
lead the way and without Makov and others to support him. In any
case, in his April 23 letter to Alexander III describing the meeting,
he concluded by saying that he believed that the disagreement was
due not to a misunderstanding but to a deeper difficulty about policy. He went on to remark that confusion could be eliminated only
by the "firm appearance" of the tsar and that a strong manifesto on

the political structure and issues was necessary. Two days later, he wrote the tsar that Loris-Melikov was wooing the Grand Duke Vladimir Alexandrovich successfully, while "all Russia" waited for leadership. "I feel that they do not want to understand me and will not listen to me, and I do not understand them. Moreover, I cannot yield to them that which I believe the truth. How many times during the life of the late tsar in my long arguments with Loris-Melikov, when he reproached me with being obstinate, did I say to him: 'I believe in one God, you, in my opinion, bow down to idols, false gods. How can you wish that we agree with each other?' "[20]

Pobedonostsev concluded his letter of April 25 with a note that he had begun work on April 24 on a draft manifesto, which he was discussing with Count Stroganov. On April 26, he mailed the manifesto to Alexander III, saying that he had weighed every word, that Count Stroganov was in full agreement, and that "all Russia waits for such a manifesto." He asserted that there was no need for the tsar to consult with any advisors about the substance or editing of the document. Early the next morning, he received a wire from the tsar that he was in full agreement and that Pobedonostsev should come to Gatchina that day. Pobedonostsev took a second copy of the paper, which his wife had copied, and spent a half-hour with the tsar, who agreed that he would issue it without further consultation on April 29. He revealed that he and the empress had both read the manifesto several times and agreed it should be issued unchanged. Pobedonostsev's wife had worked with him in drafting the paper, and Pobedonostsev told Catherine Tiutchev of it as soon as he left the tsar on April 27. Thus, three of the few people who knew of this significant paper before it was published were women.[21]

The meeting on Tuesday evening, April 28, at Loris-Melikov's was conducted in a friendly spirit. The assembled ministers quickly agreed on the establishment of a special committee of inquiry to make a study of crimes against the state and their punishment and upon a reorganization of the police. The item on "regularizing zemstvo and city institutions" led to a protest by Pobedonostsev against the electoral principle and the danger of building "local strength." However, all the others present, including Grand Duke Vladimir Alexandrovich, supported the proposal. Miliutin wrote, "That ended that." However, as the meeting ended at one in the morning, the Minister of Justice arrived with the news a manifesto had been issued, reaffirming the autocracy and thereby destroying the very foundations of the Loris-Melikov proposal. Pobedonostsev admitted that he had drafted it, while Abaza screamed that the tsar had broken his agreement with the ministers. Pobedonostsev quickly left his stunned colleagues, confident that "TRUTH is with me" but fearing that "the frenzied Asiatic Loris" might plan something foul. Loris-Melikov submitted his resignation that very day. Ignatiev succeeded him as Minister of the Interior on May 6. Within three weeks after the manifesto, Miliutin, Abaza, Grand Duke Constantine Nikolaevich, and the other supporters of Loris-Melikov had left the government, and autocratic rule had reasserted itself. Peaceful political change in Russia had been deprived the opportunity Loris-Melikov had designed, and the next changes were to come from violence.[22]

It is obvious from Pobedonostsev's letters to Alexander III and to Catherine Tiutchev that the manifesto of April 29 was his idea, that he drafted it on his own initiative, and that he persuaded Alexander III to issue it without informing any of the other ministers. However, both his own account and that of Miliutin agree that he told his stunned colleagues that the tsar had "called him to Gatchina on April 27 and ordered him to write the manifesto" so that it might be published immediately. Of course, no one asked the tsar whether this were true. Moreover, the other ministers apparently believed Pobedonostsev. Rumors did abound among them and in St. Petersburg circles for some time that Ignatiev had been a member of a conspiracy to oust Loris-Melikov and to install Ignatiev in his place, and that Katkov had been involved as well. There is no evidence whatsoever that either of these men knew of the manifesto before it was published. It is evident that Count Stroganov was consulted. However, before he died in 1883, Stroganov told Prince Meshcherskii that he had played no role whatsoever in government after March 8, 1881, and that he pitied the poor tsar, "placed between Pobedonostsev, who always knows very well what one should not do but never knows what one should do, and Ignatiev, who wants everything but can do nothing."

In 1890, Pobedonostsev told the German ambassador, General Hans von Schweinitz, that he had lost any power he had ever had and that only the strong support of Count Stroganov had helped him to persuade Alexander III not to approve proposals Alexander II had already accepted. However, when Prince Meshcherskii in 1896 ascribed full responsibility for the manifesto to Pobedonostsev alone, Pobedonostsev wrote a letter to *Grazhdanin* which denied he had overthrown the Loris-Melikov project. In this letter, he asserted that the Council of Ministers had rejected the proposal on March 8, in a meeting at which a number had attacked the project and at which the tsar had supported the critiques. The manifesto of April 29 was a completely separate act from the decision on the proposal. Indeed, Pobedonostsev argued that Alexander III repeatedly asked Loris-Melikov to prepare a manifesto reiterating the autocratic position. Loris-Melikov delayed, and "the tsar was obliged" to entrust the manifesto to Pobedonostsev. In the last months of Pobedonostsev's life, when A. A. Polovtsev reflected that adoption of an elected advisory council in 1881 might have prevented the revolution of 1905, Pobedonostsev replied that he had never seen the Loris-Melikov proposals.[23]

The April 29 manifesto is a mark of the high influence of Pobedonostsev over Alexander III. However, Pobedonostsev's contemporaries and scholars since have often been persuaded by this critical event that Pobedonostsev thereafter always exercised supreme influence over the tsar and that he guided the Russian ship of state throughout the reign of Alexander III. Pobedonostsev had considerable influence in certain fields of policy, especially those affecting the Church and education, but he sought to exercise influence only on those issues and on occasions which he thought vital. The tsar even then often chose to reject his advice. Even in 1881, when the new tsar was least sure of himself and when Pobedonostsev's influence was probably at its peak, he often failed to persuade the tsar. Thus, Abaza was allowed to remain in the Council of State several weeks after Pobedonostsev had twice insisted he be removed. A number of high appointments were made without his knowledge and others over his objections. His numerous suggestions that the tsar leave Gatchina, where he was completely isolated from the public in a way which weakened the administration and led to rumors, were all ignored. He wrote Catherine Tiutchev early in June, 1881, that he had not been invited to visit the tsar for more than three weeks. When Alexander III did visit Moscow in July and August, 1881, Pobedonostsev drafted a speech for him and wrote detailed notes concerning individuals he would encounter. However, Pobedonostsev and his friends, and presumably his enemies as well, were surprised that he was not a member of the tsar's party on this occasion or on the subsequent trip to Yaroslavl and Kostroma. Indeed, late in August Pobedonostsev had to confess that he had no knowledge concerning when the tsar would return to St. Petersburg and was even embarrassed to ask. In the middle of February, 1882, he complained that he had seen the tsar only once in the previous month.[24]

Perhaps the best illustration of the limitations upon Pobedonostsev's powers was the sudden dismissal of Captain Baranov as governor of St. Petersburg on August 13, 1881, an action of which Pobedonostsev heard only after it was common knowledge and against which his quick protests were of no avail. Baranov was brought to St. Petersburg from Kovno and named governor at Pobedonostsev's insistence, but within a month even his protector was alarmed by his wild ambition and his irresponsible actions. Once named governor, Baranov neglected Pobedonostsev and his advice, proposed an elected Grand Council in St. Petersburg to advise him as military dictator of the city, found plots against the tsar even in the highest ranks of the army, and helped frighten the tsar into staying in isolation at Gatchina. Pobedonostsev even feared that Baranov aimed to make the tsar a virtual prisoner while he became the real ruler of Russia. After Count Ignatiev was named Minister of the Interior on May 6, Baranov and Ignatiev immediately engaged in bitter conflict because of Baranov's great ambitions, his attacks on Ignatiev to the tsar, and his proposal that the Russian police system, which was Ignatiev's responsibility, be reorganized and placed under him. This conflict drove Baranov back to Pobedonostsev for support, but Ignatiev, while on tour with the tsar, persuaded him to discharge Baranov and to name him governor of Archangel, a post which Baranov accepted most reluctantly. Pobedonostsev's protest that Baranov was "the best man, indeed the only man" for St. Petersburg was ignored. The defeat became doubly bitter a year later when rumors, almost certainly without any foundation, swept St. Petersburg that Pobedonostsev's wife was going to leave him for Baranov.[25]

Ignatiev's triumph and Pobedonostsev's defeat were only temporary, for Ignatiev himself was dismissed in May, 1882, at Pobedonostsev's insistence, when Ignatiev urged the tsar to issue a manifesto calling for the election of a *zemskii sobor* (territorial assembly). Pobedonostsev had vigorously defended Ignatiev in December, 1881, against an intrigue designed to force his resignation as Minister of the Interior. However, he was annoyed when Ignatiev called representatives of the zemstvos to St. Petersburg in the summer and fall of 1881, to serve as technical advisors to committees studying the redemption payments, the head tax, and other issues of central

interest to the peasants. He was incensed when Ignatiev made proposals in some ways similar to those of Loris-Melikov a year earlier.
He was especially indignant because Ignatiev followed the same
tactic Probedonostsev had used. Ignatiev urged Alexander III to
issue, without informing or consulting his other ministers, a dramatic manifesto announcing his decision to call a *zemskii sobor* of
"the most able men" to consult with the government at the time of
his coronation. The tsar in this case disregarded his advice and
showed the draft manifesto to Pobedonostsev, who organized opposition to it in the Council of Ministers and then quickly persuaded Alexander III to dismiss Ignatiev.

Ignatiev's failure effectively destroyed the possibility for the creation of any kind of elected advisory council, one which might have
bridged the gap between government and society and which might
have established a foundation for the creation of constitutional government. Many prominent Russian conservatives favored such a
system, which was central to the beliefs and program of the Moscow
Slavophils. Indeed, Valuev and later Grand Duke Constantine
Nikolaevich in 1879 and 1880 discussed with the tsar and with other
members of his circle proposals somewhat like those of Loris-Melikov, particularly in suggesting that the gentry, the zemstvos, and the
city dumas be invited to select representatives to provide expert
advice to the Council of State concerning economic problems. However, these advocates of the *zemskii sobor* or of some form of elected
advisory council were not organized or united, and Pobedonostsev
was able to destroy their "childish fantasies" as he had the proposal
of Loris-Melikov.

On March 6, 1881, for example, Pobedonostsev was horrified to
receive a letter from Olga Novikov in which she advocated a territorial assembly, as she had in her 1880 volume, *Russia and England
from 1876–1880*, prohibited by the censor in Russia for that reason.
Five days later, Pobedonostsev received from Boris Chicherin, who
had been a friend for twenty years and who was a well-known liberal
jurist and scholar, a long memorandum for the tsar which proposed
that the Council of State be enlarged by the addition of elected
members with advisory power from the nobility and the zemstvos.
In March, 1882, Michael Katkov, the influential editor of *Moskovskiia Vedomosti* who was a close friend of Pobedonostsev, a vigorous
panslav, and a strong supporter of firm repression, wrote so frequently about the need for an elected group of advisors that he was
forbidden by the censor to continue to discuss or advocate a terri-

torial assembly. Pobedonostsev's attack upon Ignatiev and his proposal was therefore especially ruthless because he realized that Ignatiev was only reflecting a view held by many in both St. Petersburg and Moscow and one for which the tsar himself might have some sympathy. He pointed out to Alexander III that establishment even of a "purely consultative assembly" would not calm and unite the country but would have the opposite effect, strengthening the feeling of crisis and persuading the "simple people" that Russia faced threats as serious as those of 1613. The appointment of Count Dmitrii Tolstoy to replace Ignatiev as Minister of Interior reflects the degree of the change which had occurred since the spring of 1880, when Tolstoy had been removed as Director General of the Holy Synod of the Church and as Minister of Education because he was considered too conservative. Pobedonostsev and Tolstoy became close allies in fastening restrictive policies upon the body of Russia.[26]

The spring of 1881 is properly considered a crucial period in modern Russian history. Most contemporaries and observers believe that adoption of the Loris-Melikov proposals would have eased the tension in Russia, won support for the government and the state from many who were in effect neutral between the government and its revolutionary critics, isolated the revolutionaries and destroyed the atmosphere of understanding and sympathy in which they operated, and created a foundation upon which essential progress could have been made. Above all, they would have led to the creation of liberal and conservative political groups or parties twenty-five years earlier than they did in fact appear, thereby creating a far more substantial foundation for a constitutional monarchy and representative government than Russia was able to build before 1914. Pobedonostsev's success in shattering this possibility not only destroyed the bright hopes of these years, but saddled Russia for twenty-five years with a repressive and essentially sterile policy which won little support, increased the attractiveness of various proposals for revolution, frustrated individuals and groups eager to participate in a program for strengthening and improving Russia, and delayed the development of institutions on which a democratic Russia might have been built.

VIII

Director
General of the Synod

POBEDONOSTSEV's reputation in Russian history rests largely upon his actions as *Ober-Prokuror* or Director General of the Most Holy Synod of the Russian Orthodox Church from April, 1880, until October, 1905. For twenty-five years, he was in effect Minister for Religious Affairs in a state which recognized and supported a national church and in which the Church's range of responsibility and authority had always been great. Moreover, Pobedonostsev remained a member of the Council of State and of the Senate, and after November, 1880, was also a member of the Council of Ministers. These official positions and his relations with the tsars, their wives, the imperial family, and the court insured him enormous influence in Russian political life in the last quarter of the nineteenth century.*

The Code of Laws of the Russian Empire declared firmly that "the foremost and dominant faith in the Russian Empire is the Christian Orthodox Catholic Eastern Confession." As the official

---

* I have not been able to examine the archives of the Synod and of the other government departments, which contain some quantity of information concerning Pobedonostsev's activities as Director General of the Synod and as an important participant in discussions of high policy from 1880 until 1905. Moreover, Soviet scholars have devoted remarkably little attention to this period and to the institutions and issues with which Pobedonostsev was most concerned, so that even their research in these closed materials is not of much use. However, the voluminous official reports which Pobedonostsev prepared for the tsar on his responsibilities at the Synod, his correspondence and that of others, and other official reports, memoirs, and contemporary journals provide an immense amount of information concerning Pobedonostsev's career as an official during these critical years.

state religion, the Russian Orthodox Church enjoyed a number of important benefits and privileges. It was protected and promoted by the government, which also officially denied missionary work and often even ordinary parish functions to other religious groups. The Orthodox Church possessed a monopoly of religious propaganda and also had the right of censorship of literature dealing in any way with religious or moral issues. It not only enjoyed state protection and support for all its activities, but it also was represented in Russian political institutions at all levels. Thus, the Director General of the Synod gave it representation in the various organs of the central government. At the same time, the bishops had the right to name representatives of the Church to the county and provincial zemstvos and to the town councils. After 1718, the parish church was the official place for publication or announcement of laws and decrees. Parish priests were required to report to the civil authorities the confessions of those "with evil intent" toward the state or the sovereign and to report on general disaffection as well.

The state's financial contribution to the Orthodox Church was considerable. Nicholas I in 1840 had begun the practice of grants to the Church for salaries of the clergy, and later tsars gradually increased these sums. In 1892, Pobedonostsev persuaded Alexander III to grant 250,000 rubles toward raising the salaries of the clergy. Thereafter, direct grants from the state treasury for priests' salaries began to increase enormously. By 1905, funds for salaries alone from the treasury amounted to almost 12 million rubles (approximately $6 million), almost half the total cash income of the clergy. In 1897, almost 99 percent of the funds for the salaries of Pobedonostsev's Synod staff came from the state treasury. Professor Curtiss has estimated that state funds constituted about 20 percent of the Church's total income at the turn of the century.[1]

The Russian Orthodox Church was not only the officially recognized and supported religious institution in Russia, but it was also under the direct authority and control of the state. Thus, the tsar, "supreme defender and preserver of the dogmas of the ruling faith," had the right to supervise "the orthodoxy of belief and decorum in the holy Church." It appears the tsar selected and appointed Pobedonostsev as Director General of the Synod without having consulted any members of the hierarchy or the clergy on this important decision. Moreover, the tsar on occasion interfered directly in important Church affairs. As Pobedonostsev wrote to Catherine Tiutchev on February 8, 1882, Platon, the new metropolitan in Kiev, had been named "at the personal order of the tsar," an order which it was "impossible to oppose." When Platon died in October, 1891, Pobedonostsev asked the tsar for advice in the selection of his successor, as he did when other high clergymen died. On occasion, the tsar criticized Pobedonostsev for releasing messages for the clergy through the Synod without first receiving his permission. Even the empress sometimes interfered in important religious matters. In 1902 she pressed the tsar to have the hermit Serafim Sarovskii, who died in 1833 and whose biography she had just read, raised to sainthood. The tsar strongly urged this on Pobedonostsev and the Synod in order to please his wife, and he ratified the decision the following year.[2]

Under the organization established for the Church by Peter the Great in 1721, an act which in itself reveals clearly the state's authority, the supreme governing body of the Church was the Most Holy Synod. For the following two centuries, the Synod had full power over the Church, its dogma and ritual, the education of its clergymen and monks and all Church educational establishments, the diocesan administration, Church property, and discipline of both monastic and parish clergy. The hierarchy and the clergy were so subject to the rule of the Synod that they could not protest or oppose its rulings.

The Synod was composed of the *Ober-Prokuror* or Director General, the metropolitans of St. Petersburg, Moscow, and Kiev, the exarch of Georgia (who almost never attended a meeting), and eight or nine bishops nominated for short terms by the Director General, appointed by the tsar, and "summoned" to sessions by the tsar. The Synod ordinarily held three annual sessions, generally with only six prelates in attendance. These prelates were chosen by the Director General, who thereby controlled attendance at the meetings. Pobedonostsev and his staff established the agenda for the meetings, which were hasty and provided little time for discussion. Indeed, Pobedonostsev very rarely placed important items on the agenda, and the meetings of which we have record devoted a great deal of time to trivial matters which should not have come before such an apparently important body.

The Holy Synod was completely under the control of the Director General, who was a layman appointed and removed by the tsar and who was considered "the eye of the tsar" in the Church. The Director General as the representative of the all-powerful tsar reported directly to him, served as the intermediary between the Church—

including even the highest prelates—and the tsar, and alone within the Synod had the power to issue its decrees. As a result of pressure from Pobedonostsev upon Alexander II and Alexander III, the position of Director General of the Synod within the government was strengthened considerably. Thus, after November, 1880, Pobedonostsev was a member of the Council of Ministers. In 1887, he obtained the same rights as other ministers to participate in the decisions of the Senate, a right the Director General had held until sixty years earlier. Ten years later, in 1897, he persuaded Witte and the tsar that the salary of the Director General ought to be the same as that of the other ministers, 18,000 rubles a year.[3]

The prelates were isolated and weak and were so often transferred that they were unable to create bases of power. Under Pobedonostsev, for example, some bishops were transferred almost every year, and most of them spent less than four consecutive years at one post. All members of the hierarchy were monastics, or "black" clergy. Moreover, the bishops had little authority within their own dioceses, in which the administrative work was the responsibility of the religious consistory. The four or five priests in the consistory were dominated by the lay officials of the consistorial chancery. The chief of these lay officials, the secretary, was appointed by the Director General, who therefore obtained authority for the Synod in every diocese. Certainly, much of the responsibility for the red-tape and corruption which afflicted the administration of the Church, as well as of the state, was due to this highly centralized system of control.

The clergy were naturally even less able than the hierarchy to resist the Holy Synod's control. Almost all of the clergy were sons of clergymen, men of little education or culture, and they reflected that background of poverty and submissiveness. Poorly educated, overworked, generally unloved by their own parishioners, the clergy accepted meekly the orders they were given and served their people, the state, and the Church as simple bureaucrats.[4]

The services of the Church to the state were considerable. The most important was the intangible, pervasive influence which a state church can provide in an underdeveloped country in which the population feels respect and reverence for authority. The Church published and announced manifestoes and ukases, maintained important official records, solemnized official ceremonies with its rituals, and sanctified oaths and other expressions of loyalty and support. It preached submission to authority, respect for the status quo, and patriotism, particularly at times of stress or crisis, and it considered the opponents of respectability and order its enemies also.

Throughout his life, Pobedonostsev unthinkingly accepted and supported this system, as did most Russian officials and churchmen and indeed most Russians. In fact, even at the end of his life, when this arrangement was obviously crumbling, Pobedonostsev defended it as beneficial to Church and state, sanctified by tradition, and even absolutely essential. By that time, some other Russians, including a growing number of churchmen, were becoming convinced that the Church was severely handicapped by its ties and even subservience to the state. When they noted the serious deficiencies of the Church, the popular distrust of it as an instrument of the government, the advantages which other religious groups enjoyed even under state and Church harassment, and the thriving conditions of free churches in other countries, they began to propose that the Russian Orthodox Church break its ties and become independent, devoting its energies entirely to its spiritual functions. This reform movement became powerful within the Church, as it did in Russia in general, and contributed importantly to the overthrow of the system which Pobedonostsev represented.[5]

Pobedonostsev was a man of profound religious faith. He was well known to a large number of important churchmen, who in the 1870's came to consider him a kind of special representative of the future tsar for religious affairs and who visited him when in St. Petersburg. In some ways, his knowledge of the situation of the Russian Orthodox Church was excellent. He had a low opinion of the princes of the Church, many of whom he had met and others of whom he knew through official reports or comments from friends and associates. He was aware of the poverty and ignorance which afflicted the clergy and never idealized them or the role they might play. Indeed, his correspondence with members of the hierarchy and with friends from the very beginning of his career as Director General of the Synod reveals a cynical awareness of the shocking ills which beset the clergy and the Church as a whole, as well as strong suspicion that these shortcomings could not be repaired. In fact, the opinions concerning the clergy and the Church which Pobedonostsev expressed privately did not differ substantially from those of their most severe critics.[6]

Pobedonostsev's knowledge of the Church was naturally increased considerably by his work as director of Church affairs and by the visits of review he paid to different parts of Russia, particularly during the first five or six years of his service as Director General. However, even though he was uncomfortably aware of some of the Church's shortcomings, he had no conception whatsoever of the massive ills which afflicted the spirit and body of Orthodoxy, of the remarkably feeble influence of the Church upon all segments of society, including the peasants, and of the striking lack of spiritual vitality which undermined the Church's foundations. Moreover, it is clear from his official reports, the policy explanations which he issued, and his private letters and utterances, that he was completely unable to understand the effective appeal which the Old Believers, the various evangelical sects, and the mystical sects exerted.

Thus, he estimated with reasonable accuracy, indeed probably exaggerated, the power of Mohammedanism in Central Asia, of Lutheranism in Finland and along the Baltic, and of Roman Catholicism among the Poles along the western borders of the empire. However, his massive annual and biannual reports to the tsar on the Church ordinarily did not include the non-Russian, non-Orthodox inhabitants of the empire in his official statistics, as though he assigned them some kind of special status outside the Church and the state. The figures he did provide concerning these populations are sensible and probably as close to objective as the data of those years allow. He was not hopeful that the Church could make any inroads among the Lutherans and the Catholics on the western borders. In fact, he would have been delighted to keep these faiths from expanding their influence.[7]

However, Pobedonostsev, like most other official Orthodox observers, completely underestimated the number and spiritual vitality of the Russian inhabitants of the empire who rejected Orthodoxy for some other faith. Indeed, official estimates of the number of Russian non-Orthodox were grossly misleading throughout the period after the 1660's, when the Old Believers resented the efforts of Patriarch Nikon to correct the prayer books and liturgy and left the Russian Orthodox Church to remain true to the customs, gestures, and words of their fathers. During the succeeding centuries, especially in the nineteenth century, the Old Believers themselves were riven as new sects splintered. Moreover, a number of other evangelical sects appeared, such as the Molokane, the Dukhobors, and the Stundists in particular, and mystical sects, such as the Khlysty and Skoptsy, rose also.

The statistics concerning the Orthodox Church and concerning these sects as well were difficult to establish until the second half of the nineteenth century, but the sects presented special difficulties because the various penalties against non-Orthodox groups among the Russian members of the population were so heavy and because the Orthodox priests and others who helped collect the data often deliberately falsified the figures. The official statistics were in such flagrant disagreement with the knowledge and judgment of state officials that in 1858 a Statistical Committee was established under Count L. A. Perovskii to review the evidence. This committee found the official count of the non-Orthodox Russians grossly inaccurate. Indeed, when the official figure for the sects was 829,971, the Perovskii committee estimated there were 9,300,000. The previous official figure for non-Orthodox Russians in the province of Nizhni Novgorod was 20,240. The Statistical Committee concluded there were 172,600, and the Bishop of Nizhni Novgorod put his estimate at 233,323. In Yaroslavl province, the Statistical Committee found 278,417 Russian members of various sects at a time when Ivan Aksakov estimated there were 672,687 and the official figure was 7,454.[8]

In the early 1860's, approximately 15 percent of the Russian population (including White Russian and Ukrainian) of the Russian empire belonged to one or another of the sects. Professor Curtiss in his masterful study published in 1940 estimated that approximately the same percentage of the Russian population belonged to the sects in 1900. Pobedonostsev, however, refused to accept the facts and consistently underestimated the number and verve of the non-Orthodox Russians. His annual reports from 1881 through 1905 show a gradual increase in the number of Orthodox communicants, clergy, churches, and other measurable indices of Church strength, but deny any growth to the Old Believers and the other sects. His statistics for the Orthodox Church show a steady rise from 63 million in 1881, to 77 million in 1895, and 88 million in 1904. Even though his official reports indicate that the total number of converts from paganism and all faiths over this period averaged less than 15,000 a year, and even though his reports and his letters overflow with alarm concerning the vigor and power of the sects, Pobedonostsev estimated in 1903 that about 70 percent of the population held active membership in the Orthodox Church and that there were fewer than 2 million Old Believers in a total population of approximately 125 million.[9]

Pobedonostsev had many of the good qualities of the dedicated bureaucrat, but he was not competent as an administrator. He loved to work and despised those who did not, he was quick and efficient in accomplishing tasks, he was logical and clear in organizing facts and ideas, he was loyal to his superiors, and he was unusually honest in forsaking personal advantage from his work or his relationships. He confessed that he felt uneasy and even unwell when he had nothing to do. The last forty years of his life are filled with complaints about the number of reports he had to prepare and read, the meetings he was required to attend, the men and women from all classes and all parts of Russia whom he had to see, and the functions of all kinds which became his responsibility. Yet, it is clear that keeping busy was essential for him and that he accepted new responsibilities without reflection or review.

He rejoiced in 1878 when he could add another room to his apartment so that he could interview petitioners efficiently. From the early 1870's on, his apartment and his office were crowded with men and women from all over Russia seeking advice and assistance for collecting funds for a convent, for getting government permission to build a railroad, for publishing a manuscript, for aid in transferring an incompetent priest, for counsel in establishing a new school. He complained eternally in his correspondence about these visitors, who devoured his time and who filled his apartment in the afternoon and evening, but at the same time he never refused to see anyone, and it is clear that he enormously enjoyed this role. In fact, this beloved function was central to his role in the government and to his political philosophy. His obsession with bureaucratic work became greater as his interest in scholarship declined. Indeed, the lonely hours he once devoted to research and publication were then given to bureaucratic tasks, in which he revelled but which at the same time, like many administrators, he declared a waste of time.[10]

The qualities which served him and his superiors well with regard to ordinary tasks hampered him when he was given major responsibilities, such as directing the Volunteer Fleet or serving as Director General of the Synod. In these offices, he showed himself unable to define the large, long-term problems, to locate and appoint others to assist him, or to delegate authority to competent and reliable men. Thus, he retained the organization of the Holy Synod as he found it in 1880, although his predecessors had neglected to make the central office of the Church modern and effective. He simply leaped into his new position. There is no evidence that he ever studied the administration of the Church or discussed with his predecessor or with his assistants in the Holy Synod the principal problems and shortcomings. Apparently, he simply entered the Synod office and began to work as hard as he could on the papers which came across his desk.

He complained frequently that he had no one to help him, but there is no evidence that he sought assistance. Every matter which came to the Synod claimed his attention, from anonymous complaints against a bishop to the reorganization of the Church's courts. Thus, in the late fall of 1880, he confessed that he was trying by himself to create a new policy for dealing with the Uniates in the Kholm areas and on the western border, to advise the tsar on the negotiations then underway with the Papacy concerning the nomination of several Roman Catholic bishops in Russian territory, to review Church policy on remarriage after divorce in several different kinds of circumstance, to nominate secretaries for a number of consistories in various parts of Russia, to review new means of restricting the influence of the Old Believers, and to appoint a number of bishops and rectors of seminaries. While assuming full responsibility for critical questions of this kind without the assistance of an organized staff, he also found time to prepare a report urging the tsar to close all theaters during Lent and on all holidays and to examine the wisdom of continuing the manufacture of candles by diocesan factories.[11]

Pobedonostsev's own records and the memoirs of friendly and hostile prelates alike reveal that he considered the Holy Synod meetings unimportant. He rarely introduced the central issues of policy or administration to this group, and there is no evidence that the members of the Holy Synod introduced or discussed important policy problems. Indeed, the sessions were usually desultory, and Pobedonostsev complained that his colleagues rarely had studied the agenda or considered seriously any of the information he had made available to them.

During his first two years in office, he traveled extensively, especially in the northwestern part of European Russia and to the areas where Lutheranism and Catholicism were powerful. These visits gave him considerable insight into the strengths and weaknesses of the Church and into the main problems the Church faced. However, he ceased taking these trips after 1882 or 1883, although he did on occasion visit an area where especially troublesome problems had arisen. He travelled east of the Urals only twice, on brief official missions, and he entered the Caucasus only three times, on inspection tours. Moreover, he never visited some centers, and he relied on bishops' reports which he knew to be inadequate.

At the same time he developed no alternative system for collecting information and judgments from the bishops, the rectors of seminaries and other religious institutions, and other eminent religious
leaders. Indeed, he knew few of the bishops in the church well, and
he made no systematic review of their work. He organized three
sobors or councils of the hierarchy in his first eight years as head
of the Synod, but none of these meetings was fruitful and he did not
arrange even regional meetings of ecclesiastics in his last fifteen years
of service. His relations with the metropolitans were not close, and
the hierarchy in Moscow and St. Petersburg had little influence
upon him.

As the Director General of the Synod, he relied heavily upon
correspondence with particular friends in the hierarchy, men as
remote from St. Petersburg as his lay correspondents, Nicholas Ilminskii in Kazan and Sergei Rachinskii in Tatev, near Smolensk.
Indeed, just as these two men had a special interest in educating
peasants and non-Russian Moslems, so Pobedonostsev's closest associates in the hierarchy, such as Nikanor, Bishop of Ufa and later of
Odessa, Illarion, Archbishop of Poltava, and Makarii, Archbishop
of Tomsk, devoted a major part of their energy to missionary activity among the Stundists and Old Believers. These clerics, who received special honors and awards from the tsar, provided him petty
and often quite improper information about their colleagues in
both the Church and in the civil administration, especially the governors general, and they often pandered to Pobedonostsev's beliefs.
He also made heavy use of correspondence and visits from friends
in various European parts of the empire, generally men and women
who shared his political philosophy, rather than using the administrative apparatus of the Holy Synod itself. Finally, his wife and
friends of the Pobedonostsevs, particularly Catherine Tiutchev
until she died in the spring of 1882, often influenced Church policy,
especially in appointments within the Synod staff and within the
hierarchy. Indeed, analysis of the administrative procedures which
Pobedonostsev followed, particularly in obtaining information concerning prelates and in collecting recommendations for appointments and promotions, helps to explain his spectacular failures in
judgment concerning those whom he chose or recommended for
high office. In other words, he was both a bumbling leader and an
incompetent administrator for the Church.[12]

Pobedonostsev's principal shortcomings as an administrator
clearly derived from his failure to define his function and to con-

sider carefully the main problems he faced and the best means of organizing the forces available. He sought to direct a church which claimed 63 million communicants in 1881 with a staff budget as large as that of the sixth department of the Senate when he began work in Moscow in 1846. He did nothing to reorganize, enlarge, or improve his staff, except to bring Vladimir K. Sabler as counsel to the Holy Synod. Sabler, who had begun to study civil law in Moscow University during Pobedonostsev's last year there as a lecturer, had had an undistinguished record as a scholar and as a bureaucrat, moving from position to position without advancing in responsibility. Indeed, Pobedonostsev's anonymous article in *Grazhdanin* on October 29, 1873, attacking Russian jurists, especially those at Moscow University, had singled out Sabler as one of the less competent temporary members of the faculty in the field of civil law.

Pobedonostsev was privately quite critical of Sabler for his lack of organizing sense and discipline, but he admired his energy and relied on him increasingly to help administer the Church. Sabler soon was named director of the chancery, with especial responsibilities for censorship, he became associate director general in 1892, and he was named a Senator in 1896, a member of the Council of State in 1906, and Director General of the Synod in 1911. There is no evidence that Sabler possessed any administrative competence or made significant suggestions concerning Church policy. He did manage, however, to create a large number of bitter enemies among the clergy and even within the hierarchy.[13]

Pobedonostsev's definition of the Russian Orthodox Church, of the Russian empire, of the relations between the Church and the people who lived within the empire, and of the relationship between the Church and the remainder of the world is naturally at the core of his work as Director General of the Synod and of his entire philosophy. Briefly, he thought that all Russians, White Russians and Little Russians or Ukrainians as well as Great Russians, ought to be and indeed legally were members of the Russian Orthodox Church. He considered that the Church's first responsibility was to the great majority of the Russians who were active members of the Church; its main function was to provide religious services, guidance, and inspiration to these millions, and its principal problem was to increase their level of knowledge and understanding of Orthodoxy.

Unhappily, some Russians had fallen away from or been enticed away from the Russian Orthodox Church by the Old Believers or

one of the many sects. The Church's second main mission was to
return these wandering sheep to the true religious and national fold
and then to reduce and even destroy these crippling rival forces.
In fact, Pobedonostsev devoted a great deal of his time and energy
and the Church's resources to battle with the Old Believers and the
sects in an effort to create a spiritual unity among the Russians who
lived in the empire.

The third circle or community in which Pobedonostsev's Church
lived and acted was that inhabited by non-Russians, generally on
the borders of the empire or in areas such as Central Asia, far removed from Moscow and St. Petersburg. These included Finns, Germans, Poles, Jews, Uzbeks, and others who held religious beliefs
(Lutheranism, Catholicism, Mohammedanism, or Judaism) quite
different from Orthodoxy, the Old Believers, and the sects. In different degrees, men of these non-Russian nationalities and non-
Orthodox religious faiths were a threat to Orthodoxy, particularly
to those Russian Orthodox who lived among them. His goal so far
as they were concerned was to restrict their influence and their faiths
to the non-Russians and gradually to whittle down and eliminate
the religious forces, especially that of the Moslems, which had the
weakest organization and offered the least powerful intellectual
challenge.

Beyond the boundaries of Russia lived a few Russians who were
members of the Russian Orthodox Church, a few non-Russians who
were members of the same communion, and millions of Slavs who
were members of the greater family of Eastern Orthodoxy. These
peoples were also within his vision, although at the very horizon
of it, and they provided the outer pan-Orthodox ring of the series
of concentric circles in which he viewed Orthodoxy and his responsibilities.[14]

Because of his profound pessimism and growing cynicism and
because conservatism to him usually meant inaction or at least inertia, his policies for the Church have a markedly passive character.
Although he did not appreciate the profound weaknesses of Orthodoxy and its failure to exert significant influence on any part of
Russian society, he did have some understanding of the grave shortcomings of the clergy. In fact, the view from what he called his
mountain top persuaded him that a substantial reform program was
beyond consideration. The great majority of the clergy was ignorant,
isolated, overworked, and indifferent even to the most sacred of
their duties. A substantial number were disorderly and drunkards,

some were even revolutionaries, and scandal in one form or another was common. Even the good priests were passive, and the excellent ones were rare. Pobedonostsev was aware long before he became Director General that the Church had too few priests and that a considerable number of churches had been closed in the 1870's because of this shortage. Finally, he believed that fewer than half of the bishops were competent, that the Synod itself was an uncertain tool, and that ecclesiastical congresses would have little effect.[15]

Pobedonostsev quickly became convinced that creating parish schools throughout Russia to teach reading, writing, arithmetic, and religion at the most basic and elementary level was the principal means for preserving Orthodoxy. He supported this drive with an extensive program of publications, which will be discussed later.

So far as the Orthodox clergy was concerned, he sought immediately to increase its number by reducing the training required, reforming the seminaries, and finally, especially after 1893, increasing salaries substantially. Even before he became Director General, Pobedonostsev was convinced that the Church was over-training the rural clergy. He argued that the conditions of rural life were such that graduates of seminaries were not only not required but were even handicapped and frustrated in their pastoral work. He was impressed by the achievements of priests of high character but little learning, and by the vitality of Old Believer parishes whose clergy was infinitely less well trained than even those of the Church. He therefore lowered the educational requirements for the clergy, encouraged bishops to appoint to vacancies men who had not completed their seminary work, and sought to introduce into the seminaries more emphasis on elementary knowledge, on singing, and on effective simple preaching which would not be beyond the capacities of the illiterate peasant. According to the official history of the Church during the reign of Alexander III, the number of priests increased from 46,800 in 1881, to 56,900 in 1894. The School of St. Vladimir, which his wife founded and directed in St. Petersburg for daughters of rural priests who were quite likely to marry priests and to teach, was of the same character, for it emphasized home economics, singing, and the old-fashioned virtues, rather than learning.[16]

Pobedonostsev was appalled by the seminaries and religious academies when he first visited them, and during his first decade as Director General of the Synod he paid considerable attention to their improvement. He visited seminaries and tested the students orally in all of their subjects, from Russian language and literature to doctrine and choral work. He sought the appointment of rectors and faculty of high quality and strong discipline, and he tightened the system of inspection in an effort to prevent scandals, which occurred on occasion nonetheless, especially in Tver. Finally, especially in the earlier years before his attention was drawn to other problems, he urged the construction of dormitories and the creation of basic libraries.[17]

One of the critical problems for the Church and one of the main causes for the shortage of priests, their dissatisfaction, and the numerous scandals was their very low incomes. At the turn of the century, the annual cash income of the average priest was six or seven hundred rubles (approximately $350). Even this figure represented some improvement within the previous decade. In dividing the funds which he obtained for priests' salaries, Pobedonostsev gave especially large shares to rural clergy, especially those in the western border areas and in Central Asia.[18]

Of the religious groups which most alarmed him, the *Raskolniki* or Old Believers, the Stundists and Baptists, and the Pashkovists most attracted his ire. He consistently refused to accept the estimates of the Old Believers themselves and of some observers that they totalled 15 million, but at the same time he asserted that the 2 million Old Believers were a cancerous growth on the Russian body politic and must somehow be eliminated. He wrote in his official report to the tsar for 1890–91, "The characteristic features of the *raskol* remain what they always were, dark ignorance, callous stagnancy of thought marked by extreme intolerance, deceit, slyness, meanness, and frivolity. Such are the qualities of the mass of the Old Believers and of their leaders as well."[19]

His analysis of the survival and power of the Old Believers was quite different during the last years of his life from what it had been when he first became Director General of the Synod. Thus, late in life, after he had had to admit that his efforts to restrict and reduce the *raskol* had failed, he emphasized their skill in concentrating in remote areas where the Orthodox Church was weak, such as parts of Siberia, and in taking advantage and on occasion violating the provisions of the 1883 law which defined their very limited rights. Earlier, however, he had ascribed their survival to habit and their already long history; the firmness and stoutness of the rules and formalities they had created; the wealth of some Old Believers, which he said served as a magnet for poor Orthodox peasants and to bribe and enslave Orthodox Church members; and, more and more as time when on, the friendly attitude toward them shown by writers and journalists, "the liberals." On occasion, he described the Old Believers as a lower middle-class and poor peasant movement, fed by economic forces beyond the control of the state.[20]

The policies which he recommended toward the Old Believers reflected his analysis of their roots and his determination, first, to remove them and their influence from Russian life, and second, to educate the Orthodox Russian people against their attractions. His position toward the other sects among the Russians was the same, although he considered the Old Believers the greatest threat to the Church and the state and made them his major target. In this he was criticized by his good friend, Catherine Tiutchev, but she died in the spring of 1882, and thereafter few reminded him that "you do not persuade people with persecution." Instead, he relied through his years of high state service upon the views of a scholar of the Old Believers who was bitterly prejudiced against them, Professor Nicholas I. Subbotin, who had been a member of the Moscow Ecclesiastical Academy faculty in the monastery of the Holy Trinity since 1852. Subbotin, who lived from 1827 until 1905, spent his adult life studying the Old Believers and published more than four hundred articles and forty books on them. Pobedonostsev maintained a voluminous correspondence with him, sent him official data and reports concerning the Old Believers, asked his advice concerning policies and appointments, and followed his suggestions in establishing Church and state policies toward the Old Believers and the evangelical sects as well.[21]

Pobedonostsev and his advisor agreed on a two-pronged policy for restricting and destroying the power of other religious groups. First of all, they consistently urged use of the state's authority to deny the Old Believers and the sects any rights not clearly granted them under Russian law and to harass them in every way possible. Second, they created an educational and propagandistic program designed to wean Old Believers away from their church and to strengthen Orthodox hostility toward them.

Long before he became Director General of the Synod, Pobedonostsev wrote approvingly in his *Kurs grazhdanskago prava* (Course on Civil Law) that no member of the Russian Orthodox Church could legally leave "the state religious belief" for another. He believed therefore that the power of the state could be used against anyone or any group which sought to seduce members of the Orthodox faith and that state power could be used to eliminate the attractions which rival faiths offered. In fact, he wrote to Subbotin that "one can do nothing without the support of the state's authority." Therefore, he refused all petitions from the Old Believers and the sects for any rights not specifically authorized for them, from building altars in their officially tolerated cemeteries to repairing their chapels. He refused permission for Old Believers in Austria to visit their dying parents in Russia, and he sought to prevent Old Believers from settling along the Chinese Eastern Railroad in Manchuria. Finally, he used his influence to persuade other departments of the government to restrict the Old Believers in every way possible. He sought to place men who viewed these problems as he did in important government positions, particularly in the Ministry of the Interior.[22]

The position of the Old Believers and of the evangelical sects was sometimes unclear in Russian law, especially in Moscow, "the center of Church and state power." Catherine the Great had given the Old Believers the right to have two cemeteries in Moscow, one for those who had a clergy and one for those who did not. The former one, the Rogozhskoe cemetery, had become a real religious center, with chapels, a convent, and other buildings. Under Alexander II, when the judicial reforms were being created, special commissions were established to study the legal position of the Old Believers and of the various sects. Alexander III, who had a brief affection for the *raskol*, perhaps because some of Alexander II's bravest guards had been Old Believers, decided the work of these research committees should be used to clarify the position of the non-Orthodox. Count Dmitrii Tolstoy, who became Minister of the Interior in 1882, apparently agreed, perhaps because they wanted the law more carefully defined so that the Old Believers could be restricted more easily. Finally, in May, 1883, after completing the tortuous process established for imperial acts, the law was issued.

The 1883 act gave all schismatics (except the Skoptsy, who were therefore placed beyond the law) the right to hold internal passports, to engage in trade and industry, and to hold minor offices. They were authorized to hold religious services in their homes and in houses of prayer, but these buildings were not allowed to have bells or other distinguishing marks. No new places of worship could be built, and repairs of those which existed could be made only with the permission of the Ministry of the Interior and of the Synod. Funeral services could be held, but religious vestments could not be worn then or at any other time. Moreover, no public demonstrations of worship or processions were allowed, and proselytizing or missionary work was also forbidden.[23]

The May law clearly restricted the religious rights of the Old Believers and of the evangelical sects. Pobedonostsev, who had been one of its prime supporters, robustly denied that the rights of anyone were reduced in any way so far as religious belief was concerned or that the power of the state was used to defend the position of the established church, just as other adherents of intolerance in more recent times have defined restrictions as freedom. However, while the *raskol* and the sects rejoiced that they now had at least some rights defined and had even been recognized and made to some degree respectable in the eyes of the law, Pobedonostsev was pleased with the power he now had to deny the non-Orthodox everything not specifically granted in 1883. Church and state policies from 1883 until 1905 were therefore devoted to a precise interpretation of this law and to an effort to hamper the various sects in every way. Moreover, Pobedonostsev fought consistently, especially late in life, to make the law even more repressive, particularly with regard to the Old Believers' efforts to enlarge their cemeteries and to build schools and chapels.[24]

Because of his special interest in education and in propaganda, Pobedonostsev was relentless in denying other religious groups the right to publish or to import materials concerning their beliefs. He searched vigilantly for publications which portrayed the Old Believers or any of the sects in a favorable light. He made extensive use of the censor's authority to prevent publications by or for the Old Believers. He even succeeded in persuading the Ministry of Education to discharge from one of its bureaus Nicholas S. Leskov, the celebrated novelist whom he knew and whose earlier works he had enjoyed and had even recommended to Alexander III, because he portrayed the Old Believers as being a danger to no one and because Leskov preached religious tolerance. Pobedonostsev used Subbotin and Katkov in skillful attacks on Leskov, and he later persuaded his friends in the Main Administration of the Press to prevent new editions of some Leskov stories which were "extremely harmful" in their portrayals of the Old Believers.[25]

The Old Believers outnumbered by about six times all the other evangelical sects, but state policy directed toward these groups, especially the Baptists, the Stundists, and the Dukhobors, while precisely the same, attracted even more attention, perhaps because it

was more vigorously applied. Thus, in 1881 Pobedonostsev prevented a Russian translation of a German Baptist catechism, arguing that the sect was already "dangerous," that publication of a
catechism indicated they were planning an active propaganda campaign, and that the ignorant Russian peasant must be protected
against the allure of a sect which was pacifistic, elected its own clergymen, scorned the Orthodox, and advocated a number of antisocial
doctrines. Germans living in Russia could be Baptists, but "there
are and must be no Russian Baptists."[26]

The Stundists, an evangelical sect with beliefs much like the Baptists, who left the Orthodox Church about 1870 and who grew im-
pressively in number in the bishoprics of Kherson and Odessa, met
even more vigorous opposition. This movement appealed especially
to peasants and was a kind of peasant puritanism, rejecting smoking,
alcohol, and dancing, declaring the state an evil force, relying entirely on personal interpretations of the Bible, rejecting the sacra-
mental system and many of the rites of the Orthodox Church, and
even proposing communal property. The May, 1883, law allowed
the Stundists the same rights as the Old Believers, but Pobedonostsev quickly became dismayed as they grew in number in the southwestern part of Russia. He arranged a special *sobor* or conference of
the clergy and hierarchy in Kiev in 1884, in order to educate these
churchmen about the dangers the Stundists posed. When these
measures and a propaganda campaign proved ineffective and when
"the evil" continued "to grow and to spread," he called the forces
of the state into action. A new Stundist journal was closed. The hierarchy of the southwest, with his support, tried to have the meeting
houses of the Stundists closed, but was unsuccessful until 1894, when
Pobedonostsev succeeded in persuading the Council of Ministers to
declare them "an especially dangerous sect." Their schools and
chapels were then closed, they were denied internal passports and
other official documents, and the laws were applied to them as
severely as he could arrange. Thus, the peaceful farmers were persecuted because the Orthodox Church could tolerate no rivals. Both
publicly and privately, Pobedonostsev asserted that the Stundists
were persecuted not because of their religious beliefs, but because
they were hostile to all beliefs, used violence, and preached the use
of violence.[27]

An account of his efforts to destroy two other sects, one early in
his career and the other near its close, will complete this illustration
of his use of state authority against rival religious groups. The Du-

khobors, who were settled in the Caucasus in the 1840's and whom Count Leo Tolstoy helped convert to nonviolence, chastity, and vegetarianism, attracted Pobedonostsev's attention and wrath in the 1890's, at about the same time that he encouraged the seizure of the children of some of the Molokane and their conversion under pressure to Orthodoxy. Count Leo Tolstoy succeeded in attracting such attention to the Dukhobors that the policy of persecution ceased and this tiny group was allowed to emigrate, first to Cyprus and then to Canada, where they annoy Canadian officials just as they had Pobedonostsev.[28]

The followers of guards colonel Vasilii A. Pashkov were dispersed more quickly than the Dukhobors. Pashkov and a number of members of the high aristocracy in St. Petersburg, right under Pobedonostsev's eyes, had been converted to a form of Protestantism in the 1870's by Lord Radstock, a Victorian revivalist of the Plymouth Brethren persuasion. In fact, both Pobedonostsev and Dostoevsky had heard sermons of Radstock in 1874 and 1876. Neither had been impressed, but both were dismayed by the sensation Radstock created, especially among old ladies, and by the decision of Colonel Pashkov in 1876 to establish a Society for the Encouragement of Spiritual and Ethical Reading. Pobedonostsev was unsuccessful at first in getting the courts or the police to prevent Radstock's Bible readings. However, within a month after he had been named Director General of the Synod, he wrote a long memorandum to the tsar, urging that Radstock be forced to leave Russia and that his band of noble followers be broken up. Pobedonostsev noted that Pashkov was preaching without permission, that English hymns were being sung by his audience, that his sermons, which emphasized faith and love, were creating an indifference to sin among the aristocracy, and that the infection could easily spread down from the upper classes. His proposal occupied at least two hours of the time of the Council of Ministers in May, 1880; subsequently, Radstock was forced to leave Russia and Pashkov and some of his aristocratic followers were sent into exile.

A year or two later, Radstock, Pashkov, and their followers were back in St. Petersburg, upsetting Pobedonostsev because they were distributing *Pilgrim's Progress* without permission and because the special committee he had established to destroy Pashkov's sect had proved ineffective. In 1884, when Pashkov sought to ally his band with the other evangelical sects, he drew upon himself and his group the powerful wrath of the Director General. This time, Pashkov and some of his principal followers were forced to leave the country, his property was put in trust, their offices were closed, and their literature was confiscated. To Pobedonostsev's intense dismay, Alexander III allowed Colonel Pashkov to return to Russia again in 1887, but Pobedonostsev soon forced him to flee again to Paris, where he died in 1902.[29]

The Orthodox Church had been in combat with the Old Believers for more than two hundred years before Pobedonostsev became Director General of the Synod. During that long period, the Church had used the state's power and authority, especially in denying opportunities to the Old Believers to spread their beliefs and to enjoy the same limited rights and opportunities as other inhabitants of the empire. Pobedonostsev maintained these programs, continuing the restrictive measures and even defining them more clearly in the 1883 legislation. Missionary work was maintained among the Old Believers in a feeble and limited way, but conversions at no time during the period from 1880 until 1905 exceeded 7,500 a year. Debates between especially qualified Orthodox clergy and spokesmen for the Old Believers were expanded in the 1880's, but reduced in importance in the 1890's, when Pobedonostsev came to believe that the Old Believers were profiting too much from the exchange.

Pobedonostsev and Professor Subbotin, his special advisor on the Old Believers, introduced several new ideas in an unsuccessful effort to strengthen the official campaign. Thus, the 1884 congress in Kiev of the hierarchy and clergy of the southwest provinces was designed to increase understanding of the problems and to stimulate a drive in the Ukraine. Another congress in Kazan sought the same goals for the Church in that area. In 1887 and in 1890, Pobedonostsev sought to make use of the *edinoverii*, or priestless Old Believers, who accepted the rule of the Synod but used the forms and rituals of the Old Believers, by having conferences of missionaries at a monastery of the priestless Old Believers in Moscow. These meetings were small, in spite of the pressure he exerted upon the bishops to send representatives, and their recommendations emphasized more the use of the state's power against their rivals than missionary activity. Indeed, Pobedonostsev admitted that these efforts were utter failures, and the Synod organized only two conferences or congresses of this kind after 1890, one in Kazan in 1897 and the other in Odessa in 1898. His great admiration for Nicholas Ilminskii in Kazan and Sergei Rachinskii in Tatev near Smolensk no doubt reflected his wish that the Church could somehow organize missionary efforts like theirs.[30]

The failures of the conferences to excite the clergy and of the missionary congresses to organize effective diocesan campaigns against the Old Believers led Pobedonostsev and Subbotin to introduce a special effort to educate the seminarians so that they would be well prepared when they became priests. Thus, in 1887 the Synod ordered each seminary to establish within three years a chair on the history and evil influences of the *raskol* and of the sects. Later, Pobedonostsev pressed for courses on the history of the Russian Orthodox Church.

This program was supplemented by a campaign designed to produce inexpensive volumes for the seminaries, the parish schools, and the general public. In January, 1882, the Synod created a fund of 5,000 rubles (about $2,500) for publishing and distributing books and booklets about the Old Believers. This investment grew gradually throughout the decade, and by 1890, Pobedonostsev had created a twenty-five-ruble group of basic books about the Old Believers and the sects, which he tried to place in the library of every bishop and in every parish school. This imaginative scheme was a bitter failure. Pobedonostsev found it difficult to find the right kind of book or pamphlet or to persuade scholars such as Subbotin to prepare the kind of booklet needed. Subbotin, for example, preferred to write multivolume histories or collections of documents which had no appeal whatsoever, and Pobedonostsev was even unable to produce a good handbook on the Old Believers. Some of the pamphlets prepared were too polemical, and others tended to raise interest in the Old Believers. The bishops were ignorant and uninterested, and even the consistories made no use of the literature they were given. The Synod's bookstores were not successful outlets, and most commercial bookstores would not sell these products.

The effort to publish articles in journals and newspapers was equally unsuccessful. Subbotin lacked the touch necessary for essays in the popular press and vetoed the other contributors whom Pobedonostsev suggested. The polemical tone of many of the articles he arranged was self-destructive, and even Katkov's *Moskovskiia Vedomosti* (Moscow News) was usually reluctant to publish materials which Pobedonostsev and Subbotin had prepared for it.[31]

Pobedonostsev's final weapons against the Old Believers and the evangelical sects were an organization Subbotin founded in 1872,

The Brotherhood of St. Peter, and a journal, *Bratskoe slovo* (Brotherly Word), which he had edited and published briefly in 1875 and 1876. Pobedonostsev encouraged Subbotin to revive the journal in 1883 and gave it an annual subsidy of 2,000 rubles. He also advised Subbotin, urged him to collect and publish each month all of the materials concerning the *raskol* which were published in the various diocesan journals, suggested promotional ideas, drafted advertisements, forwarded materials for reprinting, urged bishops, priests, and seminaries to subscribe, and in general used his prestige and that of the office to aid Subbotin. In spite of all of their efforts, the journal, the Brotherhood, and the Brotherhood's program for distributing pamphlets were dismal failures. After six months, the journal had only one hundred and fifty subscribers, including only three priests in the entire Moscow region. In the spring of 1885, the journal still had only four hundred subscribers, and a massive effort that summer and fall by Pobedonostsev raised the number to only nine hundred, which was the peak attained. The journal sold only six or seven hundred copies each year throughout the 1890's, and it ceased publication and sold all back issues for waste paper at the end of the century.[32]

Thus, Pobedonostsev's work among the Old Believers and the sects was no more successful than his campaign to improve the quality of the Orthodox clergy and of Orthodox spiritual life. He suffered similar failures in his policies concerning the Church in the Russian borderlands and newly acquired Central Asia, areas in which non-Russians predominated and in which the majority of the population, particularly those with power and influence, were members of other faiths. As "the Russian Archbishop Laud" grew older, he saw these non-Russian, non-Orthodox groups more and more clearly as "agents of disintegration," and he considered it his mission to reduce their power and to restrict and destroy their influence. He created policies of persecution of these rival religious faiths, seeking to prevent them from proselytizing and to hamper their efforts even to survive and at the same time launching an educational and missionary campaign which was extraordinarily ineffective, in spite of the effort he and his administration organized.

For reasons rooted in Russian history and tradition, the Russian Orthodox Church has not been distinguished for the vigor and devotion of its missionary effort. The Orthodox Missionary Society was founded only in 1869. Ten years later, it had less than seven thousand members, almost a third of whom lived in Moscow, and after twenty years there were still less than ten thousand members. After thirty years, when it had only fifteen thousand members, it spent less than $150,000 a year on its activities, about half of which were concentrated in Siberia, with the rest in European Russia and Japan. Throughout this long period, it claimed a total of only 120,000 converts. Indeed, throughout the period Pobedonostsev was Director General of the Synod, all of the Church's efforts, including those of the Orthodox Missionary Society, led to the conversion of less than 400,000 men and women.[33]

The Church and its missionary affiliate found the major part of their harvest among the Old Believers, who were clearly the principal target, and among the pagans of Siberia, especially in and near Irkutsk. The border area groups with whom Pobedonostsev was most concerned, the Baltic Lutherans, the Catholic Poles, the Jews in the southwest in particular, and the Moslems along the Volga, in the Caucasus, and in Central Asia, were quite resistant to the campaigns which he launched. In fact, analysis of his annual reports reveals that only approximately 25 percent of the converts the Church claimed during his period of rule were from these four groups and that the percentage was higher in the first decade than in the last fifteen years. His campaign against these groups was designed more to reduce their compelling power among the Russian Orthodox than to attract them to Orthodoxy. Except perhaps for the Moslems, he had little hope of converting them or even of reducing significantly the menace he thought they raised for the Church and for the State.[34]

One of the border areas which most attracted his attention was the Baltic region, organized then into two *guberniias*, Estland and Livland. The Baltic provinces were then controlled by Germans, who dominated both the land and the cities, ruled intellectual and political life, and had made Lutheranism the dominant religion. In fact, Pobedonostsev's report as Director General of the Synod for 1888–89 noted that these *guberniias* and Kurland contained more than a million Lutherans and only 200,000 Orthodox, most of whom lived in the cities. Until 1887, German was the official language of instruction in the schools, as well as the language of the administration and of the courts.

A massive Russification program was launched in the Baltic region under Alexander III, with Pobedonostsev playing a central

role. During the 1880's, Russian became the language of administration and of instruction, control of the police was removed from
the local nobility and placed in the hands of the Minister of the
Interior in St. Petersburg, Dorpat was renamed Iuriev and Russian
replaced German officially as the language of instruction in the university, and the power of the Baltic barons over the peasantry was
reduced and city government was reorganized to restrict the authority of the Germans and to strengthen that of the government in St.
Petersburg. Russifying and imposing a uniform system of control
were the keynotes of this vigorous campaign, and by 1900, the rights
and privileges which had been recognized in formal agreements and
treaties in 1710 and 1712 by representatives of the nobility of Livland and Estonia and of the Russian government had been whittled
away.

This process of Russification and of extending a uniform system
of government to areas which had previously had a special status
was extended to Finland in the 1890's, under Nicholas II. Curiously, Pobedonostsev seems to have played no part in determining
policy toward Finland or even to have shown an interest in that
area, perhaps because there were only twenty-three Orthodox parishes and fifty thousand Orthodox communicants in Finland in
1890. He apparently never visited Helsinki. When troubles did arise
in Finland late in the 1890's, he was genuinely surprised and puzzled, because he thought Finland "the most happy country in the
world."[35]

Throughout the 1880's, he worked closely with Count Dmitrii
Tolstoy, Minister of the Interior, in defining and imposing laws
and rules to Russify Estland and Livland. A close associate of his
and Katkov, the renowned panslavist, Prince Sergei V. Shakhovskoi,
served as Governor General of Livland from 1885 until 1894. He
and Pobedonostsev agreed that "Russia and Orthodoxy are synonymous" and that "the whole so-called Baltic problem lies clearly in
the question of the unity of the local population to Orthodoxy."
They both believed that the Estonians and Latvians, both long
subject to German rule, were vulnerable to a program to unite them
to Orthodoxy and to Russia in a religious campaign which was
simultaneously a Russian political weapon against the rule of German Lutherans. Shakhovskoi used the police and the courts to
assist the Russian Orthodox Church; at the same time, he urged
Pobedonostsev to build new churches, to establish a new bishopric
in Reval (Tallin), and to train missionary priests who knew Esto-

nian. On his side, Pobedonostsev defended Shakhovskoi and his policies before the tsar and sought to create popular understanding and support of his Russification policy.[36]

The considerable evidence now available indicates that his original aim in Livland and Estland was simply to cleanse and rejuvenate the Orthodox Church there. His first visit to Riga in particular had been disillusioning, for he had met seminary students who could not list the gospels and he had been depressed by the ability and arrogance of the Lutheran clergy and the humility and poverty of the Orthodox clergy, most of whom were Estonian and Latvian peasants. He therefore set out to improve the seminary in Riga, to build new churches and parish schools, to launch an intensive missionary effort, to have religious books translated from Russian, and even to open a Synod bookstore in Riga. The resentment expressed by the German Lutherans, who urged the Orthodox Church to seek to convert pagans, not other Christians, to Orthodoxy, the drumfire of government acts in the political field, and perhaps the death in 1886 of Baroness Edith Raden, who had defended the Baltic Germans for twenty years, all led Pobedonostsev to become more rigorous and even vicious in his church policies and in his defense of them. Thus, he created deep irritation in 1885 when the Synod forbade mixed marriages in that region unless both parties agreed that the children should be raised in the Orthodox faith, reviving a law which had not been in effect for twenty years. The appointment that year of Shakhovskoi, a special grant of 100,000 rubles (about $50,000) from the state to the Church for missionary work among the Lutherans, the award of honors to those who converted Lutherans to Orthodoxy, and Pobedonostsev's success in transferring cases involving "fanatical" Lutheran pastors from the courts to the Ministry of the Interior sharpened antagonisms. Pobedonostsev's relations with the German leaders in the Baltic and in St. Petersburg became frigid.[37]

Pobedonostsev and Tolstoy were able to override the protests of the Lutheran gentry and clergy in Estland and Livland, but by 1886 this opposition was supported in St. Petersburg by members of the aristocracy of German origin and by other Russian conservatives who resented the treatment of one of Russia's western bastions as though it were "a Merv oasis." However, when these criticisms reached the Senate and the Council of State and when they were given wide publicity in St. Petersburg by Reverend Hermann Dalton, pastor of the Evangelical Church in the capital, and by a pamphlet by the Evangelical Alliance, an organization of evangelical churches from various parts of Europe and the United States, Pobedonostsev was forced to the defensive. Indeed, the criticism directed against him from 1887 until 1890 over Baltic policy may have preserved Finland from his attention in the next decade.[38]

The Evangelical Alliance had successfully intervened in the 1860's and 1870's to support evangelical churches in Russia against policies which it thought discriminatory, so its later protests drew particular attention. Moreover, the Alliance was strong in Germany and in Denmark, and it took advantage of the close relations between the royal families of these countries and the Romanovs. At first, the evangelical churches in the canton of Schaffhausen in Switzerland wrote to the tsar, protesting against the laws concerning the religious beliefs of children born of mixed marriages, the persecution of Lutheran pastors, and the new prohibition against leaving the Orthodox Church to join the Lutheran Church. Pobedonostsev in his reply denied there was any persecution of religion in Russia and argued that nowhere in Europe was freedom of belief as great as in Russia. He remarked then to the tsar that there were no lies about Russia which Europeans would not believe.

At Easter of 1887, therefore, the Evangelical Alliance itself entered the campaign with a more detailed letter, in fact a booklet, signed by its president Edward Naville and published in several languages, which it sent to the tsar while he was in Denmark. Pobedonostsev devoted great effort to his new reply, which he also had published in church newspapers and in pamphlet form. This January, 1888, statement and Pobedonostsev's defense to the tsar noted that the actions criticized were properly matters of Russian domestic policy and that the pastors were really serving a German political campaign directed against Russia, supported this time by Jews, fanatical Protestants, and Catholic Ultramontanes, all wildly hostile to Russia. He sought to distinguish between freedom of belief and freedom to proselytize or to spread propaganda, which he found inexplicably related to "a privileged class, jealous of its power, aspiring to absolute rule, and to a clergy allied with it, both employing a system of persecution created with the aim of preventing all rapprochement with the mother country and especially with the Orthodox Church." Pobedonostsev concluded that the state's policy was not only proper and more generous than the policies of the states of western Europe, but absolutely vital, because the survival of Russia depended upon religious unity.[39]

Publication of these open letters and extensive newspaper comment both in Russia and in Europe led to another important round which embarrassed Pobedonostsev and led to considerable tension between him and the tsar. In fact, the decline of his authority about 1890 may date from the incident over Orthodox policy in the Baltic provinces. The protagonist in 1888 and 1889 was Reverend Dalton, a distinguished scholar and clergyman of Pobedonostsev's own generation who had a wide circle of friends and acquaintances among both Russians and foreigners in the capital. He had been acquainted with Pobedonostsev for almost thirty years, had often discussed German literature with him, and had even written the preface to the German translation of a talk by Pobedonostsev in 1881.

Dalton's open letter to Pobedonostsev, which was published in 1889 in Russian, German, and English, was a powerful blow against Pobedonostsev's position and policy, delivered in a grave and scholarly manner by a man whom the tsar knew and respected and whom Pobedonostsev could not denounce as a rascal and as a servant of Germany. Moreover, Dalton was extremely well informed concerning Russian law and custom, had followed the controversy carefully, had studied the various official acts of the previous few years, and wrote from a position absolutely unassailable in its facts, historical tradition, and personal status. He was therefore able to demonstrate easily that Pobedonostsev's statements consisted of "outrage after outrage upon an entire class and upon the united clergy of a prominent portion of the realm, accompanied by proofs, the worthlessness of which is self-evident." He demonstrated that one of Pobedonostsev's charges against the Lutheran clergy was a complete fabrication, that he had twisted and distorted official reports, and that there was no basis in state or Church law for his key policies. Perhaps his most telling arguments were his quotations of vicious statements about Lutheranism from Synod publications, his accounts of rewards to Orthodox clergy who converted peasants from Lutheranism to Orthodoxy, and statements concerning the release of criminals from jail in return for their joining the Orthodox Church.[40]

The tsar was annoyed when he read Dalton's booklet, not only by the exposures of improper acts but also because he himself had been hoodwinked by his chief advisor on religious matters. He did not want to drive "Russia's Huguenots" to other countries, and he was irritated by Pobedonostsev's confession that some of his statements were in fact in error. Rumors abounded in St. Petersburg and Moscow that Pobedonostsev had been reprimanded sharply. The

London Times even noted reports that he had been given three months' leave without pay to prepare a defense against Dalton's critique. It is clear that Pobedonostsev's influence sagged noticeably at about this time.[41]

The areas of the empire in which Catholic Poles lived were even more central for Pobedonostsev than were the Baltic provinces, but there he did not encounter opposition as skillfully led as that by Dalton or influences within the court which hampered his actions.

Pobedonostsev had been brought up in Moscow during the years after the 1831 insurrection. No doubt in these early days he acquired a deep dislike of the Poles and of Catholicism, which reflected the strongly Orthodox and patriotic home atmosphere of Bread Lane and the traditional Orthodox Russian attitude toward the Poles and Catholics. His early book reviews, his conversations and correspondence with Dostoevsky, and his letters to the heir and to Catherine Tiutchev in the 1870's revealed a profound dislike and even hatred of the Poles, as Poles and as Catholics. The various editions of *Kurs grazhdanskago prava* gave favorable notice to the old and new Russian laws which restricted the right of Poles to hold or transfer landed property in the western borderlands. He was convinced that the radical and revolutionary movements were inspired by Poles, and he came to see the hand of Poles or Jews in all Russia's misfortunes. Catholics to him were always "Latins" and were generally Austrian agents against Russia.[42]

The drive against the Poles and "Polonism" was renewed immediately after the Russians had crushed the Polish uprising of 1863, but the program of Count Michael N. Muraviev in the "western provinces," the territories inhabited by Poles, Lithuanians, White Russians, and Ukrainians which Catherine the Great had annexed, was more vigorous than that applied by Prince Vladimir A. Cherkasskii to the old Kingdom of Poland, which was called the Government General of Warsaw after 1863. Pobedonostsev as the Director General of the Synod and as a member of the government also distinguished between these two areas, although he sought to protect the Orthodox Church from Polish and Catholic influence throughout Russia. However, he had no hope of converting Polish Catholics to Orthodoxy. He did harass and move Catholic priests whom he thought too active; he did close at least one Catholic monastery; he promoted the spread of Orthodox literature and the construction of Orthodox churches; he restricted education by Poles and Catholics. However, his main concern was to defend the Orthodox Church against inroads and, above all, to make certain that the Uniates (those Catholics who had been allowed to retain the rites and customs of the Orthodox Church but who had accepted the supremacy of the Pope), who had been forced to rejoin the Orthodox Church in the western provinces in 1839 or in the Kholm-Warsaw diocese of the Government General of Warsaw in 1875, remain firmly in the Orthodox Church.[43]

Just as Pobedonostsev was advised and guided on matters relating to the Old Believers by Professor Nicholas Subbotin of the Moscow Ecclesiastical Academy, so he found a mentor on the Uniates in Efimi N. Kryzhanovskii, a specialist on religious groups in the western provinces and in the Government General of Warsaw. Born near Kiev in 1831, Kryzhanovskii devoted his spare time as a bureaucrat to the study of Riga, Pskov, the Czechs in Volhynia, and, above all, the Uniates. He founded a school for Uniates in 1865, and in 1871 became the head of a *gimnaziia* or high school for boys in Warsaw. Pobedonostsev met him there in 1881, when he made a tour of the Government General, and he was immensely impressed by a memorandum Kryzhanovskii gave him on the Uniate issue. He soon brought him to St. Petersburg as a member of the Synod's Committee on Education and as his special advisor on Baltic and Uniate problems. Until he died in July, 1888, Kryzhanovskii helped form Pobedonostsev's policies on the western borderlands.[44]

At one time, there had been four Uniate bishoprics in Russia. However, during the reign of Nicholas I, many Uniates in White Russia rejoined the Orthodox Church. The most important single Orthodox conquest came in 1839, when, after long preparation, Uniate Bishop Joseph Semashko of Mstislav effected a union which involved 1,600 parishes and 1,600,000 people. At first, almost a third of the Uniate clergy refused to follow Semashko, but ultimately only about one hundred and sixty were recalcitrant. In 1875, another Uniate prelate, Marcellus Poppel, sought to follow Semashko's example by uniting the last remaining Ukrainian bishopric, that of Kholm, to Orthodoxy. Only about half of the clergy and of the laymen followed Poppel, who was made bishop of Kholm. Indeed, a quarter of the total fled across the border into Galicia in the Austrian monarchy, where they received shelter and aid.

Pobedonostsev followed these developments through Iurii Samarin and others who were especially interested in the border provinces, and he approved the efforts of Prince Cherkasskii as Governor General to crush Polish hopes for recovery and to Russify administration, education, and religion. Cherkasskii unsuccessfully sought to create a separate *guberniia* or province incorporating Kholm and the areas to the north and east in which large numbers of Uniates or former Uniates lived, so that the Russification process could be carried out with less opposition from Poles. Pobedonostsev supported the campaign to incorporate all the Uniates into the Church. He took especial pleasure in meeting former Uniates who had joined the Orthodox Church when they visited St. Petersburg in 1875, and he believed that the work of Cherkasskii and Poppel was immensely fruitful.[45]

When Pobedonostsev toured the western provinces and the Government General of Warsaw in the fall of 1881, he discovered that the Uniate issue was far more complicated and difficult than he had believed. Indeed, while he had profound admiration for the work in the Kholm area of Prince Cherkasskii, "who had opened Russian lands forgotten by the Russian government and revived the fading belief in Russian nationality among those surrounded by hostile Poles," he saw quickly that the incorporation of the Uniate church had been a serious mistake because the Uniate church had been a bridge over which Uniates could gradually be brought over to the Orthodox and Russian side from the Catholic and Polish camp. Destruction of the bridge by a hasty effort to herd all Uniates into the Orthodox Church at once had in fact widened the chasm and created a sharp dichotomy from which the rival Polish Catholics benefited heavily. In fact, many Uniates joined the Catholic Church because of the pressures created by the incorporation of the Uniate Church into Orthodoxy.

In this situation, Pobedonostsev recommended basically the same policies for the Church and the state which he had supported in the Baltic area. However, he had far less confidence in these western provinces in the power of attraction of Orthodoxy and of education and propaganda, because he realized that the strength of the Poles and of Catholicism there was greater than that of the Germans and of Lutheranism in the Baltic. Moreover, he believed that Austria-Hungary and the Vatican were far more interested and effective in assisting the Catholics than were any foreign states or religious groups in regard to the Baltic Lutherans. In fact, he saw "whole armies of Catholic priests" on Russia's western frontiers, profiting from Russian mistakes. Consequently, while he established parish schools and built new schools, he sought more to defend Orthodox strength than to expand it, and he relied more on "worldly power" against the Poles than against the Lutherans.[46]

He worked closely with Alexander III, with Minister of the Interior Tolstoy, and with the governors of the Government General of Warsaw and of the Siedlce *guberniia* to strengthen the use of state power against the Uniates, the Poles, and the Catholics. He was particularly eager to prevent the use of Polish in the schools and in the administration. He was also active in seeking to prevent marriages outside the Orthodox Church by enforcing the laws by which no marriage was recognized until it had been celebrated in the Orthodox Church. This effort, and his determined attempt to prevent secret marriages, baptisms, and burials by Uniates, encountered opposition in the Senate and in the Council of State. In fact, the Senate forced him to abandon some of his efforts to "stretch" the laws.

By the 1890's, Pobedonostsev was reconciled to a long drawn out and presumably unsuccessful struggle on the Uniate and Catholic issue, and he became almost as bitter toward Uniates as toward Catholics. He noted that the number of "the stubborn" were increasing as the century came to a close. Early in the twentieth century, he sought a reorganization of the civil structure to increase the Russification drive, by separating the Kholm area from Warsaw and creating a separate province in which an intensive campaign could be mounted against the Uniates. This effort, which was called "the fourth division of Poland," failed in 1902, in 1905, and again in the Third Duma, where a conservative nationalist group revived it.[47]

While Pobedonostsev was well informed concerning the tangled region of the western provinces and Poland and devoted enormous amounts of time and energy to his program there, the area ruled by Russia in and south of the Caucasus mountains was one about which he knew very little and to which he and the Synod applied little attention. He visited the region only three times. His first and most important review was in the fall of 1886, after the rector of the seminary in Tiflis had been murdered and a serious crisis had arisen. He saw no subtleties in the problems created by the Georgians and the Armenians: they both simply sought their independence, which was going to be denied them as forcefully as proved necessary. Pobedonostsev refused even to consider the pleas of some Georgians for the reestablishment of the independence of the Georgian church. In fact, the exarch Paul, whom he sent there in the 1880's and who was himself killed, was a Russian who spoke no Georgian and displayed no sense or tact in his relations with Georgians. Pobedonostsev did not think it unusual when he learned that the principal of the gymnasium or high school in Tiflis always carried a revolver. Instead, he told Alexander III: "The Armenians and Georgians are seeking to free themselves from Russian culture and nourish the mad dream of the reestablishment of their national independence. Only firm power can succeed in containing and crushing this mad dream." It is not surprising that Georgia produced a large number of revolutionaries.[48]

Pobedonostsev also had little knowledge of or interest in newly acquired Central Asia. He apparently did not travel along the Volga after 1868, and he was east of the Ural mountains only twice. In fact, before he became Director General of the Synod, the Moslems were not a part of his Russia, just as the American Negro was invisible to generations of American whites, and he gave no thought to their role or to a program for conversion or Russification. He not only knew little of the Moslems, but considered Mohammedanism no threat to Orthodoxy. In his annual reports, he failed even to mention the need for the use of "worldly power," which was central in his policies toward the Baltic Germans and the Poles. Church policy in the areas inhabited by Moslems during Pobedonostsev's first years as head of the Synod was therefore simply a continuation of the lethargic action of previous years.[49]

The man who turned Pobedonostsev's attention toward the Moslems and who shaped his and the Church's policy toward them for the next twenty-five years was Nicholas I. Ilminskii, who was his constant correspondent and mentor throughout the first decade of Pobedonostev's tenure as Director General of the Synod. Ilminskii was the son of a priest and was born in Penza province in 1821. He completed the Penza Seminary, where he then taught briefly, and moved in 1846 to Kazan. He spent most of the time between 1846 and 1872 on the faculty of the Kazan Ecclesiastical Academy, where he taught a wide variety of subjects—mathematics, the history of philosophy, Hebrew, Arabic, and Tartar—but he also lived from 1851 until 1854 in Cairo and Constantinople and he worked on the Orenburg Boundary Committee for a year. Apparently because of constant changes of policy with regard to the training of seminarians for missionary work among the Tartars, he was on occasion dropped from the faculty of the Academy and taught at Kazan University instead.

Ilminskii had an extraordinary gift for languages and developed a keen interest in the non-Russians who lived in and near Kazan and indeed in all of the Russian territory south, east, and north of that revered city. He apparently had perfect command of Old Church Slavonic, Greek, Latin, Arabic, Persian, some Turkic languages (Tartar, Chuvash, Bashkir, Tungusic), and some Uralic-Altaic languages (Mordvinian, Cheremiss, Votyak), and he could also read French, German, and English. In part because of his language talents and in part because he remained forever a country boy interested in the simple, homely aspects of life, Ilminskii was able to acquire a remarkable understanding of the various peoples in the vast area with which he became concerned. Profoundly Orthodox and as convinced as Pobedonostsev that Orthodoxy was and ought to be the distinguishing characteristic of Russian culture and life, he created an exciting and quite effective approach toward converting the Moslems and pagans to Orthodoxy and to what he and Pobedonostsev would have agreed to call "the Russian way of life." The system which Ilminskii perfected was accepted by Pobedonostsev and became the official policy of the Church toward the non-Christian peoples in the Volga area, Siberia, and Central Asia.[50]

Pobedonostsev visited Kazan in 1863, but apparently did not meet Ilminskii at that time. However, in July, 1869, he accompanied the heir to the throne and his wife and Count Dmitrii Tolstoy, then both Director General of the Synod and Minister of Education, on a trip through that part of Russia, during which they attended the ceremonies celebrating the opening of Ilminskii's Kazan Seminary for Non-Russians. They became acquainted in the early days of the reign of Alexander III, probably through Nikanor, Bishop of Ufa and a frequent correspondent of Pobedonostsev, who had come to know and admire Ilminskii when he had been rector of the Kazan Ecclesiastical Academy from 1868 to 1871. Pobedonostsev obtained scholarly books from St. Petersburg libraries and even from foreign bookstores for Ilminskii, procured funds to assist converts who might otherwise have slipped back to Mohammedanism, provided impressive financial support through the Synod, the Ministry of Education, and the Ministry of the Interior for Ilminskii's schools and other enterprises, helped arrange placement of the graduates of Ilminskii's institutions, helped organize the publication and distribution of Ilminskii's books, and provided recognition and honor for the educator and missionary and his supporters. In return, Ilminskii provided Pobedonostsev an immense fund of information concerning religious and political problems from Kazan to Kamchatka and to Tashkent, forwarded information concerning administrators of state and Church in whom Pobedonostsev was interested, advised him on books to publish for schools throughout the empire, and, above all, created for him a policy and a program for converting and Russifying the various peoples east and south of Kazan.[51]

Ilminskii was convinced that the various non-Russian groups could be converted to Orthodoxy and to Russian culture if Orthodox services were given in their native languages by native priests and if literature could be provided for them in their native language in the Cyrillic alphabet at the proper intellectual level. He reached this conclusion after analyzing the failure of the effort to convert these peoples from Mohammedanism or from Shamanism by Russian missionaries who spoke only Russian and who assumed that an approach effective with Russian Old Believers or with Georgians would be equally effective with the Chuvash or the Cheremiss. He soon realized that even Russian missionaries who spoke the foreign languages were unsuccessful when they were products of St. Petersburg and Moscow, when their knowledge of the peoples among whom they worked had been acquired only from books, and when they failed to realize that conversion to Orthodoxy was essential. Finally, he learned that the range of publications which could be translated for use among these peoples was very small, and that infinite care had to be exercised in making selections.

Under Ilminskii's program, the few Russians engaged in this missionary effort among the Turkic and Uralic-Altaic or Finno-Ugric language groups were thoroughly schooled in the language and the culture, as he was. They used only the native language in their missionary work. "The native tongue strongly and deeply penetrates the soul. It possesses an especially lively and powerful impact when it is used in Church doctrine and in religious preaching. . . . The primary education of foreigners in their own language is the most certain path to their adopting the Russian language and to acquiring a Russian education."[52]

He therefore sought originally to persuade the Kazan Ecclesiastical Academy to establish a Missionary Division in which instruction in the languages of that area would be emphasized. The disagreement concerning this policy, the refusal of some missionaries to learn the languages, and his growing understanding of the problem led him in 1863 to establish a school for non-Russian children who had joined the Church, the Kazan Central Christian School for Non-Russians. Five years later, he founded the Brotherhood of St. Iurii to collect funds for his program and to organize Russians interested in missionary work among the peoples who accepted

Mohammedanism or one form or another of Shamanism. In 1869, he organized the Kazan Seminary for Non-Russians, with the support of the newly organized Orthodox Missionary Society in St. Petersburg. Three years later, Ilminskii resigned from the Kazan Ecclesiastical Academy and devoted the last twenty years of his life to this institution, organized to train native priests for missionary work among the Turkic and Uralic-Altaic language groups on what he called "the frontiers of the Russian empire." Throughout these years, he directed an expanding project for translating and publishing prayer and song books, the Gospels, and simple handbooks about Orthodoxy for the people he sought to convert.[53]

Ilminskii's very first letter to Pobedonostsev, on February 11, 1882, began the process of persuading the Director General to support and expand the Ilminskii program against Mohammedanism. He pointed out that the Moslems outnumbered the Orthodox in the Ufa province, that they were wealthy and had active and able leaders, and that the Church must act quickly and systematically if it were to retain its strength. While the earlier methods had failed, his had been remarkably effective during their brief trial, and he urged that the Church adopt his program for the entire area inhabited by the Moslems. In effect, Ilminskii advocated a program which was nationalist in form, Orthodox in content. He wrote that his principal "shells" were books and religious services in non-Russian languages and that progress would be slow but certain. On his return to Kazan for a brief visit in July, 1883, Pobedonostsev wrote to Katkov that he had been immensely impressed by Ilminskii's work and was surprised to find Kazan "one of the main centers for religious education in Russia."

Pobedonostsev was soon converted by Ilminskii, and the latter's ideas became official policy throughout the vast areas inhabited by Moslems and pagans. Perhaps the central decision in Pobedonostsev's support was the announcement by the Synod in February, 1883, that Orthodox Church services could be held in non-Russian languages in the East. Pobedonostsev resolutely refused to permit translation of the Bible into Ukrainian on the ground that it would strengthen Ukrainian nationalism. On the other hand, he refused to allow sermons in Catholic churches in the western provinces or in the Government General of Warsaw to be given in Russian, on the ground that Catholicism was Latin and Polish and that the use of Russian in any part of the church service would weaken the barrier separating Orthodoxy from Catholicism. However, he endorsed the use of Finno-Ugric and Turkic languages in the Orthodox service because Ilminskii had persuaded him that this tactic would help draw these peoples into Orthodoxy and thus into "the Russian way of life."[54]

Pobedonostsev was especially impressed by the school Ilminskii had established in Kazan for Chuvash and Tartar children who had been converted to Orthodoxy. The program for these youngsters included six hours of catechism, six hours of Russian, three hours of Old Church Slavonic, four hours of the child's native language, and three hours of church songs in the native language in the total weekly schedule of thirty-one and a half hours. The program itself, the verve and charm with which the children sang the hymns, and the demonstrated impact they had on their parents and other relatives convinced Pobedonostsev that Ilminskii had found an ideal system for Russification.

The official opening of what Pobedonostsev came to call "a new epoch in Russian missionary activity" came in July and August, 1885, when the Synod arranged two meetings of the hierarchy and of missionaries, one in Kazan from July 9 until July 25, which both Pobedonostsev and Sabler attended, and the other in Irkutsk from July 23 until August 8, in which Sabler alone participated. These meetings placed missionary activity among the Moslems on the same level as among the Old Believers and then endorsed enthusiastically the Ilminskii approach. From that time forward, Ilminskii was Pobedonostsev's chief advisor on all missionary activities east of the Volga, and the Church's programs in Irkutsk, Khabarovsk, Kamchatka, Tashkent—wherever there was missionary activity—reflected Ilminskii's advice. In 1889, the Kazan Ecclesiastical Academy organized a permanent Missionary Division, with two-year courses in Tartar and Mongol. That same year, Pobedonostsev wrote that the missions in Siberia were not only converting non-Russian peoples but were transforming them "into people with an economy and a way of life like that of the Russians themselves." Stalin's Russia agreed with this verdict, when it announced that Ilminskii's work, especially in creating a Russian alphabet for some Turkic and Finno-Ugric languages, had "progressive significance" and that Ilminskii deserved praise for "contributing to spreading literacy and the Russian language among these peoples."[55]

The progress made among the non-Russians under Ilminskii's program is striking. Thus, by the early 1890's some of the graduates of his Kazan Central Christian School were teachers in other schools for non-Russians in the Kazan *uezd* or district. Indeed, between 1863 and 1881 alone this school produced 231 such teachers; it also graduated 163 youngsters between 1863 and 1913 who later became Orthodox priests and 29 who became deacons. The Central Chuvash School in Simbirsk was a success, and there were a hundred two- or four-year schools for Chuvash children in the Simbirsk district in 1890, as well as a special missionary society to support them. Each year, the Simbirsk Seminary admitted three Chuvash for study for the priesthood. A two-year school for Cheremiss children in Ufa prospered, and by 1890 a similar school for Votyaks had been established in Karlygan in Viatka province. When Ilminskii died in 1891, the Kazan district had 128 schools for non-Russian Orthodox children. In 1900, the Kazan bishoprics had 154 such schools, and there were 4,494 children in these four-year institutions, of whom more than two-thirds were Tartars or Chuvash. Pobedonostsev naturally cited this progress in blocking proposals of the Ministry of Education or of the zemstvos for establishing schools for Moslem children in Russian, with Moslem teachers and with courses on Mohammedanism.[56]

Ilminskii and Pobedonostsev hoped to create a network of schools for children and of seminaries for teachers based on the Kazan models, and tender shoots of progress were made before Ilminskii's death removed the driving force. Even by that time, however, there had been failures, as Pobedonostsev ruefully admitted. In 1887, Moslems and pagans outnumbered the Orthodox by 1,100,000 to 800,000 in the Ufa bishopric, where Pobedonostsev's correspondent, Bishop Nikanor, presided over one of the program's most active areas, and there were only forty-seven converts to Orthodoxy in that year. A school in Samara for training non-Russian teachers had to be closed in 1888 for lack of local interest. Ilminskii, at a meeting of the Synod's Committee on Education in the summer of 1891, found that the other members of the committee did not yet understand the principles of his approach. Schools in Orenburg, Tashkent, Tomsk, Perm, and Khabarovsk, built on the Ilminskii model and all supported by the Synod and the Orthodox Missionary Society, were all in a precarious position then in a sea of indifferent Orthodox and passive or hostile Moslems or pagans.[57]

Ilminskii and Pobedonostsev shared another powerful interest, that of publishing religious and moral literature for the *narod*. Ilminskii naturally had a special concern in translating, publishing, and distributing booklets in various non-Russian languages for those whom he wished to convert or to persuade to remain in the Orthodox fold. Shortly before he died, he wrote that he thought his main mission and greatest successes were in translating and publishing religious and moral literature for non-Russians. His first book, published in Kazan in 1862, was a Tartar primer. Before his death, he had translated or helped to translate more than a hundred books or pamphlets produced in a total of 1,600,000 copies. Most of this work was done through the Kazan Translation Committee of the Brotherhood of St. Iurii, which he founded in 1868 and which was later given an annual subsidy of 4,000 rubles, or about $2,000, by the Orthodox Missionary Society. Pobedonostsev and the Synod took up the support of this work, and many of Ilminskii's primers, prayer books, New Testaments, and moral guides were published and distributed by the Synod Press.

In February, 1883, the Synod gave special permission to Ilminskii alone to translate the Old and New Testaments into Tartar, Chuvash, Cheremiss, Votyak, Kalmyck, and Mordvinian, but he also translated materials into thirteen other languages, including Korean and Yakut. Ilminskii was convinced that "it is impossible to put the full Bible into the hands of the *narod*," because this would lead some to become mystical and others to become "enlightened and independent." He therefore generally published extracts, with the addition of precepts, rules, and some of the psalms. In some cases, he had to help create or enlarge a literary language. In every case, he put the translation into the Cyrillic alphabet as a means of destroying the influence of rival organizations, such as the English Bible Society, and as a means of increasing progress toward Russification.[58]

The final religious group among those in the non-Russian, non-Orthodox circle which Pobedonostsev surveyed from St. Petersburg consisted of the Jews, who were concentrated largely in the western and southwestern provinces and who were supposed to remain within the Pale of Settlement in that part of the empire. The position which Jews have occupied in Western society has often been a precarious one, and antisemitism is a significant and complicated factor in the history of every state or society in which Jews have lived. Antisemitism has been a traditional, powerful force in many parts of Europe, even in areas such as Brittany where few Jews have ever lived, and periods of tension, such as those produced by the vast social, political, and intellectual changes of the last century, have given this deeply rooted feeling compelling force and political explosiveness. Many political and intellectual leaders, in Russia as elsewhere, have thoroughly rejected and denounced the doctrines and actions of the antisemites, but many others, in some countries in times of tension a noisy and powerful group, have trumpeted antisemitism and made it a cardinal issue.

The character and strength of feeling against Jews, always fluid and elusive, is difficult to measure in nineteenth-century Russia. Our knowledge of this attitude in the various social strata and areas is inevitably limited because emotional attitudes such as this are always evanescent, and the evidence, particularly concerning the illiterate and inarticulate masses, is very imprecise. Even so, it is clear that antisemitism was a powerful force among Russian peasants, with the causes substantially those which afflicted peasants elsewhere. Similarly, it is clear that dislike and even hatred of Jews were quite general and strong, though probably not so common nor so deeply felt among the upper levels of society, the professional classes, bureaucrats, army officers, journalists, and landed nobility. Some Russian leaders were consistent opponents of antisemitism; others rejected it or fought it on occasion; others were infected in such a way that an outburst elsewhere would stimulate it among them.

In any case, antisemitism was a part of the atmosphere or climate of opinion in which Pobedonostsev lived and worked. It was particularly strong among the Slavophil, panslav, conservative nationalist circles in which he grew up and through which he progressed, and it apparently became more prevalent and more powerful in Russia from the time of the Crimean War until the 1880's. Thus during the early "thaw" under Alexander II, some state leaders discussed ways of improving the situation of the Jews throughout the empire, particularly concerning civil rights and access to education. In 1858, many St. Petersburg and Moscow leaders of thought, including the Aksakovs, Katkov, and Feoktistov, who were later active antisemites, signed a protest published in Katkov's newspaper against a journal which had ridiculed two writers because they were Jews.[59]

However, many Russian political and intellectual leaders were clearly full of animus against the Jews, although most of them believed that conversion to Orthodoxy would have eliminated the main reason and although most of them believed that the Jews should be protected against violence. The Aksakovs, for example, blamed much of the corruption and poverty of Russian rural life on the Jews. Constantine Aksakov wrote that emancipation of the Jews would "fill the Senate, the Council of State, and, I am afraid, even the post of Director General of the Holy Synod" with Jews. He declared that Russia should be emancipated from the Jews, not the reverse, and he wanted the Jewish "dissolvent" removed from traditional Russian life. Katkov urged the Jews to forget Polish and German, to become more like the Russians, and to recognize that they were responsible for the hate and violence directed against them. Olga Novikov, Pobedonostsev's London correspondent, noted that some of her best friends were Jews, but defended even the pogroms and the restrictive legislation and argued that the peasants turned against the Jews because of the oppression and plundering to which the Jews had subjected them. Baroness Edith Raden and Iurii Samarin, who disagreed about the role of the Baltic Germans and about Russian state policy in the Baltic provinces, agreed that the Jews were a menace in Russia. Grand Duchess Helen Pavlovna, so generous and humane in her other thoughts and policies, accepted antisemitism. Dostoevsky in the 1870's spoke of Jews as "Yids," saw them infecting everything they touched, and believed the legend that the revolutionary movement in the 1870's was dominated by Jews.[60]

Pobedonostsev's knowledge of the Jews in Russia was limited. The circles in which he lived and worked in Moscow and St. Petersburg included very few Jews, except perhaps for some of the merchants who supported the Volunteer Fleet. He visited the areas in which the great majority of the Jews in Russia lived only once before he had become Director General of the Synod, and even then there is no evidence that he visited any community inhabited largely by Jews. His comments about the few Jews whom he encountered in 1863 on a trip with the heir to the throne revealed no animosity whatsoever. In fact, he treated the Jews then precisely as he did members of other non-Russian nationality groups whom they met. His comments in the various volumes of his *Kurs grazhdanskago prava*, on which he had completed the research and most of the writing before he became Director General of the Synod, gave calm and measured approval to the various legal restrictions placed upon the Jews in the ownership and transfer of property, legal areas of residence, marriage rights, name changes, and employment in particular professions. He wrote the heir to the throne in February, 1863, "It seems to me that it is always necessary to exercise some caution in relations with the Jews because under their present system they hold themselves aloof from the rest of society, which treats them in large part unsympathetically." Pobedonostsev simply reflected the Orthodox Muscovite nest from which he had come. Jews lived in a different world from his, at least until the Balkan crisis of 1875–78 injected a note of passion and urgency into his thinking.[61]

Before 1875, Pobedonostsev in his published work and in his correspondence referred to the Jews as *evrei,* or Jews. His first reference to them as "Yids" or *zhidi* was in a letter from Salzburg in August, 1875, to Catherine Tiutchev, in which he denounced "the Yiddish-Jewish newspapers" which criticized the rebels in Bosnia-Herzogovina and supported the Ottoman effort to crush the rebellion. He continued to use *evrei* in his correspondence with the heir to the throne, but his letters to Catherine Tiutchev, Dostoevsky, and his other correspondents after 1875 generally used "Yid" instead. Indeed, his August 14, 1879, letter to Dostoevsky summarizes explicitly both his views and the intensity of his feelings under the impact of the wave of nationalism engendered by the Balkan crisis and his fear of revolution:

> What you write about the Yids is completely just. They have engrossed everything, they have undermined everything, but the spirit of the century supports them. They are at the root of the revolutionary socialist movement and of regicide, they own the periodical press, they have in their hands the financial markets, the people as a whole fall into financial slavery to them; they even control the principles of contemporary science and strive to place it outside of Christianity. And on top of all that—whenever anyone raises a question about them a shower of voices rises in favor of the Jews in the name of civilization and tolerance, of indifference to faith. Among the Roumanians and Serbs, and among us as well, no one dares to say a word about the simple fact that the Jews have won ownership of everything. Even our own press is becoming Jewish. *Russkaia Pravda* (Russian Truth), *Moskva* (Moscow), even *Golos* (Voice) are Jewish organs, and the Jews have even closed down their special journals, such as *Evrei* (Jews) and *Vestnik Evreev* (Jewish Herald), and *Biblioteka Evreiskaia* (Jewish Library).[62]

Pobedonostsev came to believe that "our great ulcer has penetrated everywhere," and his main, and false, charges against the Jews were typical of his generation and indeed of much of modern history. He assumed that the Jews were acquiring enormous economic power, and charged that they were buying landed estates, destroying the old nobility, and allowing the great country houses to deteriorate. Perhaps because he knew so many Moscow and St. Petersburg bankers and merchants and realized that few Jews lived in the capitals, he did not decry their economic power in banking and industry; indeed, he rejoiced that there were no Jews among those wealthy men he knew or met. However, his first concern was alleged Jewish control over much of the Russian press. He assumed that any liberal newspaper or journal, or any publication which adopted a position he did not approve, was Jewish. In fact, Jewish and liberal were synonymous for him, and he found their "mangy sheets" wherever he went in Russia. He believed that Russian Jews fed "lies" to foreign newspapers about Russia, and that foreign journals critical of Russian actions were also owned and controlled by Jews. Naturally, on occasion all Jews were considered foreign agents, as all foreign agents were Jews or servants of Jews. Finally, he believed the Jews responsible for much of the corruption, demoralization, and decline in religious and patriotic fervor which he found in Russia. In particular, he charged that Jewish ownership of public houses in the rural west and southwest and their Sunday trade were responsible for much of the immorality and crime among the peasants.[63]

Within the empire, Pobedonostsev thought that the Russian government ought to repress and isolate the Jews and at the same time to educate Russians concerning the dangers they raised. However, he also was very sensitive to foreign opinion, and he paid great attention to efforts to persuade foreign leaders that there was no persecution of the Jews in Russia. He was eager to have published in Western journals and newspapers information that was favorable to the Russian government's point of view. He maintained an extensive correspondence with Olga Novikov in London and used her as a conduit for the ears and minds of both conservative and liberal English statesmen and for liberal newspapers. He assured foreign ambassadors and visitors that no Russians hated the Jews, but that half of the world's Jews lived in Russia, that they were an active, intelligent and well-organized group with whom the simple Russian peasants could not compete, and that there were occasional spontaneous outbursts of fury, which often got out of control, directed at the local tormentors and exploiters. The government sought to protect both the Jews and the peasants in a reasonable way by restricting the Jews to certain parts of the empire and to certain professions.[64]

Pobedonostsev indicated in his first annual report as Director General of the Synod that he had no hope of spreading Christianity among the Jews because of their concept of the chosen race, the power of family ties, and their long tradition of holding fast to their religion. Moreover, he considered Jewish converts to Orthodoxy unreliable. The Church, therefore, made no organized effort to convert Jews, and less than five hundred Jews a year joined the Orthodox Church during the years Pobedonostsev was Director General. In the long run, he hoped one-third of the Jews would emigrate, one-third would be assimilated, and one-third would die out. However, this he thought a very remote and even unlikely solution.

In the meantime, he believed that the Jews should be isolated from the Russians, especially from the centers of national life, and that their influence should be limited in every way possible. Thus, he rejoiced when he found a community where there were no Jews and had been none. He supported the 1882 decrees designed to restrict residence for the Jews to the Pale in the southwest, and he later supported decrees designed to keep Jews from moving into other regions, such as the Don and Terek areas. He prohibited Jews from doing business with any part of the Church, and he tried to keep them from all government positions. He naturally approved the July, 1887, decrees which restricted the Jews' access to higher education to specific norms: 10 percent of the total in areas set aside for Jews, 5 percent outside that area, and 3 percent in St. Petersburg and Moscow. He advised Alexander III to appoint governors who were reliable and firm in dealing with Jews. He was apparently instrumental in replacing Prince Dolgorukov as Governor General of Moscow in 1891 with Grand Duke Sergei Alexandrovich, a former student of his who shared his beliefs and who within the first twelve months expelled approximately 20,000 Jews who had been living in Moscow illegally.[65]

While Pobedonostsev was eager to deny rights and opportunities to the Jews and to provide Russia's provinces with vigorous and forceful governors, he was resolutely opposed to pogroms and popular violence. In 1882, he denounced the Ministry of the Interior for allowing racist demagogues to stimulate riots and demonstrations against the Jews. The same year, he informed Ignatiev that the government must make clear that it not only disagreed with news-paper articles denouncing Russians with foreign names but that it would impose heavy fines for such articles. Later, he argued that panic-stricken crowds rioting out of control were a direct threat to the state and that such popular outbreaks should be prevented, lest they destroy state order and turn against the state itself. Thus, he was not an instigator of the pogroms directed against the Jews, if only because the Balkan crisis had taught him that popular move-ments easily got out of control. In fact, much of the ire he directed against foreign newspapers was due to their ascribing to him re-sponsibility for violent acts against the Jews, of which he thoroughly disapproved, althought he did support the official repressive acts, for which he was assigned responsibilty as well.[66]

Pobedonostsev was also opposed to the establishment of the *Sviashchennaia Druzhina*, or Holy Brotherhood, a kind of private police force founded by a number of extreme conservatives in 1881 to help prevent assassination attempts and to infiltrate revolutionary organizations. Baranov, whom Pobedonostsev had recommended to Alexander III as governor of St. Petersburg, may have had this kind of organization in mind when he proposed a Grand Council or Council of Twenty-Five. Count Illarion Vorontsov-Dashkov, who was head of the palace guard then, shortly after March 1 suggested a Guard, and Count Peter A. Valuev also proposed a volunteer or-ganization of dedicated patriots to help protect the tsar and the imperial family. Little is known of this organization, which acquired a sinister reputation, but Pobedonostsev was often de-nounced as one of its founders and supporters. He may in fact have favored the Holy Brotherhood in the panic of March, 1881, but he consistently opposed amateur organizations of this kind. A recent American analysis of the organization concluded that "there is no reason to believe Pobedonostsev was involved in it." A 1939 Soviet study reported that the only evidence in the correspondence and the archives concerning Pobedonostsev's relations with this organi-zation was his letters to the tsar in 1882 denouncing the Brother-hood and recommending that it be dissolved, as it was on January 6, 1883.[67]

As a prolific author and publicist, Pobedonostsev used the printed word to further his effort to isolate and control the Jews. Many of his publications, including his annual reports as Director General of the Synod, contained clearly antisemitic material. He also urged Feoktistov, who was in charge of censorship throughout most of the

1880's and 1890's, to allow publication of articles and books criticizing the Jews. Finally, as Director of the Synod, he encouraged the publication by the Synod Press of the collected works of an old acquaintance of his, Nikita Giliarov-Platonov, which contained vicious charges against the Jews. Born in Moscow in 1824, a graduate of the Moscow Ecclesiastical Academy, and a member of the Academy's faculty from 1848 until 1855, Giliarov-Platonov failed spectacularly at everything he tried, even though Pobedonostsev and others of his generation thought him in many ways a brilliant man. Too critical to hold his post in the Academy, too lenient with the Slavophils to retain his position on the Moscow Censorship Committee after 1863, too lax for the Ministry of Education, too inefficient to direct the Moscow office of the Synod Press, Giliarov-Platonov edited an unsuccessful journal, *Sovremennyia izvestiia* (Contemporary News), for the twenty years before his death in 1887, with the help of subsidies arranged by Pobedonostsev and others, even though his wild and untidy articles sometimes annoyed them seriously.

Giliarov-Platonov read widely and wrote about almost everything of any interest to an educated Russian. He was a profoundly Orthodox man and believed that the Orthodox doctrine of Christian love would one day bring genuine unity to Russia. From his early days in the seminary, he had been a special student of the Old Believers and of the evangelical sects. He was deeply antisemitic, accepting and publishing the usual charges about the malevolent power and influence of the Jews. The volumes of his articles which Pobedonostsev helped publish after his death contained many antisemitic essays. Indeed, the Director General of the Synod stooped to reprinting several of Giliarov-Platonov's essays which accepted the ritual murder legend, probably the most vile tale of all used against the Jews. Pobedonostsev even sent copies of these volumes to the tsar, and he advertised them extensively in Synod and Church publications.[68]

The Russian
Orthodox Church Abroad

FOR POBEDONOSTSEV, Russia meant the state, which represented the national will and to which the *narod* was attached by a powerful mystical bond. Its main functions were to ensure unity, to provide stability and harmony, and to prevent the rise of nationalisms or other divisive forces through a combination of persuasion and of force. As a servant and even weapon of the state, the Church was to maintain the essential unity in faith and belief, which he called "the community of believers." At a time when some of his contemporaries in western Europe were developing political programs labelled "integral nationalism," Pobedonostsev's might have been defined as "integral national Christendom."

Pobedonostsev considered religion the homogenizing cement of society. He assumed that a society or state was an independent organism and could therefore have only one religion, because all other beliefs and churches could only be "agents of disintegration." It was therefore senseless for a state to attempt to borrow ideas or philosophies from another state or society, just as it was for one state to seek to impose its customs and political system on another people, a process which would be harmful and destructive for all.[1]

Consequently, he was not a supporter of Russian expansion or of an aggressive or even active foreign policy. He was as conservative in his approach to international affairs as he was to political or social change. He saw Russia as a member of a European state system and as one of a number of states in the world with some of which, but only some of which, it had to maintain formal relations, and then "only at the top." However, he did not believe that Russia should participate actively in world affairs. He considered the Russian empire a jerry-built system plagued by so many fundamental problems that it could not expend energy on areas beyond its frontiers.

In other words, Pobedonostsev was an isolationist. The only exception to this stand helped solidify the rule, for in 1876 and through much of 1877 he was an ardent advocate and later supporter of war with Turkey to free the Balkan Slavs and to unite them with Russia in a Slavic federation. However, as the war progressed, Pobedonostsev reversed his opinion. From that time forward, he turned Russian state power inside, not outside. He therefore remained generally aloof from participation in the formal discussion or definition of Russian foreign policy, even in times of great tension. He was opposed to alliances, rejected panslavism after his one escapade had ended, and resisted policies actively or forcefully promoting Russian interests abroad.

At the same time, he accepted and supported programs using the Russian Orthodox Church and its agents to promote Russian culture and the interests of the secular Russian state. Thus, he considered cooperation with the Church of England and with the Old Catholics against their common enemy in Rome. In other parts of Europe, in the Americas, and in Japan, he sought to create Orthodox communities which would be cultural and political centers for Russia. In the Balkans, he apparently sought the expansion and strengthening of Orthodoxy so that the Balkan states would be cordial to Russia and might accept relaxed political links. In Galicia and trans-Carpathian Ruthenia, he took advantage of national, social, and religious discontents to harass and annoy the Austro-Hungarian monarchy. He even used subversive agents to try to bring the Ruthenians, who were generally Uniates, over to Orthodoxy, in the hope that they would one day join their Orthodox brethren in the Russian empire. Finally, in Palestine and Abyssinia he supported vigorous and often quite unscrupulous efforts to create Orthodox centers of influence which, if successful, might have significantly affected the course of international relations in the Middle East and in eastern Africa.

The nature of Pobedonostsev's ideas and policies toward Russian Orthodox colonies abroad is illuminated in a curious but direct way by his attitudes toward the other Orthodox churches, the Papacy, the Church of England, and the Old Catholics. Basically, he paid little attention to the Eastern Orthodox Church. Except for the guide book which he wrote about the history of Orthodoxy for semi-naries and church schools and except for the courses on this subject which he had the seminaries introduce, he devoted the same atten-tion to the various patriarchates as he did to Latin American coun-tries of whose existence he knew but in which he had no interest. Representatives of other Orthodox churches did attend the cele-bration in Kiev, in 1888, of the conversion nine hundred years ear-lier of Vladimir, but visiting prelates from Abyssinia received more attention than they did. In fact, the principal contact between the Russian Orthodox Church and the old centers was the subterranean campaign which Pobedonostsev helped lead and through which the Imperial Orthodox Palestine Society sought increased religious authority in the Holy Land. However, here the veiled opponent was not so much another Orthodox Church as it was the power of Greek prelates in churches and lands in which the Russian Ortho-dox Church sought increased power.

While the other Orthodox Churches were not in Pobedonostsev's field of vision, he was very much aware of the Vatican, if only be-cause millions of Catholics in the western border areas were such a constant torment. He thought of all Poles as Catholics or "Latins," and of all Catholics as Poles, and he considered them all by nature hostile to Russia. Moreover, every Catholic everywhere was an agent of Polonism, of Austria, and of the Vatican against the vital interests of Russia. In an article he wrote in 1888 seeking to prove that the various religious creeds enjoyed freedom in Russia, he wrote that the Catholic Church sought to destroy the Russian Orthodox Church, that the West was its base of operations against Russia, and that the Poles were one of the main weapons. "I would find it diffi-cult today to identify a part of Russia where there lives a Catholic who is neutral, tolerant, unmarked by a spirit of animosity against the Orthodox and not preoccupied with taking from Russia the basically Russian provinces on its western borders." Pobedonostsev loved to travel in Europe, and he visited northern Italy at least twice. However, while he was attracted by Rome and was eager to hear of others' impressions of the city, he could not bring himself to visit it, simply because it was the center of Catholicism. It is in-structive to note that Pobedonostsev never mentioned Constanti-nople or considered going there.[2]

Alexander II in general had been quite benevolent toward Cath-olics and Uniates. He issued a decree under which a Catholic or a Uniate could marry a member of the Orthodox Church without being required to promise that the children of the marriage would be raised in the Orthodox Church, he issued amnesties to several Uniate priests, he named a committee to study the problems raised by a concordat with the Vatican, and he was reasonably prompt in allowing the Vatican to fill vacant Catholic bishoprics.

When Leo XIII became pope in 1878, he sought to improve the position of the Catholics in Russia and to establish regular diplomatic relations with the Russian government. Naturally, Pobedonostsev was resolutely opposed to this, defending the imprisonment of Catholic bishops because of their open support of Polish nationalism and arguing that official relationships with the Vatican would only increase Polish arrogance and pertinacity. However, Leo XIII was able to have quiet talks begun in Vienna and in Rome in 1881. The rigorous stand of the Russian government over treatment of the Uniates and over the vacant bishoprics melted in 1883, when the pope skillfully sent Monsignor Vannutelli, a Dominican scholar well acquainted with Russia and Central Europe and a warm admirer of the Orthodox Church, which he did not consider schismatic, as his personal representative at the coronation of Alexander III. Pobedonostsev was unbending in his conversations, and the tsar insisted that Catholics must remain out of politics. Vannutelli was unable to persuade the Russians to establish a legation in Rome, but he did complete the appointment of two archbishops and six bishops in western Russia and he did establish contacts which he and other Vatican representatives were able to use later.[3]

Leo XIII reopened his campaign to improve the situation of Catholics in Russia in 1887, at about the same time that he sought similar goals in France under the policy commonly known as *ralliement*. Nicholas K. Giers, the Russian Minister of Foreign Affairs, and Soviet diplomatic historians have both concluded that the Vatican was seeking diplomatic support from Russia against Germany and Italy and that the simultaneous efforts to modify the policies of the French and Russian governments toward Catholics, and perhaps of Catholics toward those governments, were also part of a campaign to bring Russia and France together. These interpretations are almost certainly exaggerated. In any case, the Vatican let the Russian ambassador to the King of Italy know that Leo XIII would welcome a message from the tsar on the occasion of the golden anniversary of his consecration as a priest. Moreover, three of the grand dukes, Vladimir, Sergei, and Paul, all former students of Pobedonostsev, had an audience with the pope in January, 1888.

Alexander III's friendly message on the pope's jubilee annoyed many Russian nationalists, who noted that no European monarchs sent similar messages to any Russian metropolitan and that the tsar did not congratulate other religious leaders on such great occasions. However, it did allow Leo XIII to reply on January 28, 1888, thanking the tsar and expressing his esteem and friendly wishes. The pope then noted that he was concerned because the tsar's Catholic subjects were not allowed freely to practice their religion. The next month, Giers informed the embassy in Rome that quiet talks might be launched with a Vatican representative, but warned the ambassador that the Russian representative should not be tricked into formal negotiations, should not mention reestablishing relations, and should seek "certain and positive guarantees of the intentions of the Holy See and of the conduct of the Roman Catholic clergy."

The discussions between Cardinal Rampolla and Alexander P. Izvolskii in 1888 led to the filling of three more bishoprics, the restoration of another bishopric, the appointment of several suffragan bishops, and the completion of several unfulfilled promises made in 1883. The Grand Duchess Catherine Mikhailovna and her daughter then had an audience in November, 1888, with the pope, who began to work immediately for reestablishing diplomatic relations with St. Petersburg. Pobedonostsev was apparently so opposed to this that the Ministry of Foreign Affairs did not consult him during the five or six years these quiet discussions consumed, but relied instead upon the Ministry of the Interior for information and judgments concerning the effect the new relationship would produce. Izvolskii served as a special representative in Rome until May, 1894, when the Russian government officially named him minister to the Vatican. This appointment was made only after the tsar, the Minister of Foreign Affairs, and the Minister of the Interior had agreed that the pope's most recent encyclical had indicated that the Polish Catholic clergy would no longer support Polish nationalism against Russia. Thus, while *ralliement* was being undermined by conservative Catholics and, later, by the Dreyfus Affair in France, it achieved a minor success in Russia.[4]

Pobedonostsev supported the Izvolskii appointment because he thought it might dampen Polish nationalism. However, he vigorously resisted the appointment of a papal nuncio in St. Petersburg because it would bring the envoy of a hostile religion into the court, give respectability and prestige to Catholicism, and weaken Orthodoxy in the "eternal, life-and-death struggle" in the western provinces. His power and resistance were such that he was successful.[5]

At the same time, Pobedonostsev also fought successfully against a vague and woolly effort on the part of some leading members of the Church of England to establish close ties and even some kind of union between the Anglican and the Russian Orthodox Church. He welcomed English converts to Orthodoxy; indeed, probably because of his interest in England and the recommendations Olga Novikov gave to English visitors to Russia, he often met Englishmen who were interested in joining the Orthodox Church. He was an effective spokesman for his Church, and he and his wife on occasion devoted many hours to Englishmen seriously studying Orthodoxy. In doing this, of course, he was honoring the old Slavophil tradition, for the Slavophils had also had a special admiration for English life and had attracted the interest of Englishmen, such as William Palmer of Magdalen College in Oxford, who had sought communion with the Orthodox Church in Russia in 1841 and 1842 and who ultimately joined the Catholic Church and died in Rome.[6]

Between 1870 and 1875 and again in the 1890's, a handful of Anglicans, Russian Orthodox and, in the 1870's, Old Catholics, or Catholics who refused to accept the dogma of Papal infallibility announced in 1870, sought to form a united anti-Catholic front. Olga Novikov, her brother Alexander Kireev, and other enthusiastic Slavophils and panslavs were much impressed after 1870 by the opportunity for creating some kind of religious unity against Rome in an organization which they thought would surely be dominated by Russian Orthodoxy. Pobedonostsev expressed some interest in the annual conference representatives of these groups held in Germany until 1876, when the Balkan crisis at one stroke dissolved the interest of the Russian participants. However, from the very beginning he ridiculed those who believed any kind of union possible, and he refused the heir's suggestion that he participate in the Freiburg Conference in 1874 as an observer.[7]

In July, 1888, Edward Benson, Archbishop of Canterbury, was the only Western prelate who congratulated the Russian Church on the occasion of the nine hundredth anniversary of the introduction of Christianity into Russia. This gesture and the presence at the ceremonies of William J. Birkbeck, a Fellow of Magdalen College in Oxford as Palmer had been fifty years earlier, pleased the Russians. Indeed, Metropolitan Platon replied that he agreed fully with the archbishop's statement that "the Russian and Anglican Church have common foes. Alike we have to guard our independence against the Papal aggressiveness which claims to subordinate all the churches of Christ to the See of Rome . . ." However, the archbishop's proposal in 1889 that the two churches begin to progress toward union by agreeing first to admit believers in either church to communion in the other church was quietly ignored, largely because Pobedonostsev considered it nonsense, "nothing more than a dream."

However, Pobedonostsev was able to take advantage of the eager admiration of the Russian Church displayed by Birkbeck, who was an Orthodox fellow-traveller, and to use him to advance the ambitions of the Russian Church. Pobedonostsev took a special interest in Birkbeck at the Kievan celebrations, invited him to the banquets and ceremonies, entertained him at the Pobedonostsev dacha, and arranged for him to meet other leaders of Church and state, to visit several monasteries, and in general to enjoy the kind of favored treatment twentieth-century states provide important visitors. Birkbeck was completely conquered. His books and articles, his lectures in England, and his friendships with English scholars and Anglican leaders were thoroughly exploited by Pobedonostsev and his colleagues. Birkbeck "explained" panslavism to England, helped organize the Eastern Orthodox Association, demonstrated that "the Catholic press" of Austria and "the Jewish press" of Germany peddled misinformation about Russia, and ridiculed charges of "so-called persecution of the Jews" in Russia. He accompanied Mandell Creighton, Bishop of Peterborough and later of London, to Russia in 1896, and the following year guided Archbishop Maclagan of York. Both of these visitors were entertained handsomely, were introduced to Nicholas II, and left full of admiration and praise for Pobedonostsev, Orthodoxy, and Russia. Their expressions of interest in "a gradual approximation" and "eventual union" of the two state churches were warmly received, but Pobedonostsev in his private talks and correspondence with Russians ridiculed these hopes; only the golden glow remained after these visits. However, Pobedonostsev had succeeded in creating a sympathetic climate of opinion within an important segment of the British intellectual and political community.[8]

In other areas of the world, Pobedonostsev used quite different methods to promote Orthodox and Russian national interests. In some areas, such as Galicia and Carpathian Ruthenia, the Balkans, the Holy Land, and Abyssinia, he was able to use the authority of the state in an indirect way to advance toward religious and national goals. In other sections, he simply used Church funds to assist in building and maintaining Russian Orthodox churches as Russian cultural centers. He also used secret funds of the Synod to assist a handful of foreign clergymen and scholars interested in Orthodoxy. He gave annual subsidies to journals in Belgium and England, and he assisted some of the scattered Russian Orthodox Churches around the world with small annual subsidies and grants for special purchases. In addition, he arranged that Orthodox priests be attached to some of the major embassies abroad, and the Synod helped in the construction of churches attached to Russian legations.

Thus, between 1881 and 1894, the Synod gave financial assistance for the construction of at least eight Orthodox churches abroad, two in European Turkey, one in the Austrian Empire, one in Italy, two in France, one in Germany, and one in Argentina. Eight more churches were built with Synod support in the next decade, three in Germany, three in the United States, one in Korea, and one in China. Sometimes these churches were built to counteract the influence of Old Believers, as in Thrace, sometimes to serve Russians on vacation, as on the Riviera or at the baths in Bohemia, and sometimes at the request of diplomats who believed that a church would assist the legation and help attract local support, as in Seoul and Buenos Aires. At the turn of the century, the Synod was aiding about sixty churches scattered around the world.[9]

Pobedonostsev was especially interested in Orthodox mission work in Japan and the United States, although in both cases the numbers of church members involved were very small. A chaplain had been attached to the Russian consulate in Nagasaki in 1860, and the church grew very slowly in Japan in the next two decades. In 1883, the Synod reported there were 8,863 members, which grew to 19,000 in 1891 and 25,000 in 1900. Pobedonostsev had been interested in Russian Orthodoxy in Japan even before he became Director General of the Synod. He met clergymen from Japan and introduced them to the heir and to his other friends at court, and he collected money for mission work in Japan even during the Balkan crisis. Shortly after he became Director General, he raised an old acquaintance, archimandrite Nicholas, to bishop. By 1900, largely through financial support he provided, a cathedral, a bishop's residence, a seminary, and a girls' school had been built in Tokyo. Only three of the thirty-four priests were Russian, and Pobedonostsev was convinced that the subsidy of about fifty thousand rubles a year was a most fruitful one for improving understanding of Russia.[10]

The United States represented a separate series of problems and opportunities. The Bishopric of Alaska and the Aleutians was a complex issue, because of the size of the see and the stormy relations between the bishop and his flock, especially in San Francisco. There were only 17,000 Church members in the United States in 1889, but Pobedonostsev considered mission work there of considerable importance. He was particularly eager to convert Uniates who had emigrated from Galicia to cities such as Pittsburgh and Chicago, in part because this might assist his campaign among the Uniates in Galicia, the Carpatho-Ukraine, and Russia itself.[11]

He was naturally more active in seeking to extend the influence of the Russian Orthodox Church among other Slavs who were Orthodox or who had at one time been members of the Russian Orthodox Church. He became aware of the Slavs outside of Russia shortly after he moved from Moscow to St. Petersburg in 1865, and he began then to instruct the heir to the throne about their history and significance. He was especially fond of Prague, which he visited at least three times in the 1870's and which became a kind of gateway to the other Slavs for him. His interest in Orthodoxy and in history led him to intensive study of the history of Christianity, particularly of the Eastern Orthodox Church and its complicated relations with western Christianity and of the areas where the two church systems were in conflict. Thus, in the early 1870's, he studied the books and articles of Andrei N. Muraviev of Kiev, who wrote extensively from 1830 until his death in 1874 on the history of Christianity, with especial emphasis on the relations between the Russian Orthodox Church and other churches. Moreover, his visits to London and to Prague, particularly his participation in the consecration of a Russian Orthodox Church in Prague in 1874, awakened him to the importance Orthodox churches abroad would have for Russians travelling and working there and for attracting those interested in Orthodoxy and in Russia.[12]

After the Balkan crisis, he developed a two-edged program concerning the southern Slavs and the Balkans in general, seeking to increase knowledge of the southern Slavs in Russia, especially within the government and among the leaders of the Orthodox Church, and providing economic and educational assistance to Orthodox churches and monasteries in the Balkans. Thus, he sent Russian scholars and members of the Holy Synod staff into the Balkans and Central Europe to collect information, to prepare memoranda for Church and government officials, and to make the Holy Synod the central point for information on the Orthodox

Church in Slavic lands. His correspondence with Alexander III is full of data concerning Balkan politics, particularly about organized religion. Much of the information he collected and the views it reflected were naturally forwarded to the Ministry of Foreign Affairs. Thus, in December, 1884, he gave to Giers, the Foreign Minister, copies of memoranda prepared for him by Professor Trotskii of the St. Petersburg Ecclesiastical Academy concerning the position of the Orthodox Church in Bulgaria and the new hierarchy in Serbia.

He had the Holy Synod Press reprint the works of Muraviev on the Eastern Orthodox Church, he had books on Orthodoxy collected abroad for the libraries of Russian seminaries, and he obtained journals and books from Orthodox seminaries in the Balkans for Russian seminaries. He also established chairs in Russian seminaries on the history of Orthodoxy in the Slavic lands. Finally, in 1891 he published a history of the Orthodox Church for use especially in institutions training teachers. This volume, which aroused some criticism because he borrowed so heavily from the work of Alexandra Nikolaevna Bakhmetev, without acknowledgment, appeared in nine editions before he died.[13]

He was even more interested in providing financial, intellectual, and spiritual support to the Orthodox churches in the Balkans than he was in educating Russians concerning that area. Carefully selected Orthodox clergymen were invited to Moscow and St. Petersburg to receive protection, encouragement, advice, and support. Thus, Metropolitan Michael of Serbia, who had been assisted by Ignatiev for fifteen years but who was dismissed by King Milan in October, 1881, was advised by Pobedonostsev by special courier and was then brought to Russia, where he was maintained, and to some degree restrained or controlled, because the policies he proposed were considered too drastic and dangerous by Ivan Aksakov, Ignatiev, Pobedonostsev, and other Russian leaders.

In 1885, Pobedonostsev invited archimandrite Mitrofan Ban of Montenegro to Russia. He was presented to the tsar, given five handsome sets of vestments and other gifts by the Holy Synod, and honored by the Slavonic Benevolent Society in a special meeting in St. Petersburg. Moreover, the Holy Synod provided him an annual subsidy after he returned to Montenegro.

Other prelates from the Balkans were similarly treated. Pobedonostsev devoted especial efforts to making certain that the Orthodox Church in other Slavic lands be well represented at important religious ceremonies in Russia, such as the celebration in Kiev in 1888 of the nine hundredth anniversary of the introduction of Christianity into Russia. The Austrian and Roumanian governments recognized the political importance of these gestures and sought unsuccessfully to prevent the clergymen invited from attending.[14]

Pobedonostsev also continued a tradition which began about 1840 of bringing young Bulgarian and Serbian seminarians to Russia for education. In 1886, he reported that there were thirty-seven foreigners in Orthodox seminaries in Russia, eighteen of whom were Bulgars and six Serbs. Of the thirty-seven, nineteen were in Kiev and nine in Odessa, but only two in Moscow and four in St. Petersburg, because Pobedonostsev wanted to keep the seminarians away from the capital cities and in surroundings believed to be similar to those of their native lands. This program for training Orthodox priests was supplemented by grants of Russian liturgical books and of other religious publications to schools and seminaries in the Balkans. Most of the funds for these books were provided by the Holy Synod, but Pobedonostsev also allowed the Slavonic Benevolent Society, the panslav organization, to collect money after church services for sending literature to the southern Slavs.[15]

Economic assistance to significant churches and individuals or for especially important occasions was provided in a variety of ways, sometimes through grants from the Holy Synod, sometimes with funds from the Russian state treasury, and sometimes through the Slavonic Benevolent Society. Thus, in 1890 Pobedonostsev encouraged the panslav organization to collect funds for the famine in Montenegro; almost 300,000 rubles (approximately $140,000) were collected at churches and forwarded. On another occasion, he permitted an Orthodox group from the Dobrudja in Bulgaria to solicit funds in Bessarabia. Usually, however, he assigned funds from the Church itself or from other state funds, for vestments for priests in Albania and Montenegro, for bells for a church in Bulgaria, for an iconostasis in Montenegro, and for construction and repair of churches throughout the Slavic lands. Some churches which he considered particularly critical or needy, such as that in Prague, received annual subsidies from the Holy Synod, usually through a Russian diplomatic representative. The Russian ambassador in Vienna transmitted the subsidy there, while the Russian consul in Albania, who was especially trusted by Pobedonostsev, was given funds to distribute to Orthodox churches in that poor land. On occasion, when the Russian subvention was especially great (as for the construction of an Orthodox cathedral in Vienna to which the tsar may have contributed as much as $200,000 by 1899 figures), Pobedonostsev ensured that Russian aid was highly publicized. Thus, the church was consecrated by the archbishop of Kholm-Warsaw, the Russian ambassador and the entire embassy staff attended the ceremony, and Pobedonostsev sent the choir of the Synod from Moscow for the occasion.[16]

The foreign territories in which Pobedonostsev had the most intense interest and which he apparently hoped would one day be annexed were Carpathian Ruthenia or the Carpatho-Ukraine and the province the Austrians called Galicia, both then troubled parts of the Austro-Hungarian empire. Carpathian Ruthenia and Galicia were both primitive areas, with powerful magnates, a heavily exploited peasantry, and few artisans and professional people. However, the two great cities of Galicia, Lvov and Cracow, the latter of which was added to Austria only in 1846, were among the great cultural centers of Europe.

Carpathian Ruthenia in 1880 was inhabited by about 700,000 people, most of whom considered themselves Ruthenians or western Ukrainians and most of whom were Uniates, Christians of the Eastern rite who acknowledged the pope's primacy and accepted Roman Catholic doctrine, but whose liturgy was in some ways different from that of the Catholic Church and whose priests were allowed to marry. Carpathian Ruthenia was a part of Hungary. Galicia, on the other hand, had been a part of Austria since the last years of the eighteenth century. In 1910, it contained about 8 million people, of whom approximately 40 percent were registered as Ruthenians and about 60 percent as Poles. The substantial Jewish population registered generally as Poles, and the area contained about 100,000 Germans. The Poles were almost all Catholic. The Ruthenians, who were concentrated in the eastern part, were generally Uniates, but some were Orthodox and the upper class was often Catholic.

National and religious friction in these backward areas was endemic, but it became more fierce as the nineteenth century progressed. In Galicia the Catholic Church, led largely by Jesuits and assisted by the Austrian government, carried on an effective campaign to strengthen its position. Before 1867, the Austrian government had generally favored the Ruthenians against the Poles, in order to keep the larger and more threatening Polish group under control, to attract the sympathy of Ruthenians living under Russian rule, and to counter any Russian program designed to win the support of the Orthodox Ruthenians. After the *Ausgleich* in 1867, however, the government in Vienna decided to support the Polish landlords (the *szlachta*) against the peasant, whether they considered themselves Ruthenians or Polish. This policy intensified both conflicts on religion and nationality.

During the 1840's, a group known as Old Ruthenians appeared, with its base in Lvov and most of its members Uniates, and with support in both Galicia and Carpathian Ruthenia. It was represented in the Panslav Congress held in Prague in 1846, and some of its leaders came to know leading Russian panslavs, particularly Professor Michael Pogodin of Moscow University. As Austrian and Hungarian policies which the Ruthenians considered oppressive became more effective, the Old Ruthenians turned to Orthodox Russia for help and protection. However, toward the end of the nineteenth century, an even more powerful force appeared, a group that called itself the Young Ukrainians and that believed the Ruthenians were Ukrainians and ought to be a part of an independent, democratic Ukraine, in which the power of all churches should be restricted. This group naturally alarmed Pobedonostsev, who alerted the Ministry of the Interior and the censor.

Thus, Galicia and the Carpatho-Ukraine were both unsettled areas at the time Pobedonostsev became interested in them. Political and social conflict between the landlords and the peasants intensified the national and religious strife. Heavy emigration provided some outlet for the restless population. On the other hand, there was no middle class outside Lvov and Cracow, and the areas as a whole represented tense border provinces where foreign meddling could be both profitable and immensely dangerous.[17]

Pobedonostsev considered Galicia and the Carpatho-Ukraine Orthodox and Russian in culture. He was especially interested in them because they contained more than three million Ruthenians or Western Ukrainians, many of whom were members of the Uniate Church. He was convinced that the Ruthenian Uniates had been Orthodox and would have remained members of the Orthodox Church but for three centuries of Polish and Catholic oppression. Moreover, he believed that the reunion of these Uniates and Ruthenians to Russia would make easier the conversion and absorption of the Uniates in the western provinces.

He almost certainly met several Old Ruthenians in Prague in

1874, and he probably assisted one of them, Father Ivan Naumovich, to contribute an article to the first publication of the Russian panslav organization, *Slavianskii sbornik* (Slavonic Collection), which appeared in 1875. The Old Ruthenian leader, Adolf Dobriansky, visited Pobedonostsev in St. Petersburg in 1875. Twenty or thirty years earlier, Dobriansky had created a program for uniting the areas inhabited by Ruthenians in Hungary in a single unit with administrative autonomy and the right to use the Ruthenian language, rather than German or Magyar. By 1875, Dobriansky thought that this could be achieved only with powerful Russian support. Indeed, at that time, incorporation into Russia was probably his goal. Pobedonostsev, who described him as an "Ugro-russe," was impressed by his tales of persecution, by his conviction that "the Orthodox faith is the main guardian of nationality [*narodnost'*]," by his lack of interest in political theory, and above all, by the enthusiasm which he felt and showed for Russia and for Orthodoxy. Pobedonostsev arranged that Dobriansky should have a long conversation with the heir, whom he had previously instructed concerning these complicated areas, and he also introduced him to the Muscovite panslavs, who were just then launching the wave of emotional panslavism which made the Balkan crisis so intense two years later. When Pobedonostsev became the Director General of the Synod, he sent subsidies to Dobriansky and to Naumovich, mainly through Father Michael Raevskii, a Russian Orthodox priest attached to the Russian embassy in Vienna, and through the Russian consulate at Chernovitz. On at least one occasion, he went to Vienna while on vacation in the Salzburg area in order to carry funds to the Old Ruthenians. These grants may have been quite substantial: a letter to Pobedonostsev from an agent in Galicia indicates that Father Raevskii had received 42,000 rubles (approximately $21,000) from Pobedonostsev that year.[18]

Dobriansky and Naumovich fled to Russia with their families in 1883, when they and other Old Ruthenians were charged with treason in trials in which the prosecutor often referred to Pobedonostsev as the Russian official responsible. Pobedonostsev was especially irritated at the actions taken by the Austrian and Hungarian governments, not only because he was identified in the courts but also because this failure coincided with the collapse of Russian influence in liberated Bulgaria. He provided Holy Synod support for these Orthodox priests and their families, gave them useful functions to perform in Russia, and financed the preparation and publication of their writings, which he distributed through the Synod Press and which he also sought to distribute in Austro-Hungarian territory.

At the same time, he pressed Giers and Alexander III to protest to Emperor Francis Joseph and to the Austrian Foreign Ministry about the trials of Uniate and Orthodox leaders and about the treatment of the Old Ruthenians. He protested bitterly to the Austrian and German ambassadors on behalf of the Old Ruthenians and even conferred with Count Herbert Bismarck in the hope that his father would persuade the Austrian government to modify its policies, policies which were in fact less repressive than those which he was supporting on the Russian side of the border. He even introduced Father Naumovich to the German ambassador, and he refused the latter's request to cease Russian propaganda and financial support in Galicia and the Carpatho-Ukraine.

At Bismarck's suggestion, the German ambassador in the fall of 1886 talked with him about the hazards his policies raised at a time when Bismarck believed the three great conservative states of Europe should unite against the menace of revolution. This conversation apparently had no effect, but the deaths of Dobriansky and Naumovich a few years later and the apparent lack of progress did persuade Pobedonostsev to abandon his dangerous tactics in the early 1890's. After his death, in particular just before the outbreak of the First World War, the panslav and pan-Orthodox move which he had fostered was revived. A Galician Benevolent Society was founded in St. Petersburg in 1913, using the techniques he had adopted. After the Second World War, the Carpatho-Ukraine and almost all of Galicia were annexed by the Soviet Union, which immediately incorporated the Uniate church into the Russian Orthodox Church and introduced into these areas the institutions and values which characterize Soviet life.[19]

Pobedonostsev's aims and activities with regard to Galicia and the Carpatho-Ukraine reflected Russian ambitions which the Soviet regime has been able to achieve since the Second World War. In the same way, undertakings which he and his associates launched in the Holy Land have been followed since the Second World War by Soviet efforts designed to capitalize on these enterprises and to advance Soviet influence throughout the Middle East. The Orthodox Palestine Society, which Pobedonostsev helped to found in 1882 and which became the Imperial Orthodox Palestine Society in 1885, was renamed the Orthodox Palestine Society after the March, 1917, revolution, withered away in 1926 as the Russian Palestine Society, and then was revived in January, 1952, as part of the Soviet Academy of Sciences. In 1954, the Academy resumed publication of the old Society's *Palestinskii sbornik* (Palestine Collection), with the first Soviet volume and each succeeding volume bearing two numbers. (Thus, the 1954 issue is identified as volume one to indicate that it is the first of a series; however, the number sixty-three is alongside in parentheses to indicate that this is the successor to the old series, the last number of which, sixty-two, was published in 1916.) The new Soviet journal paid generous tribute to the earlier Society for its scholarly publications and its other "scientific work," such as its expeditions, its collections of archeological materials, and its library. It has also praised the Society for establishing monasteries, hostels, and clinics and for its work in education. The Soviet society has sought to continue these same activities, which is flattery indeed.[20]

Russian interest in the Holy Land was based on the veneration for consecrated territory felt by generations of devout Christians, some of whom in the nineteenth century sought to make a pilgrimage to this sanctified area. When Catherine the Great in 1774 imposed the treaty of Kuchuk Kainardji on the Ottoman Empire, won recognition for Russia's claim to protect the Orthodox Christians living under Ottoman rule, and acquired full liberty for Russian pilgrims in the Ottoman Middle East, she put into the hands of Russian rulers splendid instruments for interfering in Ottoman affairs. In particular, of course, the dramatic upsurge of Russian influence gave body to the dream of acquiring Constantinople, cradle of the Greek Orthodox Church, and thus of control of the straits, opening the Mediterranean to Russia.

Russian interest in and ability to use the tools Catherine created waxed and waned during the following century, reaching its nadir with the humiliating defeat in the Crimean War, which cost Russia its monopoly as protector of Christians living under the Turks. While the state's direct authority in the Middle East reflected the crises and wars, churchmen and scholars, with the knowledge and support of the Ministry of Foreign Affairs, began to carry forward a kind of cultural imperialism much like that waged in many areas of the world in the twentieth century. In 1841 the first Russian hostel for pilgrims was constructed in Jerusalem. Six years later, the first Ecclesiastical Mission was established in Palestine, at the suggestion of Foreign Minister Nesselrode and with a remarkable

clerical missionary-imperialist, Bishop Porfirii Uspenskii at its head.
Following the Crimean War, a second Ecclesiastical Mission was
established and Grand Duke Constantine Nikolaevich organized the
Palestine Committee, which built a center for Russian pilgrims in
Jerusalem, with a hostel, hospital, cathedral, home for a Russian
consul, and headquarters for the Mission. The Committee's work
was so successful that it was made a part of the Asiatic Department
of the Ministry of Foreign Affairs in 1864 and its name was changed
to Palestine Commission. However, these efforts were handicapped
by conflict between the Mission and the Commission and between
the Holy Synod and the Ministry of Foreign Affairs back in St.
Petersburg. Moreover, the creation of an independent Bulgarian
church, the noisy explosion of Russian panslavism in the 1870's,
and the Balkan crisis all alarmed Greek churchmen throughout the
Middle East and created suspicion and hostility among them toward
the Russians.[21]

The freezing of these efforts to expand Russian Orthodox influence attracted the attention of Pobedonostsev and others, who in
May, 1882, therefore formed the Orthodox Palestine Society, with
the aim of collecting and distributing information about the Holy
Land in Russia, encouraging and assisting pilgrims, and establishing schools, seminaries, hospitals, old age homes, monasteries, and
churches in the Holy Land. The first meeting of the Society was
called at Pobedonostsev's invitation, and he helped to draft the
organization's statutes. Most of the meetings during the first years
were held in his residence, although he was only an honorary member, probably because he believed that official support from the
Synod would increase the suspicion of the Greek clergy. Grand
Duke Sergei Alexandrovich, a witless former student and even
servitor of Pobedonostsev, was elected chairman of the Society, and
many courtiers and members of the hierarchy became members.
In 1892, for example, Alexander III, the empress, fifteen other
members of the imperial family, and almost all the hierarchy were
among the 980 members.[22]

The history of the Orthodox Palestine Society in many ways resembles that of the Slavonic Benevolent Society, the panslav organization which was founded in Moscow in 1858 by a group of scholars and bureaucrats to expand knowledge concerning the other
Slavs and to assist their religious and intellectual development. The
panslav movement soon became a noisy, wealthy, jingoist organization dominated by publicists and army officers, which helped to

create a military atmosphere in St. Petersburg and Moscow and to bring on the Balkan crisis and the wars of 1875–78. Similarly, the Palestine Society changed and became more active politically as it grew. An important part of its membership throughout its career consisted of scholars, but they played an especially important role only in the first six or eight years.

The Society's statutes in May, 1882, provided that it could have three hundred active members, who were to pay lifetime membership fees of five hundred rubles (about $250) or annual dues of twenty-five rubles; an undefined number of associate members, who were to pay lifetime membership fees of two hundred rubles or annual dues of ten rubles; and up to one hundred honorary members. At its second meeting, in December, 1882, the organization had 172 members, in the spring of 1883 it had 257. Participation grew slowly, to 674 in 1885, to 735 in 1886, and to 873 in 1887. The Synod publicized the organization widely and exerted considerable pressure upon the hierarchy to join and to persuade other leading Russians to become members or to contribute. It set aside Palm Sunday as the day on which all Russian Orthodox men and women were urged to contribute to the Society.[23]

For the first few years of its existence, the Society concentrated on scholarly activities, encouraging pilgrims—especially through reduced-rate transportation—and building and repairing schools and hospitals, particularly in and around Nazareth. However, the energy and activity of the new organization created new fears among the Greek clergy, especially the Greek hierarchs, in the Holy Land and in Syria. The new organization also collided with the second Ecclesiastical Mission and with the Palestine Commission of the Asiatic Division of the Ministry of Foreign Affairs. After considerable discussion in 1888 and 1889 within the government, Alexander III, at the request of Pobedonostsev, merged the Society and the Palestine Commission, which Grand Duke Sergei at that time also headed. In effect, the Society absorbed the Commission, over the protests of the Ministry of Foreign Affairs. It had already become "Imperial," but the 1889 merger ultimately meant that the Society was subject to direct government control. Moreover, even though the Society was required to make use of Ministry of Foreign Affairs channels for its overseas operations only in 1894, the leadership, the membership and the nature of its work, the history of other such Russian organizations, and the suspicion with which Middle Easterners viewed all such efforts by foreign powers strengthened their

conviction that the Society was in fact an arm of the Russian government, or a "front organization."

In pressing for the reorganization which led to the transformation of the Society, Pobedonostsev must have concluded that the
Society required powerful state support to overcome the harass-
ments and delays the Turks and Orthodox Greeks created. The
conflicts with the Palestine Commission, and with the Ecclesiastical
Mission were glaring examples of wasteful duplication of effort even
in a shockingly inadequate administrative system. From his earlier
experience with the Volunteer Fleet, Pobedonostsev must have concluded that even an organization under the tsar and chaired by a
grand duke could not survive against a rival institution within the
state apparatus.[24]

In the 1890's, the Society acquired a closer connection with the
government and a more clearly political tone and program. The
1889 reorganization put representatives of the Synod and of the
Ministry of Foreign Affairs on the Executive Council. After 1898,
the Ministry of Education as well was represented. The Russian
consuls in Damascus and Jerusalem, particularly in Damascus,
worked so closely with the Society that any objective observer must
have concluded that the Society was a government institution. In
fact, A. P. Beliaev, the executive secretary of the Society from 1903
until he died in 1906, had been extremely active in the Society's
behalf in the decade before 1903, when he was Russian consul in
Damascus, and he retained a position in the Ministry of Foreign
Affairs when he accepted the new position in St. Petersburg.

Moreover, the meetings of the Executive Council from 1887
through 1905 were held in the official residence of Pobedonostsev's
deputy in the Holy Synod, Vladimir K. Sabler. The Synod not only
helped collect a good part of the contributions made to the Society,
but contributed annually about 50,000 rubles. In 1899, Pobedonostsev helped persuade the Council of State to grant 30,000 rubles annually, and in 1901 the state made a loan of 500,000 rubles to the
Society. In fact, careful analysis of the Society's budgets indicates
that the Ministry of Foreign Affairs must also have been contributing substantially. Thus, even though the membership and income
from dues and from gifts rose throughout the 1890's, expenditures
considerably outweighed ordinary income. Even in the 1890's, annual income from dues was less than 50,000 rubles and at no time
did gifts exceed 300,000 rubles a year. In 1894, when the Society
had less than 2,000 members, its expenditures amounted to almost

700,000 rubles. In 1897, when the 3,139 members contributed 47,-259 rubles in dues and the Society received 230,000 rubles in gifts, it spent almost 856,000 rubles.[25]

Perhaps the Society's most permanent contribution was its impressive list of scholarly publications, most of which were collections of historical documents but some of which were research products in the fields of archeology, literature, and language. These volumes, of which thirty-one were published as early as 1891, are a great addition to knowledge of Palestine and of Byzantium as well. The several expeditions which the Society organized and financed have also stimulated research in the history of the Holy Land.[26]

Encouraging and assisting pilgrims constituted the second reason listed in the 1882 statutes for organizing the Society, which devoted approximately one-third of its income to this purpose. Here, too, the Society's work was impressive. It arranged tours for pilgrims at reduced prices, particularly through the round-trip "pilgrim's ticket"; it established hostels in Russian ports and in various cities in the Middle East; and it provided guidance, comfort, and Russian quarters or centers for the pilgrims, two-thirds of whom were peasants. Above all, after 1889 it had complete control over all Russian pilgrims; in assisting them, it protected them from the Greek Orthodox in the Middle East and used them to buttress Russian interests and institutions in the area. The flow of pilgrims naturally increased under the Society's encouragement; it rose from 2,000 in 1880 to 3,817 in 1889, 4,000 in 1894, and 6,000 in 1900 to 12,000 in 1913.[27]

The third major goal of the Society, to support and expand the influence of Russian Orthodoxy in the Holy Land, was sought mainly through building and maintaining educational, medical, and religious institutions. The Society built six primary schools within the first six years of its existence. By 1900, it was supporting and directing sixty-eight free schools in Palestine and Syria with a total of almost ten thousand students. To train teachers for these schools, the Society established an institute for teachers; it also sent a few of the most promising teachers and students to Russia for higher education. In addition, the Society operated several hostels, a hospital, four clinics, a home for the aged, and four monasteries.[28]

The Society encountered numerous difficulties, even after the merger in 1889 had eliminated much of the duplication and conflict among Russians. The Ottoman government was inevitably suspicious of such a Russian enterprise, particularly when it noted the important state positions some of its leaders occupied, the role

played by various members of the imperial family, and the cooperation between the society and Russian officials in Constantinople,
Damascus, and the Holy Land. Consequently, the Turks restricted
and harassed the Society. They refused recognition of its schools
until 1902. They delayed and sometimes refused permission to con-
struct new buildings. When the Russians sought to escape or evade
the Turks' controls, they usually only increased the difficulties.

The Greek patriarchates, especially that in Jerusalem, were also
worried about Russian expansion. Panslavism had been directed
as much against Greek rule of the Orthodox churches in the Balkans
as it had been against Ottoman political rule. The Greek Orthodox
hierarchy, therefore, was sensitive to a Russian state program that
made use of the Russian Orthodox Church in territory traditionally
dominated by the Greeks. The school program for Arab children;
the Russian effort to win the allegiance of the Arab clergy against
the Greeks; the presence of known panslavs, such as Ignatiev and
Alexei S. Suvorin, the editor of *Novoe vremia* (New Times), among
its active members; and Russian success in electing an Arab,
Meletios Doumani, Patriarch of Antioch in 1899, persuaded Greek
church leaders that the Society was continuing the panslav program
of the 1870's in the Balkans.

The Greek Orthodox hierarchy therefore supported the Ottoman
government in hampering the Society. It was so difficult after 1895
to build Russian schools in the Holy Land itself because of the opposition of the Greek Patriarch of Jerusalem that the major emphasis
was shifted to Damascus, where the Patriarch and the Arab clergy
were both friendly. By the turn of the century, two-thirds of the
Society's schools and pupils were in Syria, where the Society had
originally planned no schools.

Friction with French Catholics in the tangled web of the Holy
Land was almost inevitable. In 1893, a struggle between Russian
Orthodox pilgrims and French Franciscans on the stairway of the
Grotto of the Nativity caused a scandal and, according to the French,
the death of a Franciscan. In fact, the Russian effort could only remind the French of the history of conflict there, and lead them to
cooperate with the Greeks and the Turks in preserving the status
quo.[29]

The various forms of opposition or resistance which the Society
excited naturally reduced its capabilities to achieve its goals. Scholarly publications continued to appear, the schools remained active,
and the flow of pilgrims persisted, but the Society gradually de-

clined after the turn of the century, particularly after the Russo-Japanese war. Membership gradually declined, from 5,000 in 1900 to 3,266 in 1911, while income declined more precipitately. The principal reason was probably that the philanthropic and religious goals of the Society did not attract the interest of Russians after 1900 as they had in the 1880's and 1890's. In addition, the death of principal officers, Khitrovo in 1903, Grand Duke Sergei Alexandrovich in 1905, Beliaev in 1906, and Pobedonostsev in 1907, symbolized the aging of the organization and its vitality. In short, the organization seemed to reflect the decline of the pietistic patriotism of the generation of Pobedonostsev, which died out in the early years of the twentieth century.[30]

The other area of the world which attracted a flare of missionary zeal from Pobedonostsev was Abyssinia, and the consequences of the foolish venture he helped inspire there persuaded him to turn his back upon the world again and to concentrate upon tightening domestic controls instead. The fiasco in Abyssinia also clearly weakened Pobedonostsev's position with Alexander III and in the court in general and contributed to the deeper strain of pessimism which marks his thought and activity after 1890.

The interest of Russians in Abyssinia was several hundred years old, with its origins in the late medieval legend concerning Prester John, the mythical powerful king of the unknown, wealthy empire. In the seventeenth century, Russian monarchs, especially Peter the Great, were impressed by the advantages offered by cooperation with Christian Abyssinia against the Moslem Turks, and there was even talk of alliance with Abyssinia in the 1670's and 1680's. Porfirii Uspenskii, the dynamic cleric who headed the first Ecclesiastical Mission to Palestine after 1847, sought then to attract Russian attention to Abyssinia, pointing out that the Abyssinian Church was closer to Orthodoxy than to any other church. He urged that scientific and educational groups be sent to Abyssinia, that the Russian Church provide fraternal support of various kinds to the Abyssinian Church, and that political advice and assistance also be extended to the only Christian and still independent country in Africa. In 1848, he proposed that the Abyssinian monks living in Palestine be placed under Russian protection. His mission and later Russian missions in Palestine were especially friendly to the Abyssinians, whom they saw as natural allies against the Moslem Turks, the Orthodox Greeks, and the Catholic French. His efforts may have led King John IV of Abyssinia in 1876 to send Alexander II a gold cross as a token of friendship and hope that relations between Abyssinia and Russia would become closer.

However, Russian preoccupation with other matters and the Crimean and Balkan wars undermined Uspenskii's ambitions. In fact, the tsar did not reply to John IV's message and gift for more than a decade, when a Cossack adventurer, Nicholas I. Ashinov, reawakened some interest in Abyssinia. However, by the time Ashinov made his first visit to the African Christian kingdom in 1885 and 1886, the "congeries of feudal principalities" had attracted the attention of three other great powers, England, France, and Italy, all drawn or propelled into that part of Africa in the wave of imperialism which swept over Europe at that time. The French had occupied Obock in Somaliland in 1862 and in 1883 began to develop it as a base for operations inland. About the time that Ashinov returned to St. Petersburg, they occupied Jibuti on the Gulf of Aden, the port for a caravan route leading into the Harrar province of Abyssinia. In 1888, the British and French reached an agreement delimiting their spheres in that region. In the next year, however, Italy signed an agreement with Menelik, who had succeeded John IV earlier that year, which Italy claimed gave it a protectorate over all of Abyssinia. This definition was denounced by Menelik four years later, and in 1895 the Italians went to war with Abyssinia. French and Italian actions in this part of Africa and the great British concern with the upper Nile waters no doubt helped attract the attention of Ashinov and other Russians.[31]

Ashinov, a self-styled Cossack ataman, was typical of many of the adventurers who appear in Russian and European history in times of movement and expansion. When he met and bewitched the sober and studious Pobedonostsev, he was a handsome six-foot giant, twenty-nine years old, full of vitality and confidence. Uneducated, perhaps even illiterate, originally an Old Believer, Ashinov by 1885 had already seen a great deal of the Middle East and had picked up ideas current in that restless area. Born on the Terek in 1856, he visited Iran in 1870, was a caravan leader in Turkey in 1874, served with Russian forces in Bulgaria in 1883, and had acquired fluent Arabic and some Turkic by the time he first appeared in Moscow and St. Petersburg in 1883. His original mission was to obtain land for a Cossack group with which he proposed to guard the frontier against Turkey in the Caucasus. A man of incredible self-assurance, he took advantage of the easy ways of Petersburg officialdom to talk with Witte, Generals Otto B. Richter and Nicolas N. Obruchev, the

Minister of State Property, Prince Dondukov-Korsakov, who had been the head of Russian forces in Bulgaria, and a number of courtiers concerning his petition. In May, 1884, he was in fact given a large tract of land near Sukhumi. That fall, he was again in St. Petersburg seeking permission to name the new Cossack village Nikolaevsk. Before the summer of the next year, he had won the confidence of Ivan Aksakov and of Michael Katkov, the most vigorous panslavs in Moscow, and through them and others met Pobedonostsev, Metropolitan Isidore, and Grand Duke Sergei Alexandrovich. By 1885, he was complaining about the quality of the land he had been given and was seeking instead other territory along the Black Sea coast. He also let it be known that the English were trying to recruit him and his Cossacks for work in the Caucasus or in Afghanistan.

Ashinov may have visited Cairo and the Red Sea shore in 1884–85. In any case, he travelled through the Middle East again in the summer and fall of 1885, financed probably by the old panslav warhorse, Ignatiev. Perhaps invited by several Abyssinian priests he met in Palestine, he went to the Italian port, Massawa, on the Red Sea late in the fall of 1885 and then went inland to Abyssinia. No doubt presenting himself as an official representative of Russia, Ashinov was royally welcomed by the various local chieftains, particularly Menelik of Shoa in the south and Ras Alula in the north, and was passed on to John IV himself. The king bestowed honors upon him, promised land for him and his Cossacks, gave him icons and manuscripts for Alexander III, and asked him to convey to the tsar greetings like those sent a decade earlier.[32]

On his next visit to St. Petersburg, Ashinov created quite a stir in court circles, where Abyssinia represented something new and different. Alexander III received him, and Ashinov's suggestion that a Russian colony be established in Abyssinia was discussed in an informal way in church and court circles. In the summer of 1887, Ashinov visited Paris, where he represented John IV in an effort to obtain arms for Abyssinia. Some French nationalists were just as intrigued as the Russians had been, but Ashinov suddenly departed for Constantinople and Cairo. He later appeared at the Italian port of Tadjoura, where he met two Abyssinian priests whom he escorted to Kiev to attend the celebrations of the nine-hundredth anniversary of the introduction of Christianity into Russia, and to Moscow and St. Petersburg, where they met the tsar, the metropolitans, Pobedonostsev, other high officials of Church and state, and high members of society. This service gave Ashinov contacts and a respectability even greater than before and provided him the opportunity to win support for an expedition to Abyssinia.[33]

The ideas of Ashinov and of those who supported and financed him were not very clear. Basically, he exploited the religiosity and curiosity of pious Russian bureaucrats and merchants with eloquent descriptions of opportunities to assist a people whose religious beliefs and rituals were close to Orthodoxy, to expand the Russian Orthodox world, and to advance Russian state interests in an exciting, unknown area which might become of enormous significance. He argued that Russia needed a base and a colony in Africa "as from there she could always duly impress the English and other enemies. . . . Not without reason all the European countries are ready even to risk war in trying to secure important points on this world route. Why should not Russia seize one? We need it even more, if we wish to develop our trade with the East, as well as with Vladivostok. And Abyssinia is the key to the whole of Egypt and Africa, and those who will rule Abyssinia will also hold this main route . . . And the chief political interest can always, of course, without informing our diplomacy, be shifted from the Balkans to Africa. . . ."[34]

Pobedonostsev met Ashinov in May, 1885, through Ivan Aksakov, who asked Pobedonostsev to support his Black Sea project, as Katkov was already doing, even though he is "a swindler, but a clever one." Professor Subbotin warned that Ashinov had been a violent Old Believer and that churchmen should beware of such men, but Ashinov impressed Pobedonostsev, who noted that "as a cutthroat, he can be useful in a war." In the summer of 1888, he urged Alexander III to talk with Ashinov; Pobedonostsev compared Ashinov to Yermak and Christopher Columbus and remarked that history was made by "ruffians" like them. He corresponded about Ashinov with his old collaborator of the Volunteer Fleet and of the 1881 crisis, Captain Nicholas Baranov, who was then governor of Nizhni Novgorod. Apparently Pobedonostsev persuaded Grand Duke Sergei Alexandrovich that the Orthodox Palestine Society should launch a fund drive for Ashinov's project. Indeed, he also identified men and women in Kharkov, Kiev, Moscow, Nizhni Novgorod, and other centers who might support this effort to establish an Orthodox Russian colony in Africa.

Finally, at Ashinov's request, he located a monk who had the necessary languages, knowledge of the Middle East, and health and character to serve as prior or chaplain for the group. Paisii, a Cossack who had been born in the Urals or in Orenburg in 1822, who had fought in Central Asia in the 1840's and 1850's, who had then left the Old Believers and become a monk, and who had served Russian interests in the monastery of St. Pantheleimon on Mount Athos, was summoned to St. Petersburg by Pobedonostsev, ordained a priest and made an archimandrite within a week, and named spiritual advisor to Ashinov and his group. The appointment of Paisii and the campaign waged by the Palestine Society led many Russian and foreign observers to conclude that the Ashinov expedition had the official support of the Church, if not of the state as well.[35]

Both the French and the Italian governments had been disturbed by Ashinov's first visit to Abyssinia and by the rumors which naturally attended such a brash and hardy adventurer. The French Foreign Minister, Goblet, asked his ambassador in St. Petersburg to determine whether or not Ashinov had any official support and what his activities meant. The Italians were even more concerned, because John IV had asked Ashinov to help the Abyssinians procure arms, and there were well-substantiated rumors that Ashinov was active in Paris in gun-running activities. The Russian Ministry of Foreign Affairs, pressed by states whose friendship Russia wanted and naturally eager to assert control over activities such as these, sought to discredit Ashinov and to prevent his departure. However, his protectors were so powerful, their motives were so vague and confused, and the entire enterprise was so surrounded by an aura of unreality that Giers and Lamzdorf were unsuccessful.[36]

Financed by 40,000 rubles (approximately $20,000) obtained through the Palestine Society, given the moral support and the blessing of the Synod, and assisted also by the Ministry of the Navy, which discreetly provided equipment through its Odessa headquarters and at one time was planning to loan a ship as well, Ashinov and about one hundred and fifty men, women, and children left Odessa in December, 1888. After transferring to a Lloyd Trieste ship in Port Said, the expedition sailed through the Suez Canal and the Red Sea, followed by an Italian gunboat and observed by the British as well. After two or three brief stops, the group disembarked late in January, 1889, at Obock, on the Gulf of Aden, occupied an old Egyptian fort at Sagallo, which they named New Moscow, and settled down. The events of the next three weeks are unclear in detail. Ashinov was asked by the local French official to leave, but refused. Apparently, discipline among the Russians was not effective, and difficulties arose within the group and between it and the French. In any case, after again refusing to leave, Ashinov and his followers were bombarded on February 5, 1889, by three French gunboats. Several of his followers were killed.

Even while Ashinov and his group were en route, Giers was busy denying to the Italian, English, and French governments that Ashinov was acting for the Russian government and trying at the same time to reach him and to order him back. After the tragic incident, when telegrams began to fly between Paris and St. Petersburg, the Russian government formally disclaimed all responsibility for Ashinov and Paisii. Both Alexander III and Giers publicly announced that the French had acted correctly, and the tsar ordered Ashinov to submit to French orders. Two months later, in an effort to make certain that the French government and the informed Russian public should understand clearly the history of the incident and the Russian government's position, a full report, including Ashinov's interpretation, was published. Each member of his group was given the opportunity to proceed to Abyssinia; all were then returned to Odessa. Giers recommended that Ashinov be sent to Siberia for five years and his companions for three, but Alexander III reduced his sentence to three years in Saratov. However, in the fall of 1889, he was allowed to move to Chernigov, and all restrictions on his movements were removed in April, 1890. Father Paisii was stationed in Alexander Nevsky monastery in St. Petersburg for a year and then rewarded by being named head of a wealthy monastery in Nizhni Novgorod.[37]

In the unfolding of European diplomatic history, the Ashinov expedition does not occupy an important place. The flurry of concern in the various foreign offices was followed by muted expressions of dissatisfaction in Moscow and St. Petersburg about the government's yielding to the French, but many Russian nationalist leaders had been involved in the idiotic incident and were therefore delighted to have it forgotten. Some extreme French nationalists criticized the French administration, particularly after Ashinov escaped to France in 1891 and was petted by Madame Juliette Adam and other critics of the Third Republic. However, the shelling of New Moscow was followed so quickly by the collapse of Boulangism in the spring of 1889 that French criticism quickly became silent. In fact, the efficiency with which the French had acted and the candor and good will displayed on both sides during the tension may have contributed to Franco-Russian rapprochment and to the Franco-Russian alliance.[38]

However, this incident did increase Russian interest in Abyssinia and in Africa. Less than a year later, Metropolitan Platon of Kiev sent an emissary to King Menelik, probably to thank the ruler for the representatives sent to the Kievan celebration in 1888, and a geographical expedition was sent in 1891. The Ethiopians then sent an ecclesiastical mission in 1895 which was received with full honors and remained in Russia six weeks. Diplomatic recognition was extended in 1896, and Russia established a medical mission the following year which soon became a permanent fixture in Addis Ababa.[39]

Ashinov threw a quick light upon the chaotic and ineffective way in which Russia's international relations were managed, as did the coming of the war with Japan in 1904. Alexander III was so distressed by this ridiculous incident that he ordered a review made. The analysis within the government was not searching and press comment also was shallow, but Alexander III did remember that Pobedonostsev had described Ashinov as another Yermak or Christopher Columbus and did learn that he had introduced him to high clergy and wealthy merchants. Moreover, the Foreign Minister described the use Pobedonostsev and Grand Duke Sergei Alexandrovich had made of the Palestine Society to collect funds for Ashinov. Documents from the expedition itself and from the Ministry of the Navy revealed that Pobedonostsev had been an eager supporter of the expedition. When Prince Vladimir P. Meshcherskii published much of this information in *Grazhdanin* (The Citizen), to which Pobedonostsev had been a contributor fifteen years earlier, he blackened Pobedonostsev's reputation for careful judgment in the court. Pobedonostsev's efforts to deny his responsibility only increased the zeal of Giers and his deputy, Lamzdorf, to fasten responsibility on him. Coming as it did at the same time that Pobedonostsev was so rudely shaken by the criticism presented by the Evangelical Alliance and Pastor Dalton on Church policy in the Baltic area, this incident undermined his position with the tsar and at the same time increased his bitterness and pessimism.[40]

X

Russian Political
and Intellectual Life

POBEDONOSTSEV's relationship with Alexander III, his role in the
Church in a society where the Church was deeply involved in all
political and intellectual questions, and his membership in the central organizations of the state in a loosely organized autocratic system provided him splendid opportunities for influencing state policies. As this study indicates, his authority over Russian life during
the 1880's was considerable. In particular, the decisive role he played
in the spring of 1881 in destroying the possibility for creating a base
for greater participation in state affairs by at least the educated elite
proved a decisive point in Russian history. His actions throughout
the next quarter-century, particularly the next decade, reinforced
the 1881 decision. Moreover, he set the tone or controlled the climate of Russian state policy throughout the 1880's in particular
and helped create the invisible web which made change or reform
in St. Petersburg almost impossible.

Pobedonostsev's influence has been considerably exaggerated,
both by his contemporaries and by later observers, especially those
critical of or hostile to him. This inaccuracy is due to a number of
factors: the crucial role he did play at the very outset of the reign
of Alexander III; the nature of the tsarist government, whose methods of operations were often so inscrutable as to encourage devilish
theories concerning its workings; Pobedonostsev's forbidding character and personality and his lack of concern about public opinion;
and the powerful discontents and dissatisfactions which wracked
Russian society throughout these years.

238

Pobedonostsev's influence could have been considerably greater than it was and could easily have become as substantial as most observers considered it. However, while he possessed remarkable capabilities as a politician, he lacked the open zest for power and the ambition to use the authority he had acquired. He was so much a man of the study, a man who preferred to read books than to deal with men, and a man of the past rather than of the present or future, that he failed to seize and exercise the authority within his reach. He believed in government by men, not by laws or institutions, and he was much more interested in affecting appointments than in molding or revising important institutions. His mind was much more clear on policies he opposed than on those he favored. He did exercise considerable influence in Russian political and intellectual life, especially in the 1880's, but this was achieved in a fitful and unsystematic way, reflecting the kind of man he was and his approach to government. More and more after 1880, he devoted his energy simply to maintaining the status quo, from the system of government to internal passports, from religious marriage to the old system of property rights. In addition, he became increasingly pessimistic about what could be done to preserve the Russia he revered. He referred to himself even in the 1870's as "the last of the Mohicans," and his defensive efforts became more feeble as he grew older.[1]

His main responsibility and interest were the Russian Orthodox Church and its effort to restrict the number and power of other religious groups in Russia. The Church's power ramified throughout Russian society because of the nature of the state, so his actions as Director General of the Synod often led him into issues not considered of a religious or moral character in the West. Aside from the Church and its extensive responsibilities, he was especially interested in the appointment of ministers of departments and of governors, because he thought the character and views of those in important positions were decisive. He was also especially attentive to the administration of justice, in part because of his training and his work as a jurist, in part because of the role he had played in preparing the 1864 reform, and in part because he thought the courts could and should play an important part in defending authority and in throttling discontent. Education, particularly at the university level and in primary school, was also a burning concern for him, because he was convinced that training the elite and indoctrinating the peasant masses would help ensure stability for Russia. Finally, because of his concern with ideas and information, he devoted great attention to control of the flow of information, particularly through censorship, and to spreading abroad or publicizing what he considered the proper point of view.

Pobedonostsev's triumph in the spring of 1881 over the Loris-Melikov plan for bridging the gap between the government and society were followed quickly by the resignation of Loris-Melikov and those who supported him. Pobedonostsev was then able to advise Alexander III concerning the new ministers, most of whom were appointed at his suggestion. A year later Count Ignatiev was replaced by Count Dmitrii Tolstoy as Minister of Interior, when Ignatiev made the mistake of advocating that a *zemskii sobor,* or territorial assembly, meet on the occasion of Alexander III's coronation. Moreover, Baron Alexander P. Nikolai proved unsatisfactory as Minister of Education and had to be replaced by Ivan D. Delianov. Early in the reign of Nicholas II, Pobedonostsev set the tone for the new administration by drafting the famous speech for the tsar which referred to hopes "about the participation of representatives of the zemstvos in matters of internal administration" as "senseless dreams." While he showed no interest in the appointment of the Minister of Foreign Affairs at any time, even late in life he played a decisive role in selecting other ministers he thought central. Thus, in 1895, when Nicholas II asked him to choose between Viacheslav K. von Plehve and Dmitrii S. Sipiagin as Minister of Interior, he said that one was a scoundrel and the other a fool and recommended instead Ivan L. Goremykin, who was at least a lawyer. When Goremykin resigned in 1899, Pobedonostsev recommended Sipiagin, who was assassinated in 1902. Von Plehve, who then succeeded him, was assassinated in 1904.[2]

Pobedonostsev's preoccupation with the western border areas, inhabited largely by non-Russians who were usually not members of the Orthodox faith and who were becoming increasingly nationalistic and restive under Russian and Orthodox rule, led him to emphasize to the tsar the need to appoint strong and firm men who were both Russian and Orthodox as governors general in these territories. His influence on the selection of the governors for the borderlands in particular was therefore considerable. He probably had more authority in these important appointments, especially during the reign of Alexander III, than any other member of the government, even the Minister of the Interior, to whom these administrators were responsible. In fact, it is evident that most governors were recommended by him and that none was named without his approval. In 1887, and again in 1888, he reviewed the administration of the Baltic and western provinces for the tsar. His detailed comments then on problems, policies, and individual administrators no doubt were the primary influences upon the tsar so far as these territories were concerned.[3]

The principal new institution introduced into the Russian administration during the reign of Alexander III was the *zemskii nachalnik*, or land captain or rural leader, a salaried central government agent who was made virtual ruler over the peasants in his district. This office was established in 1889, largely to undermine or destroy the authority among the peasants of the justice of the peace and to reduce the significance of the zemstvo, the representative institution of local self-government allowed in 1864 and granted limited financial authority to build roads, schools, bridges, and hospitals. It was also a belated effort on the part of the autocracy to rebuild the position and authority of the landowning nobility, which had been weakened by the emancipation of the serfs in 1861 and which had gradually deteriorated since.

The effort to establish the rural leaders took more than three years to achieve, even though the principal government leaders all sought such an institution. Alexander D. Pazukhin in the Ministry of Justice made the original proposal late in the winter of 1885–86, and Pobedonostsev was a member of a committee established in April, 1886, to review the proposal and to recommend the reorganization of local government and of the administration of justice at the local level. Apparently the only disagreements were over whether the rural leader should have judicial as well as administrative authority and whether he should be elected by the landowners of the area or named by the tsar through the Minister of the Interior. Pobedonostsev's letters, the published accounts of the discussions within the Ministries of Justice and of the Interior, and a Soviet study based on the archives of the Council of State all agree that Pobedonostsev triumphed in having the rural leader named by the tsar and in giving him both administrative and judicial powers. Pobedonostsev drew up the decree of July 12, 1889, for the tsar, and the final document reflects closely the draft which he prepared for discussion by the Council of State. A decade later he was dissatisfied with the way the new institution operated and with the failure of the landed nobility to recover its strength. Moreover, at that time he was convinced that the very principles on which the

zemstvo was based were immoral and that the zemstvo institution
and the city duma or legislature should be eliminated if Russia
were to survive. However, by that time he was unwilling to attack
that problem and left it to Count Witte and others more energetic
than he.[4]

Pobedonostsev's most impressive achievements as a young liberal
were his numerous studies critical of the administration of justice
and his work in helping to draft the judicial reform legislation of
1864. A decade later, he was a vociferous critic of the jury trial in
particular. His venom against this "Western institution" continued
to increase after 1875. However, preoccupied by other matters he
considered even more important, he began to consider revision of
the 1864 law only in 1882 or 1883. At that time, he urged the Minister of Justice, Vladimir A. Nabokov, one of the few ministers who
had survived the overturn of 1881, to draft changes, particularly to
abolish the irremovability of judges and the right to jury trial. Nabokov, while agreeable to this, was reluctant to accept several other
Pobedonostsev proposals and seemed slow, so Pobedonostsev in
November, 1885, persuaded Alexander III to replace him with Senator Nicholas A. Manasein, who had just drawn Pobedonostsev's
attention by his rigorous review of policy in the Baltic provinces.[5]

At the same time that Pobedonostsev succeeded in putting Manasein into Nabokov's position as Minister of Justice, he forwarded
the tsar a memorandum suggesting a comprehensive revision of
Russia's judicial procedures. This was probably his own work, because it reflects his views accurately and is written in his style, and
there is no indication that others worked with him. In any case, it
established government policy for the next few years, because it
proposed the ending of permanent tenure for judges, which was
achieved in 1889, the denial of public trials in cases which the state
considered harmful to public morals, reduction of the role and influence of the lawyer, the withdrawal of cases from the regular courts
which the state considered sensitive, restrictions on the kinds of
case which should go before juries, and the increased use of written
evidence in trials. The 1864 reform was so appreciated even within
the administration itself, the lawyers were so skillful and well organized in their defense of the earlier law, and the Ministry of
Foreign Affairs was so opposed to some of Pobedonostsev's proposals
because of the damage they did to Russia's rights and reputation in
other countries, that he was not able to achieve all the goals outlined
in the 1885 memorandum. Indeed, in 1894, after Pobedonostsev

and his friends had assailed the jury trial in Russia for two decades, a committee of judges and prosecutors named by the Minister of Justice disagreed with his view that the jury handed down an exaggerated number of acquittals. The committee in fact reported that courts with a jury were even more repressive than those without and that "the activities of the jury correspond perfectly to its aims and that it has an ennobling influence on the people's sense of equity."[6]

Pobedonostsev fought strenuously to withdraw cases involving crimes against the state from jury trial and to have cases such as those involving marital problems and charges of religious proselytizing kept from public view. He campaigned rigorously within the Council of State. He made use of newspapers, including Katkov's *Moskovskiia Vedomosti* (Moscow News), to win support for his position. He insisted that the new *zemskii nachalnik* have both administrative and judicial powers, thus violating one of the cardinal principles of the 1864 reform. He also urged the tsar simply to transfer some cases from public trial to military courts. While he was not completely successful, he did reduce the effectiveness of the reform legislation and strengthen the hand of the autocracy.[7]

There had been rumors in the late 1870's that Pobedonostsev was to be named either Director General of the Synod or Minister of Education, positions which Count Dmitrii Tolstoy held at that time. When Tolstoy was removed in April, 1880, Pobedonostsev replaced him at the Synod and Alexander A. Saburov at the Ministry of Education. Saburov, who had recently been Russian ambassador in Berlin and who was known to be an honorable man of moderately liberal views, soon alarmed Pobedonostsev and other conservatives by associating zemstvo and city duma leaders with discussions in the Ministry and, above all, by proposing that disorders in the universities could best be handled by allowing student organizations more freedom and by increasing the authority of the administration of the university, rather than that of the Ministry or of the police. Pobedonostsev, who then considered students "crowds of monsters and scoundrels with whom nothing could be done, no matter how university life was administered," opposed Saburov in Council of Ministers' meetings and privately urged the heir and later the tsar to remove Saburov, who was replaced by Baron Nikolai only three weeks after Alexander III became tsar.

The new minister was recommended to the tsar by Pobedonostsev, who then had to overcome Nikolai's heavy reluctance to accept the position and who soon discovered he had erred. Nikolai in January, 1882, planned a meeting of representatives of the zemstvo and city schools to discuss reorganization of the system of education, a proposal Pobedonostsev considered so close to the *zemskii sobor* and other ideas concerning representative institutions that he persuaded the tsar to order that the meeting not be held. A few days later, he had to intervene to prevent a meeting of teachers in Pskov *guberniia* because of the precedent that might establish. The final straw came in March, when Nikolai proposed that Professor Nicholas A. Liubimov be retired from the Department of Physics at Moscow University. According to the regulations of the Ministry and of the University, Liubimov should have been retired in 1877. However, his close friend, Michael Katkov, had persuaded the heir to the throne to intervene, set aside University rules, and allow Liubimov to remain on the faculty another five years. When Nikolai chose to end Liubimov's career, both Katkov and the professor vehemently denounced Nikolai and his "reform programs" in Katkov's powerful newspaper, and Katkov, who had opposed Nikolai's appointment before it was made, asked the tsar to renew Liubimov's appointment. In this instance, Pobedonostsev sought to persuade the Minister of Education to accept another violation of the regulations and, failing that, had to ask him to resign after less than a year of service.

The new minister, Delianov, who had been Pobedonostsev's first recommendation in 1881 but whom Loris-Melikov had rejected as "a man of limited intelligence and an extreme reactionary," had been an associate of Pobedonostsev for about ten years. They had worked together in the Senate and on a special committee established in 1875 to review Russian education. An extreme conservative who was in full agreement with Pobedonostsev concerning university education, Delianov sought and accepted his advice often, survived as Minister of Education for fifteen years, and was made Count Delianov as a reward.[8]

Student disorders in the late 1870's and early 1880's, the sympathy demonstrated by many university professors and teachers for radicals and revolutionaries and their ideas, the constant suspicion of educators as soft and dangerous liberals, and the atmosphere of fear and tension, especially after the assassination of Alexander II, led to another intensive reorganization of university regulations. The decree issued by the tsar on August 25, 1884, was a day of triumph for those like Pobedonostsev and Delianov who believed that the state had to exert firm and exacting control over the universities. However, it was a part of the zig-zag pattern of the position of higher education in Russia in the nineteenth century. Thus, the relatively relaxed and open system established by Alexander I in 1804 was replaced early in the reign of Nicholas I by a statute which restricted access to the *gimnazii* or high schools and the universities to the "free orders of society," with those few local and parish schools "to afford the children of tradesmen, artisans, and other town dwellers such instruction as would be most useful to them, having regard to their manner of life and their special needs and customs." Under this ruling, the universities lost their autonomy and were put under the direct rule of the Ministry of Education. After the revolutions of 1848 racked western and central Europe, regulation of university life was made even more strict: courses in constitutional and state law were prohibited, and only priests were allowed to teach philosophy and psychology. By the time of the outbreak of the Crimean War, travel abroad for scholars was prohibited, and foreign scholars were not allowed to teach in Russian universities, which in 1855 had only 3,659 students. No student organizations were allowed, meetings of students could be held only with special permission, and students from poor families were no longer exempted from tuition. Russian university life was thus very tightly controlled by a fearful state.[9]

In 1863, both the Ministry of Education itself and the university statutes were revised. Each of the six universities was given autonomy, and the rector, deans, inspectors, and professors were elected by the faculty, which also governed itself through an elected university council. The chairs abolished after 1848 were restored, tuition was lowered, and poor students were given tuition exemptions. Tolstoy, who was Minister of Education from 1866 until 1881, tried to whittle down these rights and succeeded on occasion in violating them with irregular appointments and dismissals. However, until the great fear of 1881 and the decree of 1884, the universities retained a considerable amount of independence and freedom.

Pobedonostsev thought that most Russian professors were a menace to society because of their irreligiousness and their political liberalism. To him, the student demonstrations reflected a chronic weakness in the state. He used his authority in the Synod to send unruly seminarians into the army, and he urged the Council of State to adopt such a policy for all troublesome students. He and Delianov were in complete agreement on state policy toward the universities. He apparently helped to draft the original proposal for the 1884 decree, he recommended it to the tsar, he defended its most repres-

Portrait of Pobedonostsev painted by Repin in 1903 for canvas, "Meeting of the Council of State." Now in Russian Museum, Leningrad. (From Igor E. Grabor, *Repin* [Moscow, 1964], II, 132.)

sive measures in the Council of State, against even Katkov, who thought it too extreme, and he persuaded the tsar to issue the decree although the majority of the Council of State did not support it. Consequently, he bears a considerable amount of responsibility for the ruling which kept Russian higher education in shackles until another decree in September, 1905, restored autonomy to the universities and allowed students to hold meetings.

Briefly, in 1884, the Russian universities lost the independence and freedom they had acquired only two decades earlier. The Ministry of Education received authority to name all rectors, deans, and inspectors and to approve all appointments and promotions. Student organizations were forbidden again, membership in a student organization was declared a crime, and special uniforms were required. Tuition rates were raised, the curriculum was revised in order to reduce the number of students from classes below the gentry and bureaucracy, and control of examinations was given to committees named by the Ministry of Education. New efforts were made to expand vocational education for those who might otherwise have entered a university.[10]

The 1884 decree did not eliminate the tension and disorder nor give the universities the class character Delianov and Pobedonostsev thought they ought to have, so they continued their activities. Thus, they delayed establishment of a new university in Tomsk. Convinced that allowing high school education "for the lower classes" was harmful to them and to Russia, they asked the tsar in 1887 for permission to allow into high schools only children of those estates not lower than second guild merchants. When Alexander III refused because he feared foreign reaction would weaken Russia's unstable credit, Delianov then issued the famous "cooks' children decree" in June, 1887, the language of which is like that of many of Pobedonostsev's statements on this subject.

> Gymnasiums and progymnasiums are freed from receiving the children of coachmen, servants, cooks, launderers, small tradesmen, and the like, whose children, with the exception, perhaps, of those who are gifted with extraordinary capacities, ought by no means to be transferred from the sphere to which they belong, and thus be brought, as many years' experience has shown, to slight their parents, to feel dissatisfied with their lot, and to conceive an aversion to the existing inequality of fortune, which is in the nature of things unavoidable.[11]

Pobedonostsev believed firmly that woman's place was in the home. He was a warm supporter of his wife's effort to provide elementary education and home economics training for the daughters of priests who would then marry priests and work with them in the countryside, and he lavished praise on other women who founded and directed schools of that kind. He was willing to admit that some particularly talented young ladies of high birth should receive the equivalent of a high school education. However, even though Dostoevsky and his good friend, Baroness Edith Raden, advocated higher education for women, and even though the baroness wrote several memoranda for the tsar advocating it, Pobedonostsev remained adamant. As a member of a committee named by Alexander in 1882 to review proposals for establishing a medical school for women, he not only wrote a stiff negative report, but persuaded the tsar to close the courses established for midwives by military hospitals. These were reopened when some St. Petersburg social leaders and several zemstvo units collected the necessary funds and petitioned the tsar for permission. In 1891, when the supporters of these schools sought permission to establish a medical school for women, Pobedonostsev succeeded in persuading Alexander III to deny their request. He had to fight the same struggle again in 1895.[12]

The policies and administrative appointments which he recommended for higher education were an accurate reflection of his policy toward Russian cultural development and toward access to information. Even though at one point in his career at least he considered opening mail and denying educated Russians the opportunity to read Western books childish and ridiculous, his positions with regard to freedom were almost instinctively restrictive. In the third volume of his *Kurs grazhdanskago prava* (Course on Civil Law), which was published in 1880 but which he had written and corrected during the previous five years, he made an elaborate defense of the system of internal passports. He admitted that "the fact that no one among us can absent himself from his regular residence without his passport" is restrictive, "but on the other hand, the conditions of our life make this a comparative convenience." The passport serves "as a graphic and visible certificate of personality," of enormous importance in a vast and disorganized land. It reduced the likelihood that some local government would arrest and hold an unwary traveller unable to identify himself or to prove his good intentions. It ensured both the worker and the employer that the worker complete his task before becoming free to move on.

In other words, the restrictions inherent in the internal passport system were a blessing for which all Russians should be grateful, just as they should appreciate the other benefits of autocratic government.[13]

While he was writing and correcting this volume and reading proof on it, Pobedonostsev and Catherine Tiutchev complained bitterly in private to each other about the restrictions which invaded their own reading and correspondence. Both of them, especially Pobedonostsev, had come to know well Sir Donald MacKenzie Wallace, the most competent and celebrated correspondent of the *London Times*, and author of a remarkably perceptive book on Russia, the first edition of which Pobedonostsev himself called a classic and which he recommended to the tsar. In fact, both of them had spent long evenings with Wallace between 1875 and 1877, correcting what they considered his errors in understanding Russia, especially the character and role of the Church. Wallace sent Miss Tiutchev a copy of the first edition of his volume early in 1877, but the censor seized it. She then appealed to Pobedonostsev and other friends at court in order to obtain the book, which even in that troubled year in Anglo-Russian relations she found of "remarkable fidelity, precision, and accuracy." However, before she was allowed to obtain it, she had to submit to the ultimate indignity of signing an agreement that she would not give or lend the book to anyone else.

Pobedonostsev had even more difficulty, because he had to spend more than two months prying his copy from the Main Administration of the Press in St. Petersburg. He noted that "something needs to be done about the insanity of our censorship," the main characteristics of which are "ignorance and bureaucratic cowardice." He wrote two letters, one of which he called an ultimatum, to censorship officials and made at least two visits to the main office, "a scandal through all of Europe," before he could get his copy.

He was dismayed that the government should have at least three men read a book written in English and prohibitively expensive (twelve rubles, or six 1877 dollars) before releasing it, with some pages removed, to a Senator and a member of the Council of State. At the same time, he accepted the system of censorship, simply resenting the stupid and capricious decisions made concerning books in which he himself was especially interested.[14]

However, even more annoying and humiliating than these incidents involving the Wallace book, or than the troubles he often had in obtaining copies of Carlyle and other favorite Western authors, was their suspicion that their private correspondence was opened and read by state officials and the need therefore to have friends carry their letters by hand between St. Petersburg and Moscow.[15]

In short, Pobedonostsev resented the ignorance, stupidity, and inefficiency of the censorship when it affected his own affairs, yet he accepted without question the authority of the state over all information. After he had achieved a position of influence, he used his authority to strengthen the state's control over access to information. The archives of the Synod in Leningrad reveal that he worked closely with Count Ignatiev, Minister of the Interior, in drafting the rules of August, 1882, which tightened severely the state's control over the press and other media of information and which gave the government the right to prevent publication of a newspaper or journal, without redress.[16]

The first instrument which he used in his campaign as guardian of political loyalty, public morality, and good taste was the Office for Ecclesiastical Censorship in the Synod, which he reorganized and expanded and the powers of which he sought to extend beyond what had been considered issues affecting the Church and religion. This office kept all publications dealing with religious affairs under close review, closing down those which ignored admonitions and often denying the right to publish to groups not associated with the Russian Orthodox Church. Lutherans in the Baltic area, for example, were often prevented from publishing hymnals. Journalists and dramatists beyond the authority of the Synod were often warned; if the warnings proved ineffective, Pobedonostsev then turned to the Main Administration of the Press, the Minister of the Interior, or the tsar himself.[17]

Generally, however, he relied on the Main Administration of the Press, a part of the Ministry of the Interior, which had the principal responsibility then for most forms of censorship or control of information. The Director of this branch of the Ministry from January 1, 1883, until May, 1896, was a contemporary and a close associate of Pobedonostsev, Evgenii M. Feoktistov, who served his official and private interests during his years in office. A graduate of the law faculty of Moscow University in 1851, and a special admirer there of the celebrated Granovskii, Feoktistov worked as a chancery clerk for three years in the provinces and then joined the office of the Governor General of Moscow in 1854. After the Crimean War, he travelled in western Europe, returning to Russia during the exciting days of "the thaw" of Alexander II. At that time, he was an advocate of the various reforms and wrote essays in the liberal press advocating that Russia should become more Western. In fact, his principal associate at that time was apparently Katkov, who was also then in his liberal phase. Late in 1862, Feoktistov joined the Ministry of Education, where he worked for twenty years, serving from 1871 to January, 1883, as the editor of the Ministry's important journal, *Zhurnal Ministerstva narodnago prosveshcheniia* (The Journal of the Ministry of National Education).

Count Dmitrii Tolstoy, as Minister of Education, gave Feoktistov his important position in 1871. Feoktistov's views changed during the middle of the 1860's, apparently along the same lines and at about the same time as those of Katkov, Pobedonostsev, and others of that generation. In any case, he abandoned his 1861 dream of a free press in Russia and of a Russian Tory party, joined Tolstoy, and became known as a staunch conservative. In 1882, he worked with Pobedonostsev to increase the role of the Church in the zemstvo primary schools. After he was put in charge of censorship in 1883, with Pobedonostsev's warm approval, they worked very closely together. In fact, Pobedonostsev wrote him seventy-nine letters between 1883 and 1896, even though their offices were close to each other and they met often at various committee meetings. Feoktistov executed Pobedonostsev's requests concerning censorship, he turned to him often for advice, and he made no major decisions without making certain first of Pobedonostsev's support. Some of his principal assistants were former employees of the Synod whom Pobedonostsev had recommended for positions where he thought their judgment could be trusted. Moreover, his successor, Michael P. Soloviev, was nominated by Pobedonostsev, had been a student of Pobedonostsev at the law faculty of Moscow University, and had later, as a competent painter, prepared illustrations for publications issued by the Press of the Synod. Thus, from 1883 until 1900, the main official responsible for censorship in Russia was a nominee and collaborator of Pobedonostsev.[18]

His service as guardian of the state was by no means restricted to review of the newspapers, and the historical record provides much evidence that no aspect of Russian cultural life was beyond his attention. Thus, in the fall of 1881 he persuaded the Governor General of Moscow to remove photographs of Old Believer priests from shop windows. Four years later, he wrote to Alexander III denouncing the "disgusting, critical, accusatory" painting, "Ivan the Terrible and the Corpse of His Son," one of Elia E. Repin's most famous, and persuaded the tsar not only to order that it be removed from the exhibition but that its owner, Paul M. Tretiakov, not be allowed to show it in public. In 1890, he found Nicholas N. Ge's "What Is the Truth," even more revolting, and asked the tsar to remove it from an exhibition of Russian art which was to tour provincial cities. Two years later, he appealed to the tsar concerning another painting by Ge, but then learned that Grand Duke Vladimir Alexandrovich had already acted.[19]

A great lover of the theater as a young man, Pobedonostsev saw only one play in the last three or four decades of his life. However, he was devout in his attention to the hazards the theater raised. He sometimes appealed directly to the tsar to close a play which affronted his view of Russian history, and he helped prevent tours of plays which escaped the censor's watch in St. Petersburg. Finally, he urged Feoktistov to establish a special division within his office to review and inspect the theater.

Books, journals, libraries, and bookstores were also the subject of careful scrutiny. He had few complaints to make concerning Russian literature, except for Count Leo Tolstoy, apparently because Feoktistov was alert and active in this area of traditional concern. However, he did identify popular novels which insidiously glorified banditry or threatened to undermine public morality. He was particularly alert concerning foreign literature, perhaps because he read so widely and had so low an opinion of the censor's judgment when dealing with unfamiliar issues and scenes. Thus, he cautioned against careless permissions to publish translations of novels printed in the *Revue des Deux Mondes*. He was outraged that bookstores were not allowed to sell the works of Thomas Carlyle, one of his favorite authors, whose works were "thoroughly penetrated by moral principles," at a time when it was possible to buy Russian translations of *Das Kapital*, "one of the most incendiary books," but the second volume of which the censor had passed in 1885 as "serious economic research, available, though only to specialists, because of its contents and its exposition." Pobedonostsev wrote to Delianov in November, 1887, that he knew from several sources that "many" seminarians and students in ecclesiastical academies were reading Marx.

He urged Feoktistov to "take all necessary measures" to prevent the publication of a Russian translation of *Germinal*, even though he considered it Zola's finest novel. When the censor asked his advice, he urged that *In Praise of Folly*, by Erasmus, not be published in translation. Boccaccio's *Decameron* he agreed might be printed in one hundred copies at a price of one hundred rubles ($50), with a larger edition with a number of excisions priced at ten rubles. But he resolutely opposed an inexpensive edition.[20]

He called the attention of the Minister of the Interior to a reading room in Tomsk because harmful Russian and translated foreign books might be placed there. In 1894, when he heard that the director of the principal Synod bookstore in Moscow was planning to establish a reading room for workers, he insisted that a catalogue or full list of the books be sent to him for approval. Even the reading rooms and libraries of seminaries were not exempt. In December, 1883, he asked Nikanor, Bishop of Ufa, to inspect the library of the seminary there because he had heard it contained books by men such as Goncharov, Daudet, and Hugo.[21]

The foreign and dead authors whose works were prohibited or were allowed only in limited or censored editions were, of course, unable to protest against his actions. Moreover, neither Repin, who later painted his portrait, nor the director of the reading room in Tomsk could defend himself with success, although both were able to increase the unpopularity of Pobedonostsev and of the regime by drawing attention to the censorship. However, Pobedonostsev's efforts to control or hamper the circulation of the works and the actions of more distinguished and independent artists and philosophers encountered serious difficulties and, in fact, hampered his program for maintaining full control over the course of Russian culture.

Pobedonostsev was critical of all systematic philosophers, because he was convinced that their thought inevitably became remote from life, abstract, and therefore dangerous. Fortunately for him as guardian of the purity of Russian life, Russian philosophy was not notably distinguished in the last quarter of the nineteenth century. Indeed, the influence which Marxism began to acquire in the last years of the century reflected in part the poverty of Russian philosophical thought. One of the most dramatic and exotic Russian philosophers from the 1870's until his death in 1892 was Constantine Leontiev, who was employed as a censor in Moscow from 1880 until 1887, almost certainly with the knowledge and consent of Pobedonostsev, some of whose views he appreciated. Thus, while Leontiev was critical of Pobedonostsev's lack of imagination and historical perspective, he thought him a competent administrator of the Church and approved his emphasis on discipline and on autocratic rule. However, much of Leontiev's writing, especially his cult of beauty and the panegyrics he devoted to Byzantium, had no appeal for Pobedonostsev, who approved Leontiev in principle but kept him at a distance.[22]

Vladimir Soloviev was more influential in Russia during these years, and was viewed with hostility by Pobedonostsev. Soloviev, who was born in Moscow in 1853, was the son of Sergei M. Soloviev, the eminent historian whom Pobedonostsev admired as one of the few professors at Moscow University in the 1860's and 1870's who was "of Russian soul and mind." He used to obtain archival material in St. Petersburg for the professor, and he visited him in his Moscow home just before he died in 1879. At that time, they almost certainly discussed the brilliant prospects facing Vladimir Soloviev, who in 1874 had published a brilliant thesis at St. Petersburg University attacking positivism. Pobedonostsev, who was bored by most lectures and who attended few in his life, heard each one of a series of twelve which young Soloviev gave in St. Petersburg in 1878, and found his discussion of the philosophy of religion most stimulating. Dostoevsky was at the same time an admirer and friend of the young philosopher, whose future seemed very bright indeed to these conservatives.[23]

However, from the early 1880's until his death in 1900, Soloviev was an accursed problem for Pobedonostsev and the censor. Pobedonostsev was appalled when Soloviev in a public lecture in 1881 urged that the murderers of Alexander II not be executed. He persuaded the Minister of the Interior to prevent a lecture by Soloviev in February, 1883, because he thought he would criticize the government for its policies toward the various religious sects. He had articles published in Katkov's *Moskovskiia Vedomosti* criticizing Soloviev's philosophical views and his proposals for greater freedom in Russia. He had some Soloviev books transferred from the Main Administration of the Press to the censor of the Synod because they were so critical of Orthodox doctrine and of the hierarchy and because they could be more easily quashed there. When Soloviev began to publish abroad, especially in Zagreb, he intervened to make certain that none of these "Papist" publications with their "disgusting verbiage" was admitted into Russia. Soloviev's vigorous defense of his freedom to write, his condemnation of religious persecution and of the use of pressure to convert others to Orthodoxy, and his skillful criticisms of Pobedonostsev in his poetry only made the conflict more bitter. Pobedonostsev was especially irritated because Soloviev defended liberty of expression, while writing as a religious philosopher, and thus to some associated liberty and religion, which Pobedonostsev thought inevitably in conflict.[24]

Some of Russia's great writers created even more serious problems. Dostoevsky, of course, was a friend during the last decade of the author's life, and their views were close. Chekhov, for some reason, never attracted Pobedonostsev's attention or interest. Tolstoy and Turgenev, however, roused his effort to control the directions of Russian cultural life to its peak. Turgenev spent most of his time abroad and died in 1883, but Pobedonostsev despised him, welcomed his long residence abroad, and sought to isolate him while he was in Russia. In 1879, before he had authority to prevent such incidents, he was enraged when "so-called writers," most of them "bribed by Poles," gave a banquet for the popular novelist, a "gray-haired idiot, like a crow flattered by the fox." When Turgenev returned to Russia in 1881, Pobedonostsev asked an old acquaintance, the poet Iakov P. Polonskii, who was on the staff of the censor in St. Petersburg, to persuade him to leave the city for his country estate quickly and quietly. Polonskii refused categorically, just as Metropolitan Isidore and Father Sokolov did later, when Pobedonostsev proposed that Turgenev should not be given a Church funeral and, above all, that he should receive no eulogy.[25]

Count Leo Tolstoy was, of course, the giant of Russian literature during Pobedonostsev's lifetime, as he remains today. His views, especially after 1880, were such that conflict between Tolstoy and the state, with its self-appointed spiritual guardian, was inevitable. In his conversations with foreigners, Pobedonostsev often reflected Russian national pride in Tolstoy as one of the glories of his country. He read *War and Peace* for the first time only while he was in Salzburg on vacation in 1875, five years after it had been published in book form, but he thought it a splendid novel and a great intellectual achievement. *Anna Karenina*, which he read as it appeared, did not please him so much because he thought Anna unreal, an artificial puppet. Later, both he and Rachinskii came to admire Tolstoy's schools, which were in fact very much like those of Rachinskii, except that Tolstoy ignored the heavy emphasis Rachinskii gave to religion.[26]

However, after 1881, Pobedonostsev was a relentless, if careful, tormentor of Tolstoy, whose influence within Russia he sought to restrict in every way possible. The original spark for this prolonged and bitter hostility was a request which Tolstoy sent directly to

Pobedonostsev and which he also asked Nicholas N. Strakhov, a well-known St. Petersburg publicist, to give Pobedonostsev for the new tsar, asking him to pardon those who had just assassinated Alexander II. Pobedonostsev was incredulous and from that time forward considered Tolstoy a dangerous lunatic out to destroy the very bases of the Russian state. He refused to forward the request to the new tsar and then denounced it when the tsar received a copy through Grand Duke Sergei Alexandrovich. Three months later, he wrote Tolstoy that their religious beliefs and goals were obviously quite different. Indeed, he remarked that in Tolstoy he thought he "detected the features of one who is feeble and himself needs to be cured."[27]

Pobedonostsev devoted his main campaign against Tolstoy to preventing publication of his books and the appearance of his plays, especially of those which seemed to him most subversive of the Church and of morality. He alerted Feoktistov to rumors early in 1883 that Tolstoy was going to publish a new philosophical work. When Tolstoy published *V chem moia vera* (What I Believe) in only fifty copies in order to evade the censor, Pobedonostsev had even this limited edition seized, although he had Feoktistov forward him two copies so that he himself might read the volume and add it to his library. Three years later, he was unable to persuade Feoktistov to prohibit publication of Tolstoy's play, *The Power of Darkness*, but as soon as he had read it and had heard reliable rumors that the tsar had authorized production of the play in both St. Petersburg and Moscow, he made such a blistering attack to both the tsar and Feoktistov that this permission was immediately and categorically withdrawn. Pobedonostsev saw the play as an "abasement of art" which would persuade the educated people in the capitals that the popular masses wallowed without resistance in sin and which would lead foreigners to believe Russia was a foul and decadent country. The very fact that evil was not resisted and that the play offered no ideals was a shattering demonstration to him of the moral degradation of Tolstoy and of the threat he posed for Russia.

The Kreutzer Sonata in 1890 disturbed Pobedonostsev so much that he could complete reading it only after he had made three resolute efforts. He considered it a "very powerful work, . . . all true, as though in a mirror." At the same time, he insisted that changes be made and requested that one entire chapter be eliminated before he would give approval for even a limited edition. Moreover, he complained the next year when Alexander III gave Tolstoy's wife permission to include *The Kreutzer Sonata* in the new complete edition of Tolstoy's work which she was publishing. He quickly warned Feoktistov that this decision affected only the full edition and that *The Kreutzer Sonata* could not be printed separately, particularly in an inexpensive version.[28]

Pobedonostsev also condemned Tolstoy's books and ideas in his annual reviews and in the journals and newspapers published by the Synod. He published rumors about his extravagance and laziness which he almost certainly knew to be untrue. He personally translated for publication by the Synod press an English attack on Tolstoy in order to demonstrate that foreigners shared his critical view of the great Russian writer. In his translation, he carefully omitted the praise given Tolstoy, a suggestion that Tolstoy really did love and respect the Orthodox Church, and the remark that "he is not more unorthodox than thousands in and out of his own country who live and die at peace with their Established Churches, to the comfort of their friends and relatives."

By 1890, Pobedonostsev had come to recognize that prohibiting publication "does not attain its aim in one time. It is impossible to prevent in any way the distribution and reading of the works of Tolstoy." One could only hope to limit the damage. Moreover, he believed that the work of Tolstoy had already had a profound influence on faith, the Church, society, and the state. At the turn of the century, when student disorders like those at the end of the reign of Alexander II received Tolstoy's sympathetic support, and when Pobedonostsev decided that neither the state nor the Church could prevent Tolstoy's actions, he accepted a suggestion that Tolstoy's influence be reduced by a formal announcement separating him from the Russian Orthodox Church, but without labeling him a heretic. On February 24, 1901, the official Church paper, *Tserkovnyia Vedomosti* (Church News) published an announcement signed by the three metropolitans, the archbishop of Kholm and Warsaw, and four bishops, which identified the principal attacks that Tolstoy, "seduced by intellectual pride," had made on the established Church and faith. "Therefore the Church does not consider him a member and cannot consider him one so long as he does not renew relations with it."

Although Pobedonostsev was the Director General of the Synod and had in fact drafted the announcement, he did not join the other members of the Synod in signing the decree, probably in the hope that the absence of his layman's signature would strengthen the weight of the Church's charge as a religious document. The announcement of the separation, which was not formally an excommunication, was reprinted by most Russian newspapers and of course caused a tremendous sensation within Russian and abroad. Tolstoy, who had in fact separated himself from the Church and had therefore justified the Synod's action, received wide publicity for his charge that the decision was arbitrary, without foundation, and illegal. Although the Synod reiterated that Tolstoy had removed himself from the Church and that the Church was only recognizing his action, Tolstoy won the sympathy and support of most Russians, as Pobedonostsev himself confessed. Even before the tempest became a storm, Pobedonostsev had to apologize to Nicholas II for publishing the Synod communication without his approval, although he had agreed in principle. Later in the year, when Tolstoy was seriously ill, the Synod sent instructions through the Minister of the Interior to all governors and police chiefs that no memorial services in Tolstoy's honor were to be allowed. In January, 1902, Pobedonostsev even planned to have a priest join the Tolstoy household and announce at his death that he had recanted in his last hour and had rejoined the Church. Tolstoy's survival wrecked this perfidious plan, just as his towering strength and international prestige destroyed Pobedonostsev's other efforts to reduce or destroy his influence.[29]

While Pobedonostsev was unsuccessful in caging or controlling the great force which Count Leo Tolstoy represented in the world, he did achieve substantial triumphs in limiting the press, which he despised for spreading what he considered deliberate falsehoods and political poison. His efforts to restrict the power of this "monster" reflected a deeply held philosophy, for he thought the press overpowering in its crushing or swallowing customs and laws and more characteristic of his era than even technology. As a convinced believer in autocracy and that the Russian Orthodox Church possessed "the one and only truth," he concluded that the government had an obligation "to guard the little ones who believe in it" and that tolerating views other than those of the state and the Church was like bringing a mistress into one's home. Public opinion, on the other hand, was derided and denounced as a creation of the press, a new and powerful conformism which could create wars and revolutions but had no responsibility or sense of responsibility. Since anyone with sufficient funds could purchase or found a newspaper, virtue and ability were not required or even allowed. In fact, Pobedonostsev thought that all journalists were chatterboxes and liars, that they were men "who see one thing and write another," and that they inevitably pandered to the base instincts of the readers. He generally referred to the press as "the father of lies," and was convinced that history would view press attacks upon him as "a sample of the falseness of so-called public opinion fabricated by newspapers and journals." The press as a whole therefore constituted a "basic disintegrating force," and the public opinion it created threatened the institutions and values he held central to survival.[30]

Pobedonostsev believed that foreign newspapers and journals should not be allowed within Russia, except for those like him who had a responsibility to remain informed about foreign opinion. In fact, he viewed the foreign press much as Soviet rulers do in their efforts to maintain ideological purity and to prevent publication of the picture of Soviet reality. He also sought to ensure that the discussion of critical issues by government officials be safeguarded from the press and even that no government action or consideration be mentioned in the press without official permission. Third, he worked for complete and fully effective control of all the press through the Main Administration of the Press in the Ministry of the Interior. Finally, he urged state financial support and special privileges for those editors and journalists who supported the state's position and who could be relied upon to represent its point of view faithfully.

Some newspapers and journals Pobedonostsev considered so filthy that he could not read them and had to learn of their vices and crimes only from friends. Except for that, he read consistently not only the principal St. Petersburg and Moscow papers but also the English and French press. He even kept an eye on the provincial press through members of the hierarchy and priests who corresponded with him about "the local devils." While he was on vacation abroad, he often sent the Minister of Interior clippings from German and English newspapers, with the suggestion that their correspondents in Russia be censored and that those who ignored warnings should be forced to leave the country. His correspondence with the tsar, the Minister of the Interior, and Feoktistov was peppered with exhortations to tighten controls; denunciations of particular newspapers and journalists who deserved punishment; complaints because of the treatment given Church appointments, the Old Believers, difficulties within the schools, strikes or disorders, or even scandals; and suggestions that the government be far more rigorous in its policies toward those who distributed information and opinion. In the spring of 1881, the Minister of the Interior dedended himself by pointing out he had already closed more than fifty newspapers and journals. In August, 1882, he wrote that he would like to prohibit all newspapers but that they both realized this would be impossible. Pobedonostsev remained relentless; even advertisements did not escape his attention in the publications he denounced as the work of liberals, Polish agents, or "Yids."[31]

He fought relentlessly to maintain absolute state control over the press, but he was aware that this negative policy was not sufficient and that the state had also to use the press if it wished to ensure that its point of view prevail. Therefore, just as he sought to discredit and restrict the influence of men such as Turgenev and Tolstoy, so also he sought honors and awards for those whose views he shared or whom he thought brought both stability and honor to Russia. Dostoevsky was therefore provided the connections and recognition from the court which pleased him so much. Pobedonostsev similarly urged the tsar to attend a concert in St. Petersburg by Anton Rubinstein, "a real Russian, by his birth, education, social connections and family, habits, and way of life." He persuaded the tsar also to provide financial assistance to Tchaikovsky and to Rimsky-Korsakov, as well as to other authors and artists less known but equally loyal, and he helped conservative journals, such as *Russkoe obozrenie* (Russian Review) obtain subsidies.[32]

Pobedonostsev's service for *Grazhdanin* (The Citizen), both as a protector against the censor and as a frequent contributor while Dostoevsky was editor, began his education as a participant in the struggle within the bureaucracy for and against the right to print. Long before he emerged as a power in the reign of Alexander III, he was approached by colleagues and acquaintances for help against the censor and for intercession for government subsidies. He assisted Dostoevsky by having his journal released from an official critic. He also intervened to protect Nikita P. Giliarov-Platonov, whose Moscow newspaper was being harassed by the Main Administration of the Press, although the publication had "a fundamentally sound policy and stood on serious principles." He realized that censors lacked a sense of proportion and were alarmed by phrases, and he therefore frequently intervened to assist a paper or journal which shared his views, but which had committed a minor slip. He also on occasion used Katkov's paper or *Grazhdanin* to attack a state leader or bureaucrat whose actions he especially disliked and which he could bring to the attention of the court in no other way.[33]

Aside from his own extensive publications and the outpouring of the Press of the Synod, his principal weapon in his war as a publicist for the mind of Russia was Michael Katkov, who was without doubt the best-known journalist in Russia from early in the 1860's until his death in 1887. Pobedonostsev read Katkov's newspaper every day. They were close associates as early as 1862 when they were both on the side of reform, especially the reform of the judicial system, and were both ardent admirers of England. In the 1870's, the pan-slav movement and the subsequent war fever of 1876–77 affected them both, and they were both frightened conservatives in the 1880's. Katkov did have a romantic attachment to the *zemskii sobor*, and his advocacy of this in the troubled months after the assassination of Alexander II annoyed Pobedonostsev and caused constant friction with the censor, who at Pobedonostsev's orders forbade even Katkov to mention this ancient institution. They disagreed also in the early 1880's on state policy on university education. Moreover, Katkov wished to be Minister of Education and had some support for this in high circles. However, Pobedonostsev considered him a jewel as a journalist but impossible as a state official, and blocked the appointment.

Pobedonostsev utilized Katkov very effectively and also provided him important services. In addition to lending his name as a contributor on a number of occasions, he ensured that the tsar, the empress, and other members of the court read Katkov daily. He warned Katkov of particular sensitivities and of attacks on him which were brewing within the court. He sent him items of information which he found in the foreign press, tips or even "leaks" in twentieth-century terminology, government reports and unclassified documents of limited circulation, and general news about the court and Russia's leaders which a newsman would find useful, not only for background information but also for avoiding errors. He gave Katkov's son-in-law, Prince Sergei V. Shakhovskoi, a position as his administrative assistant with the Volunteer Fleet. Later, he helped Shakhovskoi to move to the Ministry of the Interior and then obtain appointment as Governor General in Reval, where he promoted the Russification program. Finally, he helped Katkov obtain regular subsidies through the Ministry of Education for his newspaper, and for a school which the journalist established in

Moscow. He intervened twice—in 1875, when the Minister of Finance was reluctant to continue the annual subsidy of 23,000 rubles (approximately $11,500) for the school, and in 1883, when some of Katkov's critiques of government officials led to a delay in the newspaper subsidy. The size of Katkov's subsidy is not known, but Witte noted that Prince Meshcherskii received 80,000 rubles each year in 1892 and 1893 for *Grazhdanin*, which was considerably less significant than Katkov's journal.[34]

Katkov's services to Pobedonostsev and the Russian government were just as significant, though perhaps more difficult to measure, as Pobedonostsev's assistance to him. Probably his greatest contribution was his providing a platform from which "the Russian Truth" could be purveyed. *Moskovskiia Vedomosti* not only served as the unofficial government newspaper, but it also denounced other newspapers as unfree and claimed for itself the virtue of independence, just as Soviet papers do today. Thus, in December, 1886, Katkov wrote that the press in Russia was freer than anywhere else. "We do not know a single organ of the foreign press which can truthfully call itself independent. In the so-called constitutional states, in contrast to Russia, there are parties which struggle for power and to participate in power. The political press in those countries serves as organs for those contesting parties. . . . In Russia, where there are no such parties, a newspaper can be completely independent."[35]

On the personal level, Katkov arranged that a niece of Pobedonostsev be admitted to his Moscow *gimnaziia* with a 50 percent reduction in tuition. He called prompt attention to Pobedonostsev's books and gave them long and favorable reviews. During the crisis of 1876–78 and throughout the period when Pobedonostsev was in charge of the Volunteer Fleet, he gave ample publicity to the Red Cross, in which Pobedonostsev and his wife were both interested, and to the Volunteer Fleet. When Pobedonostsev in 1883 launched the drive to establish parish schools throughout European Russia, Katkov called attention to this movement and praised its creators. Above all, Katkov skillfully published the hints, rumors, and leaks which Pobedonostsev fed him and which were designed to support a particular maneuver or policy.[36]

The last year of Katkov's life was a troubled one, for his exuberant and headstrong actions created minor crises for Russian diplomacy and seriously annoyed the tsar and some of his advisors. After the Congress of Berlin in 1878, and after 1881 in particular, Katkov and a number of other noisy patriots had become critical of Germany and Bismarck and flirted with the idea of a friendlier relation with France. In fact, Pobedonostsev once or twice had had to warn Katkov to be cautious and had had to defend him at the court for some of his less temperate comments about Germany. The humiliating loss of Russia's privileged position in Bulgaria, where the Bulgars themselves turned against the Russians who had helped them to gain their freedom, led Katkov to urge that Russia occupy and administer Bulgaria, abandon her traditional alliance with conservative Germany and Austria-Hungary, and ally with radical and republican France. By late 1886, Tolstoy, the Minister of the Interior, and some other Russian leaders agreed with Katkov, arguing that Germany was likely to absorb Austria-Hungary and assume her position as the enemy of Russia and the other Slavs in the Balkans. The tsar and Foreign Minister Giers not only disagreed with this thesis, but thought that discussion of it in the press was most unwise. Katkov, old and perhaps even less responsible than usual, was carried away by fervor to assault the motives of some of his critics, some of whom were especially infuriated because they were aware that he was subsidized by the government. Pobedonostsev intervened in this situation to defend Katkov, arranged an audience for him with the tsar, and succeeded in limiting his punishment to an oral reprimand.[37]

This tempest had hardly settled when Katkov became involved in two other storms, both of which might have had important diplomatic repercussions. In the first of these, Katkov in May, 1887, published secret information he had just acquired from Senator Saburov concerning the creation of the League of Three Emperors in 1880, thereby destroying Saburov's career, annoying Giers and Alexander III, and raising new problems between Russia and Germany, which were just then discussing another treaty. That crisis had hardly subsided when Katkov was denounced by his rivals, probably unjustly, for a letter he supposedly had written to Premier Floquet of France proposing an alliance between Russia and France.

The scandal raised by public charges concerning Katkov's direct intervention into Russian foreign policy at the very highest level had hardly subsided when Katkov died. Just as he had done at Dostoevsky's death, Pobedonostsev drafted a telegram from Alexander III to the widow, declaring that "all true Russians mourn." He apparently also asked the tsar to provide Mrs. Katkov a pension. Finally, he and Delianov advised the tsar to name Sergei A. Petrovskii, a former student and a close acquaintance of Pobedonostsev, the new editor of the paper, of which the Minister of Education admitted the Ministry was generally considered the owner. Perhaps the best illustration of the alleged independence of Katkov's paper and of the role Pobedonostsev played in manipulating the press is the correspondence within the government concerning selection of the new editor.[38]

Pobedonostsev's influence on Katkov's newspaper did not end with Katkov's death. He continued to defend Katkov from attack or even criticism in obituary articles through his influence with Feoktistov. He served as an advisor to Petrovskii, sending him warnings, scoldings, tips, and materials written by members of the Synod staff for anonymous publication. He advised Petrovskii on sensitive subjects, and he defended the paper against the censor when particular articles caused offense. Above all, he placed his imprimatur on the paper by publishing several articles in it, particularly his moving eulogy of Alexander III.[39]

Ivan Aksakov, who died just a year before Katkov and who was the other stormy petrel of Russian journalism, was more volatile and less subject to control and official use than Katkov. During the first few years after Aksakov married Anna Tiutchev in 1866, his relations with Pobedonostsev were apparently close. Pobedonostsev was the godfather for their first child, in 1867. He was an enthusiastic reader of a journal, *Moskva* (Moscow), which Aksakov founded in 1867, and he persuaded a number of the grand dukes to subscribe. He visited the Aksakovs whenever he was in Moscow in the late 1860's, and he advised Aksakov through his sister-in-law of issues which were sensitive at the court.

However, while Pobedonostsev's relations with Catherine Tiutchev became closer and they began to write to each other two or three times a month, his connections with Aksakov dwindled and cooled. Only a few letters between the two men have survived, and apparently no more than these were written. This drift was probably due principally to the inevitable development of new interests by two newly married couples living in separate cities, but Pobedonostsev by 1868 or 1870 was also alarmed by Aksakov's lack of sensitivity and tact in dealing with political questions. Pobedonostsev warned him on a number of occasions to avoid potentially troublesome issues and criticized him for drafting the petition to the tsar from the Moscow Duma in November, 1870. This petition, which might be called the last act of the Slavophil movement, supported the autocracy and government policy, but asked for freedom of the press and of religious belief and for what Ivan Aksakov called "respect for our spiritual freedom, our personal quality." Pobedonostsev considered the tone aggressive and the requests beyond possibility. Aksakov in turn protested bitterly against Pobedonostsev's "bureaucratic conservatism" and the influence he had used in St. Petersburg to discredit him, Samarin, and the other signers.

Pobedonostsev did not seek to interfere with the censor, as he often did for friends, when Aksakov's biography of his father-in-law, Fedor Ivanovich Tiutchev, was confiscated in 1874. While he did intercede in 1876 to support Aksakov's application for permission to produce a newspaper "defending Slavic interests," he was not enthusiastic or vigorous in his support and indeed he and Catherine were isolated from Ivan and his wife because of their unsuccessful efforts to dissuade him from launching the new publication. In 1880, Aksakov apparently won permission from Loris-Melikov for a new weekly, *Rus'* (Russia), and did not even seek Pobedonostsev's support. Pobedonostsev was critical of this venture, even of the title Aksakov chose.[40]

Some of the positions Aksakov adopted in *Rus'* seriously strained relations with Pobedonostsev and the court and illustrated precisely the delicate problems raised in an autocratic state by an energetic and somewhat irresponsible journalist who was a vigorous nationalist and conservative, who at the same time disagreed openly with important government policies, and who had powerful support and personal friends at court. Aksakov fully appreciated the reluctance of the government to warn or reprimand a prominent nationalist journalist, and Pobedonostsev admitted privately that "there is no point in talking with him—he is out of his mind." Some of his essays on the Old Believers, on religious freedom, on the great virtues of the 1864 reform of the judicial system, and on standing up vigorously against the Germans annoyed Pobedonostsev and other powerful St. Petersburg figures. In December, 1885, a particularly vigorous Aksakov attack upon the censorship itself led Feoktistov and Pobedonostsev to discuss some policy which would quiet Aksakov without making matters worse. At this critical point, Aksakov suddenly died.

The memorial essay which Pobedonostsev wrote after Aksakov's death said little about him and was really a glowing tribute to the Aksakov family, to the Slavophils, and to the Moscow which Pobedonostsev had known as a child and young man. The Slavophils he described as "honorable and pure Russians, native sons of their land, rich in Russian intelligence, sensitive to the feelings of the Russian heart, full of love for their people and their land . . ." [who] "sought truth in the eternal principles of the rule of God and in the basic conditions of the nature of the Russian man." Ivan Aksakov was "an heir of this tradition, a guardian of the testament left by his ancestors," and a man whom "the great majority of the simple Russian people" felt "burned with a true fire for the interests of the Russian land." However, Pobedonostsev did not refer to any of Ivan Aksakov's journalistic activities or to the ideas with which he was most closely connected before his death.[41]

The care which Pobedonostsev lavished on Katkov and Aksakov as voices of the true Russia, regardless of the discordant notes which on occasion they sounded, was less important in his efforts as a publicist than his own writings, the vigor he instilled into the Holy Synod Press and its publication program, and his campaign to establish parish schools throughout Russia. His own extensive work as a writer, editor, and translator reflects accurately his political interests, his concern with public issues, and his inherited devotion to the printed word, if not to the life of the scholar, which he had so enjoyed for the two decades in Moscow between 1846 and 1866. It also helps to explain his failure as a policy-maker or "grey eminence" for Alexander III and as the Director General of the Synod, because he was so actively engaged in front-line sniping that he failed to concentrate on his principal role and on the main problems at hand.

Pobedonostsev was lured from his principal responsibilities into labors as a publicist by elements deep in his character and solidly established by the time he became Director General of the Synod. However, his various endeavors as a publicist and propagandist in the last thirty years of his life reflected above all the fear which dominated him after 1877 and his obsession with defending the values and institutions which he saw threatened. On the official level, he therefore devoted especial care to writing, printing, and distributing his annual and biannual reports to the tsar on his work as Director General of the Synod. These volumes described what he considered the great achievements of the Church and the weaknesses of the other religious groups and of the sects. He also arranged to have his principal state papers and speeches reprinted in the Russian press, reproduced and sold as pamphlets, and published in translation abroad, especially in England, France, and Germany. Indeed, he revealed some of the instincts of the modern politician in his efforts to make certain his point of view received wide publicity.[42]

A high percentage of his publications during the last two or three decades of his life was sheer, low-quality propaganda, but some of it had a more enduring quality or is at least of considerable interest to the scholar. Thus, reading several French and American books about the American farm, especially the Midwestern homestead, convinced him that a possible solution to Russia's political, economic, and social problems was the establishment of small, independent family farms. He published an essay about this in 1889 in *Russkii vestnik*, reprinted it as a pamphlet in 1892, and included it as an appendix in the final edition of the first volume of *Kurs grazhdanskago prava* in 1896.[43]

The issues on which he sought to influence Russian opinion were naturally the same as those with which he was concerned as a government leader and as a part-time philosopher, the role of religion in society, the position of the Russian Orthodox Church in Russia, the necessity for expanding the attention given to sound moral instruction in primary school education, and the need to emphasize the central role the family must play in a healthy society. These themes are an index to his political philosophy. They are reflected in his principal writings, especially in *Moskovskii sbornik* (Moscow Collection), as well as in his efforts devoted to instructing and edifying those who helped shape Russian state policy.

Pobedonostsev as a publicist sought to demonstrate that religion was the foundation of civilized life and that modern civilization, especially the rise of parliamentary government, democracy, and the various freedoms associated with liberal political institutions, posed a dreadful threat to the very core of the institutions and values all should cherish. His own books and articles in this drive were supplemented by translations from a wide range of European authors published in a variety of ways. Thus, he published part of an essay from Gladstone's *The Impregnable Rock of Holy Scripture* in a conservative journal, *Russkoe obozrenie*, as well as in *Moskovskii sbornik*. In 1896, he translated and published in a 160-page booklet part of the American government's *Report of Statistics on Churches*, printed six years earlier in Washington, apparently to prove that democratic government led to a crazy proliferation of religious sects and that the existence of 117 churches in the United States inevitably reflected and contributed to the decline of religious faith. In the early 1890's, he published a volume of which ten editions appeared before 1906, which included part of St. Augustine's *Confessions* as well as chapters from two books by an Anglican cleric, William Samuel Lilly, *Christianity and Modern Civilization* and *A Century of Revolution*. Lilly's books, as well as selections from the work of a Brussels professor, Adolphe Prins, *De l'esprit du gouvernement démocratique*, Pobedonostsev used to support his attack on constitutional and democratic government, both in books and in pamphlets. On the other hand, in the official Synod newspaper, *Tserkovnyia Vedomosti*, he combined an attack on the French government for its anticlerical policies with praise of the views of Theodore Roosevelt on the role of religion in human society, as expressed in *The Strenuous Life*.[44]

Almost everything he published was directed toward strengthening and glorifying the Russian Orthodox Church and its role in Russian history. In the summer of 1891, he published a volume, *Istoriia pravoslavnoi tserkvi do nachala razdeleniia tserkvei* (History of the Orthodox Church before the Beginning of the Separation of the Churches) designed especially to increase understanding of the Church's history and to demonstrate that throughout its history the Church "had overcome all obstacles and still preserved in itself that holy fire which our Saviour Himself brought down to earth," and that it was in the nineteenth century as it had been in the first centuries of Christianity. This volume was prepared by Pobedonostsev, with the help of his wife, for seminaries and for institutions training teachers for the parish schools. However, the first edition of one thousand copies sold so quickly that a revised and enlarged edition appeared in 1892, and nine editions had been published before his death.[45]

Pobedonostsev's *Istoriia pravoslavnoi tserkvi* was a great success, but the way in which he prepared the book sheds most valuable illumination upon his character and also led to sharp criticism among Russian scholars and even among Russian churchmen. In short, this volume, the first edition of which appeared as his own work and which he described to the tsar as his own, was really only an abbreviated edition of a two-volume set published first in 1883 by Alexandra N. Bakhmetev, *Razskazi iz russkoi tserkovnoi istorii* (Stories from Russian Church History), from which Pobedonostsev borrowed without the original author's knowledge or consent. Miss Bakhmetev, a resident of Moscow born two years before he was, a good friend of Catherine Tiutchev, and an earlier admirer of Pobedonostsev as an author and administrator, was a successful author of religious books for children. In fact, one volume of her life of Christ for children appeared in eighteen editions, and the history of the Church from which Pobedonostsev borrowed so heavily was published in four editions. She naturally resented his action, and criticism became so sharp that he stopped advertisements and decided not to produce a second edition, even though the first edition was quickly exhausted. When the demand became overwhelming (three printings were published in 1892 alone), he added other materials to the original version and placed a note on the page after the title page acknowledging that "some pages were borrowed from other books, especially from *Razskazi iz russkoi tserkovnoi istorii* by Bakhmetev."[46]

He was deeply engrossed in educational problems in Russia, particularly at the primary school level. He devoted enormous amounts of time and energy and a substantial portion of the Church's funds to expanding the parish school system. At the same time, many of his publications described schools and views which he approved and which he recommended for Russia. Perhaps the most interesting of these volumes is his wife's translation of *The Mighty Atom*, a sentimental novel by Minnie Mackay. The dedication inscribed in the American edition reveals the point and the tone of this volume:

> To those self-styled "Progressivists," who by precept and example assist the infamous cause of Education Without Religion and who, by promoting the idea, borrowed from French atheism, of denying to the children in board-schools and elsewhere, The Knowledge and Love of God as the true foundation of noble living, are Guilty of a worse crime than Murder."[47]

The Pobedonostsev translation of *The Mighty Atom* appeared in five editions and was even translated from Russian into Serbian. Another collection of translated essays about primary school education appeared in six editions. In fact, in the last decade of his life in particular, he released a veritable flood of books, articles, and pamphlets on the kind of education Russian children ought to receive. Most of these publications were translations of books and articles describing particular schools or educational systems of France or England or his summaries of information he had acquired about education of a religious kind in various countries of western Europe.[48]

The family was an institution he considered central for any sound society, and his published works during his last years sought to persuade Russian leaders that the state ought to concentrate upon re-building this critical social organism. In 1901, therefore, he pro-duced a second edition of his translation of Heinrich Thiersch's *Uber christliches Familienleben*, which he had first translated in 1861. In addition, he wrote an essay describing in flattering terms the work of Frederick Le Play, the French Catholic sociologist who devoted most of his research and writing to the family and who founded a school of thought which had considerable influence in France in the last half of the nineteenth century and again in the 1940's and 1950's. He also translated and published in 1897 Le Play's principal work on the family, *La Constitution essentielle de l'humanité*.[49]

Even the most relentlessly careful search cannot ensure the scholar that he has located all of Pobedonostsev's publications or that he has been able to find and identify the materials he had published as books or articles or that he forwarded to editors of newspapers or journals for insertion. His letters indicate often that he transmitted original or translated materials to editors. Olga Novikov on occa-sion translated original essays or articles he found and forwarded to her and had them published anonymously in the *London Times* or in another English journal or newspaper. Sometimes direct evi-dence in the correspondence, or indirect information from these or other letters, or from other sources, have enabled discovery of the essay or article. Even then, it has sometimes been impossible to de-termine whether or not the material was written by Pobedonostsev or was simply transmitted by him after translation. It is clear, though, that he thoroughly appreciated public opinion and worked skillfully to influence it.

In his struggle to direct the mind of Russia, Pobedonostsev ac-quired a useful instrument in 1880 when he became Director Gen-eral of the Synod, because the Synod owned and directed a Press, with printshops in Moscow and in St. Petersburg, a number of bookstores, and a thriving business, particularly in theological works, catechisms, and books for various kinds of religious service. In fact, the Press in 1880 published more than 400,000 copies of books and almost 5 million leaflets, as well as 172,400 copies of books and 6,948 leaflets which it printed on a commercial basis for private individuals. As a devout member of the Church and as a man interested both in intellectual and Church life, Pobedonostsev must have been well acquainted with the Moscow printery and bookstore on Nikolskii Street near Red Square. His acquaintance,

Nikita Giliarov-Platonov, had been director of the Moscow print-shop from 1863 until 1867, and an old neighbor who became an important correspondent, S. D. Voit, was the business manager of the shop for a number of years.

Pobedonostsev was immensely interested in the work of the Synod Press and was closely engaged in the decisions made concerning the works it published. In 1889, which was an exceptional year because of the celebration of the fiftieth anniversary of the return of the Uniates in the western provinces to Orthodoxy, the Press published 6 million books and pamphlets and 17 million leaflets. Income from sales leaped from almost 400,000 rubles (about $200,000) in 1881 to more than a million rubles in 1894. After an advisory committee in 1896 recommended special emphasis on books for parish schools and the creation of a kind of basic, package Parish School Library, production of books and booklets for school use and for supplementary reading became a substantial part of the Press's expanded operations. For example, in 1900, the Press published in the Parish School Library series fourteen books for school use and ten for home use in a total of 2,700,000 copies. In 1901, it produced forty-two books for this series in a total of 3,600,000 copies.[50]

The Synod Press's published *Catalogue* in 1886 was 142 pages long and listed 858 titles. Less than half of the titles were sacred scriptures, theology, prayers, and publications for religious services; the majority were spiritual and moral volumes, documents, and learned tomes which Pobedonostsev had published.

He was just as interested in the printing part of the Press's operations as he was in selecting titles. Thus, he boasted in 1889 that one of the new machines in the shop in Moscow was the only one of its kind in Russia. By the time he retired in 1905, the Moscow shop employed 347 skilled workers in a modern plant which included more than one hundred fifty different machines capable of printing 30 million pages a year. The shop owned 180 tons of Old Church Slavonic, Russian, and foreign type. The St. Petersburg branch was approximately the same size, though probably not so modern or efficient. During the labor troubles in the fall of 1903 and the revolution in the fall of 1905, Pobedonostsev displayed more interest in the attitudes of the workers in the print shops than he did in government policy. He was predictably opposed to Voit's proposal in January, 1904, that the Press establish a pension system for the workers: "to create rules and reports, even for ten years' service. God deliver us!"[51]

Pobedonostsev and the administrators with whom he worked at the Press were alert and imaginative in their approach to producing and distributing literature. The Press was a semi-autonomous part of the Synod. It was self-supporting, and it invested its profits in new equipment, rather than in financing some other part of the Synod's program. It not only established the Parish School Library, but it made bulk sales to diocesan offices in a successful effort to place its publications in the hands of children and other readers. Teachers received special discounts for all books, and primitive bookstores were established by the consistories in more than five hundred cities and villages. Pobedonostsev made an especially intensive effort to distribute the Press's publications in the Baltic region, where the Synod established six bookstores in the Riga bishopric alone, and in the western provinces, where he was convinced that Jews controlled the book trade. In addition, beginning in 1888, the Press published and sold a weekly newspaper, *Tserkovnyia Vedomosti*, as an official organ for the Church, publishing news of Church affairs and Russian life which Pobedonostsev and its editor thought should be made available. He used this paper frequently to reprint essays he had written or essays he had read or translated and thought should have wide distribution. By the early 1890's, the Press was publishing a group of weekly papers or journals, each aimed at a special part of the Orthodox audience.[52]

Pobedonostsev also used the Synod Press as a kind of hobby, publishing books which had some interest or value to churchmen in Russia but which could not have sold well or even paid the cost of publication. Thus, in 1897, he had his good friend Prince Shakhovskhoi edit and the Synod Press publish a two-volume selection of the essays of Nikita Giliarov-Platonov. Even more striking was his decision to publish an edition of the letters of Metropolitan Filaret of Moscow, who was born in 1782 and who died in 1867 after more than four decades in that important position. Pobedonostsev was an admirer of Filaret. He was especially impressed by his firm will, his patriotism, and his asceticism, but Filaret's rooted opposition to change must also have been a factor. In fact, Filaret had opposed both emancipation and the campaign to end flogging in the army. As soon as he became Director General of the Synod, Pobedonostsev began to study the papers of Filaret, which had been stored in the Synod safe after his death. He assigned the director of the Synod archives, Nicholas S. Grigorovich, the task of putting the letters and papers in order, and asked Bishop Savva of Tver to edit the letters, a selection of which alone filled ten volumes. Pobedonostsev paid close attention to the production of these volumes and even edited one volume of Filaret's papers himself. There is no evidence that these had any influence on Russian intellectual life, because Filaret was truly a voice of the distant past and had no relevance even for conservative churchmen in the 1880's and 1890's.[53]

The Press of the Holy Synod became a major instrument in his effort to reshape Russian intellectual life. On a different level, the parish schools he promoted vigorously while he was Director General of the Synod represented another major endeavor to change both the spirit and the intellectual content of peasant life and to strengthen popular respect for and belief in autocracy and Orthodoxy. This massive program, which became an official part of Church and state policy in 1884, reflected a sharp change in his view of primary education and of the means of strengthening the Church's position in the countryside.

A "city boy" throughout his long life, Pobedonostsev was remarkably uninformed concerning the peasantry and concerning primary education in Russia. In fact, as late as 1875, he was opposed to primary school education. He thought compulsory elementary education a mistake even for England, and believed that any effort to introduce elementary education into rural Russia reflected great ignorance of peasant life and would lead to resentment and even to violence on the part of the peasants. However, both then and later in his life, he praised warmly the efforts of women whom he knew who had established schools for peasant girls. He applauded Catherine Tiutchev's efforts to establish a school on the Tiutchev estate, and he enthusiastically supported the work of Nicholas Ilminskii in organizing Orthodox primary schools for non-Russians in and near Kazan. In 1881, he was one of a number of leading state officials and churchmen who founded a society to promote technical training for peasants and workers. The announcement of this organization declared that "spreading general education or book learning among the *narod* frequently creates more harm than good; it excites dissatisfaction with their position among the masses." At about the same time, his letters to Catherine Tiutchev and to the new tsar revealed that Russian primary and secondary schools were dangerous because they "pulled" many beyond their class and their means. However, by 1880, he was beginning to believe that primary education could not be denied and that the Orthodox Church must be placed in full control of it.[54]

The belief that the Church should found and maintain a national system of primary schools, particularly in European Russia, was, of course, not a new one in the 1880's. Peter the Great had toyed with the concept briefly, and Nicholas I had in fact promoted parish schools systematically. Thus, in 1830, Russia had approximately one hundred parish schools with 1,860 pupils. These figures leaped to 2,500 schools with 19,000 pupils in 1840, to 4,610 schools with 88,512 pupils in 1850, and to 7,907 schools with 133,666 pupils in 1860. In 1861, the Synod sought a monopoly of primary school education and insisted that the clergy obtain in elementary education "the natural preponderance which is due them." However, the tsar ruled in January, 1862, that the Synod should control only those schools founded by the clergy. The Church's schools declined heavily in number and significance during the next two decades, due in part to the vigor shown by the new zemstvo institutions and by the peasant communities in establishing schools under the Ministry of Education and in part to the disinterest or even opposition to parish schools shown by Count Dmitrii Tolstoy. The number of parish schools declined gradually under Tolstoy; there were only 7,402 with 205,559 pupils in 1875, and 4,348 with 108,990 in 1880.[55]

Pobedonostsev was convinced of the importance of having a school system under Church control by the very successes of the zemstvo schools. Like many other frightened Russian leaders, he saw a connection between the flourishing zemstvo schools and the rising revolutionary movement. He may also have been influenced by Giliarov-Platonov, who in the 1860's had sought to persuade the empress and some of her ladies-in-waiting, whom Pobedonostsev knew well, to press for the creation of a national system of primary schools under the control of the Church, with a school in each parish. Pobedonostsev may have been reminded of this idea by its author in the critical days after the assassination of the tsar. He did reprint several essays on this subject by Giliarov-Platonov, who complained just before his death in 1887 that he had never received the credit due him for this concept.[56]

However, Sergei A. Rachinskii was probably the Russian most responsible for persuading Pobedonostsev of the virtues of the parish school system and for the growth of that system throughout European Russia before 1905, a development which consumed much of Pobedonostsev's time and energy. One might describe Rachinskii as a Christian Populist or as the leader of a one-man Christian going-to-the-people movement, because he had the same respect and even veneration for the peasant as the Populists had and the same burning interest to assist in uplifting the peasants. In fact, the three decades of work he accomplished in and near the village of Tatev in Smolensk province reveal a missionary fervor which was generally lacking in the Orthodox Church in the nineteenth century.

Soviet scholars in the 1930's ridiculed Rachinskii, to whom they devoted much attention, as a clerical reactionary who sought to preserve the autocracy and a class system and who opposed the introduction of natural science in the secondary schools. He was lampooned for believing that literacy is "the key to secret prayer, to eternal life, and to heavenly wisdom" and for allegedly asserting that enlightenment would reach the Russian peasant "by the incredible but firm belief in the story of the dark wanderer, by travel to a distant monastery, by long readings of the sacred scriptures or of the lives of the saints in the moonlight on endless winter evenings." More recently, however, Rachinskii has been honored for helping to inspire and educate poor peasant children, such as Nicholas P. Bogdanov-Bel'skii, an eminent Russian painter born of landless peasants in 1868 who studied under Rachinskii, who attended his funeral in 1902, and whose 1895 painting of Rachinskii among his eager young pupils now hangs in the Tretiakov Gallery in Moscow.[57]

Rachinskii was a Muscovite just six years younger than Pobedonostsev. After receiving his education at Moscow University and studying at the University of Berlin, he returned to his alma mater as a member of the faculty in botany. A scholar of some merit, if one can judge by his early publications, he joined Professor Boris N. Chicherin and others in 1866 and 1867 in protesting the appointment of Professor V. N. Leshkov as dean of the Faculty of Law. When Minister of Education Tolstoy supported what they considered a violation of the rights of the university corporation, Chicherin and Rachinskii resigned from the faculty. A few years later, Rachinskii left Moscow for life among the peasants, founded the first of several successful schools for peasant boys and girls in a village where even the news of Alexander III's death was not known for four days, and began by example and by publication to urge the establishment of parish schools for the masses of peasant children.

Pobedonostsev was acquainted with Rachinskii when they were both members of the Moscow University faculty, and they were in constant contact after 1878. Catherine Tiutchev in 1879 wrote that a letter from Rachinskii was "like a breath of fresh air," while Pobedonostsev the following year feared that Rachinskii was being extreme in leaving his home to dress like a peasant and to live with the children he was educating. However, he often quoted Rachinskii to Alexander III as "a simple, good, and honorable man," one of the true Russians and voices of Russia who worked "in the dark corners" and who offered faith and hope. Rachinskii wrote Pobedonostsev 895 letters between 1880 and 1902, a measure of their relationship. He visited the Pobedonostsevs for several days on three occasions during the last decade of his life and was apparently the only house guest they ever entertained.[58]

It appears likely that Rachinskii interested Pobedonostsev in the parish schools, just as Ilminskii did in schools for children converted from Mohammedanism in the Kazan area. Pobedonostsev began to advocate the establishment of such schools shortly after he had heard of Rachinskii's successes. In 1882, he named Rachinskii a member of the Synod committee which recommended the parish school system, and in 1883 he had the Synod Press publish and give one of Rachinskii's principal books on the subject to every bishop and seminary, as it did his later volumes as well.

Rachinskii was aware that the influence of the landed gentry in the countryside was declining, and he proposed to use his schools and the priests who served as instructors to fill the vacuum left, and to prevent the infiltration of Western ideas and institutions through the zemstvo schools. He sought to create boarding schools for both boys and girls which operated throughout the year, combining a careful and highly disciplined schedule with the loving care of the priest who was to take the place of the parents. The four-year school was to emphasize character, honor, duty, and responsibility as much as formal education, and the Christian spirit was to be its distinguishing characteristic. The principal subject was "the law of God," which was to infuse all courses and every hour of the day. In addition to Church doctrine, the boys and girls were to study Old Church Slavonic, Russian literature, arithmetic, and church songs. Rachinskii assumed that the pupils would remain in the geographical area and class into which they had been born, so he included physical work as part of the curriculum. He believed that only extraordinary children should be allowed to continue their schooling beyond four years, and he urged instruction in the industrial arts for children of workers and peasants. Indeed, he thought that the teachers should also be peasants, preferably trained by him or in a

seminary but certainly not in a teachers' college. The Russian literature he selected included little written after Pushkin and emphasized the work of conservative nationalists. He neglected history and
anything connected with politics or government, and even nature
drew little attention.

Rachinskii's single school in 1875 had increased to four in 1883,
with five priests serving with him as teachers. By 1900, he was responsible for the founding of thirteen such schools in the Smolensk
province and had trained forty priests to serve as teachers. He had
also become prominent in the effort to improve church singing and
to abolish drunkenness, both causes that were dear to the heart of
Pobedonostsev. Ivan Aksakov, Katkov, and conservative journals
publicized his work as that of an unsung hero, while Pobedonostsev
lavished praise on him, forwarded him funds on his request, and reprinted one of his last essays in the fifth edition of *Moskovskii
sbornik*. One of his books describing his work, *Sel'skaia shkola*
(The Rural School), appeared in five editions, and others also were
published in several editions.[59]

As soon as he was convinced that a system of elementary schools
under the Synod with the parish priest as the teacher was "the rock
on which our salvation shall be achieved," Pobedonostsev began to
describe its virtues to the then heir to the throne, who later became
Alexander III. Within six months after he had been made a member of the Council of Ministers, he succeeded in persuading Minister of Education Nikolai to provide funds for the parish schools,
where "people of the lowest class could receive the basic education
necessary for life, but not for learned science, to which not all can
devote themselves." His campaign with the tsar and his colleagues
in the Council of Ministers and in the Council of State led to the
Council decision in November, 1882, to provide 50,000 rubles (approximately $25,000) to the Synod for priests to start such schools.
He continued to argue for the vital necessity of a powerful spiritual
element in elementary education and for the need to have a parish
school in every village, which provided the natural school unit, with
the priest and the Church in full authority. A special committee he
had established early in the fall of 1882 reported to the Synod in
April, 1884, proposing a national system of parish schools directed
by the Church and supported by the state. Early in June, 1884,
Alexander III issued a decree supporting this program, encouraging the clergy to play an active role, and indirectly promising that
the state would provide the money necessary.[60]

The 1884 announcement of the Statute on Parish Schools indicated that the aim was "to strengthen the Orthodox faith and Christian morality among the people and to impart useful elementary knowledge." In January, 1885, Pobedonostsev named a Council within the Synod to provide general direction for the schools. He used Mogilev province as a kind of laboratory in the early years, but sought to spread the system throughout European Russia. Thus, he had each seminary establish a model parish school and organize courses to train priests how to direct them and to teach. He naturally viewed these schools as rivals of those established by the zemstvos, which often neglected the religious aspect of education, and he sought unsuccessfully to persuade Alexander III in 1891 to decree that no other schools could be established without the permission of the Church.[61]

The parish schools which Pobedonostsev spread so vigorously throughout the villages of European Russia were much like those which Rachinskii had established in and near Tatev, although they were not boarding schools and few had more than one teacher and two years of study. Each parish was to have a school, and each school was to be the responsibility of a parish. Thus, the school was designed to strengthen the parish unit, which was its base, and to increase the role and influence of the priest, who was the teacher. The entire chain of schools was placed under a School Council within the Synod, with a Council in each diocese responsible to the Synod group. In effect, the Synod's School Council by 1900 had become a separate Ministry of Education, with the full approval of the Minister of Education.

The Statute on Parish Schools provided detailed instructions which every school was to follow. Each school was to emphasize Christian doctrine and the creation of Christian character and discipline. The one-class, two-year schools provided each week seven hours of Christian doctrine, Bible, and prayers, four hours of Church songs, four of Old Church Slavonic, seven of Russian language and literature, six of arithmetic, and three of writing. They were in effect literacy schools and were not a considerable advance beyond the "alphabet schools" which had appeared in some Russian villages earlier in the century. The two-class, four-year schools, of which there were only one hundred in 1885 and 602 in 1905 and which ordinarily had two teachers, simply extended this program and added a little Russian geography and history. All of these schools placed heavy emphasis upon singing, one of the few subjects about which Pobedonostsev ever displayed genuine enthusiasm.

Pobedonostsev and his School Council worked hard to expand and advance the parish schools. Courses were established in the seminaries to train priests, and three additional seminaries and three schools for teachers were founded. He established the weekly Synod newspaper, *Tserkovnyia Vedomosti*, to help persuade the clergy to assist in establishing schools and to provide them significant information. In 1896, the Synod began to publish a special monthly journal, *Narodnoe obrazovanie* (National Education), for the teachers and all those interested in the parish schools. He persuaded the tsar to give special honors to particularly deserving priests, and he also awarded financial prizes to those who had notably distinguished themselves.

Interest in education of any kind was often high in Russian villages, so the parish schools met a genuine need and impressive progress was made between 1884 and 1905. The Synod's statistics were not handled with the accurate attention common in advanced countries in the twentieth century, and various scholars have compiled different sets of statistics, but it is obvious that growth was extraordinarily rapid. Thus, while there were 4,348 parish schools in 1880 with 108,990 students, and 4,540 schools with 112,114 students in 1884, there were 21,840 schools with 626,100 pupils in 1890, 42,604 schools with 1,634,461 pupils in 1900, and 43,407 schools with almost 2 million students in 1905. According to one compilation, the number of pupils in parish schools increased by 265 percent in the 1890's and another 27 percent between 1900 and 1914. At the turn of the century, approximately half of the primary schools in Russia were parish schools under the Synod, and slightly more than one-third of all the children receiving a primary school education were in parish schools. (The others were in schools founded by peasant communities or by zemstvos and officially under the Ministry of Education.) All but a handful of the children, less than ten thousand each year throughout the 1890's, were Orthodox, and the great majority were boys.

Pobedonostsev's success in persuading the tsars to grant state funds to the parish schools helps explain their rapid growth. The 50,000 rubles granted in 1882 rose in 1886 to 175,500 rubles, all given through the Ministry of Education, in 1900 to 6,821,150 rubles, and in 1902 to 10,338,916 rubles. According to the calculations of Professor Curtiss, these state funds in 1900 accounted for almost half of the total cost of the parish school system, since of the total of 14,552,775 rubles, local taxes contributed 826,947; gifts from rich and poor, 6,335,358; and the Synod itself, 569,320.[62]

The parish school system reached its height in 1905, after which the number of schools gradually declined, and the number of pupils remained relatively stable. Thus, the 43,841 schools had 1,924,900 pupils in 1904, the 42,836 schools had 1,990,300 in 1905, the 38,226 schools had 1,949,100 pupils in 1910, and the 37,528 schools had 2,079,900 in 1914. However, while the number of pupils in the Synod's schools remained relatively fixed between 1905 and 1914, the number in schools financed locally but under the administrative control of the Ministry of Education rose by 65.2 percent. In 1898, the parish schools had 1,476,124 pupils and the primary schools under the Ministry of Education, 2,650,058. In 1911, the figures were 1,976,900 and 5,900,000, respectively.[63]

In spite of the impressive expansion of the system of parish schools during the period when Pobedonostsev was Director General of the Synod, the achievement had only a shallow foundation and little substantial progress was made. The principal reason for this was the Russian Orthodox Church's ages-old disinterest in education, one of the characteristics that distinguishes its history from that of the Christian churches in western Europe. Pobedonostsev, Rachinskii, and the other crusaders could not overcome attitudes based on centuries of history. Moreover, even they were interested only in the most elementary forms of education for children living in the countryside, where the handicaps were most grave and the resources most feeble. In addition, the massive illiteracy which the parish schools and the other elementary schools were seeking to reduce was such a heavy weight and the annual increase in the size of the population was so great that even the rapid growth of the parish schools in the 1890's did not reduce the number of illiterates.

Pobedonostsev relied heavily on the rural priests to administer his schools and to serve as teachers, but even he realized that they were both unqualified and disinterested. A few priests welcomed the new crusade and were competent to serve, but most lacked the ability and the sense of dedication necessary. Most of the rural clergy saw the parish school as an additional and unwanted burden, and their participation was half-hearted at best. They were particularly unqualified to compete with the zemstvo schools, which usually had eager leadership and considerable popular support, and which offered more effective instruction. Moreover, many educated Russians were reserved about, if not hostile to, the kind of elementary education the parish schools offered, particularly with their emphasis on Christian doctrine, prayer, and church songs. The parish schools paid teachers so poorly, in more than a quarter of the cases less than one hundred rubles a year, and offered so few other advantages, that the level of instruction was very low. In 1899, more than a third of the teachers failed to complete their first year with a school. In that year, only 5 percent of the teachers had taught more than ten years, 20 percent more than five years, and 37 percent more than three years.

XI

Political
and Social Thought

POBEDONOSTSEV's view of the world and his political and social philosophy remained remarkably constant throughout his long life,
particularly the last forty years. Indeed, between 1890 and 1910,
he reprinted without change several books he had written or translated originally in the 1860's. There were exceptions, of course, and
there were variations in his views from time to time as new issues
arose and as the political atmosphere changed. Moreover, the years
of crisis from 1876 through 1881 introduced both a sharp rigidity
and a fervor not previously characteristic of him. However, the
variations and new concepts were almost invariably developments
of well-established judgments. Thus, when he advocated the parish
school system in the 1880's and 1890's, he was in fact expressing in
practical and concrete form ideas he had adumbrated twenty years
earlier concerning education by the Church. Even his most daring
essay, his bitter indictment of Count V. N. Panin's administration
of the Ministry of Justice, which was published anonymously in
London in 1859 in Herzen's *Golosa iz Rossii*, was a faithful representation of views he held throughout his life concerning sound
administrative principles. In short, his statements in the Council
of State in 1880 and 1896 supported positions similar to those he
had advocated in 1859, even though his role and the nature of the
problems facing the government had both changed immeasurably.[1]

The thought of most conservative philosophers tends to be unsystematic and sometimes even unclear, in part because of the very
nature of conservatism and in part because of conservatives' rooted

opposition to the expression of political philosophy in neat, pithy formulas or theories which ignore and confuse the realities of life and politics and seek to substitute wishes and even dreams for the institutions and practices which in fact shape man's destiny. Inevitably, the observations of conservatives reflect the society in which they are produced, its social forces, its problems, reactions to these issues and strains, and its very atmosphere. This is true for Pobedonostsev, who as a conservative took on the coloration of the society in which he lived and who borrowed somewhat indiscriminately in his effort to create a policy which would justify and defend the *status quo*.

His views naturally not only represent and reflect the circumstances in which he lived and worked and the qualities of the system he sought to preserve, but also the particular family atmosphere in which he grew up and his personal qualities. He wrote a great deal and reflected occasionally on the nature of man. Indeed, his views concerning the permanent and indelible qualities of man are at the core of his philosophy. It is therefore ironic that his ideas should echo so clearly his own personal virtues and shortcomings and that his role as a statesman and conservative spokesman should reflect so well his character and personality. Some description of his qualities and temperament will help explain the character and temper of his thought.

Pobedonostsev was essentially a plain, simple, colorless, humorless man, in dress and in personality not unlike Calvin Coolidge. Tall, thin, pale, dry, he dressed in black and always wore a black bow tie. The German ambassador, General Hans von Schweinitz, said that he reminded him of a French professor, while the pastor of the Evangelical Church in St. Petersburg, Hermann Dalton, who was acquainted with Pobedonostsev for more than thirty years, thought he resembled a German research scholar. He was almost as invisible as G. K. Chesterton's postman. He had no interest in the little things of life. In the immense material which he preserved and in the memoir literature about him, there is no reference to the ordinary pleasures. He never mentioned clothing. In all of his papers and books, he referred to food only once, and then to mention a wine he had tasted while visiting the Don Cossack country with the heir to the throne in 1863. Even English cooking failed to elicit a comment.

In short, Pobedonostsev as a man was an enlarged and older version of the lad in the School of Jurisprudence, whose diary for the

1840's reveals a serious, hard-working, joyless young man interested only in work and possessing study habits which today would label him a "grind." The grave and impersonal young boy grew up to the mature "man of the study" without warmth or affection for other human beings. The Pobedonostsevs entertained very rarely and paid little attention to their comfort or the quality of their furnishings. In fact, they lived a thoroughly plain, simple, and even frugal life. Apparently, they gave no more than a half-dozen dinner parties in the forty years they were married. Dostoevsky, for example, was surprised that their apartment was so barren and that they had only one servant. The German ambassador found him ascetic both in appearance and in life.[2]

Throughout his life, except for plagiarism and other forms of intellectual dishonesty which he skillfully concealed, Pobedonostsev was a person of exemplary character and conduct, completely foreign to improper social behavior. He became a great admirer of Emerson during the 1860's, and the standards of the proper New Englander supplemented those he had acquired in the strict and severe home on Bread Lane. He apparently did not drink vodka or wine. However, until he was about fifty, he did not censure those who did, even to excess. He was naturally to some degree indignant concerning the wasteful and immoral behavior of St. Petersburg society, but he recognized that "purity exists only in the desert" and that false idols have always tempted some men successfully. As late as February, 1877, he wrote with gentle irony of a conversation in the heir's study during a party at Anichkov Palace. He was amused to hear Grand Duke Vladimir Alexandrovich and Princess Maria Vasil'evna Vorontsov condemn contemporary luxury and reminisce on the simplicity of earlier days, on an occasion when the princess was dressed in great luxury and wore many diamonds and the Grand Duke wore an elegant uniform. However, Pobedonostsev went on to say that the princess was "one of our most remarkable and attractive women," that he loved her lively spirit and sensible conversation, and that she belonged to those "who have loved much even though they have perhaps sinned."[3]

Pobedonostsev was a moralist throughout his life, and the puritanical viewpoint pervades all of his work. However, the Balkan crisis turned him into a savage critic of society and gave his puritanism the sharp edge which thereafter he turned against the world and which provides an essential flavor to his thought. He railed at senseless luxury, particularly among women who spent a thousand

rubles for a gown while collecting a hundred rubles for the Red
Cross. The strain of the Balkan war led him to denounce all waste
and to urge the establishment of a league against luxury in dress by
women of good character, who would agree on what could be worn,
select and educate dressmakers, and establish drawing rooms to
which only women in simple dress would be invited. Later, dances,
fancy balls, and elaborate banquets came under his criticism. In the
late 1880's and in the 1890's, he worked hard to establish teetotalling
societies, convinced by then that drunkenness was a national scandal
and that temperance societies were ineffective. Ambassador von
Schweinitz wrote in February, 1882, shortly after he had met Pobedonostsev, that he talked like an anchorite and had the point of
view of a medieval monk. An English observer noted that he was
"a man who would have sent his own son to Siberia."[4]

He had always a reflective, pessimistic, and melancholy cast of
mind. Secular celebrations did not excite his interest, although funerals and cemeteries attracted both him and his wife. He wrote on
a number of occasions that the beginning of a new year was always
a melancholy day and that he could not understand why others celebrated. Even in early middle age, he was obsessed by the flight of
time and the approach of death. On January 4, 1875, he wrote:
"Why rejoice, when another drop has disappeared from the cup and
one can hear a deep echo from the dark chasm into which it fell?"
A year earlier, writing in the summertime about the Russian countryside, he declared that a Russian village was the best place in the
world in summer, "especially when it stands on old foundations,
or memorials to fathers and grandfathers, on old graves, on an old
church and a homestead filled with old people. Alas, few such corners remain."

He loved funerals and often wrote about those he attended. He
told Catherine Tiutchev in August, 1881, that his wife had returned
enthusiastic from a funeral celebrated in Sergiev monastery, near
Peterhof, because the day and the singing had been so beautiful and
the burial ceremony so peaceful, "a holiday not to death but to life."
Long before he became old and very pessimistic, melancholy poetry
fascinated him. He loved verses about twilight, such as this one:

> The radiant colours in the West are paling,
> Fast fades the gold, and green, and crimson light,
> And softly comes, each trivial object veiling,
> The all-ennobling mystery of night.[5]

There are few elements in human affairs more difficult to measure with any confidence than the depth and sincerity of a man's most private religious beliefs and feelings. So far as we can tell, Pobedonostsev throughout his life was a man of deep religious faith; Orthodoxy was the central fact of existence both for him and for his wife. He prayed devoutly every day, he attended religious services every Sunday, preferably in small churches and at early Mass so he could be among those who came to worship reverently and quietly, and he very often attended services Saturday evenings. Throughout his adult life, he spent Easter Week and a few days before Christmas at a monastery, and he frequently spent other periods in monasteries for reflection and rest. Long before he became Director General of the Synod, he had acquired such a reputation as a man of faith and as a churchman that clerics visiting St. Petersburg always called on him. However, he showed remarkably little interest in doctrine. He emphasized heavily the emotional and ceremonial aspects of Orthodox Christianity: the church bells, the splendor of the services, particularly the choral singing, and the cherished memories particular churches and holidays held for him. Throughout his life, he preferred the "Christian" early morning Mass, evening vespers, opportunities for quiet prayer in deserted churches or ancient monasteries, which he sometimes referred to as "green islands," and the beauty of services in which deacons of especially devout bearing and excellent voice participated. Thus, in some ways the Russian Orthodox Church provided the romance and majesty and splendor which were otherwise absent from his life. It also brought him among the Russian people, from whom he isolated himself in his study, and it renewed his faith in himself and in man. Indeed, in a quite uncharacteristic turn of phrase, he once wrote Catherine Tiutchev that "a sea of Orthodox people embraced us and poured prayers over us" in a most impressive Trinity Sunday service.[6]

His asceticism and puritanism are reflected in his life and thought, and the forbidding visage he presented to the ordinary world was to some degree responsible for the reputation he acquired as the Grand Inquisitor. He had a softer, gentler side, however, which was almost never shown to the public. For example, in 1865 he founded an organization to support a school for orphans, in memory of the Grand Duke Nicholas Alexandrovich. He devoted the proceeds of his translation of Thomas à Kempis, *The Imitation of Christ*, of which eight editions were published between 1869 and 1899, to this organization and its school. He drafted the constitution of the Red Cross, although late in his life he considered it and its work fraudulent, and he also helped to support a number of other charitable institutions. He contributed a translation of a favorite Emerson essay, "Works and Days," to a volume of essays edited by Goncharov, Kraevskii, and others to collect funds for those affected by the 1873 famine. The income from the sale of 20,000 copies of a lecture he gave in 1880 in memory of Empress Maria Alexandrovna, the wife of Alexander II, was assigned to assist poor seminarians.

Letters to his closest friends indicate that his private charities, especially to aged poor whom he had known for a long time, were very considerable. Dostoevsky's widow has even recalled the successful effort he made to delay the exile of a woman who was ill and whose husband was considered a dangerous criminal. His most private letters reveal that he was especially generous with poor teachers and professors and that he helped support a number of old ladies who had no other means of assistance.[7]

During his last few months, when he had less than a year's salary in a savings account and considered selling the family home on Bread Lane, one of his principal concerns was the problems those whom he had assisted would face after his death. He wrote in October, 1906, that he had given 47,000 rubles (approximately $23,500) to people in need between 1890 and 1905. His salary in 1897 was raised to 18,000 rubles a year and was 22,000 rubles when he was retired in 1905. Moreover, between 1890 and 1905 he received a total of 58,217 rubles in royalties from the sale of his books. In other words, his private charities were considerable. His knowledge of them was also precise.[8]

His charitable actions began in the late 1860's and probably represented in part the humanizing influence of Grand Duchess Helen Pavlovna, Baroness Edith Raden, and the other generous women whom he knew at court and who were deeply engaged in charitable enterprises of one kind or another. At the same time, they no doubt sprang from the deep Christian spirit he had imbibed at home and which strongly affected his view of life around him, though perhaps not of Russian life in general. His generosities are especially noteworthy because he was so obsessed with money and kept such a precise and niggardly account of his income and expenditures. He refused to borrow money, hated the very idea of credit, and felt insecure unless he had no financial worries, attitudes which almost certainly had their roots in his childhood, when his father had worked so hard to educate his large family and to provide them a respectable life in a society in which the Pobedonostsevs did not possess social standing. Genteel poverty and jollity need not be associated, although they often are, especially in fiction, and ambition may also be clothed in casual and relaxed approaches. However, the Pobedonostsev family atmosphere was austere and even grim, and the puritanical training he received at home colored and strengthened his precise, pedantic approach toward life. This approach helps to explain both his scorn for idlers and his venomous criticism of abstract ideas.

Not only were Pobedonostsev's personal accounts meticulously detailed, but he displayed a remarkably petty interest in the income from his various publications. Authors are traditionally sensitive to every action which can affect the sales and influence of the works which have consumed their time and intellectual energy. However, the abundant material available concerning Pobedonostsev's direction of the Synod Press, the attention he devoted to advertising his publications, his correspondence with the business manager of the Moscow office of the Press, and other evidence reveal that he was almost scandalously involved in the sale of his books, and possessed an extraordinary interest in increasing income from them. In the last twenty years of his life, he had the Synod Press advertise his publications on the covers of all of its books and pamphlets. He pressed Michael Katkov, Sergei Petrovskii, and other newspaper editors to ensure that his books and pamphlets received attention early, and he devoted careful effort to the advertisements for which he paid. He harassed his printers and publishers about bookstores which were deficient in making his publications available, about the frequency and accuracy of their accounts for each volume, and about suggestions designed to increase sales, from more attractive jackets to a range of discounts. In short, his concern with money was considerably greater than one would expect and sheds some illumination upon his attitudes and ideas.[9]

The petty puritanism and the zeal and care Pobedonostsev devoted to his finances help explain the style of his thought and the thrust of his thinking and actions. The fervor he devoted to his cause is also reflected in the intellectual dishonesty which marred the work of the last three decades of his life. In fact, his righteousness may have become fierce because of his own secret shame at transgressions he would have denounced in anyone else. A frank person, never touched personally by the breath of corruption, ruthless for what he believed the good of Russia, he often deliberately distorted the meaning of some of the books and articles he translated and edited. Although he had been trained as a lawyer and was himself a competent historian, he often failed to indicate in any way that he was not translating the original fully and accurately. Those passages which he did not distort by omissions were translated correctly. This quality is a great aid for anyone who seeks to understand Pobedonostsev, because his omission of sentences, paragraphs, and even pages often revealed his views perhaps more clearly than what he actually wrote or translated.

Perhaps a few examples will suffice to demonstrate how his zeal as a publicist or propagandist overcame his training and the high intellectual and moral standards he claimed for himself and required of others. Some of these unmarked excisions are revealing in their very pettiness; others illuminate his whole philosophy by their significance. Thus, his translation of Emerson's essay, "Works and Days," omitted election day and Thanksgiving Day from the list of American national holidays Emerson had included. His translation of Edmond Demolins' *A quoi tient la supériorité des Anglo-Saxons* included the critique made by William II of the German school system for allegedly neglecting character and failing to prepare for a life of struggle, but eliminated the passage in which Demolins attacked the German emperor for asserting that the function of schools was to produce tools of the state. Similarly, his version of Demolins' *L'Education nouvelle* omitted Demolins' criticism of a French law prohibiting foreigners from teaching other languages in France.[10]

When publishing translations which dealt with the church and the state, he was similarly precise in his excisions, without any indication of this fact. Thus, his translation of a part of Herbert Spencer's *The Study of Sociology* did not include Spencer's criticism of the drift toward increased government action in social fields and toward a more centralized government. In the same chapter, Pobedonostsev omitted, also without any indication of this fact, a brief section in which Spencer declared that morals could not be taught, even by the school or by the church. Finally, in his translation from a chapter in Gladstone's *The Impregnable Rock of Holy Scripture*, which he deeply admired, he omitted Gladstone's very last paragraph, with no indication of this fact:

I have yet one more closing word. I have desired to make
this humble offering at the shrine of Christian belief in general,
and have sought wholly to avoid the questions which concern
this or that particular form of it. For there is a common cause,
which warrants and requires common efforts. Far be from me
the intention hereby to undervalue particular beliefs. I have
not intentionally said a word to disparage any of them. It will
in my view be an evil day, and a day of calamity, when men are
tempted, even by the vision of a holy object, to abate, in any
region or in the smallest fraction, the authority of conscience,
or to forget that the supreme title and the supreme efficacy of
truth lies in its integrity.[11]

He not only grossly misrepresented, by omissions, the thoughts
of those whose works he "translated," but he was also guilty of deliberate distortion of the words of others and of plagiarism. Thus,
in January, 1887, he requested that Bishop Savva, who was editing
the works of Metropolitan Filaret, remove from one of Filaret's letters an indication that a member of the imperial family had not been
a member of the Orthodox Church. Two years later, when Alexander III in some anger asked him to explain his policies toward the
Baltic Lutherans, for which the Russian government was being bitterly attacked, in his defense he fabricated a damaging quotation
from a sermon supposedly made by a Lutheran bishop in Riga in
1864 and misrepresented an official report of the same year on the
Baltic area. He admitted this privately when queried by the German
ambassador, but argued that no one could expect such a busy man
as he to go to the sources for every statement he made.[12]

His "borrowing" from Bakhmetev's book on the history of the
Church is only one of several examples of plagiarism. Perhaps the
most interesting illustration is revealed by comparing the final section of the fourth chapter of Max Nordau's popular *Die conventiollen Lügen der Kulturmenschheit*, which was published in 1883,
and Pobedonostsev's chapter in *Moskovskii sbornik* (Moscow Collection) entitled "The Great Lie." Pobedonostsev clearly borrowed
ideas, phrases, and even entire sentences from Nordau, without
acknowledgment. Moreover, his correspondence reveals that he had
also inserted translations of sections of Nordau's "remarkable book,
... which contains a masterly critique of both parliamentarism and
of the press," into *Grazhdanin*, without indicating the source. The
irony is that Pobedonostsev was antisemitic and thought positivism
a mortal danger for Russia. However, he was willing to use, without

credit, the words of a Jew whom he also recognized as "a great radical and positivist."[13]

Pobedonostsev's personal qualities and temperament help explain both the fundamentals and the style of his political philosophy, which was in the Karamzin tradition of Russian thought in its attitude toward the state. He thought first of the state as naturally as an American thinks first of the individual. The individual, indeed humanity itself, had less significance in his thinking than did the state, and was relegated to fourth place behind the state, the Church, and the family. The state, and the Church in union with the state, were the foundations upon which his political philosophy was erected, with the family a cooperating instrument of these senior agencies, to all of which the individual was subject. Even so, and perhaps because of this, his philosophy can best be explained by beginning with his view of the nature of man, of Russian man in particular, and of the evils of his age.

Pobedonostsev was an eternal foe of abstractions or general theories and of those who used them. At the same time, his own views inevitably hardened into abstract theories which became sharply defined as he grew older and more conservative. For him, as for all reactionaries, man by nature was "weak, vicious, worthless, and rebellious." Like Hobbes, who has been called "the Baroque forerunner of the modern police state" and like the philosophers and practitioners of authoritarianism, he "vilified the human nature." His writings are saturated with descriptions of the frailties and follies of man and of the particular evils of the age which nourished these inherent weaknesses. In some private meditations, he wrote in November, 1860, "Every man is a lie, and every word said by him is an idle word of self-delusion." This quotation from Thomas à Kempis reflected his views concerning the "nothingness" of man when he was young. Maurice Bompard, the French ambassador to St. Petersburg from 1903 to 1908, found the old statesman still convinced that man was fundamentally and basically weak and that all his instincts led him to evil. In fact, Pobedonostsev viewed man with a combination of pity and horror and was mildly surprised that humanity had survived.[14]

Russians constituted a particular case, because he thought he was well acquainted with the nature of the Russian man and because he was convinced that Russians by nature had peculiar flaws. Thus, he believed that "inertness and laziness are generally characteristic of the Slavonic nature" and that for these reasons Russians

292 POBEDONOSTSEV: HIS LIFE AND THOUGHT

more than most people required relentlessly firm and vigorous leadership. He thought Russians were particularly obsessed with money, power, and drink and that they were marked by "decomposition and weakness and untruth." He once declared that outside the imperial palaces lay Russia, "an icy desert and an abode of the Bad Men." When pressed by foreigners in private conversations to justify his policies, he cited particular weaknesses of Russian character, made worse by the simple fact that Russia was a century behind even Central Europe.[15]

A corollary to his assumption that man was by nature evil and weak was his condemnation of those who assumed that man could reason or that reason could be an effective tool for any but a tiny minority, whom he called "the aristocracy of intellect." Except for the minority, he saw man as a vessel, an object of soft wax molded and formed by three forces utterly beyond his control: the unconscious, land, and history. Probably no statesman in modern times, not even Hitler, so directly and openly glorified the unconscious as he did. Noting that "the healthy do not think about health," he urged that society be allowed by men to operate as an organ of the body does, "simply and unconsciously." He declared that "true, sound intelligence is not logical, but intuitive, because the aim of intelligence consists not in finding or showing reasons but in believing and trusting."

Under this philosophy, of course, knowledge itself is evil, except for knowledge of one's national history. He would have accepted the apothegm of Barrès that the necessary foundation of a state is a cemetery, for he saw the "congenial seed" of a nationality in "the unconscious sphere of feeling, accumulated from our ancestors." Since the capabilities of all but the minority are so limited, man must realize simply that his roots are in the past and that he derives from his ancestors. More he cannot understand. The man who is not satisfied with instinctive feeling and who by himself seeks truth and his own equilibrium automatically idolizes reason and becomes a dangerous fanatic, threatening the unity and the very existence of society. The great, essential, and living truths are above the mind, and the great mass of men can receive ideas only through feeling. The will of man is hidden deep in the soul, where the intellect cannot penetrate. The only supports of man's will can be faith and religious feeling, and the Christian faith alone can perforate the principles of egotism and pride, reach the core of man, and give him true freedom in his recognition of necessity. Pobedonostsev so viewed the nature of man that, although he wished ardently to end drinking and drunkenness and supported teetotalling societies, he admitted that prohibition was impossible. In short, society was forced to tolerate sin and evil.[16]

There were exceptions, of course, and his view was not always that bleak. He had a special affection for childhood and believed either that children did not possess the faults and frailties he noted among their elders or that corrupt society was responsible for the flourishing of these hidden qualities after childhood. Pobedonostsev's "good society," if he could envision one, was like Carlyle's, with freedom in discipline, no sense of time, rest and sleep, and a mother's love.

Some few individuals also escaped the fatal flaw which affected all other humans. Grand Duchess Helen Pavlovna, Baroness Edith Raden, Nicholas Ilminskii, and Sergei Rachinskii were among these few. Others, who lived quietly as unsung heroes in the countryside, had been born with or had somewhere learned the harmony and equilibrium of thought and action, and had come to recognize that the body works best without thought, silently, "without system." These sound and sensible men and women unknowingly and unconsciously lived blameless lives and developed unmatched character.[17]

He knew little of the peasant or of rural life, had no especial veneration for established peasant traditions or institutions, and indeed was far removed from the ideas of the Slavophils, who had had particular respect for the *narod* and their institutions. Given his view of human nature, he could hardly idolize the people in mass when he had such scorn for them as individuals. However, on his first trip through European Russia, one made in the summer of 1863 with the then heir to the throne, he was deeply impressed by the enthusiastic respect shown for the heir "by the *Rus* of Moscow and of Suzdal from the depths of the Russian heart, . . . with their purely Russian blood, clear eyes, satisfied faces, radiant with happiness, beauty, and intelligence." This view of the *narod* was evanescent, but it did return on occasion when he read the letters and books of Rachinskii and Ilminskii, who were working daily among the peasantry. Above all, however, the *narod* appear in his letters to Alexander III, for in times of crisis he identified himself as the true interpreter of the *narod*, that mystical body of Muscovites and of the Russian rural population who supported all of the policies he advocated and who were the reservoir of the pure and good from which the salvation of Russia would ultimately come. In purporting to speak for the simple and unspoiled, he was of course simply using old-fashioned Slavophil nationalism against a simple-minded tsar who had already been led to believe that Russia's problems were due to feeble leadership, scheming bureaucrats, and ambitious intellectuals.[18]

Like most dour and pessimistic philosophers and statesmen, he was convinced that his own age was subject to particularly corrosive evils, all thriving because of the basic weakness of Russian character and of Russian society. The principal danger he fought was the presumption that man was perfectible, which led to doubt, discontent, irritation, and fantasies on one hand, and explained laziness, the vogue of credit, and other modern and artificial approaches to life on the other. At the heart of this basic misconception and in part responsible for it was the belief that man was a rational creature and that "the fanaticism of formal logic" could resolve the problems the state faced. He urged that knowledge was the root of evil, and that doubt provided access to it. He considered speculative thought "destructive, suicidal, and sinful." Proud, sophisticated intellectuals in particular did not recognize that rationalism is an art and not a science. They were instead seduced by arguments, abstractions, and swollen self-interest into attitudes which were irrelevant, subject to vast and rapid fluctuations, and highly dangerous. He would have accepted Iurii Samarin's phrase, "Revolution is nothing else but rationalism in action," and he would have agreed with Pascal that most problems arose "because of man's inability to sit still in a room." The belief that man and society could be improved by individual or group action and that reason, not faith, should guide Russia was responsible for most of Russia's problems, particularly for the subversive doctrines concerning parliamentary and democratic government and concerning unbelief.[19]

The vogue of rationalism, which corroded all of Russia's healthy values and beliefs, was also responsible for the vanity and vulgarity of Russian life, the increasing hypocrisy, and the spread of drunkenness, even among the clergy. The press was a reflection of these vices as well as a significant contributor. He considered newspapers "the most irresponsible and violent despotism," "the fatal disintegrating force," one of the causes of "decomposition and weakness and untruth." Throughout his life, as a profoundly anti-intellectual moralist, he found Russia characterized by falsehood, irresponsible talk, deceit, injustice, cupidity, hypocrisy, and vulgarity. These and the human foibles which so annoyed him—the theater during Lent, gambling, ostentatious dress, excessive drinking—were all due to the cult of rationalism. "Vanity, vanity, all is vanity" was his perpetual croak of despair. "All fades, all vanishes, all disintegrates, all deceives."[20]

In this grim picture, he identified three institutions which might save Russia and even enable her to provide guidance for other threatened peoples. These institutions, which were at the heart of his philosophy, were the state, the Russian Orthodox Church, and the family, with their functions and authority overlapping and intermingled, but with the state central. As a highly educated, widely read intellectual who came from an academic family, he was also much interested in the educational system as a contributor to the establishment of a stable society. However, he was convinced that an educational system reflected a society, its character, its history, and its climate, and that it neither could nor should be used to transform it. He did agree that "learning is light," but he ridiculed the proposal that Russia should consider the establishment of compulsory and free primary education. He thought laws restricting child labor were unreasonable and senseless. He was certain that the educational system in its every aspect should remain under the direct control of the state and the Church, as the 1884 regulations established for Russian universities and his active campaign for parish schools reveal. He believed fervently that "a university in the true meaning of the word must serve society with its high authority for analyzing, testing, and controlling all ideas rising in that society."[21]

His views with regard to the character and role of education were consistent throughout his life, except for his recognition after 1880 that elementary education of a primitive kind was a necessity and for the lively interest he developed in his last decade in secondary school education for the elite. He paid remarkably little attention to higher education until the 1890's, apparently because he did not believe that some of the ills of which he complained within the government could be eliminated by improved training for bureaucrats. When he did begin to direct his attention to the secondary and higher education of Russia's future ruling group, he borrowed heavily from studies of England's public schools, which impressed him in every way. For the future statesmen and the "enlightened minority," a detailed knowledge of their family, nation, and Church, and of the climatic and geographic conditions of Russian society were vital. Since they were to be educated for important state duties, they were to know foreign languages, literatures, and societies, though not so well as their own. They were to acquire knowledge of the antagonistic states and racial groups surrounding their nation. They were not only to be learned, but they were also to be experienced "social authorities," sagacious, intelligent, and respected. They should, moreover, possess wives who would read together with them evenings and who would cooperate in charitable work in the neighborhood.

Pobedonostsev was very precise not only in his insistence upon "the harmonious development of all the human faculties" of the ruling group, but also in his prescription of pedagogical methods. Thus, he advocated that this elite be educated in boarding schools for nine months of the year and live with their families the remaining three months. Life at school was to resemble family life, for a small group of students was to live in the home of each instructor. The faculty was to consist not of learned specialists, but of well-rounded men who would dress as the students did, join in their games, and act as fathers as well as instructors. The curriculum was to create character as well as intelligence, to stimulate incentive and loyalty to duty, and to ensure both physical health and clarity of expression. Learning was to be acquired by seeing, doing, and travelling, not by lectures or memory.

He did not develop so fully his ideas with respect to the highest levels of formal education, but his ideas for university life, the curriculum, the faculty, and pedagogical methods were similar to those for the secondary school. The ideal professor was one who devoted his entire life to his students, with great patience, enthusiasm, and love for them and for his service. He was specifically not to be an intellectual, because this frequently led to irreligion, to liberalism, and to poisoning the entire educational system.[22]

So far as the mass of the Russian people was concerned, he declared that "schools must fit the people." Since most children in the community must earn their living, most of their education must be conducted at home, where they should master their father's work. Sons of miners should become miners, sons of sailors, sailors, and sons of peasants, peasants. The only formal education of these millions should be provided by the Church in a brief period of primary school, which should not be a step to higher education. Knowledge should not be the goal: indeed, no well-ordered schools should have examinations. In fact, the pupils should first learn, "know thyself," which to him meant their "milieu, their country, their nature, their people with its soul." The main purpose of primary education was to instruct the youngsters to know, love, and fear God, to love their native land, and to honor and obey their parents. The emphasis was therefore moral, rather than intellectual, and the brief period of primary school should therefore concentrate on the "four R's," reading, writing, arithmetic, and religion. He would have agreed with Wellington that "instruction without religion produces only clever devils," and he was convinced that "educated and unemployed fools," marred by vanity and conceit, constituted a tremendous danger for Russia.

Thus, for Pobedonostsev, the primary school should provide Russian children with "the basic elements of intellectual and moral culture" and should also "leave them in that place and in the milieu in which they belong." He emphasized that everyone should remain "in that place, in that area, in that corner where fate has placed him." The place of women was therefore in the home. He feared lest primary education excite a love of learning or create "discontent and ambition." He would have approved the statement of Nicholas I, "Instruction must never be given except to teach one to fill better the office to which the pupil is destined. In the countryside, the school sometimes does more harm than good. By teaching peasants to read, one exposes them to knowing bad books."[23]

Just as the curriculum of the primary school should emphasize virtue and native Russian skills, so should the teacher exemplify the best qualities of his country. He should naturally be an Orthodox Christian from the same stratum of society as his pupils. He should be concise, clear, patient, lively, attentive, well mannered, highly disciplined, and well prepared. Finally, he should be completely absorbed by and dedicated to his work, not a "hireling" who considers his position a "temporary stage toward a better arrangement of his own life." Like Socrates, or an unsung hero, he should love his work and should be prepared to give his life to his calling.[24]

The family for Pobedonostsev was clearly a more central institution than was the primary school. Indeed, he saw the family as the fundamental instrument for educating and controlling man. He referred to it as "the spiritual and cultural nursery of citizens," "the foundation of the state," and "the eternal element of prosperous societies." For him, the family was "the ultimate social institution." It also reflected the character of the society of which it was a part and therefore served as a perfect illustration of it.

During the years in which he was a scholar in the field of Russian

civil law, he devoted a great deal of attention to marriage, the powers
and responsibilities of the parents, especially the husband, the problems connected with separation and divorce, the rights of children,
issues raised by illegitimacy and adoption, and all of the complications connected with inheritance. His *Kurs grazhdanskago prava*
(Course on Civil Law) reflected enormous learning not only on the
history and position of the Russian family, but also on the family
among the national minorities on the western frontiers and in central Asia, among other Slavic peoples, in western Europe, and in
antiquity. He even read carefully and summarized the views of
Lewis Morgan, whose study of kinship relations and rights among
the Seneca Indians was published by the Smithsonian Institute in
1871. Morgan's *Systems of Consanguinity and Affinity in the Human
Family* was studied carefully by Marx and Engels and heavily influenced the views of Engels in particular on the family.[25]

Pobedonostsev translated two important French and German
studies into Russian, Heinrich Thiersch's *Uber christliches Familienleben*, published originally in 1854 and produced in Russian in
two editions, one in 1861 and the second forty years later, and
Frederick Le Play's *La Constitution essentielle de l'humanité*, published originally in 1881 and translated in 1897. Thiersch was a conservative Protestant theologian and humanist from Marburg who
emphasized the religious and social character of marriage and the
family. Pobedonostsev was especially impressed by Thiersch's ideas
concerning the personal qualities required and produced by marriage and family life, the powers of the husband in a Christian marriage, and the role the state church should play.

Le Play was a conservative French Catholic engineer and sociologist who travelled widely throughout Europe in particular and
whose books, articles, journal, and organization helped create the
Social Catholic movement in France in the last decade of the nineteenth century. Le Play's ideas had considerable influence in France
during the dark days after 1870 and again during the 1930's and
1940's, when Marshall Pétain and his government sought to emphasize some of the institutions and values Le Play had. Pobedonostsev may have been introduced to Le Play and his work by Count
Sergei G. Stroganov, who had met the Frenchman in 1837. He particularly appreciated Le Play's concept of the role the family should
play in a stable society. He wrote an essay about Le Play, sought to
persuade Count Dmitrii Tolstoy when he was Minister of Interior
of the virtues of Le Play's view, and through Olga Novikov called

Le Play to the attention of Gladstone. The great English liberal politician thought highly of Le Play, except for his attitudes toward the Old Regime, Napoleon, and the Papacy. Pobedonostsev agreed with these criticisms, but considered Le Play one of the most profound minds Europe produced in the nineteenth century.[26]

Pobedonostsev was convinced that the family was "the foundation of all social life and order," that moral development and all human welfare were based upon it, that it was "the foundation of all enduring happiness," and that it even resembled and "anticipated" the Kingdom of God. In Russia and among Russians, "for all those familiar with our history and conditions of life," it had its origins both in Christian doctrine and in history. It was based upon religious faith and upon a religious ceremony. Marriage therefore was an indissoluble contract of a sacred character, broken at peril to society when that society allowed "personal egotism" to triumph over higher values. Pobedonostsev opposed civil marriage, separation, and divorce. He considered divorce a blow against the highest interests of the state, as well as a violation of a solemn contract sanctified by the Church, recognized by the state, and approved by society. He agreed that women might suffer because of such views, but he reasoned that this religious definition of marriage defended their "high moral position" and dignity better than did or could any other marriage system.[27]

For Pobedonostsev, the family was responsible for repressing the nature of the child, harnessing and controlling one of man's most fundamental instincts, providing for the orderly perpetuation of the human race, ensuring social stability, and maintaining history and tradition. He believed, as did Le Play, that the child from birth was weak and that God in entrusting it to the parents gave them the choice of raising either a dutiful or a parasitic and destructive child. The parental power, "the only power established by God in the Decalogue, is the highest power," and "willing obedience . . . is the only virtue of the child." The function of the parents, particularly the father, was to repress the child's instincts firmly and surely, through force, love, and fear. "Faithfulness, love, sacrifice, and obedience" should be learned by the child in the home. The father should also instill into the child knowledge of and respect for the Decalogue and provide him the physical and moral education to enable him to assume his alloted place in society.

Pobedonostsev recognized that economic and other worldly considerations were important factors in marriage and in family life.

He also believed that the state's role and interest in marriage and in the family placed upon it some responsibilities and duties, with regard to defending the sanctity of the religious bond and to guarding the interests of minors. It should, in short, seek to ensure that relationships between parents and children were of a Christian character, like those between Christian masters and servants. In fact, the Pobedonostsev translations of Thiersch and Le Play included several strong declarations concerning the responsibility of the state to promote social reform through assisting in the establishment of cooperatives and of workers' associations. The European Social Christian view of society and the family led Pobedonostsev to urge upon the state active social policies which he ordinarily rejected, probably because he thought carrying out such policies beyond the capacities of the Russian state system.[28]

Pobedonostsev's research into the position of the family in various societies led him naturally to study various forms of communities, such as the *obshchina* or commune in Russia, the *zadruga* among some of the southern Slavs, and other such groups in other societies. He read a great deal about the commune and other such organizations, but his knowledge was not clear or precise. In fact, as a city boy throughout his life, he knew almost nothing of the Russian countryside and its problems. Except as a member of the Church or of one of the sects or as a statistic, the Russian peasant did not exist for him. Moreover, he wrote nothing significant about the commune until 1875. From the beginning, he was a supporter of it, but believed that "different political and economic conditions" would undermine it as soon as "the economic laws" visibly at work in western Europe began to have an effect within Russia. To him, the commune had many virtues for Russia's stage of development at that time. It had kept central the idea that land was "the base of the state's strength, the foundation of the whole structure, the main store of economic strength, the repository of the natural elements of nationality in all their basic characteristics." It preserved the belief that the land was the peasants', it provided the optimum form for economic development by pooling labor and capital at the necessarily primitive level, it satisfied the primary needs of all, and it ensured the government a reasonably effective system for collecting taxes and recruiting soldiers. As long as the commune operated satisfactorily, the family would remain a lively institution and Russia would manage to avoid perils which harassed some European states.[29]

On the other hand, he recognized that the commune was both a primitive and a temporary institution which would wither away when more powerful economic forces appeared. In fact, even before 1880, he noted briefly that what he came to call *semeinye uchastki*, or family farms, would and should replace the commune. By the late 1880's, he concluded that the state should seek to hasten the dismantling of the commune and its replacement by small, free farms. This view is presented in considerable detail in an article in 1889 in *Russkii vestnik* (Russian Herald), which he inserted later into the last edition of his *Kurs grazhdanskago prava*. In effect, he urged that the Russian government seek the creation of farms much like the American homesteads, of which he read a great deal and which impressed him enormously. He was in fact advocating "the wager on the strong" which Stolypin launched in 1906.

Pobedonostsev was concerned far more with the peasants in the communes than with the large landowners, whose estates were breaking up in the last third of the nineteenth century. Convinced that the old regime on the land could not survive, he urged a national policy of establishing a landholding system in which each peasant family would receive property, "sufficient to satisfy the needs of the family so that its members do not have to go elsewhere for seasonal work to support themselves." His definition of the size of the property was always vague, in part because of the nature of the problem and in part because he was so poorly informed concerning rural life. He wrote several times of a small holding, "according to the type developed in North America in the Homestead farm," and he apparently had in mind from one hundred to three hundred *desiatin*, or from three hundred to eight hundred acres.[30]

According to Pobedonostsev, the problem was not that the system of landholding had to be changed—economic change was inevitable, as he thought it had been in western Europe—but the way in which it was achieved and timed. Thus, while convinced that the commune was doomed, he also wrote that "it would be extremely dangerous to adopt measures which would lead *artificially* [sic] to the decay of the commune." First of all, the state had to direct and control the reorganization. The essential economic and social information was not available, and only the central state authorities could collect and analyze these data. The transfer should also be directed in such a way as to prevent "merchants, Jews, and kulak-usurers, a great evil for the state and for the local population," from acquiring land. The government should establish a peasant class with "indivisible and inalienable" ownership of property and with a fixed domicile and roots in a particular hearth. Finally, the state should make provisions for capital and credit for the new landowners, so that the change should be economically and socially productive and so that emigration to the cities could be controlled. This would prevent the creation of an urban landless and unemployed proletariat with a high crime rate. In short, he produced a program for Russia's rural population which he hoped would maintain and strengthen the autocratic system of government and at the same time adapt Russia's land system to new economic forces.[31]

The Church was incomparably more important for Pobedonostsev than even the family, the institutions related to the family, or the organization of economic life in the countryside. In fact, the Church and religion were central to his life and saturated his beliefs and policies. Orthodoxy meant the membership of the Russian Orthodox Church or the ethnic Great Russians when he spoke or wrote in general terms about Russia or about the state. While he did recognize that Russia contained other religious groups and many national minorities, he saw the Russians in the Russian Orthodox Church, with those White Russians and Little Russians who were also Orthodox, at the center of his world. The Old Believers and the sects resided in an outer circle, and the non-Russians—Finns, Germans, Poles, Jews, Uzbeks, and others—lived on the empire's borders in a shadowy, distant circle, given serious thought only when he had to consider issues or policies involving them. Doctrine simply was not a subject of discussion for him, in part because he was not interested in doctrine and in part because he thought it such a rooted matter for any religious group that it was beyond discussion.[32]

He was convinced that Russia was more than a country, that Orthodoxy was more than a religion, and that they together constituted a world. He considered Russia not necessarily superior to other societies and cultures, but different, so different that perhaps only a Russian could understand his religion and country, just as perhaps only an Englishman could understand his religion and country. He was convinced that churches, like races or ethnic groups, had distinct virtues and defects, reflecting their history and tradition. The Russian Orthodox Church, for example, was weakened by ignorance, superstition, and inactivity, but these were temporary and reflected the country's backwardness. Similarly, Roman Catholicism, Anglicanism, and other forms of Protestantism had particular weaknesses which reflected their histories. Whatever its shortcomings, he saw the Russian Orthodox Church as "the church of all of the people," one which answered a deep-seated popular need, and "a living organism held together by sentiment and conscience."

The Church became "identical with and inseparable from the history of the Russian *narod*" in the ninth century and had since then been the "life, truth, and full foundation of our existence." He believed that "the power of the state is based solely on the unity of consciousness between the people and the state, on the national faith." Because the history of the Church and the state had been so entwined for almost a thousand years, the Church was and should always be the state or national church, with no other religious groups allowed or tolerated. In fact, he sought to reduce and ultimately to destroy the power of all other religious groups within the empire. He thought that the Russian state should ignore and refuse to provide official recognition of beliefs other than Orthodoxy, because recognition gave legal status, which strengthened the rival religions and helped delay the day when everyone in Russia would share the same faith. However, while he vigorously advocated forceful policies with regard to the religious minorities, he recognized that elimination of these groups would inevitably require time, because "even lies should be removed slowly."[33]

Pobedonostsev believed so strongly that the character and fate of each state were determined by religion and that sooner or later one religious group would acquire absolute dominance that he could not understand the policy of the American government regarding religious toleration. Indeed, he predicted that the Catholic Church would take advantage of the freedom the American Protestant rulers granted and would one day seize power, establish Catholicism as the state religion, and seek to root out all other faiths.[34]

Just as he believed that the nature of society and religion made coexistence of two or more religions in one state inconceivable, so also he was convinced that the union or even the close cooperation of two creeds was impossible. He declared that each racial group possessed distinctive customs and traditions, that these shaped their religious beliefs and their political institutions as well, and that it was both impossible and dangerous for one society to attempt to borrow ideas and beliefs from another or to impose its values upon another.[35] Faith is "parcelled out according to nationalities," and is "intolerant and uncompromising." Moreover, the most important elements of a faith cannot be defined, expressed, or separated, even by an articulate believer.[36]

The role of the Russian Orthodox Church was to maintain the unity in faith and belief essential for the maintenance of stability. In other words, religion was to act as a cement for society. The strong and stable society should therefore have only one religion, regardless of the number of races it contained. He wrote that "there are and there must be no Russian Baptists." He often said that he who deserts Orthodoxy "ceases to be Russian, not only in his thoughts and work, but also in his way of living and in his dress."[37]

Pobedonostsev believed that "the Church and the Church alone has allowed us to remain Russians and to unite our scattered strength." In fact, the greatest quality of the Church was its unity with the *narod*. He was persuaded that Orthodoxy alone could provide the unity without which no one would have confidence in the government or in the state. He considered that one of the greatest advantages deriving from this system was the equality provided by the unity. "Our Church is the house of the Russian man, the most hospitable house, the house where all are equal." The Church in thus satisfying one of man's elemental desires helped at the same time to strengthen the stability of society.

The Church was to accomplish its mission through providing and supporting the traditions, the loved ceremonies and spectacles, and the revered superstitions and beliefs. Pobedonostsev thought the "majestic, simple, unifying" rituals of Orthodoxy the embodiment of religious and national principles. He was enormously interested in religious song, which he valued most highly. In other words, the Church was to link society with the past and to consecrate the national history. He had great contempt for those who opposed or ridiculed his philosophy, and he considered intellectuals, those without faith who exalted reason, as Russia's most dangerous citizens. He argued that the fall of the Roman Empire was due largely to the decline of faith among the intellectuals. Indeed, his principal series of essays, *Moskovskii sbornik*, identified intellectuals and unbelief as the greatest single danger facing Russia and Europe. He so emphasized tradition and unconscious acceptance of ritual and ceremony that he considered colorful, eloquent, and even notably spiritual priests dangerous. He preferred priests who quietly promoted "unconscious conservatism." For this, the best type of priest was one firm in his beliefs and in his adherence to traditions, modest, quiet, unlearned, and devoted to his simple duties.[38]

The character and temper of Pobedonostsev's approach to the problems of government are as important as his ideas themselves. He had a positive dislike and distaste for any kind of enthusiasm or liveliness. He was extremely critical of imaginative literature, he was savage concerning eloquence, he lacked a sense of humor, and passion or high feeling was completely remote from him. Even his hatreds were cold and bureaucratic, and he lacked originality, system, or organization. In his political philosophy he was critical of anything original. In many ways, he was a Plyushkin of Russian political institutions and thought, jealously guarding all the scraps and rags of history, so long as they were old. He was not only suspicious and resentful of anything new, but, as an ambassador once noted, he saw "the work of the devil everywhere."[39]

Most, if not all, of Pobedonostsev's ideas after 1880 were borrowed directly from others. More than half of his publications during the period after 1880 were translations of others' works, and in his own writings he frequently reiterated or rephrased the ideas of other people. Moreover, he did this without any deep understanding or system. In fact, to understand Pobedonostsev's view of the state and of the Russian government, one must note carefully the position he occupied in the 1860's and 1870's and the view this gave him of the governing process. First of all, he had no close friends, above all male friends of his own age. Prince Odoevskii and Fedor Tiutchev, for example, were both a quarter of a century older than he. Dostoevsky, who cooperated closely with him in 1873 and who saw him frequently between 1877 and 1881, was only six years older than Pobedonostsev, but their friendship was quite brief and never truly close. None of the men with whom he worked, at Moscow University, in the judicial reform campaign, or in various administrative offices, became a friend. The memoirs and documents of these years reveal that he set himself apart behind an invisible social wall and had no close friendships with other Senators or members of the Council of State or with any of the leading statesmen of the day. His connections with other government leaders were remarkably slight. For example, when he joined the Council of Ministers in November, 1880, he had not met some of his new colleagues, even though they had all been high government officials in St. Petersburg for more than a decade.

The contemporaries besides Catherine Tiutchev with whom he had the warmest relations were two men who lived far from Moscow and St. Petersburg and with whom he carried on extensive correspondence. Sergei Rachinskii, a professor of botany at Moscow University until he resigned in 1866, spent the last twenty-five years of his life in the village of Tatev, near Smolensk. There he established a rural school and trained teachers for country schools, emphasizing reading, writing, arithmetic, and religious instruction. Between 1880 and his death in 1902, he wrote almost nine hundred letters to Pobedonostsev. His other closest friend, Nicholas Ilminskii, spent his adult life in Kazan, first at the seminary and later at a special school he started for training teachers to work among the non-Russian Moslem groups around Kazan. His correspondence with Pobedonostsev, most of which was published in 1895, was just as intensive as Rachinskii's. In fact, Pobedonostsev considered these distant men the voice of true Russia and often cited their views when he wished to persuade Alexander III that the Russian people supported a particular position.[40]

During his first fifteen years in St. Petersburg, his closest friends were women, generally ladies-in-waiting whom he had come to know because their function and status originally resembled his. They were almost all a generation older than he, and their greatest days of influence had ended before he came to know them. Thus, his closest confidante for twenty years was Catherine Tiutchev, who was a lady-in-waiting at the court with her sister when Pobedonostsev became a tutor there. In the 1860's and 1870's, he became known to those who did help rule Russia largely through the salons of the Grand Duchess Helen Pavlovna, the aunt of Alexander II, who died in 1873; her daughter Catherine Mikhailovna, who died twenty years later; Countess Bludov, whose salon was one of the most important in the decade after 1873; and Baronness Edith Raden. Finally, he was a favorite of the Empress Maria Fedorovna, the wife of Alexander III, and of the last empress, Alexandra Fedorovna, often breakfasting with these influential women while waiting to see their husbands. He advised them and their children on books to read or places to visit, and walked and talked with them more than with the tsars when he stayed at Tsarskoe Selo or at Yalta in the Crimea.

Thus, the people Pobedonostsev knew well at court tended to be women and most were members of an earlier generation. The collection of nine essays about departed friends which Pobedonostsev published in 1896 is quite revealing: four (including the first three) are devoted to women; one to the Aksakov family; one to Nicholas Ilminskii; one to Senator Nicholas Kalachov, who had published some of his first articles forty years earlier; and two to Alexander III. The four women about whom he wrote included three of those in whose salons he found refuge during these years, Grand Duchess Helen Pavlovna, her daughter Catherine Michailovna, and Baroness Raden.[41]

Pobedonostsev's view of the imperial family and of court life was also affected by the manner in which he entered the court and reached high position in the bureaucracy. He was introduced as a tutor, a bright and promising young university lecturer and government bureaucrat with no great connections and no important family. His rise in many ways was spectacular, but it was due to his own ability, to grinding hard work, and to simple good fortune. He remained an outsider, he lacked defenders, he was always aware that even his intellectual merit might not ensure his position, and he was surrounded by men of inferior ability who usually owed their rank and power to family connections or court intrigue. If it is difficult for a man to be a hero to his valet, it is even more demanding for him to acquire distinction in the eyes of his tutor. Thus, the views of the court which Pobedonostsev received were not attractive ones; the salons of the grand old ladies and the tutor's chair both served to disillusion him about the character of the St. Petersburg government.

Finally, the peculiarities of the angle at which Pobedonostsev was introduced to high position gave him a singular definition of authority or power and of the way in which the government worked. The contempt he had for the bureaucracy, his faith in autocratic rule and his scorn for the autocrats he knew and their advisors, his belief that power ought to be husbanded and sheltered from the view of the public or its representatives, his conviction that "curves rule" in human affairs and that the central art of government is manipulation, and his conclusion that only a highly trained and knowledgeable elite could govern effectively—all these attitudes and ideas were shaped to some degree by the women who drew him into their circles and by his service as a tutor to the future tsars.[42]

During the twenty-five years he was under continuous attack as the man most responsible for the government's repressive policies, even his most violent critics did not accuse him of profiting from his position, of assisting friends and relatives to advance in the bureaucracy or to profit from business with the state, or of being devoted to anything but his principles, harmful though they may have been. Even his most bitter critics admitted that Pobedonostsev neither sought power nor was grasping and ambitious. He preferred the power behind the throne or the role of invisible governor to that of ruling directly. Shortly after being named Director General of the Synod, the only important official administrative position he held, he wrote to the heir that he had always envied those who had minor and undemanding positions in which they could work quietly.

> But people are so insane that they always try to enlarge their destiny and to extend their fate. I am not guilty in this. I have always feared to widen my responsibilities, but, against my will, fate has carried me further and further from my quiet enclosures and brought me to my present activity. I am not complaining, because I see in this the will of God, but I tremble before the great test, and I consider my life ended, that is, my life for my own sake. Now, I am bound hand and foot by fate.[43]

Somewhat later, Pobedonostsev wrote to Catherine Tiutchev, "I have always looked on it [power] as on a calamity, knowing that one in power must lose his freedom and become a servant to all." He was often compared to Speransky, both by his contemporaries and by later observers, because both were the sons and grandsons of priests, were interested in reform of the judicial system, were well-educated Westerners, translated Thomas à Kempis, and acquired important positions in the Russian administration. Pobedonostsev always professed to be flattered by these comparisons and declared he had high admiration for Speransky's intellectual ability and energy, even though his policies were "not always to my taste" and "his moral character did not always excite my sympathy." However, he wrote that he could not understand Speransky's "passionate drive for power," his pining in quiet positions, his suffering when removed from power, and "his eagerness to grovel to be let out again." Pobedonostsev could see no strength or greatness in the possession of power, and was stunned by the egoism and violence of those who sought it. He was always reverent of autocratic power and eager to serve as an advocate or advisor in its shadows, but he was a reluctant and unimaginative official.[44]

Since Pobedonostsev did not develop his thought into a consistent philosophic system, he did not describe with any systematic clarity his view of the nature and purpose of society and of government. Most of his work as a member of the governing class dealt with pressing practical problems, and much of his writing, particularly in his letters, was concerned with daily affairs. Nevertheless, even in these records, there is a considerable amount of data concerning his political philosophy, due to his custom frequently to describe the basic, fundamental, even "eternal" principles by which he believed governments and societies should operate. He did this particularly in his letters to Alexander III, who was, in fact, always a student of Pobedonostsev.

There was, of course, a very clear distinction in Pobedonostsev's mind between the best procedure to adopt under given circumstances and the ideal practice under ideal circumstances. There was, too, a clear recognition of the distinction between the present community and the best attainable human community. This distinction for him was not so great as it has been for most people interested in politics. First of all, as a conservative he believed that the society which he surveyed contained many highly satisfactory institutions and that the changes which should be made were by no means drastic or revolutionary. In addition, and this is certainly even more significant, his view of human capabilities was not high. He ridiculed any idea of an "ideal society," and he would certainly have used the word "utopian" as a term of ridicule. He sought the best attainable society, not the unattainable perfect community.

It is important also to recognize that Pobedonostsev's Russia was not a secure or unchanging society. He believed that stability was the supreme virtue of a social organism, and his entire system was one which glorified static relationships. However, he did not believe that the struggle between good and evil, right and wrong, darkness and light, would cease, even in the best attainable society. Actually, even the best attainable society would not be reached. Even this finite community would always be "becoming," would never "be."

It should be clear now what the principal function or purpose of the autocratic state was: simply to provide balance, stability, or equilibrium, and to supply "the daily interests and needs of society." These were its ultimate goals. To reach these goals, the absolute government was to provide "rational direction" by means of a "calm, humane, indulgent, and arbitrary administration." It was to distinguish between light and dark, good and evil. It was, above all, to prevent the rise of nationalisms in the multinational Russian empire, through providing both force and equality. It was to override established laws and institutions whenever those laws and institutions interfered with the maintenance of equilibrium.

From this peace and quiet, he believed that splendid fruits would

develop. These fruits, of course, compared to those envisoned by
Aristotle or Sir Thomas More or Edward Bellamy—or even the
makers of the American Constitution—are quite meager. Pobedonostsev declared that the first great consequence of the "establishment" of a well-organized and stable state would be reliance upon
inertia, which he considered a vastly underrated force. Once stability had been obtained, inertia would work its slow magic, the
"good side" of man would flower, and there would be a "slow moral
improvement and uplift of the soul in society."[45]

If one compares Pobedonostsev's aims with those expressed in the
preamble of the American Constitution, it becomes apparent that
two of the goals sought by the American leaders, unity and tranquility, were also sought by Pobedonostsev. For the founders of the
United States, however, unity and tranquility were not ends to the
same degree that they were for him. They were also, to a considerable degree, means to the acquisition of three of the other expressed
aims, justice, the general welfare, and the blessings of liberty. Of
these, Pobedonostsev says nothing.

It is not surprising, given his view of the nature of man and his
philosophy of government, that he viewed the Russian state in some
ways as a family, with absolute parental authority and paternal care
on one hand and unquestioning obedience and love on the other.
He was certain that the ideal time for each individual was his childhood, and his state was designed to make that era permanent. As a
child, with no responsibilities or sense of time, with firm but gentle
parental care and direction, surrounded by love and certain truth,
and above all, with instinct and feeling ruling over the illusions of
reason and freedom, man is truly happy. The short spiritual essays
which he published in 1894 but which were written between 1856
and 1864 reveal that in his early thirties, as well as late in life, he
frequently looked back upon his own childhood in Moscow as the
time in which he had been happiest. He and his wife translated and
published Minnie Mackay's *The Mighty Atom* in 1897 because it
demonstrated how modern pedagogical methods were destroying
this paradise while at the same time failing to instill the necessary
moral attitudes in children. His political philosophy in many ways
represented an effort to create conditions under which the *narod*
could live as a child lived.[46]

His translations of Frederick Le Play, Edmond Demolins, St.
Augustine, and commentaries on St. Augustine and the *City of God*
reveal that models for Pobedonostsev's society had existed. He

hoped to organize a Christian society such as the one which for a thousand years had made religion more important than race, except that the Christendom he sought was simply a national Christendom. He would have agreed with Ammianus Marcellinus that "life is never sweeter than under a pious king." His ideal monarch was Louis IX, King of France in the second half of the thirteenth century, when everyone in each of the "estates" knew his place, social peace prevailed, the Church and the state ruled in harmony, and the king, a saint, sat under a tree and decided those few disagreements which arose within the society. In the 1880's, he thought the reign of Nicholas I one of the "most clear and brilliant periods" of Russian history, with few and simple problems, clear policies, gifted advisors for the tsar, and a government strong enough to persuade the lion to lie down with the lamb. The reign of Alexander III, during which Pobedonostsev played a very important role, was a highly satisfactory one, though far from perfect, because it at least had preserved the principle of divine right and "the rule of the fittest."[47]

The state, and the Church in union with the state, were the foundations upon which his political philosophy was erected. Although he wrote a great deal about the vital question of the sanctions of authority, his ideas were not completely clear. He wrote on occasion that the Russian ruler derived his power from divine right, but more frequently and insistently he spoke of the power of the tsar as "based solely on the unity of consciousness between the people and the state, on the national faith." In his most important statement of this philosophy, the impassioned attack upon the proposals of Loris-Melikov which he gave at the Council of Ministers meeting on March 8, 1881, he asserted that "Russia was strong, thanks to the autocracy, thanks to the unlimited mutual confidence and intimate relationship between the *narod* and the tsar." The most important justification for autocracy, of course, was historical, but he so clearly assumed this that he wrote little about it. The family played an important connecting role in the relationship between the *narod* and the state, especially in the essays he wrote in the last decade of his life. However, the idea of *sobornost'*, or community, so dear to the Slavophils, he never mentioned. Moreover, he did not seek to provide a legal rationale for the autocracy and would have scorned the very idea that this was necessary or even useful. Thus, the state for him was an expression of truth. "Power is founded on truth, and truth on power." The state, power, good, and the *narod* were, thus, all connected in one indissoluble and blurred unity.[48]

Pobedonostsev recognized that autocracy was not a perfect form of government, but it was built on Russian history and tradition and "the evils of autocracy are the evils of society itself." He vigorously opposed a *zemskii sobor* (territorial assembly) or other arrangements to provide some kind of representation for the most important and most highly educated groups in Russia. During the last ten or fifteen years of his life, the best defense of autocracy he could devise was a series of blistering attacks upon other forms of government, especially parliamentarism, in which the "personal ambition, vanity, and self-interest" of the members prevailed, eloquence and ambition were the most important qualities required, and "manipulators" acquired rule. They combined bribery and dogma in maintaining control, and the national interest was not even considered. Constitutions for him were "the instruments of the unrighteous, the weapon of intrigue." Popular sovereignty was "the great falsehood of our time," and democratic government was the most complex and difficult form of government known to man. It could not survive in a state which contained a number of nationalities, and it led inevitably to a Napoleonic dictatorship by way of materialism, infidelity, disorder, violence, and anarchy.[49]

In short, autocracy was the best form of government and the only conceivable one for Russia. It operated most effectively when the monarch was a dutiful father or shepherd for his country, distinguished by high moral standards. The autocrat was to represent the *narod's* interests. By his travels and his presence at ceremonies, he was to strengthen the love of the *narod* for the state. In addition, he was to select able and energetic executive aids and to accept their advice in directing the state. These executive agents for Pobdonostsev were the principal instruments of rule, and efficient operation of the system depended upon them. Essentially, he sought to modernize the autocracy. His advice to Alexander III was, "Cherchez des capables." His letters to the tsar and his correspondence with Catherine Tiutchev constantly reiterated that a few able men in responsible positions could resolve Russia's principal problems.

These executives were first of all to be men of courage, willing to accept responsibility and to speak frankly to the tsar. They were to be hard-working, practical, sagacious, efficient; they were to have organizing ability; they were to operate with clear lines of authority and responsibility. In their advice to the Russian ruler, they were to consider "history, tradition, the actual position of the state, and the needs of national life." Thoroughly schooled in the history and tra-

dition of their nation, they were also to ignore and smash its binding laws and institutions when they believed this was required in the
state's interest. He justified violent and arbitrary government action
and angrily denounced the moralistic interpretation of history and
of political action for ignoring or giving insufficient weight to the
national interest, which should always be the main concern of the
state and its rulers. He defended "the conscious lie" of the statesman in a world which inevitably contained a considerable amount
of evil, and he believed that superior men should be beyond criticism in life as well as in recorded history.[50]

In short, while he was a supporter of autocracy, he really believed
in the forms of absolutism and in rule by an "aristocracy of intellect" or by men whom Le Play called "social authorities." This
group was quite different from those whom Burke called a "true
natural aristocracy" and "an essential integral part of any large
body rightly constituted," because Pobedonostsev neglected the cultural framework or social institutions within which they would
work. Authority by men such as these in a strong and respected centralized government would insure stability, just as the absence of
such men and confusion in policy had led to a series of disasters and
destroyed popular faith in the system.

Pobedonostsev's admiration for bold men of energy and action,
such as Captain Nicholas M. Baranov, Nicholas I. Ashinov, General
Michael D. Skobelev, and Count Nicholas P. Ignatiev reflected his
central views. It was unfortunate for him and for Russia that his
judgments on men were so unsound, but his search for leaders of
this type represented his own philosophy accurately, as did his scorn
for the bureaucracy. Throughout his years of service in the Russian
state system, he poured scorn on the bureaucrats, from the notaries
he encountered in the Senate in 1846 and Panin and the others who
sought to block the judicial reform in 1864 to the men with whom
he had to deal in the last years of his career. He wrote that "all the
evil from which we suffer came up from the bureaucracy, not down."
He remarked that "paper will tolerate all things." He declared that
one of the great curses of Russia was the spineless government official who was smooth and polished, solved small and unimportant
problems, eliminated personality and efficiency from government,
and skillfully and perpetually evaded major issues. One of them he
noted "resembled an inadequate meal." He did not identify any
relationship between the size and quality of the Russian bureaucracy and the autocracy, although he did wonder why the English

were successful in identifying immensely able men and in giving them authority. In fact, of course, his proposal for a kind of dictatorship of the few within the autocracy was a proposal to resolve the problems the government itself created.[51]

He wrote remarkably little about the landowning nobility. He apparently visited a landed estate only rarely, and then for brief visits to his father-in-law's Smolensk property when he and his wife were en route to Salzburg for vacation. In fact, industrialists and merchants were much more the subject of his comment than were landowners, and he clearly preferred representatives of the middle class (but not intellectuals!) for executive positions. Indeed, he stated in the fifth edition of *Moskovskii sbornik* (Moscow Collection) in 1901 that the landed nobility as a class had ceased to have power and influence in Russia. However, he did believe that the nobility had acquired a special place of honor for their labors throughout Russian history, and he was convinced that they were more loyal to the state than were the bureaucrats, intelligentsia, merchants, or peasants.

Pobedonostsev was certain that "it is important in the highest degree that the landowning nobility remain on their estates within Russia and not crowd into the capitals." He resisted those who sought to arrange congresses of the nobility, but he urged that their economic and political position be strengthened in every way possible and that they retain their preponderant position in the administration of justice, in the army, and in the creation of national ideals. It is significant that he urged that the landed nobility live in the country and did not propose that their role in the central administration or even at the highest levels of provincial administration be increased or even maintained. In short, the "aristocracy of intellect" and the "social authorities" could include members of the aristocracy, but that class should not dominate the government and should instead be one of the pools of talent from which the state should select its leaders. Pobedonostsev explicitly opposed on grounds of efficiency a system restricting the possibility of attaining positions of authority to only one class, and he did believe that merit should ideally be the determining factor.[52]

The base of the triangle of the Russian state system was the *narod*, a word he used frequently but failed to define clearly. The virtues he considered desirable and necessary for this group were duty and sacrifice, obedience, love of work and of order, Christian love for one's fellow man, and submission to one's inner, unconscious balance. He recognized that a man with these virtues would be considered uncreative by many, but he reiterated that a stable society, composed of placid and obedient citizens "who knew their place," would develop a force more productive of enduring achievement than any other kind of society. In summary, then, his ideal citizen was the unsung hero, working constantly, quietly, and peacefully in his own sphere, seeking no reward but life itself, uncomplaining, and devoted to service to his community. The most frequent examples he offered were the rural teacher and the rural priest, poorly paid, unrewarded by the authorities for their contributions, but blindly devoted to their work and to service.[53]

A brief analysis of Pobedonostsev's political philosophy and a quick survey of his state's armory of instruments reveals several striking characteristics. To begin with, his ideas concerning the nature of man were fundamental to his entire philosophy and "justified" the arbitrary and authoritarian government he advocated. In addition, his belief that the character of the state was shaped by its national religious faith and by its traditional political and social institutions provided a base from which he could oppose "alien" ideas and institutions.

Nevertheless, Pobedonostsev's system was not so well organized or traditional as it appeared. Perhaps this can be shown most clearly by neglecting for the moment the obvious weapons in the state's hands and by identifying some of the principal instruments or elements he ignored or slighted. Neither justice nor the general welfare were of great significance to him. He did not appreciate the significance of a political façade, and there is a striking absence of color and trappings, except for the song and ceremony of the Church. Neither the army nor the police played an important role. However, it is in his treatment of the established nineteenth-century political trinity, the throne, the altar, and the aristocracy, that the most serious lacunae appear. For Pobedonostsev, of course, the main bulwark of the state was the Orthodox Church. The other two members of the trinity, though, were very shaky indeed. He was a fervent supporter of autocracy, but his advocacy was based neither on functional nor on religious grounds, and his arguments were generally vague. His autocrat was in effect a figurehead, and Pobedonostsev sought to replace the landed nobility with a group of middle-class executive managers and efficiency experts, the technocrats of the twentieth century.

XII

Philosophy of History

DURING THE FIRST two decades of his adult life, Pobedonostsev was a devoted, competent, and productive historian of Russian law and institutions. His scholarship and his teaching were so impressive that he could surely have achieved a satisfying and distinguished career as a university professor, if he had chosen to do so. His interest in learning and in research remained high throughout his life, not only because he was by nature an avid reader, but also because he was convinced that no one could understand the present who did not possess a profound knowledge of the past.

On the other hand, he thought that systematic philosophy and general, abstract ideas were among the curses of the nineteenth century. He read Comte, Marx, Carlyle, Emerson, Spenser, Darwin, and Fourier, among other nineteenth century philosophers, and he had a proper appreciation of their intellectual achievements. At the same time, he thought that the Russian Orthodox Church possessed the truth and that a determined intellectual search for truth was both wasteful and dangerous. His own political and social philosophy was itself an eclectic hodge-podge, never systematically put together and even today somewhat difficult to unravel. However, at the core of his thoughts and actions lay a coherent political position, which remained fundamentally consistent throughout his life.

He had a genuine interest in the history of his native land, which is reflected in the spirit and the quantity of his historical scholarship. He had been raised with a strong sense of history and tradition, and he loved to visit old churches, museums, archives, and monuments. His most pleasant hours were spent reading and writing history, which he considered "the teacher and tutor of a people." He thought that revealed history and accepted tradition were the two greatest authorities, more illuminating and reliable than the minds and ideas of even the most intelligent critics. "For a person, for a people, for a society, the whole value of history consists of represented self- consciousness." In fact, "there is no better school than the dead."[1]

As an historian, he thought that his greatest goal, and that of any conscientious scholar, was to discover and relate "how it actually happened." His knowledge of his time and his research in the tangled thickets of Russian legal history persuaded him that providing a clear and accurate description of an event or of the changing character of an institution was itself a remarkable achievement. His research on serfdom and on the history of Russian civil law convinced him that institutions, social concepts, and values "grew" organically in Russia, and therefore presumably elsewhere, in an extremely complicated way, about which it was impossible to create succinct conclusions or crisp theories. He was certain that no straight or simple explanation could describe the labyrinthian histories he had sought to explain. In fact, he came to believe that any effort to create a general theory which could explain these institutions and ideas was ludicrous. He was, therefore, as contemptuous of philosophies of history as he was of other general theories or abstract conceptions.[2]

He naturally would have ridiculed Comte's belief that there are "general laws governing the course of events which it was history's business to recount." He would also have considered preposterous the proposal that one could create "a conception or picture of the whole course of human events as a continuous unitary play in which successive eras or generations play distinctive parts." He would have urged that no effort "to sum up past history, to grasp it as a whole, and to decipher its ultimate meaning" could possibly succeed because of the very nature of man and of the historical process.[3]

Indeed, he was not interested in the philosophy of history and would perhaps have been surprised to learn that he had put one together. For example, while he read and enjoyed the great Russian historians of his times, such as Soloviev and Kliuchevsky, and foreign scholars, such as Ranke and Taine and Macaulay, he did not comment upon the philosophical views they held. Similarly, he did not discuss the views of Chaadaiev or Mikhailovsky or Lavrov, whose views concerning the nature and destiny of Russia were important

in the last two-thirds of the nineteenth century. Neither the doctrines of the Slavophils nor the later ones of the panslavs affected
him significantly, even though he shared some of the basic ideas of
the Slavophils and became a fervent panslav during the Balkan
crisis from 1875 to 1878. Thus, he did not join the Slavophils in
describing Russia's golden past or bright future. Even the ideas of
Professor Nicholas J. Danilevsky, which emphasized the decay of
the West and the youthfulness and vitality of the Orthodox Slavic
East, failed to impress him, although these general concepts were
closely related to some of his own.

He was equally remote from a Christian philosophy of history, in
which the work of God explained and summarized past history and
deciphered its ultimate meaning. In fact, it is striking how little
significance moral or ethical considerations played in his view of
historical developments. Finally, the idea of progress, with the victory of reason the highest goal for humanity, annoyed and frightened him. His father had believed in progress, accepted unwittingly
the Enlightenment and its main concepts, and devoted his life to uplifting and improving those near him, but Pobedonostsev vigorously
rejected this liberal view of history. Man was weak, if not evil; survival, not progress, was the attainable goal. A critical study of history
revealed that the more things changed, the more likely they were
to remain the same.

Even so, Pobedonostsev himself created a coherent philosophy of
history, analysis of which helps illumine his entire philosophy and
the age in which he lived. This was as home-made and composed of
as many ill-fitting, assorted parts acquired from many sources as was
his political philosophy. It was a natural extension of his political
philosophy, which it served to support. First of all, his views concerning government reflect both his concept of man and his ideas
concerning the nature and character of societies and the differences
between societies. He equated society and religion, and he would
have accepted Professor Toynbee's thesis that the great religions
have created the different characteristics which make one "civilization" distinct from another. He would also have agreed with Carlyle, whom he warmly admired: "Every society, every Polity, has a
spiritual principle, which is the embodiment, tentative or more or
less complete of an Idea; all its tendencies of endeavor are prescribed
by an Idea and flow naturally from it, as movements from the living
source of motion."[4] The most important single fact about Russia,
that which made it unique and impervious to external influences,

was Orthodoxy, which shaped the political system and bound Russia into a united body, saturated and permeated by love.

He believed that each society or state possessed distinctive political and social beliefs and institutions which helped to shape its character. Each nation's development represented an organic process based on immutable laws. Each state was thus a "mysterious organism" and a prisoner of history, which determined that the various states had different philosophies and institutions. Thus, he explained that some states, such as Russia, had highly centralized, authoritarian governments because the necessary emphasis in their distant past had been upon communal life and upon firm control over the family by the father or by the patriarch; consequently, each person remained dependent, political power was respected and became ever more highly concentrated, and strong central government inevitably developed.

Several particular historical developments explained Russia's political and social system. The first, which appeared constantly in his conversation and in his writing from 1859 until his death, was the character of the population, inert, lazy, primitive, and often barbaric. The qualities of the Russian people, of course, reflected the national history. They also enforced restrictions upon policy which he believed binding upon Russia's reformers and critics as well as upon its rulers. He explained in 1858, for example, that Russia could not at that time adopt Western judicial institutions because "all law must conform to the basic needs of a given society," which derived from specific local conditions. The characteristics of Russian national life, the economy, the level of education, and the customs were such that any new institutions planned would have to reflect those qualities. In 1880, he described the Russian economy as "in many places primitive and in other places extremely undeveloped." The feeble state of local institutions and the basic inability of the population to supply local needs made centralized power a necessity. This was strengthened by the absence of a sound educational system, the large number of nationalities and of interest groups sprinkled throughout the huge country, and the constant external pressures. Russian backwardness cut it off, too, from the capacity to borrow Western ideas and institutions and thereby to overcome "our history, our life, the poverty of our science and education."[5]

When pressed by hostile critics to defend widely unpopular government measures, such as those directed against the Baltic Germans in the 1880's, Pobedonostsev also asserted that the critical role Rus-

sia had played in world history helped to explain the political system and the state's evolution. Thus, Christianity in the West had
been lured into active political life and power, with the Papacy
seeking ever unsuccessfully to fasten its rule and its language upon
all Christians. This caused conflict, revolt, and the collapse of Christianity in the West. At the same time, the isolated Russian Orthodox
Church maintained the true and pure faith it had received and
brought all members into one communion in one language. Moreover, Providence had placed Russia to guard the passage against
migrant groups from Asia "so that Christian Europe could devote
itself in peace to the work of a new civilization, a Christian civilization." Only "its fidelity to the immutable principles of its national
spirit" enabled Russia and its Church to prevent Europe from being
overrun. At the same time, the state and the Church together had
to fight the Poles and the Germans in the West. These pressures
above all explained the backward but pristine nature of Russian
society, the character of its government, and its place in world
history.[6]

On the other hand, "the Anglo-Saxon and Scandinavian states"
had decentralized, democratic governments with an independent
judiciary and an effective jury system because the emphasis throughout their long history had been upon individualism. The father had
not acquired absolute power in the family; consequently, local government developed, and the central authority remained compara-
tively weak. From this base came an educated and self-disciplined
citizenry. These human qualities and the institutions established in
the long run produced a different "national soul" in England and
in Scandinavia than in Russia.

He emphasized that democratic institutions were a consequence
of historical developments more than a cause of them. Late in life,
he wrote approvingly that parliament in England "thus consists of
active representatives of local interests, closely tied to the land; that
is why their voice can be considered exactly as the voice of the land
and as the organ of the national interest." At that time, he came to
believe that Belgium might succeed in adopting democratic institutions which had their roots in England, because the size of the country and the quality of the population made this possible.

He included the United States in the "Anglo-Saxon and Scandinavian" world and thought it would survive and prosper as a
democratic country with free institutions because it was building
upon English stock and upon English models in particularly fruitful

soil. Indeed, he considered the United States a "dreamland." Such institutions for France and the other states of continental Europe, though, were poisonous. He interpreted the French revolution in 1789 and the later revolutions and efforts inevitably doomed to failure because they sought to implant a foreign institution in a soil unprepared for it. Similarly, he interpreted the Decembrist revolt of 1825 as "an insane attempt of aristocratic dreamers who knew neither their own people nor their own history" to attain British ideals on Russian soul. All other efforts to borrow foreign institutions were likewise foolish and fatal. In short, he was convinced that constitutional and democratic government would flourish in those states in which it developed from historical roots. Thus, all systems were consecrated by history. The principal problem rose when a state such as France or Russia sought to graft an alien institution upon its ancient foundations.[7]

Throughout the last fifteen or twenty years of his life in particular, he saw Western political ideas as the principal threat to Russia. However, he was not resistant to economic change within Russia. In fact, throughout his adult life and increasingly as he grew older, he welcomed the gradual, directed transformation of the Russian economy by modernizing ideas and techniques introduced from western Europe. However, the autocracy and Orthodoxy were to remain unaffected foundations surrounded by a world of change. He was never asked to explain this anomaly, perhaps because his critics did not appreciate or understand his relaxed attitude toward controlled economic innovation. Perhaps he himself did not realize the strangeness of his view of the permanent and unchanging character of the state system and of the role of the Church in a society inevitably in flux. In any case, the political system was permanent and indelible. In an undramatic and inglorious fashion, for he saw neither a glorious past nor a magnificent future for Russia, it had provided and should continue to assure harmony, unity, and homogeneity for a satisfied Russia. So long as the state and Church remained fixed stars, "Naught shall make us rue, if 'Russia' to itself do rest but true."[8]

With these exceptions, he recognized change in history and assumed it would continue, whether or not any individuals, groups, or states opposed. However, historical developments within a particular state, such as Russia, were shaped and controlled by the institutions and values of the past, which insured the preeminence of a sort of manifest destiny. Thus, the history of a country ran like a slow-flowing river, between banks which determined the course of the channel so that the flow could not be diverted by will or chance. "Man makes history but it is not less true and perhaps it is still more important to realize that history makes man." Change in established societies was and should remain slow, organic, conditioned by history and the character of life, because "nature does not produce results quickly." The history of a country was therefore created in layers and inevitably was characterized by a kind of incoherence.

This view of course reflects his political philosophy, but it also represents his work as an historian of institutions. He often repeated that the historian must remember that customs and beliefs of historical ages and of countries differed and that he errs grievously who criticizes the acts of one age or country according to the standards of another. He was a resolute critic of the moralistic interpretation of history:

> The moral feeling is insulted by violence, but moral feeling alone cannot serve as a guide and instrument for the historian studying the political activity of an historical person; otherwise, the historian would judge and declare pernicious a government measure simply because it was accompanied by violence. This would be unjust. It is true that the greatest transformations in the soul of man have been effected by peaceful means, by people strong in soul but lowly and even base in social position. But these were exceptional occurrences. The rulers of the world usually act through material force, by external and internal authority. It has always been so, and it will always be so, at least as long as moral force does not acquire decisive rule over material force in the rules of all society.[9]

His ideas concerning the nature of change in history can perhaps best be explained through an analysis of his fear of subversive ideas and forces, which led him to create a kind of "plot theory" of history; of the role which Peter the Great and other outstanding individuals had played; of the way in which serfdom has been fastened upon and then removed from the backs of the Russian people; of the history of various forms of property ownership in Russia; and finally, in most detail, of his conception of the role of modern economic forces.

Convinced that history unfolds in a slow, organic way, unaffected by the theories of intellectuals or by foreign values, Pobedonostsev, like most reactionaries, was fearful lest this inevitable, stately process be upset by chance or by the ideas or actions of a handful of skillful, malevolent men. Curiously, he was not alarmed by the work of particular Russian radical and revolutionary individuals or groups. He never even noticed the views of the various kinds of socialists which appeared in Russia in the last third of the nineteenth century, and he devoted far more attention to the work of western European liberals and radicals than he did to their Russian counterparts. At the same time, he continually expressed alarm concerning the supposed threat to his society posed by hostile concepts. Superstitious, generally fearful, he thought that the Jews, the Old Believers, and the Stundists were conspiring against the regime and were acquiring economic power in order to mount an insidious attack. The main dangers, though, were Western ideas and the soft-headed professors, journalists, and amateur politicians who had swallowed them. The great threat, then, was internal and intellectual. "We are betrayed by what is false within." As Professor Morris Cohen noted, "It is curious that those who insist that human ideas cannot influence the course of history are almost continually complaining of how people are misled by false views."[10]

The history of Russia for him resembled somewhat a slow, majestic, dignified advance, on occasion achieving a higher rate of speed when challenge and outstanding leadership occurred at the same time. His father was an enthusiastic admirer of Peter the Great, Catherine the Great, and Alexander I, and Pobedonostsev grew up in a household which had great reverence for the state and for its most vigorous rulers. When still a young scholar, he remarked that "the great ruler of the Russian land had to take the clumsy Russian people" in hand to lead them to significant achievements. As a believer in a strong central government, in firm rule, and in a powerful state, he expressed great admiration for Peter the Great in particular.

He wrote favorably of Peter because Peter had placed the interests of the state first, "collected all the power around one center and directed it toward one goal," and made Russia a larger, stronger, and more industrial power. His appraisal was sharply critical of those who believed that Russia had enjoyed a golden age before Peter. He was particularly critical of the Slavophils (although he never mentioned them as a group) because in their attacks on Peter the Great they were "carried away by their historical ideal, the features of which they find in the ancient history of Russia before Peter." He was also critical of the Westerners, whom he denounced for interpreting Peter's age and actions according to their own pre-conceived ideas and for asserting that Peter wanted to make Russia a Western state.

According to Pobedonostsev, Peter did not wish to give Russia new institutions and was not opposed to the old ones. He strength-ened the power of the *pomestchik* only when it was to the interest of the state. He was personally opposed to serfdom, but recognized that he could not eliminate it or even reduce its significance. On the one hand, he made more severe the decrees concerning runaway serfs and tightened internal passport regulations. On the other hand, he eliminated abuses when he could. He was a great man because he saw the needs of his age clearly and undertook nothing which was in sharp contradiction with the concepts then generally held. He was unaffected by moral or philosophical principles. He simply acted in the interest of the state, using the established institutions when possible to increase the state's power and authority and revising the established institutions when necessary.

Frederick the Great was acclaimed for precisely the same reasons, although he too "must answer for every outrage he committed." Both were properly national heroes. Alexander I, on the other hand, was as patriotic as they, "but his education had not furnished him the means for understanding the history of his country or of his people." Alexander scorned the *narod*, was dazzled by the Enlight-enment and preferred its charms to those of the Russian Orthodox Church, and did not have the national interest as his highest ideal. He even dreamed of the restoration of Poland, "knowing nothing of history, which would have told him that the existence of the Polish kingdom would mean slavery and oppression for all the Rus-sian nation."

In short, even when discussing Russia's leaders, he saw the history of Russia as the history of the state as it was affected by blind, organic historical forces. He saw all Russian institutions and leaders as the unconscious instruments or even weapons of the state. "History is explained not by chance alone, nor by personal arbitrary power alone, but by the whole course of history." No Russian ruler emerges from his writings as a giant causing sharp breaks in the continuity of Russian history, which flows on eternally as the history of the state, its course determined by the "law of historical and political necessity."[11]

His analysis of the origins and establishment of serfdom, as well as of the process which led finally to its abolition in 1861, serves as a most clear illustration of his views concerning the nature of the historical process and change in history. In fact, he noted that the study of institutions such as serfdom was both natural and essential for anyone who sought to understand Russia and who realized that history was more than a chronological collection of political facts. He also admitted that his own way of viewing Russian history had been powerfully affected by his research on serfdom and other institutions.

Serfdom, in fact, grew; it "was formed little by little." It filled a political, economic, and social vacuum. It was not an evil or an obstacle to the material and spiritual growth of the *narod*. It was instead a sign that full personal development then was impossible. The Code of 1649 was not significant in fastening serfdom upon Russia, for juristic principles were not valued then and were understood only late in the eighteenth and in the nineteenth century. Neither Peter the Great nor any other Russian ruler was an important abettor of serfdom, because the rulers only recognized and accepted the conditions of life in which they had to live. Serfdom did bring misfortunes and even evils to many Russians, but these were inevitable. Moreover, one should not project nineteenth century standards of conduct into earlier periods or assume either that laws were always vigorously enforced. He even argued that there were few protests against serfdom until late in the eighteenth century, because no one in the seventeenth century thought of himself as a citizen or had any "sense of independent civic personality" or "personal freedom." Abstract ideas, notions of complex juridical problems, and economic and spiritual criticisms of serfdom also appeared much later. Even the Church failed to resist or criticize the establishment of serfdom, in part because slavery and serfdom were not explicitly condemned in the Bible or in Orthodox doctrine and in part because the Church leaders, inevitably imbued with the ideals of the age, accepted its institutions and concentrated upon spreading love and peace throughout society and upon keeping alive for better days the ideas of personal independence.

The state had played a very important role in establishing serfdom. Its main interest was in "order and organization." It utilized and strengthened serfdom because it wanted the landowner to serve the state, it sought to prevent vagabondage to assist the landowner, and it wanted assurance concerning state finances. In fact, in the conditions of that time, it had no alternatives. Similarly, the state in the nineteenth century participated in the dismantling of serfdom because its interests remained the same at a time when conditions of life had changed. Thus, "that same law of historical and political necessity, according to which serfdom was formed, has led to its abolition. . . ." The barge of history moves on, relatively unaffected by heads of state or philosophers or accident.[12]

His analysis of the historical career of serfdom in Russia was paralleled exactly and in even greater detail in his more complicated study of the history of the various forms of property ownership, to which he naturally devoted a great deal of time and energy in his works on the history of Russian civil law. His review of property-holding was remarkably disinterested and practical. He apparently was concerned only with its legal aspects. Even though he was writing at a time of quiet revolutionary change in the fortunes of the large landowners, he failed to comment on the political significance of that important development. Although he was intensely conservative, he recognized the values of banking and of new credit institutions. He even approved the introduction in Russia of joint stock companies, although he recognized the fundamental impact they would surely have. This characteristic of his approach toward one of his country's most central problems illuminates his entire political philosophy.

Thus, throughout his career as a scholar and conservative statesman, he identified private property as "a clear expression of the human personality" and "the most definite and absolute of civil rights." He saw the human record, including that of the Russian people, as "the uninterrupted striving for personal ownership" and as part of "the natural struggle of the individual for freedom." After reviewing the political history of Russia, he explained that the civil history of private property began, and could begin to grow, only with Catherine the Great, when the internal political system and Russia's place in the European state system began to change. The position of private property therefore depended upon the political fate of the era and the special history of the various parts of Russia, where the systems of land ownership and control inevitably differed from each other. Change came so rapidly in his own lifetime that in 1883 he defined private property as "among the most rooted and fundamental institutions of our time."[13]

His knowledge of the economic changes taking place in western Europe and in Russia as well was not substantial or systematic, but it was greater than one would assume and it was superior to his knowledge concerning rural Russia. He lived throughout his life in Moscow and St. Petersburg, Russia's two largest and most important cities and those most visibly affected by economic change. His several trips throughout European Russia with the young grand dukes took him into workshops, factories, and mines, gave him some understanding of the importance of improved transportation facilities, and introduced him to a large number of merchants and manufacturers and their views. He was made aware of the impact industrialization was having upon transportation in Europe and Russia by his travelling.[14]

Similarly, his years of service as director of the Volunteer Fleet were an education in transportation, commerce, and international trade. In addition, in his years in the Senate, the Council of State, and the Council of Ministers, he participated in many discussions concerning state policies on economic problems of national importance. He had a deep interest in his own financial situation and prospects, and his personal concerns no doubt led him to place special emphasis in his work in civil law upon financial issues. Indeed, it is obvious that his knowledge of civil law, particularly of its history in more advanced countries, enormously multiplied his interest in and knowledge of modern economic developments and problems. He wrote a great deal concerning property ownership and rights, taxes, rent, contracts, insurance, interest, credit, bills of exchange, and various forms of commercial and industrial organization, so he acquired considerable knowledge concerning the labyrinths of the growing capitalist economy.

Finally, some of the Western scholars who especially impressed him, such as Emerson, Spencer, and Carlyle, were particularly concerned with industrialization and effects it had produced and was likely to produce. Frederick Le Play, the French sociologist he so admired, was an engineer, wrote at considerable length concerning the changes he saw taking place in various parts of Europe, and created a philosophy of history which had the bases for a rudimentary theory of development or modernization and which Pobedonostsev absorbed and made his own.

In short, he was both knowledgeable about and interested in the Russian economy. In fact, he came to believe that the principal motor behind the gradual changes visible in history was economic. By 1890, he became convinced that the system of landholding in Russia must be changed, that Russia must become an industrialized state, that the state must assume responsibility for the direction and pace of this change, and that the pattern of Russian history was and should be such that the state could be transformed into a modern industrial power without modification of the political system. Thus, the course of the stream should continue within the banks long established and consecrated by history, the ship or barge of state should maintain its progress through the established channel, the pilot of the ship and the administrative and spiritual arrangements should remain unchanged, and only the motive power should be altered. His philosophy of history was therefore blended with his political philosophy in such a way as to enable him to reject all change in Russia except that brought on by economic forces and to propose direction of that change in such a way as to maintain the cherished political system.

Throughout his life he was acutely aware that the Russian economy was primitive and backward. On occasion he referred to it as "extremely underdeveloped" and "even medieval." He was convinced that the gap which separated Russia from France, Germany, and England was much greater in 1900 than it had been when he first began to write forty years earlier. The capital and the institutions for making Russia more fruitful were both absent. The Russian people lacked skills and ambition, and there was no visible means for educating or training them to work as Western peoples did. Trade was primitive, transport was feeble, and social institutions reflected a premodern society. The country possessed no economic unity, and the authorities could not even hope to acquire the information necessary for sensible national economic policies. Most important, because of their history, the Russians lacked a concept of personal responsibility and any interest in or ambition for improvement.[15]

However, throughout his life Pobedonostsev believed that the economic transformation of Russia was both inevitable and fruitful. He saw that industrial growth was necessary if Russia was to remain a European power. As a young man, he was impressed by the instruments of modernization, such as the telegraph and the railroad. He approved of limited liability companies, and he was interested in expanding credit facilities so that economic growth could be stimulated. After visiting a mine near Kostroma in 1863, he wrote, "Please God that the time will come soon when the wealth in the womb of our dear country will be brought into the light and when our capital will eagerly put itself to work." Above all, he saw economic change as inevitable. He often quoted Le Play and Emerson on the nature of the new historical era into which France and the United States were entering, and he clearly believed that Russia would and should follow the same path.[16]

At the same time, like the Western philosophers he studied and admired, he regretted the withering away of cherished values and institutions and resented the crudities and ugly flaws of economic change. He had little genuine affection for "old Russia," and he was heartily in favor of railroads, but he did deplore that railroads would end the isolation of cities such as Kostroma and Kazan and thereby reduce their virtues as lovely centers of old culture. He thought "the new aristocracy" excessively avid in its search for wealth and honor. He was savagely critical of speculators and "usurers," and he was dismayed by the moral dissolution which he thought factory life introduced for many Russians lured from their rural homes and parishes into industrial centers. In 1903, he exulted concerning the benefits the machine was bringing his country, but was depressed by the way it was "exhausting and dissolving the strength of the national soul and drying up the living sources of life." Even so, he was far less critical and concerned than Emerson or Carlyle about similar developments in their countries.[17]

The most impressive illustration of his views concerning the economic transformation of Russia is provided by the gradual change in his policy toward the commune or *mir* and his advocacy after 1889 of its replacement in the Russian countryside by family farms similar to the American homesteads. He did not participate at any time in the debate between the Westerners and the Slavophils concerning whether or not the commune was unique to the Slavic peoples, and he never demonstrated either admiration or contempt for the peasants. He noted that the factual data necessary for a decision were not available and that the dispute between "political doctrinaires" on one hand and "dreamers" on the other was therefore senseless. The role the commune should play was simply a practical problem. It did possess unquestioned advantages, but it also suffered from serious flaws. The essential fact about the commune was that it could not be separated "from the temporary economic conditions in which it grew and by which it has been supported."

Thus, he kept the commune's role under observation, always emphasizing that national interest must be the decisive consideration and that economic forces and trends, not men, would make the final judgment. Even in the 1870's, he wrote that all rural collectives were ultimately doomed because they "did not provide sufficient strength and scope for enterprise and for the production of new

value and new capital." His historical analyses of the various forms
of landholding which had prevailed at one time or another in Russia and in western Europe led him to conclude that "natural causes"
had led to the gradual disappearance of each system. In 1883, he
judged that the time had not yet come for the withering away of the
commune, but he added:

> This time will come by itself, with the natural development
> of productive forces and with the change of economic condi-
> tions. The experience visible in the history of all other people
> will not escape us, because all have proceeded through the same
> stages of economic life and through the same forms of land-
> holding, even though in different climatic, geographical, and
> political conditions of economic development. The growth of
> all was not identical, but it would have been a serious error,
> although unfortunately a very common one, to imagine that it
> is possible to stop or to quicken growth by artificial measures
> of legislation without violating the physical conditions of
> growth.[18]

In short, he valued the commune as the framework for the rural
family, but saw that it was being undermined by powerful economic
forces which were going to eliminate it as they had other institutions
in other countries. No individual should tamper with this ineluc-
table process, the impact of which would be so tremendous that only
the state should seek to influence the flow of events. Even state intervention should be directed with great caution and only after economic conditions themselves had changed. Above all, the state in its
actions should recognize that the future interest of the entire nation
should be its central concern. By 1889, he came to believe that the
historical forces which operated everywhere had so influenced the
structure of the Russian economy that he urged the state to hasten
the dismantling of the commune and the creation of a large peasant
proprietor class. This was philosophy of history in action.

The blending of his philosophy of history and his political philosophy is reflected also in other policies he recommended concerning the Russian economy and economic development. From the very
beginning, the core of his interest in economic growth was a nationalistic approach toward the economy and toward economic relations
with other states. He considered the economic transformation of
both the city and countryside not only unavoidable, but also necessary to enable Russia to resist the pressures exerted by the more advanced economies of England and Germany. One of the reasons he

admired Peter the Great was the tsar's actions to advance the economic strengthening of Russia and to expand its frontiers in the west and in the south. His 1863 tour helped make him understand the importance of machines and machine tools. From that time forward, he was a strong believer in tariffs for Russian industries, for the merchants and industrialists he met then and later demonstrated to him the need for protecting their infant industries against competition from foreigners, especially Germans. He therefore urged that foreigners be prohibited from building and operating grain elevators, oil wells, pipe lines, coastal shipping concerns, and banks. He proposed that foreign capital be allowed only under strict supervision.[19]

Similarly, while he clearly lacked the understanding and interest of men such as Witte in industrialization, he was active in supporting the economic transformation of the country, with the constant insistence that this be directed and controlled by the state, which should remain the supreme and unquestioned authority. In fact, he urged that the state consider the economic strength of the country more important than the army. As the "guardian of the highest interest," he believed it should promote the construction of railroads and of a network of roads to strengthen the country. It should maintain firm control over credit and currency to insure a flow of beneficent resources at controlled interest rates into the main stream of the economy. It should restrict the influence of "Jewish usurers" and assure opportunities and aid for small businesses.[20]

His statist policy was also reflected in his view of the position and role of the working class, which he first noticed in his 1863 tour of European Russia. Throughout his life, his attitudes remained traditionally patriarchal. He was appalled by the conditions in which some workers lived and worked. He was convinced that the crowding of masses of Russians into ugly cities—removed from their homes and parishes, provided occasional empty holidays, and offered no hope—was a national danger which the government should act to eliminate. At the same time, he supported the passport or workbook system and opposed workers' organizations. When he chaired a committee in 1897 to review a report critical of conditions in which workers lived, he opposed the eight-hour day, recognition of May Day as a holiday, and state inspection of factories. In short, while on occasion he recognized the evils and the hazards, he believed that the solution lay in submission to the forces of history, as they might be directed or influenced by the state. "Whatever will be, will be."[21]

XIII

Russia and the West

For Pobedonostsev, and for most Russians of his generation and indeed of this century as well, one of Russia's central problems was its relationship with the West. There may be no better method of illustrating his thought than describing and analyzing his knowledge of and attitude toward this critical geographical and cultural area. It is naturally difficult, perhaps impossible, to provide a clear definition of "the West," although Pobedonostsev and others very frequently used the word. Moreover, the definition used by any one person changes from year to year. Similarly, the West itself is not a constant: the West of Hitler or Picasso is not that of Gladstone or Goethe.

Generally, most informed Russians and Europeans throughout the nineteenth century assumed that Russia was a part of the European state system and a leading member of the concert of Europe. This had probably been so since the time of Catherine the Great, and the role of Russia in the Napoleonic wars, in the peace settlement in 1815, and in international affairs in general ensured it. In fact, Russia became a world power during the nineteenth century, because of her powerful position in Europe and because of the conquest, during the century, of the Caucasus, Central Asia, and substantial areas in the Pacific Far East.

At the same time, there was a serious gap between Russia's apparent position and the foundation of this position. During the first half of the nineteenth century, Russia's reputation rested generally upon her massive size and upon her large parade-ground army. This reputation was pricked by the Crimean War, and the new economic foundations which underlay British and German power as the century progressed exposed Russia further. Moreover, the growing dichotomy between the congealed political system of Russia and the changing forms of western Europe contributed to the gap between Russia and the West. Finally, as more Russians appreciated the significant differences which distinguished Russia from the West, they became critical of their own government and society. In other words, Russia in the nineteenth century was in the West, but not of it. Even those Russians who believed that Russia was and ought to remain distinct from the West recognized Western superiority in some fields and borrowed from it.

Pobedonostsev's knowledge of the West, his definition of it, and his attitudes toward it inevitably reflected the age in which he lived and its inheritance. As Russia more and more became a part of Europe in the nineteenth century, the knowledge which educated Russians had of Europe increased. Despite the backwardness of Russian culture, the level of Russian education, the censorship and controlled isolation which generally prevailed, and the ignorance of the rest of the world of the vast group which Avvakum in the seventeenth century had described as "the ignorant, self-sufficient majority untouched by any cultural influence," Russians among the aristocracy in particular began to develop clearly defined views of Europe and of its various parts. However, even the best-educated Russians were poorly or inaccurately informed, so that their views on occasion were both shallow and indefinite and changed in remarkable ways from time to time as political and other crises affected the country.

The interest some educated Russians developed concerning Europe began in the Middle Ages, but it was only in the middle of the eighteenth century that a handful, most of them in the aristocracy and residents of Moscow or St. Petersburg, began to acquire the kinds of knowledge from travel and study that enabled them to create coherent views. Interest originally, especially in the seventeenth and eighteenth centuries, concentrated upon France. French influence probably reached its apogee during the period from 1780 to 1815, but it grew remarkably after 1740 and it remained high throughout the nineteenth century.

The reign of Catherine the Great was, of course, the great landmark for intellectual relations between Russia and Europe, and the age of the Enlightenment therefore occupies a central position. It has been estimated that three-quarters of the books which were imported into Russia in the last third of the eighteenth century were published in France and that most of these books represented the philosophy of the Enlightenment. Thus, by the beginning of the nineteenth century, the established tradition reflected both in reading and in travel made France and its culture the principal subject of study in the Russian empire.

Basically, "the boneless man of Europe" was afflicted then by "idol worship" with regard to France, in large part because the Russian aristocracy lacked well-established beliefs of its own. This enthusiasm about every aspect of French culture survived the powerful waves of disenchantment created by the violence of 1793 and the invasion of 1812. Thus, even during the French revolutionary period and during the period of the most strict censorship, several journals were published in St. Petersburg and in Moscow which translated articles from French newspapers and magazines and selections from the classics of the age of Louis XIV and of the eighteenth century. As has been discussed earlier,* Pobedonostsev's father, a pious member of the Orthodox Church, a nationalistic Russian, a professor of Russian literature, and a founder of the Society of the Lovers of Russian Literature, devoted a good part of his time and energy to publishing journals, the main function of which was the dissemination of material from Western (mainly French) books, journals, and newspapers. One mark of the changes in the Russian view of Europe which unfolded as the nineteenth century progressed was the contrast between Professor Pobedonostsev and his distinguished son, who learned early to read French and who read the *Revue des Deux Mondes* consistently as an adult, but who refused to visit Paris and who turned to the English and Germans rather than to those whose works his father had published or to French writers of his own era.[1]

Throughout the nineteenth century, the court played an important part in shaping the Russian view of other parts of the world. The St. Petersburg court was basically a German institution, most of the princesses whom Russian state leaders married after Peter the Great were German, and Germans, usually from the Baltic area, occupied many important state positions. The education of the court was German throughout the eighteenth and nineteenth centuries, and the German state system very often served as the court's model. Sumner has pointed out that four of the nine Russian ambassadors to the Court of St. James between 1812 and 1917 were

* See pp. 5-9.

Baltic Germans and that these four men served Russia in London for a total of eighty-three of the one hundred and five years. In other words, the court when looking westward tended to concentrate on Germany, while the aristocracy when looking in the same direction tended to see only France.[2]

The court's attitude was inevitably affected by the French revolution and by the invasion of Napoleon. During the era of reaction after 1815, both Alexander I and Nicholas I tightened the censorship to a degree beyond that practiced even during the revolution. Nicholas I in 1830 was prepared to invade France to crush the revolution which broke out in that year, and he abandoned this intention only when he realized such an action was not possible. Alarmed by developments in France and fearful that the infection would spread from Paris, after 1830 he in effect closed Paris and France to Russian tourists and students. Indeed, he began to send Russian students to Berlin for their studies, particularly after 1840. It was in Berlin, of course, that young Russians encountered the doctrines first of Hegel and later of Marx. Ironically, therefore, the policies of Nicholas I led to the importation of doctrines from Berlin which proved more dangerous than the ideas which Russian scholars would have imported from Paris.[3]

The efforts of Nicholas I to isolate Russia from France failed because the culture of the aristocracy had been so powerfully shaped in earlier years. The libraries which had been imported in the eighteenth century and which continued to grow in the nineteenth century included many French volumes, particularly the classics of the age of the Enlightenment. These collections in the great homes of the aristocracy and in homes such as that of Professor Pobedonostsev proved to be time bombs, because the Herzens and the Kropotkins in reading these volumes as youngsters imbibed doctrines and information which Nicholas I was trying to obliterate.

For the cultivated aristocracy of St. Petersburg and Moscow, France occupied quite a different position from the one it held at the court. Of course, most of the Russian nobility in the first half of the nineteenth century, and even in the first part of the twentieth century, were no more cultivated or educated than the English gentry whom Macaulay ridiculed in the famous third chapter of his *History of England*. However, the educated aristocrats, who tended to spend their winters at least in St. Petersburg and Moscow, were highly cultured people, in many ways more French than Russian. Almost all of them spoke French, they had travelled often in France, most of their reading was in French books, journals, and newspapers, and they traditionally had their children educated by French tutors.

For them, France was the France of the eighteenth century, the era of the Enlightenment. It was not just a country or a people, but a corps of ideas which should affect the lives of all men. It represented the belief in the excellence of natural man, the importance of the individual and of the individual's rights, and the power of reason. It meant the great literature of the eighteenth century, the city of Paris as the City of Light, and, perhaps above all, the fashions and luxuries of Paris. Their readings and travel, their ideals and sympathies, and their definition of France in general therefore produced quite a different view of France and Europe from that held by Nicholas I and the court. For the nobility, the West began west of Berlin and Vienna, while for the court and the state officials, Berlin and Vienna were the centers of the Western world. For the nobility, Victor Hugo, George Sand, and Father Felicité de Lamennais represented the Western giants of the nineteenth century, standing on the shoulders of the great Frenchmen of the eighteenth century.

In short, some of the cultivated aristocracy in the nineteenth century were more French than Russian. They had no real roots in Russian society, the main cultural influences upon them came from abroad, their minds and hearts were always directed westward, they lacked understanding of or sympathy for their native land, and their tradition and upbringing had destroyed many of the beliefs which their ancestors had held. This helps to account for the "betrayal" of Russian tradition by the nobility, a handful of whom turned in revolt against the regime in 1825 and others of whom helped to lead the revolutionary movement later in the nineteenth century.[4]

Probably the most critical period in shaping the view of educated Russians in the nineteenth century was the 1840's, when the celebrated debate took place between the Slavophils and the Westerners about the nature of Russia and about Russia's position in the world. This discussion went back, of course, at least to Peter the Great. It was launched by the publication in French in a Russian journal of the *Philosophical Letters* of Peter Chaadaiev, who argued that Russia had no past, no present, and no future and that Russia had to become a part of Europe if it were to make a significant contribution in world history. This series of essays led to the creation of two schools of the philosophy of history which have had a profound impact on Russian intellectual history and on definitions of Russia and of Russia's attitude toward the rest of the world.

The Slavophils, who were much influenced by the German romantics, in effect tended to glorify Russia, emphasizing the qualities which separated it from other peoples and other countries and arguing that Russia should remain true to its historical traditions. They glorified the Russian Orthodox Church, the saintly quality of the Russian people, the peace and tranquility which prevailed in Russian social and political relations, and the Christian, peasant kingdom which Russia had always been. This glorification of rural Russia and of the Old Regime influenced the Slavophils' view that Russia should remain isolated from other cultures and that in borrowing Russia would only poison the springs of its distinctive civilization. Alexis Khomiakov, the Kireevskys, and the Aksakovs also became convinced that Russia had a mission to the rest of the world and that the outstanding qualities which had characterized the history of the Russian people and of the Russian state should be recognized and adopted by others.

The Slavophils had great admiration for England, partly because Khomiakov and his associates believed that England shared some of the fine qualities they found in Russia. In fact, they saw in England a kind of advanced or progressive Russia, a society which respected conservative institutions, the past, and authority, and which possessed the kind of peaceful relations among classes which they thought existed in Russia.

The Slavophils' view of France was quite different. They thought France an artificial, rational, abstract, depraved, and cruel society, one ruled on occasion by a fierce Catholic monopoly and on other occasions by a bureaucratic and parliamentary despotism. They were convinced that the French people, or at least their rulers, were the prisoners of an abstract rationalism which led them to glorify materialism and cruel despotic rule. One of the Aksakovs wrote that France was "the miserable land called to warn by her fate the rest of mankind, a country flinging herself about between Papacy and atheism, between superstition and disbelief, between slavery and revolt."[5] In short, the Slavophils despised France and feared French influence. The only Frenchmen of their generation whom they admired were de Tocqueville and Montalembert, whom they called "western Slavophils" and whom they considered almost English in their view of the state and society.

The Westerners had a different view. Led by Vissarion Belinsky, the celebrated critic of the 1840's, Herzen, and Nicholas P. Ogarev, they developed a concept of the world which emphasized that Russia was a backward and underdeveloped country which could progress only if it recognized that it was a part of a larger civilization and borrowed effectively from other European countries. The Westerners were in general great admirers of France, particularly of the French Enlightenment and of French socialist thought. They were much influenced by Fourier and Louis Blanc, and they revered Hugo and George Sand, whom Belinsky called "the first poetic glory of the contemporary world" and "the Joan of Arc of our time." While they were occasionally critical of particular French institutions, they generally considered the French "an heroic and noble people." They thought that Russia could progress only if it continued to revise its institutions and values along the lines established clearly by France.

Belinsky reflected some of the principal changes which were occurring in the Russian view of Europe in the second quarter of the nineteenth century. He represents what Vladimir Weidlé has called "the coming of the clerks," because he was of the non-noble class, did not complete his formal education, read French poorly and did not speak it at all, and was more attracted by socialist and radical thought than by the writers of the Enlightenment. In short, he reflected the group which included sons of priests, expelled students, and censored journalists, and which began to have a powerful impact on Russian thinking by the middle of the nineteenth century.[6]

Another important turning point in the Russian view of Europe occurred between 1848 and 1870, when the views of the court, of the leading statesmen, and of the Russian "establishment" became sharply anti-French. The 1848 revolution which spread throughout most of western and central Europe alarmed Russian conservatives. The rise to power of Napoleon III frightened them even more, both because the name of Napoleon meant invasion and because of the radical social policy and the reorganization of Europe which he advocated. Russian failure in the Crimean War, the ensuing "thaw" and reforms, and the unsuccessful revolt of the Poles in 1863 pushed the official Russian view of France even further toward hostility, particularly because of the diplomatic support Napoleon III provided the Poles and because of the traditional Russian fear of the Catholic powers, Poland and France.

Consequently, the official Russian position during the years before the Franco-Prussian War helped Bismarck to create a situation in which he was able to isolate and attack France. The Russian court and most Russian leaders supported Germany in the war. So far as can be determined, most educated Russians not involved in the court or in official activities provided sentimental support for France in 1870, and popular sympathy as well seemed to favor the French against the Germans. However, this popular support for France, which had no effect on state policy, was for the "ideal, imaginary France" of the eighteenth and first part of the nineteenth centuries and not for the France of Napoleon III, for whom there was little affection or sympathy.

While the court and the government were becoming more clearly critical of France during the middle years of the nineteenth century, an important change was also occurring among the aristocracy and among a new class, the intelligentsia. One splendid example of this was provided by Herzen, who left Russia in 1847 but who had a powerful influence on Russian thought and political development during the next quarter-century through his journalistic and other activities abroad. Herzen had been brought up to believe in the France of the great century, but residence in western Europe after 1847 disillusioned him. By 1854, he was almost as critical of France as was Nicholas I, although for quite different reasons. His letters, particularly those written between 1847 and 1854, reveal his disenchantment with France and with Europe in general and his growing conviction that the salvation of Russia had to reflect Russian history and tradition and must be found within Russia itself.[7]

Herzen became convinced that France had little to offer Russia, because he was appalled by the role which the petty bourgeoisie played, because the power of Catholicism as an organized religion filled him with alarm, and because parliamentary government as he saw it practiced by Napoleon III in France and by Palmerston in England depressed him. He was so dismayed by French economic development that he denounced "the small, dirty milieu of petty bourgeoisie, which covers all of France like a green slime." He remarked as early as the 1850's that he had begun "the moral return to my own country." Indeed, he began to have great faith in Russian man and in the likelihood that the Russians might form a society superior to anything with which he was familiar in western Europe. It is no doubt symbolic that Herzen wrote most of his letters in French in 1847, that he began then to write some in German, and that he usually wrote in Russian after 1854.[8]

The Populists, or *narodniki*, whose writings and ideas dominated the Russian social movement in the 1860's, were also critical of France. One of the leading Populists, Peter Lavrov, referred to France as "the republic of humbug." They were much impressed by peasant institutions and believed that the future of socialism could be built on native Russian foundations. They were also more affected by philosophers from England and from Germany than they were by those of France. For example, Herbert Spencer and Darwin had much more influence upon their thinking in the 1860's than the earlier French philosophers or the French Socialists, or even Taine and Comte and Renan, whose writings were among those most popular then in Paris.

Further to the right in the Russian political spectrum, views of France rested on quite different grounds and were even more critical and hostile. The panslavs, the great Russian nationalists who began in the 1860's and 1870's to advocate that "big brother" Russia help lead the other Slavic peoples to independence and to some form of federation under Russian leadership, were more critical of France than were the Populists and were more influenced by England and by Germany than by France. Katkov and other panslavs like him were so mesmerized by the rise of German power and by what they considered the threat the Germans raised in the Balkans that France almost ceased to exist for them. Count Nicholas Ignatiev, the Russian ambassador to Constantinople during most of the 1870's, for example, devoted most of his attention to England and Germany and thought that France was an unimportant power in European politics. Nicholas Danilevsky, whose important volume *Russia and Europe* was published in 1869, so concentrated on Germany that other European states to some degree ceased to exist. General Rostislav Fadeev dismissed France as a power of no importance and wrote that "Russia's chief enemy is by no means western Europe, but the German race and its enormous pretensions." The poet, Fedor Tiutchev, who lived twenty years in Germany, whose two wives were German, and who wrote very often in French, was so consumed by the German problem that he thought France of little importance either politically or culturally.[9]

Dostoevsky illustrates another attitude which fits into this general pattern. He was a great admirer of French literature, read Fourier, George Sand, and Hugo, and was much influenced by Balzac. At the same time, he lived more in Germany than in France, and he was more impressed by German thought and German power than he was by those of the French. For Dostoevsky, Paris was Nineveh, a dying power. In 1868, he criticized a niece who sought a French governess for her daughter because he thought French should no longer be spoken in Russia and because the little girl would learn "vile things" from such a governess. Moreover, France to him represented Roman Catholicism and the idea of force in religion, while Russia represented Orthodoxy and unity in freedom. Dostoevsky saw Catholicism, socialism, the corrupting power of the bourgeoisie, and Western civilization in general as the principal threats to Russia, with France in every case the principal culprit.

Leo Tolstoy represented still another view, but one within this pattern. As a young man, he often read French literature and was particularly impressed by Stendhal. In his teens, he was so influenced by Rousseau that he carried his picture in a locket around his neck. However, Tolstoy visited Paris only twice, in 1857 and 1860. In 1870, he wrote that "civilization and progress are on the side of the Prussians" in the Franco-Prussian war. Although he remained interested and informed about French literature and culture, he became more and more possessed by Russian problems and turned more and more to the Russian peasant and the Russian people for solutions of critical issues. As a consequence, France had little significance in the last forty or fifty years of Tolstoy's life and thought, reflecting in part the great change which had come over the Russian view of Europe in the course of the nineteenth century.[10]

After 1870 and the establishment of the Third Republic, Russian views of Europe again underwent a significant turn. For the court and those involved in guiding the Russian state, the Third Republic was more dismal and even disgusting than the France of Napoleon III. Before the formation of the Russian-French alliance in 1894, the Third Republic was considered a "hot-bed of republicanism, atheism, and anarchy" by those who were engaged in directing Russian destinies. Alexander III once defined France as "nothing but atheists and radicals." In the two decades of history before the alliance was formed in 1894, there was more friction than friendship between the two countries. The outstanding French intellectuals of the time, such as Taine and Renan, had remarkably little influence in Russia.[11]

In short, while French culture retained some influence on Russian society after Napoleon's invasion in 1812, German social thought appears to have attained greater influence than French after approximately 1830. By and large, liberals and conservatives tended to look to England throughout the nineteenth century, and radicals to France and Germany. In addition, those who were most influenced by England tended to be most interested in political ideas, those who turned to France and Germany, in social philosophy and in socialism. Government circles were most influenced by Germany (Iurii Samarin, for example, made a study of the Prussian administrative system), but by the German system of rule rather than by German political and social philosophy.

Late in the nineteenth century, men such as Count Witte began to appear in the Russian state apparatus, men who by character, training, and experience had been affected by Western values and by the Western emphasis upon efficiency and economic progress. Many Russians after the Crimean War began to acquire a new kind of knowledge from Europe, as Russia carried out its reforms and imported capital and technique for industry and transportation. This view of the West came from no one country, though England and Germany were probably the most important single sources, but it had a powerful influence upon Russian action and thought.

Pobedonostsev's position with regard to the West must be considered in the perspective of this historical background. However, his attitude was based also upon his knowledge of his own country and upon the way he defined or thought of his native land. He was a man of the study who isolated himself even from St. Petersburg society. His knowledge of Russia was based largely upon his voluminous reading, on his correspondence with a few friends and with Church officials, and on talks in his office with men and women who sought his advice or aid. He consumed several Russian daily newspapers, including several he despised and thought dangerous. He was thoroughly acquainted with the great writers of his own generation, including Tolstoy, Turgenev, and Chicherin, whose writings he often thought pernicious. He devoured historical novels, the Russian classics, pamphlet literature on contemporary issues, and journals of all varieties.[12]

He was and remained a Muscovite, and his knowledge of Moscow was extraordinary. St. Petersburg never attracted his attention or his affection, and he was acquainted with very little of it outside the area in which the official world lived and worked. He made four trips of several months' duration through European Russia, two in the 1860's when he served as a tutor and two in the 1880's, when he visited a number of church centers. He was well acquainted with many of the monasteries in European Russia, and he especially enjoyed visiting the old churches in Vladimir, Yaroslavl, Suzdal, and Kostroma. Early in their married life, the Pobedonostsevs spent parts of several summers on the Baltic coast near Narva, and they later often spent Septembers in the Crimea.

However, his information concerning Russian life and conditions was limited. He ventured beyond the Urals only twice, in 1885 and 1889 on official missions, and he never travelled east of Irkutsk or into Central Asia. He travelled into the Caucasus only three times, on each occasion on an official trip which he combined with a holiday. He was forty-two years old before he visited Kiev, and fifty-four before he stayed in Warsaw. When he travelled, he acquired only the knowledge a contemporary businessman does, for he limited himself to his hotel and the church or office in which he was interested. He had no interest in the life of the city or its inhabitants. The worlds of the merchant or of the worker were equally unknown to him. Moreover, he read constantly while he travelled by train and did not view the countryside. In his youth, he visited several times the country place of Lazhechnikov, the historical novelist who had been a student of his father. He paid several short visits to the estate of his father-in-law near Smolensk, he once visited Ilminskii in that same area, and he once visited the country place of an acquaintance near Moscow. Yet except for his research and writing on legal and economic problems affecting rural life, there is no evidence of knowledge of or concern with peasant life. In other words, like Marx, he was a city boy. Indeed, he was in this way a "typical" member of the Russian intelligentsia.

His lack of concern for the countryside and the peasant help mark him off from the Slavophils, who had a special veneration for the peasant and for the *narod* and who had a dual image of Russia in which the state, an unavoidable evil, played an artificial and often arbitrary role. They saw Russia as a harmonious organic country, without classes or class divisions, distinguished by vigor, simplicity, love, Orthodoxy, and peaceful change, and they considered the Orthodox Church free from and superior to the Romanov state. The Slavophils spoke often of Holy Russia; Pobedonostsev never used the phrase. Indeed, the Slavophils would have considered him and most other bureaucrats and members of the intelligentsia in the last third of the nineteenth century, conservative or radical, as non-Russians, city-dwellers who had been corrupted by Western ideas without realizing it.

In short, for Pobedonostsev Russia meant the state, the various organs of the state apparatus, and the ideas which held the state together and gave it distinctive meaning. He was convinced that Orthodoxy and the Russian Orthodox Church provided the doctrine and the cement which held society together and gave it meaning and substance. They were at the heart of the distinct and superior Russian way of life. He also saw Russia as a member of a European state system and as one of a number of states in the world, with some of which it should maintain formal relations. Moreover, he did not believe Russia should participate actively in world affairs. Indeed, there is some evidence that he resented and opposed all foreign alliances. In other words, he was an isolationist. During the Balkan war of 1876 and 1877, he adopted a position which was an exception to his basic one and which in fact helped to solidify his view or policy. From that time forward, he turned the interest and the power of the state inside. He opposed entangling alliances or collisions with other states. He assigned to the Orthodox Church and to economic imperialism whatever strength and influence Russia was to have beyond her borders. He profoundly believed that it was impossible and dangerous for one society to attempt to borrow ideas and institutions from another or to impose its customs and system upon another. Each society, in short, was an independent organism.[13]

Both the Slavophils and the panslavs thought Russia was unique in having a messianic role to play in the history of Europe and the world—a different role was envisaged by each group—but Pobedonostsev, and many of his generation, after 1880 believed that Russia's destiny was simply to preserve and save the territory, institutions, and beliefs which he then cherished.

The education he received from his father was both Muscovite and Western. His family life, religious training, and early education were all heavily impregnated by Russian history and tradition. At the same time, in the little house on Bread Lane he learned to read, write, and speak German, Latin, and French, as well as Old Church Slavonic. He learned Greek and English at the School of Jurisprudence in St. Petersburg, and he learned to read Polish and Czech, probably at home from his brother Sergei. He was able to translate from all of these languages and to speak and write all except English, in which he could converse but which his wife mastered much more fluently than he. During the two decades in which he devoted enormous time and energy to research in the field of civil law, the emphasis he inevitably placed upon Western systems, principles, concepts, and sources enormously increased his understanding of other societies. This was supplemented during those years devoted to improving the Russian judicial system, for he concentrated then upon an analysis of the legal arrangements in France, England, and the German states. He even considered learning Italian at that time so that Russia could benefit from any improvements which could be borrowed from Italy.

Throughout his life, he had an intense curiosity concerning intellectual life in western Europe, and he clearly enjoyed and valued the months he spent there. The range of his interests was immense. He read book reviews with extraordinary care. He visited libraries and bookstores in every city to which he travelled, both Russian and foreign, to scan the old and new books and journals. Even on his first trip to London, he became acquainted with some of the staff members of the British Museum.

Similarly, he was eager to meet foreigners who came to Moscow and St. Petersburg. He especially enjoyed quiet chats concerning intellectual developments with the Greek, German, and English ambassadors, with the American minister, and with interesting junior men on their staffs. Journalists and scholarly observers of the Russian scene, such as MacKenzie Wallace of the *London Times*, author of the classic volume in English on Russia in the nineteenth century, were occasional evening companions and correspondents. Eugene Schuyler, whose volumes on Central Asia created great interest in the English-speaking world in the 1870's and 1880's; Anatole Leroy-Beaulieu, who later angered Pobedonostsev by referring to him as "The Russian Torquemada" but whose books helped increase French interest in Russia after 1880; George Kennan, "who arrived with most impressive credentials" but whose book in 1885, *Siberia and the Exile System*, candidly exposed the horrors of Russian treatment of the political opposition—these men and their colleagues in journalism and scholarship attracted the interest and attention of Pobedonostsev, who was always eager to meet them. Visiting statesmen and clergymen, regardless of their national origin and faith, were invited to his study for conversation. In short, he was intensely interested in learning from European and American visitors and informing them of his views concerning Russia and the world.[14]

His knowledge of the West was derived mainly from omnivorous and constant reading, however, and, to a much lesser but still significant degree, from travel and holidays in western Europe. He loved to be busy, but he resented the arrival of visitors "who took the books" from his hands. He sometimes took a train from St. Petersburg to Moscow in order to acquire an opportunity for uninterrupted reading. He read consistently the *London Times*, the *Daily News*, the *Manchester Guardian*, *Blackwood's*, the *Review of Reviews*, *Fraser's*, *The Nineteenth Century*, and the *Revue des Deux Mondes*. During times of tension, such as the period from 1876 through 1878, he devoted particular attention to the foreign press. When he was abroad, he read all of the newspapers he could purchase in or near his hotel.

Books, however, were the main staple of his diet of Western publications, with Victorian England the principal contributor. He was a great admirer and constant reader of Thomas Carlyle, whose views concerning the nature of man, of government, and of peoples (for example, the Jews) very much resembled his own. During the last twenty years of his life, he was especially interested in the writings of William Morris, whom he called "the finest of all contemporary writers" and whose photograph he obtained for his desk through Olga Novikov. He enjoyed the Whig historian Macaulay and the Tory Froude, the work of great liberals, such as Gladstone, John Morley, and John Stuart Mill, and the volumes of rooted conservatives, such as Sir Henry Maine and Kinglake. Spencer, Seeley, and Darwin were balanced by the novels of Marie Corelli and Mrs. Humphrey Ward. Browning, Shelley, and Swinburne were among his favorite English poets.[15]

American literature was, of course, less rich then and less well known, even in western Europe. He had very high admiration for Emerson, some of whose essays he translated. In fact, he tried to read a little of Emerson every day, and he told the American minister that he always had a copy of an Emerson volume on his desk. Hawthorne, Lowell, Mark Twain, and James Fenimore Cooper were also among his favorites.[16]

Although his research in civil law reflects extensive study of German law and of work in German on the history of civil law, he read considerably less in German than in English. The great scholar in the history of law, Savigny, was one of his early mentors and had a profound influence upon his view of institutional history. In fact, he referred to Savigny's *System des heutigen römischen Rechts* as "a book unequalled in the strictness of its juristic analysis, for the soundness of its conclusions, for the simplicity of its organization

and method of thought, and for the grace and elegance of its style."
He also read Max Nordau, Schopenhauer, and Schiller, as well as
Goethe, Heine, and Lessing. Late in life, he was delighted to have
many of his views confirmed by the volumes of Houston Stewart
Chamberlain, whose *Die Grundlagen des XIX Jahrhunderts* had a
significant impact upon Wagner and Hitler and upon the Nazi
movement. However, there is no evidence that he ever read
Treitschke or Nietzsche.[17]

His range of reading in French was also not so wide as that in
English. As a young man, he had been deeply moved by Lamartine
and by the "sentimental socialists," especially Fourier, whom he
later called "an insane genius." Le Play was a constant favorite, as
was Fustel de Coulanges. He was immensely impressed by Taine's
Les Origines de la France contemporaine and by Taine's other
work, which supported his own theses concerning intellectual and
political developments in Europe in the eighteenth and nineteenth
centuries. The novels of Zola in a different way also confirmed his
views, while Molière, Montaigne, and Racine represented the good
old France which had been swept away by the Revolution.[18]

In short, Pobedonostsev's reading reveals that he was in many
ways a highly cultivated European, as much a European as Gladstone, Bismarck, Pius IX, or Andrassy. One should note, however,
that Europe or the West to him really included only England, the
United States, Germany, and France. He read nothing written in
Scandinavia, except for Ibsen. Italian literature, even Dante, did
not exist for him, and neither did Spanish. Even the other Slavs
were neglected. In fact, the Europe in which he was interested and
about which he read was largely the "Anglo-Saxon Europe" of
which he often wrote. Moreover, he concentrated almost entirely
upon the writings of his contemporaries, even of his own generation, both in his scholarly research and in his general reading. Thus,
he did not read such writers as Hobbes, Burke, and de Maistre, who
might have been expected to have appealed to him. Finally he
read almost entirely in *belles lettres*, philosophy, and intellectual
history. Politics, economics, international relations, and science,
for example, were almost completely absent from his fare.

His travels reflect the same interests and qualities and help to
illuminate both his knowledge of Europe and his attitude toward it.
He wrote Anna Tiutchev in November, 1864, that he could not
imagine himself "outside my native air," particularly because
"they" hated, despised, and ridiculed Russia and Russians. He was

forty-one years old before he went abroad, but he visited Europe for a month or six weeks in the summer in more than half of the remaining years of his life, in every case with his wife. His last trip, to Marienbad, was made when he was seventy-five years old.

England was his first interest and affection, and he spent parts of the summers of 1868, 1869, and 1873 there, largely in London and on the Isle of Wight. He wrote Catherine Tiutchev that he went to England first "because England after Russia pleases me most." He was fascinated by the British Museum, the monuments, and, above all, Westminster Abbey and the variety of churches. His summers in England may have significantly influenced his philosophy, for they led him to reflect on the nature of institutions, the differences between societies, and the special qualities which set Russia off from even England and which dictated her future course.[19]

In 1874, he spent a month in Salzburg, which was thereafter his favored vacation center, even though it did not offer a Russian Orthodox Church. He was impressed by its trees and flowers, its marvelous views, its museums and churches, its libraries and bookstores, and the old portraits one found everywhere. He wrote that he liked Salzburg more than any other place in the world except Moscow. Salzburg, Marienbad, and Wiesbaden thereafter were his European vacation centers. From these sites, he travelled to Prague to meet interesting Czech priests and statesmen, to Bayreuth to hear *Lohengrin*, to Vienna to give assistance to Ruthenians living under Austrian or Hungarian rule, and to northern Italy to see the golden city of Venice and the mosaics at Ravenna.[20]

The Europe to which he travelled and in which he spent his holidays resembles the Europe whose literature he read. He did not visit Prague after 1876, and he never travelled in the Balkans. He did not visit any part of Scandinavia, except for six days in Copenhagen in 1873, when the Pobedonostsevs travelled with the children of Grand Duke Alexander on their way to England. He never visited Helsinki, even though it was then a part of the Russian empire. Moreover, he never travelled to France or to any part of French territory, even though he visited Brussels in 1873. He was much pleased in 1888 by his being elected a corresponding member of the Académie des Sciences Morales et Politiques of the Institut de France, even though the other foreigner so honored that year was Sir James Stephens, whose views he abhorred. He kept the Academy informed concerning his achievements and honors, and he forwarded it copies of his publications. He even considered going to Paris to attend the celebration of the two hundredth anniversary of the founding of the Academy. However, he could never bring himself to step on French soil, particularly to visit Paris.[21]

Similarly, he enjoyed hearing foreigners and other Russians describe Rome, and he was immensely interested in that great city. He wrote that he often dreamed of going there, and he spoke enviously to Angelicans who had attended services in St. Peter's. However, even before he became Director General of the Synod, he thought it was impossible, "almost illegal," to visit the center of the Roman Catholic Church. As he wrote to one English acquaintance, he was so much a Russian that he could not also become a citizen of the world, which an Orthodox visitor to Rome inevitably became.[22]

He travelled to Europe for a rest and a renewal of his health and spirits, but he also went because of his powerful interest in the West. His vacations were devoted in part to reading and in part to tours of places of historical significance. He attended Catholic churches where there was no Orthodox Church, he studied carefully churches of other denominations, and he attended services of many denominations, Anglican, Lutheran, Methodist, Unitarian, and Deist. He even studied the Salvation Army, visited missions and soup kitchens in the slums of London, and analyzed various nonconformist sects. He commented on the architecture, seating plans, organ music, choirs, sermons, and financing of churches. He concluded that the various churches in England, for example, revealed the differences between "the Russian and the Anglo-Saxon world." In the Anglican church, he was alienated by the seating arrangements, the individual prayer, the absence of a sense of union or communion, and the stiff and uncomfortable character of the services. The preferment system he considered outrageous, and the flourishing of so many varieties of churches in England proved to him that none met the national need. Even so, the English seemed satisfied, which showed that "all institutions are shaped by history, grow out of historical conditions, and develop in a logical and necessary way from the past."

He was impressed by parts of the Catholic services he attended, but he was appalled by the apparent isolation of the priest from the parishioners. Moreover, he considered most of the service "theatrical mimicking." The *kulturkampf*, on the other hand, he described as "one of the most interesting and important events of our time."

In short, travel abroad, conversations and correspondence with ministers of faiths other than Orthodoxy, and study combined to persuade him that Russia and the West possessed two different ways of life. Above all, the ignorance and hostility he found concerning Orthodoxy and Russia convinced him that neither side could hope to influence the other or even to trust the other. "This ignorance of the Latins about the Russian Church and people is astonishing. It of course comes from their contemptuous attitude toward the East in general, and from the pride of their own culture." Since the West thought it possessed light and the East darkness, and since the West did not see or understand national peculiarities and differences between races, relationships between Russia and the West would have to remain stiff and reserved.[23]

In his definition of the West, he was no more clear or consistent than we are today. Generally, however, for him the West meant that part of Europe west of Vienna and Berlin. Geographically and culturally, the West did not include the Balkans or any territories inhabited by Poles or other Slavs. Scandinavia was a part of Europe and therefore of the West, but it was generally neglected. Italy and Spain were naturally Western and European geographically and culturally, but Italy smelled too strongly of the Papacy and Spain was too forlorn and backward to deserve serious consideration. Pobedonostsev and his generation, of all political groupings, had much interest in American politics, economic development, and literature. Indeed, when he referred to Anglo-Saxon ideas and institutions in the last decade of his life, he often seemed to include the United States, although he did not make it explicit. In fact, he believed that England and the United States would succeed in maintaining constitutional and democratic government, which would fail elsewhere.

However, he defined the West not in terms of geography, but in terms of institutions, values, and ideas. The West to him meant that part of western Europe, including the British Isles, where four significant ideas were widely accepted: the concept of the excellence of natural man and the belief that man was a rational being, which he thought fundamental to Catholicism and to Protestantism and which he considered the foundation of Western political institutions; the idea that the individual was important, perhaps even more important than the state or society; the belief in the effectiveness and propriety of government by law and parliamentary democracy; and the emphasis upon freedom and diversity. Pobedonostsev believed that none of these ideas and values could or should be adopted in Russia. Indeed, borrowing in this case could only be destructive, perhaps fatal.

In addition, however, as he grew older and travelled more extensively, the West for him also meant industrialization: the telegraph, the railroad, electric power, the comforts of Western hotels, and the inevitable growth of national economic and military power and status. He was well aware of the social consequences the transformation of western Europe was producing, but he was equally convinced that the achievements and promise of industrialization must be imported from the West.

He could not have agreed with Chaadaiev, or with the Westerners in general, that "not one useful thought has germinated on the barren soil of our country; not one great truth has sprung up in our midst." He would have disagreed strongly with Nicholas Turgenev, who wrote in 1847: "In Europe, in most civilized countries, institutions have developed by stages; everything that exists there has its source and roots in the past; the Middle Ages still serve, more or less, as the basis for everything that constitutes the social, civic, and political life of the European states. Russia has had no Middle Ages; everything that is to prosper there must be borrowed from Europe; Russia cannot graft it on her own ancient institutions."[24]

In other words, Pobedonostsev did not have the Westerner's view of Russia and of the West. He did not consider the West as the cradle of a superior universal civilization which could flourish anywhere. He did think Russia had a national culture with its own distinct personality. At the same time, he was neither a Slavophil nor a Eurasian: he could not have said that "Russia has preserved the childhood of Europe" nor that it is "a world apart." Russia to him was simply another one of the world's societies or civilizations. It had been heavily influenced by the West since Peter and Catherine, but these influences had been limited to the structure and operation of the central government and to the process of industrialization. The effort to maintain the old system, especially the old values, in the face of economic change and of the rise of liberal and radical political ideas which flourished in part because of these changes, was extremely difficult for him and others like him. Indeed, this was largely responsible for his pessimistic assumption that a revolution would sweep away the Russia he knew and bring in European ideas and institutions.[25]

His old friend in the country near Smolensk, Nicholas Ilminskii,

wanted to abandon the accepted system of musical notation, because he considered it an "Italian, Catholic, and foreign" creation
which "had brought evil and corruption into our Church." Nicholas
Ilminskii, in Kazan, was opposed to the construction of railroads,
even though he recognized that a railroad would bring "golden
rain." Pobedonostsev viewed the West and importations from it
through the same kind of spectacles, but his hostility and fear were
concentrated upon political and religious ideas and upon some of
the main intellectual currents then dominant in western Europe,
especially positivism and secularism. The main hazards the West
posed were unbelief, which threatened to dissolve the very foundations of the Russian state, and western political systems, with their
growing emphasis upon constitutional government, universal suffrage, equality, liberty, and the rule of parties. The last four decades
of his life were devoted to the defense of Russia against these elements from the West. Even the Salvation Army constituted a
threat.[26]

Thus, basically he rejected the Europe of the second half of the
nineteenth century, just as Pius IX did in the Syllabus of Errors. He
was contemptuous of the idea that an individual had sacred rights
and that all should participate in government: the rights of the
state and society must always prevail over those of the individual.
He saw constitutional government as "the tyranny of the mass" and
the "weapon of the unrighteous." Parliamentary government and
democracy to him meant party rule, which produced the division
and weakening of the state, rule by party ministries dominated by
eloquent and ambitious scoundrels, the predominance in society
of party machines and corruption, and the triumph of general ideas,
meaningless and destructive but attractive to ambitious and unscrupulous politicians and to the ignorant masses. He was opposed
even to advisory councils, such as the *zemskii sobor*. He believed
that the greatest dangers for Russia derived from intellectuals and
the ideas they produced and carried. Freedom of the press was a
Western device for inundating Russia with lies.

On the other hand, his hostility to the West was not so blind or
consistent as to prevent him from admiring some aspects of European life and from seeking benefit for himself and for Russia from
Europe. One of the satisfactions which he enjoyed, but which he
thought should always be restricted to the trusted intellectual elite,
which he labelled "the aristocracy of intellect," was access to the
learning and information of the West. His beloved Russia clearly

provided him little intellectual excitment; this he found in Western newspapers, journals, and books. His holidays abroad also represent a part of his exploitation of the West. He used ideas and information acquired from the West in his scholastic debates with other Russians concerning the nature and future of Russia and the most fitting policies for the government. In fact, the West was a kind of reserve armory or storehouse of ammunition for him, and Le Play, Thiersch, Emerson, Carlyle, and Thomas à Kempis were quarried for arguments he used in defense of the old regime. At the same time, of course, he denounced other ideas and beliefs as "foreign" and therefore dangerous for the Russian body politic.

His attitudes toward the West were therefore marked by a number of paradoxical ambivalences. Although he resented and despised much of the West, it was at the same time the hub of his universe, as Boston was the center of the universe for Emerson and his fellows. He was simultaneously a Westerner and a Westernizer, and an Orthodox, fundamentalist, Russian nationalist. He was opposed to Western influence, but wished to use Western innovations to strengthen state power. He sought to preserve the state system and the privileged position of Orthodoxy in a system guided by religious faith, while he also sought to have the patriarchal, absolute state introduce reforms from the top. He was excited and inspired by the West, although at the same time he hated and feared it. Russia was superior to the West, and yet he believed the state should increase its efforts to "catch up" with the West without affecting society or philosophy. Indeed, he almost seems to prove Chaadaiev's charge that "only Russia's government is Western."[27]

In the history yet to be written of Russia's intellectual relations with the West since the eighteenth century, Pobedonostsev represents a critical stage in the transition from the "idol worship" which generally characterized the aristocracy in the eighteenth century to the combination of relentless and frightened hostility with intensive scientific and technological borrowing, which are important parts of the Soviet position. He reflects the transition from the Slavophils through the panslavs to the Russian nationalism of the period just before the First World War. He also represents the decline of religion and of the religious framework through which the West was viewed. In addition, the dry and dusty character of his feeling for Russia and the Russian people is demonstrated by the absence of enthusiasm on his part for the nobility, the *narod*, or any identifiable Russian group or class.

His role in the transition can be demonstrated perhaps most effectively by comparing his views with those of one of his predecessors and of several of the men just one generation younger than he. Thus, Nicholas I and his chief administrator in cultural affairs, Count Uvarov, were hostile not to Europe, but only to a particular definition of Europe. Uvarov, the symbol of the repressive policy toward culture and education in the 1830's and 1840's, considered himself a true European. He spoke several European languages, and he had received the kind of education which Nicholas I considered dangerous for other Russians. He was a great admirer of Europe, but of the Europe that existed before 1789. He feared the French revolution with its secularism and liberalism and its effort to destroy the old France, which he considered the soul of Europe. Consequently, just like Pobedonostsev, he sought to preserve the regime which he and others like him had cherished, but to destroy the Europe of the first half of the nineteenth century, which he considered a perversion of European history and tradition.

The character of the changes which had taken place can be demonstrated by comparing Uvarov's views with those of outstanding Russians of the quarter-century before the First World War, such as Count Sergei Witte, who began the massive industrialization of Russia and who represented the new businessman's spirit at the very highest levels of the government. Witte was born in Tiflis, which was quite removed from European influence and the rise of which illustrates the growing significance of areas remote from Moscow and St. Petersburg. His early career was based on important achievements in the railroad industry. As he rose to power over the railroad system and then to a commanding position over Russian finance and economic development, his view of Europe began to be impressed upon the Russian state.

Uvarov, who had sought to resist European influence, was in many ways more European in culture than Witte, who did not read easily or well in any foreign language, and who did not travel extensively. However, Witte was interested in making Russia a modern European power and in borrowing from the new Europe as effectively as he could. The Europe from which he borrowed was industrial Germany. For many members of the educated aristocracy in the first third of the nineteenth century, such as Uvarov, Berlin was on the easternmost fringe of the frontiers of Europe. For Witte, however, Berlin and all of Germany were the very heart of Europe, even though France became an ally of Russia and French funds helped the Russian drive toward industrialization. To him, German industrial power constituted the heart and the future of Europe.

Peter Stolypin, who was the principal political leader in Russia from 1906 until his death in 1911, represented in many ways the same kind of development. Born in Dresden and resident of that part of the empire closest to East Prussia, Stolypin's view of Europe concentrated upon Germany. He was particularly influenced by the agricultural progress he saw in East Prussia when he set out to "wager on the strong" by abolishing the *mir* and by seeking to establish an independent farming class. Stolypin, in other words, looked first of all to Germany, and to a lesser degree to the United States, when he sought to reorganize the Russian rural economy and social system. France was a very minor power indeed, so far as Stolypin and his generation of those remaking Russia were concerned, and the qualities which had attracted the attention and affection of earlier generations did not interest them.

Lenin provides another example. He was born in Simbirsk on the Volga in a family in which French and German were read and spoken. He was well educated within Russia and spent an important part of his life abroad, being as much at home in London, Paris, and Capri as he was in Moscow or St. Petersburg. However, he had very little regard for France or England and was very little influenced by French or English thought. As a disciple of Marx, he was especially learned in German thought, and he declared Germany "the classical country of capitalism and of socialism." The central point of Europe had therefore moved east from Paris, where it had been earlier in the century for most educated Russians, and the focus was now on economics rather than *belles lettres*.

For most educated Russians, France remained "old France" and had less intellectual and political impact and effect than did "new Germany." The rise of Germany and its place in the Russian view of Europe is also naturally reflected in philosophy and in statecraft. For example, Hegel had replaced Voltaire by the middle of the nineteenth century in Russian political thought. Bismarck clearly had more influence on the Russian state and on Russian politics in the latter part of the nineteenth century than did Napoleon III or any of the statesmen of the Third Republic. Consequently, when the modernization of Russia was begun, particularly under Count Witte, and when Russia's army, industry, and state system were reorganized during the course of the last part of the nineteenth century, the Russians almost inevitably turned to Germany rather than to France.

This changing attitude is represented clearly in the Russian state structure and in institutional developments. The Napoleonic Code had considerable influence outside France during the first part of the nineteenth century, even in Russia, and Michael Speransky, to whom Alexander I assigned the responsibility for planning the reorganization of the central government in the first decade of Alexander I's reign, turned to French institutions as his models. The institute established by Prince Peter Oldenburg in St. Petersburg in 1836 to provide training in law for future Russian bureaucrats paid as much attention to the Napoleonic Code as it did to Roman law. However, by the middle of the nineteenth century, Russian law professors were studying under Savigny in Berlin, and it was German and English, rather than French, influence which helped to shape the judicial reform of 1864 and the legal institutions and attitudes which developed in Russia following that momentous change.

This new view of Europe naturally was a result of a number of changes within Russia, particularly the decline of the aristocracy and the various waves of social revolution which swept over the country. As the nobility lost its influence and power, its view of Europe became less significant. At the same time, the new radical view of the West which began to develop after the 1840's and the increasing effort to modernize Russia led to a view which was quite critical of France as a bourgeois country and as one which possessed very little dynamism. Even the court, especially the men with power in the higher levels of government, such as Witte and Stolypin, had a low regard for France as a model for Russia, and turned more to Germany and even to the United States for patterns of development which Russia might follow.

This change naturally derived to some degree from changes which occurred within France during the course of the century. The Old Regime and the Enlightenment had a clear and powerful attraction for Russians, one which diminished as France became less stable and more bourgeois. The rise to power of the middle class in France occurred at the same time that the anti-bourgeois tradition in Russia increased in strength, both among the nobles and among the lower classes as they achieved intellectual and political significance. In fact, it is illuminating to note the similarities between the views of many Russian radicals and of Pobedonostsev with regard to the

West. As Professor Venturi's masterful study of the Populists has
shown, their attitude was quite similar to his toward prominent
Western ideas and institutions: constitutional government, political
democracy, the party system, Western judicial procedures, Darwinism, Spencer, and capitalism. Moreover, the similarities of view between Pobedonostsev and even later Russian radicals, including
the Bolsheviks, were even more remarkable, for they not only
shared attitudes toward liberalism and its institutional forms but
also saw Russia as a model society surrounded by hostile states and
threatened by cultural infection from abroad.[28]

There were and remain dissimilarities, however. The most important of these is the contrast between the verve and optimism of
the Bolsheviks and the gloomy pessimism of Pobedonostsev. He
emphasized the historical origins of the society he was defending
and believed the creative forces were all in the West. He was confident that constitutional forms of government would not survive on
the continent of Europe, except perhaps in Belgium and in
the Scandinavian states, but he also believed that Russian society
and the Russian state would soon collapse because of the hollowness
of its internal strengths and the persistence of powerful external
pressures.

XIV

Fading Away

THROUGHOUT the twenty-five years in which he was Director General of the Most Holy Synod, Pobedonostsev was generally considered the man most responsible for Russian domestic policy, particularly for those decisions which affected education, access to information, civil rights, and national and religious minorities. This view is reflected in the memoir literature of that time and is firmly implanted also in the histories of that era. His influence was decisive during the critical spring of 1880, and it was important in the 1880's in the appointment of officials in the Ministeries of Education, Interior, and Justice in particular. He also had considerable authority then on policies affecting Russian intellectual life. However, his interest in and influence upon policies outside his own special spheres of interest, such as foreign policy, were minimal. Moreover, after 1890, especially after 1896, his influence throughout the government declined perceptibly. During the last decade or so of his official life, except for a few key appointments with which he was concerned, he had virtually no power.

His decline was concealed because the outward trappings of authority remained the same. He retained his conspicuous positions in the Synod and the Council of State, the Council of Ministers, and the Senate, and his role at the court appeared unchanged. He was honored on a number of occasions by the last two tsars: Alexander III bestowed a number of awards upon him, of which the most important was the Order of Saint Alexander Nevsky in 1888, and he appointed him a secretary of state, or a kind of privy councillor, in 1894. Nicholas I gave him the Order of Vladimir, first class, and

Portrait of Pobedonostsev made in 1902 by Serov. (From Igor E. Grabor, *Valentin Aleksandrovich Serov. Zhizn' i tvorchestvo* [Moscow, 1913], 159.)

also arranged a special celebration in 1896 in honor of his fifty years of service in the bureaucracy. Later he was given the highest award the government could then give a civilian. Both in 1898 and at his retirement in October, 1905, he was honored with an imperial rescript.[1]

The laurels and awards on one hand were balanced by criticism and attacks on the other. His imagined power created such obloquy that he was widely blamed among political and intellectual circles for every unpopular action or inaction of the government. He received a large number of threatening letters. He was the gloomy, forbidding symbol of the Old Regime even for Lenin.[2] Moreover, in an era when several Russian political leaders were assassinated, five attempts were made to kill him, all during those years of his political life when his authority had gravely diminished. He escaped a number of other such attacks only because he failed to attend funerals or other public gatherings that he had been scheduled to attend.[3]

The evidence of his declining influence is clear. The rich archival materials simply indicate that both his interest and authority disintegrated. Except over the Church, education, and access to information, in which his power also declined to some degree, he failed to exert any jurisdiction. During the last decade of his life, he rarely attended sessions of the Council of State or other high institutions, often sending his deputy, Sabler, to represent him. He was not appointed to the significant committees of the Council of State. His correspondence with the tsars declined progressively, and his private meetings with them became rare. After 1896, he consulted with Nicholas II only on Church affairs. During the last ten years of his life, he lamented the way in which the tsar and his ministers failed to consult him on matters on which he had once had the decisive voice. In 1896, he did assist Witte in persuading Nicholas II to reject a proposal by the ambassador in Constantinople, Nelidov, that the Russians seize the Bosporus during the Armenian crisis in order to ensure a strong position when the anticipated disintegration of the Ottoman Empire occurred. Privately, he was bitterly opposed to Russian policy in the Far East, but his views were not sought or considered. The policy of rapid industrialization carried out by the energetic Witte during the years he was Minister of Finance, from 1892 until 1903, was not influenced in any way by Pobedonostsev, although he was convinced the system of landholding had to be revised along American lines and that modern industrial technology had to be introduced.[4]

The reasons for his declining influence after 1890 and the precipitate collapse of it after 1896 are quite obvious. Alexander III had been deeply annoyed by his role in the fiasco of Ashinov in the Abyssinian project in 1889 and by the way in which the government was embarrassed at the same time by Pobedonostsev's policies toward the Baltic Germans and Lutheranism.* Shortly thereafter, the rise of Witte and the new concentration of government interest and policy on economic development inevitably reduced his significance. Similarly, the death of most of Pobedonostsev's retainers in the administration and their replacement by younger men whom he did not know crippled his influence, which was almost always exercised behind the scenes. The decline and death of Alexander III removed his faithful pupil from the throne. Pobedonostsev had been the tutor of Nicholas II as well as of Alexander III, but their first meetings took place a year after he had been appointed, which reveals much concerning their importance. The relationship was never so close as it had been between Alexander III and Pobedonostsev, and he did not acquire the same ascendance over his new charge's mind. Nicholas II did not have the same interests as his father, particularly in religion and in the Orthodox Church. He was in fact indifferent to most of his professor's concerns.[5]

In addition, Pobedonostsev about 1890 began progressively to lose the burning concern he had previously felt. One cause of this was the disaffection which grew between him and the tsars. Another was his resigned annoyance with the public criticism and the private gossip about his political fortunes which floated around the St. Petersburg world, which he had always despised. He was so wearied by criticisms he considered petty and misguided that he ceased defending himself. Finally, his health, which was never robust, became increasingly delicate. He was seventy years old in 1897, but he was infirm several years before that.

The state of his health may explain much concerning Pobedonostsev's ideas and actions. He was always slight. Even as a boy, he had frequently been ill. He possessed no physical reserve strength, so that minor colds often were prolonged and kept him in bed for a week or even several weeks. His correspondence and that of his

* See pp. 187-92, 231-37.

friends is filled with references to his being unwell. He was ordinarily in bed for a week with a cold after his return from his summer
vacations, whether they were on the Baltic coast, in the Crimea, or in
Salzburg. February and March were always months of sickness for
him, and his correspondence for these months had a particularly
baneful and gloomy character. He always disliked St. Petersburg,
in part because its weather was not salubrious. It is likely that the
colds and influenza from which he suffered, which often affected
his eyes, were due in part to the damp climate of the capital city.
The various frequent illnesses from which his wife suffered no
doubt influenced his own health and also contributed to his morose
view of the world.[6]

Often unwell, a hypochondriac with a sickly wife who was also a
hypochondriac, he apparently suffered from poor health with increasing frequency during the last fifteen years of his life. He aged
quickly after 1890; his acquaintances noticed that he complained
bitterly about trifles and that his voice had become a constant whine.
He failed to attend an ever larger number of official meetings because of illness. He did not even visit Moscow at any time in 1900.
He often remained at home simply because he was exhausted. He
spoke and talked frequently of resigning from his various posts, but
inertia so gripped him that he failed to act. He took a holiday from
May through September in 1896, in part to celebrate the golden
anniversary of his years of service and in part because he was simply
decrepit. In effect, except for a flash of resistance to reform within
the Church in 1905, he resigned in 1896.[7]

He had always had a somber view of human nature and of man's
prospects in this world. The gloom and pessimism which pervaded
his view became even more bleak in his last years. As early as 1881,
when he was only fifty-four years old, he became depressed by the
death of colleagues and began to wonder how long he would live.
He was always a frightened and fearful man, but even the German
ambassador was perplexed by his fear of war when not a cloud
threatened the horizon of international politics. As his political influence waned and he felt ever more neglected and isolated, his pessimism deepened. He was ever more impressed that the growing
"maladies of our time" would overwhelm Russia and the world.
His old fears concerning constitutional and democratic government,
freedom of the press, and religious freedom were swollen by concern over the growing number of suicides, the sensual appetites of
the young, the rule of the false and artificial and meaningless. "All

fades, all vanishes, all disintegrates, all deceives." The sensible goal
of the state was to delay the collapse of society because it could not
be prevented. "There is no light visible anywhere, and the horizons
are closed."[8]

The revolutionary events of 1904 and 1905 naturally confirmed
the correctness of these pessimistic views. Ill much of the winter of
1904–1905 and embittered because no one visited or asked his advice, he was convinced that the unrest he could hear from his windows would lead to disorders such as Russia had never seen and to
slaughter throughout the country. He was especially moved by the
assassination of Grand Duke Sergei Alexandrovich, who had been
his favorite pupil and the one over whom he had had the greatest
influence. He confessed in February, 1905, that he had long since
given up hope for restoring sanity in Russia. When he talked with
the Empress dowager in May, he told her that all was lost and that
she should "go back home and cry."[9]

His role during the exciting days of 1904 and 1905 was unimportant, except for one briefly successful intervention with Nicholas II
in March, 1905, to preserve the established system of Church administration. He had ignored the vigorous campaign of leading
churchmen and religious journals which, after 1902 in particular,
urged review and reorganization of the Church's administration
and its role in the state. Indeed, he ignored the crucial Council of
Ministers meetings in November, 1904, which led to the ukase of
December 12 that promised religious toleration and gave assurance
that this would be defined soon in legislation. In 1905, he did not
attend the sessions of the high institutions of which he was a member, except for the October 3 meeting of the Council of State, when
the situation was most critical and a decision had to be made concerning the form of government Russia was to have. During these
crucial months, when the position of the Church was being debated,
he did not call a meeting of the Synod or consult at any time with
leading clerics. He sent Sabler to the special committee chaired by
Witte in January, February, and March, 1905, to discuss the
Church's role and the principle of toleration. He made only one or
two brief attempts to sway Nicholas II, an approach quite different
from the one he had adopted in the spring of 1881 with Alexander
III. He did redraft the manifesto of February 18, 1905, which he
made into a critique of reform and a rousing old-fashioned defense
of autocracy. He also presided over a committee which on July 30
reviewed a draft of the August 6 manifesto on electoral procedures,

but neither his role nor the manifesto itself was important. In short, the mounting pressure for change, which seemed irresistible as Russia stumbled from one disaster to another in its war against Japan, paralyzed his will.[10]

The official campaign to revise radically the Orthodox Church's role within the government and to reorganize the structure and spirit of the Church itself was initiated by the ukase of December 12, 1904. Nicholas II named a special committee under the chairmanship of Witte to recommend the specific legislation necessary. This released the floodgates. When Pobedonostsev failed to attend these committee meetings during the first ten weeks of 1905, Witte summoned Metropolitan Antonii of St. Petersburg to speak for the Church. A humane, generous, educated, and knowledgeable man, Antonii in memoranda and in oral discussion emphasized that the December ukase, which he approved, placed the Orthodox Church in a disadvantageous position in competing with other religious groups, because it was paralyzed and "chained" by its relationship with the state. Antonii even suggested that the arrangements made possible by the December ukase would create a state church on one hand and popular, national beliefs on the other, with the state church eternally at a disadvantage in the struggle. Antonii, a number of Orthodox bishops and directors of seminaries, a large number of priests and interested laymen, and some of the most important religious journals asserted that every aspect of the Church and its activities required searching review to enable it to face the new challenges. The relationship between the Church and the state, the central administration of the Church, administrative arrangements within the Church, the role and strength of the parishes, the system of education for priests, the kind of education provided by the parish schools—all, Antonii and others suggested, were shoddy and decaying. He therefore recommended that a *sobor* (or council) of bishops, priests elected within each bishopric, and interested laymen be called immediately to conduct a careful review and to transform the Church from a dusty government department ruled throughout by bureaucrats into the ancient, free, canonical institution which Peter the Great had abolished, with a patriarch again at the head.

Witte's views were generally identical to those of Antonii. He was quickly persuaded of "the urgency of establishing the canonical freedom of the Russian Orthodox Church," particularly because he was convinced that the government in such a crisis could no longer continue to ignore vivid and powerful expressions of public demand. The memorandum Witte submitted to the committee and the reports of the committee's work which he presented to Nicholas II recommended the steps which Antonii and his supporters had proposed.[11]

Witte was a great admirer of Pobedonostsev, whom he considered the most highly cultured and intelligent Russian he knew and whom he also called "the last of the Mohicans." As soon as the Witte committee was appointed, the two men engaged in a vigorous and frank private correspondence and series of talks, in which their opposing views were clearly outlined. Pobedonostsev agreed that ideally Church and state should be separated, but argued that this was and would remain impossible in Russia. In fact, separation would be dangerous and perhaps even fatal for both. The establishment of the Synod by Peter had been a necessary and fruitful act. No Church Council could administer such a large body in such a disorganized country. The patriarchate was not a Russian institution, but an importation from Byzantium. The most serious weakness within the Church was not administrative, but the quality of the clergy, who were what they had always been and who must continue their role as servants of the state, even as policemen and detectives. The absence of vitality within parishes was inevitable and would not be affected by administrative changes, because the parishes reflected faithfully the character and quality of Russian life. Education of the clergy and of children was forever being expanded and improved. In short, anyone who advocated significant changes simply did not understand conditions within Russia.[12]

His memorandum to the Witte committee was late and ineffective. He gave no instructions to Sabler concerning his views, in part because Sabler apparently disagreed with him and in part because he wanted to preserve the fiction that the Synod had not been represented in the committee discussions. He carefully maintained no relations with Antonii and other leading churchmen who were invited by Witte to present their views.

When it was clear that the committee report would override his position and reflect fully the views of Witte and Antonii, he made his last effort to affect state policy, temporarily a successful one, by sending a memorandum and a long letter to Nicholas II. These documents combined all of his skills in delaying or preventing action. He emphasized that the committee's considerations were grossly improper, because Church affairs by law and tradition were the sole responsibility of the Church. The Director General of the Synod, the responsible body, had attended none of the sessions, and the appearance of Antonii and other churchmen was without precedent or sanction. Antonii's proposals had never been discussed with him or by the Synod. If the committee's apparent recommendations should be adopted, the tried and effective arrangements created by Russia's greatest tsar would be hastily overturned. Reestablishment of the patriarchate would surely sometime lead to the rise of another Nikon, who might use his authority and the ambitions of social groups to rival the power of the tsar, threatening Russia with disunity at a time when hostile states encircled her. Among the immediate consequences would be the eruption of Catholic influence to power in provinces "Russian since time immemorial," and the expansion throughout the Volga and in Central Asia of the authority of Mohammedanism, assisted mightily by the English. Kazan, one of Russia's most sacred cities, would become a Moslem center. The tsar must therefore stand strong and true. He should not yield to a "panic-stricken crowd." He should "guard the ideals and the principles of power, because without these there is no salvation anywhere, especially in Russia."[13]

This last appeal, on March 12, 1905, persuaded Nicholas II to surrender to the Synod the functions concerning the Orthodox Church which the Witte committee had assumed. The tsar therefore asked the Synod to arrange a review of the Church's position and role. Pobedonostsev's tactics were thus much like those of 1881 and of 1894, and the tsar's response was initially the same also.

However, in 1905, the power and determination of Witte were such that Pobedonostsev's victory was a fleeting one. Witte informed the tsar that the Synod had no canonical foundation in law and was only an inefficient bureaucratic college. The clergy had been the cultural leaders of Russia in the seventeenth century; in the twentieth century, everyone agreed that they lagged in a nation which itself trailed other countries. Any religious organization which would die if it were separated from the state must surely be a feeble one. The demand for reform from within and without the Church was powerful. It was supported by any candid review of the situation, so reform there must be.[14]

Pobedonostsev's victory quickly evaporated. On April 17, the tsar yielded to Witte's arguments and announced that anyone might leave the Orthodox Church and join another faith, with no penalty or loss of rights. Within two years, more than 300,000 officially made this decision. Moreover, the meetings within the bishoprics which Pobedonostsev organized quietly under the guardianship of the Synod and which were attended by clerics whom he trusted themselves adopted Witte's proposals. They urged the calling of a Council like that proposed by Antonii, the naming of a patriarch, reform of diocesan administration and courts, improvement of the seminaries, and provision of greater autonomy for the parishes. These suggestions received wide support from ecclesiastical journals and papers, and some high clerics in the summer and fall bypassed Pobedonostsev and the Synod and presented their views directly to the tsar.[15]

The height of the revolution in the fall of 1905 led to the overthrow of autocratic government in Russia and the apparent establishment on October 17 of a constitutional monarchy, with civil liberties and an extended franchise for a new legislative assembly. Pobedonostsev played no role in the crisis during which Nicholas II chose between trying to preserve the system through a military dictatorship or yielding some of his authority. The series of decisions made in those crucial days introduced institutions and values he had unceasingly resisted and indicated that Pobedonostsev could no longer remain as Director General of the Synod. At Witte's suggestion, he was therefore quietly replaced two days after the October Manifesto. Witte arranged that he remain in the Council of State, that his full salary be continued, and that he be allowed to live in his official residence. After Pobedonostsev's death, he also arranged for a generous pension for his wife. During the height of the uproar in St. Petersburg, while crowds poured along the streets beneath his windows, Pobedonostsev in his study peacefully worked upon his translation of the New Testament. His last day of service, October 24, he called one of "sorrowful happiness." He said goodbye to the Synod staff and from that time forward was not even informed or consulted concerning the changes made at the upper levels of the Synod's administration.[16]

His last days were pitiful. He was exhausted and hopeless. Both he and his wife were almost constantly ill. Except for a few weeks in a dacha on the Gulf of Finland in the summer of 1906, and occasional visits to St. Vladimir's School, which his wife still directed, he did not leave his rooms. He had no visitors. His only correspondent was S. D. Voit, the business manager of the Synod bookstore in Moscow. He was wracked by worry concerning his wife, and his letters were full of worried financial calculations. Apparently, while his salary was continued, he was not certain that this practice would be followed until his death, and he had no other source of income. He owned no property, except for the family home on Bread Lane in Moscow, which was heavily mortgaged. He had about 20,000 rubles (about $10,000) in a reserve fund, but he had no pension and no provision for one for his wife. Moreover, he felt a moral obligation to continue to assist some orphans and aged teachers whom he had helped to support for years.

He felt so dispirited and ill that on occasion he could not even read. However, he did summon the energy to read the current Russian press and several Russian and foreign journals. He even found time and energy to translate and arrange for the publication of two essays, one attacking the Church *sobor* or council and the other parliamentary government, precisely symbolizing two of his permanent concerns. He also thoroughly enjoyed reading Kliuchevsky's *Kurs russkoi istorii* (Course of Russian History), the several volumes of which were published at his suggestion by the Synod Press and all of which he hoped would be published before he died.[17]

He chose the garden of St. Vladimir's School for his final resting place. He was bedridden throughout the winter of 1906–1907 and succumbed to pneumonia on March 10, 1907. As his will had insisted, his funeral was simple and modest. Metropolitan Antonii presided over one of the services, which were attended by the Wittes but by few others. The tiny cortège was surrounded by priests and policemen as it made its way from the church to the schoolyard, thus providing a final accurate symbol of his position in Russia. The members of the Council of State stood briefly when his death was officially announced. For a few days, newspapers throughout Russia commented at length concerning the importance of the role he had played, but then the quiet of the graveyard descended over him and his career.

Bibliography

FEW PERIODS IN THE HISTORY of any country are richer in the quantity of well-organized materials for historical research than is the nineteenth century in Russia, and there are few statesmen or men of letters for whose study the historical record is more complete than for Pobedonostsev. He lived in a period in which the government and the educated members of society were acutely conscious of the need to preserve historical records, and succeeding generations in the Soviet Union have shown remarkable thoroughness and care in preserving these materials, putting them into good order, publishing substantial quantities of significant source material, and providing guides and bibliographies. Soviet archivists are exceeded by none in the skill and cordiality with which they have organized their resources and have made them available to scholars, except where political considerations still intervene. Since 1956, most archives in Moscow and Leningrad (but few outside these two cities) have been open to American scholars, who have therefore profited enormously in their efforts to expand and improve our understanding of Russian history.

The information available concerning Pobedonostsev is particularly rich. He began his career as a scholar-bureaucrat and remained a prolific author, translator, and editor throughout his long life. He kept all of his letters and papers throughout the last forty years of his life and most of them for the previous decade. During his last fifteen years, he gave many letters to him and by him to scholars and to friends for publication, and he arranged for the publication of many himself. His will provided for the transfer of his surviving records to the Rumiantsev Museum in Moscow, now a part of the Lenin Library. Many of these letters and other materials have been published. Others are well catalogued, as are those of the other men and women of his time who kept their private papers.

The nature of Pobedonostsev's interests, his acquaintances, and his work required me to use every possible type of bibliographical tool. Indeed, the thorough and careful search for all data developed into an education in itself, since Russian bibliographical data are not so well organized as are those for studies in the histories of most western European countries or the United States. The foundations on which this volume was built therefore consist of exacting work in bibliographies of bibliographies; bibliographies of many kinds; lists of books published annually; the *Zhurnal Ministerstva narodnago prosveshcheniia* for the years from 1837 through 1868, the *Pravitel'stvennyi vestnik* from 1869 through 1906, and the various manifestations of *Knizhnaia Letopis'* since 1907. The dreary task of plodding through these last two chronicles was relieved by catalogues which for a few years list the books published in Russia during those years. Pobedonostsev was a frequent contributor to *Russkii arkhiv* and *Istoricheskii vestnik*, so these historical journals were studied with great care. *Russkaia starina* in the second half of the nineteenth century and *Krasnyi arkhiv* during the first two decades of the Soviet period were also reviewed systematically because of the valuable documents, letters, memoirs, and other vital source material they contained. Biographical collections, guides to periodical literature, encyclopedias, and similar tools in various languages were also systematically consulted. Guides to libraries and to archives, particularly in the Soviet Union, helped locate other data.

The impressive growth in quality of American library collections in the field of Russian history is demonstrated by the fact that almost every published work of Pobedonostsev was obtainable in the United States. Moreover, almost all of the other published volumes and articles, from memoirs to state papers, were also available here. Some European libraries, notably the British Museum and the Bibliothèque National, were also splendid resources. Soviet archives, particularly those in the manuscript divisions of the Lenin Library, the Library of the Academy of Sciences in Moscow, and the Saltykov-Shchedrin Library in Leningrad, were remarkably rich in the letters and other papers of Pobedonostsev and his generation. These archives were supplemented by the Manuscript Division of the Institute of Russian Literature (Pushkinskii Dom) and the Central State Historical Archive of the U.S.S.R., both in Leningrad.

This volume is based on careful analysis of all the material which a thorough and imaginative survey could produce, except for a few letters to and from Pobedonostsev and the archival materials in the Central State Historical Archive concerning the Council of State, the Senate, the Synod, and the Ministry of Education, which I was not able to obtain. This deficiency is repaired to a considerable extent by the mass of other data, some published and some unpublished, dealing with the work of these institutions. For example, the large and thorough annual reports which Pobedonostsev published concerning his work as Director General of the Holy Synod, his letters to the tsars and to leading churchmen in particular, the essays he wrote on religious issues and affairs, and the documents he published provide an immense amount of information concerning the Synod and its operations. None of the Soviet scholars who have had access to the archival materials I was not able to see has thus far produced any information not known to me from other sources, although my understanding of Pobedonostsev's role in these state institutions would clearly have been enriched by these data.

PRIMARY SOURCES

Publications of Pobedonostsev

1. BOOKS

Dlia nemnogikh. Otryvki iz shkol'nago dnevnika, 1842–1845 g. St. Petersburg, 1885. Diary published in a limited edition. Peter Bartenev published selections from this in *Russkii arkhiv*, I (1907), 636-52.

Grazhdanskoe sudoproizvodstvo. Lektsii. Moscow, 1863. Lithographed lectures given at Moscow University, January 15–March 25, 1863.

Istoriia pravoslavnoi tserkvi do nachala razdeleniia tserkvei. St. Petersburg, 1892. This volume, of which nine editions were published, was an abbreviated version of *Razskazy iz russkoi tserkovnoi istorii*, by Alexandra N. Bakhmetov, published originally in 1883 in two volumes.

Istoricheskiia izsledovaniia i stat'i. St. Petersburg, 1876. Collected historical essays.

Istoriko-iuridicheskie akty perekhodnoi epokhi XVII-XVIII vekov. Moscow, 1887. Documents collected and edited by Pobedonostsev.

Kurs grazhdanskago prava. St. Petersburg, 1868–80, three vols. Four editions of two and three editions of one of these volumes were produced. This is Pobedonostsev's principal publication in the field of Russian civil law.

Moskovskii sbornik. Moscow, 1896. His most important and best-known work. It appeared in five editions before 1901, and it has been translated, never fully, into English (1898), French (1897), German (1897 and 1904), Serbian (1899), and Spanish. It is a collection of essays, some of which appeared as early as 1873. Some essays are translations, or mis-translations, from Ralph Waldo Emerson, *Society and Solitude* (Boston, 1870); Herbert Spencer, *The Study of Sociology* (New York, 1873); William Ewart Gladstone, *The Impregnable Rock of Holy Scripture* (Philadelphia, 1896); and Max Nordau, *Die conventiollen Lügen der Kulturmenschheit* (sixth edition, Chicago, 1884).

Prazdniki Gospodni. St. Petersburg, 1894. A series of religious essays written between 1857 and 1864. The seventh edition of this volume appeared in 1905.

Sudebnoe rukovodstvo. Sbornik pravil, polozhenii i primerov. St. Petersburg, 1872. Handbook concerning principles, rules, and examples of court procedure designed to assist judges and lawyers.

Uchenie i uchitel'. Pedagogicheskiia zametki. St. Petersburg, 1901–1904, two vols. Series of little essays on education and methods of instruction. Five editions of the first volume and two of the second were published.

Vechnaia pamiat'. Vospominaniia o pochivshikh. Moscow, 1896. Series of most informative essays written to honor several departed friends. A second edition appeared in 1899. Most of these essays were previously published in journals.

Voprosy zhizni. Moscow, 1904. Contains some of the essays already published in *Moskovskii sbornik.*

Vsepoddanneishii otchët ober-prokurora Sviateishago sinoda K. Pobedonostseva po vedomstvu Pravoslavnago Ispovedaniia. St. Petersburg, 1881–1909. These are the massive official reports, usually annual but sometimes for two years, which Pobedonostsev prepared and published on his stewardship as Director General of the Synod. Most valuable.

With Ivan K. Babst. *Pis'ma o puteshestvii gosudaria naslednika tsesarevicha po Rossii ot Peterburga do Kryma.* Moscow, 1864. This volume of letters was originally published in Katkov's *Moskovskiia Vedomosti* between June and October, 1863.

2. PAMPHLETS

A Monsieur Edouard Naville, Président du comité central suisse de l'Alliance évangélique. St. Petersburg, 1888. Pobedonostsev's defense of the treatment of the Lutherans in the Baltic provinces. It was also published in *Tserkovnyia Vedomosti, Grazhdanin, Vera i razum,* and *Svet.*

Chelovecheskii rod. St. Petersburg, 1902.

Dlia nemnogikh. Vospominanie ob Edite Radene. St. Petersburg, 1893. Most interesting essay. This was also included in the book, *Dlia nemnogikh.*

Dobroe Slovo vospitatel'nikam Dukhovnykh Seminarii i Akademii po povodu nyneshnikh strashnykh sobytii. St. Petersburg, 1881. Speech Pobedonostsev gave at Yaroslavl June 9, 1880. It appeared also in *Moskovskiia Vedomosti* and was published in 1882 in Bremen in a German translation made by Baroness Raden.

N. I. Ilminskii. St. Petersburg, 1892. This was also published in *Dlia nemnogikh.*

Khristianskoe verouchenie. St. Petersburg, 1904.

Mery k povsemestnomu rasprostraneniiu gramotnosti v narod. St. Petersburg, 1892.

Nachala semeinoi zhizni. St. Petersburg, 1904.

Prizvanie zhenshchiny v shkole i obshchestve. St. Petersburg, 1902.

Rechi i tosti g. ober-prokurora Sv. sinoda K. P. Pobedonostseva, skazannye na obede, dannom gorodom v den iubileinago torzhestva 900-letiia kreshcheniia Rusi. Kiev, 1888.

3. ARTICLES

"Aksakovy," *Sbornik statei, napechatannykh v raznykh periodicheskikh izdaniiakh po sluchaiu konchiny I. S. Aksakova* (Moscow, 1886), Part II, 1-7. This was included in *Dlia nemnogikh.* It also appeared in *Grazhdanin* in 1886.

"Akty, otnosiashchikhsia do iuridicheskago byta drevnei Rossii," *Arkhiv istoricheskikh i prakticheskikh svedenii otnosiashchikhsia do Rossii,* IV, Book IV (1859), 25-60.

"Anekdoty iz XVIII stoletiia. 1. Moskovskaia volokita. 2. Ochistitel'naia pytka," *Arkhiv istoricheskikh i prakticheskikh svedenii otnosiashchikhsia do Rossii,* IV, Book IV (1859), supplement, 1-22. Most valuable. This was reprinted in *Istoricheskiia izsledovaniia i stat'i* in 1876.

"Anekdoty iz XVIII stoletiia. Ubiistvo Zhukovikh," *Russkii vestnik,* XXX (1860), 462-501. Also reprinted in 1876 volume.

"Bor'ba gosudarstva s tserkoviu v Germanii," *Grazhdanin,* Number 34, August 20, 1873, 915-18. On Kulturkampf; signed Z. Z.

"9 ianvaria 1873 goda," *Grazhdanin,* Number 3, January 15, 1873, 57-58. Memorial article on Grand Duchess Helen Pavlovna. Signed K. P.

"Eshchë na pamiat' o kniaze V. F. Odoevskom," Obshchestvo liubitelei rossiiskoi slovesnosti. Moscow, *V pamiat' o kniaze Vladimire Fedoroviche Odoevskom* (Moscow, 1869), 79-86. This was reprinted from the March 19, 1869, issue of *Moskovskiia Vedomosti.*

"Frantsiia. Vzgliad na tepereshnee eia sostoianie," *Grazhdanin,* Number 35, August 27, 1873, 939-42. Signed Z. Z.

"Gosudar' Imperator Aleksandr Aleksandrovich," *Russkii arkhiv,* I (1906), 619-24. This was a speech given in October, 1894, in memory of Alexander III. It was printed originally in *Moskovskiia Vedomosti* on November 1, 1894, and also appeared in Sergei A. Petrovskii (editor), *Pamiati Imperatora Aleksandra III* (Moscow, 1894), 88-89, and in the *Revue Anglo-Romaine,* I (1895), 40-44.

"Graf V. N. Panin," *Golosa iz Rossii,* VII (1859), 1-142. Anonymous.

"Imenie rodovoe i blagopriobretennoe," *Zhurnal Ministerstva iustitsii,* VIII, Part II (1861), 3-75.

"Irvingity v Londone. Deisty i unitarii v Londone," *Grazhdanin,* Number 35, August 27, 1873, 949-51. Signed V.

"Ispaniia," *Grazhdanin,* Number 37, September 10, 1873, 991-94. Signed Z. Z.

"Iuridicheskiia zametki i voprosy po nasledstvennomu i zaveshchatel'nomu pravam," *Zhurnal Ministerstva iustitsii,* XXII, Part II (1864), 169-210; XXVII, Part II (1866), 25-44.

"Iz chernovykh bumag K. P. Pobedonostseva," *Krasnyi arkhiv,* XVIII (1926), 203-207. Drafts of the celebrated speech of Nicholas II on "senseless dreams" and of the manifestoes of February 18 and April 17, 1905.

"Iz dalekago proshlago (o sudebnoi volokite v doreformennykh sudakh); iz zapisok K. P. Pobedonostseva," *Sudebnoe obozrenie,* II (1903), 593-98. Extract from *Istoricheskiia izsledovaniia i stat'i.*

"Iz dnevnika odnogo gosudarstvennago deiatelia. Zasedanie Gosudarstvennago soveta 8 marta 1881 g.," *Byloe,* Number 1 (1906), 189-94. Speech Pobedonostsev made at the important meeting of the Council on March 8,

1881, reconstructed from notes made at the meeting by another participant. This was printed under another title, "Rech' K. P. Pobedonostseva o konstitutsii," *Russkii arkhiv*, II (1907), 103-105.

"Iz Londona," *Grazhdanin*, Number 27, July 2, 1873, 750-52. Unsigned.

"Iz vospominanii o N. I. Ilminskom," *Russkii vestnik*, CCXVIII (1892), 142-52. This also appeared in *Vechnaia pamiat'*.

"K voprosu o vozsoedinenei tserkvei," *Grazhdanin*, Number 33, August 13, 1873, 893-96. Signed V.

"Kartina vysshago vospitaniia. Avtobiografiia Dzh. Stiuarta Millia," *Grazhdanin*, Number 45, November 5, 1873, 1190-93. Signed V.

"Knizhnyia zagranichnyia vesti o Rossii," *Russkii arkhiv*, IV (1866), 260-62. Review article of several French and English books on Russian history.

"Kritika i bibliografiia. Svoboda, ravenstvo, i bratstvo," *Grazhdanin*, Number 35, August 27, 1873, 958-62; Number 36, September 3, 1873, 976-79; Number 37, September 10, 1873, 1007-1010. Signed * * *. Review of Sir James Stephen, *Liberty, Equality, Fraternity* (London, 1873).

"Le-Plè," *Russkoe obozrenie*, XXIII (1893), 5-30.

"Lionskiia grazhdanskiia pokhorony," *Grazhdanin*, Number 31, July 30, 1873, 848. Signed V.

"La Lutte contre l'alcoolisme en Russie," *La Réforme sociale*, XXVII (1894), 947-48.

"Mestnoe naselenie Rossii," *Russkii vestnik*, XL (1862), 5-34. Long book review.

"Nadezhda Pavlovna Shults," *Grazhdanin*, Number 25-26, October 21, 1877, 618-20. Signed K. P. Also published in *Vechnaia pamiat'*.

"Nekotorye voprosy, voznikaiushchie po dukhovnym zaveshchaniiam," *Arkhiv istoricheskikh i prakticheskikh svedenii otnosiashchikhsia do Rossii*, I, Book I (1859), supplement, 1-27; II, Book II (1859), supplement, 1-22.

"Novaia kniga russkoga avtora v anglii po vostochnomu voprosu," *Grazhdanin*, Number 38-40, December 14, 1877, 854. Review of volume by Olga Novikov. Unsigned.

"Novaia vera i novye braki," *Grazhdanin*, Number 39, September 24, 1873, 1047-1050. Signed V.

"Noveishaia angliiskaia literatura po vostochnomu voprosu," *Grazhdanin*, Number 1, January 8, 1877, 20-25.

"Novyia puteshestvyia po vostoku," *Russkii vestnik*, XLIII (1863), 489-548. Review of volumes in German and in English.

"Nravstvennyi kharakter grazhdanina v khristianskom obshchestve," *Tserkovnyia Vedomosti*, March 23, 1902, 415-16. Attack on secularism of French government policy and commendation for Theodore Roosevelt.

"O chrezpolosnom vladenii," *Iuridicheskii vestnik*, III (1867), 3-18.

"O preobrazovanii tserkovnago upravleniia v Rossii na sobornom nachale," *Tserkovnyia Vedomosti*, November 5, 1905, 1897–1905. Pobedonostsev's proposals of March, 1905, concerning administration of the Church. These were adopted by the Synod later that month.

"O reformakh v grazhdanskom sudoproizvodstve," *Russkii vestnik*, XXI (1859), 541-80; XXII (1859), 5-34, 153-90. His master's thesis and most important attack on the unreformed judicial system.

"O iuridicheskoi dostovernosti telegraficheskikh izvestii," *Iuridicheskii vestnik*, I (1860), 39-46.

"Ob universitetskom prepodavanii," *Moskovskiia Vedomosti*, June 26, 1899.

"Obozrenie chastnikh trudov po sobraniiu zakonov i po sostavleniiu ukaznikh slovarei do izdaniia Polnago Sobraniia Zakonov Rossiiskoi Imperii," *Arkhiv istoricheskikh i prakticheskikh svedenii otnosiashchikhsia do Rossii*, V (1863), 51-84.

"Odin iz psevdonimov v russkoi zhurnalistike," *Bibliograficheskie zapiski*, Number 8 (1892), 574. Note on Sergei P. Pobedonostsev.

"Odnodvorcheskiia zemli i nachalo spetsialnago mezhevaniia v Rossii," *Zhurnal Ministerstva iustitsii*, XV, Part II (1863), 85-104.

"Opyt iuridicheskago kommentariia na nekotoryia stat'i zakonov o zaveshchaniiakh," *Arkhiv istoricheskikh i prakticheskikh svedenii otnosiashchikhsia do Rossii*, II, Book II (1859), 52-71.

"Otvet russkago cheloveka Kropotkinu," *Moskovskiia Vedomosti*, October 15, October 16, 1901. Signed * * *. This was published also as "Russia and Popular Education. A Reply to Prince Kropotkin," *North American Review*, CLXXIII (1901), 349-54.

"Pamiat' velikoi kniagini Ekateriny Mikhailovny," *Moskovskiia Vedomosti*, June 8, 1894. Also published in *Vechnaia pamiat'*.

"Pamiati Fedora Mikhailovicha Dmitrieva," *Russkii arkhiv*, I (1894), 634-37.

"Podlezhit li zemstvo po zakonu otvetstvennosti za nepriniatie mer protiv goloda?" *Grazhdanin*, Number 52, December 29, 1873, 1380. Signed V. P-ch.

"Preobrazovanie suda prisiazhnykh," *Grazhdanin*, Number 51, December 22, 1873, 1371-72. Signed V.

"Prichiny nepravosudiia i provolochki v prisutstvennikh mestakh," *Zhurnal Ministerstva iustitsii* XXVII (1866), 33-34. Part of an article printed in the same journal in 1864.

"Priobretenie sobstvennosti i pozemel'nyia knigi," *Russkii vestnik*, XXVIII (1860), 5-39, 193-230.

"Protivorechiia v anglikanskoi tserkvi," *Grazhdanin*, Number 34, August 20, 1873, 921-23. Signed V.

"Russkoe grazhdanskoe sudoproizvodstvo v istoricheskom ego razvitii ot Ulozheniia 1649 goda do izdaniia Svoda Zakonov," *Arkhiv istoricheskikh i prakticheskikh svedenii otnosiashchikhsia do Rossii*, I, Part I (1859), 1-62. Review of a volume by M. M. Mikhailov.

"Semeinye uchastki," *Russkii vestnik*, CCIV (1889), 56-72. This important essay was reproduced in 1892 as a pamphlet and in *Kurs grazhdanskago prava* (fourth edition, Moscow, 1896), I, 730-45.

"La Société et le sentiment religieux," *Revue des Revues*, XXIV (1898), 14-15.

"Sovremennaia Letopis'," *Sovremennaia Letopis' Russkago vestnika*, II (1861), 11-13. Unsigned.

"Statistiki angliiskikh grazhdanskikh sudov za 1858 god," *Iuridicheskii vestnik*, V (1860–61), 46-54.

"S'ezd iuristov v Moskve," *Grazhdanin*, Number 44, October 29, 1873, 1173–75. Signed * * *.

"Tserkov' i gosudarstvo v Germanii," *Grazhdanin*, Number 40, October 1, 1873, 1064-66. Signed Z. Z.

"Tserkovnyia dela v Germanii," *Grazhdanin*, Number 51, December 22, 1873, 1367-69. Signed Z. Z.

"Utverzhdenie krepostnago prava v Rossii v XVIII stoletii," *Russkii vestnik*, XXXV (1861), 223-53. This was reprinted in *Istoricheskiia izsledovaniia i stat'i*.

"V protestanskikh khramakh," *Grazhdanin*, Number 31, July 30, 1873, 849. Signed V.

"Vechnaia pamiat'. (Posviashchaetsia pamiati N. V. Shenshina)," *Russkaia beseda*, V (1859), Part I, 5-7. Signed K. P.

"Veshchnyi kredit i zakladnoe pravo," *Russkii vestnik*, XXXIII (1861), 409-451.

"Vestminsterskoe abbatstvo," *Grazhdanin*, Number 32, August 6, 1873, 870-73. Signed V.

"Vorovskii uzhin," *Grazhdanin*, Number 36, September 3, 1873, 974-76. Signed V. On Salvation Army.

"Vospominanie o Nikolaie Vasilieviche Kalachove," *Vestnik arkheologii i istorii*, V (1886), 75-78. Reprinted in *Vechnaia pamiat'*.

"Vospominanie o V. P. Zubkove," *Russkii arkhiv*, I (1904), 301-305.

"Zametka o Beniovskom iz angliiskoi knigi ob ostrove Madagaskare," *Russkii arkhiv*, III (1865), 859-62.

"Zametki dlia istorii krepostnago prava v Rossii," *Russkii vestnik*, XV (1858), 209-48, 459-98; XVI (1858), 537-82. This was reprinted, with minor changes, in *Istoricheskiia izsledovaniia i stat'i*.

"Zapisnaia knizhka," *Grazhdanin*, Number 17, February 27, 1886.

4. TRANSLATIONS (arranged alphabetically by translated title)

"Chernogoriia. Stat'ia Gladstona," *Grazhdanin*, Number 32-33, November 22, 1877, 741-49. Translation of Gladstone, "Montenegro. A Sketch," *Nineteenth Century*, I (1877), 360-69. The translation was unsigned.

Deianiia sviatikh apostolov i soborniaia poslaniia v novom russkom perevode. St. Petersburg, 1905. Translation of Acts of the Apostles.

Ralph Waldo Emerson, "Dela i dni," in *Skladchina; literaturnyi sbornik* (St. Petersburg, 1874), 217-40. Translation of "Works and Days," in Emerson, *Society and Solitude* (Boston, 1870), 149-77.

Fomy Kempiiskago o podrazhanii Khristu. St. Petersburg, 1869. This translation of Thomas à Kempis, *The Imitation of Christ* (in Latin), appeared in six editions, the last in 1896.

"Gladstone ob osnovakh veri i neveriia," *Russkoe obozrenie,* XXVI (1894), 32-41. Translation of the last chapter of Gladstone's *The Impregnable Rock of Holy Scripture* (Philadelphia, 1892), 279-325.

Heinrich W. Thiersch, *Khristianskiia nachala semeinoi zhizni.* Moscow, 1861. Translation of *Uber christliches Familienleben* (Frankfurt-am-Main, 1854). A second edition of the translation appeared in 1901. Thiersch was also translated into English and French.

Edmond Demolins, *Novaia shkola.* Moscow, 1898. Translation of parts of *L'Education nouvelle* (Paris, 1897) and of *A quoi tient la supériorité des Anglo-Saxons* (Paris, 1897).

Novyi zavet Gospoda nashego Iisusa Khrista v novom russkom perevode. St. Petersburg, 1907. Translation of the New Testament.

Heinrich W. Thiersch, "O khristianskom brake," *Pravoslavnoe obozrenie,* IV (1861), 307-34. Translation of part of *Uber christliches Familienleben.*

Pierre Le Play, *Osnovnaia konstitutsiia chelovecheskago roda.* Moscow, 1897. Translation of *La Constitution essentielle de l'humanité* (Tours, 1881). The preface to this volume is especially valuable.

Pobeda, pobedivshaia mir. Moscow, 1898. This includes sections from *The Confessions of Saint Augustine* and from William S. Lilly's *Christianity and Modern Civilization* (London, 1886), and *A Century of Revolution* (London, 1889).

George L. Calderon, *Pravda o gr. Leve Tolstome.* Moscow, 1901. Translation of "The Wrong Tolstoi," *The Monthly Review,* III (1901), 129-41.

Wenceslas Wratislaw, *Prikliucheniia cheshkago dvorianina Vratislava v Konstantinopole i v tiashkoi nevole u Turok, s avstriiskim posol'stvom 1591 g.* St. Petersburg, 1877. Translation of *Prihody W. W., swabodného Pána z Mitrowic, kteréz w Tureckém hlawnjm městě Konstantinopoli widěl, w zagetj sevém, zkusyl* (Prague, 1807). A second edition of the translation appeared in 1904.

Sekty i veroucheniia v Soedinennykh Shtatakh Severnoi Ameriki. St. Petersburg, 1896. Translation of part of Department of the Interior, U.S. Census Office, *Report on Statistics of Churches in the United States at the Eleventh Census: 1890* (Washington, 1894).

"Starye listia," *Russkaia beseda,* II, Part I (1859), 7-8. Poems.

"Vospitanie kharaktera v shkole," *Narodnoe obrazovanie,* Number 2 (1900), 3-12. Translation of parts of Canon Samuel Barnett, *Common Sense in Education and Teaching* (London, 1899).

Vseobshchaia podacha golosov (Suffrage Universel). St. Petersburg, 1906. Translation of Adolphe Prins, *De l'esprit du gouvernement démocratique* (Brussels, 1905), 159-232.

"Zapisnaia knizhka. Velikaia lozh' nashego vremeni," *Grazhdanin,* Number 4, January 22, 1884; Number 19, May 6, 1884; Number 24, June 10, 1884. Translation of parts of Max Nordau, *Die conventiollen Lügen der Kulturmenschheit* (second edition, Naumburg, 1884). Unsigned.

With Constantine N. Bestuzhev-Riumin, William E. Gladstone. *Bolgarskie Uzhasy i Vostochnyi Vopros.* St. Petersburg, 1876. Translation of *Bulgarian Horrors and the Questions of the East.* London, 1876.

5. EDITING

"Anekdot o Didro," *Russkii arkhiv,* III (1893), 128. Effort to demonstrate Diderot was upset by proof of existence of God.

"Iz pisem Ego Imperatorskago Vysochestva Velikago Kniaz'ia Konstantina Nikolaevicha k stats-sekretariu A. V. Golovninu," *Russkii arkhiv,* I (1895), 439-45. 1886 letters.

"K istorii snoshenii s inovertsami," *Russkii arkhiv,* II (1894), 5-27.

"Materialy dlia istorii Akademii nauk," *Letopis' russkoi literatury i drevnostei,* V, Part III (1863), 3-36.

Materialy dlia istorii prikaznago sudoproizvodstva v Rossii. Moscow, 1890.

"O vnutrennem sostoianii Rossii pri votsarenii Imperatora Nikolaia Pavlovicha," *Russkii arkhiv,* I (1895), 161-76. 1826 letter of a Decembrist to Nicholas I.

Perepiska Iu. F. Samarina s baronessoiu E. F. Raden, 1861–1876 g. Moscow, 1893.

"Pis'ma baronessy Raden k g. Berkgoltsu," *Russkoe obozrenie,* XXXVII (1896), 317-26; XXXVIII (1896), 786-94; XXXIX (1896), 781-88; XL (1896), 800-809.

"Russkii novyi god v Prage," *Moskovskiia Vedomosti,* January 11-12, 1877. Letters from a Czech acquaintance to Pobedonostsev describing the arrival in Prague of General Chernaiev in December, 1876. Unsigned.

Sbornik myslei i izrechenii mitropolita Moskovskago Filareta, 1782–1867. Moscow, 1897. Unsigned.

Vypiski iz Polnago Sobraniia Zakonov. St. Petersburg, 1895.

Manuscripts

1. LENIN LIBRARY

1. Mnenie ego po povodu zapiski Predsedatel'ia komiteta G. g. Ministrov IU. Vitte po voprosu ob uchrezhdenii patriarshestva v Rossii. 2. K voprosu o predstavlenii vysshim predstaviteliam tserkovnoi Ierarkhii prava uchastiia v zasedaniiakh vysshikh gosudarstvenno-zakonodatelnykh uchrezhdenii. St. Petersburg, 1905.

Predlozhenie po voprosu o sozvanii Sobora eparkhialnykh episkopov dlia uchrezhdeniia patriarshestva. St. Petersburg, 1905. Important documents on discussion concerning Church organization in 1905.

2. SALTYKOV-SHCHEDRIN LIBRARY

O rabotakh Komissii dlia izyskaniia glavneishikh osnovanii luchshei postanovki zhenskago obrazovaniia v Rossii. St. Petersburg, 1888?.

O zhalobakh na deistviia dolzhnostnykh lits administrativnago vedomstva. St. Petersburg, 1864.

Obozrenie inostrannykh zakonov o zaveshchaniakh. St. Petersburg, 1872.

Proekt pravil ob obezpechenii iskov s obiiasneniiami redaktora. St. Petersburg, 186?.

Zapiska o grazhdanskom sudoproizvodstve. St. Petersburg, December, 1861.

Pobedonostsev Letters

1. PUBLISHED (arranged alphabetically by addressee)

Panteleev, Longin F. (editor), "Pis'mo K. P. Pobedonostseva k N. S. Abazie," *Golos minuvshago*, VI (1914), 231-32.

Presniakov, A., "Moskovskii adres Aleksandru II v 1870 g. Iz perepiski K. P. Pobedonostseva s I. S. Aksakovym," *Krasnyi arkhiv*, XXXI (1928), 144-54.

Pobedonostsev, Constantine P., *Pis'ma Pobedonostseva k Aleksandru III*. Moscow, 1925–26, two vols. Most valuable. The second volume also contains the letters to Nicholas II and Grand Duke Sergei.

"Pobedonostsev and Alexander III," *Slavonic Review*, VII (1928–29), 30-54. Translation of about forty letters published in the two volumes listed above.

"Iz pis'ma K. P. Pobedonostseva k izdateliu 'Russkago arkhiva,'" *Russkii arkhiv*, I (1904), 189.

Grossman, Leonid, "Dostoevskii i pravitel'stvennye krugi 1870-kh godov," *Literaturnoe nasledstvo*, Number 15 (1934), 83-162. This includes 40 letters which Pobedonostsev wrote to Dostoevsky. Excellent analysis.

"Pis'ma K. P. Pobedonostseva k E. M. Feoktistovu," *Literaturnoe nasledstvo*, Number 22-24 (1935), 497-560. Important letters concerning the censorship.

Kantor, R. M. (editor), "Pis'ma K. P. Pobedonostseva k grafu N. P. Ignatievu," *Byloe*, Number 27-28 (1925), 50-89. 57 letters between May, 1881, and May, 1882, when Ignatiev was Minister of the Interior.

Petrovskii, Sergei A. (editor), "Pis'ma K. P. Pobedonostseva preosviashchennomu Illarionu, arkhiepiskopu Poltavskomu," *Russkii arkhiv*, LIV (1916), 129-71, 360-80. Letters between 1886 and 1898.

Parkhomenko, Vladimir (editor), "Dopolnenie k stat'e 'Pis'ma K. P. Pobedonostseva preosviashchennomu Illarionu, arkhiepiskopu Poltavskomu,'" *Russkii arkhiv*, III (1916), 281-85.

38 Pisem byvshago Ober-Prokurora Sviateishago sinoda K. P. Pobedonostseva

k vysokopreosviashchenneishemu Makariiu, arkhiepiskopu Tomskomu.
Tomsk, 1910. 1887–1906 correspondence, mostly concerning missionary
work.

"Iz zapisok arkhiepiskopa Nikanora," *Russkii arkhiv*, I (1909), 209-276; II
(1909), 19-77.

Petrovskii, Sergei A. (editor), "Perepiska K. P. Pobedonostseva s preosviashchennym Nikanorom, episkopom Ufimskim," *Russkii arkhiv*, I (1915),
458-73; II (1915), 68-111, 244-56, 335-84, 501-28; III (1915), 81-108, 249-68.
147 letters.

Yakobson, Sergius (editor), "Pis'ma K. P. Pobedonostseva k V. K. Putsykovichu," Kruzhok liubitelei russkoi stariny, *Stat'i i materialy* (Berlin, 1932),
72-78. Putsykovich was briefly editor of *Grazhdanin*. These thirteen letters
were written between 1877 and 1903.

Miller, P. N. (editor), "Melochi iz museia P. I. Shukina v Moskve. Dva pis'ma
K. P. Pobedonostseva k N. P. Poliakovu. Nastroenie K. P. Pobedonostseva
v 1902 g.," *Minuvshie gody*, Number 10 (1908), 48.

Pobedonostsev, "Privetstvie starago vospitatelia Velikomu Kniaz'iu v den' ego
sovershennoletiia," *Starina i novizna*, XII (1907), 1-9. Most interesting letter of the late 1860's to Grand Duke Sergei.

Markov, Vladimir S., *K istorii raskola-staroobriadchestva vtoroi poloviny
XIX stoletiia. Perepiska prof. N. I. Subbotina.* Moscow, 1915. Includes 187
letters from Pobedonostsev to Subbotin, and 234 in return, between 1880
and 1903.

Istomin, K. (editor), "Pis'mo g. ober-prokurora Sv. sinoda K. P. Pobedonostseva k Pateru V. Vannutelli," *Vera i razum*, I (1893), 353-86. Significant on
relations with Vatican.

"Perepiska Vitte i Pobedonostseva, 1895–1905," *Krasnyi arkhiv*, XXX (1928),
89-116. Most useful.

"Pis'ma K. P. Pobedonostseva k S. D. Voitu," *Russkii arkhiv*, I (1917), 77-101;
II (1917), 112-24. 110 letters written between 1892 and 1895. Unfortunately,
the other 800 letters to Voit have disappeared.

Mel'gunov, S. (editor), "K. P. Pobedonostsev v dni pervoi revoliutsii. Neizdannyia pis'ma k S. D. Voitu," *Na chuzhoi storone*, VIII (1924), 177-202.
Mel'gunov brought these selected letters from the 1901–1906 period with
him when he left Russia in 1922.

"Pis'mo K. P. Pobedonostseva," *Istoricheskii vestnik*, LXV (1896), 553-54.

2. UNPUBLISHED

Manuscript Division, Lenin Library. In his will, Pobedonostsev gave all of
the letters he had received, plus many he had written, to the Rumiantsev Museum, now the Manuscript Division of the Lenin Library, which has added to
these materials and now contains the largest single collection of source materials
concerning him, and indeed concerning many other nineteenth century Russians. Of those which have not been published, the most valuable letters were

the 330 he wrote to his closest confidante, Catherine Tiutchev, between 1866 and her death early in 1882. These were particularly important during two of the most critical years, 1880 and 1881, when he wrote her forty-six and sixty-nine letters, respectively, some of remarkable candor and detail. A few of these letters were published in *Russkii arkhiv*, II (1907), 88-102. According to Academician Iurii V. Gotie, he regained 550 letters to her sister, Anna Tiutchev, who became the wife of Ivan Aksakov, but only 31 remain in the Lenin Library.

Other most important letters in this collection were 20 he wrote to Boris Chicherin, a liberal professor whom he first met on the Moscow University faculty, between 1864 and 1903; 71 to Dostoevsky's widow between 1881 and 1906, when he was executor of her will and her business advisor; 68 to Michael Katkov, the renowned panslav journalist, between 1862 and 1887; 183 between 1876 and 1904 to Olga Novikov, who was usually in London, which are particularly revealing concerning Pobedonostsev's activities in 1877–78 and his views on international affairs; 39 between 1890 and 1896 to Sergei A. Petrovskii, who was then editor of *Grazhdanin;* and 5 in 1856 to Mrs. Elizabeth A. Zhukovskii, which are particularly important for a period of Pobedonostsev's life on which little other information is available. This collection also contains letters from Mrs. Pobedonostsev to Catherine Tiutchev and to Olga Novikov, generally written in French.

Less significant correspondence was directed to Amvrosii, archbishop of Kharkov; Tertii and Sergei Filippov, who were prominent officials and courtiers under Alexander III; Count Dmitrii A. Miliutin, who was Minister of War under Alexander II; Professor Michael P. Pogodin, prominent Moscow historian; Dmitrii F. Samarin, son of the renowned Slavophil, Iurii Samarin; Savva, archbishop of Tver; Prince Alexander V. Shakhovskoi; Professor Sergei M. Soloviev, distinguished Moscow historian and father of Vladimir Soloviev; Count Dmitrii A. Tolstoy, who was Pobedonostsev's predecessor as Director General of the Holy Synod and Minister of the Interior from 1882 until his death in 1889; and Prince I. I. Vorontsov-Dashkov, who was a high court official under Alexander III.

Institute of Russian Literature (Pushkinskii Dom). The most valuable of the letters in this collection were one written in 1866 to his sister, Elizabeth, the only letter to a brother or sister which has survived; and others to Ivan Aksakov, most of whose correspondence with Pobedonostsev has disappeared; Constantine A. Gubastov, director of a music school in St. Petersburg; Prince V. P. Meshcherskii, who had introduced him to Dostoevsky but from whom Pobedonostsev broke bitterly; and Sergei I. Zarudnyi, with whom Pobedonostsev had worked on the reform of the Russian judicial system in 1864.

Saltykov-Shchedrin. The manuscript collection of this library contained Pobedonostsev's letters to fifteen different Russians, but only those to Prince Vladimir Odoevskii were valuable. Unfortunately, the unpublished letters to Ivan Aksakov in this collection were missing. However, twelve letters from Sergei Pobedonostsev to Professor Michael Pogodin, written between 1841 and

1849, were obtainable and were full of interest. According to S. L. Evenchik, *Reaktsionnaia deiatel'nost' Pobedonostseva v 80-kh gg. XIX-go veka* (a Moscow University thesis for the Candidate Degree in History, 1939), the manuscript collection of this library then possessed about seven hundred letters to Sergei Rachinskii of especial value on religious and educational matters. These could not be located.

Central State Historical Archive, Leningrad, and Central State Literary Archive, Moscow. The first of these archives contained several valuable letters to Count Peter A. Valuev and the second, five letters to Ivan Aksakov and one hundred to Peter I. Bartenev, editor of *Russkii arkhiv*, written between 1865 and 1906. The latter I was not able to use.

Letters to Pobedonostsev
(arranged alphabetically by author)

1. PUBLISHED

"Ob istoricheskikh bumagakh ostavshikhsia posle A. N. Popova. Iz pis'ma I. S. Aksakova k K. P. Pobedonostsevu," *Russkii arkhiv*, I (1894), 103-104.

Aksakov, Ivan S., "Pis'ma I. S. Aksakova k K. P. Pobedonostsevu, 1876–1885," *Russkii arkhiv*, III (1907), 163-92.

"Pis'mo I. S. Aksakova k K. P. Pobedonostsevu," *Russkii arkhiv*, II (1905), 591-92. A letter of November 29, 1877.

Pobedonostsev, Constantine P., *K. P. Pobedonostsev i ego korrespondenty. Pis'ma i zapiski. Novum Regnum.* Moscow, 1923, two vols. in one. Edited by Pokrovsky, this is most valuable, particularly for the letters from Alexander III and Nicholas II. A 1927 French edition was not complete and did not indicate where entire letters or memoranda had been omitted or where sections of letters or memoranda had been eliminated. (*L'Autocratie russe. Constantine Pobiédonostsev ... Mémoires politique, correspondance officielle et documents inédits.*)

"Iz biografii tsesarevicha Nikolaia Aleksandrovicha. Dva pis'ma B. N. Chicherina k K. P. Pobedonostsevu," *Russkaia starina*, II (1910), 311-12.

Dostoevskii, Fedor M. *Pis'ma.* Moscow, 1928–59, four vols. This includes all the Dostoevsky letters in the Manuscript Division of the Lenin Library and therefore probably all Dostoevsky wrote to him. Some of these were published in *Byloe*, Number 15 (1919), 99-134, under the title, "Dostoevskii o 'Bratiakh Karamazovykh', Neizdannyia pis'ma, 1879–1881 gg."

Ilminskii, Nicholas I. *Pis'ma Nikolaia Ivanovicha Ilminskago k ober-prokuroru Sviateishago sinoda Konstantinu Petrovichu Pobedonostsevu.* Kazan, 1895. Includes 137 letters written between 1882 and 1891.

Pobedonostsev, Constantine P. (editor), "Pis'ma I. I. Lazhechnikova k S. P. i K. P. Pobedonostsevym," *Russkoe obozrenie*, XXXII (1895), 881-87.

"Dva pis'ma Andreia Nikolaevicha Muravieva k K. P. Pobedonostsevu," *Russkii arkhiv*, II (1905), 415–16.

Palimpsestov, I. U., "Pis'mo I. U. Palimpsestova k ober-prokuroru Sv. sinoda K. P. Pobedonostsevu," *Russkaia starina*, II (1910), 607-608.

"Briefwechsel zwischen Arnold von Tideböhl, Redakteur der Baltischen Monatschrift, und K. P. Pobedonoszego, Prokureur des Hl. Synod," *Baltische Monatshefte*, 1934, 571-77. 1895 correspondence on Baltic area.

Bartenev, Peter I. (editor), "Bolezn' i konchina naslednika-tsesarevicha Nikolaia Aleksandrovicha, 1865. Pis'ma Anny Fedorovny Tiutchevoi v Moskve k K. P. Pobedonostsevu i k sestre eia Ekaterine Fedorovne," *Russkii arkhiv*, II (1905), 283-304. Very interesting.

Tverskoi, P., "Iz delovoi perepiski s K. P. Pobedonostsevym," *Vestnik evropy*, XII (1907), 651-68.

2. UNPUBLISHED

The Manuscript Division of the Lenin Library contains a large collection of unpublished letters written to Pobedonostsev, as well as hundreds which have been published. The most important of these were the 179 letters from Catherine Tiutchev, written between 1866 and 1882 and reflecting the closest kind of intellectual relationship. There are also six letters from her to Mrs. Pobedonostsev, in French. Other significant correspondence includes eight letters from Captain Nicholas M. Baranov between 1881 and 1888; forty from Count Nicholas P. Ignatiev in 1881 and 1882; eight from Nicholas Giers in the Foreign Ministry between 1877 and 1886; four each from Katkov and Loris-Melikov, and a number from men and women active in the campaign sponsored by Pobedonostsev among the Uniates in Galicia.

This collection also contained almost nine hundred letters from Sergei Rachinskii, written between 1880 and 1902, and forty-nine letters and other materials from Savva, archbishop of Tver.

Publications of Peter V. Pobedonostsev

1. ARTICLES

"Iz dnevnika 1812 i 1813 godov," *Russkii arkhiv*, XXXIII (1895), 213-24.

"K chitateliam," *Novosti russkoi literatury*, Number 12 (1805), 409-412.

"Liubov' k otechestvu," *Trudy Obshchestva liubitelei rossiiskoi slovesnosti pri Imperatorskom Moskovskom universitete*, XV (1819), 5-26.

Slovo o sushchestvennykh obiazannostiakh vitii i o sposobakh k priobreteniiu uspekhov v krasnorechii. Moscow, 1831.

"Vospominanie o Petre Alekseeviche Plavilshchikove," *Trudy Obshchestva liubitelei rossiiskoi slovesnosti pri Imperatorskom Moskovskom universitete*, XI (1818), 87-135.

"Zaslugi Kheraskova v otechestvennoi slovesnosti," *Trudy Obshchestva liubitelei rossiiskoi slovesnosti pri Imperatorskom Moskovskom universitete*, I (1812), 111-47.

2. EDITING AND TRANSLATIONS

Anekdoty i dostopamiatnye izrecheniia velikikh osob. Moscow, 1816.

Detskii vestnik. Moscow, 1813. Monthly journal.

Drug iunosti. Moscow, 1821, four vols. Journal.

Ippokrena, ili utekhi liubosloviia. Moscow, 1799–1801, eleven vols. Journal superseded by *Novosti russkoi literatury.*

Istinnoe i lozhnoe schastie. Sochinenie slavnago Gellerta. Moscow, 1799.

Izbrannyia nravouchitel'nyia povesti, udobnyia vlivat' v serdtse chuvstvo nravstvennoi krasoty. Perevod iz luchshikh inostrannykh pisatelei. Moscow, 1815, four vols.

Kratkoe rukovodstvo k Estetik Eshenburga. Moscow, 1829.

Minerva. Zhurnal rossiiskoi i inostrannoi slovesnosti. Moscow, 1806–1807, five vols. Superseded *Novosti russkoi literatury.*

Napravlenie uma i serdtsa k istine i dobrodeteli. Moscow, 1830–31, three vols. Journal.

Novaia nauka naslazhdat'sia zhizn'iu. Poema v 4 pesniakh, s prisovokupleniem luchshikh sochinenii Kroneka, Gallera, Kramera, Klopstoka, Vilanda, i Kleista. Moscow, 1799.

Novosti russkoi literatury. Moscow, 1802–1805, fourteen vols. Superseded *Ippokrena*, succeeded by *Minerva.*

Novyi Panteon otechestvennoi i inostrannoi slovestnosti. Moscow, 1819, four vols. Journal. Reprinted much from *Minerva.*

Plody melankholii. Moscow, 1796, two vols.

Sokrovishche poleznykh uveselenii, ili lekarstvo vrachaiushchee liudei, predannykh pechali i skuke. Moscow, 1800.

Starinnyi drug, vozvrativshiisia iz puteshestviia i razskazyvaiushchii vse, chto videl, slyshal i chuvstvoval, s nemetskago. Moscow, 1802, two vols. This was reprinted in 1816.

Tsvetnik, izbrannykh stikhotvorenii v pol'zu i udovol'stvie iunosheskago vozrasta. Moscow, 1816, two vols.

Publications of Mrs. Catherine A. Pobedonostsev

(Translator). Minnie Mackay (Marie Corelli, *pseud.*), *Istoriia detskoi dushi. Mogushchestvennyi Atom. Povest'* (third edition, Moscow, 1897). Translation of *The Mighty Atom.* Philadelphia, 1896.

(Editor). *Severnye tsvety. Vybor iz stikhotvorenii A. S. Pushkina.* St. Petersburg, 1888.

Publications of Pobedonostsev's Brothers and Sisters

1. SERGEI P. POBEDONOSTSEV: ORIGINAL WORKS

(Sergei Neitralnyi, *pseud.*). "Iz 'Zapisok neizvestnago'," *Otechestvennyia zapiski*, XXXI (1843), 281-316.

"Kazimir Vladislav Voinitskii," *Russkii vestnik*, Numbers 5 and 6 (1842), 112-36.

"Mam'zel Babett i eia al'bom," *Biblioteka dlia chteniia*, LIV, Part I (1842), 161-92. Sentimental story.

"Milochka. Povest'," *Otechestvennyia zapiski*, XL (1845), 283-368. This was published as a book in 1867 in St. Petersburg.

"Niania," *Otechestvennyia zapiski*, XLIII (1845), 1-73.

"Nikolai Kopernik. Golos za pravdu," *Moskvitianin*, Number 9 (1843), 108-125. This is the essay which caused the controversy with Herzen.

Novesti. St. Petersburg, 1856. This volume includes five of his stories or novelettes.

"Pokhodnaia baryshnia. Povest'," *Otechestvennyia zapiski*, XLIX, Part I (1846), 1-78.

"Pol'skii teatr. Istoricheskii vzgliad na teatr v Pol'she so vremeni ego osnovaniia," *Repertuar russkago i Panteon inostrannykh teatrov*, IV (1843), 63-80.

"Prazdnik v Moskovskom kadetskom korpuse," *Moskvitianin*, Part II, Number 11 (1842), 255-56.

"Putevyia zapiski russkago po Evrope v 1847-m godu," *Otechestvennyia zapiski*, LVIII (1848), 1-56. Most interesting essay on his travels in western Europe in 1847.

"Starinnyia poveria polskiia i russkiia," *Moskvitianin*, Part I, Number 2 (1842), 49-59.

"Torzhestvo pereneseniia ikony Smolenskoi Bogoroditsy iz Semiezernoi Pustyni v Kazan'," *Moskvitianin*, Part IV, Number 9 (1842), 241-46.

"Ukazatel' goroda Kazani," *Moskvitianin*, Part IV, Number 8 (1842), 383-95.

"Zapiski Paseka," *Moskvitianin*, Part I, Number 2 (1842), 618-27.

2. SERGEI P. POBEDONOSTSEV: EDITING AND TRANSLATIONS

"Kolishchizna i stepi. Razskaz Eduarda Tarshy," *Moskvitianin*, Part II, Number 4 (1842), 357-94.

"Luchshe-by Ia byla sirotoi! Drama v trekh deistviiakh grafa Fridrikha Skarbeka," *Repertuar russkago i Panteon inostrannykh teatrov*, VII (1844), 4-42.

"Parizhskie teatralnye nravy. Mat' aktrisy," *Repertuar russkago i Panteon inostrannykh teatrov*, XVI, Part II (1842), 9-21.

"Pozhar Moskvy," *Moskvitianin*, Part IV, Number 8 (1843), 13-21. Selection from Alexander Dumas on 1812.

"Zakulisnye nravy. Opernaia krysa. Stat'ia Teofilia Got'e," *Repertuar russkago i Panteon inostrannykh teatrov*, I, Part III (1843), 176-88.

3. OTHERS

Pobedonostsev, Alexander (translator). *Rech' konsula Marka Portsiia Katona v zashchishchenie Oppieva zakona. (Perevod iz Tita Liveia).* Moscow, 1830.

Pobedonostsev, Kat. "Chuvstvovaniia detei pri vosvrashchenii materi. Nashestvie tatar na Rossiiu," *Russkii vestnik*, VI (1819), 5-47.

Pobedonostsev, Maria P. (translator). "Sel'skii prikhod. Roman Rodol'fa Tepfera," *Moskvitianin* (supplement), Numbers 5-8, 10-15 (March-August, 1852), 1-437.

Pobedonostsev, Olga P. (editor). "Ivan Ivanovich Lazhechnikov. Pis'mo ego k professoru P. V. Pobedonostsevu, 1823 g.," *Russkaia starina*, LXXII (1891), 230-31.

Collected Works of Prominent Russians

Aksakov, Constantine S. *Polnoe sobranie sochinenii.* Moscow, 1861–80, three vols.

Aksakov, Ivan S. *Sochineniia.* Moscow, 1886–91, seven vols.

Dostoevsky, Fedor M. *Sobranie sochinenii.* Paris, 1945–46, sixteen vols.

Herzen, Alexander. *Polnoe sobranie sochinenii i pisem.* Petrograd-Leningrad, 1919–25, twenty-two vols.

Khomiakov, Alexei S. *Polnoe sobranie sochinenii.* Moscow, 1900–1904, eight vols.

Leontiev, Constantine. *Sobranie sochinenii.* Moscow, 1912-14, nine vols.

Samarin, Iurii F. *Sochineniia.* Moscow, 1911, eleven vols.

Soloviev, Vladimir S. *Sobranie sochinenii.* St. Petersburg, 1901–1907, nine vols.

Tolstoy, Count Leo. *Polnoe sobranie sochinenii.* Moscow, 1928–58, ninety vols.

Memoirs

Aksakov, Constantine S. *Vospominanie studentstva, 1832–1835 godov.* St. Petersburg, 1911.

Grand Prince Alexander Mikhailovich. *Vospominaniia.* Paris, 1933. This appeared also in English, *Once a Grand Duke* (New York, 1932).

Annenkov, Paul V. *P. V. Annenkov i ego druzh'ia. Literaturnyia vospominaniia i perepiska, 1835–1885 godov.* St. Petersburg, 1892, two vols.

——. *Literaturnye vospominaniia.* Moscow, 1960.

Beliaev, A. P. "Vospominaniia dekabrista A. P. Beliaeva o perezhitom i perekuvstvovannom s 1803 goda," *Russkaia starina*, XXIX (1880), 599-661, 823-50; XXX (1881), 27-42, 487-518, 799-838; XXXI (1881), 329-70; XXXII (1881), 1-46, 251-86, 679-704; XLI (1884), 67-86; XLII (1884), 67-86, 303-324.

Bogdanovich, Alexandra V. *Dnevnik, 1880–1912.* Moscow, 1924. Part of this memoir was published in French, *Journal de la générale A. V. Bogdanovitch* (Paris, 1926). It is filled with "gutter gossip."

Bogoliubov, Alexei P. *Vospominaniia o pochivshem Imperatore Aleksandre III.* St. Petersburg, 1895. Bogoliubov was one of the tutors of Alexander III.

Bompard, Maurice. *Mon Ambassade en Russie, 1903–1908.* Paris, 1937. Useful memoirs of French ambassador in St. Petersburg.

Buslaev, Fedor I. "Moi vospominaniia," *Vestnik evropy,* Number 10 (1890), 645-84; Number 11 (1890), 5-55; Number 12, (1890), 513-48; Number 2 (1891), 469-92; Number 3 (1891), 183-225, 563-95; Number 4 (1891), 177-219; Number 5 (1891), 612-48; Number 6 (1891), 138-62; Number 1 (1892), 569-93; Number 2 (1892), 160-91. Moscow University professor closely acquainted with Pobedonostsev.

Chicherin, Boris N. *Vospominaniia.* Moscow, 1929–34, four vols. Valuable memoirs of a liberal acquaintance of the 1860's and 1870's.

Crispi, Francesco. *The Memoirs of Francesco Crispi.* London, 1912–14, three vols. Translated from Italian.

Curtin, Jeremiah. *Memoirs.* Madison, Wis., 1940. American who knew Pobedonostsev well.

Dalton, Hermann. *Lebenserinnerungen.* Berlin, 1906–1908, three vols. Evangelical minister in St. Petersburg who knew Pobedonostsev well and who resisted his policies in the Baltic provinces.

Douglas, Norman. *Looking Back. An Autobiographical Excursion.* New York, 1933. English novelist who met Pobedonostsev.

Egorov, Anatole. "Stranitsii iz godov moei zhizni," *Russkaia starina,* CIL (1912), 139-43.

Esipovich, Senator Iakov G. "Zapiski senatora Esipovicha," *Russkaia starina,* CXXXVII (1909), 123-44, 259-78, 555-64; CXXXVIII (1909), 146-60, 301-310, 493-501; CXXXIX (1909), 35-43, 215-28, 397-409; CXL (1909), 63-78, 287-96. Some information on Pobedonostsev as a member of the Senate in the 1870's.

Evlogii, Metropolitan of Western Europe. *Put' moei zhizni. Vospominaniia.* Paris, 1947. Information on Church policy in territories inhabited largely by Polish Catholics.

Feoktistov, Evgenii M. *Vospominaniia. Za kulisami politiki i literatury, 1848–1896.* Leningrad, 1929. Very valuable on Pobedonostsev's influence concerning censorship.

Glinskii, Boris B. "Iz tsenzurnago proshlago. Stranichka vospominanii," *Istoricheskii vestnik,* CIV (1906), 186-201. An editor's problems with the censor.

Golitzyn, Prince V. M. "Moskovskii universitet v 60-kh godakh," *Golos minuvshago,* V (1917), 173-240.

Gradovskii, Grigorii K. "Iz minuvshago. Vospominaniia i vpechatleniia literatura, 1867–1897 g.," *Russkaia starina,* CXXXIII (1908), 77-86, 323-30, 637-44; CXXXIV (1908), 148-57, 293-302; CXXXVI (1908), 57-74, 553-62; CXXXVII (1909), 529-35. Information on Church policies.

Gurko, Vladimir. *Features and Figures of the Past. Government and Opinion in the Reign of Nicholas II.* Stanford, 1939. Memoirs of a high official.

Heidler, Jan (editor). *Příspěvky k listáři Dra. Frant. Lad. Riegra.* Prague, 1924-26, two vols. Valuable on Pobedonostsev's relations with Czech leaders.

Herzen, Alexander. *Memoirs. My Past and Thoughts.* London, 1924–27, six vols.

———. *Pis'ma iz Frantsii i Italii, 1847–1852.* Moscow-Leningrad, 1934. This was published originally in 1854. There is a French edition, *Lettres de France et d'Italie, 1847–1852.* Geneva, 1871.

Ianzhul, Ivan I. "Vospominaniia," *Russkaia starina,* CXL (1909), 33-57, 249-72, 495-518; CXLI (1910), 133-48, 271-306, 475-507; CXLII (1910), 67-101, 307-328; CXLIV (1910), 3-20, 258-72, 485-500; CXLV (1911), 41-58, 257-69, 501-520; CXLVI (1911), 43-70, 267-89, 488-506. Some data on the Volunteer Fleet.

Ignatiev, Count Nicholas P. "Zapiski grafa N. P. Ignatieva, s primechaniiami A. A. Bashmakova," *Istoricheskii vestnik,* CXXXV (1914), 49-75, 441-62, 805-836; CXXXVI (1914), 50-85, 430-68, 825-63; CXXXVII (1914), 54-93.

———. "Posle San-Stefano. Zapiski gr. N. P. Ignatieva, s primechaniiami A. A. Bashmakova," *Istoricheskii vestnik,* CXLIII (1916), 35-58, 357-79, 654-78.

Jirásek, Josef. *Rusko a my.* Prague, 1945–46, four vols. in two. Some information concerning relations with Czech leaders.

Koni, Anatole F. "Iz zametok i vospominanii sudebnago deiatelia," *Russkaia starina,* CXXXVII (1909), 5-27, 233-55; CXL (1909), 3-29, 231-47, 461-85; CXLIV (1910), 231-57, 469-83.

———. *Na zhiznennom puti.* Moscow-Riga, 1912–29, five vols. Valuable memoirs of a distinguished jurist who was a student of Pobedonostsev in the early 1860's.

Kovařík, Fedor. *Zážitky a dojmy ruského Čecha za cárství.* Prague, 1932. Czech teacher who was aided by Pobedonostsev in Russia.

Kryzhanovskii, Sergei E. *Vospominaniia. Iz bumag S. E. Kryzhanovskogo, poslednago gosudarstvennago sekretaria Rossiiskoi Imperii.* Berlin, 1938.

Kuropatkin, A. N. "Dnevnik A. N. Kuropatkina," *Krasnyi arkhiv,* II (1922), 5-117; V (1924), 82-101; VII (1924), 55-69; VIII (1925), 70-100.

Lamzdorf, Count Vladimir N. *Dnevnik V. N. Lamzdorfa, 1886–1890.* Moscow, 1926.

———. *Dnevnik, 1891–1892.* Moscow, 1934. Valuable information concerning Pobedonostsev's role in the Holy Land and in Abyssinia.

Lebedev, V. A. "Iz zhizni Fedora Ivanovicha Buslaeva," *Russkaia starina,* CXXXIII (1908), 298-306.

"Kniaz'ia tserkvi. Iz dnevnika A. N. Lvova," *Krasnyi arkhiv,* XXXIX (1930), 108-148; XL (1930), 97-124. Librarian of Holy Synod, quite critical of Pobedonostsev and his associates in the Synod.

Mavor, James. *My Windows on the Street of the World.* London, 1923, two vols.

Meshcherskii, Prince Vladimir P. *Moi vospominaniia.* St. Petersburg, 1897–1912, three vols. Interesting information from an early acquaintance.

Miliutin, Count Dmitrii A. *Dnevnik.* Moscow, 1947–50, four vols. in three. Valuable memoirs of Minister of War under Alexander II.

Naumovich, Father Ivan. *Piatidesiatiletie (1839–1889) vozsoedineniia s pravoslavniiu tserkoviiu zapadno-russkikh uniatov. Istoricheskii ocherk.* St. Petersburg, 1889. Valuable memoirs and history by priest Pobedonostsev subsidized in Galicia.

Nazimova, M. "Dvor velikoi kniagini Eleny Pavlovny, 1865–1867," *Russkii arkhiv,* X (1899), 311-18. Data on Pobedonostsev in early years at court.

Novikova, Olga A. *Russian Memories.* London, 1917.

Panaev, Valereian A. "Iz vospominanii V. A. Panaeva," *Russkaia starina,* CXXVIII (1906), 397-442. Information on Ashinov.

Panteleev, Longin F. *Vospominaniia.* Moscow, 1958.

Pares, Sir Bernard. *My Russian Memoirs.* London, 1931.

———. *A Wandering Student. The Story of a Purpose.* Syracuse, 1948. Pares, outstanding liberal English historian, met Pobedonostsev.

Peretts, Egor A. *Dnevnik E. A. Perettsa, 1880–1883.* Moscow-Leningrad, 1927. Valuable diary for these critical years.

Pfeil und Klein-Ellguth, Count Richard von. *Das Ende Kaiser Alexanders II. Meine Erlebnisse in russischen Diensten, 1878–1881.* Berlin, 1903.

———. *Neun Jahre in russischen Diensten unter Kaiser Alexander III. Erinnerungen.* Leipzig, 1907. Prussian in Russian military service.

Polonskii, Iakov P. "Dnevnik. Rossiia v 1876 godu," *Na chuzhoi storone,* IV (1924), 88-100.

———. "Iz dnevnika Ia. P. Polonskago 1878 g.," *Na chuzhoi storone,* V (1924), 41-49.

Polovtsev, Alexander A. "Dnevnik," *Krasnyi arkhiv,* III (1923), 75-172; IV (1923), 63-128. Covers 1901–1908. Interesting.

"Iz dnevnika A. A. Polovtsova," *Krasnyi arkhiv,* XLVI (1931), 110-32.

Polovtsov, Alexander A. *Dnevnik gosudarstvennogo sekretaria A. A. Polovtsova v dvukh tomakh.* Moscow, 1966, two vols. Diary covers 1883–92, when Polovtsov was State Secretary. Very valuable.

Radziwill, Princess Catherine. *Memories of Forty Years.* New York, 1915.

Rozanov, Nicholas. "Vospominaniia o Danile Mikhailoviche Vellanskom," *Russkii vestnik,* LXXII (1867), 99-137.

Rozanov, Vasilii V. (editor) "Iz perepiski S. A. Rachinskago," *Russkii vestnik,* CCLXXXI (1902), 603-629; CCLXXXII (1902), 143-57.

Rubinstein, Anton. *Autobiography of Anton Rubinstein, 1829–1889.* Boston, 1890.

Savva, Archbishop of Tver. *Khronika moei zhizni.* Sergiev Posad, 1897–1911, nine vols. Much information on Pobedonostsev and Church administration.

Schilovsky, P. P. "Reminiscences of K. P. Pobedonostsev," *Slavonic and East*

European Review, XXX (1952), 364-75. Interesting insight on Pobedonostsev's interest in legal scholarship.

Schweinitz, General Hans von. *Briefwechsel des Botschafters General v. Schweinitz*. Berlin, 1928.

——. *Denkwürdigkeiten des Botschafters General v. Schweinitz*. Berlin, 1927, two vols. Memoirs of German ambassador in St. Petersburg, 1878–92.

Shelgunov, Nicholas V. *Vospominaniia*. Moscow, 1923.

Shevelev, A. A. "Puteshestviia po Rossii ego Imperatorskago Vysochestva naslednika tsesarevicha Aleksandra Aleksandrovicha," *Russkoe obozrenie*, XLVI (1897), 52-92; IL (1898), 821-32. Information on 1867 and 1869 trips.

Shtakenshneider, Elena A. *Dnevnik i zapiski, 1854–1886*. Moscow, 1934.

Simpson, J. Y. (editor). *The Saburov Memoirs, or Bismarck and Russia*. Cambridge, England, 1929.

Spasovich, Wlodzimierz D. *Za mnogo let, 1859–1871*. St. Petersburg, 1872. Distinguished jurist who commented on *Kurs grazhdanskago prava*.

Stead, William T. (editor). *The M.P. for Russia. Reminiscences and Correspondence of Madame Olga Novikoff*. London, 1909, two vols. Most valuable.

——. *Truth about Russia*. London, 1889. Result of a trip to Russia.

Suvorin, A. S. *Dnevnik A. S. Suvorina. Redaktsiia, predislovie i primechaniia Mikh. Krichevskogo*. Moscow-Petrograd, 1923. Suvorin was editor of *Novoe Vremia*. This was translated into French, *Journal intime d'Alexis Souvorine* (Paris, 1927).

Tanaevskii, Father S. *Pamiati Sergeia Aleksandrovicha Rachinskago*. Kazan, 1904. Excellent on Rachinskii.

"Tekushchaia khronika i osobye proizshestviia. Dnevnik V. F. Odoevskogo, 1859–1869 gg.," *Literaturnoe nasledstvo*, Number 22-24 (1935), 79-308. Quite valuable, with excellent notes by B. Koz'min.

Tiutcheva, Anna F. *Pri dvore dvukh imperatorov. Dnevnik, 1855–1882*. Moscow, 1928–29, two vols. Fragments of her copious diary.

"Tolstoi v 1880-e gody. Zapiski I. M. Ivakina," *Literaturnoe nasledstvo*, Number 69, Part 2 (1961), 21-124.

Valuev, Count Peter A. *Dnevnik, 1877–1884*. Petrograd, 1919. Valuable on critical period.

Vogüé, Viscount Eugène de. *Les Routes*. Paris, 1910. Valuable chapter on Pobedonostsev.

Voronov, A. "Vospominaniia byvshago studenta Kharkovskago universiteta 60-kh godov," *Russkaia starina*, CLIV (1913), 571-95.

Wemyss, Rosslyn (editor). *Memoirs and Letters of the Right Hon. Sir Robert Morier, G. C. B. from 1826 to 1876*. London, 1911, two vols.

White, Andrew D. *Autobiography*. New York, 1905, two vols. American minister in St. Petersburg, 1892–94. See also White, "A Statesman of Russia: Constantine Pobedonostsev," *Century Magazine*, LVI (1898), 110-18.

Witte, Count Sergei IU. *Vospominaniia.* Moscow, 1923, two vols. A new three-volume edition with splendid notes by A. L. Sidorov was published in Moscow in 1960.

Zhirkevich, A. V. "Arkhiepiskop Ierononinim. Opyt' kharakteristiki," *Istoricheskii vestnik,* CXIII (1908), 881-915.

Letters

Aksakov, Ivan S. *Ivan Sergeevich Aksakov v ego pismakh.* Moscow, 1888–96, four vols. This does not include all his letters.

Belchikov, N. F. (editor). *Pis'ma F. M. Dostoevskogo k zhene.* Moscow-Leningrad, 1926.

Frank, V. S. (editor). "Iz neizdannoi perepiski Imp. Aleksandra III i Nikolaia II s kn. V. P. Meshcherskim," *Sovremennyia zapiski,* LXX (1940), 165-88.

"Iz razorenoi Moskvy. Pis'ma I. M. Snegireva k P. V. Pobedonostsevu," *Russkii arkhiv,* I (1897), 110-12. 1813 letters.

Konovalov, Serge (editor). "The Emperor Alexander II and Princess Ekaterina Dolgorukaya (Yurievskaya): Nine Letters," *Oxford Slavonic Papers,* XI (1964), 94-100.

Kovalevskii, Maxim M. *Konstitutsiia grafa Loris-Melikova i ego chastnye pis'ma.* Berlin, 1904. Very valuable.

Lazarev, E. E. *Gavaiskii Senator i vozhdi russkago pravoslaviia, episkop Vladimir i K. P. Pobedonostsev.* Geneva, 1902. Russian exile whose correspondence contains interesting information on Russian Orthodox Church in San Francisco.

Mustafin, V. (editor). "Mikhail Nikiforovich Katkov i graf Petr Aleksandrovich Valuev v ikh perepiske, 1863–1879 gg.," *Russkaia starina,* CLXIII (1915), 279-300, 403-413; CLXIV (1915), 91-95, 247-51, 416-30; CLXVI (1916), 346-65. Some data on 1863.

"Perepiska Aleksandra III s gr. Loris-Melikovym, 1880–1881 gg.," *Krasnyi arkhiv,* VIII (1925), 101-131. Significant letters.

"Perepiska P. D. Golokhvastova s I. S. Aksakovym o zemskom sobore," *Russkii arkhiv,* I (1913), 93-111; II (1913), 181-204.

Radziwill, Princess Marie. *Lettres de la princesse Radziwill au général de Robilant, 1889–1914.* Bologna, 1933–34, four vols. Valuable information.

Repin, Il'ia E. *I. E. Repin i V. V. Stasov. Perepiska.* Moscow, 1948-50, three vols.

Staal, Baron Egor F. *Correspondance diplomatique de M. de Staal, 1884–1900.* Paris, 1929, two vols. Ambassador in London, 1884–1902.

Stankevich, Aleksei (editor). *Perepiska Nikolaia Vladimirovicha Stankevicha, 1830–1840.* Moscow, 1914. Reference to Professor Pobedonostsev as a teacher.

"Vozhd' reaktsii 60-80-kh godov. Neizdannyia pis'ma M. N. Katkova Aleksandru II i Aleksandru III," *Byloe*, Number 4 (1917), 1-32.

Jakobson, Sergius. "Pis'ma Iv. Serg. Aksakova k V. F. Putsykovichu," *Na chuzhoi storone*, V (1924), 129-58. Fifteen letters written between 1878 and 1886.

Zilbershtein, Il'ia S. (editor). *F. M. Dostoevskii i I. S. Turgenev. Perepiska*. Leningrad, 1928.

Some Official Documents and Reports

"M. N. Katkov i Aleksandr III v 1886–1887 gg.," *Krasnyi arkhiv*, LVIII (1933), 58-85. Memoranda from Katkov to Alexander III on foreign policy.

Chuloshnikov, N. (editor). "K istorii manifesta 6 avgusta 1905 goda," *Krasnyi arkhiv*, XIV (1926), 262-70. Documents and drafts.

Iasevich-Borodaevskaia, Varvara I. (editor). *Materialy k vysochaishemu ukazu 12 dekabria 1904 g*. St. Petersburg, n.d., five vols.

Russia. Gosudarstvennyi sovet. *Otchët po deloproizvodstvu Gosudarstvennago soveta za sessiiu 1892/1893–1905/1906*. St. Petersburg, 1893–1906, fourteen vols. in eighteen.

———. *Otchët po Gosudarstvennomu sovetu, 1869–1891*. St. Petersburg, 1870–92, twenty-three vols.

———. *Gosudarstvennyi sovet, 1801–1901. Istoriko-iuridicheskii ocherk*. St. Petersburg, 1901.

———. *Stenograficheskie ochëti, ses. 1-13 (28 apr. 1906 g.– 14 fevr. 1917 g.)*. St. Petersburg, 1906–1917, thirteen vols.

Russia. Komitet ministrov. *Zhurnaly Komiteta ministrov po ispolneniiu ukaza 12 dekabria 1904 g*. St. Petersburg, 1905.

Russia. Ministerstvo iustitsii. *Ministerstvo iustitsii za sto let, 1802–1902. Istoricheskii ocherk*. St. Petersburg, 1902.

———. *Obshchii obzor deiatel'nosti Ministerstva iustitsii i pravitel'stvuiushchago Senata za tsarstvovanie Imperatora Aleksandra III*. St. Petersburg, 1901.

Russia. Ministerstvo vnutrennykh del. *Obshchii obzor Ministerstva vnutrennykh del za vremia tsarstvovaniia Aleksandra III*. St. Petersburg, 1901.

Sudebnoe preobrazovanie v 1863 i 1864 g. St. Petersburg, 1867, six vols. This is a set of documents concerning the judicial reform. It was apparently prepared by S. I. Zarudnyi.

Zarudnyi, S. I. (editor). *Materialy po sudebnomu preobrazovaniiu 1864 goda*. St. Petersburg, 1864?, seventy-four vols. Documents collected by S. I. Zarudnyi, one of those most responsible for the reform of the judicial system. These memoranda, reports, and drafts include all the official materials leading to the reform between 1861 and 1864. They include Pobedonostsev memoranda in volumes 12, 13, 17, and 26. One set of these volumes is in the Saltykov-Shchedrin Library in Leningrad.

SECONDARY SOURCES

Studies of Pobedonostsev

Adams, Arthur E. "The Ideology and Influence of K. P. Pobedonostsev, 1881–1905," Cornell University, Thesis for Doctorate in History, 1951.

———. "Pobedonostsev and the Rule of Firmness," *Slavonic and East European Review*, XXXII (1953), 132-39.

———. "Pobedonostsev's Religious Politics," *Church History*, XXII (1953), 314-26.

———. "Pobedonostsev's Thought Control," *Russian Review*, XI (1953), 241-46.

Amfiteatrov, Alexander V., and Evgenii Anichkov. *Pobedonostsev*. St. Petersburg, 1907.

d'Avril, Adolphe. "Pensées d'un homme d'état," *Revue des questions historiques*, XX (1898), 525-31. Basically, a review of *Moskovskii sbornik*.

Borzenko, A. "Pacta sunt servanda," *Russkoe obozrenie*, VI (1890), 455-64.

Courtney, William L. "A Reactionary Statesman," in *The Development of Maurice Maeterlinck and other Sketches of Foreign Writers* (London, 1904), 163-72. *Daily Telegraph* correspondent.

Dillon, E. J. (E. B. Lanin, *pseud.*). "Constantine Pobedonostseff," *Contemporary Review*, LXIII (1893), 584-608. *Daily Telegraph* correspondent.

Dobrosaabskii, V. *Konstantin Petrovich Pobedonostsev v svoikh pedagogicheskikh vozzreniakh*. Kharkov, 1911.

Evenchik, S. L. "Reaktsionnaia deiatel'nost' Pobedonostseva v 80-kh gg. XIX-go veka." Moscow University Thesis for Candidate Degree in History, 1939. This thesis was based in part on archival materials of the Holy Synod which I was not able to use.

Fet, A. "K. P. Pobedonostsev o semeinykh uchastkakh," *Nabliudatel'*, Number 10 (1889), 31-33.

Firsov, N. N. "Pobedonostsev. Opyt kharakteristiki po pis'mam," *Byloe*, Number 25 (1924), 246-70. Based largely on his published letters.

Gavrilov, Alexander V. "Konstantin Petrovich Pobedonostsev v ego pis'makh," *Tserkovnyia Vedomosti*, March 24, 1907, supplement, 541-44.

Glinskii, Boris B. "Konstantin Petrovich Pobedonostsev. Materialy dlia biografii," *Istoricheskii vestnik*, CVIII (1907), 247-74. Valuable.

Gnevyshev, M. *Konstantin Petrovich Pobedonostsev*. Kiev, 1907.

Golovin, K. F. "K voprosu o semeinykh uchastkakh," *Russkoe obozrenie*, III (1890), 280-99, 540-58.

Golubov, Sergei. *Den' Konstantina Petrovicha. Povest'*. Moscow, 1941. Novel which ridicules Pobedonostsev as a cuckold.

Görlitz, Walter. *Russische Gestalten*. Heidelberg, 1940.

Gotie, Iurii V. "K. P. Pobedonostsev i naslednik Aleksandr Aleksandrovich, 1865–1881," *Publichnaia Biblioteka SSSR imeni V. I. Lenina. Sbornik*, II (1929), 107-134. Excellent analysis based on thorough, objective research.

Hunterberg, Max. *The Russian Mephistopheles.* Glasgow, 1909. Novel.

Kaminka, A. "K. P. Pobedonostsev," *Pravo,* I (1907), 822-25.

Kizevetter, Alexander A. "Pobedonostsev," *Na chuzhoi storone,* IV (1924), 257-81. Review of *Novum Regnum* by eminent Russian historian.

Kopina, Liudmila. *Stranitsy bolshoi zhizni.* Moscow, 1953. Novel on Pobedonostsev and Count Leo Tolstoy.

Korolenko, V. "K. P. Pobedonostsev i V. I. Askochenskii," *Russkoe bogatstvo,* Number 3 (1907), 133-39.

Medvedskii, K. "Piatidesiatiletie sluzhebnoi deiatel'nosti K. P. Pobedonostseva," *Russkii vestnik,* CCXLV (1896), 280-82.

Mesniaev, G. "Dostoevskii i Pobedonostsev," *Rossiia,* June 27, 1959, 2, 4.

Nikol'skii, Boris V. "Literaturnaia deiatel'nost' K. P. Pobedonostseva," *Istoricheskii vestnik,* LXV (1896), 711-32. Excellent bibliographical article.

———. "Moskovskii sbornik," *Novoe Vremia,* June 12, 1896. Review.

Nikol'skii, N. "K. P. Pobedonostsev," *Tserkovnyi vestnik,* XXXIII (1907), 381-83.

Nolde, Baron Alexander E. *K. P. Pobedonostsev i sudebnaia reforma.* Petrograd, 1915. Very valuable study.

———. "Obzor nauchnoi iuridicheskoi deiatel'nosti K. P. Pobedonostseva," *Zhurnal Ministerstva narodnago prosveshcheniia,* VIII (1907), 93-116. Excellent.

Orshanskii, Il'ia G. "Kurs grazhdanskago prava," *Zhurnal grazhdanskago i ugolovnago prava,* Book II (1876), 258-82.

"50-Letie sluzhebnoi deiatel'nosti K. P. Pobedonostseva," *Istoricheskii vestnik,* LXV (1896), 253-56. Important for bibliography and record of government service.

"50-letnii iubilei K. P. Pobedonostseva," *Sudebnaia gazeta,* June 9, 1896, 10-11.

Preobrazhenskii, I. V. *Konstantin Petrovich Pobedonostsev, ego lichnost' i deiatel'nosti v predstavlenii sovremennikov ego konchiny.* St. Petersburg, 1912. Thorough record of obituaries at time of Pobedonostsev's death.

Preobrazhenskii, P. "Russkii papa. O perepiski Pobedonostseva," *Pechat' i Revoliutsiia,* Book I (1924), 61-67. Review of his correspondence.

de Proyart, Jacqueline. "Le Haut-Procureur du Saint-Synode Constantin Pobedonoscev et le coup d'état du 29 avril 1881," *Cahiers du monde russe et soviétique,* III (1962), 408-458. Sound analysis, based on published data.

———. "Pobedonoscev et Dostoevsky. Un amitié littéraire," *Revue des études slaves,* XXXVIII (1961), 151-63. Based on published letters.

Rappoport, A. S. "Pobiedonostzev, the Apostle of Absolutism and Orthodoxy," *Fortnightly Review,* LXXXI (1907), 868-78.

Rozanov, Vasilii V. *Okolo tserkovnykh sten.* St. Petersburg, 1906, two vols. Contains an analytical essay.

Schaper, Edzard H. *Attentat auf den Mächtigen. Roman.* Frankfurt, 1957.

Shoob, Leo. "Konstantin Petrovich Pobedonostsev: A Study in Reaction," University of California, Berkeley, Thesis for Doctorate in History, 1947.

Slavik, Jan. "Zhoubny obránce samoderžavi (K 25. výročí smrti K. P. Pobĕdonosceva.)," *Slovansky přehled*, XXIV (1932), 207-214, 257-63.

Slonimski, L. *O velikoi lzhi nashego vremeni. K. P. Pobedonostsev i kniaz' V. P. Meshcherskii.* St. Petersburg, 1908.

Spasovich, Wlodzimierz D. "Kurs grazhdanskago prava K. Pobedonostseva, Chast' vtoraia," *Zhurnal grazhdanskago i torgovago prava*, Book I (1871), 134-57. One of the most penetrating reviews.

Steinmann, Friedrich, and Elias Hurwicz. *Konstantin Petrovitsch Pobjedonoszew, der Staatsmann der Reaktion unter Alexander III.* Königsberg, 1933. Largely an analysis of his influence on Alexander III, plus translations of some of their correspondence.

Tal'berg, N. D. *Muzh' vernosti i razuma. K 50-letniiu konchiny K. P. Pobedonostseva.* Jordanville, New York, 1957. Favorable; based largely on letters.

———. " 'Uchenie i uchitel' v izobrazhenii K. P. Pobedonostseva," *Pravoslavnaia Zhizn'*, Number 3 (1960), 18-23. Study of his views on education, supported by quotations.

Vengerov, Semen. *Ocherki po istorii russkoi literatury. S epokhi Belinskago do nashikh dnei.* St. Petersburg, 1907. Contains an essay on Pobedonostsev.

Volkhovsky, F. V. "The Philosophy of Reaction," *Free Russia*, X (1899), 90-91; XI (1900), 4-5.

Voroshilov, A. "O sootnoshenii prav votchinago i krepostnago," *Otechestvennyia zapiski*, CXXV (1859), 63-94. Excellent study of a Pobedonostsev article.

Wren, Melvin C. "Pobedonostsev and Russian Influence in the Balkans, 1881–1888," *Journal of Modern History*, XIX (1947), 130-41. Misinterprets Pobedonostsev's policies in the Balkans.

Studies of Dostoevsky

Belchikov, N. F. (editor). "Dostoevskii o Pushkinskikh torzhestvakh," *Krasnyi arkhiv*, I (1922), 367-405. Largely letters.

———. "Dostoevskii i Pobedonostsev," *Krasnyi arkhiv*, II (1922), 240-55.

Cheshikhin, Vasilii (Ch. Vetrinskii, *pseud.*). *F. M. Dostoevskii v vospominaniiakh sovremennikov.* Moscow, 1912.

Dostoevsky, Anna G. *Bibliograficheskii ukazatel' sochinenii i proizvedenii iskusstva, otnosiashchikhsia k zhizni i deiatel'nosti F. M. Dostoevskogo.* St. Petersburg, 1906.

Ermilov, Vladimir V. *F. M. Dostoevskii.* Moscow, 1956.

Gibian, George. "C. G. Carus' *Psyche* and Dostoevsky," *American Slavic and East European Review*, XIV (1955), 371-82. Valuable.

Grossman, Leonid P. "Dostoevskii i pravitel'stvennye krugi 1870-kh godov," *Literaturnoe nasledstvo*, Number 15 (1934), 83-162. Excellent analysis, plus forty letters Pobedonostsev wrote to Dostoevsky.

———. *Dostoevskii na zhiznennom puti.* Moscow, 1928, two vols.

396   BIBLIOGRAPHY

──. *Seminarii po Dostoevskomu. Materialy, bibliografiia i kommentarii.* Moscow, 1922.

──. *Tvorchestvo Dostoevskogo, 1821–1881–1921. Sbornik stat'ei i materialov.* Odessa, 1921.

──. *Zhizn' i trudy F. M. Dostoevskogo.* Moscow-Leningrad, 1935. Includes detailed chronology of Dostoevsky's life.

Izkoz, Arkadii S. (A. S. Dolinin, *pseud.*). *F. M. Dostoevskii. Materialy i issledovaniia.* Leningrad, 1935.

──. *V tvorcheskoi laboratorii Dostoevskogo.* Leningrad, 1947.

Mochul'skii, Constantine V. *Dostoevskii. Zhizn' i tvorchestvo.* Paris, 1947.

Nechaeva, Vera S. (editor). *Opisanie rukopisei F. M. Dostoevskogo.* Moscow, 1957.

Oksman, Iulian G. "F. M. Dostoevskii v redaktsii *Grazhdanina*," *Tvorchestvo Dostoevskogo. Stat'i i materialy pod red. Grossmana* (Odessa, 1921), 63-82.

Seduro, Vladimir. *Dostoyevski in Russian Literary Criticism, 1846–1956.* New York, 1957.

Simmons, Ernest J. *Dostoevsky, The Making of a Novelist.* London, 1950. Excellent biography.

Studies of Russian Literature

Ovsianiko-Kulikovskii, Dmitrii N. (editor). *Istoriia russkoi literatury XIX v.* Moscow, 1918–23, five vols. Useful information on Russian journals.

Poggioli, Renato. *The Poets of Russia, 1890–1930.* Cambridge, 1960.

Smirnovski, Peter V. *Istoriia russkoi literatury deviatnadtsatago veka.* St. Petersburg, 1899–1904, eight vols.

Tkhorzhevskii, Ivan I. *Russkaia literatura.* Paris, 1946, two vols. in one. A second edition of this was published in 1950.

Biographies and Critical Studies

Aksakov, Ivan S. *Biografiia Fedora Ivanovicha Tiutcheva.* Moscow, 1886.

Alekseev, Anatole D. (editor). *Letopis' zhizni i tvorchestva I. A. Goncharova.* Moscow-Leningrad, 1960.

Andreevskii, I. E. "O Kalachove, kak iurist, arkheolog i uchreditel' Arkheologicheskago Instituta," *Vestnik arkheologii i istorii,* V (1886), 1-14.

Barsukov, Nicholas P. *Zhizn' i trudy M. P. Pogodina.* St. Petersburg, 1880–1910, twenty-two vols. Valuable information.

Baylen, Joseph O. "Madame Olga Novikov: Defender of Imperial Russia, 1880–1900," *Historia,* I (1951), 133-56.

──. "Madame Olga Novikov, Propagandist," *American Slavic and East European Review,* X (1951), 255-71.

Berdyaev, Nicholas. *Constantin Leontieff.* Paris, 1936.

Birkbeck, Rose J. *Life and Letters of W. J. Birkbeck.* London, 1922. Very valuable.

Bowers, Claude G. *Beveridge and the Progressive Era.* Cambridge, Mass., 1932. Beveridge met Pobedonostsev in 1901.

Bowman, Herbert. *Vissarion Belinski, 1811–1848.* Cambridge, Mass., 1954. Sound study.

Bullock, George. *Marie Corelli. The Life and Death of a Best-Seller.* London, 1940.

Creighton, Louise. *Life and Letters of Mandell Creighton.* London, 1904, two vols. Valuable information on Bishop of London.

Danilov, I. G. "O trudakh Kalachova po krestianskomu delu," *Vestnik arkheologii i istorii,* V (1896), 15-24.

Firsov, Nicholas N. "Alexandr III. Lichnaia kharakteristika chast'iu po ego neizdannym dnevnikam," *Byloe,* Number 29 (1925), 85-108. Based on diary of Alexander III.

Gorbov, N. M. "S. A. Rachinskii," *Zhurnal Ministerstva narodnago prosveshcheniia,* CCCXLIV (1902), 67-107.

Gratieux, Albert. *A. S. Khomiakov et le mouvement slavophile.* Paris, 1939, two vols. Good analysis.

Katz, Martin. *Mikhail N. Katkov. A Political Biography.* The Hague, 1967. Based on sources available in United States and Finland.

Klevenskii, M. "Gertsen-izdatel' i ego sotrudniki," *Literaturnoe nasledstvo,* Number 41-42 (1941), 572-620.

Knorring, N. N. *General Mikhail Dmitrievich Skobelev.* Paris, 1939–40, two vols. in one.

Koliupanov, Nil P. *Biografiia Aleksandra Ivanovicha Kosheleva.* Moscow, 1889–92, two vols. in three.

Koni, Anatole F. "Velikaia kniaginia Elena Pavlovna," *Velikaia reforma,* V (1911), 14-34.

Kovalewski, Pierre, *N. S. Leskov. Peintre méconnu de la vie nationale russe.* Paris, 1925.

Labry, Raoul. *Alexandre Ivanovič Herzen, 1812–1870.* Paris, 1928.

Leroy-Beaulieu, Anatole. *Un Homme d'état russe, Nicholas Miliutine.* Paris, 1884.

Lisicki, Henryk. *Le marquis Wielopolski, sa vie et son temps, 1803–1877.* Vienna, 1880, two vols.

Liubavskii, Matvei K. "Vasilii Osipovich Kliuchevskii," in *V. O. Kliuchevskii. Kharakteristiki i vospominaniia* (Moscow, 1912), 5-25.

Liubimov, Nicholas A. *Mikhail Nikiforovich Katkov i ego istoricheskaia zasluga.* St. Petersburg, 1889. Illuminating biography by close collaborator.

———. *Pamiati N. A. Liubimova.* St. Petersburg, 1897.

Livov, Grégoire. *Michel Katkoff et son époque.* Paris, 1897.

Lukashevich, Stephen. *Ivan Aksakov, 1823–1886.* Cambridge, Mass., 1965.

MacMaster, Robert E. *Danilevsky: A Russian Totalitarian Philosopher.* Cambridge, Mass., 1967. Careful study.

Maiakovskii, I. L. "N. V. Kalachov," Moskovskii istoriko-arkhivnyi institut. *Trudy*, IV (1948), 161-80. Praises Kalachov as patriotic archivist.

Maikov, Leonid N. "E. M. Feoktistov," *Zhurnal Ministerstva narodnago prosveshcheniia*, CCCXVII (1898), 26-44.

Maude, Aylmer. *The Life of Tolstoy*. London, 1953, two vols.

Mazon, André. *Un Maître du roman russe. Ivan Gontcharov, 1812-1891* Paris, 1914.

Morley, John. *The Life of William Ewart Gladstone*. London, 1903, three vols.

Moskvinov, V. N. *Repin v Moskve*. Moscow, 1955.

Nicolaevski, Boris. *Aseff*. London, 1934.

Nikolaeva, T. "Deti sela Tateva," *Ogonëk*, Number 50, December, 1963, 24-25. Interesting as Soviet view in 1963 of Rachinskii.

Nikon, Bishop of Florida. *Zhizneopisanie blazhennieishago Antonii, metropolita Kievskago i Golitskago*. New York, 1957–63, ten vols.

Notovich, Nicholas. *L'Empereur Alexandre III et son entourage*. Paris, 1893.

Obninski, Victor. *Poslednyi samoderzhets. Ocherk zhizni i tsarstvovaniia Imperatora Rossii Nikolaia II-go*. Berlin, 1912. Splendid photographs.

Piatkovskii, Alexander P. *Kniaz' V. F. Odoevskii i D. V. Venevitinov*. St. Petersburg, 1901.

Platonov, Sergei F. *Konstantin Nikolaevich Bestuzhev-Riumin*. St. Petersburg, 1897.

Pypin, Alexander N. *Belinskii, ego zhizn' i perepiska*. St. Petersburg, 1908, second edition. Some information on Professor Peter V. Pobedonostsev.

Raeff, Marc. "A Reactionary Liberal: M. N. Katkov," *Russian Review*, XI (1952), 157-67.

Sakulin, Paul N. *Iz istorii russkago idealizma: Kniaz' V. F. Odoevskii*. Moscow, 1913, two vols. in one.

Sidorskii, Iosif. "Efimi Mikhailovich Kryzhanovskii, 1865–1888 gg.," *Russkaia starina*, LXVI (1890), 717-26.

Simmons, Ernest J. *Leo Tolstoy*. Boston, 1946.

Smith, Charles E. "The Young Czar and His Advisers," *North American Review*, CLX (1895), 21-28.

Stremooukoff, Dmitri. *La Poésie et l'idéologie de Tiouttchev*. Paris, 1937.

———. *Vladimir Soloviev et son oeuvre messianique*. Paris, 1935.

Tatishchev, Sergei S. (S. Nevedenskii, *pseud.*). *Katkov i ego vremia*. St. Petersburg, 1888.

Thomas, Louis. *Frédéric Le Play, 1806–1882*. Paris, 1943, second edition.

Vengerov, Semen A. "Ivan Ivanovich Lazhechnikov. Kritiko-biograficheskii ocherk," *Polnoe sobranie sochinenii I. I. Lazhechnikova*. (St. Petersburg, 1899–1900), I, i-cxxxi. Some data on Professor Peter V. Pobedonostsev.

Religion and the Russian Orthodox Church

1. GENERAL

Arseniev, Constantine C. *Svoboda sovesti i veroterpimost'. Sbornik stat'ei*. St. Petersburg, 1905. Based largely on Pobedonostsev's official reports.

Bolshakoff, Serge. *The Doctrine of the Unity of the Church in the Works of Khomyakov and Moehler*. London, 1946.

――――. *Russian Nonconformity*. Philadelphia, 1950. Excellent.

Curtiss, John S. *Church and State in Russia: The Last Years of the Empire, 1900–1917*. New York, 1940. First-rate study.

Dalton, Hermann. *Der Stundismus in Russland*. Gütersloh, 1896. Critical of Pobedonostsev policies.

Giliarov-Platonov, Nikita P. *Sbornik sochinenii*. Moscow, 1899, two vols.

――――. *Voprosy very i tserkvi*. Moscow, 1905–1906, two vols. Devoted largely to Church affairs.

Izmailov, A. "Novosti istorii," *Istoricheskii vestnik*, CXLI (1915), 629-36; CXLII (1915), 668-69. Information on Pobedonostsev as administrator of Church.

K tserkovnomu soboru. Sbornik. St. Petersburg, 1906. Documents on 1905 discussion.

"Kievskii sobor 1884 goda. Poslanie k vysokopreosviashchennomu Pavlu, eksarkhu Gruzii. Zapiski arkhiepiskopa Nikanora," *Russkii arkhiv*, II (1908), 554-74; III (1908), 86-138. Much information on Pobedonostsev's position toward the Stundists.

Latimer, Robert S. *Under Three Czars. Liberty of Conscience in Russia, 1856–1907*. London, 1909. Valuable.

2. THE HOLY SYNOD

Avidonov, N. (editor). "9 ianvaria 1905 goda i Sinod," *Byloe*, Number 29 (1925), 51-57. Pobedonostsev's reaction to Bloody Sunday.

Barsov, Timofei V. *Sinodal'nyia uchrezhdeniia preshniago vremeni*. St. Petersburg, 1897. Good description of Synod institutions.

Conseil Scolaire de Saint-Synode. *Ecoles paroissales en Russie*. Boulogne-sur-Seine, 1900. Information on parish schools prepared by Synod for international exposition in Paris in 1900.

Istoricheskaia perepiska o sud'bakh pravoslavnoi tserkvi. Moscow, 1912. Memoranda on 1904–1905 crisis in Church.

Kamenev, S. IU. "S. IU. Vitte i K. P. Pobedonostsev o sovremennom polozhenii pravoslavnoi tserkvi," *Vestnik evropy*, II (1909), 651-91. Quite informative.

Moscow. Sinodal'naya tipografiia. *Katalog knig, prodaiushchikhsia v sinodal'nykh knizhnykh lavkakh v S. Peterburge i Moskve*. Moscow, 1896.

Myshtsyn, V. N. "K istorii tserkovno-preobrazovatel'nago dvizheniia," *Bogoslovskii vestnik*, III (1905), 6, 359-83. Documents concerning 1904–1905 crisis in Church.

"Prebyvanie g. ober-prokurora Sv. sinoda K. P. Pobedonostseva v Tveri," *Pravoslavnoe obozrenie*, III (1882), 631-34.

Russia. Sviateishii pravitel'stvuiushchii sinod. *Obzor deiatel'nosti vedomstva Pravoslavnago Ispovedaniia za vremia tsarstvovaniia Imperatora Aleksandra III*. St. Petersburg, 1901.

――――. *Pravila i programmy dlia tserkovno-prikhodskikh shkol i shkol gra-moty*. St. Petersburg, 1894, second edition.

――――. *Tsirkuliarnye ukazy Sviateishago pravitel'stvuiushchago sinoda, 1867–1900 gg*. St. Petersburg, 1901. Most useful. Well organized.

Soloviov, A. N. *Moskovskii pechatnyi dvor*. Moscow, 1917.

Titlinov, B. V. *Tserkov' vo vremia revoliutsii*. Petrograd, 1924. Largely on controversy between Witte and Pobedonostsev in 1904–1905.

"Zapiski prisutstvuiushchago v Sviateishem pravitel'stvuiushchem vserossii-skom sinode. (Arkhiepiskopa Khersonskago Nikanora)," *Russkii arkhiv*, III (1906), 5-37, 161-213, 321-57, 481-504.

3. THE BALTIC LANDS

Dalton, Hermann. *On Religious Liberty in Russia*. Leipzig, 1890. Translation of Dalton's famous 1889 Open Letter to Pobedonostsev.

Dukmeyer, Friedrich. *Aus Anlass des offenen Sendschreibens an den Ober-prokureur des Synods K. Pobedonoszeff, von H. Dalton und des offenen Briefes an Pastor Dalton von A. D.* St. Petersburg, 1889.

Durnovo, N. *Nechto o russkoi tserkvi v ober-prokurorstve K. P. Pobedonos-tseva*. Leipzig, 1889.

Evangelical Alliance. *Rapport présenté aux branches de l'Alliance évan-gélique par le comité de Genève, sur des démarches faites au près de S. M. l'Empereur de Russie rélativement à la liberté religieuse dans l'empire russe de 1887 à 1889*. Geneva, 1889.

Loeoeralt, W. *Baltenhetze. Die Verfolgung von Glauben, Sprache und Recht in den Ostseeprovinzen Russlands*. Leipzig, 1890.

Pravoslavnaia tserkov' v Finlandii, napechatano po rasporiazheniiu g. ober-prokurora Sviateishago sinoda. St. Petersburg, 1893. Taken from an official Holy Synod report. Quite objective.

Shakhovskoi, Prince Sergei V. *Iz arkhiva Kniazia S. V. Shakhovskogo. Mate-rialy dlia istorii nedavniago proshlago Pribaltiiskoi okrainy, 1885–1894 gg*. St. Petersburg, 1909–1910, three vols. in one. Very illuminating on policy by governor of Estland, 1885–94.

Tobien, Alexander. *Die livlaendische Ritterschaft in ihrem Verhältnis zum Zarismus und russischen Nationalismus*. Riga, 1925–30, two vols.

Wurstemberger, L. von. *Die Gewissensfreiheit in den Ostsee-Provinzen Russ-lands*. Leipzig, 1872.

4. GALICIA AND RUTHENIA

Andrusiak, N. "Ruthène (église)," *Dictionnaire de théologie catholique*, XIV (1939), 382-407.

Kryzhanovskii, Efimi. *Russkoe zabuzh'e*. St. Petersburg, 1911. Collection of articles by one of Pobedonostsev's advisers.

Pelipenko, Alexis. "Die politische Propaganda des russischen Heiligen Synod in Galizien vor dem Kriege," *Berliner Monatshefte*, XII (1934), 825-38.

Soloviev, Father I. "Otets Ivann Naumovich," *Russkoe obozrenie*, XXII (1893), 290-93, 791-803. Useful.

5. THE HOLY LAND AND ABYSSINIA

Constantin, Viscount Jean Robert de. *L'Archimandrite Paisi et l'ataman Achinoff. Une Expédition religieuse en Abyssinie*. Paris, 1891. French defender of Ashinov project.

d'Alonzo, Alphonse. *La Russie en Palestine*. Paris, 1901. Valuable, by former French consul in Jerusalem.

Jesman, Czeslaw. *The Russians in Ethiopia. An Essay in Futility*. London, 1958.

Otchët Pravoslavnago Palestinskago Obshchestva. St. Petersburg, 1883–91, 1908–1911. Very useful.

Russkiia uchrezhdeniia v Sviatoi Zemlie i pochivskie deiateli Imperatorskago Pravoslavnago Palestinskago Obshchestva, 1882–1907. St. Petersburg, 1907.

Smolitsch, Igor. "Zur Geschichte der Beziehungen zwischen der russischen Kirche und dem Orthodoxen Osten," *Ostkirchliche Studien*, VII (1958), 1-47.

Stavrou, Theofanis. *Russian Interests in Palestine, 1882–1914*. Thessaloniki, 1963. Most useful history and analysis.

6. THE WEST

Birkbeck, William J. *Birkbeck and the Russian Church*. London, 1917.
———. *The Prospect of Reunion with Eastern Christendom*. London, 1894.
———. *Russia and the English Church in the Last Fifty Years*. London, 1895.
Birkbeck was an English clergyman who visited Russia and became a great admirer of Pobedonostsev and an advocate of the union of the Anglican Church with the Russian Orthodox.

Bolshakoff, Serge. *The Foreign Missions of the Russian Orthodox Church*. New York, 1943.

Smirnov, Eugene. *A Short Account of the Historical Development and Present Position of Russian Orthodox Missions*. London, 1903.

7. COUNT LEO TOLSTOY

Birkett, G. A. "Official Plans for Tolstoy's Funeral in 1902," *Slavonic and East European Review*, XXX (1951), 2-6. Excellent short article.

Graf Lev Tolstoi i Svyatyeishi-sinod. Berlin, 1901. Documents and letters concerning the excommunication of Tolstoy.

Ioann, Archimandrite. *Tolstoi i tserkov'*. Berlin, 1939. Well documented.

Poslanie Sviateishago sinoda o grafe Leve Tolstome. Moscow, 1901. Defense of the Synod's action with regard to Tolstoy.

Education

Darlington, Thomas. *Education in Russia*. London, 1909.

Eimontova, R. G. "Universitetskaia reforma 1863 g.," *Istoricheskie zapiski,* Number 70 (1961), 163-96. Excellent study based on thorough research.

Hans, Nicholas. *History of Russian Educational Policy, 1701–1917.* London, 1931. Based on materials available in England.

Ilminskii, Nicholas I. *Besedy o russkoi shkole.* Kazan, 1889.

Johnson, William H. *Russia's Educational Heritage.* Pittsburgh, 1950.

Konstantinov, Nicholas A. *Ocherki po istorii srednei shkoly.* Moscow, 1947. Concentrates on 1890–1917 period.

Leary, Daniel B. *Russian Education. Organization, History, Statistics.* New York, 1918.

Liubavskii, Matvei K. "Moskovskii universitet v 1812 godu," *Obshchestvo istorii i drevnostei rossiiskikh. Moscow. Chteniia,* Book IV, Part I (1912), 57-122.

Medynskii, Evgenii N. *Istoriia russkoi pedagogiki do Velikoi Oktiabrskoi Sotsialisticheskoi Revoliutsii.* Moscow, 1938, second edition. Excellent and most valuable.

Rachinskii, Sergei A. "La Lutte contre l'alcoolisme en Russie," *La Réforme sociale,* XXI (1891), 718-21.

———. *Pis'ma S. A. Rachinskago k dukhovnomu iunoshestvu o trezvosti.* Moscow, 1899.

———. *Sel'skaia shkola. Sbornik stat'ei.* Moscow, 1902, fifth edition.

———. *1001 zadacha dlia umstvennago schëta. Posobie dlia uchitelei sel'- skikh shkol.* Moscow, 1892.

———. "Tserkovnaia shkola," *Russkoe obozrenie,* XXXIII (1895), 541-56; XXXV (1895), 437-54; XXXVII (1896), 6-19.

———. Uchitelia i uchitelnitsy," *Russkoe obozrenie,* L (1898), 422-36.

———. *Zametki o sel'skikh shkolakh.* St. Petersburg, 1883.

Rashin, A. G. "Gramotnost' i narodnoe obrazovanie v Rossii v XIX i nachale XX v.," *Istoricheskie zapiski,* Number 37 (1951), 28-80. Contains much statistical information.

Rozhdestvenskii, S. V. (editor). *Istoricheskii obzor deiatel'nosti Ministerstva narodnago prosveshcheniia, 1802–1902.* St. Petersburg, 1902. Official history.

Saddler, R. E. "National Education and Social Ideals," in R. D. Roberts (editor), *Education in the Nineteenth Century* (Cambridge, England, 1901), 210-39.

Shakhovskoi, Prince Nicholas V. "N. P. Giliarov-Platonov, kak initsiator tserkovno-prikhodskoi shkoly," *Russkoe obozrenie,* XXXVIII (1896), 572-89.

Udal'tsov, Ivan D. (editor). *Ocherki po istorii Moskovskogo universiteta.* Moscow, 1940, two vols.

Zaionchkovskii, Peter A. and A. N. Sokolov (editors). *Moskovskii universitet v vospominaniiakh sovremennikov.* Moscow, 1956.

The Nineteenth Century

1. GENERAL

Almazova, N. "K dvatsatipiatiletiu Rossiiskago Obshchestva krasnago kresta," *Russkii arkhiv*, II (1892), 360-81. Some information on Pobedonostsev's activities in the 1860's.

Istoriia pravitel'stvuiushchago Senata za dvesti let, 1711–1911 g. St. Petersburg, 1911, five vols. in four. Valuable.

Jane, Frederick T. *The Imperial Russian Navy. Its Past, Present, and Future.* London, 1899.

Kucherov, Samuel. *Courts, Lawyers and Trials under the Last Three Tsars.* New York, 1953. Excellent study.

Kulomzin, A. N. (editor). *Istoricheskii obzor deiatel'nosti Komiteta Ministrov. K stoletiiu Komiteta Ministrov, 1802–1902.* St. Petersburg, 1902–1903, eight vols.

Monas, Sidney. *The Third Section. Police and Society in Russia under Nicholas I.* Cambridge, Mass., 1961.

Ozerov, Ivan Kh. *Politika po rabochemu voprosu v Rossii za poslednye gody.* Moscow, 1906. Useful information, some of it from archives of Ministry of Finance.

Shtrange, Mikhail. *La Révolution française et la société russe.* Moscow, 1960. Translation of a useful Soviet study.

Strakhovsky, Leonid I. "Constitutional Aspects of the Imperial Russian Government's Policy toward National Minorities," *Journal of Modern History*, XIII (1941), 467-92.

Sumner, Benedict H. *Peter the Great and the Emergence of Russia.* New York, 1951.

Veselovskii, Boris. *Istoriia zemstva za sorok let.* St. Petersburg, 1909–1911, three vols.

2. INTELLECTUAL HISTORY

Barghoorn, Frederick C. "Some Russian Images of the West," in Cyril E. Black (editor), *The Transformation of Russian Society* (Cambridge, Mass., 1960), 574-87.

Berdiaev, Nicholas A. *Dukhovnyi krizis intelligentsii. Stat'i po obshchestvennoi i religioznoi psikhologii, 1907–1909 gg.* St. Petersburg, 1910. Includes a pointed analysis of Pobedonostsev as a nihilist.

Berline, Paul. "Russian Religious Philosophers and the Jews," *Jewish Social Studies*, IX (1947), 271-318.

Brianskii, A. M. *"Repertuar i Panteon, 1839–1856," Russkii bibliofil,* Number 2 (1916), 54-76.

Carr, E. H. " 'Russia and Europe' as a Theme of Russian History," in Richard Pares and A. J. P. Taylor (editors), *Essays Presented to Sir Lewis Namier* (London, 1956), 357-93.

Dement'ev, Alexander G. *Ocherki po istorii russkoi zhurnalistiki, 1840–1850 gg.* Moscow, 1951.

Duff, James D. (editor). *Russian Realities and Problems*. Cambridge, England, 1917.

Haumant, Emile. *La Culture française en Russie, 1700–1900*. Paris, 1910.

Lappo-Danilevsky, Alexander S. "The Development of Science and Learning in Russia," in James D. Duff (editor), *Russian Realities and Problems* (Cambridge, England, 1917), 153-229.

Leningrad University. *Ocherki po istorii russkoi zhurnalistiki i kritiki*. Leningrad, 1950.

Malia, Martin. *Alexander Herzen and the Birth of Russian Socialism, 1812–1855*. Cambridge, Mass., 1961.

Mansuy, Abel. *Le Monde slav et les classiques français au XVIe-XVIIe siècles*. Paris, 1912.

Masaryk, Thomas G. *The Spirit of Russia. Studies in History, Literature, and Philosophy*. London, 1919, two vols. Translation of an early masterpiece on Russian intellectual history.

Miliukov, Paul N. *Le Mouvement intellectuel russe*. Paris, 1918. Translation.

Molok, A. "Tsarskaia Rossiia i iiul'skaia revoliutsiia 1830 g.," *Literaturnoe nasledstvo*, Number 29-30 (1937), 727-62.

Samarin, Iurii F., and O. Dmitriev. *Revoliutsionnyi konservatizm*. Berlin, 1875.

Samarine, Yuri. *Préface aux Oeuvres théologiques de A. S. Khomiakov*. Paris, 1939.

Sanine, Kyra. *Les Annales de la patrie et la diffusion de la pensée française en Russie, 1868–1884*. Paris, 1953.

Schelting, Alexander von. *Russland und Europa im russischen Geschichtsdenken*. Bern, 1948. Splendid and central book.

Sumner, B. H. "Russia and Europe," *Oxford Slavonic Papers*, II (1951), 1-16.

Volk, Stepan S. "Dekabristy o burzhuaznom Zapade," *Izvestiia. Akademiia Nauk SSSR, Seriia istorii i filosofii*, VIII (1951), 78-81.

Venturi, Franco. *Roots of Revolution*. New York, 1960. Translation from Italian.

Zenkovskii, Vasilii V. *Russian Thinkers and Europe*. Ann Arbor, Mich., 1953. Translation.

3. THE 1860's

Bazileva, Z. P. *"Kolokol" Gertsena, 1857–1867 gg.* Moscow, 1949.

Dzhanshiev, Grigorii A. *Epokha velikikh reform*. Moscow, 1900, eighth edition. Significant and most valuable study, first published in 1892.

———. *Osnovy sudebnoi reformy k 25-ti letiiu novago suda*. Moscow, 1891.

————. "Pervyia stranitsy v istorii sudebnoi reformy v Rossii, 1862–1867 gg.," *Russkaia starina,* XLVII (1885), 481-94.

Gessen, Iosif V. *Sudebnaia reforma.* St. Petersburg, 1903.

Hammer, Darrell P. "Russia and the Roman Law," *American Slavic and East European Review,* XVI (1957), 1-13.

Iakovlev, Vasilii I. *Khronologicheskiia dannyia k istoriiu sostavleniia sudebnykh ustavov 20 noiabria 1864.* Petrograd, 1914.

Kapnist, Count Ivan S. *Code d'organisation judiciare de l'Empire de Russie de 1864.* Paris, 1893.

Russia. Ministerstvo iustitsii. *Sudebnye ustavy 20 noiabria 1864 g. za piat'desiat let.* Petrograd, 1914, two vols. in three parts.

Shershenevich, Gabriel F. *Uchebnik russkago grazhdanskago prava.* St. Petersburg, 1907, sixth edition.

Zaionchkovskii, Peter A. *Voennye reformy 1860–1870 godov v Rossii.* Moscow, 1952. Excellent study.

4. 1876–82

Bagurin, A. *Dobrovol'nyi flot i ego zadachi.* St. Petersburg, 1888. Defense of Volunteer Fleet.

Golitsyn, Prince Nicholas V. "Konstitutsiia grafa Loris-Melikova. Materialy dlia eia istorii," *Byloe,* Number 10-11 (1918), 125-86. Includes important documents.

"P. D. Golokhvastov o Russkom gosudarstvennom stroenii i Zemskom sobore," *Russkii vestnik,* Number 2 (1905), 745-62. Useful data extracted from memoranda and letters to Pobedonostsev and to Ivan Aksakov.

Gotie, Iurii V. "Bor'ba pravitel'stvennykh gruppirovok i manifest 29 aprelia 1881 g.," *Istoricheskie zapiski,* II (1938), 240-99. Superb analysis based on thorough research on materials then available.

"Gr. Loris-Melikov i imp. Aleksandr II o polozhenii Rossii v sentiabre 1880 g.," *Byloe,* Number 4 (1917), 33-37. Loris-Melikov memorandum of September, 1880, and Alexander II's comments.

Heilbronner, Hans. "The Administrations of Loris-Melikov and Ignatiev, 1880–1882," University of Michigan, Thesis for Doctorate in History, 1954. Sound study, but based only on published materials available in the United States and western Europe.

Iakovlev, Vasilii I. (V. Ia. Bogucharskii, *pseud.*). *Iz istorii politicheskoi bor'by v Rossii v 70-kh i 80-kh godakh XIX veka.* Moscow, 1912.

Ignatiev, Count Nicholas P. *Proekt manifesta o sozyve Zemskogo Sobora vo vremiia koronatsionnykh torzhestv 1883 g.* May 6, 1882. Ignatiev proposal for *zemskii sobor,* in Pobedonostsev's handwriting.

Kovalevskii, M. M. *Konstitutsiia grafa Loris-Melikova.* London, 1893. The Loris-Melikov proposal and some comments upon it.

Lukashevich, Stephen. "Holy Brotherhood: 1881–1883," *American Slavic and East European Review,* XVIII (1959), 491-509.

Nolde, Baron Boris E. "Sovet ministrov 8 marta 1881 goda. Razskaz grafa Loris-Melikova V. A. Bil'basovu," *Byloe*, Number 10-11 (1918), 187-94. Bil'basov diary of March 12, 1881, after talk with Loris-Melikov.

Pervyi s'ezd russkikh iuristov v Moskve v 1875 godu. Moscow, 1882. Essays presented at congress which Pobedonostsev ridiculed.

Poggenpol', M. IU. (editor). *Ocherk vozniknoveniia i deiatel'nosti dobrovol'nago flota za vremia XXV-ti letnago ego sushchestvovaniia*. St. Petersburg, 1903.

Shchegolev, P. E. "Iz istorii konstitutsionnykh veianii v 1879–1881 godakh," *Byloe*, Number 12 (1906), 261-84. Based largely on Valuev diary.

———. "K delu 1 marta 1881. Neizdannye doklady grafa Loris-Melikova, V. K. Pleve, zhand. gen. Komarova i rezoliutsii Aleksandra III," *Byloe*, Number 10 (1918), 12-69. Based on documents in police archives.

Shuvalov, P. P. "Konstitutsionnaia zapiska grafa P. P. Shuvalova (k istorii russkogo osvoboditel'nogo dvizheniia v 80-kh godakh XIX stoletiia). Publ. I. D. Shishmanova," *Vestnik evropy*, Number 8 (1913), 136-66.

Zaionchkovskii, Peter A. *Krizis samoderzhaviia na rubezhe 1870–1880 godov*. Moscow, 1964. First-rate study based on analysis of all archival materials.

5. THE SLAVOPHILS

Christoff, Peter K. *An Introduction to Nineteenth-Century Russian Slavophilism. Volume I. A. S. Xomjakov*. The Hague, 1961.

Miliukov, Paul N. "Slavianofilstvo," *Entsiklopedicheskii slovar'*, XXX (1900), 307-314.

Riasanovsky, Nicholas. *Russia and the West in the Teaching of the Slavophiles*. Cambridge, Mass., 1952. Excellent and important book.

6. PANSLAVISM

Danilevsky, Nicholas J. *Rossiia i Evropa*. St. Petersburg, 1889, fourth edition. Significant book, particularly because of impact it produced in western Europe.

Fadeev, Rostislav A. *Mnenie o vostochnom voprose*. St. Petersburg, 1870.

Harris, David. *Britain and the Bulgarian Horrors of 1876*. Chicago, 1939.

Istomin, Fedor M. *Kratkii ocherk deiatel'nosti S. Peterburgskago slavianskago blagotvoritel'nago obshchestva za 25 let ego sushchestvovaniia, 1868–1893*. St. Petersburg, 1893.

Kohn, Hans. *Pan-Slavism. Its History and Ideology*. Notre Dame, 1953.

Petrovich, Michael B. *The Emergence of Russian Panslavism, 1856–1870*. New York, 1956. Fine study.

Portier d'Arc, Alfred (A. Dovérine, *pseud.*). *L'Esprit nationale russe sous Alexandre III*. Paris, 1890.

Pypin, Alexander N. *Panslavism v proshlom i nastoiashchem*. St. Petersburg, 1913.

Sinclair, Sir Tollemache. *A Defence of Russia and the Christians of Turkey.* London, 1877. Volume by an Englishman more panslav than the Russian panslavs. This was translated into Russian in 1878, except for its suggestion for reconstructing the Byzantine empire.

Strakhovsky, Leonid I. "General Count N. P. Ignatiev and the Pan-Slav Movement," *Journal of Central European Affairs*, XVII (1957), 223-35.

Sumner, Benedict H. "Ignatyev at Constantinople, 1864–1874," *Slavonic Review*, XI (1933), 341-53, 556-71.

———. *Russia and the Balkans, 1870–1880.* Oxford, 1937. Classic study.

———. "Russia and Pan-Slavism in the Eighteen-Seventies," *Transactions of the Royal Historical Society*, Fourth Series, XVIII (1935), 25-52.

Vrba, Rudolf. *Russland und der Panslavismus. Statistische und sozialpolitische Studien.* Prague, 1913, two vols.

7. INTERNATIONAL RELATIONS

Adamov, Evgenii A. *Diplomatiia Vatikana v nachalnuiu epokhu imperializma, 1887–1900.* Moscow, 1931.

Black, Cyril E. *The Establishment of Constitutional Government in Bulgaria.* Princeton, N. J., 1943.

Boudou, Adrien. *Le Saint-Siège et la Russie.* Paris, 1922–25, four vols.

Dansette, Adrian. *Le Boulangisme.* Paris, 1946.

Dorpalen, Andreas. "Tsar Alexander III and the Boulanger Crisis in France," *Journal of Modern History*, XXIII (1951), 122-36.

Erusalimsky, Arkadii S. *Vneshnaia politika i diplomatiia germanskago imperializma v kontse XIX veka.* Moscow, 1951, second edition. Excellent.

France. Ministère des Affaires Etrangères. *Documents diplomatiques français, 1871–1914.* Paris, 1929–51, thirty-two vols.

Khvostov, Vladimir M. "Problemy zakhvata Bosfora v 90-kh godakh XIX veka," *Istorik marksist*, XX (1930), 100-129.

Knaplund, Paul. *Gladstone's Foreign Policy.* New York, 1935.

Langer, William L. *The Diplomacy of Imperialism, 1890–1902.* New York, 1935, two vols.

———. *The Franco-Russian Alliance, 1890–1894.* Cambridge, Mass., 1929. These studies by Langer are of very high quality and great importance.

Mosse, Werner E. "Russia and the Levant, 1856–1862. Grand Duke Constantine Nikolaevich and the Russian Steam Navigation Company," *Journal of Modern History*, XXVI (1954), 39-48.

Novikova, Olga A. *Russia and England from 1876–1880.* London, 1880.

Pigarev, K. "F. I. Tiutchev i problemy vneshnei politiki tsarskoi Rossii," *Literaturnoe nasledstvo*, Number 19-21 (1935), 177-256.

"Proekt zakhvata Bosfora v 1896 g.," *Krasnyi arkhiv*, XLVII-XLVIII (1931), 50-70.

"Proekt zakhvata Bosfora v 1897 godu," *Krasnyi arkhiv*, I (1922), 152-62. Largely documents.

Schwertfeger, Bernhard H. (editor). *Zur europäischen Politik. Unveröffentlichte [Belgische] Dokumente.* Berlin, 1919, five vols.

Seton-Watson, Robert W. *Disraeli, Gladstone, and the Eastern Question.* London, 1935.

Skazkin, Sergei D. *Konets avstro-russko-germanskogo soiuza.* Moscow, 1928. First-rate study based on careful archival research.

Winter, Eduard. *Russland und die slawischen Völker in der Diplomatie des Vatikans, 1878–1903.* Berlin, 1950. Based largely on Vienna archives.

Yakobson, Sergius. "Russia and Africa," *Slavonic Review,* XVII (1937–38), 623-37; XIX (1939), 158-74. Fascinating and valuable.

Histories and Philosophy of History

Cohen, Morris R. *The Meaning of Human History.* La Salle, llinois, 1947.

Collingwood, R. G. *The Idea of History.* Oxford, 1946.

Kann, Robert. *The Multinational Empire.* New York, 1950, two vols.

Kliuchevsky, Vasilii O. *Kurs russkoi istorii.* Moscow, 1904–1910, four vols.

Mandelbaum, Maurice. "Can There Be a Philosophy of History?" *American Scholar,* IX (1939–40), 74-84.

May, Arthur. *The Hapsburg Monarchy, 1867–1914.* Cambridge, Mass., 1951.

Miliukov, Paul, Charles Seignebos, and Louis Eisenman. *Histoire de Russie.* Paris, 1932–33, three vols.

Shishkin, T. "Arkhiv istoricheskikh i prakticheskikh svedenii otnosiashchikhsia do Rossii," *Otechestvennyia zapiski,* CXXIV (1859), 47-64.

Sumner, Benedict H. *A Short History of Russia.* New York, 1943.

Weidlé, Wladimir. *Russia: Absent and Present.* New York, 1952.

Guides and Indexes

Adresnaia i spravochnaia kniga goroda Moskvy na 1894 god. Moscow, 1894.

Eck, Alexandre. "Introduction bibliographique à l'histoire du droit russe," *Archives d'histoire du droit oriental,* II (1938), 403-430.

Golitsyn, Nicholas N. (editor). *Bibliograficheskii slovar' russkikh pisatel'nits.* St. Petersburg, 1888–89.

Institut de France, Paris. Académie des sciences morales et politiques. *Table alphabétique et bibliographique des matières et des auteurs figurant dans les volumes 131 à 154 (1889–1900) du Compte rendu.* Paris, 1901.

Institut de France, Paris. Académie des sciences morales et politiques, "Séances et travaux," *Annales,* CXXXI (1889), 359-60; CIL (1898), 418, 703-705.

Moscow University. *Bibliograficheskii slovar' professorov i prepodavatelei Imperatorskago Moskovskago universiteta, 1755–1855.* Moscow, 1855, two vols.

Neustroev, Alexander N. *Istoricheskoe rozyskanie o russkikh povremennykh izdaniiakh i sbornikakh za 1703–1802.* St. Petersburg, 1874.

Nikitin, Sergei A. *Istochnikovedenie istorii SSSR; XIX v. (do nachala 90-kh godov).* Moscow, 1940.

Obshchestvo liubitelei rossiiskoi slovesnosti pri Moskovskom universitete. *Istoricheskaia zapiska i materialy za sto let.* Moscow, 1911.

———. *Slovar' chlenov.* Moscow, 1911.

Pogodin, Aleksandar. *Rusko-srpska bibliografija, 1800–1925. I.* Belgrade, 1932.

Povorinskii, Andrei F. (editor). *Sistematicheskii ukazatel' russkoi literatury po sudoustroistvu i sudoproizvodstvu grazhdanskomu i ugolovnomu.* St. Petersburg, 1896–1905, two vols.

Royal Society of London. *Catalogue of Scientific Papers, 1800–1900.* London, 1867–1925, nineteen vols.

Russia. Gosudarstvennyi sovet. *Opis' del arkhiva Gosudarstvennago soveta,* St. Petersburg, 1908–1913, twenty-one vols.

Russkii biograficheskii slovar'. St. Petersburg, 1896–1918, twenty-five vols.

Spravochnik k II i III izdaniiam sochinenii V. I. Lenina. Moscow, 1935.

Veniukov, M. I. "Russkie vo 'Frantsuzskom Institute' v 1892 g.," *Russkaia starina,* LXXIII (1892), 808.

Miscellaneous

Dillon, Emile J. *The Eclipse of Russia.* New York, 1918. *Daily Telegraph* correspondent.

Engels, Friedrich. *The Origin of the Family, Private Property, and the State.* Chicago, 1902.

Gsovski, Vladimir. *Soviet Civil Law.* Ann Arbor, Michigan, 1948–49, two vols.

Kalachov, Nicholas V. "O zhilishchakh dlia rabochikh," *Arkhiv istoricheskikh i prakticheskikh svedenii otnosiashchikhsia do Rossii,* I (1859), supplement, 90-91.

Le Play, F. *Oeuvres de F. Le Play. Principes de paix sociale. La Famille.* Paris, 1941.

Morgan, Lewis. *Systems of Consanguinity and Affinity in the Human Family.* Washington, 1868.

Von Laue, Theodore H. "Die Revolution von aussen als erste Phase der russischen Revolution von 1917," *Jahrbücher für Geschichte Osteuropas,* IV (1956) 138-58.

———. "Tsarist Labor Policy, 1895–1903," *Journal of Modern History,* XXXIV (1962), 135-45.

Yaney, George. "The Concept of the Stolypin Land Reform," *Slavic Review,* XXIII (1964), 275-93.

Zimmerman, Carle C. and Merle E. Frampton. *Family and Society. A Study of the Sociology of Reconstruction.* New York, 1935. Study of the Le Play method of social investigation.

Notes

The following abbreviations are used in the notes:

CPP —Constantine P. Pobedonostsev
KA —*Krasnyi arkhiv*
MDLL—Manuscript Division, Lenin Library
RA —*Russkii arkhiv*

I. *The Pobedonostsev Family*

1. Peter I. Bartenev (editor), "Iz dnevnika K. P. Pobedonostseva," *RA*, I (1907), 652; MDLL, CPP letter to Anna Tiutchev, September 19, 1867; December 18, 1868.

2. Moscow University, *Bibliograficheskii slovar' professorov i prepodavatelei Imperatorskago Moskovskago universiteta, 1755–1855* (Moscow, 1855), II, 228-29; Peter V. Pobedonostsev, "Iz dnevnika 1812 i 1813 godov," *RA*, XXXIII (1895), 213-18; Matvei K. Liubavskii, "Moskovskii universitet v 1812 godu," *Obshchestvo istorii i drevnostei rossiiskikh. Moscow. Chteniia*, Book IV, Part I (1912), 76-78, 88-90.

3. Peter V. Pobedonostsev, "K chitateliam," *Novosti russkoi literatury*, Number 12 (1805), 409; CPP (editor), "Pis'ma I. I. Lazhechnikova k S. P. i K. P. Pobedonostsevym," *Russkoe obozrenie*, XXXII (1895), 881-86; Nicholas P. Barsukov, *Zhizn' i trudy M. P. Pogodina* (St. Petersburg, 1888–1910), I, 46; II, 242, 288; III, 79, 354; XII, 199-200; Semen A. Vengerov, "Ivan Ivanovich Lazhechnikov. Kritiko-biograficheskii ocherk," in *Polnoe sobranie sochinenii I. I. Lazhechnikova* (St. Petersburg, 1899–1900), I, x, xxvii, cxiii, cxxxi; MDLL, Sergei P. Pobedonostsev letter to Michael P. Pogodin, November 15, 1841.

4. Obshchestvo liubitelei rossiiskoi slovesnosti pri Moskovskom universitete, *Istoricheskaia zapiska i materialy za sto let* (Moscow, 1911), 7-11, 16-22, 40, 43, 56, 76-80; Nil P. Koliupanov, *Biografiia Aleksandra Ivanovicha Kosheleva* (Moscow, 1889–92), I, Book I, 156-58; Book II, 334-72; Peter V. Pobedonostsev, "Liubov' k otechestvu," *Trudy Obshchestva liubitelei rossiiskoi slovesnosti pri Imperatorskom Moskovskom universitete*, XV (1819), 5-26; Peter V. Pobedonostsev, "Vospominaniia o Petre Alekseeviche Plavil'shchikove," *Trudy Obshchestva liubitelei rossiiskoi slovesnosti pri Imperatorskom Moskovskom universitete*, XI (1818), 87-135; Pobedonostsev, "Zaslugi Kheraskova v otechestvennoi sloves-

nosti," *Trudy Obshchestva liubitelei rossiiskoi slovesnosti pri Imperatorskom Moskovskom universitete*, I (1812), 111-47.

5. Peter V. Pobedonostsev (translator and editor), *Plody melankholii* (Moscow, 1796), two vols.; Peter V. Pobedonostsev (editor), *Ippokrena, ili utekhi liubosloviia* (Moscow, 1799–1801), eleven vols.; Peter V. Pobedonostsev (translator), *Novaia nauka naslazhdat'sia zhizn'iu* (Moscow, 1799); Peter V. Pobedonostsev (translator), *Istinnoe i lozhnoe schastie. Sochinenie slavnago Gellerta* (Moscow, 1799); Peter V. Pobedonostsev (editor), *Sokrovishche poleznykh uveselenii, ili lekarstvo vrachuiushchee liudei, predannykh pechali i skuke* (Moscow, 1800); Peter V. Pobedonostsev (translator), *Starinnyi drug, vozvrativshiisia iz puteshestviia i razskazyvaiushchii vse, chto videl, slyshal i chuvstvoval, s nemetskago* (Moscow, 1802), two vols.; Peter V. Pobedonostsev (editor), *Izbrannyia nravoutchitel'nyia povesti, udobnyia vlivat' v serdtse chuvstvo nravstvennoi krasoty. Perevod iz luchshikh inostrannykh pisatelei* (Moscow, 1815), four vols.; Peter V. Pobedonostsev (translator and editor), *Anekdoty i dostopamiatnye izrecheniia velikikh osob* (Moscow, 1816); Peter V. Pobedonostsev (editor), *Tsvetnik izbrannykh stikhotvorenii v pol'zu i udovol'stvie iunosheskago vozrasta* (Moscow, 1816), two vols.; Peter V. Pobedonostsev (editor), *Novosti russkoi literatury* (Moscow, 1802–1805), fourteen volumes; Peter V. Pobedonostsev (editor), *Minerva. Zhurnal rossiiskoi i inostrannoi slovesnosti* (Moscow, 1806–1807), five vols.; Peter V. Pobedonostsev (editor), *Novyi Panteon otechestvennoi i inostrannoi slovesnosti* (Moscow, 1819), four vols.; Peter V. Pobedonostsev (editor), *Drug iunosti* (Moscow, 1821), four vols.; Peter V. Pobedonostsev (editor), *Napravlenie uma i serdtsa k istine i dobrodeteli* (Moscow, 1830–31), three vols.; Koliupanov, *Biografiia Kosheleva*, I, 158.

6. Peter V. Pobedonostsev (editor), *Novosti russkoi literatury*, Number 12 (1805), 409-410; Alexander N. Neustroev, *Istoricheskoe rozyskanie o russkikh povremennykh izdaniiakh i sbornikakh za 1703–1802 gg.* (St. Petersburg, 1874), 850-55; Koliupanov, *Biografiia Kosheleva*, I, 73-79.

7. Peter V. Pobedonostsev, "Liubov' k otechestvu," 14-25; Peter V. Pobedonostsev, "Iz dnevnika 1812 i 1813 godov," 218; Koliupanov, *Biografiia Kosheleva*, I, 68-73.

8. Sergei P. Pobedonostsev, "Putevyia zapiski russkago po Evrope v 1847-m godu," *Otechestvennyia zapiski*, LXVII (1848), 12, 15, 20.

9. Peter V. Pobedonostsev, "Liubov' k otechestvu," 25; Peter V. Pobedonostsev, "Zaslugi Kheraskova," 112-14; Peter V. Pobedonostsev (editor), *Slovo o sushchestvennykh obiazannostiakh vitii i o sposobakh k priobreteniiu uspekhov v krasnorechii* (Moscow, 1831), 26; Peter V. Pobedonostsev (editor), *Novosti russkoi literatury*, Number 9 (1804), 212-14.

10. Peter V. Pobedonostsev, "Vospominaniia," 129-32; Peter V. Pobedonostsev, "Zaslugi Kheraskova," 111-14, 118, 140-46; Peter V. Pobedonostsev, *Slovo o sushchestvennykh obiazannostiakh vitii*, 7-9.

11. Constantine S. Aksakov, *Vospominanie studentstva, 1832–1835 godov* (St. Petersburg, 1911), 12; André Mazon, *Un Maître du roman russe. Ivan*

Gontcharov, 1812–1891 (Paris, 1914), 21-22; Alexander N. Pypin, *Belinskii, ego zhizn' i perepiska* (second edition, St. Petersburg, 1908), 53-56; Peter A. Zaionchkovskii and A. N. Sokolov (editors), *Moskovskii universitet v vospominaniiakh sovremennikov* (Moscow, 1956), 77, 103-104.

12. Anatole F. Koni, *Na zhiznennom puti* (Moscow-Riga, 1912–29), III, 170; Raoul Labry, *Alexandre Ivanovič Herzen, 1812–1870* (Paris, 1928), 94; Barsukov, *Pogodin*, I, 46.

13. "Iz razorenoi Moskvy. Pis'ma I. M. Snegireva k P. V. Pobedonostsevu," *RA*, I (1897), 111-12.

14. CPP, *Kurs grazhdanskago prava* (fourth edition, Moscow, 1896), I, 730-45; II, 445, 656; CPP (translator), Frederick Le Play, *Osnovnaia konstitutsiia chelovecheskago roda* (Moscow, 1897), preface, 1-6, 82-87; CPP (translator), Heinrich W. Thiersch, *Khristianskiia nachala semeinoi zhizni* (Moscow, 1861) and (second edition, Moscow, 1901); CPP, "Le Plè," *Russkoe obozrenie*, XXIII (1893), 5-30; CPP, "Semeinye uchastki," *Russkii vestnik*, CCIV (1889), 56-72; CPP, *Pis'ma Pobedonostseva k Aleksandru III* (Moscow, 1925–26), II, 147-48.

15. *Russkii biograficheskii slovar'* (St. Petersburg, 1896–1918), XIV, 141; Nicholas N. Golitsyn (editor), *Bibliograficheskii slovar' russkikh pisatel'nits* (St. Petersburg, 1888–89), 198-99; *Sbornik Imperatorskago russkago istoricheskago obshchestva*, LXII (1888), 162; Olga P. Pobedonostsev, "Ivan Ivanovich Lazhechnikov. Pis'mo ego k professoru P. V. Pobedonostsevu, 1823 g.," *Russkaia starina*, LXII (1891), 230-31; Maria P. Pobedonostsev (translator), "Sel'skii prikhod. Roman Rodol'fa Tepfera," *Moskvitianin* [supplement], Numbers 5-8, 10-15 (March–August, 1852), 1-437; Barsukov, *Pogodin*, XII, 199-200; MDLL, CPP letter to Anna Tiutchev, December 24, 1863; CPP letters to Catherine Tiutchev, June 15, September 10, 1878; October 17, November 24, 1881.

16. CPP, *Prazdniki Gospodni* (seventh edition, Moscow, 1905), 16-17, 48-51; MDLL, CPP letter to Anna Aksakov, September 19, 1867; Sergei P. Pobedonostsev letters to Michael Pogodin, November 15, 1841–March 8, 1849.

17. Obshchestvo liubitelei rossiiskoi slovesnosti pri Moskovskom universitete, *Slovar' chlenov* (Moscow, 1911), 223-24; Obshchestvo liubitelei rossiiskoi slovesnosti, *Istoricheskaia zapiska i materialy*, appendix, 59, 83; Barsukov, *Pogodin*, XII, 199-200; MDLL, CPP letter to Mrs. Elizabeth Alexandrovna Zhukovskii March 24, 1856. A letter to Catherine Tiutchev on June 15, 1878, refers to a brother in Riazan, but it has been impossible to identify him further.

18. CPP, "Odin iz psevdonimov v russkoi zhurnalistike," *Bibliograficheskie zapiski*, Number 8 (1892), 574; CPP, "Pis'ma Lazhechnikova k S. P. i K. P. Pobedonostsevym," 881-87; Paul N. Sakulin, *Iz istorii russkago idealizma: Kniaz' V. F. Odoevskii* (Moscow, 1913), II, 331.

19. Sergei P. Pobedonostsev, "Pozhar Moskvy," *Moskvitianin*, Part IV, Number 8 (1843), 13-21; Sergei P. Pobedonostsev, "Torzhestvo pereneseniia ikony Smolenskoi Bogoroditsy iz Semiezernoi Pustyni v Kazan'," *Moskvitianin*, Part IV, Number 9 (1842), 241-46; Sergei P. Pobedonostsev, "Ukazatel' goroda

Kazani," *Moskvitianin*, Part IV, Number 8 (1842), 383-95; Barsukov, *Pogodin*, VII, 258-60; VIII, 166; X, 364; *Russkii biograficheskii slovar'*, XIV, 143.

20. Alexander G. Dement'ev, *Ocherki po istorii russkoi zhurnalistiki, 1840– 1850 gg.* (Moscow, 1951), 61, 78-79, 82-85; Leningrad University, *Ocherki po istorii russkoi zhurnalistiki i kritiki* (Leningrad, 1950), I, 467-69, 472-74, 531-33; Peter V. Smirnovski, *Istoriia russkoi literatury deviatnadtsatago veka* (St. Petersburg, 1899–1904), II, 394-98; A. M. Brianskii, *"Repertuar i Panteon*, 1839–1856," *Russkii bibliofil*, Number 2 (1916), 55-58.

21. Sergei P. Pobedonostsev, "Starinnyia poveria polskiia i russkiia," *Moskvitianin*, Part I, Number 2 (1842), 49-59; Sergei P. Pobedonostsev, "Zapiski Paseka," *Moskvitianin*, Part I, Number 2 (1842), 618-27; Sergei P. Pobedonostsev (translator), "Kolishchizna i .stepi. Razskaz Eduarda Tarshy," *Moskvitianin*, Part II, Number 4 (1842), 357-94; Sergei P. Pobedonostsev, "Kazimir Vladislav Voinitskii," *Russkii vestnik*, Number 5 and 6 (1842), 112-36; Sergei P. Pobedonostsev, "Pol'skii teatr. Istoricheskii vzgliad na teatr v Pol'she so vremeni ego osnovaniia," *Repertuar russkago i Panteon inostrannykh teatrov*, IV (1843), 63-80; Sergei P. Pobedonostsev (translator), "Luchshe-by Ia byla sirotoi! Drama v trekh deistviiakh grafa Fridrikha Skarbeka," *Repertuar russkago i Panteon inostrannykh teatrov*, VII (1844), 4-42.

22. Sergei P. Pobedonostsev, "Nikolai Kopernik. Golos za pravdu," *Moskvitianin*, Number 9 (1843), 108-125; Alexander Herzen, *"Moskvitianin* o Kopernike," in Herzen, *Polnoe sobranie sochinenii i pisem* (Petrograd-Leningrad, 1919–25), III, 269-73; Herzen, *"Moskvitianin* o Kopernike," *Otechestvennyia zapiski*, XXXI (1843), 56-58; Barsukov, *Pogodin*, VII, 79-80.

23. Sergei P. Pobedonostsev, "Mam'zel Babett i eia al'bom," *Biblioteka dlia chteniia*, LIV, Part I (1842), 161-92; Sergei P. Pobedonostsev, "Milochka. Povest'," *Otechestvennyia zapiski*, XL (1845), 283-368; Sergei P. Pobedonostsev, "Niania," *Otechestvennyia zapiski*, XLIII (1845), 1-73; Sergei P. Pobedonostsev, "Pokhodnaia baryshnia. Povest'," *Otechestvennyia zapiski*, XLIX, Part I (1846), 1-78. *Milochka* was published in book form in 1867. These four novels, except for *Niania*, and two other novels by Sergei were published in one volume in 1856 in St. Petersburg.

24. Sergei P. Pobedonostsev (translator), "Parizhskie teatralnye nravy. Mat' aktrisy," *Repertuar russkago i Panteon inostrannykh teatrov*, XVI, Part II (1842), 9-21; Sergei P. Pobedonostsev (translator), "Zakulisnye nravy. Opernaia krysa. Stat'ia Teofilia Got'e," *Repertuar russkago i Panteon inostrannykh teatrov*, I, Part III (1843), 176-88; Sergei P. Pobedonostsev, "Putevyia zapiski russkago," 1-56.

25. MDLL, CPP letter to Catherine Tiutchev, March 6, 1880.

26. Benedict H. Sumner, *Peter the Great and the Emergence of Russia* (New York, 1951), 41.

II. *The Young Scholar*

1. Peter V. Pobedonostsev (editor), *Slovo o sushchestvennykh obiazannostiakh*

vitii i o sposobakh k priobretenii uspekhov v krasnorechii (Moscow, 1831), 27-31.

2. Peter V. Pobedonostsev, "Liubov' k otechestvu," *Trudy Obshchestva liubitelei rossiiskoi slovesnosti pri Imperatorskom Moskovskom universitete,* XV (1819), 5-18; Peter V. Pobedonostsev, *Slovo o sushchestvennykh obiazannostiakh vitii,* 27-33; CPP (editor), "Pis'ma I. I. Lazhechnikova k S. P. i K. P. Pobedonostsevym," *Russkoe obozrenie,* XXXII (1895), 881-86; Alexander N. Pypin, *Belinskii, ego zhizn' i perepiska* (second edition, St. Petersburg, 1908), 137-38; Claude G. Bowers, *Beveridge and the Progressive Era* (Cambridge, Mass., 1932), 147-48; Hermann Dalton, *Lebenserinnerungen* (Berlin, 1906–1908), III, 98-99; Louise Creighton, *Life and Letters of Mandell Creighton* (London, 1904), II, 150-55; Evgenii M. Feoktistov, *Vospominaniia. Za kulisami politiki i literatury, 1848– 1896* (Leningrad, 1929), 129-221; S. Mel'gunov (editor), "K. P. Pobedonostsev v dni pervoi revoliutsii. Neizdannyia pis'ma k S. D. Voitu," *Na chuzhoi storone,* VIII (1924), 178; Alexander A. Polovtsev, "Dnevnik," *KA,* III (1923), 94.

3. CPP, *Dlia nemnogikh. Otryvki iz shkol'nago dnevnika, 1842–1845 g.* (St. Petersburg, 1885), supplement, 1-5; Peter I. Bartenev (editor), "Iz dnevnika K. P. Pobedonostseva," *RA,* I (1907), 636-52; *Obshchii obzor deiatel'nosti Ministerstva iustitsii i pravitel'stvuiushchago Senata za tsarstvovanie Imperatora Aleksandra III* (St. Petersburg, 1901), 143; *Istoriia pravitel'stvuiushchago Senata za dvesti let, 1711–1911* (St. Petersburg, 1911), III, 40.

4. CPP, *Pis'ma Pobedonostseva k Aleksandru III* (Moscow, 1925–26), I, 339; CPP, *Dlia nemnogikh, passim;* Baron Alexander E. Nolde, "Obzor nauchnoi iuridicheskoi deiatel'nosti K. P. Pobedonostseva," *Zhurnal Ministerstva narodnago prosveshcheniia,* VIII (1907), 95-97; MDLL, CPP letters to Catherine Tiutchev, December 30, 1871; December 18, 1875.

5. Samuel Kucherov, *Courts, Lawyers and Trials Under the Last Three Tsars* (New York, 1953), 44; Sergei A. Nikitin, *Istochnikovedenie istorii SSSR XIX v. (do nachala 90-kh godov)* (Moscow, 1940), II, 7-8; *Istoriia pravitel'stvuiushchago Senata,* III, 308; V, 69-70.

6. CPP, "Vospominaniia o V. P. Zubkove," *RA,* I (1904), 301-303; Nolde, "Obzor," 84-86; *Sudebnaia gazeta,* June 9, 1896, 10; S. L. Evenchik, "Reaktsionnaia deiatel'nost' Pobedonostseva v 80-kh gg. XIX-go veka," Moscow University Thesis for Candidate Degree in History, 1939, 49-50; MDLL, CPP letters to Mrs. Elizabeth Alexandrovna Zhukovskii, March and April, 1856.

7. CPP, "Vospominaniia o Zubkove," 301-304; Senator Iakov G. Esipovich, "Zapiski senatora Esipovicha," *Russkaia starina,* CXXXIX (1909), 36-37.

8. CPP, *K. P. Pobedonostsev i ego korrespondenty. Pis'ma i zapiski. Novum Regnum* (Moscow, 1923), 823; "Pis'ma K. P. Pobedonostseva k E. M. Feoktistovu," *Literaturnoe nasledstvo,* Number 22-24 (1935), 542; MDLL, CPP letter to Catherine Tiutchev, November 30, 1868.

9. CPP, *Pis'ma k Aleksandru III,* I, 292; CPP, "Vospominaniia o Zubkove," 302-303; Boris N. Chicherin, *Vospominaniia* (Moscow, 1929–34), IV, 102-103; Nolde, "Obzor," 102; MDLL, CPP letters to Anna Tiutchev, December 24,

1862; February 12, February 16, 1864; CPP letter to Catherine Tiutchev, July 8, 1876.

10. CPP (translator), "Starye listia," *Russkaia beseda*, II, Part I (1859), 7-8; CPP (translator), Heinrich W. Thiersch, *Khristianskiia nachala semeinoi zhizni* (Moscow, 1861); CPP, "Novyia puteshestvyia po vostoku," *Russkii vestnik*, XLIII (1863), 489-548; CPP, "Zametka o Beniovskom iz angliiskoi knigi ob ostrove Madagaskare," *RA*, III (1865), 859-62; CPP, "Materialy dlia istorii Akademii nauk," *Letopis' russkoi literatury i drevnostei*, V, Part III (1863), 3-36; CPP, "Knizhnyia zagranichnyia vesti o Rossii," *RA*, IV (1866), 260-62; CPP and Ivan K. Babst, *Pis'ma o puteshestvii gosudaria naslednika tsesarevicha po Rossii ot Peterburga do Kryma* (Moscow, 1864).

11. CPP, "Zametki dlia istorii krepostnago prava v Rossii," *Russkii vestnik*, XV (1858), 209-248, 459-98; XVI (1858), 537-82; CPP, "Utverzhdenie krepostnago prava v Rossii v XVIII stoletii," *Russkii vestnik*, XXXV (1861), 223-53; CPP, "Graf V. N. Panin," *Golosa iz Rossii*, VII (1859), 1-142; M. Klevenskii, "Gertsen-izdatel' i ego sotrudniki," *Literaturnoe nasledstvo*, Numbers 41-42 (1941), 605.

12. CPP, "O reformakh v grazhdanskom sudoproizvodstve," *Russkii vestnik*, XXI (1859), 541-80; XXII (1859), 5-34, 153-90; CPP, "Anekdoty iz XVIII stoletiia. 1. Moskovskaia volokita. 2. Ochistitel'naia pytka," *Arkhiv istoricheskikh i prakticheskikh svedenii otnosiashchikhsia do Rossii*, IV, Book IV (1859), supplement, 1-22; CPP, "Anekdoty iz XVIII stoletiia. Ubiistvo Zhukovikh," *Russkii vestnik*, XXX (1860), 462-501; CPP, "Prichiny nepravosudiia i provolochki v prisutstvennikh mestakh," *Zhurnal Ministerstva iustitsii*, XXVII (1866), 33-44.

13. Boris B. Glinskii, "Konstantin Petrovich Pobedonostsev. Materialy dlia biografii," *Istoricheskii vestnik*, CVIII (1907), 255-57; Boris V. Nikol'skii, "Literaturnaia deiatel'nost' K. P. Pobedonostseva," *Istoricheskii vestnik*, LXV (1896), 724-25; Nolde, "Obzor," 95-98, 106-114; Gabriel F. Shershenevich, *Uchebnik russkago grazhdanskago prava* (sixth edition, St. Petersburg, 1907), 18. Several editions of each volume of the "Course on Civil Law" were published. The final complete edition appeared in 1896, on the fiftieth anniversary of Pobedonostsev's entry into government service. The principal articles in the field of Russian civil law which Pobedonostsev published in the decade after 1858 include: "Opyt iuridicheskago kommentariia na nekotoryia stat'i zakonov o zaveshchaniiakh," *Arkhiv istoricheskikh i prakticheskikh svedenii otnosiashchikhsia do Rossii*, II, Book II (1859), 52-71; "Nekotorye voprosy, voznikaiushchie po dukhovnym zaveshchaniiam," *Arkhiv istoricheskikh i prakticheskikh svedenii otnosiashchikhsia do Rossii*, I, Book I (1859), supplement, 1-27; II, Book II (1859), supplement, 1-22; "Priobretenie sobstvennosti i pozemel'nyia knigi," *Russkii vestnik*, XXVIII (1860), 5-39, 193-230; "Veshchnyi kredit i zakladnoe pravo," *Russkii vestnik*, XXXIII (1861), 409-451; "Imenie rodovoe i blagopriobretennoe," *Zhurnal Ministerstva iustitsii*, VIII, Part II (1861), 3-75; "Odnodvorcheskiia zemli i nachalo spetsialnago mezhevaniia v Rossii," *Zhurnal Minis-*

terstva iustitsii, XV, Part II (1863), 85-104; "Iuridicheskiia zametki i voprosy po nasledstvennomu i zaveshchatel'nomu pravam," *Zhurnal Ministerstva iustitsii,* XXII, Part II (1864), 169-210; XXVII, Part II (1866), 25-44.

14. CPP, *Pis'ma k Aleksandru III,* II, 330; CPP, "Pamiati Fedora Mikhailovicha Dmitrieva," *RA,* I (1894), 634-37; Anatole F. Koni, *Na zhiznennom puti* (Moscow-Riga, 1912–29), III, 173-94; Fedor I. Buslaev, *Moi vospominaniia* (Moscow, 1897), 330; Nolde, "Obzor," 84-88; Chicherin, *Vospominaniia,* III, foreword; IV, 102-103; MDLL, CPP letters to Boris N. Chicherin, September 18, October 10, 1864.

15. CPP, *Pis'ma k Aleksandru III,* II, 330; CPP and Babst, *Pis'ma, passim;* Alexei P. Bogoliubov, *Vospominaniia o pochivshem Imperatore Aleksandre III* (St. Petersburg, 1895), 5-12; A. Voronov, "Vospominaniia byvshago studenta Kharkovskago universiteta 60-kh godov," *Russkaia starina,* CLIV (1913), 590–91; Nicholas P. Barsukov, *Zhizn' i trudy M. P. Pogodina* (St. Petersburg, 1888–1910), XXI, 69; XXII, 1-3; "Iz biografii tsesarevicha Nikolaia Aleksandrovicha. Dva pis'ma B. N. Chicherina k K. P. Pobedonostsevu," *Russkaia starina,* II (1910), 311-12; Russia. Ministerstvo iustitsii, *Sudebnye ustavy 20 noiabria 1864 g. za piat'desiat let* (Petrograd, 1914), I, 73; I. V. Preobrazhenskii, *Konstantin Petrovich Pobedonostsev, ego lichnost' i deiatel'nosti* (St. Petersburg, 1912), 20-21; Nolde, "Obzor," 86.

16. CPP, *Vechnaia pamiat'. Vospominaniia o pochivshikh* (Moscow, 1896), 3-6; Anatole F. Koni, "Velikaia kniaginia Elena Pavlovna," in *Velikaia reforma,* V (1911), 14-33; Prince Vladimir P. Meshcherskii, *Moi vospominaniia* (St. Petersburg, 1897–1912), I, 149-50, 207-209, 266-67; II, 14; III, 55-56, 333-34; Count Sergei IU. Witte, *Vospominaniia* (Moscow, 1923), II, 468-70; MDLL, CPP letter to Anna Tiutchev, August 19, 1864.

17. MDLL, CPP letters to Anna Tiutchev, September 26, 1864; February 2, 1865; CPP letters to Catherine Tiutchev, April 24, May 1, August 21, 1865; CPP letter to Alexei D. Zheltukhin, June 5, 1862; Anna Tiutchev letter to CPP, February 26, 1865.

18. CPP, *Kurs grazhdanskago prava* (second edition, Moscow, 1873), I, 280; (third edition, Moscow, 1883), I, 301; (fourth edition, Moscow, 1896), I, 311-14, 730-35; (second edition, Moscow, 1875), II, 120-215; (fourth edition, Moscow, 1896), II, 140-42, 248-52.

19. CPP, *Grazhdanskoe sudoproizvodstvo. Lektsii* (Moscow, 1863); CPP, *Kurs grazhdanskago prava* (third edition, Moscow, 1883), I, 720; Matvei K. Liubavskii, "Vasilii Osipovich Kliuchevskii," in *V. O. Kliuchevskii. Kharakteristiki i vospominaniia* (Moscow, 1912), 7; Nolde, "Obzor," 84-88, 91-92, 104-105; Andrei F. Povorinskii (editor), *Sistematicheskii ukazatel' russkoi literatury po sudoustroistvu i sudoproizvodstvu grazhdanskomu i ugolovnomu* (St. Petersburg, 1896–1905), I, 80-81; Koni, *Na zhiznennom puti,* III, 191-92.

20. CPP, *Sudebnoe rukovodstvo. Sbornik pravil, polozhenii i primerov* (St. Petersburg, 1872); CPP, *Istoriko-iuridicheskie akty perekhodnoi epokhi XVII-XVIII vekov* (Moscow, 1887), introduction, i-vi; CPP (editor), *Materialy dlia*

istorii prikaznago sudoproizvodstva v Rossii (Moscow, 1890), introduction; CPP, *Vypiski iz Polnago Sobraniia Zakonov* (St. Petersburg, 1895); Nolde, "Obzor," 94-95, 102-103.

21. CPP, "Anekdot o Didro," *RA*, III (1893), 128; CPP, "K istorii snoshenii s inovertsami," *RA*, II (1894), 5-27; CPP, "O vnutrennem sostoianii Rossii pri votsarenii Imperatora Nikolaia Pavlovicha," *RA*, I (1895), 161-76; CPP (editor), "Iz pisem Ego Imperatorskago Vysochestva Velikago Kniaz'ia Konstantina Niko-laevicha k Stats-sekretariu A. V. Golovninu," *RA*, I (1895), 439-45; CPP, "Odin iz psevdonimov v russkoi zhurnalistike," *Bibliograficheskie zapiski*, Number 8 (1892), 574; William J. Birkbeck, *Russia and the English Church in the Last Fifty Years* (London, 1895), 182.

22. CPP, *Moskovskii sbornik* (third edition, Moscow, 1896), 111, 125, 188-89, 207-208; CPP, *Pis'ma k Aleksandru III*, II, 64-65; "Pis'ma K. P. Pobedonostseva k S. D. Voitu," *RA*, I (1917), 77; "Pis'ma K. P. Pobedonostseva k E. M. Feoktis-tovu," 530-31; Vasilii O. Kliuchevsky, *Kurs russkoi istorii* (first edition, Moscow, 1904–1910); Mel'gunov, "Pobedonostsev v dni pervoi revoliutsii," 183-84, 196; Moscow. Sinodal'naya tipografiya, *Katalog knig, prodaiushchikhsia v sinodal'-nykh knizhnykh lavkakh v S. Peterburge i Moskve* (Moscow, 1896).

23. CPP, *Pis'ma k Aleksandru III*, II, 29; CPP, *Novum Regnum*, 979; "Pis'ma K. P. Pobedonostseva k E. M. Feoktistovu," 557; CPP (editor), *Perepiska Iu. F. Samarina s baronessoiu E. F. Raden, 1861–1876 g.* (Moscow, 1893).

24. Ivan I. Ianzhul, "Vospominaniia," *Russkaia starina*, CXLIV (1910), 10-11; Nicholas I. Ilminskii, *Pis'ma Nikolaia Ivanovicha Ilminskago k ober-prokuroru Sviateishchago sinoda Konstantinu Petrovichu Pobedonostsevu* (Kazan, 1895), iii-iv; Sergei A. Petrovskii (editor), "Perepiska K. P. Pobedonostseva s preo-sviashchennym Nikanorom episkopom Ufimskim," *RA*, I (1915), 458; Petrovskii (editor), "Pis'ma K. P. Pobedonostseva preosviashchennomu Illarionu, arkhie-piskopu Poltavskomu," *RA*, LIV (1916), 129-71, 360-80; Vladimir S. Markov, *K istorii raskola-staroobriadchestva vtoroi poloviny XIX stoletiia. Perepiska prof. N. I. Subbotina* (Moscow, 1915), CPP, *Vechnaia pamiat'*, 74-94.

25. Bartenev, "Iz dnevnika," 635.

26. CPP, *Prazdniki Gospodni* (St. Petersburg, 1894); CPP (translator), Thiersch, *Khristianskiia nachala semeinoi zhizni* (second edition, Moscow, 1901); CPP (translator), *Fomy Kempiiskago o podrazhanii Khristu* (sixth edi-tion, St. Petersburg, 1896).

27. CPP, *Pis'ma k Aleksandru III*, II, 275-77; Alexander A. Kizevetter, "Pobe-donostsev," *Na chuzhoi storone*, IV (1924), 257-58; Iurii V. Gotie, "K. P. Pobe-donostsev i naslednik Aleksandr Aleksandrovich, 1865–81," *Publichnaia biblio-teka SSSR imeni V. I. Lenina. Sbornik*, II (1929), 108-109.

28. Chicherin, *Vospominaniia*, IV, 102-103; MDLL, CPP letters to Boris N. Chicherin, September 18, October 10, 1864; February 8, February 24, March 16, 1873; December 20, 1877; November 3, 1879.

29. CPP, *Vechnaia pamiat'*, 57-58; CPP, *Kurs grazhdanskago prava* (third edi-tion, St. Petersburg, 1883), I, 713-17; (second edition, St. Petersburg, 1875), II,

441; CPP, "Russkoe grazhdanskoe sudoproizvodstvo v istoricheskom ego razvitii ot Ulozheniia 1649 goda do izdaniia Svoda Zakonov," *Arkhiv istoricheskikh i prakticheskikh svedenii otnosiashchikhsia do Rossii*, I, Part I (1859), 5-8.

30. Il'ia G. Orshanskii, "Kurs grazhdanskago prava," *Zhurnal grazhdanskago i ugolovnago prava*, Book II (1876), 260-62, 271-82; Wlodzimierz D. Spasovich, "Kurs grazhdanskago prava K. Pobedonostseva. Chast' vtoraia," *Zhurnal grazhdanskago i torgovago prava*, Book I (1871), 134-57; A. Borzenko, "Pacta sunt servanda," *Russkoe obozrenie*, VI (1890), 455-64; *Iuridicheskii vestnik*, XXXIX (1890), 701-703.

31. CPP, *Istoricheskiia izsledovaniia i stat'i* (St. Petersburg, 1876), 1-2; CPP, "Russkoe grazhdanskoe sudoproizvodstvo," 1-4; CPP, *Kurs grazhdanskago prava* (second edition, St. Petersburg, 1873), I, preface, 717-19; (second edition, St. Petersburg, 1875), II, 441.

32. Nikol'skii, "Literaturnaia deiatel'nost' Pobedonostseva," 724-25; Wlodzimierz D. Spasovich, *Za mnogo let, 1859–1871* (St. Petersburg, 1872), 161; Alexander S. Lappo-Danilevsky, "The Development of Science and Learning in Russia," in James D. Duff (editor), *Russian Realities and Problems* (Cambridge, England, 1917), 198-99; Nolde, "Obzor," 109-111.

33. CPP, "Russkoe grazhdanskoe sudoproizvodstvo," 1-62. See also, CPP, "Obozrenie chastnikh trudov po sobraniiu zakonov i po sostavleniiu ukaznikh slovarei do izdaniia Polnago Sobraniia Zakonov Rossiiskoi Imperii," *Arkhiv istoricheskikh i prakticheskikh svedenii otnosiashchikhsia do Rossii*, V (1863), 51-84, especially 68-73; CPP, "Akty, otnosiashchikhsia do iuridicheskago byta drevnei Rossii," *Arkhiv istoricheskikh i prakticheskikh svedenii otnosiashchikhsia do Rossii*, IV (1859), Book IV, 25-60; CPP, "Mestnoe naselenie Rossii," *Russkii vestnik*, XL (1862), 5-34.

34. CPP, *Istoricheskiia izsledovaniia*, 124-25, 175-80.

III. *The Liberal Reformer*

1. CPP, *Pis'ma Pobedonostseva k Aleksandru III* (Moscow, 1925–26), II, 330-31; CPP, *Pobedonostsev i ego korrespondenty. Pis'ma i zapisky. Novum Regnum* (Moscow, 1923), I, 68-69, 455-86; MDLL, CPP letter to French Academy of Sciences, 1892.

2. CPP, *Dlia nemnogikh. Otryvki iz shkol'nago dnevnika, 1842–1845* (St. Petersburg, 1885), 10, 12, 17, 23, 32, 68-76, 105-119; Peter I. Bartenev (editor), "Iz dnevnika K. P. Pobedonostseva," *RA*, I (1907), 636-52.

3. CPP, "Vospominaniia o V. P. Zubkove," *RA*, I (1904), 301-305; MDLL, CPP letter to Catherine Tiutchev, November 30, 1868.

4. CPP, "Zametki dlia istorii krepostnago prava v Rossii," *Russkii vestnik*, XV (1858), 209-248, 459-98; XVI (1858), 537-82; CPP, "O reformakh v grazhdanskom sudoproizvodstve," *Russkii vestnik*, XXI (1859), 541-80; XXII (1859), 5-34, 153-90; CPP, "Anekdoty iz XVIII stoletiia. Ubiistvo Zhukovikh," *Russkii*

vestnik, XXX (1860), 462-501; CPP, "Utverzhdenie krepostnago prava v Rossii v XVIII stoletii," *Russkii vestnik,* XXXV (1861), 223-53; Nicholas A. Liubimov, *Mikhail Nikiforovich Katkov i ego istoricheskaia zasluga* (St. Petersburg, 1889), 67-68; MDLL, CPP letter to Michael N. Katkov, March 31, 1862. The four articles noted here were all reprinted by Pobedonostsev in 1876 and constituted the bulk of a volume, *Istoricheskiia izsledovaniia i stat'i,* which he published in honor of his being made a member of the Moscow Society of Russian History and Antiquities. This would indicate that Pobedonostsev considered them among the most important articles he had written at that time.

5. Sergei S. Tatishchev (S. Nevedenskii, *pseud.*), *Katkov i ego vremia* (St. Petersburg, 1888), 1-97; Grégoire Livov, *Michel Katkoff et son époque (Paris,* 1897), 11-24; Liubimov, *Katkov,* 128.

6. Grigorii A. Dzhanshiev, *Epokha velikikh reform* (eighth edition, Moscow, 1900), 118; Tatishchev, *Katkov,* 159, 412-23, 464-68; Livov, *Katkoff,* 61-68, 190-95.

7. Viscount Eugène de Vogüé, *Les Routes* (Paris, 1910), 136; Louise Creighton, *Life and Letters of Mandell Creighton* (London, 1904), II, 153; Marc Raeff, "A Reactionary Liberal: M. N. Katkov," *Russian Review,* XI (1952), 160-67; Liubimov, *Katkov,* 24, 31-41, 70-71; MDLL, CPP letters to Catherine Tiutchev, October 18, 1868; June 25, 1869; August 14, 1873.

8. CPP, *Vechnaia pamiat'. Vospominaniia o pochivshikh* (Moscow, 1896), 56-60; *Russkii biograficheskii slovar'* (St. Petersburg, 1896–1918), VIII, Part 2, 394-99.

9. CPP, *Vechnaia pamiat',* 59-60; Alexandre Eck, "Introduction bibliographique à l'histoire du droit russe," *Archives d'histoire du droit oriental,* II (1938), 406-412; T. Shishkin, "Arkhiv istoricheskikh i prakticheskikh svedenii otnosiashchikhsia do Rossii," *Otechestvennyia zapiski,* CXXIV (1859), 47-64; I. E. Andreevskii, "O Kalachove, kak iurist, arkheolog i uchreditel' arkheologicheskago instituta," *Vestnik arkheologii i istorii,* V (1886), 3-10; *Arkhiv istoricheskikh i prakticheskikh svedenii otnosiashchikhsia do Rossii,* I (1858), iii-viii.

10. *Arkhiv istoricheskikh i prakticheskikh svedenii otnosiashchikhsia do Rossii,* I (1858), iii-iv; I. G. Danilov, "O trudakh Kalachova po krestianskomu delu," *Vestnik arkheologii i istorii,* V (1886), 15-24; I. L. Maiakovskii, "N. V. Kalachov," *Moskovskii istoriko-arkhivnyi institut. Trudy,* IV (1948), 163-64; Nicholas V. Kalachov, "O zhilishchakh dlia rabochikh," *Arkhiv istoricheskikh i prakticheskikh svedenii otnosiashchikhsia do Rossii,* I (1859), supplement, 90-91; "Opisanie doma dlia rabochikh liudei v S. Skopine," *Arkhiv istoricheskikh i prakticheskikh svedenii otnosiashchikhsia do Rossii,* IV (1859), 59-60.

11. CPP (translator), Heinrich W. Thiersch, *Khristianskiia nachala semeinoi zhizni* (Moscow, 1861), preface, 3-6; Heinrich W. Thiersch, *On the Christian Commonwealth* (Edinburgh, 1877), 15-43, 149-86.

12. CPP, "Russkoe grazhdanskoe sudoproizvodstvo v istoricheskom ego razvitii ot Ulozheniia 1649 goda do izdaniia Svoda Zakonov," *Arkhiv istori-*

cheskikh i prakticheskikh svedenii otnosiashchikhsia do Rossii, I, Part I (1859), 1-3; CPP, *Istoricheskiia izsledovaniia i stat'i* (St. Petersburg, 1876), 1-2, 14-17, 118-19; CPP, "Utverzhdenie krepostnago prava," 223-53.

13. Z. P. Bazileva, *"Kolokol" Gertsena, 1857–1867 gg.* (Moscow, 1949), 71, 86, 122-26, 134-49; M. Klevenskii, "Gertsen-izdatel' i ego sotrudniki," *Literaturnoe nasledstvo*, Numbers 41-42 (1941), 581-82, 605-608, 614-15; Alexander A. Polovtsev, "Dnevnik," *KA*, III (1923), 79; Baron Alexander E. Nolde, *K. P. Pobedonostsev i sudebnaia reforma* (Petrograd, 1915), 11-12; Paul N. Miliukov, Charles Seignebos, and Louis Eisenman, *Histoire de Russie* (Paris, 1932-33), III, 842; Alexander G. Dement'ev, *Ocherki po istorii russkoi zhurnalistiki, 1840– 1850 gg.* (Moscow, 1951), 423, 432, 489.

14. CPP, "Graf V. N. Panin," *Golosa iz Rossii*, VII (1859), 1-142, especially 3-12, 15-25, 34-36, 45-53, 62-63, 76-82, 96-124. Dzhanshiev, in *Epokha velikikh reform* (eighth edition, 372), described Panin in this way: "A slave at heart, he was at the same time a despot who put the fancies of his extravagant arbitrariness and dream phantasy higher than law and justice. He was a vehement defender of serfdom, the whip, the branding iron, censorship—in one word, an inveterate conservative, a typical representative of the stupid stagnation which lasted thirty years. . . ." Panin was replaced by Dmitrii N. Zamiatin on October 21, 1862.

15. Count Ivan S. Kapnist, *Code d'organisation judiciare de l'Empire de Russie de 1864* (Paris, 1893), xv, lxxix-lxxxiv; Samuel Kucherov, *Courts, Lawyers and Trials under the Last Three Tsars* (New York, 1953), 3-9, 14; Miliukov, Seignebos, and Eisenman, *Histoire*, III, 870-72; Darrell P. Hammer, "Russia and the Roman Law," *American Slavic and East European Review*, XVI (1957), 7-10.

16. CPP, "O reformakh," 541-52, 560-78.

17. Ibid., 162-63; Manuscript Division, Saltykov-Shchedrin Library, CPP memorandum, "Zapiska o grazhdanskom sudoproizvodstve," December, 1861, *passim*.

18. CPP, "O reformakh," 9-20, 153-90, 541-60; CPP, *Istoricheskiia izsledovaniia*, 233-325.

19. Nolde, *Pobedonostsev i sudebnaia reforma*, 13.

20. CPP, *Grazhdanskoe sudoproizvodstvo. Lektsii* (Moscow, 1863), *passim*, especially 1-15, 117-34; Baron Alexander E. Nolde, "Obzor nauchnoi iuridicheskoi deiatel'nosti K. P. Pobedonostseva," *Zhurnal Ministerstva narodnago prosveshcheniia*, VIII (1907), 91-93; Nolde, *Pobedonostsev i sudebnaia reforma*, 10-11; Anatole F. Koni, *Na zhiznennom puti* (Moscow-Riga, 1912–29), III, 191-92.

21. CPP and Ivan K. Babst, *Pis'ma o puteshestvii gosudaria naslednika tsesarevicha po Rossii ot Peterburga do Kryma* (Moscow, 1864), 12-20; Nicholas V. Shel'gunov, *Vospominaniia* (Moscow, 1923), 225; Longin F. Panteleev, *Vospominaniia* (Moscow, 1958), 260-61; "Tolstoi v 1880-e gody. Zapiski I. M. Ivakina," *Literaturnoe nasledstvo*, Number 69, Part 2 (1961), 59, 110; *Moskov-*

skiia Vedomosti, April 19, 1861; MDLL, CPP letter to Prince Vladimir F. Odoevskii, January 12, 1865.

22. Miliukov, Seignebos, and Eisenman, *Histoire*, III, 871-72; Kucherov, *Courts, Lawyers and Trials*, 16; Dzhanshiev, *Epokha velikikh reform*, eighth edition, 365-72.

23. *Sudebnoe preobrazovanie v 1863 i 1864 g.* (St. Petersburg, 1867?), Part III, Section 1, 1-3; Russia. Ministerstvo iustitsii, *Sudebnye ustavy 20 noiabria 1864 g. za piat'desiat let* (Petrograd, 1914), I, i-ii, 123-26, 179-80; Iosif V. Gessen, *Sudebnaia reforma* (St. Petersburg, 1903), 77-78; Grigorii A. Dzhanshiev, *Osnovy sudebnoi reformy k 25-ti letiiu novago suda* (Moscow, 1891), introduction, xii-xiii; supplement, 8-10; Dzhanshiev, *Epokha velikikh reform*, eighth edition, 380-88; Nolde, *Pobedonostsev i sudebnaia reforma*, 16-17; Kucherov, *Courts, Lawyers and Trials*, 16, 23-25; Kapnist, *Code d' organisation judiciare*, lxxxiv-c.

24. CPP, "Statistiki angliiskikh grazhdanskikh sudov za 1858 god," *Iuridicheskii vestnik*, V (1860–61), 51-53; CPP, "Mestnoe naselenie Rossii," *Russkii vestnik*, XL (1862), 18-19; CPP, *Pis'ma k Aleksandru III*, II, 330-31; Nolde, *Pobedonostsev i sudebnaia reforma*, 6-14; Dzhanshiev, *Epokha velikikh reform*, eighth edition, 365-68; Dzhanshiev, *Osnovy sudebnoi reformy*, 27-29; Vasilii I. Iakovlev, *Khronologicheskiia dannyia k istoriiu sostavleniia sudebnykh ustavov 20 noiabria 1864* (Petrograd, 1914), 27-28, 33.

25. Nolde, *Pobedonostsev i sudebnaia reforma*, 15, 35, 41-42; Nolde, "Obzor," 94; Russia. Ministerstvo iustitsii, *Sudebnye ustavy 20 noiabria 1864*, I, 213.

26. Nolde, *Pobedonostsev i sudebnaia reforma*, 39-42; Nolde, "Obzor," 91-94; *Istoriia pravitel'stvuiushchago Senata za dvesti let, 1711–1911 g.* (St. Petersburg, 1911), IV, 467-68; *Sudebnoe preobrazovanie v 1863 i 1864*, Part III, Section I, 5-183, 265-78.

27. CPP, "O reformakh," 184-89; *Istoriia pravitel'stvuiushchago Senata*, IV, 468-70.

28. Russia. Ministerstvo iustitsii, *Sudebnye ustavy 20 noiabria 1864*, I, 118-119.

29. *Istoriia pravitel'stvuiushchago Senata*, IV, 471-72; Russia. Ministerstvo iustitsii, *Sudebnye ustavy 20 noiabria 1864*, I, 154, 294; Miliukov, Seignebos, and Eisenman, *Histoire*, III, 875-76; Kucherov, *Courts, Lawyers and Trials*, 32; Dzhanshiev, *Epokka velikikh reform*, eighth edition, 477.

30. CPP, *Grazhdanskoe sudoproizvodstvo. Lektsii*, 15-18, 57-64; Nolde, *Pobedonostsev i sudebnaia reforma*, 10-11, 25-35; *Sudebnoe preobrazovanie v 1863 i 1864*, Part III, Section I, 151-66; Manuscript Division, Saltykov-Shchedrin Library, CPP memorandum, "O zhalobakh na deistviia dolzhnostnykh lits administrativnago vedomstva," 1864, 1-15.

31. Russia. Ministerstvo iustitsii, *Sudebnye ustavy 20 noiabria 1864*, I, 294; Kapnist, *Code d' organisation judiciare*, lxxxvi-lxxxvii; Dzhanshiev, *Epokha velikikh reform*, eighth edition, 454-57, 477; Miliukov, Seignebos, and Eisenman, *Histoire*, III, 874.

32. Nolde, *Pobedonostsev i sudebnaia reforma*, 17-23, 35-38; Nolde, "Obzor,"

88-90; *Sudebnoe preobrazovanie v 1863 i 1864*, Part III, Section I, 302-28; Manuscript Division, Saltykov-Shchedrin Library, CPP memorandum, "Zapiska o grazhdanskom sudoproizvodstve," December, 1861, 14-24.

33. Nolde, *Pobedonostsev i sudebnaia reforma*, 41; *Istoriia pravitel'stvuiushchago Senata*, IV, 469-72.

34. CPP and Babst, *Pis'ma o puteshestvii*, 526-30; MDLL, CPP letters to Anna Tiutchev, November 8, December 14, 1864; February 2, February 7, 1865; Central State Historical Archive of the USSR, Leningrad, CPP letters to Alexei D. Zheltukhin, June 5, June 7, 1862.

35. CPP, "Iuridicheskiia zametki i voprosy po nasledstvennomu i zaveshchatel'nomu pravam," *Zhurnal Ministerstva iustitsii*, XXVII, Part II (1866), 33-40; CPP, *Kurs grazhdanskago prava* (first edition, St. Petersburg, 1880), III, 56-58; Russia. Ministerstvo iustitsii, *Sudebnye ustavy 20 noiabria 1864*, II, 597-600.

36. CPP, *Sudebnoe rukovodstvo. Sbornik pravil, polozhenii i primerov* (St. Petersburg, 1872), *passim*; "Sudebnoe rukovodstvo," *Zhurnal grazhdanskago i torgovago prava*, III (1872), 514-26; "Sudebnoe rukovodstvo," *Sudebnyi vestnik*, April 26, April 28, 1872.

37. CPP, "Preobrazovanie suda prisiazhnykh," *Grazhdanin*, Number 51, December 22, 1873, 1371-72; Prince Vladimir P. Meshcherskii, *Moi vospominaniia* (St. Petersburg, 1897–1912), II, 55-60, 157-69; III, 333-34; Leonid Grossman, "Dostoevskii i pravitel'stvennye krugi 1870-kh godov," *Literaturnoe nasledstvo*, Number 15 (1934), 100-104, 127-28; Nolde, *Pobedonostsev i sudebnaia reforma*, 13.

38. CPP, *Moskovskii sbornik* (third edition, Moscow, 1896), 53-56; CPP, *Pis'ma k Aleksandru III*, I, 18; II, 173-74; Alexander A. Polovtsov, *Dnevnik gosudarstvennogo sekretaria A. A. Polovtsova* (Moscow, 1966), I, 147; II, 13, 14, 16, 26; Dzhanshiev, *Epokha velikikh reform*, eighth edition, 463-64; Kucherov, *Courts, Lawyers and Trials*, 81; Russia. Ministerstvo iustitsii, *Sudebnye ustavy 20 noiabria 1864*, II, 604-605.

39. CPP, "S'ezd iuristov v Moskve," *Grazhdanin*, Number 44, October 29, 1873, 1173-75; *Pervyi s'ezd russkikh iuristov v Moskve v 1875 godu* (Moscow, 1882), i-viii, 7-14, 119-28, 252-72; R. G. Eimontova, "Universitetskaia reforma 1863 g.," *Istoricheskie zapiski*, Number 70 (1961), 182-83; MDLL, CPP letter to Catherine Tiutchev, February 27, 1875.

40. Count Dmitrii A. Miliutin, *Dnevnik* (Moscow, 1947–50), I, 111; MDLL, CPP letter to Catherine Tiutchev, February 16, 1874.

41. CPP, *Pis'ma k Aleksandru III*, I, 277-78, 346; II, 9-13; CPP, *Novum Regnum*, 68-69, 171-72, 398; MDLL, CPP letters to Catherine Tiutchev, October 11, October 16, 1877; March 28, 1881; Catherine Tiutchev letters to CPP, April 10, 1878; March 29, 1881.

42. CPP, "Podlezhit li zemstvo po zakonu otvetstvennosti za nepriniatie mer protiv goloda?," *Grazhdanin*, Number 52, December 29, 1873; Grossman, "Dostoevskii i pravitel'stvennye krugi," 129.

IV. The Petersburg Tutor

1. CPP, *Pis'ma Pobedonostseva k Aleksandru III* (Moscow, 1925–26), II, 330-31; Russia. Ministerstvo iustitsii, *Sudebnye ustavy 20 noiabria 1864 g. za piat'desiat let* (Petrograd, 1914), I, 73; Nicholas P. Barsukov, *Zhizn' i trudy M. P. Pogodina* (St. Petersburg, 1888–1910), XXI, 69; XXII, 1-3; MDLL, CPP letters to Anna Tiutchev, September 26, 1864; February 2, April 12, April 24, May 1, August 21, September 22, December 28, 1865.

2. A. A. Shevelev, "Puteshestviia po Rossii Ego Imperatorskago Vysochestva naslednika tsesarevicha Aleksandra Aleksandrovicha," *Russkoe obozrenie,* XLVI (1897), 52-92; IL (1898), 821-22; Prince Vladimir P. Meshcherskii, *Moi vospominaniia* (St. Petersburg, 1897–1912), II, 3-11, 55-60; Iurii V. Gotie, "K. P. Pobedonostsev i naslednik Aleksandr Aleksandrovich, 1865–1881," *Publichnaia biblioteka SSSR imeni V. I. Lenina. Sbornik,* II (1929), 110-12, 120-21, 127-28; MDLL, CPP letters to Anna Aksakov, February 2, March 21, 1867; October 20, December 12, 1868; March 17, 1869; CPP letters to Catherine Tiutchev, October 18, December 2, 1866; October 18, 1868; December 30, 1871; December 22, 1874; February 25, September 22, 1880; September 20, 1881; Catherine Tiutchev letters to CPP, December 7, 1866; November 29, 1875.

3. CPP, *K. P. Pobedonostsev i ego korrespondenty. Pis'ma i zapiski. Novum Regnum* (Moscow, 1923), 23, 1004-1006, 1014-16, 1097-98; CPP, *Pis'ma k Aleksandru III,* I, 4-7, 19-21, 31-32, 36, 42-43, 212, 230-37, 255-58, 277-78, 280-81, 402-406, 419; CPP, "Proshchanie Moskvy s Tsarem svoim," in Sergei A. Petrovskii (editor), *Pamiati Imperatora Aleksandra III* (Moscow, 1894), 88-89; CPP, "Gosudar'Imperator Aleksandr Aleksandrovich," *RA,* I (1906), 620-22; Egor A. Peretts, *Dnevnik E. A. Perettsa, 1880–1883* (Moscow-Leningrad, 1927), 5; Count Peter A. Valuev, *Dnevnik, 1877–1884* (Petrograd, 1919), 128-29; V. S. Frank (editor), "Iz neizdannoi perepiski Imp. Aleksandra III i Nikolaia II s kn. V. P. Meshcherskim," *Sovremennyia zapiski,* LXX (1940), 187; Nicholas N. Firsov, "Aleksandr III. Lichnaia kharakteristika chast'iu po ego neizdannym dnevnikam," *Byloe,* Number 29 (1925), 90-104; Meshcherskii, *Vospominaniia,* II, 3-11, 99; III, 7; Gotie, "Pobedonostsev i naslednik," 125-27; MDLL, CPP letters to Anna Aksakov, March 21, 1867; October 20, 1868; CPP letters to Catherine Tiutchev, March 31, 1877; August 8, August 27, October 17, 1879.

4. Russia. Gosudarstvennyi sovet, *Opis' del arkhiva Gosudarstvennago soveta* (St. Petersburg, 1908–1913), XVI, 172; XVII, 745; Russia. Gosudarstvennyi sovet, *Otchëtiza 1872–1881* (St. Petersburg, 1874–83), 1872, 319-20; 1876, supplement, 22; 1877, supplement, 13-21, 31-32; 1878, supplement, 20; 1879, supplement, 30; 1880, supplement, 32, 45; 1881, supplement, 61; "50-letnii iubilei K. P. Pobedonostseva," *Sudebnaia gazeta,* June 9, 1896, 10-11; Baron Alexander E. Nolde, "Obzor nauchnoi iuridicheskoi deiatel'nosti K. P. Pobedonostseva," *Zhurnal Ministerstva narodnago prosveshcheniia,* VIII (1907), 87; MDLL, CPP letters to Catherine Tiutchev, December 14, 1868; March 22, 1869; December 15, 1877; December 29, 1879; February 25, 1880; October 17, 1881.

5. MDLL, CPP letter to Catherine Tiutchev, August 9, 1880.

6. B. Koz'min, "Odoevskii v 1860-e gody," *Literaturnoe nasledstvo*, Numbers 22-24 (1935), 79-82; Alexander P. Piatkovskii, *Kniaz' V. F. Odoevskii i D. V. Venevitinov* (St. Petersburg, 1901), 9-53.

7. Anatole D. Alekseev (editor), *Letopis' zhizni i tvorchestva I. A. Goncharova* (Moscow-Leningrad, 1960), 142, 239, 248; CPP, "Eshchë na pamiat' o kniaze V. F. Odoevskom," in Obshchestvo liubitelei rossiiskoi slovesnosti, Moscow, *V pamiat' o kniaze Vladimire Fedoroviche Odoevskom* (Moscow, 1869), 78-82; Evgenii N. Medynskii, *Istoriia russkoi pedagogiki do Velikoi Oktiabrskoi Sotsialisticheskoi Revoliutsii* (second edition, Moscow, 1938), 150-51; "Tekushchaia khronika i osobye proisshestviia. Dnevnik V. F. Odoevskogo, 1859–1869 gg.," *Literaturnoe nasledstvo*, Numbers 22-24 (1935), 162, 180, 193, 202-203, 216, 255; "Iz pis'ma K. P. Pobedonostseva k izdateliu 'Russkago arkhiva'," *RA*, I (1904), 189; Prince V. M. Golitzyn, "Moskovskii universitet v 60-kh godakh," *Golos minuvshago*, V (1917), 233; Koz'min, "Odoevskii," 82-86; Piatkovskii, *Odoevskii*, 54-98; MDLL, CPP letters to Prince Vladimir F. Odoevskii, January 12, July 22, 1865; undated letters.

8. Anatole Leroy-Beaulieu, *Un Homme d'état russe, Nicholas Miliutine* (Paris, 1884), 27-32, 37-41, 44-49, 124-26; Anatole F. Koni, "Velikaia kniaginia Elena Pavlovna," in *Velikaia reforma*, V (1911), 14-34; Meshcherskii, *Vospominaniia*, II, 205-216.

9. CPP, *Pis'ma k Aleksandru III*, I, 13, 402; CPP, *Vechnaia pamiat'. Vospominaniia o pochivshikh* (Moscow, 1896), 3-7, 18, 95-97; CPP, "9 ianvaria 1873 goda," *Grazhdanin*, Number 3, January 15, 1873, 57-58; MDLL, CPP letter to Catherine Tiutchev, January 12, 1873.

10. CPP (editor), *Perepiska Iu. F. Samarina s baronessoiu E. F. Raden, 1861–1876 g.* (Moscow, 1893), 2-29, 34-37, 46-48, 53-61, 85-144, 170-78; CPP (editor), "Pis'ma baronessy Raden k g. Berkgoltsu," *Russkoe obozrenie*, XXXVII (1896), 318-22; XXXVIII (1896), 786-94; XXXIX (1896), 781-88; XL (1896), 800-809; CPP, *Pis'ma k Aleksandru III*, I, 84-87; CPP, *Vechnaia pamiat'*, 21-25; "Pis'ma K. P. Pobedonostseva k E. M. Feoktistovu," *Literaturnoe nasledstvo*, Number 22-24 (1935), 542-43, 557; "Briefwechsel zwischen Arnold von Tideböhl, Redakteur der Baltischen Monatschrift, und K. P. Pobedonoszego, Prokureur des Hl. Synod," *Baltische Monatshefte*, 1934, 571-77; Anton Rubinstein, *Autobiography of Anton Rubinstein, 1829–1889* (Boston, 1890), 58-61; MDLL, CPP letters to Catherine Tiutchev, January 4, 1875; December 15, 1877.

11. Yuri Samarine, *Préface aux Oeuvres théologiques de A. S. Khomiakov* (Paris, 1939), 11-19; Iurii Samarin and O. Dmitriev, *Revoliutsionnyi konservatizm* (Berlin, 1875), 10-11; CPP, *Perepiska Samarina*, 153-54, 238-42; Nicholas Riasanovsky, *Russia and the West in the Teaching of the Slavophiles* (Cambridge, Mass., 1952), 85-86; MDLL, CPP letters to Catherine Tiutchev, March 22, April 6, 1876.

12. Peter I. Bartenev (editor), "Bolezn' i konchina naslednika-tsesarevicha Nikolaia Aleksandrovicha, 1865. Pis'ma Anny Fedorovny Tiutchevoi v Moskve

k K. P. Pobedonostsevu i k sestre eia Ekaterine Fedorovne," *RA*, II (1905), 283-304; Ivan S. Aksakov, "Pis'ma I. S. Aksakova k K. P. Pobedonostsevu, 1876–1885," *RA*, III (1907), 163-92; "Pis'mo I. S. Aksakova k K. P. Pobedonostsevu," *RA*, II (1905), 591-92; Gotie, "Pobedonostsev i naslednik," 108-109; Manuscript Division, Institute of Russian Literature (Pushkinskii Dom), CPP letter to Ivan Aksakov, June 27, 1878.

13. CPP, *Perepiska Samarina*, 206-207; CPP, *Pis'ma k Aleksandru III*, I, 147; Dmitri Stremooukhoff, *La Poésie et l'idéologie de Tiouttchev* (Paris, 1937), *passim*, especially 13-25, 51-60, 109-119, 139-49; Ivan S. Aksakov, *Biografiia Fedora Ivanovicha Tiutcheva* (Moscow, 1886), 242-45, 317-18; K. Pigarev, "F. I. Tiutchev i problemy vneshnei politiki tsarskoi Rossii," *Literaturnoe nasledstvo*, Number 19-21 (1935), 240; Alexander von Schelting, *Russland und Europa im russischen Geschichtsdenken* (Bern, 1948), 182-85; MDLL, CPP letters to Catherine Tiutchev, October 18, October 20, 1868; April 22, 1875; July 8, 1876; March 12, 1879.

14. Vladimir S. Markov, *K istorii raskola-staroobriadchestva vtoroi poloviny XIX stoletiia. Perepiska prof. N. I. Subbotina* (Moscow, 1915), 208-209, 219, 224, 229, 448; Aksakov, "Pis'ma," 176-77; Ivan S. Aksakov, *Ivan Sergeevich Aksakov v ego pis'makh* (Moscow, 1886–96), I, 28-32, 37; CPP, *Pis'ma k Aleksandru III*, I, 107, 176-77; CPP, *Novum Regnum*, 275-77, 556; CPP, *Vechnaia pamiat'*, 63-73; Samuel Kucherov, *Courts, Lawyers and Trials under the Last Three Tsars* (New York, 1953), 98-99; Riasanovsky, *Russia and the West*, 52; MDLL, CPP letters to Anna Aksakov, July 15, 1867; March 21, July 17, October 20, November 23, 1868; CPP letters to Catherine Tiutchev, November 10, 1876; March 12, November 4, 1877; July 6, 1878; September 20, December 8, 1881.

15. Markov, *K istorii raskola-staroobriadchestva*, 229-33, 239; MDLL, CPP letter to Anna Aksakov, March 18, 1882; CPP letters to Catherine Tiutchev, February 12, 1867; November 24, 1869; November 22, December 5, December 20, 1870; October 12, October 31, November 21, 1874; November 17, 1875; January 29, September 16, 1877; May 30, December 14, 1878; February 25, July 23, August 9, December 29, 1880; June 5, July 21, 1881; January 8, January 10, February 15, 1882; Catherine Tiutchev letters to CPP, December 8, 1870; October 10, December 31, 1875; February 23, July 23, September 27, December 23, 1877; November 6, 1878; July 16, September 7, September 20, 1881.

16. MDLL, CPP letter to Anna Tiutchev, July 15, 1865.

17. CPP, *Novum Regnum*, 997; Rose J. Birkbeck, *Life and Letters of W. J. Birkbeck* (London, 1922), 29, 166; William J. Birkbeck, *Birkbeck and the Russian Church* (London, 1917), 123; William T. Stead, *Truth About Russia* (London, 1889), 324; "Kievskii sobor 1884 goda. Poslanie k vysokopreosviashchennomu Pavlu, eksarkhu Gruzii. Zapiski arkhiepiskopa Nikanora," *RA*, III (1908), 112; Friedrich Steinmann and Elias Hurwicz, *Konstantin Petrowitsch Pobjedonoszew, der Staatsmann der Reaktion unter Alexander III* (Königsberg, 1933), preface, viii; Royal Society of London, *Catalogue of Scientific Papers, 1800–*

1900 (London, 1867–1925), XIV, 844-46; MDLL, CPP letter to Anna Tiutchev, August 19, 1864.

18. Catherine A. Pobedonostsev (translator), Minnie Mackay (Marie Corelli, *pseud.*), *Istoriia detskoi dushi. Mogushchestvennyi Atom. Povest'* (fifth edition, Moscow, 1911); Catherine A. Pobedonostsev (editor), *Severnye tsvety. Vybor iz stikhotvorenii A. S. Pushkina* (St. Petersburg, 1888); CPP, *Novum Regnum,* 823-37, 867, 1084; Jeremiah Curtin, *Memoirs* (Madison, Wisconsin, 1940), 467-68, 486-87, 781; Boris V. Nikol'skii, "Literaturnaia deiatel'nost' K. P. Pobedonostseva," *Istoricheskii vestnik,* LXV (1896), 722; MDLL, CPP letters to Olga Novikov, January 28, 1877; April 26, 1888.

19. I. V. Preobrazhenskii, *Konstantin Petrovich Pobedonostsev, ego lichnost' i deiatel'nosti* (St. Petersburg, 1912), 22-23; "Pis'ma Pobedonostseva k Feoktistovu," 550; *Lettres de la princesse Radziwill au général de Robilant, 1889–1914* (Bologna, 1933–34), II, 21-22; MDLL, CPP letters to Anna Aksakov, February 2, 1867; October 20, 1868; CPP letters to Catherine Tiutchev, February 12, May 14, 1868; September 21, 1879.

20. Sergei A. Petrovskii (editor), "Pis'ma K. P. Pobedonostseva preosviashchennomu Illarionu, arkhiepiskopu Poltavskomu," *RA,* LIV (1916), 374-80; Petrovskii (editor), "Perepiska K. P. Pobedonostseva s preosviashchennym Nikanorom episkopom Ufimskim," *RA,* III (1915), 252, 258; Harry de Windt, *The New Siberia* (London, 1896), 67; William T. Stead, *The M.P. for Russia. Reminiscences and Correspondence of Madame Olga Novikoff* (New York, 1909), II, 332, 336; S. Mel'gunov (editor), "K. P. Pobedonostsev v dni pervoi revoliutsii. Neizdannyia pis'ma k S. D. Voitu," *Na chuzhoi storone,* VIII (1924), 186; MDLL, CPP letters to Catherine Tiutchev, February 1, March 13, August 16, November 28, 1880; CPP letters to Olga Novikov, July 3, 1891; July 25, 1895.

21. Petrovskii, "Pis'ma Pobedonostseva," 131-34, 361-64; MDLL, CPP letters to Catherine Tiutchev, April 19, 1872; November 23, 1873; January 16, February 2, March 17, April 21, May 26, December 22, 1874; December 25, 1875; January 23, May 25, 1876; March 31, May 11, August 3, November 22, November 24, 1877; January 19, August 19, 1878; July 1, September 21, 1879; February 25, 1880; June 3, October 24, November 12, November 20, November 24, November 28, December 30, 1881; CPP letters to Olga Novikov, November 30, 1876; October 11, 1877; December 21, 1881; April 6, November 13, 1890; June 30, 1893; Catherine Tiutchev letters to CPP, January 11, December 31, 1876; April 11, August 31, November 19, 1877; Sergei A. Rachinskii letters to CPP, October 10, 1889; October 17, 1890; July 11, 1891; October 11, 1892; April 17, May 31, 1895; April 4, April 26, 1896. Pobedonostsev's correspondence with Catherine Tiutchev and with Olga Novikov contains many references to his wife's being unwell.

22. CPP, *Pis'ma k Aleksandru III,* I, 182, 252, 350-51; Valuev, *Dnevnik,* 213; MDLL, CPP letters to Catherine Tiutchev, June 29, December 14, December 21, 1878; December 17, 1879; August 15, 1881; Manuscript Division, Library,

University of California, Berkeley, Count Vladimir N. Lamzdorf letter to Nicholas K. Giers, November 28, 1882. Sergei Golubov, a Soviet historical novelist, published a novella in 1941 designed to ridicule Pobedonostsev. In the novel, Golubov described the Pobedonostsev home as a cold and broken one after the early 1870's. Her brother was described as their idiot son, and Mrs. Pobedonostsev was given Sonya's habits of dress and of eating chocolates, while Baranov appeared as a lieutenant general who was in fact having an affair with her which Pobedonostsev decided to ignore. Golubov's description of the Pobedonostsev family life was grossly inaccurate, but it is clear that their lives did suffer heavy personal strain. (*Den' Konstantina Petrovicha. Povest'* [Moscow, 1941], *passim*, especially 9-18, 72, 142-43.)

23. Boris N. Chicherin, *Vospominaniia* (Moscow, 1929–34), IV, 104-105, 328; CPP, *Pis'ma k Aleksandru III*, II, 29-31; Petrovskii, "Pis'ma Pobedonostseva," 131; MDLL, CPP letters to Catherine Tiutchev, June 7, July 22, September 21, 1881; February 15, March 3, 1882; Catherine Tiutchev letters to CPP, June 12, July 21, 1881; February 17, 1882.

V. Dostoevsky

1. CPP, *Pis'ma Pobedonostseva k Aleksandru III* (Moscow, 1925–26), I, 310-11; Leonid Grossman, "Dostoevskii i pravitel'stvennye krugi 1870-kh godov," *Literaturnoe nasledstvo*, Number 15 (1934), 89; Vasilii Y. Cheshikhin (Ch. Vetrinskii, *pseud.*), *F. M. Dostoevskii v vospominaniiakh sovremennikov* (Moscow, 1912), 162-63; N. F. Belchikov (editor), "Dostoevskii o Pushkinskikh torzhestvakh," *KA*, I (1922), 375.

2. Vladimir V. Ermilov, *F. M. Dostoevskii* (Moscow, 1956), 163, 201-202; Grossman, "Dostoevskii i pravitel'stvennye krugi," 83-84, 86, 89-90, 114.

3. So far as relations between Dostoevsky and Pobedonostsev are concerned, the principal published Dostoevsky materials are the Dostoevsky *Pis'ma*, published in four volumes in Moscow in the years 1928–59, under the editorship of Arkadii S. Izkoz (A. S. Dolinin, *pseud.*); Dostoevsky, *Dnevnik pisatelia*, published in volumes IV-VI in the Dostoevsky *Sobranie sochinenii* (Paris, 1945–46); the studies of Dostoevsky by Leonid Grossman, in addition to that listed above: *Dostoevskii na zhiznennom puti* (Moscow, 1928), two vols.; *Seminarii po Dostoevskomu. Materialy, bibliografiia i kommentarii* (Moscow, 1922); *Tvorchestvo Dostoevskogo, 1821–1881–1921. Sbornik stat'ei i materialov* (Odessa, 1921); and *Zhizn' i trudy F. M. Dostoevskogo* (Moscow-Leningrad, 1935); Iulian G. Oksman, "F. M. Dostoevskii v redaktsii *Grazhdanina*," *Tvorchestvo Dostoevskogo. Stat'i i materialy pod red. Grossmana* (Odessa, 1921), 63-82; and Arkadii S. Izkoz (A. S. Dolinin, *pseud.*), *F. M. Dostoevskii. Materialy i issledovaniia* (Leningrad, 1935).

Careful examination of the Dostoevsky and Pobedonostsev archives in the Manuscript Division of the Lenin Library in Moscow indicated that the four-volume edition of the Dostoevsky letters published between 1928 and 1959 is complete so far as the letters of Pobedonostsev to Dostoevsky are concerned.

These archives also contain seventy-one unpublished letters written by Pobedonostsev to Dostoevsky's widow between 1881 and 1906.

The principal published sources on this relationship, on the Pobedonostsev side, are CPP, *Pis'ma k Aleksandru III*, and CPP, *Pis'ma i zapiski. Novum Regnum* (Moscow, 1923), two volumes in one. Pobedonostsev's twenty-two articles in *Grazhdanin* in 1873 are, of course, very important, for Dostoevsky was the editor of the journal at that time. Finally, the immense mass of unpublished Pobedonostsev correspondence in the Manuscript Division of the Lenin Library in Moscow is valuable, if only for the paucity of references to Dostoevsky.

4. N. F. Belchikov, "Dostoevskii i Pobedonostsev," *KA*, II (1922), 245-47; Dostoevsky, *Pis'ma*, III, 308; Grossman, "Dostoevskii i pravitel'stvennye krugi," 89-90, 103-104, 114, 138-39, 145; Ernest J. Simmons, *Dostoevsky* (London, 1950), 300.

5. Anna G. Dostoevsky, *Bibliograficheskii ukazatel' sochinenii i proizvedenii iskusstva, otnosiashchikhsia k zhizni i deiatel'nosti F. M. Dostoevskogo* (St. Petersburg, 1906), 240-41, 263; N. F. Belchikov (editor), *Pis'ma F. M. Dostoevskogo k zhene* (Moscow-Leningrad, 1926), 77, 339-40, 379; Prince Vladimir P. Meshcherskii, *Moi vospominaniia* (St. Petersburg, 1897–1912), II, 14, 55-60, 157-69; III, 333-34; A. A. Shevelev, "Puteshestviia po Rossii Ego Imperatorskago Vysochestva naslednika tsesarevicha Aleksandra Aleksandrovicha," *Russkoe obozrenie*, XLVI (1897), 55; CPP, *Pis'ma k Aleksandru III*, I, 232, 233, 325; "Pis'ma K. P. Pobedonostseva k E. M. Feoktistovu," *Literaturnoe nasledstvo*, Number 22-24 (1935), 530-32.

6. Grossman, "Dostoevskii i pravitel'stvennye krugi," 128; Oksman, "Dostoevskii," 64-67.

7. Alexandra V. Bogdanovich, *Dnevnik, 1880–1912* (Moscow, 1924), 44; "Dostoevskii o 'Bratiakh Karamazovykh.' Neizdannyia pis'ma, 1879–1881 gg.," *Byloe*, Number 15 (1919), 125; Dostoevsky, *Pis'ma*, III, 61, 69, 202, 273; Anna Dostoevsky, *Bibliograficheskii ukazatel'*, 263; CPP, *Pis'ma k Aleksandru III*, I, 311; Grossman, *Seminarii*, 13, 16, 17, 30-40, 45, 50, 65; Grossman, *Zhizn'*, 207, 245-324, *passim;* Grossman, "Dostoevskii i pravitel'stvennye krugi," 92, 121, 124, 129, 134-39, 143-44, 146, 149; Belchikov, *Pis'ma Dostoevskogo*, 85-86, 277, 340, 360, 373-75.

8. Il'ia S. Zilbershtein (editor), *F. M. Dostoevskii i I. S. Turgenev. Perepiska* (Leningrad, 1928), 9; Vera S. Nechaeva (editor), *Opisanie rukopisei F. M. Dostoevskogo* (Moscow, 1957), 543-44; Elena A. Shtakenshneider, *Dnevnik i zapiski, 1854–1866* (Moscow, 1934), 449; CPP, *Novum Regnum*, 285, 681-82; Grossman, *Zhizn'*, 336; Grossman, "Dostoevskii i pravitel'stvennye krugi," 118, 121; Grossman, *Seminarii*, 65; Belchikov, "Dostoevskii o Pushkinskikh torzhestvakh," 373-74; MDLL, CPP letters to Anna Dostoevsky, June 5, August 27, November 18, 1881; May 22, December 10, December 15, 1882; July 18, December 11, 1883; January 8, March 26, 1885; April 9, 1888; September 19, 1889; February 14, 1892; January 26, 1893; January 3, 1902.

9. MDLL, CPP letters to Catherine Tiutchev, September 5, December 18, 1875; March 15, 1876; February 19, 1878; October 9, 1879.

10. Boris N. Chicherin, *Vospominaniia* (Moscow, 1929–34), IV, 104; Grossman, "Dostoevskii i pravitel'stvennye krugi," 88, 134; Oksman, "Dostoevskii," 69-82.

11. Count Sergei IU. Witte, *Vospominaniia* (Moscow, 1923), II, 468-70; Grossman, *Zhizn'*, 256, 324; Grossman, "Dostoevskii i pravitel'stvennye krugi," 88, 124-25, 132-34; CPP, *Pis'ma k Aleksandru III*, I, 62; CPP, *Novum Regnum*, 1008-1010, 1026.

12. Grossman, *Zhizn'*, 207; Grossman, "Dostoevskii i pravitel'stvennye krugi," 83-86, 90-92, 114, 136, 159-60; MDLL, CPP letters to Catherine Tiutchev, February 5, October 11, 1877.

13. "Dostoevskii o 'Bratiakh Karamazovykh,'" 100-101; Vladimir Seduro, *Dostoevsky in Russian Literary Criticism, 1846–1956* (New York, 1957), 310; Nechaeva, *Opisanie rukopisei*, 451-52; Constantine V. Mochul'skii, *Dostoevskii. Zhizn' i tvorchestvo* (Paris, 1947), 445; Dostoevskii, *Sobranie sochinenii*, V, 134; Grossman, *Zhizn'*, 245, 248, 277; Grossman, "Dostoevskii i pravitel'stvennye krugi," 130-36, 138, 141-46, 245.

14. Dostoevsky, *Sobranie sochinenii*, V, 179-80; Dostoevsky, *The Diary of a Writer* (New York, 1949), I, 301-302; Grossman, *Zhizn'*, 259, 287-88, 298, 307; Grossman, "Dostoevskii i pravitel'stvennye krugi," 89-90, 120-21, 138-39, 146; Belchikov, "Dostoevskii i Pobedonostsev," 247-52; Belchikov, "Dostoevskii o Pushkinskikh torzhestvakh," 374-75.

15. Vladimir V. Ermilov, "F. M. Dostoevskii," *Novyi mir*, XXXI (1955), 163, 201-202; Dostoevsky, *Pis'ma*, III, 308; "Dostoevskii o 'Bratiakh Karamazovykh,'" 100; Grossman, *Zhizn'*, 282, 286; Grossman, "Dostoevskii i pravitel'stvennye krugi," 103-104, 134-39, 145; Belchikov, "Dostoevskii i Pobedonostsev," 242-47.

16. Dostoevsky, *Sobranie sochinenii*, V, 384-85; Dostoevsky, *Pis'ma*, II, 87; Grossman, "Dostoevskii i pravitel'stvennye krugi," 88, 124-29, 135-36; *Grazhdanin*, September 10, 1873, 991.

17. CPP, "Iz Londona," *Grazhdanin*, Number 27, July 2, 1873, 750-52; CPP, "Lionskiia grazhdanskiia pokhorony," *Grazhdanin*, Number 31, July 30, 1873, 848; CPP, "V protestantskikh khramakh," *Grazhdanin*, Number 31, July 30, 1873, 849; CPP, "Vestminsterskoe abbatstvo," *Grazhdanin*, Number 32, August 6, 1873, 870-73; CPP, "K voprosu o vozsoedinenei tserkvei," *Grazhdanin*, Number 33, August 13, 1873, 893-96; CPP, "Protivorechiia v anglikanskoi tserkvi," *Grazhdanin*, Number 34, August 20, 1873, 921-23; CPP, "Vorovskii uzhin," *Grazhdanin*, Number 36, September 3, 1873, 974-76; CPP, "Irvingity v Londone. Deisty i unitarii v Londone," *Grazhdanin*, Number 35, August 27, 1873, 949-51.

18. CPP, "Bor'ba gosudarstva s tserkov'iu v Germanii," *Grazhdanin*, Number 34, August 20, 1873, 915-18; CPP, "Tserkov' i gosudarstvo v Germanii,"

Grazhdanin, Number 40, October 1, 1873, 1064-1066; CPP, "Tserkovnyia dela v Germanii," *Grazhdanin*, Number 51, December 22, 1873, 1367-69; Dostoevsky, *Sobranie sochinenii*, IV, 384-85, 409-414; Grossman, "Dostoevskii i pravitel'-stvennye krugi," 125-26.

19. CPP, "Kritika i bibliografiia. Svoboda, ravenstvo i bratstvo," *Grazhdanin*, Number 35, August 27, 1873, 958-62; Number 36, September 3, 1873, 976-79; Number 37, September 10, 1873, 1007-1010; CPP, "Kartina vysshago vospitaniia. Avtobiografiia Dzh. Stuarta Millia," *Grazhdanin*, Number 45, November 5, 1873, 1190-93.

20. CPP, "Frantsiia. Vzgliad na tepereshnee eia sostoianie," *Grazhdanin*, Number 35, August 27, 1873, 939-42; Pobedonostsev, "Ispaniia," *Grazhdanin*, Number 37, September 10, 1873, 991-94; Dostoevsky, *Sobranie sochinenii*, IV, 367, 379, 400-408, 415-61. In a footnote to Pobedonostsev's article on the Third International in Spain, Dostoevsky sought to direct the readers' attention to its analysis "of one of the most interesting and important phenomena in the history of contemporary Europe."

21. CPP, "S'ezd iuristov v Moskve," *Grazhdanin*, Number 44, October 29, 1873, 1173-75; CPP, "Preobrazovanie suda prisiazhnykh," *Grazhdanin*, Number 51, December 22, 1873, 1371-72; CPP, "Podlezhit li zemstvo po zakonu otvet-stvennosti za nepriniatie mer protiv goloda?," *Grazhdanin*, Number 52, December 29, 1873, 1380; Dostoevsky, *Pis'ma*, III, 313-14.

22. Dostoevsky, *Sobranie sochinenii*, IV, 194-208; V, 71-73, 78-101; Dostoevsky, *The Diary of a Writer*, I, 16-22, 30, 213-38; Samuel Kucherov, *Courts, Lawyers and Trials under the Last Three Tsars* (New York, 1953), 169-71; Grossman, "Dostoevskii i pravitel'stvennye krugi," 100-104, 107, 115-19, 146-48.

23. General Hans von Schweinitz, *Denkwürdigkeiten des Botschafters General v. Schweinitz* (Berlin, 1927), II, 424; "Pis'ma K. P. Pobedonostseva k grafu N. P. Ignatievu," *Byloe*, Number 27-28 (1924), 55, 71, 73, 78-79; CPP, *Pis'ma k Aleksandru III*, I, 343, 345; II, 12, 153, 191-92, 220, 230, 299; CPP, *Novum Regnum*, 250, 770-76, 937-38, 1021; Dostoevsky, *Sobranie sochinenii*, VI, 97-101; Dostoevsky, *The Diary of a Writer*, II, 637-53; Grossman, "Dostoevskii i pravitel'stvennye krugi," 142-43; Belchikov, "Dostoevskii i Pobedonostsev," 244-45; Paul Berline, "Russian Religious Philosophers and the Jews," *Jewish Social Studies*, IX (1947), 271-318.

24. Dostoevsky, *Sobranie sochinenii*, V, 249-63, 393-413; VI, *passim;* CPP, *Pis'ma k Aleksandru III*, II, 26-27, 65-68; CPP, *Novum Regnum*, 314-15, 896; "Pis'ma Pobedonostseva k Ignatievu," 73-74; Anatole F. Koni, *Na zhiznennom puti* (Moscow-Riga, 1912–29), I, 592-93; Grossman, "Dostoevskii i pravitel'-stvennye krugi," 108-112; Simmons, *Dostoevsky*, 252-53, 319-32.

25. Arkadii S. Izkoz (A. S. Dolinin, *pseud.*), *V tvorcheskoi laboratorii Dostoevskogo* (Leningrad, 1947), *passim;* Sergei D. Skazkin, *Konets avstro-russko-germanskogo soiuza* (Moscow, 1928), 184-85; Count Peter A. Valuev, *Dnevnik, 1877–1884* (Petrograd, 1919), 15, 281; Sergius Yakobson (editor), "Pis'ma K. P.

Pobedonostseva k V. F. Putsykovichu," in Kruzhok liubitelei russkoi stariny, *Stat'i i materialy* (Berlin, 1932), 73; "Pis'mo I. S. Aksakova k K. P. Pobedonostsevu," *RA*, II (1905), 591-92; CPP, "Noveishaia angliiskaia literatura po vostochnomu voprosu," *Grazhdanin*, Number 1, January 8, 1877, 20-25; CPP and K. N. Bestuzhev-Riumin (translators), William E. Gladstone, *Bolgarskie Uzhasy i Vostochnyi Vopros* (St. Petersburg, 1876), ix-xi; CPP, *Pis'ma k Aleksandru III*, I, 34, 40-41, 49-60, 80-87, 89-120, 405-408; CPP, *Novum Regnum*, 562-63, 607, 1016-21; von Schweinitz, *Denkwürdigkeiten*, I, 22.

VI. *Panslavism and the Balkan Crisis*

1. Sergei P. Pobedonostsev, "Putevyia zapiski russkago po Evrope v 1847-m godu," *Otechestvennyia zapiski*, LVIII (1848), 17-18.
2. This is a brief analysis of Slavophil thought as it is reflected in the works of Ivan Aksakov, Constantine Aksakov, Alexei Khomiakov, and Iurii Samarin in particular. Their collected works have all been published: Ivan S. Aksakov, *Sochineniia* (Moscow, 1886–91), seven vols.; Constantine S. Aksakov, *Polnoe sobranie sochinenii* (Moscow, 1861–80), three vols.; Alexei S. Khomiakov, *Polnoe sobranie sochinenii* (Moscow, 1900–1904), eight vols.; Iurii F. Samarin, *Sochineniia* (Moscow, 1911), eleven vols. The most useful secondary works are Serge Bolshakoff, *The Doctrine of the Unity of the Church in the Works of Khomyakov and Moehler* (London, 1946); Albert Gratieux, *A. S. Khomiakov et le mouvement slavophile* (Paris, 1939), two vols.; Nicholas Riasanovsky, *Russia and the West in the Teaching of the Slavophiles* (Cambridge, Mass., 1952); Paul N. Miliukov, "Slavianofilstvo," *Entsiklopedicheskii slovar'*, XXX (1900), 307-314; Miliukov, *Le Mouvement intellectuel russe* (Paris, 1918); Peter K. Christoff, *An Introduction to Nineteenth-Century Russian Slavophilism. Volume I. A. S. Xomjakov* (The Hague, 1961).
3. This general survey of the background and principal characteristics of Russian panslavism is based largely on Hans Kohn, *Pan-Slavism. Its History and Ideology* (Notre Dame, 1953); Thomas G. Masaryk, *The Spirit of Russia* (London, 1919), I, 237-335; Michael B. Petrovich, *The Emergence of Russian Panslavism, 1856–1870* (New York, 1956); Alexander N. Pypin, *Panslavism v proshlom i nastoiashchem* (St. Petersburg, 1913); and Benedict H. Sumner, *Russia and the Balkans, 1870–1880* (Oxford, 1937).
4. Ivan S. Aksakov, "Pis'ma I. S. Aksakova k K. P. Pobedonostsevu, 1876–1885," *RA*, III (1907), 163-64, 173-74; CPP, *Pis'ma Pobedonostseva k Aleksandru III* (Moscow, 1925–26), I, 66, 124-27; CPP, *K. P. Pobedonostsev i ego korrespondenty. Pis'ma i zapiski. Novum Regnum* (Moscow, 1923), 1018; MDLL, CPP letters to Catherine Tiutchev, March 12, March 31, October 16, November 4, 1877; June 29, July 6, July 12, 1878; Catherine Tiutchev letters to CPP, March 2, September 28, 1877; July 13, 1878.
5. Fedor M. Istomin, *Kratkii ocherk deiatel'nosti S. Peterburgskago slavianskago blagotvoritel'nago obshchestva za 25 let sushchestvovaniia, 1868–1893* (St.

Petersburg, 1893), 12-25; Olga Novikova, *Russia and England from 1876–1880* (London, 1880), 32; Sumner, *Russia and the Balkans*, 60-62; Petrovich, *The Emergence of Russian Panslavism, passim*, especially 129-53, 198-289.

6. Nicholas J. Danilevsky, *Rossiia i Evropa* (fourth edition, St. Petersburg, 1889), *passim*, especially 25-60, 73-85, 172-83, 283-323, 388-419, 426, 468, 472-510.

7. Rostislav A. Fadeev, *Mnenie o vostochnom voprose* (St. Petersburg, 1870); Benedict H. Sumner, "Russia and Pan-Slavism in the Eighteen-Seventies," *Transactions of the Royal Historical Society*, Fourth Series, XVIII (1935), 40-45. Fadeev's book was translated into English in 1871; a second edition of this translation was published in 1876, when many Englishmen were becoming alarmed about Russian policy in the Balkans.

8. Benedict H. Sumner, "Ignatyev at Constantinople, 1864–1874," *Slavonic Review*, XI (1933), 343-44, 569-71; Leonid I. Strakhovsky, "General Count N. P. Ignatiev and the Pan-Slav Movement," *Journal of Central European Affairs*, XVII (1957), 223-35.

9. Count Nicholas P. Ignatiev, "Zapiski grafa N. P. Ignatieva s primechaniiami A. A. Bashmakova," *Istoricheskii vestnik*, CXXXVI (1914), 827-28; MDLL, CPP letter to Catherine Tiutchev, June 29, 1876.

10. CPP, *Pis'ma k Aleksandru III*, I, 9-10, 34-40, 402, 405-406; CPP, *Novum Regnum*, 1015-16; V. S. Frank (editor), "Iz neizdannoi perepiski Imp. Aleksandra III i Nikolaia II s kn. V. P. Meshcherskim," *Sovremennyia zapiski*, LXX (1940), 184-88; MDLL, CPP letters to Catherine Tiutchev, May 25, June 19, 1876.

11. CPP, *Pis'ma k Aleksandru III*, I, 23-30; MDLL, CPP letters to Catherine Tiutchev, August 11, 1874; September 5, 1875; June 22, July 27, July 29, 1876.

12. Fedor Kovařík, *Zážitky a dojmy ruského Čecha za cárství* (Prague, 1932), 23-24, 44-47, 50-54, 136-37, 341; Jan Heidler (editor), *Příspévky k listáři Dra. Frant. Lad. Riegrá* (Prague, 1924–26), II, 61, 68, 84; Robert Kann, *The Multinational Empire* (New York, 1950), II, 136-38; CPP, *Pis'ma k Aleksandru III*, I, 68, 408-409; Ignatiev, "Zapiski," 827-28; MDLL, CPP letter to Catherine Tiutchev, October 22, 1877.

13. CPP (translator), Wenceslas Wratislaw, *Prikliucheniia cheshskago dvorianina Vratislava v Konstantinopole i v tiashkoi nevole u Turok, s avstriiskim posol'stvom 1591 g.* (St. Petersburg, 1877), (second edition, Moscow, 1904), *passim*, especially 27, 239-41; *Moskovskiia Vedomosti*, July 10, 1877; MDLL, CPP letters to Catherine Tiutchev, August 3, August 28, 1877; CPP letter to Olga Novikov, October 26, 1877; Catherine Tiutchev letter to CPP, August 12, 1877. These memoirs have been translated into German, French, Hungarian, and English, sometimes in full and sometimes considerably abbreviated.

14. CPP, *Pis'ma k Aleksandru III*, I, 45-58, 62-66; CPP, *Novum Regnum*, 1016-18; MDLL, CPP letters to Catherine Tiutchev, May 28, June 22, June 29, October 30, November 10, 1876; April 16, 1877; Catherine Tiutchev letters to CPP, July 14, November 20, 1876.

15. CPP, *Pis'ma k Aleksandru III*, I, 66, 97-98, 124-27; CPP, *Novum Regnum*,

1018; Aksakov, "Pis'ma k Pobedonostsevu," 163-67, 172-74; MDLL, CPP letters to Michael N. Katkov, April 26, May 26, June 21, 1877; January 8, February 14, February 21, 1878; CPP letters to Catherine Tiutchev, September 5, 1876; April 27, March 12, March 31, September 3, September 6, September 9, September 30, November 4, 1877; June 29, July 6, July 12, 1878; Catherine Tiutchev letters to CPP, September 12, 1876; January 15, March 2, March 23, April 27, June 13, September 28, 1877; July 13, 1878.

16. William E. Gladstone, *The Bulgarian Horrors and the Question of the East* (London, 1876); Robert W. Seton-Watson, *Disraeli, Gladstone, and the Eastern Question* (London, 1935), 51-101; David Harris, *Britain and the Bulgarian Horrors of 1876* (Chicago, 1939), 160-61, 182-86, 200-208, 231-33, 252-53, 303, 369; Paul Knaplund, *Gladstone's Foreign Policy* (New York, 1935), 71, 132-33; John Morley, *The Life of William Ewart Gladstone* (London, 1903), II, 551-54, 560; MDLL, CPP letter to Catherine Tiutchev, November 10, 1876.

17. CPP and Constantine N. Bestuzhev-Riumin (translators), William E. Gladstone, *Bolgarskie Uzhasy i Vostochnyi Vopros* (St. Petersburg, 1876), preface; Sergei F. Platonov, *Konstantin Nikolaevich Bestuzhev-Riumin* (St. Petersburg, 1897), 11, 13; Istomin, *Kratkii ocherk*, 27; *Pchela*, October 17, October 24, 1876; MDLL, CPP letter to Catherine Tiutchev, September 11, 1876; CPP letter to Olga Novikov, November 18, 1876.

18. William E. Gladstone, "Montenegro. A Sketch," *Nineteenth Century*, I (1877), 360-69; Pobedonostsev (translator), William E. Gladstone, "Chernogoriia. Stat'ia Gladstona," *Grazhdanin*, Number 32-33, November 22, 1877, 741-49; Sir Tollemache Sinclair, *A Defense of Russia and the Christians of Turkey* (London, 1877), preface, iv, xi-xxiv, appendix, 112-54; CPP, "Noveishaia angliiskaia literatura po vostochnomu voprosu," *Grazhdanin*, Number 1, January 8, 1877, 20-25; CPP, "Novaia kniga russkago avtora v anglii po vostochnomu voprosu," *Grazhdanin*, Number 38-40, December 14, 1877, 854; CPP, *Pis'ma k Aleksandru III*, I, 63-64, 407-408; Sergius Yakobson (editor), "Pis'ma K. P. Pobedonostseva k V. F. Putsykovichu," in Kruzhok liubitelei russkoi stariny, *Stat'i i materialy* (Berlin, 1932), 73-74; Yakobson (editor), "Pis'ma Iv. Serg. Aksakova k V. F. Putsykovichu," *Na chuzhoi storone*, V (1924), 153; MDLL, CPP letter to Catherine Tiutchev, November 10, 1876; CPP letters to Olga Novikov, January 28, March 2, October 11, November 15, 1877; Catherine Tiutchev letter to CPP, January 15, 1877.

19. CPP, *Pis'ma k Aleksandru III*, II, 292-94; MDLL, CPP letters to Catherine Tiutchev, November 26, 1875; February 25, November 4, 1877; February 23, 1878; Catherine Tiutchev letters to CPP, November 12, 1876; February 23, March 2, March 23, November 2, 1877; January 4, 1881.

20. William T. Stead (editor), *The M.P. for Russia. Reminiscences and Correspondence of Madame Olga Novikoff* (London, 1909), I, 7-12, 37-40, 184, 310; II, 6, 7, 59, 77, 123-24, 300-313; CPP, *Novum Regnum*, 179-80, 398, 874, 887; CPP, "Noveishaia angliiskaia literatura," 25; Iakov P. Polonskii, "Iz dnevnika Ia. P. Polonskago 1878 g.," *Na chuzhoi storone*, V (1924), 42; Joseph O.

Baylen, "Madame Olga Novikov: Defender of Imperial Russia, 1880–1900," *Historia*, I (1951), 133-56; Baylen, "Madame Olga Novikov, Propagandist," *American Slavic and East European Review*, X (1951), 256-58; MDLL, CPP letters to Catherine Tiutchev, June 29, July 6, July 10, July 14, July 15, November 10, November 18, November 22, November 27, 1876; February 5, 1877; December 14, 1878; March 6, 1881; January 6, 1882; Catherine Tiutchev letters to CPP, July 14, 1876; January 15, March 2, April 27, October 14, November 19, 1877; June 22, 1879; March 2, March 14, 1880; CPP letters to Olga Novikov, October 20, November 6, November 13, November 18, November 30, 1876; January 28, March 2, October 11, 1877.

21. Count Dmitrii A. Miliutin, *Dnevnik* (Moscow, 1947–50), III, 210, 236-37; CPP, *Pis'ma k Aleksandru III*, I, 127, 253-54, 273-74, 413.

22. CPP, *Pis'ma k Aleksandru III*, I, 73-118, 170, 193-96, 206-209, 236-37, 250-52, 416-18; CPP, *Novum Regnum*, 1017; Sumner, *Russia and the Balkans,* 334-37; Novikova, *Russia and England*, 52; MDLL, CPP letters to Catherine Tiutchev, July 2, July 23, August 3, August 28, August 29, August 30, September 9, September 24, October 22, November 4, November 28, 1877; February 19, 1878; CPP letter to Olga Novikov, May 27, 1878; Catherine Tiutchev letters to CPP, October 14, November 2, 1877; Manuscript Division, Institute of Russian Literature (Pushkinskii Dom), CPP letter to Ivan Aksakov, June 27, 1878. The diary of Count Valuev contains a very revealing critical comment upon Pobedonostsev's sudden transformation (Count Peter A. Valuev, *Dnevnik, 1877–1884* [Petrograd, 1919], 281).

23. CPP, *Pis'ma k Aleksandru III*, I, 49, 124-27; CPP, *Novum Regnum*, 562-63; Sumner, *Russia and the Balkans*, 554-55; Sergei D. Skazkin, *Konets avstro-russko-germanskogo soiuza* (Moscow, 1928), 185; General Hans von Schweinitz, *Denkwürdigkeiten des Botschafters General v. Schweinitz* (Berlin, 1927), II, 275.

24. General Hans von Schweinitz, *Briefwechsel des Botschafters General v. Schweinitz* (Berlin, 1928), 225-26, 287; von Schweinitz, *Denkwürdigkeiten*, II, 290, 301; Andrew Dickson White, *Autobiography* (New York, 1905), II, 55-71; CPP, *Pis'ma k Aleksandru III*, II, 88-89; CPP, *Novum Regnum*, 874; Jeremiah Curtin, *Memoirs* (Madison, Wis., 1940), 780.

25. CPP, *Pis'ma k Aleksandru III*, II, 123-26; CPP, *Novum Regnum*, 554, 576-79, 606-609, 617-18, 637-39, 653-55, 695-99, 705-709, 733-37, 757-58, 796-97, 844, 846, 1068-1069.

26. CPP, *Pis'ma k Aleksandru III*, II, 321-22; Count Sergei IU. Witte, *Vospominaniia* (Moscow, 1923), I, 80-85; "Perepiska Vitte i Pobedonostseva, 1895–1905," *KA*, XXX (1928), 89, 98; Vladimir M. Khvostov, "Problemy zakhvata Bosfora v 90-kh godakh XIX veka," *Istorik marksist*, XX (1930), 117, 127-218; William L. Langer, *The Diplomacy of Imperialism, 1890–1902* (New York, 1935), I, 330-49; Emile J. Dillon, *The Eclipse of Russia* (New York, 1918), 233-44.

27. M. IU. Poggenpol' (editor), *Ocherk vozniknoveniia i deiatel'nosti dobrovol'nago flota za vremia XXV-ti letniago ego sushchestvovaniia* (St. Peters-

burg, 1903), 3-32, 44, 252-71; CPP, *Pis'ma k Aleksandru III*, I, 131-33, 177-80, 200, 209-211, 281-84, 412; Sumner, *Russia and the Balkans*, 486; MDLL, CPP letters to Catherine Tiutchev, April 30, May 3, 1878.

28. Poggenpol', *Ocherk*, 41-43, 106, 251. The Russian Steam Navigation Company, founded under the same impulses at the end of the Crimean War, suffered from the same rapid decline of enthusiasm. See Werner E. Mosse, "Russia and the Levant, 1856–1862; Grand Duke Constantine Nicolaevich and the Russian Steam Navigation Company," *Journal of Modern History*, XXVI (1954), 39-48.

29. Leonid Grossman, "Dostoevskii i pravitel'stvennye krugi 1870-kh godov," *Literaturnoe nasledstvo*, Number 15 (1934), 137-38; MDLL, CPP letters to Catherine Tiutchev, August 30, 1878; May 8, 1879.

30. CPP, *Pis'ma k Aleksandru III*, I, 122-45, 154-55, 163-64, 171, 181-85, 188-92, 196, 202-206, 211, 217-31, 238, 264-65, 298-301, 312-14; Poggenpol', *Ocherk*, 46-62, 97; MDLL, CPP letters to Catherine Tiutchev, June 15, July 12, 1878; May 2, June 1, June 16, July 18, 1879; May 11, 1880.

31. Frederick T. Jane, *The Imperial Russian Navy. Its Past, Present, and Future* (London, 1899), 333-34; (London, 1904), 334; A. Bagurin, *Dobrovol'nyi flot i ego zadachi* (St. Petersburg, 1888), 3-37; CPP, *Pis'ma k Aleksandru III*, I, 146-53, 158-59, 163, 184, 253-54, 273-74, 281-83, 301-303; II, 13-23; CPP, *Novum Regnum*, 310-11; Miliutin, *Dnevnik*, III, 210, 236-37; MDLL, CPP letters to Catherine Tiutchev, November 11, 1878; January 31, 1880.

32. CPP, *Pis'ma k Aleksandru III*, I, 182, 244-45; MDLL, CPP letters to Catherine Tiutchev, June 29, October 1, October 6, November 27, December 14, December 21, December 25, December 30, 1878; April 6, April 14, June 16, July 8, 1879; Catherine Tiutchev letters to CPP, July 13, December 24, 1878.

33. CPP, *Pis'ma k Aleksandru III*, I, 244-45, 252, 265-66; MDLL, CPP letters to Catherine Tiutchev, August 27, December 17, December 18, December 29, 1879; January 31, February 1, 1880.

34. CPP, *Pis'ma k Aleksandru III*, I, 233-37, 240-42; Iurii V. Gotie, "Bor'ba pravitel'stvennykh gruppirovok i manifest 29 aprelia 1881 g.," *Istoricheskie zapiski*, II (1938), 253; Egor A. Peretts, *Dnevnik E. A. Perettsa, 1880–1883* (Moscow-Leningrad, 1927), 5; Miliutin, *Dnevnik*, IV, 41, 172; Mosse, "Russia and the Levant," 40-43.

35. Iurii V. Gotie, "K. P. Pobedonostsev i naslednik Aleksandr Aleksandrovich, 1865–1881," *Publichnaia biblioteka SSSR imeni V. I. Lenina. Sbornik*, II (1929), 124.

VII. *1881*

1. Peter A. Zaionchkovskii, *Krizis samoderzhaviia na rubezhe 1870–1880 godov* (Moscow, 1964), 151, 215-16, 232; MDLL, CPP letters to Catherine Tiutchev, April 6, August 27, 1879; February 12, February 25, March 1, March 13, July 23, August 9, August 18, 1880.

2. CPP, *Pis'ma Pobedonostseva k Aleksandru III* (Moscow, 1925–26), I, 23;

Baron Boris E. Nolde, "Sovet ministrov 8 marta 1881 goda. Razskaz grafa Loris-Melikova V. A. Bil'basovu," *Byloe*, Number 10-11 (1918), 189; Nicholas A. Konstantinov, *Ocherki po istorii srednei shkoly* (Moscow, 1947), 18-26; Alexandra V. Bogdanovich, *Journal de la générale A. V. Bogdanovitch* (Paris, 1926), 38; MDLL, CPP letters to Catherine Tiutchev, October 16, 1875; April 30, December 14, December 30, 1878; March 2, 1880.

3. Count Dmitrii A. Miliutin, *Dnevnik* (Moscow, 1947–50), III, 243-44; Count Peter A. Valuev, *Dnevnik, 1877–1884* (Petrograd, 1919), 86-89; Evgenii M. Feoktistov, *Vospominaniia. Za kulisami politiki i literatury, 1848–1896* (Leningrad, 1929), 219; Konstantinov, *Ocherki po istorii srednei shkoly*, 18-66; Iurii V. Gotie, "K. P. Pobedonostsev i naslednik Aleksandr Aleksandrovich, 1865–1881," *Publichnaia biblioteka SSSR imeni V. I. Lenina. Sbornik*, II (1929), 116-22; Hans Heilbronner, "The Administrations of Loris-Melikov and Ignatiev, 1880–1882," University of Michigan, Thesis for Doctorate in History, 1954, 145-52; MDLL, CPP letter to Anna Aksakov, October 20, 1868; CPP letters to Catherine Tiutchev, October 16, 1875; April 30, December 30, 1878; Central State Historical Archive, Leningrad, Count Peter A. Valuev note of December 2, 1875.

4. CPP, *Pis'ma k Aleksandru III*, I, 69-73, 111-13, 193-95, 288-99, 303-304; Alexander A. Polovtsev, "Dnevnik," *KA*, III (1923), 170; Valuev, *Dnevnik*, 113-14, 121, 128-219; A. N. Kulomzin (editor), *Istoricheskii obzor deiatel'nosti Komiteta Ministrov* (St. Petersburg, 1902–1903), IV, 465-66; Serge Konovalov (editor), "The Emperor Alexander II and Princess Ekaterina Dolgorukaya (Yurievskaya): Nine letters," *Oxford Slavonic Papers*, XI (1964), 94-100; Gotie, "Pobedonostsev i naslednik," 117-22; MDLL, CPP letters to Catherine Tiutchev, September 24, December 15, 1877; December 29, 1879; February 25, June 15, July 2, September 16, November 3, November 4, November 17, November 28, 1880; January 2, January 25, January 26, 1881.

5. CPP, *Pis'ma k Aleksandru III*, I, 84-87, 119-20, 276-77, 283-89; CPP, *K. P. Pobedonostsev i ego korrespondenty. Pis'ma i zapiski. Novum Regnum* (Moscow, 1923), 8-9; MDLL, CPP letters to Catherine Tiutchev, August 3, 1877; February 19, April 20, 1878; CPP letter to Michael N. Katkov, December 29, 1879.

6. Egor A. Peretts, *Dnevnik E. A. Perettsa, 1880–1883* (Moscow-Leningrad, 1927), 22; P. E. Shchegolev, "Iz istorii konstitutsionnykh veianii v 1879–1881 godakh," *Byloe*, Number 12 (1906), 264-76; Jacqueline de Proyart, "Le Haut-Procureur du Saint-Synode Constantin Pobedonoscev et le 'coup d'état' du 29 avril 1881," *Cahiers du monde russe et soviétique*, III (1962), 411; CPP, *Pis'ma k Aleksandru III*, I, 206-209, 302-303, 416-17.

7. Viscount Eugène de Vogüé, *Les Routes* (Paris, 1890), 137-39; MDLL, CPP letters to Catherine Tiutchev, November 3, 1880; January 2, January 7, January 15, February 4, 1881; Catherine Tiutchev letter to CPP, January 15, 1881; CPP letter to Katkov, January 9, 1881. The information concerning these February meetings was obtained from a thesis for the Candidate degree at Moscow State University completed in 1939 by S. L. Evenchik, who had access to the

archives of the Ministry of the Interior and who found there important data on these days (S. L. Evenchik, "Reaktsionnaia deiatel'nost' Pobedonostseva v 80-kk gg. XIX veka," chapter 3, 3).

8. Prince Nicholas V. Golitsyn, "Konstitutsiia grafa Loris-Melikova. Materialy dlia eia istorii," *Byloe*, Number 10-11 (1918), 125-86, especially 162-73; Maxim M. Kovalevskii, *Konstitutsiia grafa Loris-Melikova i ego chastnye pis'ma* (Berlin, 1904), 45-47; "Perepiska Alexandra III s gr. Loris-Melikovym, 1880–1881 gg.," *KA*, III (1925), 101-131; "Gr. Loris-Melikov i imp. Aleksandr II o polozhenii Rossii v sentiabre 1880 g.," *Byloe*, Number 4 (1917), 33-37; Evenchik, "Reaktsionnaia deiatel'nost' Pobedonostseva," chapter 3, 1.

9. MDLL, CPP letter to Catherine Tiutchev, March 3, 1881.

10. CPP, *Pis'ma k Aleksandru III*, I, 315-16.

11. Zaionchkovskii, *Krizis samoderzhaviia*, 304-305; MDLL, CPP letter to Catherine Tiutchev, March 3, 1881; Catherine Tiutchev letters to CPP, March 2, March 4, March 9, March 12, 1881; Captain Nicholas M. Baranov letter to CPP, March 2, 1881.

12. CPP, *Pis'ma k Aleksandru III*, I, 319-24; CPP, *Novum Regnum*, 48, 155-58; Miliutin, *Dnevnik*, IV, 43; de Vogüé, *Les Routes*, 156; Zaionchkovskii, *Krizis samoderzhaviia*, 339; MDLL, CPP letters to Catherine Tiutchev, January 2, January 15, February 4, March 3, March 4, 1881; Catherine Tiutchev letters to CPP, March 2, March 4, March 9, March 19, March 20, 1881; CPP letter to Michael N. Katkov, March 24, 1881.

13. CPP, *Pis'ma k Aleksandru III*, I, 317, 327-29; CPP, *Novum Regnum*, 226-29, 240, 251-55; 273-74; "Pis'ma K. P. Pobedonostseva k grafu N. P. Ignatievu," *Byloe*, Number 27-28 (1925), 66-69, 85; Peretts, *Dnevnik*, 29, 118, 128-29; MDLL, CPP letters to Catherine Tiutchev, March 6, March 12, March 24, April 18, 1881.

14. Prince Vladimir P. Meshcherskii, *Moi vospominaniia* (St. Petersburg, 1897–1912), I, 149-50, 207-209; CPP, *Pis'ma k Aleksandru III*, I, 314-16, 318, 324-26; CPP, *Novum Regnum*, 45-46; Gotie, "Pobedonostsev i naslednik," 127-32; MDLL, CPP letters to Catherine Tiutchev, March 3, March 6, March 11, March 31, November 2, December 9, 1881.

15. CPP, *Pis'ma k Aleksandru III*, I, 275-76, 343-44, 356-78; CPP, *Novum Regnum*, 48.

16. "Iz dnevnika odnogo gosudarstvennago deiatelia. Zasedanie Gosudarstvennago soveta 8 marta 1881 g.," *Byloe*, Number 1 (1906), 189-94; Miliutin, *Dnevnik*, IV, 32-37; Peretts, *Dnevnik*, 39-45; Valuev, *Dnevnik*, 152-54; Zaionchkovskii, *Krizis samoderzhaviia*, 331-32; MDLL, CPP letter to Catherine Tiutchev, March 11, 1881; CPP letter to Michael N. Katkov, April 18, 1881.

17. CPP, *Pis'ma k Aleksandru III*, I, 324, 327-29; Miliutin, *Dnevnik*, IV, 40; MDLL, CPP letters to Catherine Tiutchev, March 29, April 18, 1881; CPP letter to Katkov, April 18, 1881.

18. CPP, *Pis'ma k Aleksandru III*, I, 325; Miliutin, *Dnevnik*, IV, 55; MDLL, CPP letter to Catherine Tiutchev, April 18, 1881.

19. CPP, *Pis'ma k Aleksandru III*, I, 327-29; Miliutin, *Dnevnik*, IV, 57-59;

Peretts, *Dnevnik*, 63-64; MDLL, CPP letter to Catherine Tiutchev, April 27, 1881.

20. CPP, *Pis'ma k Aleksandru III*, I, 327-30.

21. Ibid., 331-33; Zaionchkovskii, *Krizis samoderzhaviia*, 371; MDLL, CPP letter to Catherine Tiutchev, April 27, 1881.

22. CPP, *Pis'ma k Aleksandru III*, I, 337-38; CPP, *Novum Regnum*, 51-52, 63; Miliutin, *Dnevnik*, IV, 61-63, 72; MDLL, CPP letters to Catherine Tiutchev, April 29, May 1, 1881; CPP letter to Katkov, May 19, 1881.

23. CPP, "Pis'mo K. P. Pobedonostseva," *Istoricheskii vestnik*, LXV (1896), 553-54; K. Medvedskii, "Piatidesiatiletie sluzhebnoi deiatel'nosti K. P. Pobedonostseva," *Russkii vestnik*, CCXLV (1896), 280-81; General Hans von Schweinitz, *Denkwürdigkeiten des Botschafters General v. Schweinitz* (Berlin, 1927), II, 395-96; Miliutin, *Dnevnik*, IV, 65-67; Meshcherskii, *Vospominaniia*, III, 65-66; Polovtsev, "Dnevnik," 84-85; Valuev, *Dnevnik*, 164; Feoktistov, *Vospominaniia*, 198; MDLL, CPP letters to Catherine Tiutchev, April 29, May 1, 1881. The thesis that Katkov was a collaborator of Pobedonostsev in 1881 was accepted by Sergei D. Skazkin, in his excellent *Konets avstro-russko-germanskogo soiuza* (Moscow, 1928), 90-92. Skazkin does point out that Bismarck's views may have played some role in the crisis, because he frequently told the Russian ambassador in Berlin that he believed the autocratic government should regain its prestige and authority before considering reforms. "Russia is a horse which must be made to feel today the bridle of its master."

24. CPP, *Pis'ma k Aleksandru III*, I, 347-49; Gotie, "Pobedonostsev i naslednik," 134; MDLL, CPP letters to Catherine Tiutchev, June 3, July 16, July 22, July 23, August 23, August 25, December 9, 1881; February 15, February 22, 1882; Catherine Tiutchev letters to CPP, July 7, July 20, 1881.

25. CPP, *Pis'ma k Aleksandru III*, I, 350-51; CPP, *Novum Regnum*, 78-79, 95, 99-102; Valuev, *Dnevnik*, 213; Miliutin, *Dnevnik*, IV, 41; MDLL, CPP letters to Catherine Tiutchev, March 3, March 31, July 22, August 15, August 25, August 26, 1881; February 15, 1882; Catherine Tiutchev letters to CPP, March 2, March 4, March 9, March 12, March 29, August 21, 1881; February 5, 1882; Captain Baranov letters to CPP, March 2, May 1, June 16, June 20, July 5, August 2, 1881; Archives, University of California, Berkeley, Count Vladimir N. Lamzdorf letter to Nicholas K. Giers, November 28, 1882.

26. Boris N. Chicherin, *Vospominaniia* (Moscow, 1929–34), IV, 130-32, 220-23; Olga A. Novikova, *Russia and England from 1876–1880* (London, 1880), 231-32, 244-51; William T. Stead (editor), *The M. P. for Russia. Reminiscences and Correspondence of Madame Olga Novikoff* (London, 1909), II, 300-306; "Perepiska P. D. Golokhvastova s I. S. Aksakovym o zemskom sobore," *RA*, I (1913), 93-111; II (1913), 181-204; Shchegolev, "Iz istorii konstitutsionnykh veianii," 261-84; CPP, *Pis'ma k Aleksandru III*, I, 350-51, 379-81, 426; CPP, *Novum Regnum*, 104-120, 132-50, 179-80, 247, 261-63, 274-75, 392, 399, 410; Peretts, *Dnevnik*, 137-38; Miliutin, *Dnevnik*, IV, 139; Meshcherskii, *Vospominaniia*, III, 40-42, 336, 337; Valuev, *Dnevnik*, 199-200; Feoktistov, *Vospo-*

minaniia, 206-212; von Schweinitz, *Denkwürdigkeiten*, II, 193, 198-200; Zaionch-kovskii, *Krizis samoderzhaviia*, 41, 280-83, 411-12, 463-71; MDLL, CPP letters to Catherine Tiutchev, March 6, December 20, December 22, 1881; Catherine Tiutchev letters to CPP, March 12, 1881; January 7, 1882. The Manuscript Division of the Lenin Library has two copies of Ignatiev's draft manifesto in Pobedonostsev's handwriting.

VIII. *Director General of the Synod*

1. John S. Curtiss, *Church and State in Russia. The Last Years of the Empire, 1900–1917* (New York, 1940), 35-39, 123-24, 130; Timofei V. Barsov, *Sinodal'nyia uchrezhdeniia prezhniago vremeni* (St. Petersburg, 1897), 20-21.

2. CPP, *Pis'ma Pobedonostseva k Aleksandru III* (Moscow, 1925–26), II, 34-36, 249-50, 263-66, 328-29; Count Sergei IU. Witte, *Vospominaniia* (Moscow, 1960), II, 238, 269-71, 273; Alexander A. Polovtsev, "Dnevnik," *KA*, III (1923), 157, 170; Curtiss, *Church and State*, 41; MDLL, CPP letter to Catherine Tiutchev, February 8, 1882.

3. *Istoriia pravitel'stvuiushchago Senata za dvesti let, 1711–1911 g.* (St. Petersburg, 1911), IV, 449; "Perepiska Vitte i Pobedonostseva, 1895–1905," *KA*, XXX (1928), 100; Count Peter A. Valuev, *Dnevnik, 1877–1884* (Petrograd, 1919), 113-14, 121; Archbishop Savva of Tver, *Khronika moei zhizni* (Sergiev Posad, 1897–1911), VIII, 303, 786-90; Thomas Darlington, *Education in Russia* (London, 1909), 219.

4. "Zapiski prisutstvuiushchago v Sviateishem pravitel'stvuiushchem vserossiiskom sinode (Arkhiepiskopa Khersonskago Nikanora)," *RA*, III (1906), 5-7; Curtiss, *Church and State*, 44-72.

5. Curtiss, *Church and State*, 72-78; *Istoricheskaia perepiska o sud'bakh pravoslavnoi tserkvi* (Moscow, 1912), 32-47. For examples of the Church's efforts to express religious and patriotic feeling and to organize demonstrations of popular support for the monarch and the monarchy, see CPP, *Vsepoddanneishii otchët ober-prokurora Sviateishago sinoda K. Pobedonostseva po vedomstvu Pravoslavnago Ispovedaniia za 1888–1889* (St. Petersburg, 1891), 1-3; CPP, *Vsepoddanneishii otchët za 1890–1891* (St. Petersburg, 1893), 1-2.

6. Sergei A. Petrovskii (editor), "Perepiska K. P. Pobedonostseva s preosviashchennym Nikanorom episkopom Ufimskim," *RA*, I (1915), 463-64; II (1915), 351-52, 374-75; Boris B. Glinskii, "Konstantin Petrovich Pobedonostsev. Materialy dlia biografii," *Istoricheskii vestnik*, CVIII (1907), 263-64; "Kievskii sobor 1884 goda. Poslanie k vysokopreosviashchennomu Pavlu, eksarkhu Gruzii. Zapiski arkhiepiskopa Nikanora," *RA*, III (1908), 86-87; Vladimir S. Markov, *K istorii raskola-staroobriadchestva vtoroi poloviny XIX stoletiia. Perepiska prof. N. I. Subbotina* (Moscow, 1915), 329-53; MDLL, CPP letters to Catherine Tiutchev, July 23, September 16, 1880; June 12, June 13, July 22, November 24, 1881; Catherine Tiutchev letter to CPP, February 7, 1882.

7. CPP, *Vsepoddanneishii otchët za 1888–1889*, 7-8.

8. Serge Bolshakoff, *Russian Nonconformity* (Philadelphia, 1950), 15; Curtiss, *Church and State*, 136-38.

9. CPP, *Izvlechenie iz vsepoddanneishago otchëta ober-prokurora Sviateishago sinoda K. Pobedonostseva po vedomstvu Pravoslavnago Ispovedaniia za 1881* (St. Petersburg, 1883), 46-47; CPP, *Vsepoddanneishii otchët za 1894–1895* (St. Petersburg, 1898), 86; CPP, *Vsepoddanneishii otchët za 1903–1904* (St. Petersburg, 1909), 130; Curtiss, *Church and State*, 136-38. The statistics presented in the Holy Synod reports must be used with caution. Thus, the figures given in the annual report for 1881 differ somewhat from those for 1881 used in the volume published to review the work of the Orthodox Church during the reign of Alexander III, from 1881 to 1894. (Russia. Sviateishii pravitel'stvuiushchii sinod, *Obzor deiatel'nosti vedomstva Pravoslavnago Ispovedaniia za vremia tsarstvovaniia Imperatora Aleksandra III* [St. Petersburg, 1901], 7-8; CPP, *Izvlechenie iz vsepoddanneishago otchëta za 1881*, 46-47.)

10. "Pis'ma K. P. Pobedonostseva k S. D. Voitu," *RA*, I (1917), 180; Petrovskii, "Perepiska Pobedonostseva s Nikanorom," II, 251, 253; MDLL, CPP letters to Anna Tiutchev, September 26, November 8, 1864; CPP letters to Catherine Tiutchev, October 18, 1866; November 11, 1878; January 7, 1881.

11. Barsov, *Sinodal'nyia uchrezhdeniia prezhniago vremeni*, 20-21; Petrovskii, "Perepiska Pobedonostseva s Nikanorom," III, 365-68; "Kievskii sobor 1884 goda," II, 560; III, 88; "Zapiski arkhiepiskopa Khersonskago Nikanora," 91; MDLL, CPP letters to Catherine Tiutchev, July 23, September 2, September 16, November 17, December 16, 1880; September 20, 1881; Catherine Tiutchev letter to CPP, September 7, 1880.

12. Savva, *Khronika moei zhizni*, VII and VIII, *passim*; Petrovskii, "Perepiska Pobedonostseva s Nikanorom," I (1915), 458-73; II, 68-111, 244-56, 335-84, 501-528; III, 81-108, 249-68, *passim*; Sergei A. Petrovskii (editor), "Pis'ma K. P. Pobedonostseva preosviashchennomu Illarionu, arkhiepiskopu Poltavskomu," *RA*, LIV (1916), 129-71, 360-80, *passim*; Vladimir Parkhomenko, "Dopolnenie k stat'e, 'Pis'ma K. P. Pobedonostseva preosviashchennomu Illarionu, arkhiepiskopu Poltavskomu,'" *RA*, III (1916), 281-85; "Iz zapisok arkhiepiskopa Nikanora," *RA*, I (1909), 209-276; II, (1909), 19-77; "Zapiski arkhiepiskopa Khersonskago Nikanora," 189-90; *38 Pisem byvshago Ober-Prokurora Sviateishago sinoda K. P. Pobedonostseva k vysokopreosviashchenneishemu Makariiu, arkhiepiskopu Tomskomu* (Tomsk, 1910), 1-38; A. Izmailov, "Novosti istorii," *Istoricheskii vestnik*, CXLI (1915), 629-36; CXLII (1915), 668-69; "Kniaz'ia tserkvi. Iz dnevnika A. N. Lvova," *KA*, XXXIX (1930), 101-103, 122-23; MDLL, CPP letters to Catherine Tiutchev, May 20, June 15, June 19, August 4, September 24, September 28, October 10, October 23, November 17, 1880; June 3, June 12, July 22, September 12, September 20, October 17, November 24, 1881; Catherine Tiutchev letter to CPP, February 7, 1882.

13. CPP, "S'ezd iuristov v Moskve," *Grazhdanin*, Number 44, October 29, 1873, 1173; Leonid Grossman, "Dostoevskii i pravitel'stvennye krugi 1870-kh godov," *Literaturnoe nasledstvo*, Number 15 (1934), 127-28; Petrovskii, "Pis'ma

Pobedonostseva Illarionu," 165-67; S. Mel'gunov (editor), "K. P. Pobedonostsev v dni pervoi revoliutsii. Neizdannyia pis'ma k S. D. Voitu," *Na chuzhoi storone,* VIII (1924), 179; Markov, *K istorii raskola-staroobriadchestva,* 308, footnote; Savva, *Khronika moei zhizni,* VIII, 303; Alexandra V. Bogdanovich, *Journal de la générale A. V. Bogdanovitch* (Paris, 1926), 69, 93-94, 100-108; "Kniaz'ia tserkvi," XXXIX, 101-103, 108-117, 121, 129; XL, 106-107, 113-16, 123.

14. Russia. Sviateishii pravitel'stvuiushchii sinod, *Obzor deiatel'nosti vedomstva Pravoslavnago Ispovedaniia za vremia Aleksandra III,* 7-8; CPP, *Vsepoddanneishii otchët za 1884–1885* (St. Petersburg, 1887), 206. In his report to the tsar for 1888–89, Pobedonostsev described the main sources of Orthodox strength and the main domestic hazards in this way: "In this huge mass of the Orthodox *narod,* the bishoprics in the interior of Russia with all the Great Russian and part of the Little Russian population form the main strength of both the Church and the state. After them follow the Little Russians and White Russians of the western *guberniias,* both exposed heavily to foreign influence, especially Latin influence. On the border areas of the state, the Orthodox are surrounded by millions of other nationalities and of other religions. They are frequently exposed to the influence of these millions of others and are lost in their mass, to the harm of their nationality and of their faith." (CPP, *Vsepoddanneishii otchët za 1888–1889,* 8.)

15. CPP, *K. P. Pobedonostsev i ego korrespondenty. Pis'ma i zapiski. Novum Regnum* (Moscow, 1923), 779-81; CPP, *Pis'ma k Aleksandru III,* I, 23; Petrovskii, "Perepiska Pobedonostseva s Nikanorom," I, 463-64; II, 345-46, 351-52; III, 87-89, 101; "Pis'ma K. P. Pobedonostseva k E. M. Feoktistovu," *Literaturnoe nasledstvo,* Numbers 22-24 (1935), 506; Grossman, "Dostoevskii i pravitel'stvennye krugi," 144-45; "Kievskii sobor 1884 goda," 88-89; Savva, *Khronika moei zhizni,* VIII, 507; IX, 202-204, 294-97; Glinskii, "Pobedonostsev," 263-64; Curtiss, *Church and State,* 62-70, 80-86; MDLL, CPP letters to Catherine Tiutchev, June 13, July 22, 1881.

16. CPP, *Pis'ma k Aleksandru III,* II, 69-70; Petrovskii, "Perepiska Pobedonostseva s Nikanorom," 468-69; CPP, *Vsepoddanneishii otchët za 1883* (St. Petersburg, 1885), 282-88, 299-302; CPP, *Vsepoddanneishii otchët za 1888–1889,* 52-53; *Obzor deiatel'nosti vedomstva Pravoslavnago Ispovedaniia za vremia Aleksandra III,* 7, 387-411; Rose J. Birkbeck, *Life and Letters of W. J. Birkbeck* (London, 1922), 166.

17. CPP, *Pis'ma k Aleksandru III,* I, 340-41; CPP, *Vsepoddanneishii otchët za 1880* (St. Petersburg, 1882), 125-28; CPP, *Vsepoddanneishii otchët za 1883,* 319-56; Markov, *K istorii raskola-staroobriadchestva,* 340-41; Savva, *Khronika moei zhizni,* VII, 925-26; IX, 32-36, 62.

18. CPP, *Novum Regnum,* 968-69; CPP, *Vsepoddanneishii otchët za 1885* (St. Petersburg, 1887), 229; Russia. Sviateishii pravitel'stvuiushchii sinod, *Tsirkuliarnye ukazy Sviateishago pravitel'stvuiushchago sinoda, 1867–1900 gg.* (St. Petersburg, 1901), 426-31; Curtiss, *Church and State,* 123-24.

19. CPP, *Vsepoddanneishii otchët za 1890–1891*, 172; CPP, *Vsepoddanneishii otchët za 1901* (St. Petersburg, 1904), 198-200.

20. CPP, *Vsepoddanneishii otchët za 1885*, 86-87; CPP, . . . *za 1887* (St. Petersburg, 1889), 15, 50-52; CPP, . . . *za 1888–1889*, 32-33; CPP, . . . *za 1890–1891*, 188-97; CPP, . . . *za 1900* (St. Petersburg, 1903), 210-12; CPP, . . . *za 1902* (St. Petersburg, 1905), 157-66; Alexander A. Polovtsov, *Dnevnik gosudarstvennogo sekretaria A. A. Polovtsova* (Moscow, 1966), I, 49-50; Markov, *K istorii raskola-staroobriadchestva*, 89; "Vnutrennee obozrenie," *Vestnik Evropy*, CLXVII-CLXVIII (1894), 388-403.

21. Markov, *K istorii raskola-staroobriadchestva, passim*; MDLL, Catherine Tiutchev letters to CPP, April 5, December 12, 1881; January 16, February 3, 1882.

22. CPP, *Kurs grazhdanskago prava* (second edition, St. Petersburg, 1875), II, 469-74, 564; CPP, *Novum Regnum*, 580-82, 1062; Markov, *K istorii raskola-staroobriadchestva*, 13, 188-91, 194-201, 291-92, 301-306, 559-60, 598-602, 655-732; "Perepiska Vitte i Pobedonostseva," 99-100; V. I. Iasevich-Borodaevskaia (editor), *Materialy k vysochaishemu ukazu 12 dekabria 1904 g.* (St. Petersburg, n.d.), III, 205-224; Curtiss, *Church and State*, 141-42.

23. CPP, *Novum Regnum*, 263-64; Markov, *K istorii raskola-staroobriadchestva*, 110-11, 283-85, 295, 298-300, 311-13, 321; Egor A. Peretts, *Dnevnik E. A. Perettsa, 1880–1883* (Moscow-Leningrad, 1927), 144-45; Curtiss, *Church and State*, 28, 42, 132-36.

24. CPP, *Vsepoddanneishii otchët za 1883*, 209-271, especially 209-219; "Pis'ma Pobedonostseva k Feoktistovu," 529; Polovtsev, *Dnevnik*, 109; Curtiss, *Church and State*, 135-60; Iasevich-Borodaevskaia, *Materialy*, III, 205-224; Markov, *K istorii raskola-staroobriadchestva*, 191-201, 222-23, 296-98, 306-308, 352-54, 397-402, 450, 467-69, 478, 485, 528-30, 547-50, 733-80.

25. CPP, *Pis'ma k Aleksandru III*, I, 44; "Pis'ma Pobedonostseva k Feoktistovu," 534, 537; Pierre Kovalewski, *N. S. Leskov. Peintre méconnu de la vie nationale russe* (Paris, 1925), 65-70, 128-62; Ivan I. Tkhorzhevskii, *Russkaia literatura* (Paris, 1946), I, 301-305; Constantine C. Arseniev, *Svoboda sovesti i veroterpimost'* (St. Petersburg, 1905), 86-141; Markov, *K istorii raskola-staroobriadchestva*, 20, 223-25, 228, 232, 240-44, 250-68.

26. "Pis'ma K. P. Pobedonostseva k grafu N. P. Ignatievu," *Byloe*, Number 27-28 (1925), 66-67; Curtiss, *Church and State*, 170.

27. CPP, *Pis'ma k Aleksandru III*, II, 54; Petrovskii, "Pis'ma Pobedonostseva Illarionu," 153; Petrovskii, "Perepiska Pobedonostseva s Nikanorom," 352, 361-65, 373-74, 520-27; "Kievskii sobor 1884 goda," II, 555-56, 562-66; III, 90-107; Anatole F. Koni, *Na zhiznennom puti* (Moscow-Riga, 1912–29), III, 465-88; Curtiss, *Church and State*, 164-70; Bolshakoff, *Russian Nonconformity*, 113-18; MDLL, CPP letter to Olga Novikov, January 13, 1892.

28. P. Tverskoi, "Iz delovoi perepiski s K. P. Pobedonostsevym," *Vestnik Evropy*, XII (1907), 651-68; Ernest J. Simmons, *Leo Tolstoy* (Boston, 1946), 515-16, 530-32; Curtiss, *Church and State*, 161-65.

29. CPP, *Pis'ma k Aleksandru III*, I, 284-85; II, 53-54, 158-60; "Pis'ma Pobe-donostseva k Ignatievu," 52, 70, 76; Petrovskii, "Perepiska Pobedonostseva s Nikanorom," II, 360; Valuev, *Dnevnik*, 93-94; William T. Stead, *Truth about Russia* (London, 1889), 324-78; "Kievskii sobor 1884 goda," 554-55; Fedor M. Dostoevsky, *Sobranie sochinenii* (Paris, 1945–46), IV, 256-60; V, 137-39; VI, 11-15; Bolshakoff, *Russian Nonconformity*, 115-16; MDLL, CPP letters to Catherine Tiutchev, March 1, 1874; July 22, 1881; CPP letters to Olga Novikov, January 5, 1889; December 21, 1890; November 22, 1891; October 23, 1892. Pobedonostsev was equally resolute against the Salvation Army and the Quakers.

30. CPP, *Vsepoddanneishii otchët za 1880*, 39-74; CPP, . . . *za 1885*, 105-114; CPP, . . . *za 1886* (St. Petersburg, 1888), 74-94; CPP, . . . *za 1887*, 65-73; CPP, . . . *za 1888–1889*, 79-106, 122-23; CPP, . . . *za 1890–1891*, 210-19; CPP, . . . *za 1899* (St. Petersburg, 1902), 140; Markov, *K istorii raskola-staroobriadchestva*, 416-23, 461, 484-85, 642-45.

31. CPP, *Vsepoddanneishii otchët za 1885*, 226; CPP, . . . *za 1886*, 143-46; Markov, *K istorii raskola-staroobriadchestva*, 93-94, 134-35, 189-91, 201-206, 210-14, 225-30, 234-36, 240-44, 265-67, 272-75, 281-82, 294, 298-300, 309-314, 334-35, 358-60, 374, 423-38, 444-46, 452, 466, 478-84, 516-27, 533-35, 539-45, 577-78, 580-88, 608-619, 615, 626-30.

32. Markov, *K istorii raskola-staroobriadchestva*, 28, 78-85, 183-85, 209, 247-48, 309-312, 317-18, 337-45, 352-60, 382, 386-87, 404-405, 412-14, 441, 465, 486-98, 516, 522, 606, 615-16, 649.

33. CPP, *Izvlechenie iz vsepoddanneishago otchëta za 1881*, 8-11, 62-63; CPP, *Vsepoddanneishii otchët za 1879* (St. Petersburg, 1882), 11-21, 59-61; CPP, . . . *za 1888–1889*, 59-60; CPP, . . . *za 1899*, 49-78; "Kniaz'ia tserkvi," 143, fn.

34. CPP, *Pis'ma k Aleksandru III*, II, 294-302; CPP, *Novum Regnum*, 947-50; CPP, *Vsepoddanneishii otchët za 1880*, 4-37, 62-63; CPP, . . . *za 1883*, 160, 179-81; CPP, . . . *za 1885*, 49-51; appendix, 63-65; CPP, . . . *za 1886*, 94-127; CPP, . . . *za 1887*, 67-69; CPP, . . . *za 1888–1889*, 83-85, 163-65; CPP, . . . *za 1890–1891*, appendix, 65-67, 185-87; CPP, . . . *za 1894–1895*, appendix, 46-47, 124; "Kniaz'ia tserkvi," 116, 143-44.

35. Prince Sergei V. Shakhovskoi, *Iz arkhiva Kniazia S. V. Shakhovskogo. Materialy dlia istorii nedavniago proshlago Pribaltiiskoi okrainy, 1885–1894 gg.* (St. Petersburg, 1909–1910), I, 3-324; II, 3-311; Leonid V. Strakhovsky, "Constitutional Aspects of the Imperial Russian Government's Policy toward National Minorities," *Journal of Modern History*, XIII (1941), 471-72, 482; CPP, *Vsepoddanneishii otchët za 1890–1891*, 166.

36. Shakhovskoi, *Iz arkhiva*, I, 126-28; III, v-vii, xlvi-li, 5-7, 26-39, 44-47, 85-86, 139-42, 162-70; CPP, *Pis'ma k Aleksandru III*, II, 257-59.

37. CPP, *Pis'ma k Aleksandru III*, II, 51-53, 58-59, 119-20, 162-67; CPP, *Novum Regnum*, 622-24, 658, 836, 921-23, 1070, 1074; CPP, *Kurs grazhdanskago prava* (fourth edition, Moscow, 1896), II, 180-81; CPP, *Vsepoddanneishii otchët za 1880*, 87-90; CPP, . . . *za 1883*, 100-110; CPP, . . . *za 1886*, 24; CPP, . . . *za 1888–1889*, 192-96; Russia. Sviateishii pravitel'stvuiushchii Sinod, *Obzor deiatel'-*

nosti vedomstva Pravoslavnago Ispovedaniia za vremia Aleksandra III, 131, 148; General Hans von Schweinitz, *Denkwürdigkeiten des Botschafters General v. Schweinitz* (Berlin, 1927), II, 388; Stead, *Truth about Russia*, 327.

38. CPP, *Pis'ma k Aleksandru III*, II, 51-53, 58-59; CPP, *Novum Regnum*, 921-23; CPP, *Vsepoddanneishii otchët za 1896–1897* (St. Petersburg, 1899), 79; Alexander Tobien, *Die livlaendische Ritterschaft in ihrem Verhältnis zum Zarismus und russischen Nationalismus* (Riga, 1925–30), I, 86-102, 195, 206; *Pravoslavnaia tserkov' v Finlandii, napechatano po rasporiazheniiu g. ober-prokurora Sviateishago sinoda* (St. Petersburg, 1893), 1-166, *passim*.

39. CPP, *Pis'ma k Aleksandru III*, II, 137-38; CPP, *Novum Regnum*, 861-65, 1038, 1088; CPP, *Vsepoddanneishii otchët za 1888–1889*, 464-67; CPP, *A Monsieur Edouard Naville, Président du comité central suisse de l'Alliance évangélique* (St. Petersburg, 1888); Evangelical Alliance, *Rapport présenté aux branches de l'Alliance évangélique par le comité de Genève, sur des démarches faites au près de S. M. l'Empereur de Russie rélativement à la liberté religieuse dans l'empire russe de 1887 à 1889* (Geneva, 1889), 1-71; Friedrich Dukmeyer, *Aus Anlass des offenen Sendschreibens an den Oberprokureur des Synods K. Pobedonoszeff, von H. Dalton und des offenen Briefes an Pastor Dalton von A. D.* (St. Petersburg, 1889); L. von Wurstemberger, *Die Gewissensfreiheit in den Ostsee-Provinzen Russlands* (Leipzig, 1872), foreword; MDLL, CPP letters to Olga Novikov, December 13, 1887; November 26, 1889; January 7, 1890.

40. Hermann Dalton, *Lebenserinnerungen* (Berlin, 1906–1908), III, 40-41, 108-124, 128-60; Dalton, *Otkrytoe poslanie ober-prokuroru pravitel'stvuiushchago sinoda* (Leipzig, 1890), *passim*; Dalton, *Der Stundismus in Russland* (Gütersloh, 1896), 47-58; CPP, *Ein herzliches Wort an unsere Jugend* (Bremen, 1882), preface; W. Loeoeralt, *Baltenhetze. Die Verfolgung von Glauben, Sprache und Recht in den Ostseeprovinzen Russlands* (Leipzig, 1890), 1-49; Tobien, *Dit livlaendische Ritterschaft*, I, 206.

41. CPP, *Pis'ma k Aleksandru III*, II, 333-34; Bogdanovich, *Journal*, 43; Dalton, *Lebenserinnerungen*, III, 154-55, 158-60; Bernhard H. Schwertfeger (editor), *Zur europäischen Politik. Unveröffentlichte [Belgische] Dokumente* (Berlin, 1919), V, 33; *London Times*, November 16, 1889.

42. CPP, *Kurs grazhdanskago prava* (third edition, St. Petersburg, 1883), I, 707, 712-13; (fourth edition, St. Petersburg, 1896), I, 33-34, 599, 612-13; (second edition, St. Petersburg, 1875), II, 524-31, 601; (fourth edition, St. Petersburg, 1896), II, 65-66; Count Vladimir N. Lamzdorf, *Dnevnik V. N. Lamzdorfa, 1886–1890* (Moscow, 1926), 36; F. V. Volkhovsky, "The Philosophy of Reaction," *Free Russia*, X (1899), 90-91; MDLL, CPP letter to Catherine Tiutchev, October 7, 1879; Catherine Tiutchev letter to CPP, March 25, 1878.

43. CPP, *Pis'ma k Aleksandru III*, II, 26-27, 65-68; CPP, *Novum Regnum*, 239, 314-15; CPP, *Vsepoddanneishii otchët za 1890–1891*, 133-35, 324-30; CPP, . . . *za 1899*, 44-46; CPP, . . . *za 1902*, 100-106; Petrovskii, "Perepiska Pobedonostseva s Nikanorum," 470-72; "Zapiski arkhiepiskopa Khersonskago Nikanora," 174-76; "Pis'ma Pobedonostseva k Ignatievu," 72; *Obzor deiatel'nosti vedomstva*

Pravoslavnago Ispovedaniia za vremia Aleksandra III, 55-64; A. N. Kulomzin (editor), *Istoricheskii obzor deiatel'nosti Komiteta Ministrov. K stoletiiu Komiteta Ministrov, 1802–1902* (St. Petersburg, 1902–1903), IV, 107-110; Paul Miliukov, Charles Seignebos, and Louis Eisenman, *Histoire de Russie* (Paris, 1932–33), II, 913.

44. CPP, *Pis'ma k Aleksandru III*, II, 191-92; Iosif Sidorskii, "Efimi Mikhailovich Kryzhanovskii v 1865–1888 gg.," *Russkaia starina*, LXVI (1890), 717-26; Efimi M. Kryzhanovskii, *Russkoe zabuzh'e* (St. Petersburg, 1911), preface, xxviii-xlv; Petrovskii, "Perepiska Pobedonostseva s Nikanorom," III, 264-65.

45. Cyril E. Black, *The Establishment of Constitutional Government in Bulgaria* (Princeton, 1943), 52-54; Bolshakoff, *Russian Nonconformity*, 138-39; Curtiss, *Church and State*, 178-79; Kryzhanovskii, *Russkoe zabuzh'e*, iii-viii; MDLL, CPP letters to Catherine Tiutchev, January 4, March 25, 1875; February 18, 1878; October 4, 1881.

46. CPP, *Pis'ma k Aleksandru III*, I, 354-56; CPP, *Vsepoddanneishii otchët za 1880*, 76-86; "Pis'ma Pobedonostseva k Ignatievu," 63, 73-74; MDLL, CPP letters to Catherine Tiutchev, January 15, October 4, October 17, 1881; January 10, 1882.

47. CPP, *Kurs grazhdanskago prava* (fourth edition, St. Petersburg, 1896), II, 65-66; CPP, *Vsepoddanneishii otchët za 1883*, 88-100; CPP, . . . *za 1885*, 155-59; CPP, . . . *za 1888–1889*, 138-42, 169-72, 186-92; CPP, . . . *za 1894–1895*, 153-67; CPP, . . . *za 1896–1897*, 70-71; Evlogii, Metropolitan of Western Europe, *Put' moei zhizni. Vospominaniia* (Paris, 1947), 90-126; Koni, *Na zhiznennom puti*, I, 590-93; Koni, "Iz zametok i vospominanii sudebnago deiatelia," *Russkaia starina*, CXXXVII (1909), 249-51; CXL (1909), 239-40; "Kniaz'ia tserkvi," *KA*, XXXIX, 123; Birkbeck, *Life*, 280; Miliukov, Seignebos, and Eisenman, *Histoire*, III, 1161.

48. CPP, *Pis'ma k Aleksandru III*, II, 115-17; CPP, *Novum Regnum*, 515-17, 612-17, 980, 993-94; CPP, *Vsepoddanneishii otchët za 1892–1893* (St. Petersburg, 1895), 110-19; "Zapiski arkhiepiskopa Khersonskago Nikanora," 23-24, 32-36; N. Durnovo, *Nechto o russkoi tserkvi v ober-prokurorstve K. P. Pobedonostseva* (Leipzig, 1887), *passim*.

49. CPP, *Vsepoddanneishii otchët za 1883*, 124-57; Russia. Ministerstvo vnutrennykh del, *Obshchii obzor Ministerstva vnutrennykh del za vremia tsarstvovaniia Aleksandra III* (St. Petersburg, 1901), 201-213, 226-28, 229-33.

50. Peter V. Znamenskii, *Istoriia Kazanskoi dukhovnoi akademii za pervyi (doreformennyi) period eia sushchestvovaniia, 1842–1870 gg.* (Kazan, 1891–92), II, 28-30, 89-90, 146, 162-63, 172, 238-39, 304-305; Evgenii N. Medynskii, *Istoriia russkoi pedagogiki do Velikoi Oktiabrskoi Sotsialisticheskoi Revoliutsii* (second edition, Moscow, 1938), 350-52; Eugene K. Smirnov, *A Short Account of the Historical Development and Present Position of Russian Orthodox Missions* (London, 1903), 27-47; *Bol'shaia sovetskaia entsiklopediia* (second edition, 1952), XVII, 551.

51. CPP, *Pis'ma k Aleksandru III*, II, 78-83, 108-110; Nicholas I. Ilminskii,

Pis'ma Nikolaia Ivanovicha Ilminskago k ober-prokuroru Sviateishchago sinoda Konstantinu Petrovichu Pobedonostsevu (Kazan, 1895), 1-62, 78-87, 93, 101-115, 124-34, 138-229, 239-42, 250-54, 266-71, 286-315, 320-41, 347-52, 361-91, 396, 400-404; Petrovskii, "Perepiska Pobedonostseva s Nikanorom," 105, 250-51; Markov, *K istorii raskola-staroobriadchestva*, 428, 556.

52. Quoted in Medynskii, *Istoriia russkoi pedagogiki*, 352.

53. Ibid., 350-52; Ilminskii, *Pis'ma*, 116-17; William J. Birkbeck, *Birkbeck and the Russian Church* (London, 1917), 210-12; Smirnoff, *Short Account*, 27-47.

54. Kulomzin, *Istoricheskii obzor*, IV, 107-110; Ilminskii, *Pis'ma*, 1-6, 13, 177-80; MDLL, CPP letter to Katkov, July 21, 1883.

55. CPP, *Pis'ma k Aleksandru III*, II, 78-84, 102-104, 108-110; CPP, *Vechnaia pamiat'. Vospominaniia o pochivshikh* (Moscow, 1896), 74-94; CPP, *Vsepoddanneishii otchët za 1885*, 17-33; CPP, . . . *za 1888–1889*, 216-18, 293-94; Petrovskii, "Perepiska Pobedonostseva s Nikanorom," 250-51, 510-12; Ilminskii, *Pis'ma*, 112-24, 177-87, 195-202, 353-59, 395-400; Ilminskii, *Besedy o russkoi shkole* (Kazan, 1889); Kulomzin, *Istoricheskii obzor*, IV, 434-35; Markov, *K istorii raskola-staroobriadchestva*, 555-56; *Bol'shaia sovetskaia entsiklopediia* (second edition, 1952), XVII, 551.

56. CPP, *Vechnaia pamiat'*, 77-79; CPP, *Vsepoddanneishii otchët za 1900*, 152-53; Medynskii, *Istoriia russkoi pedagogiki*, 353-55.

57. CPP, *Vsepoddanneishii otchët za 1885*, 35-42; CPP, . . . *za 1887*, 35; Ilminskii, *Pis'ma*, 28-30, 191-202, 247-50, 259-60, 271-86, 335-44, 397-400; Medynskii, *Istoriia russkoi pedagogiki*, 355-56.

58. CPP, *Pis'ma k Aleksandru III*, II, 259-60; CPP, *Vsepoddanneishii otchët za 1883*, 132-39; CPP, . . . *za 1885*, 43-49; Ilminskii, *Pis'ma*, 11-28, 53-57, 130-32, 136-38, 143-45, 169-73, 180-87, 191-202, 243-46, 265-66, 326-33, 354-61, 365-66, 374-78; Russia. Sviateishii pravitel'stvuiushchii sinod, *Tsirkuliarnye ukazy*, 181-83; Smirnoff, *Short Account*, 48; Znamenskii, *Istoriia Kazanskoi dukhovnoi akademii*, I, 304-305; Birkbeck, *Birkbeck and the Russian Church*, 210-12.

59. Nicholas A. Liubimov, *Mikhail Nikiforovich Katkov i ego istoricheskaia zasluga* (St. Petersburg, 1889), 126; Medynskii, *Istoriia russkoi pedagogiki*, 190-91.

60. Nicholas Riasanovsky, *Russia and the West in the Teaching of the Slavophiles* (Cambridge, Mass., 1952), 116-17; Sergei S. Tatishchev (S. Nevedenskii, pseud.) *Katkov i ego vremia* (St. Petersburg, 1888), 328-33; Paul Berline, "Russian Religious Philosophers and the Jews," *Jewish Social Studies*, IX (1947), 271-72; William T. Stead (editor), *The M.P. for Russia. Reminiscenses and Correspondence of Madame Olga Novikoff* (London, 1909), I, 11-12; II, 277-88; CPP (editor), *Perepiska IU. F. Samarina s baronessoiu E. F. Raden, 1861–1876 g.* (Moscow, 1893), 238-42; N. F. Belchikov, "Dostoevskii i Pobedonostsev," *KA*, II (1922), 244-45; Fedor M. Dostoevsky, *The Diary of a Writer* (New York, 1949), II, 637-53; Grossman, "Dostoevskii i pravitel'stvennye krugi," 108-112; MDLL, CPP letter to Catherine Tiutchev, March 15, 1876.

61. Sergei P. Pobedonostsev, "Putevyia zapiski russkago po Evrope v 1847-m godu," *Otechestvennyia zapiski*, LVIII (1848), 12, 15; CPP and Ivan K. Babst,

Pis'ma o puteshestvii gosudaria naslednika tsesarevicha po Rossii ot Peterburga do Kryma (Moscow, 1864), 73-75, 565; CPP, *Pis'ma k Aleksandru III*, I, 13-14; CPP, *Istoriia pravoslavnoi tserkvi do nachala razdeleniia tserkvei* (second edition, St. Petersburg, 1892), 5, 35-42, 120-21; Fedor Kovařík, *Zážitky a dojmy ruského Čecha za cárství* (Prague, 1932), 53-54.

62. CPP, *Pis'ma k Aleksandru III*, I, 44; CPP, *Novum Regnum*, 1016, 1021; Grossman, "Dostoevskii i pravitel'stvennye krugi," 142-43; MDLL, CPP letters to Catherine Tiutchev, August 11, 1875; March 17, 1879.

63. CPP, *Moskovskii sbornik* (third edition, Moscow, 1896), 60; CPP, *Pis'ma k Aleksandru III*, II, 12, 72-74, 111-13, 154, 191-92, 220, 249, 320; CPP, *Novum Regnum*, 695-99, 770-72, 877-82; "Pis'ma Pobedonostseva k Feoktistovu," 539, 543-44; "Pis'ma Pobedonostseva k Ignatievu," 71; CPP, *Vsepoddanneishii otchët za 1888–1889*, 143-47; CPP, . . . *za 1890–1891*, 123-26; CPP, . . . *za 1893*, 76; CPP, . . . *za 1894–1895*, 169-70; Markov, *K istorii raskola-staroobriadchestva*, 196-97, 201, 297, 307.

64. CPP, *Novum Regnum*, 937-38; Andrew D. White, "A Statesman of Russia: Constantine Pobedonostzeff," *Century Magazine*, LVI (1898), 110-18; Baron Egor F. Staal, *Correspondance diplomatique de M. de Staal, 1884–1900* (Paris, 1929), II, 123-214; William J. Birkbeck, *The Prospect of Reunion with Eastern Christendom* (London, 1894), 16-19; Tverskoi, "Iz delovoi perepiski," 665-66; von Schweinitz, *Denkwürdigkeiten*, II, 424; Volkovsky, "The Philosophy of Reaction," 90.

65. CPP, *Pis'ma k Aleksandru III*, II, 72-74, 249; CPP, *Novum Regnum*, 250, 569-70, 937-38; CPP, *Vsepoddanneishii otchët za 1886*, 226-27; CPP, . . . *za 1888–1889*, 293; "Pis'ma Pobedonostseva k Feoktistovu," 499-543; Peretts, *Dnevnik*, 130-32; S. L. Evenchik, "Reaktsionnaia deiatel'nost' Pobedonostseva v 80-kh gg. XIX-go veka," Moscow University Thesis for Candidate Degree in History, 1939, 114-15; Medynskii, *Istoriia russkoi pedagogiki*, 339; Miliukov, Seignebos, and Eisenman, *Histoire*, III, 1056; MDLL, CPP letters to Olga Novikov, November 24, 1890; December 15, 1891; November 7, November 20, 1892; December 27, 1893; January 4, 1894.

66. CPP, *Pis'ma k Aleksandru III*, I, 343-45; 424; "Pis'ma Pobedonostseva k Ignatievu," 53, 55, 58-58, 73, 78-80, 88; Tverskoi, "Iz delovoi perepiski," 665-66.

67. Vasilii I. Iakovlev (V. Ia. Bogucharskii, *pseud.*), *Iz istorii politicheskoi bor'by v Rossii v 70-kh i 80-kh godakh XIX veka* (Moscow, 1912), 268-85, 297-98, 304-305; CPP, *Novum Regnum*, 247-48, 289-94, 344, 389, 408; Steven Lukashevich, "Holy Brotherhood: 1881–1883," *American Slavic and East European Review*, XVIII (1959), 491-509; Evenchik, "Reaktsionnaia deiatel'nost' Pobedonostseva," 49-54; MDLL, CPP letter to Catherine Tiutchev, March 8, 1881. See also, Hans Heilbronner, "The Administrations of Loris-Melikov and Ignatiev, 1880–1882," University of Michigan, Thesis for Doctorate in History, 1954, 65-66, 122, 199, 370-78, 475, 491-93.

68. CPP, *Pis'ma k Aleksandru III*, II, 319-20; "Pis'ma Pobedonostseva k Feoktistovu," 522-24, 543; Nikita P. Giliarov-Platonov, *Sbornik sochinenii*

(Moscow, 1899), I, introduction; II, 236-70; Giliarov-Platonov, *Evreiskii vopros v Rossii* (St. Petersburg, 1906); Giliarov-Platonov, *Voprosy very i tserkvi* (Moscow, 1905–1906), I, *passim*, especially 135-37; II, *passim*, especially 46-49, 92-96; Grossman, "Dostoevskii i pravitel'stvennye krugi," 135; Markov, *K istorii raskola-staroobriadchestva*, 434, 469, 471, 488-90.

IX.   *The Russian Orthodox Church Abroad*

1. CPP, *Pis'ma Pobedonosteva k Aleksandru III* (Moscow, 1925–26), I, 170-71; II, 3-4, 46-47, 79-82, 102-104, 108-110, 145, 191-92, 259-60, 308-309; CPP, *K. P. Pobedonostsev i ego korrespondenty. Pis'ma i zapiski. Novum Regnum* (Moscow, 1923), 832-35, 1004-1006; CPP, *Moskovskii sbornik* (Moscow, 1896), 3-9, 12-16, 20-23, 154-56, 216-21; General Hans von Schweinitz, *Denkwürdigkeiten des Botschafters General v. Schweinitz* (Berlin, 1929), II, 243-44, 275, 302, 388, 395-96.

2. CPP, *A Monsieur Edouard Naville, Président du comité central suisse de l'Alliance évangélique* (St. Petersburg, 1888); Evangelical Alliance, *Rapport présenté aux branches de l'Alliance évangélique par le comité de Genève, sur des démarches faites au près de S. M. l'Empereur de Russie rélativement à la liberté religieuse dans l'empire russe* (Geneva, 1889), 36; Rose J. Birkbeck, *Life and Letters of W. J. Birkbeck* (London, 1922), 113; Princess Marie Radziwill, *Lettres de la princesse Radziwill au général de Robilant, 1889–1914* (Bologna, 1933–34), II, 42; Igor Smolitsch, "Zur Geschichte der Beziehungen zwischen der russischen Kirche und dem Orthodoxen Osten," *Ostkirchliche Studien*, VII (1958), 40-41.

3. CPP, *Novum Regnum*, 961; Count Peter A. Valuev, *Dnevnik, 1877–1884* (Petrograd, 1919), 135; Adrien Boudou, *Le Saint-Siège et la Russie* (Paris, 1922–25), II, 537-44; Henryk Lisicki, *Le marquis Wielopolski, sa vie et son temps, 1803–1877* (Vienna, 1880), II, 21-27; K. Istomin (editor), "Pis'mo g. ober-prokurora Sv. sinoda K. P. Pobedonostseva k Pateru V. Vannutelli," *Vera i razum*, I (1893), 353-86.

4. CPP, *Novum Regnum*, 859-60; Sergei A. Petrovskii (editor), "Perepiska K. P. Pobedonostseva s preosviashchennym Nikanorom episkopom Ufimskim," *RA*, III (1915), 258-61; Evgenii A. Adamov, *Diplomatiia Vatikana v nachalnuiu epokhu imperializma, 1887–1900* (Moscow, 1931), 16-17, 41-48, 64-77, 81-95; Russia. Gosudarstvennyi sovet, *Otchët po deloproizvodstvu Gosudarstvennago soveta za sessiiu 1894–1895 gg.* (St. Petersburg, 1895), 123-26.

5. CPP, *Pis'ma k Aleksandru III*, II, 323-26; Edouard Winter, *Russland und die slawischen Völker in der Diplomatie des Vatikans, 1878–1903* (Berlin, 1950), 99-100; Adamov, *Diplomatiia Vatikana*, 130-34.

6. Serge Bolshakoff, *The Foreign Missions of the Russian Orthodox Church* (New York, 1943), 78-121; Nicholas Riasanovsky, *Russia and the West in the Teaching of the Slavophiles* (Cambridge, Mass., 1952), 34, 36, 62, 94-95, 131; MDLL, CPP letters to Catherine Tiutchev, February 5, 1872; October 16,

1875; February 7, May 11, 1877; June 11, June 17, June 29, 1881; Catherine Tiutchev letters to CPP, June 13, 1877; June 23, July 10, 1881.

7. CPP, *Pis'ma k Aleksandru III*, I, 29, 404; William T. Stead (editor), *The M.P. for Russia. Reminiscences and Correspondence of Madame Olga Novikoff* (London, 1909), I, 135-38; MDLL, CPP letters to Catherine Tiutchev, October 23, 1871; April 19, 1872; August 11, October 12, 1874; August 11, 1875.

8. CPP, *Novum Regnum*, 868-70; William J. Birkbeck, *The Prospect of Reunion with Eastern Christendom* (London, 1894), 3-30; Birkbeck, *Birkbeck and the Russian Church* (London, 1917), preface, 2-16, 70, 103, 106-164; Birkbeck, *Russia and the English Church in the Last Fifty Years* (London, 1895), preface; Birkbeck, *Life*, 22, 29, 42, 142, 177-79.

9. CPP, *Pis'ma k Aleksandru III*, II, 317-18; CPP, *Novum Regnum*, 455-57, 821-22; CPP, *Vsepoddanneishii otchët ober-prokurora Sviateishago sinoda K. Pobedonostseva po vedomstvu Pravoslavnago Ispovedaniia za 1883* (St. Petersburg, 1885), 420; CPP, . . . *za 1886* (St. Petersburg, 1888), 28-29; CPP, . . . *za 1887* (St. Petersburg, 1889), 91-92; CPP, . . . *za 1888–1889* (St. Petersburg, 1891), 246-47; CPP, . . . *za 1890–1891* (St. Petersburg, 1893), 505-511; CPP, . . . *za 1901* (St. Petersburg, 1904), 207, 214-18, 227; CPP, . . . *za 1903–1904* (St. Petersburg, 1909), 165-67; Russia. Sviateishii pravitel'stvuiushchii sinod, *Obzor deiatel'nosti vedomstva Pravoslavnago Ispovedaniia za vremia tsarstvovaniia Imperatora Aleksandra III* (St. Petersburg, 1901), 369-71; Vladimir S. Markov, *K istorii raskola-staroobriadchestva vtoroi poloviny XIX stoletiia* (Moscow, 1915), 293-94, 578-80.

10. CPP, *Pis'ma k Aleksandru III*, I, 261-62; CPP, *Vsepoddanneishii otchët za 1883*, 200-202; CPP, . . . *za 1890–1891*, 305-316; Eugene K. Smirnov, *A Short Account of the Historical Development and Present Position of Russian Orthodox Missions* (London, 1903), 80-83; MDLL, CPP letter to Catherine Tiutchev, October 7, 1879.

11. CPP, *Pis'ma k Aleksandru III*, II, 270-72; CPP, *Novum Regnum*, 982-84; CPP, *Vsepoddanneishii otchët za 1888–1889*, 254-55; E. E. Lazarev, *Gavaiiskii Senator i vozhdi russkago pravoslaviia, episkop Vladimir i K. P. Pobedonostsev* (Geneva, 1902), 13-34, 57-69.

12. Michael Semenov, *Vospominanie ob A. N. Muravieve* (Kiev, 1875), 187-91; "Dva pis'ma Andreia Nikolaevicha Muravieva k K. P. Pobedonostsevu," *RA*, II (1905), 415-16.

13. CPP, *Pis'ma k Aleksandru III*, II, 64-65, 70-72, 89-93, 308-309; CPP, *Novum Regnum*, 93-94, 824-28, 1084; CPP, *Vsepoddanneishii otchët za 1887*, 288-89; Pobedonostsev, *Istoriia pravoslavnoi tserkvi do nachala razdeleniia tserkvei* (second edition, St. Petersburg, 1892), 11, 219-24; Markov, *K istorii raskola-staroobriadchestva*, 315, 558; Boris B. Glinskii, "Konstantin Petrovich Pobedonostsev. Materialy dlia biografii," *Istoricheskii vestnik*, CVIII (1907), 259; A. N. Kulomzin (editor), *Istoricheskii obzor deiatel'nosti Komiteta Ministrov* (St. Petersburg, 1902–1903), IV, 59-61; Boris N. Chicherin, *Vospominaniia* (Moscow, 1929–34), IV, 105-106; MDLL, CPP letters to Catherine Tiutchev,

October 24, 1881; January 28, 1882; CPP letter to Sergei A. Petrovskii, January 5, 1892.

14. CPP, *Pis'ma k Aleksandru III*, II, 70-72, 92-93, 178-85; CPP, *Novum Regnum*, 93-94; CPP, *Vsepoddanneishii otchët za 1885* (St. Petersburg, 1887), 281-82; Pobedonostsev, . . . *za 1888–1889*, 5-7; CPP, . . . *za 1899* (St. Petersburg, 1902), 163-64; MDLL, CPP letters to Catherine Tiutchev, October 24, 1881; January 28, 1882.

15. Cyril E. Black, *The Establishment of Constitutional Government in Bulgaria* (Princeton, N. J., 1943), 29-31; CPP, *Vsepoddanneishii otchët za 1880* (St. Petersburg, 1883), 191-94; CPP, . . . *za 1883*, 408-417; CPP, . . . *za 1885*, 220-22; CPP, . . . *za 1886*, 135-37, 173-74, 206, 237; CPP, . . . *za 1890–1891*, 510-11; Bernard H. Schwertfeger (editor), *Zur europäischen Politik. Unveröffentlichte [Belgische] Dokumente* (Berlin, 1919), V, 236.

16. CPP, *Pis'ma k Aleksandru III*, II. 291-92; CPP, *Izvlechenie iz Vsepoddanneishago otchëta ober-prokurora Sviateishago sinoda K. Pobedonostseva po vedomstvu Pravoslavnago Ispovedaniia za 1881* (St. Petersburg, 1883), 104; CPP, *Vsepoddanneishii otchët za 1885*, 220-22, 285-86; CPP, . . . *za 1888–1889*, 456-72; CPP, . . . *za 1890–1891*, 504-505; CPP, . . . *za 1899*, 146-49; 163-65; CPP, . . . *za 1900* (St. Petersburg, 1903), 273-74; CPP, . . . *za 1903–1904*, 158; MDLL, CPP letter to Catherine Tiutchev, winter, 1875; CPP letters to Olga Novikov, November 13, 1890; April, 1899.

17. This account of the political and other problems in Galicia and the Carpatho-Ukraine in the nineteenth century was derived largely from Robert Kann, *The Multinational Empire* (New York, 1950), I, 221-31, 299-302, 318-27, 413-14, 443; Arthur May, *The Hapsburg Monarchy, 1867–1914* (Cambridge, Mass., 1951), 216-17, 432, 500; N. Andrusiak, "Ruthène (église)," *Dictionnaire de théologie catholique*, XIV (1939), 382-407; Serge Bolshakoff, *Russian Nonconformity* (Philadelphia, 1950), 139-40.

18. Alexander A. Polovtsov, *Dnevnik gosudarstvennogo sekretaria A. A. Polovtsova* (Moscow, 1966), I, 70, 142, 485-86; MDLL, Adrian I. Mazur letter to CPP, September, 1886.

19. CPP, *Pis'ma k Aleksandru III*, I, 406; II, 9-13, 34-39; CPP, *Novum Regnum*, 302, 309, 330-31, 420, 499-500, 507, 536-37; "Pis'ma K. P. Pobedonostseva k E. M. Feoktistovu," *Literaturnoe nasledstvo*, Number 22-24 (1935), 504-505, 537-38; Petrovskii, "Perepiska Pobedonostseva s Nikanorom," 525-27; Father Ivan Naumovich, *Piatidesiatiletie (1839–1889) vozsoedineniia s pravoslavniiu tserkoviiu zapadno-russkikh uniatov. Istoricheskii ocherk* (St. Petersburg, 1889), 1-62; Father I. Soloviev, "Otets Ivann Naumovich," *Russkoe obozrenie*, XXII (1893), 270-93, 781-803; Alexis Pelipenko, "Die politische Propaganda des russischen Heiligen Synod in Galizien vor dem Kriege," *Berliner Monatshefte*, XII (1934), 825-38; von Schweinitz, *Denkwürdigkeiten*, II, 275, 302; von Schweinitz, *Briefwechsel des Botschafters General v. Schweinitz* (Berlin, 1928), 225-26, 362; Jan Heidler (editor), *Příspěvky k listáři Dra. Frant. Lad. Riegra* (Prague, 1924–26), II, 61, 68; Fedor Kovařík, *Zážitky a dojmy ruského Čecha za*

cárstvi (Prague, 1932), 25; Paul Miliukov, Charles Seignebos, and Louis Eisenman, *Histoire de Russie* (Paris, 1932–33), III, 1245; MDLL, Nicholas K. Giers letters to CPP, April 26, 1885; October 10, 1886.

20. *Palestinskii Sbornik*, I (LXIII) (1955), cover page, 3-5; *The New York Times*, August 14, 1952; *Christian Science Monitor*, October 1, 1955. The new Soviet institution immediately claimed the earlier organization's property in Jerusalem, repaired Orthodox churches in both Israel and Jordan, sent clerical and lay representatives to assume care of the aged Russian monks and nuns living in monasteries and convents in and around Jerusalem, reinforced the staffs of the Russian Orthodox churches, and distributed large quantities of religious books. In short, it resumed earlier Russian efforts to weaken the position of the Greek hierarchy and to replace it by Russians, who could then use the Orthodox Church base for influence in the Middle East and in the Orthodox world. The Soviet agents have followed the tactics of the Imperial Orthodox Palestine Society by seeking to persuade the Arab clergy that their role in the Church should be greater and would indeed become greater when that of the Greeks in the hierarchy had been reduced or eliminated. According to newspaper reports, the Soviet Minister to Israel and his staff in 1952 even began to attend Orthodox services regularly.

21. Theofanis Stavrou, *Russian Interests in Palestine, 1882–1914* (Thessaloniki, 1963), 10-17, 31-55; Alphonse d'Alonzo, *La Russie en Palestine* (Paris, 1901), 83-90.

22. "Pis'ma K. P. Pobedonostseva k grafu N. P. Ignatievu," *Byloe*, Number 27-28 (1925), 76; CPP, *Vsepoddanneishii otchët za 1883*, 419-20; Archbishop Savva of Tver, *Khronika moei zhizni* (Sergiev Posad, 1897–1911), VII, 196, 220, 223; VIII, 572; *Otchët Pravoslavnago Palestinskago Obshchestva za 1906–1907 god* (St. Petersburg, 1908), 11-12; *Russkiia uchrezhdeniia v Sviatoi Zemlie i pochivshie deiateli Imperatorskago Pravoslavnago Palestinskago Obshchestva, 1882–1907* (St. Petersburg, 1907), v-vii; Stavrou, *Russian Interests in Palestine*, 64-69.

23. CPP, *Vsepoddanneishii otchët za 1885*, 290-92; CPP, . . . *za 1888–1889*, 455; Stavrou, *Russian Interests in Palestine*, 70-76, 87-88, 129-30; *Otchët Pravoslavnago Palestinskago Obshchestva za 1882–1883 god* (St. Petersburg, 1883), 2, 31; *Otchët . . . za 1885–1886* (St. Petersburg, 1886), 200; *Soobshcheniia Palestinskago Obshchestva*, III (1892), 260, supplement, 1-2, 17-28, 60-61; V (1895), supplement, 135, 155-56; VI (1896), 167; VII (1897), supplement, 196, 222.

24. CPP, *Pis'ma k Aleksandru III*, II, 188-92; Count Vladimir N. Lamzdorf, *Dnevnik V. N. Lamzdorfa, 1886–1890* (Moscow, 1926), 199-203; Stavrou, *Russian Interests in Palestine*, 115-30.

25. CPP, *Vsepoddanneishii otchët za 1885*, 290-92; CPP, . . . *za 1888–1889*, 455; CPP, . . . *za 1894–1895* (St. Petersburg, 1898), 280-81; CPP, . . . *za 1899*, 150; *Otchët Pravoslavnago Palestinskago Obshchestva za 1906–1907*, 18; *Otchët . . . za 1908–1909* (St. Petersburg, 1909), 16; Stavrou, *Russian Interests in Palestine*, 115-36, 168-74, 212.

26. Stavrou, *Russian Interests in Palestine*, 89-99, 194-99; *Russkiia uchrezhdeniia v Sviatoi Zemlie*, v-vi.

27. Stavrou, *Russian Interests in Palestine*, 99-105, 131, 149-57.

28. Ibid., 105-111, 162-64, 187-89; CPP, *Vsepoddanneishii otchët za 1885*, 290-92; CPP, . . . *za 1887*, 217-18; CPP, . . . *za 1888–1889*, 455, 466; *Russkiia uchrezhdeniia v Sviatoi Zemlie*, xii-lvii; d'Alonzo, *La Russie en Palestine*, 58-65, 70-73.

29. Stavrou, *Russian Interests in Palestine*, 136, 157-69, 188-89, 192-94, 212; Lamzdorf, *Dnevnik*, 348-49; d'Alonzo, *La Russie en Palestine*, 17-18, 34-51, 74-82.

30. *Otchët Pravoslavnago Palestinskago Obshchestva za 1906–1907*, 11-12, 18; *Otchët . . . za 1908–1909*, 16; *Otchët . . . za 1910–1911* (St. Petersburg, 1911), iv, 3; Stavrou, *Russian Interests in Palestine*, 174-85.

31. William L. Langer, *The Diplomacy of Imperialism, 1890–1902* (New York, 1935), I, 103-105, 108-109, 129-31, 271-74; Sergius Yakobson, "Russia and Africa," *Slavonic Review*, XVII (1937–38), 625-36; XIX (1939), 162-66.

32. Valerian A. Panaev, "Iz vospominanii V. A. Panaeva," *Russkaia starina*, CXXVIII (1906), 421-35; Czeslaw Jesman, *The Russians in Ethiopia. An Essay in Futility* (London, 1958), 18-23; Viscount Jean Robert de Constantin, *L'Archimandrite Paisi et l'ataman Achinoff. Une Expédition religieuse en Abyssinie* (Paris, 1891), 4-45.

33. Jesman, *The Russians in Ethiopia*, 23-28; de Constantin, *L'Archimandrite Paisi*, 57-72.

34. Quoted in Yakobson, "Russia and Africa," XIX, 164.

35. CPP, *Pis'ma k Aleksandru III*, II, 186-88; CPP, *Novum Regnum*, 828-30, 846-47, 1085; Ivan S. Aksakov, "Pis'ma I. S. Aksakova k K. P. Pobedonostsevu, 1876–1885," *RA*, III (1907), 185-86; Markov, *K istorii raskola-staroobriadchestva*, 472-73; Schwertfeger, *Zur europäischen Politik*, V, 245-46; Lamzdorf, *Dnevnik*, 157-58; de Constantin, *L'Archimandrite Paisi*, 73-111; Panaev, "Iz vospominanii," 435-37; Jesman, *The Russians in Ethiopia*, 23-31; Alfred Portier d'Arc (A. Dovérine, *pseud.*), *L'Esprit national russe sous Alexandre III* (Paris, 1890), 31, 39-43.

36. France. Ministère des Affaires Etrangères, *Documents diplomatiques français, 1871–1914* (Paris, 1929–51), first series, VI, 510-11; VII, 132; Francesco Crispi, *The Memoirs of Francesco Crispi* (London, 1912–14), II, 337; Jesman, *The Russians in Ethiopia*, 4; de Constantin, *L'Archimandrite Paisi*, 73-83, 113-31; Lamzdorf, *Dnevnik*, 114, 122, 146, 227.

37. France. Ministère des Affaires Etrangères, *Documents diplomatiques français, 1871–1914*, first series, VII, 314, 335, 344-45, 347-51, 380-81, 392; Baron Egor F. Staal, *Correspondance diplomatique de M. de Staal, 1884–1900* (Paris, 1929), II, 17; Polovtsov, *Dnevnik*, II, 184; Andreas Dorpalen, "Tsar Alexander III and the Boulanger Crisis in France," *Journal of Modern History*, XXIII (1951), 134; Panaev, "Iz vospominanii," 436-37; Jesman, *The Russians in Ethiopia*, 1-16; de Constantin, *L'Archimandrite Paisi*, 133-36, 167, 255-77, 320-27.

38. France. Ministère des Affaires Etrangères, *Documents diplomatiques français*, first series, VII, 347-49, 380-81, 392, 594; VIII, 371-72; Adrian Dansette, *Le Boulangisme* (Paris, 1946), 234-95; Dorpalen, "Tsar Alexander III and the Boulanger Crisis," 134; Jesman, *The Russians in Ethiopia*, 16; de Constantin, *L'Archimandrite Paisi*, preface, 201-222, 225-53, 277-311, 330-36; Portier d'Arc, *L'Esprit national russe*, 37.

39. CPP, *Pis'ma k Aleksandru III*, II, 308-310; Jesman, *The Russians in Ethiopia*, 118-46, 167-94; d'Alonzo, *La Russie en Palestine*, 80-81.

40. CPP, *Novum Regnum*, 903, 922; Lamzdorf, *Dnevnik*, 122-23, 137, 142-46, 168, 227; Savva, *Khronika moei zhizni*, VIII, 598-601; Nicholas Notovich, *L'Empereur Alexandre III et son entourage* (Paris, 1893), 267-69.

X. Russian Political and Intellectual Life

1. This view is accepted by Michael Pokrovsky, eminent Bolshevik historian, who edited and published some of the papers of Pobedonostsev and the letters of the last two tsars to him, and by S. L. Evenchik, whose thesis for the degree of Candidate in History at Moscow University in 1939 benefited from research in the archives, particularly those of the Orthodox Church and of the Ministry of the Interior (Pokrovsky preface to CPP, *Konstantin P. Pobedonostsev i ego korrespondenty. Pis'ma i zapiski. Novum Regnum* [Moscow, 1923], I, preface; S. L. Evenchik, "Reaktsionnaia deiatel'nost' Pobedonostseva v 80-kh gg. XIX veka," Moscow University Thesis for Candidate Degree in History, 1939).

2. CPP, "Iz chernovykh bumag K. P. Pobedonostseva," *KA*, XVIII (1926), 203-207; Count Sergei IU. Witte, *Vospominaniia* (Moscow, 1960), II, 32-35; "Iz dnevnika A. A. Polovtsova," *KA*, XLVI (1931), 124; Paul Miliukov, Charles Seignebos, and Louis Eisenman, *Histoire de Russie* (Paris, 1932–33), III, 1037, 1052; *Pravitel'stvennyi vestnik*, January 18, 1895.

3. CPP, *Pis'ma Pobedonostseva k Aleksandru III* (Moscow, 1925–26), I, 176; II, 152-57, 197-201, 257-59; "Pis'ma K. P. Pobedonostseva k E. M. Feoktistovu," *Literaturnoe nasledstvo*, Number 22-24 (1935), 499; MDLL, CPP letter to Catherine Tiutchev, June 16, 1879.

4. CPP, *Pis'ma k Aleksandru III*, II, 46-47, 104-106, 203-208; CPP, *Novum Regnum*, 452-53, 521-22; "Perepiska Vitte i Pobedonostseva, 1895–1905," *KA*, XXX (1928), 101-103; Alexander A. Polovtsov, *Dnevnik gosudarstvennogo sekretaria A. A. Polovtsova* (Moscow, 1966), I, 411-13, 540-41; II, 96, 108, 117-19, 136, 159-61, 411-13, 540-41; Prince Vladimir P. Meshcherskii, *Moi vospominaniia* (St. Petersburg, 1897–1912), III, 335; Russia. Ministerstvo vnutrennykh del, *Obshchii obzor Ministerstva vnutrennykh del za vremia tsarstvovaniia Aleksandra III* (St. Petersburg, 1901), 18-28; Russia. Ministerstvo iustitsii, *Sudebnye ustavy 20 noiabria 1864 g. za piat'desiat let* (Petrograd, 1914), II, 697-701; Evenchik, "Reaktsionnaia deiatel'nost' Pobedonostseva," chapter 5, 15-45.

5. CPP, *Pis'ma k Aleksandru III*, II, 91-92; Maxim M. Kovalevskii, *Konstitutsiia grafa Loris-Melikova i ego chastnye pis'ma* (Berlin, 1904), 90-91; MDLL, CPP letters to Catherine Tiutchev, March 11, April 27, April 29, 1881.

6. Quoted in Samuel Kucherov, *Courts, Lawyers and Trials under the Last Three Tsars* (New York, 1953), 81.

7. CPP, *Pis'ma k Aleksandru III*, II, 74-76, 114-17, 128, 140, 173-74, 214-18; CPP, *Novum Regnum*, 463-64, 485-86, 495, 508-514, 598-601, 610-11, 645-47, 683-84, 702-704, 839-40, 915-21, 1072; Egor A. Peretts, *Dnevnik E. A. Perettsa, 1880–1883* (Moscow-Leningrad, 1927), 141; A. N. Kulomzin (editor), *Istoricheskii obzor deiatel'nosti Komiteta Ministrov. K stoletiiu Komiteta Ministrov, 1802–1902* (St. Petersburg, 1902–1903), IV, 275; Russia. Ministerstvo iustitsii, *Ministerstvo iustitsii za sto let, 1802–1902. Istoricheskii ocherk* (St. Petersburg, 1902), 186-87; Kucherov, *Courts, Lawyers and Trials*, 79, 90; Russia. Ministerstvo iustitsii, *Sudebnye ustavy 20 noiabria 1864*, II, 670-671.

8. CPP, *Pis'ma k Aleksandru III*, I, 305-306, 315-21, 422; II, 335-38; CPP, *Novum Regnum*, 48, 155-58, 197-99, 226-29, 240, 251-55, 273-74, 281-86, 461-80, 588-89, 677-79, 745-48, 1076; "Pis'ma K. P. Pobedonostseva k grafu N. P. Ignatievu," *Byloe*, Number 27-28 (1925), 66-69, 85; Count Dmitrii A. Miliutin, *Dnevnik* (Moscow, 1947–50), IV, 12-15, 43; Iurii V. Gotie, "K. P. Pobedonostsev i naslednik Aleksandr Aleksandrovich, 1865–1881," *Publichnaia Biblioteka SSSR imeni V. I. Lenina. Sbornik*, II (1929), 133-34; Polovtsov, *Dnevnik*, I, 154, 172-73; Peretts, *Dnevnik*, 118, 128-29; Nicholas A. Konstantinov, *Ocherki po istorii srednei shkoly* (Moscow, 1947), 29-34; S. V. Rozhdestvenskii (editor), *Istoricheskii obzor deiatel'nosti Ministerstva narodnago prosveshcheniia, 1802–1902* (St. Petersburg, 1902), 611; "Vozhd' reaktsii 60-80-kh godov. Neizdannyia pis'ma M. N. Katkova Aleksandru II i Aleksandru III," *Byloe*, Number 4 (1917), 19-20; MDLL, CPP letters to Catherine Tiutchev, October 7, 1874; November 17, 1875; February 4, 1881; February 1, February 4, February 7, 1882; CPP letter to Michael N. Katkov, March 24, 1881.

9. Evgenii N. Medynskii, *Istoriia russkoi pedagogiki do Velikoi Oktiabrskoi Sotsialisticheskoi Revoliutsii* (second edition, Moscow, 1938), 140–41; William H. Johnson, *Russia's Educational Heritage* (Pittsburgh, 1950), 138-40; Daniel B. Leary, *Russian Education. Organization, History, Statistics* (New York, 1918), 62-64.

10. CPP, *Pis'ma k Aleksandru III*, I, 99-100; CPP, *Novum Regnum*, 272, 279-80, 346-50, 461-80, 500-501; "Pis'ma Pobedonostseva k Feoktistovu," 533; "Vozhd' reaktsii 60-80-kh godov," 6-29; Evenchik, "Reaktsionnaia deiatel'nost' Pobedonostseva," chapter 6, 86-95; Savva, Archbishop of Tver, *Khronika moei zhizni. Avtobiograficheskiia zapiski* (Sergiev Posad, 1897–1911), VII, 291-92; "Kievskii sobor 1884 goda. Poslanie k vysokopreosviashchennomu Pavlu, eksarkhu Gruzii. Zapiski arkhiepiskopa Nikanora," *RA*, III (1908), 114; Nicholas Hans, *History of Russian Educational Policy, 1701–1917* (London, 1931), 142-53; Thomas Darlington, *Education in Russia* (London, 1909), 428-49; Medynskii, *Istoriia russkoi pedagogiki*, 344; Johnson, *Russia's Educational Heri-*

tage, 141-43, 153-54; MDLL, CPP letters to Catherine Tiutchev, December 9, December 12, 1878.

11. CPP, *Pis'ma k Aleksandru III*, II, 99-100, 168-73; Medynskii, *Istoriia russkoi pedagogiki*, 338-39; Hans, *History of Russian Educational Policy*, 142-53; Johnson, *Russia's Educational Heritage*, 154-55.

12. CPP, *Pis'ma k Aleksandru III*, II, 42-44, 236-43; CPP, *Novum Regnum*, 26-28, 264-68, 294-96, 938-42, 947-48, 1093; CPP, *Vechnaia pamiat'. Vospominaniia o pochivshikh* (Moscow, 1896), 9-20; Fedor M. Dostoevsky, *The Diary of a Writer* (New York, 1949), I, 368; Polovtsov, *Dnevnik*, II, 411, 510; Manuscript Division, Saltykov-Shchedrin Library, CPP memorandum, "O rabotakh Komissii dlia izyskaniia glavneishikh osnovanii luchshei postanovki zhenskago obrazovaniia v Rossii," 1888?, 1-34; MDLL, CPP letter to Catherine Tiutchev, June 9, 1880; CPP letter to Sergei A. Rachinskii, October 14, 1895.

13. CPP, *Kurs grazhdanskago prava* (first edition, Moscow, 1880), III, 393-94.

14. CPP, *Pis'ma k Aleksandru III*, II, 292-94; MDLL, CPP letters to Catherine Tiutchev, November 26, 1875; February 25, March 17, November 4, 1877; February 23, 1878; Catherine Tiutchev letters to CPP, November 12, 1876; February 23, March 2, March 23, November 2, 1877; January 4, 1881; CPP letters to Olga Novikov, February 14, March 2, 1877.

15. MDLL, CPP letters to Catherine Tiutchev, October 16, 1877; June 5, 1881; January 10, 1882; Catherine Tiutchev letters to CPP, September 28, December 23, 1877.

16. Evenchik, "Reaktsionnaia deiatel'nost' Pobedonostseva," chapter 6, 99-100.

17. "Pis'ma Pobedonostseva k Feoktistovu," 503-504; Hermann Dalton, *On Religious Liberty in Russia* (Leipzig, 1890), 59-60; Savva, *Khronika moei zhizni*, VIII, 716-717; S. Mel'gunov (editor), "K. P. Pobedonostsev v dni pervoi revoliutsii. Neizdannyia pis'ma k S. D. Voitu," *Na chuzhoi storone*, VIII (1924), 181.

18. CPP, *Novum Regnum*, 533; "Pis'ma Pobedonostseva k Feoktistovu," *passim*, especially 497, 499, 552-53; Evgenii M. Feoktistov, *Vospominaniia. Za kulisami politiki i literatury, 1848–1896* (Leningrad, 1929), vii-xxv; Vladimir I. Gurko, *Features and Figures of the Past* (Stanford, 1939), 188-89, 638-39; Anatole Egorov, "Stranitsii iz godov moei zhizni," *Russkaia starina*, CIL (1912), 139-40; Boris B. Glinskii, "Iz tsenzurnago proshlago. Stranichka vospominanii," *Istoricheskii vestnik*, CIV (1906), 186-89, 194-95; Leonid N. Maikov, "E. M. Feoktistov," *Zhurnal Ministerstva narodnago prosveshcheniia*, CCCXVIII (1898), 26-42.

19. CPP, *Pis'ma k Aleksandru III*, I, 230-37, 322; II, 6-9, 34-36, 41-42; CPP, *Novum Regnum*, 308-311, 498-99, 858, 908-909, 934, 963; Il'ia E. Repin, *I. E. Repin i V. V. Stasov. Perepiska* (Moscow, 1948–50), II, 320; V. N. Moskvinov, *Repin v Moskve* (Moscow, 1955), 56-57; Vladimir S. Markov, *K istorii raskola-staroobriadchestva vtoroi poloviny XIX stoletiia. Perepiska prof. N. I. Subbotina* (Moscow, 1915), 210, 216.

20. CPP, *Pis'ma k Aleksandru III*, II, 211-14; "Pis'ma Pobedonostseva k Feoktistovu," 514-15, 518-20, 530-31, 539, 549, 560; Savva, *Khronika moei zhizni*,

VIII, 578-80; Longin F. Panteleev, *Vospominaniia* (Moscow, 1958), 648; Evenchik, "Reaktsionnaia deiatel'nost' Pobedonostseva," chapter 6, 109-110.

21. "Pis'ma K. P. Pobedonostseva k S. D. Voitu," *RA*, I (1917), 87; Sergei A. Petrovskii (editor), "Perepiska K. P. Pobedonostseva s preosviashchennym Nikanorom episkopom Ufimskim," *RA*, II (1915), 254-56; Evenchik, "Reaktsionnaia deiatel'nost' Pobedonostseva," chapter 6, 109-110.

22. CPP, *Pis'ma k Aleksandru III*, I, 277-78; Constantine Leontiev, *Sobranie sochinenii* (Moscow, 1912–14), VIII, 206-207; Nicolas Berdyaev, *Constantin Leontieff* (Paris, 1936), *passim*, especially 8-10, 74, 119-22, 188.

23. Leonid Grossman, "Dostoevskii i pravitel'stvennye krugi 1870-kh godov," *Literaturnoe nasledstvo*, Number 15 (1934), 145; Sergei M. Soloviev, *Zapiski Sergeia Mikhailovicha Solov'eva* (Petrograd, 1915), *passim*, especially 5-21; Dmitri Stremooukhoff, *Vladimir Soloviev et son oeuvre messianique* (Paris, 1935), 10; MDLL, CPP letters to Catherine Tiutchev, February 19, 1878; October 7, 1879; CPP letter to Olga Novikov, January 14, 1877; CPP letters to Boris N. Chicherin, October 10, 1864; March 16, 1873.

24. CPP, *Novum Regnum*, 323-24, 828, 956-57, 969-70, 1084-1085, 1094; "Pis'ma Pobedonostseva k Feoktistovu," 545; Stremooukhoff, *Soloviev*, 192, 218-19, 296, 301-302; E. L. Radlov (editor), *Pis'ma Vladimira Sergeevicha Solovieva* (St. Petersburg, 1908–11), III, 131-33, 142; MDLL, CPP letter to Catherine Tiutchev, March 29, 1881.

25. CPP, *Novum Regnum*, 172-73, 398; "Kniaz'ia tserkvi. Iz dnevnika A. N. Lvova," *KA*, XXXIX (1930), 133-34; Iakov P. Polonskii, "Iz dnevnika Ia. P. Polonskago 1878 g.," *Na chuzhoi storone*, V (1924), 41-49; Grigorii K. Gradovskii, "Iz minuvshago. Vospominaniia i vpechatleniia literatura, 1867–1897 g.," *Russkaia starina*, CXXXVII (1909), 529-31; MDLL, CPP letter to Catherine Tiutchev, March 17, 1879.

26. Sergei A. Rachinskii, *Zametki o sel'skikh shkolakh* (St. Petersburg, 1883), 57-58; Andrew D. White, "A Statesman of Russia: Constantine Pobedonostzeff," *Century Magazine*, LVI (1898), 114; MDLL, CPP letters to Catherine Tiutchev, September 5, 1875; March 15, 1876.

27. CPP, *Novum Regnum*, 171; Ernest J. Simmons, *Leo Tolstoy* (Boston, 1946), 335-38; MDLL, CPP letter to Catherine Tiutchev, March 29, 1881.

28. CPP, *Pis'ma k Aleksandru III*, II, 130-34, 251-54; CPP, *Novum Regnum*, 643-50, 687; "Pis'ma Pobedonostseva k Feoktistovu," 502-503, 508-509, 524-27, 540-41, 547-48, 553; Feoktistov, *Vospominaniia*, 242-43; Simmons, *Tolstoy*, 395, 420, 448-50, 572; Aylmer Maude, *The Life of Tolstoy* (London, 1953), II, 30-31; MDLL, Sergei A. Rachinskii letters to CPP, March 17, June 17, June 23, 1894.

29. CPP, *Pis'ma k Aleksandru III*, II, 251-54, 328-29; "Pis'ma Pobedonostseva k Feoktistovu," 540; CPP, *Vsepoddanneishii otchët ober-prokurora Sviateishago sinoda K. Pobedonostseva po vedomstvu Pravoslavnago Ispovedaniia za 1886* (St. Petersburg, 1888), 201-202; George L. Calderon, "The Wrong Tolstoi," *The Monthly Review*, II (1901), 129-41; CPP (translator), George L. Calderon, *Pravda o gr. Leve Tolstome* (Moscow, 1901); *Poslanie Sviateishago sinoda o*

grafe Leve Tolstome (Moscow, 1901), 5-20; *Graf Lev Tolstoi i Svyatyeishi sinod* (Berlin, 1901), 7-42; Archimandrite Ioann, *Tolstoi i tserkov'* (Berlin, 1939), 120-37; G. A. Birkett, "Official Plans for Tolstoy's Funeral in 1902," *Slavonic and East European Review*, XXX (1951), 2-6; John S. Curtiss, *Church and State in Russia. The Last Years of the Empire, 1900–1917* (New York, 1940), 41; Simmons, *Tolstoy*, 593-99, 608; Maude, *Tolstoy*, II, 289; MDLL, CPP letters to Olga Novikov, March 17, June 17, June 23, 1894.

30. CPP, *Moskovskii sbornik* (third edition, Moscow, 1896), 57-74; CPP, *Pis'ma k Aleksandru III*, I, 189-90; P. Tverskoi, "Iz delovoi perepiski s K. P. Pobedonostsevym," *Vestnik Evropy*, XII (1907), 657-59; MDLL, CPP letters to Catherine Tiutchev, September 24, November 17, 1880; January 9, 1881; CPP letters to Olga Novikov, January 4, January 11, 1889; July 3, October 27, November 21, 1891; February 13, 1892; December 27, 1893; January 4, 1894; Catherine Tiutchev letter to CPP, January 13, 1881; N. Chernyshek memorandum, "Razgovor s ober-prokurorom Sv. sinoda K. P. Pobedonostsevym 1881 dek. 28."

31. CPP, *Pis'ma k Aleksandru III*, I, 255-58, 419; CPP, *Novum Regnum*, 69-70, 86-89, 94, 170-71, 264-66, 271-72, 318, 353-55, 369-74, 424; "Pis'ma k Feoktistovu," 502, 508-523, 527-28, 533, 538-39; "Pis'ma Pobedonostseva k Ignatievu," 61; Peretts, *Dnevnik*, 114-15; Polovtsov, *Dnevnik*, I, 380-82, 534; Markov, *K istorii raskola-staroobriadchestva*, 426-29; Vasilii V. Rozanov (editor), "Iz perepiski S. A. Rachinskago," *Russkii vestnik*, CCLXXXI (1902), 603-629; V. A. Labedev, "Iz zhizni Fedora Ivanovicha Buslaeva," *Russkaia starina*, CXXXIII (1908), 302.

32. CPP, *Pis'ma k Aleksandru III*, I, 342-44, 403-404; CPP, *Novum Regnum*, 557-58, 562-63, 936-37, 1061; "Pis'ma Pobedonostseva k Feoktistovu," 554; Dmitrii N. Ovsianiko-Kulikovskii (editor), *Istoriia russkoi literatury XIX v.* (Moscow, 1918–23), V, 436; MDLL, CPP letter to Catherine Tiutchev, February 4, 1881.

33. CPP, *Novum Regnum*, 728-29, 851-52; "Pis'ma Pobedonostseva k Feoktistovu," 515-16; Login F. Panteleev (editor), "Pis'mo K. P. Pobedonostseva k N. S. Abazie," *Golos minuvshago*, VI (1914), 231-32; "Dostoevskii o 'Bratiakh Karamazovykh.' Neizdannyia pis'ma, 1879–1881 gg.," *Byloe*, Number 15 (1919), 104-106; Nikita P. Giliarov-Platonov, *Sbornik sochinenii* (Moscow, 1899), I, preface; Ovsianiko-Kulikovskii, *Istoriia russkoi literatury*, V, 436; Sergius Yakobson (editor), "Pis'ma K. P. Pobedonostseva k V. F. Putsykovichu," in Kruzhok liubitelei russkoi stariny, *Stat'i i materialy* (Berlin, 1932), 74-76.

34. CPP, *Pis'ma k Aleksandru III*, I, 39-40, 176, 405; II, 257-59; CPP, *Novum Regnum*, 169-70, 415, 460-61, 1050, 1054; "Pis'ma Pobedonostseva k Feoktistovu," 507; Grossman, "Dostoevskii i pravitel'stvennye krugi," 136; Nicholas A. Liubimov, *Pamiati N. A. Liubimova* (St. Petersburg, 1897), 26; Sergei S. Tatishchev (S. Nevedenskii, *pseud.*), *Katkov i ego vremia* (St. Petersburg, 1888), 107-135; Witte, *Vospominaniia*, III, 578; Polovtsov, *Dnevnik*, I, 193, 389, 536, 590; II, 44; MDLL, CPP letter to Catherine Tiutchev, June 16, 1879; CPP letters to Katkov, July 20, 1866; August 18, 1869; January 8, February 14, February 21,

1878; March 3, March 30, April 1, April 18, 1880; February 17, June 28, August 21, October 17, October 21, December 6, 1882; May 16, 1883; March 1, March 13, July 19, November 3, November 5, 1884; October 27, November 3, 1885.

35. Quoted in Liubimov, *Pamiati*, 1-2.

36. MDLL, CPP letters to Catherine Tiutchev, February 5, 1874; July 8, August 27, 1879; October 23, 1880; CPP letters to Katkov, April 11, 1873; April 26, May 26, June 21, 1877; July 7, October 16, 1881; Catherine Tiutchev letters to CPP, June 6, August 19, 1879.

37. CPP, *Pis'ma k Aleksandru III*, II, 141-44; CPP, *Novum Regnum*, 585-86, 610, 644-45; "M. N. Katkov i Aleksandr III v 1886–1887 gg.," *KA*, LVIII (1933), 58-85; MDLL, CPP letter to Katkov, March 18, 1887.

38. CPP, *Pis'ma k Aleksandru III*, II, 151-52, 161-62; CPP, *Novum Regnum*, 676, 684-92, 705, 711-20, 744-45, 795-96, 1076-1078, 1081.

39. CPP, *Novum Regnum*, 721-22, 1081; CPP, "Pamiat' velikoi kniagini Ekateriny Mikhailovny," *Moskovskiia Vedomosti*, June 8, 1894; CPP, "Proshchanie Moskvy s tsarem svoim," *Moskovskiia Vedomosti*, November 1, 1894; CPP, "Ob universitetskom prepodavanii," *Moskovskiia Vedomosti*, June 26, 1899; CPP, "Otvet russkago cheloveka Kropotkinu," *Moskovskiia Vedomosti*, October 15, October 16, 1901; CPP, "Russia and Popular Education. A Reply to Prince Kropotkin," *North American Review*, CLXXIII (1901), 349-54; "Pis'ma Pobedonostseva k Feokistovu," 546-47; MDLL, CPP letters to Sergei A. Petrovskii, April 16, July 12, 1890; February 25, February 28, March 16, September 4, October 13, November 1, November 21, 1891; January 4, January 19, January 24, March 10, May 6, November 25, 1892; February 18, March 20, June 22, August 31, 1893; June 3, June 17, October 30, November 18, 1894; March 7, 1896.

40. CPP (editor), *Perepiska Iu. F. Samarina s baronessoiu E. F. Raden, 1861–1876* (Moscow, 1893), 150-55; CPP, *Vechnaia pamiat'*, 63-73; CPP, *Novum Regnum*, 178-79, 399; Ivan S. Aksakov, *Ivan Sergeevich Aksakov v ego pis'makh* (Moscow, 1888–96), IV, 294-97; A. Presniakov, "Moskovskii adres Aleksandru II v 1870 g.," *KA*, XXXI (1928), 144-54; MDLL, CPP letters to Catherine Tiutchev, November 23, 1868; November 20, December 15, December 20, 1870; August 11, 1874; November 10, November 18, 1876; January 17, 1877; September 6, September 7, September 28, November 30, 1880; March 21, 1881; CPP letters to Anna Aksakov, March 21, July 17, 1867; October 20, December 12, 1868; CPP letter to Ivan Aksakov, June 27, 1878; Catherine Tiutchev letters to CPP, December 8, 1870; November 12, November 13, 1876; September 7, 1880; January 4, January 13, March 12, July 24, 1881. Pobedonostsev wrote 550 letters to Anna Aksakov, but only forty have survived. (Gotie, "Pobedonostsev i naslednik," 108.)

41. CPP, *Novum Regnum*, 275-77, 556; "Pis'ma Pobedonostseva k Feoktistovu," 520-21; Ivan S. Aksakov, "Pis'ma I. S. Aksakova k K. P. Pobedonostsevu, 1876–1885," *RA*, III (1907), 176-77; Markov, *K istorii raskola-staroobriadchestva*, 208-209, 219, 224, 229, 448; Kucherov, *Courts, Lawyers and Trials*, 98-

99; MDLL, CPP letters to Catherine Tiutchev, September 20, December 8, 1881; February 4, February 8, 1882; Catherine Tiutchev letter to CPP, October 21, 1881.

42. A good illustration of his interest and skill in arranging for publication in several journals of a speech he thought especially important is the treatment provided the talk he gave in memory of Alexander III in 1894: *Proshchanie Moskvy s tsarem svoim* (Moscow, 1894), which was published in *Moskovskiia Vedomosti* and reprinted in Sergei A. Petrovskii (editor), *Pamiati Imperatora Aleksandra III* (Moscow, 1894), 88-89; in *Vechnaia pamiat'. Vospominaniia o pochivshikh* (Moscow, 1896), 101-104; and in *RA*, I (1906), 619-24. It was translated and published in French in the *Revue Anglo-Romaine*, I (1895), 40-44. It was also translated into Serbian. (Aleksandar Pogodin, *Rusko-srpska bibliografiia, 1800–1925* [Belgrade, 1932], I, 146.)

43. CPP, "Semeinye uchastki," *Russkii vestnik*, CCIV (1889), 56-72; *Semeinye uchastki* (St. Petersburg, 1892); "Semeinye uchastki," *Kurs grazhdanskago prava* (fourth edition, Moscow, 1896), I, 730-45.

44. CPP, *Pis'ma k Aleksandru III*, I, 353-54; "Pis'ma Pobedonostseva k Voitu," 79-84, 113-14; William E. Gladstone, *The Impregnable Rock of Holy Scripture* (Philadelphia, 1896), 279-325; CPP (translator), "Gladstone ob osnovakh veri i neveriia," *Russkoe obozrenie*, XXVI (1894), 32-41; CPP (translator), *Sekty i veroucheniia v Soedinennykh Shtatakh Severnoi Ameriki* (St. Petersburg, 1896); Department of the Interior, U.S. Census Office, *Report on Statistics of Churches in the United States at the Eleventh Census: 1890* (Washington, 1894); CPP (translator), *Pobeda, pobedivshaia mir* (tenth edition, Moscow, 1905); *The Confessions of St. Augustine* (New York, 1927), 1-40; William S. Lilly, *Christianity and Modern Civilization* (London, 1903), 131-61; Lilly, *Chapters in European History* (London, 1886), I, 49-97; CPP, "Nravstvennyi kharakter grazhdanina v khristianskom obshchestve," *Tserkovnyia Vedomosti*, March 23, 1902; Adolphe Prins, *De l'esprit du gouvernement démocratique. Essai de science politique* (Brussels, 1905), 159-232; CPP (translator), *Vseobshchaia podacha golosov (Suffrage Universel)* (St. Petersburg, 1906); CPP, *Voprosy zhizni* (Moscow, 1904); MDLL, CPP letter to Olga Novikov, June 17, 1900.

45. CPP, *Istoriia pravoslavnoi tserkvi do nachala razdeleniia tserkvei* (St. Petersburg, 1891), preface; (ninth edition, St. Petersburg, 1905).

46. CPP, *Novum Regnum*, 965-66, 998; CPP, *Istoriia pravoslavnoi tserkvi* (second edition, St. Petersburg, 1892), page after title page; Alexandra N. Bakhmetev, *Razskazy iz russkoi tserkovnoi istorii. Chtenie dlia detei starshago vozrasta* (fourth edition, Moscow, 1904); Boris N. Chicherin, *Vospominaniia* (Moscow, 1929–34), IV, 105; MDLL, CPP letters to Sergei A. Petrovskii, January 5, January 10, 1892; Catherine Tiutchev letters to CPP, May 20, 1880; September 16, 1881.

47. Minnie Mackay (Marie Corelli, *pseud.*), *The Mighty Atom* (Philadelphia, 1896), dedication; Catherine A. Pobedonostsev (translator), *Istoriia detskoi dushi (Mogushchestvennyi Atom)* (third edition, Moscow, 1897).

48. Ibid. (fifth edition, Moscow, 1911); Pogodin, *Rusko-srpska bibliografiia*, I, 13; CPP, *Uchenie i uchitel'* (sixth edition, St. Petersburg, 1906); CPP (translator), *Vospitanie kharaktera v shkole* (St. Petersburg, 1900); CPP (translator), "Vospitanie kharaktera v shkole," *Narodnoe obrazovanie*, Number 2 (1900), 3-12; CPP (translator), *Novaia shkola* (second edition, Moscow, 1899); Edmond Demolins, *L'Education nouvelle* (Paris, 1899); CPP, *Prizvanie zhenshchiny v shkole i obshchestve* (St. Petersburg, 1902); CPP, *Mery k povsemestnomu rasprostraneniiu gramotnosti v narod* (St. Petersburg, 1892).

49. CPP (translator), Heinrich W. Thiersch, *Khristianskiia nachala semeinoi zhizni* (Moscow, 1861); (second edition, Moscow, 1901); CPP (translator), Heinrich W. Thiersch, "O khristianskom brake," *Pravoslavnoe obozrenie*, IV (1861), 307-334; Heinrich W. Thiersch, *Uber christliches Familienleben* (Frankfurt-am-Main, 1854); CPP (translator), Frederick Le Play, *Osnovnaia konstitutsiia chelovecheskago roda* (Moscow, 1897); Frederick Le Play, *La Constitution essentielle de l'humanité* (Tours, 1881); CPP, *Nachala semeinoi zhizni* (St. Petersburg, 1904); CPP, "Le Plè," *Russkoe obozrenie*, XXIII (1893), 5-30.

50. CPP, *Vsepoddanneishii otchët ober-prokurora Sviateishago sinoda K. Pobedonostseva po vedomstvu Pravoslavnago Ispovedaniia za 1880* (St. Petersburg, 1882), 92-93; CPP, *Izvlechenie iz vsepoddanneishago otchëta za 1881* (St. Petersburg, 1883), 97-98; CPP, *Vsepoddanneishii otchët za 1883* (St. Petersburg, 1885), 70-72; CPP, . . . *za 1885* (St. Petersburg, 1887), 138-41; CPP, . . . *za 1886* (St. Petersburg, 1888), 53-59, 170-79, 218; CPP, . . . *za 1888–1889* (St. Petersburg, 1891), 403; CPP, . . . *za 1894–1895* (St. Petersburg, 1898), 72; CPP, . . . *za 1896–1897* (St. Petersburg, 1899), 246-47; CPP, . . . *za 1900* (St. Petersburg, 1903), 5-7, 356-57; Mel'gunov, "Pobedonostsev v dni pervoi revoliutsii," 190-91; Boris B. Glinskii, "Konstantin Petrovich Pobedonostsev. Materialy dlia biografii," *Istoricheskii vestnik*, CVIII (1907), 259; Giliarov-Platonov, *Sbornik sochinenii*, I, preface, xxix-xxxi.

51. Moscow. Sinodal'naya tipografiya, *Katalog knig, prodaiushchikhsia v sinodal'nykh knizhnykh lavkakh v S. Peterburge i Moskve* (Moscow, 1896); A. N. Soloviev, *Moskovskii pechatnyi dvor* (Moscow, 1917); Markov, *K istorii raskola-staroobriadchestva*, 521; Mel'gunov, "Pobedonostsev v dni pervoi revoliutsii," 182-84, 188-91.

52. CPP, *Pis'ma k Aleksandru III*, II, 88-90, 137-38; CPP, *Novum Regnum*, 885-86, 1088; Petrovskii, "Perepiska Pobedonostseva s Nikanorom," 244-46, 250-52, 338; Markov, *K istorii raskola-staroobriadchestva*," 323; CPP, *Vsepoddanneishii otchët za 1883*, 72-77; CPP, . . . *za 1885*, 141; CPP, . . . *za 1887* (St. Petersburg, 1889), 293-94; CPP, . . . *za 1888–1889*, 390-400; Russia. Sviateishii pravitel'stvuiushchii sinod, *Obzor deiatel'nosti vedomstva Pravoslavnago Ispovedaniia za vremia tsarstvovaniia Imperatora Aleksandra III* (St. Petersburg, 1901), 206; Conseil Scolaire de Saint Synode, *Ecoles paroissales en Russie* (Boulogne-sur-Seine, 1900), 7-9; William J. Birkbeck, *Birkbeck and the Russian Church* (London, 1917), 20-21; Curtiss, *Church and State in Russia*, 252.

53. CPP, *Pis'ma k Aleksandru III*, II, 319-20; "Pis'ma Pobedonostseva k Feok-

tistovu," 522-24; Mel'gunov, "Pobedonostsev v dni pervoi revoliutsii," 201; CPP, *Vsepoddanneishii otchët za 1887*, 149; "Dva pis'ma Andreia Nikolaevicha Muravieva k K. P. Pobedonostsevu," *RA*, II (1905), 415-16; CPP (editor), *Sbornik myslei i izrechenii mitropolita Moskovskago Filareta, 1782–1867* (Moscow, 1897), 3-4; Filaret, Metropolitan of Moscow, *Mneniia, otzyvy i pis'ma Filareta* (Moscow, 1905), foreword; Grigorii A. Dzhanshiev, *Epokha velikikh reform* (eighth edition, Moscow, 1900), 4-5, 61-63, 73, 193-99; Prince Nicholas V. Shakhovskoi, "N. P. Giliarov-Platonov, kak initsiator tserkovno-prikhodskoi shkoly," *Russkoe obozrenie*, XXXVIII (1896), 572-89; Savva, *Khronika moei zhizni*, VII, 68-72, 77; VIII, 214, 226, 257-60, 277, 287, 295-96, 351-59, 371-81, 388, 437-39, 452, 462-66, 517-18, 527-29, 532-35; IX, 62, 244-45; Markov, *K istorii raskola-staroobriadchestva*, 469-71, 488-90; Curtiss, *Church and State in Russia*, 31; MDLL, CPP letters to Catherine Tiutchev, November 27, 1867; February 28, 1868; November 11, December 8, December 17, December 22, 1872; February 11, 1874; December 22, 1881.

54. CPP, *Pis'ma k Aleksandru III*, I, 323; CPP, *Kurs grazhdanskago prava* (second edition, St. Petersburg, 1875), II, 155, 169; (fourth edition, St. Petersburg, 1896), II, 186; Rozhdestvenskii, *Istoricheskii obzor deiatel'nosti Ministerstva narodnago prosveshcheniia*, 549-50; Boris Veselovskii, *Istoriia zemstva za sorok let* (St. Petersburg, 1909–1911), III, 296-97; MDLL, CPP letter to Catherine Tiutchev, September 3, 1877; Catherine Tiutchev letter to CPP, October 21, 1881.

55. Miliukov, Seignebos, and Eisenman, *Histoire*, III, 878; Johnson, *Russia's Educational Heritage*, 282; MDLL, CPP letters to Olga Novikov, July 3, 1881; July 25, 1895; Sergei Rachinskii letters to CPP, June 1, December 7, 1894.

56. Nikita P. Giliarov-Platonov, *Voprosy very i tserkvi* (Moscow, 1905–1906), I, 135-37; II, 46-49, 92-96.

57. Medynskii, *Istoriia russkoi pedagogiki*, 324-28, 374; T. Nikolaeva, "Deti sela Tateva," *Ogonëk*, Number 50, December, 1963, 24-25; MDLL, CPP letter to Olga Novikov, May 3, 1902.

58. CPP, *Pis'ma k Aleksandru III*, I, 275-76; "Pis'ma Pobedonostseva k Feoktistovu," 532; Medynskii, *Istoriia russkoi pedagogiki*, 323-24; Ivan D. Udal'tsov (editor), *Ocherki po istorii Moskovskago universiteta* (Moscow, 1940), I, 69-70; MDLL, CPP letters to Catherine Tiutchev, December 25, 1878; February 4, 1881; CPP letters to Olga Novikov, March 5, 1895; June 20, 1899; December 21, 1901; Catherine Tiutchev letter to CPP, November 1, 1879; Rachinskii letters to CPP, January 26, March 17, November 2, 1894. Rachinskii published at least six articles in *Russkii vestnik* while he was in Germany in 1857–58.

59. CPP, *Pis'ma k Aleksandru III*, II, 5-6, 38-41, 223-25; CPP, *Moskovskii sbornik* (fifth edition, Moscow, 1901); CPP, *Vsepoddanneishii otchët za 1902* (St. Petersburg, 1905), 24-33; Sergei A. Rachinskii, *Sel'skaia shkola* (fifth edition, Moscow, 1902), introduction, 80-91; Rachinskii, "Tserkovnaia shkola," *Russkoe obozrenie*, XXXIII (1895), 541-56; XXXV (1895), 437-54; XXXVII (1896), 6-19; Rachinskii, "Uchitelia i uchitelnitsy," *Russkoe obozrenie*, L (1898), 422-36;

Rachinskii, "La Lutte contre l'alcoolisme en Russie," *La Réforme sociale*, XXI (1891), 718-21; Rachinskii, *Pis'ma S. A. Rachinskago k dukhovnomu iunoshestvu o trezvosti* (Moscow, 1899); Rachinskii, *1001 zadacha dlia umstvennago schëta. Posobie dlia uchitelei sel'skikh shkol* (Moscow, 1892); Father S. Tanaevskii, *Pamiati Sergeia Aleksandrovicha Rachinskago* (Kazan, 1904), *passim;* Rozanov, "Iz perepiski S. A. Rachinskago," 603-604, 610-11; N. M. Gorbov, "S. A. Rachinskii," *Zhurnal Ministerstva narodnago prosveshcheniia*, CCCXLIV (1902), 80; Kulomzin, *Istoricheskii obzor deiatel'nosti Komiteta Ministrov*, IV, 419; Markov, *K istorii raskola-staroobriadchestva*, 321, 359-60; Medynskii, *Istoriia russkoi pedagogiki*, 324-27, 346; MDLL, Rachinskii letters to CPP, January 19, January 26, February 4, February 17, February 23, March 3, March 11, June 21, July 8, August 9, October 6, November 17, November 28, December 7, 1894.

60. CPP, *Pis'ma k Aleksandru III*, II, 27-28, 322-24; CPP, *Novum Regnum,* 339-42, 452, 1048; CPP, *Vsepoddanneishii otchët za 1883*, 55-70; Petrovskii, "Perepiska Pobedonostseva s Nikanorom," 106-107, 245; Tanaevskii, *Pamiati Rachinskago*, 125-30; Evenchik, "Reaktsionnaia deiatel'nost' Pobedonostseva," chapter 6, 68-71; MDLL, CPP letters to Rachinskii, December 18, 1881; August 8, 1882.

61. Hans, *History of Russian Educational Policy*, 158-63.

62. CPP, *Vsepoddanneishii otchët za 1885*, 178-86; CPP, . . . *za 1886*, 128-54, 181-82; CPP, . . . *za 1890–1891* (St. Petersburg, 1893), 424; CPP, . . . *za 1894–1895*, 361-98; CPP, . . . *za 1896–1897*, 221; CPP, . . . *za 1902*, 4-5; Russia. Sviateishii pravitel'stvuiushchii sinod, *Obzor deiatel'nosti*, 691-715; Russia. Sviateishii pravitel'stvuiushchii sinod, *Pravila i programmy dlia tserkovno-prikhodskikh shkol i shkol gramoty* (St. Petersburg, 1894), 3-112; Russia. Sviateishii pravitel'stvuiushchii sinod, *Tsirkuliarnye ukazy Sviateishago pravitel'stvuiushchago sinoda, 1867–1900 gg.* (St. Petersburg, 1901), 191, 248-53; Hans, *History of Russian Educational Policy*, 155-63; Curtiss, *Church and State in Russia*, 182-84; Johnson, *Russia's Educational Heritage*, 192, 282; Alexander A. Polovtsev, "Dnevnik," *KA*, III (1923), 113; MDLL, Rachinskii letter to CPP, August 9, 1894.

63. CPP, *Vsepoddanneishii otchët za 1888–1889*, 382-83; CPP, . . . *za 1902*, 244-45; A. G. Rashin, "Gramotnost' i narodnoe obrazovanie v Rossii v XIX i nachale XX v.," *Istoricheskie zapiski*, Number 37 (1951), 64-67; Savva, *Khronika moei zhizni*, VIII, 581-89; Conseil Scolaire de Saint Synode, *Ecoles paroissales*, 5; Johnson, *Russia's Educational Heritage*, 192, 208-209; Curtiss, *Church and State in Russia*, 183-84.

XI. *Political and Social Thought*

1. CPP, *Pis'ma Pobedonostseva k Aleksandru III* (Moscow, 1925–26), II, 27-28, 271; CPP, *K. P. Pobedonostsev i ego korrespondenty. Pis'ma i zapiski. Novum Regnum* (Moscow, 1923), 452, 1048; CPP, *Kurs grazhdanskago prava* (second edition, Moscow, 1875), II, 155-69; CPP, *Vsepoddanneishii otchët ober-pro-*

kurora Sviateishago sinoda K. Pobedonostseva po vedomstvu Pravoslavnago Ispovedaniia za 1883 (St. Petersburg, 1885), 55-70; CPP and Ivan K. Babst, *Pis'ma o puteshestvii gosudaria naslednika tsesarevicha po Rossii ot Peterburga do Kryma* (Moscow, 1864), 519-20; CPP (translator), Heinrich W. Thiersch, *Kristianskiia nachala semeinoi zhizni* (Moscow, 1861); (second edition, Moscow, 1901); CPP (translator), Heinrich W. Thiersch, "O khristianskom brake," *Pravoslavnoe obozenrie*, IV (1861), 307-334; CPP (translator), *Fomy Kempiiskago o podrazhanii Khristu* (St. Petersburg, 1869), (sixth edition, St. Petersburg, 1896). *Prazdniki Gospodni*, a series of intensely personal religious meditations which Pobedonostsev wrote between 1858 and 1869, was published for the first time in St. Petersburg in 1894. "Starye listia," a poem he translated in *Russkaia beseda*, II (1859), Part I, 7-8, reappeared in *Moskovskii sbornik* (fifth edition, Moscow, 1901), 233.

2. General Hans von Schweinitz, *Briefwechsel des Botschafters General v. Schweinitz* (Berlin, 1928), 362-63; Louise Creighton, *Life and Letters of Mandell Creighton* (London, 1904), II, 150, 155; Hermann Dalton, *Lebenserinnerungen* (Berlin, 1906–1908), III, 98-99; Princess Catherine Radziwill, *Memories of Forty Years* (New York, 1915), 247-48; Boris B. Glinskii, "Konstantin Petrovich Pobedonostsev. Materialy dlia biografii," *Istoricheskii vestnik*, CVIII (1907), 273-74; I. V. Preobrazhenskii, *Konstantin Petrovich Pobedonostsev, ego lichnost' i deiatel'nosti v predstavlenii sovremennikov ego konchiny* (St. Petersburg, 1912), 11; MDLL, CPP letter to Catherine Tiutchev, December 18, 1875.

3. MDLL, CPP letter to Anna Tiutchev, May 1, 1865; CPP letter to Catherine Tiutchev, February 5, 1877. This point of view reappears in Pobedonostsev's principal work, *Moskovskii sbornik* (third edition, Moscow, 1896), 238.

4. CPP, "La Lutte contre l'alcoolisme en Russie," *La Réforme sociale*, XXVII (1894), 947-48; CPP, *Pis'ma k Aleksandru III*, I, 230-31, 302; II, 5-9, 34-41, 223-26; CPP, *Novum Regnum*, 308, 858, 908-909; "Perepiska Vitte i Pobedonostseva, 1895–1905," *KA*, XXX (1928), 98-100, 114; Vladimir S. Markov, *K istorii raskola-staroobriadchestva vtoroi poloviny XIX stoletiia. Perepiska prof. N. I. Subbotina* (Moscow, 1915), 504-505, 521-22; Robert S. Latimer, *Under Three Tsars. Liberty of Conscience in Russia, 1856–1909* (London, 1909), 133, 138; General Hans von Schweinitz, *Denkwürdigkeiten des Botschafters General v. Schweinitz* (Berlin, 1927), II, 185; MDLL, CPP letters to Catherine Tiutchev, February 14, 1874; February 10, 1876; April 16, 1877; February 26, 1880; January 26, 1881; Catherine Tiutchev letter to CPP, November 1, 1879.

5. MDLL, CPP letters to Catherine Tiutchev, February 19, 1869; December 30, 1871; June 12, 1874; January 4, 1875; July 21, August 29, 1881; February 4, 1882; Catherine A. Pobedonostsev letter to Catherine Tiutchev, June 16, 1880.

6. CPP, *Prazdniki Gospodni, passim;* CPP, *Pis'ma k Aleksandru III*, II, 271; Andrew D. White, "A Statesman of Russia: Constantine Pobedonostzeff," *Century Magazine*, LVI (1898), 115; Preobrazhenskii, *Pobedonostsev*, 20. The three hundred thirty letters from Pobedonostsev to Catherine Tiutchev, written between 1866 and 1882, now in the Manuscript Division of the Lenin Library,

are a reservoir of information concerning Pobedonostsev's religious beliefs.

7. CPP, *Novum Regnum*, 681-82; Sergei A. Petrovskii (editor), "Pis'ma K. P. Pobedonostseva preosviashchennomu Illarionu, arkhiepiskopu Poltavskomu," *RA*, LIV (1916), 371-73; S. Mel'gunov (editor), "K. P. Pobedonostsev v dni pervoi revoliutsii. Neizdannyia pis'ma k S. D. Voitu," *Na chuzhoi storone*, VIII (1924), 185-89; Ivan S. Aksakov, "Pis'ma I. S. Aksakova k K. P. Pobedonostsevu, 1876–1885," *RA*, III (1907) 169-71; N. Almazova, "K dvadtsatipiatiletiu Rossiiskago Obshchestva krasnago kresta," *RA*, II (1892), 360-67; *Adresnaia i spravochnaia kniga goroda Moskvy na 1894 god* (Moscow, 1894), 750-77, 793; Preobrazhenskii, *Pobedonostsev*, 18-22; MDLL, CPP letters to Anna Tiutchev, September 22, December 28, 1865; CPP letter to Catherine Tiutchev, December 22, 1877.

8. CPP, *Dobroe Slovo vospitatelnikam Dukhovnykh Seminarii i Akademii po povodu nyneshnikh strashnykh sobytii* (St. Petersburg, 1881); CPP, *Pis'ma k Aleksandru III*, I, 285-88, 344; CPP (translator), *Fomy Kempiiskago o podrazhanii Khristu* (fifth edition, St. Petersburg, 1893), 358; CPP (translator), Ralph Waldo Emerson, "Dela i dni," in *Skladchina; literaturnyi sbornik* (St. Petersburg, 1874), 217-40; Peter I. Bartenev (editor), "Iz dnevnika K. P. Pobedonostseva," *RA*, I (1907), 652; Prince Vladimir P. Meshcherskii, *Moi vospominaniia* (St. Petersburg, 1897–1912), II, 231, 244-45; Leonid Grossman, "Dostoevskii i pravitel'stvennye krugi 1870-kh godov," *Literaturnoe nasledstvo*, Number 15 (1934), 145-46; MDLL, CPP letter to Catherine Tiutchev, June 3, 1881.

9. "Pis'ma K. P. Pobedonostseva k S. D. Voitu," *RA*, I (1917), 82-88, 91-99; II (1917), 112-24; MDLL, CPP letters to Catherine Tiutchev, August 27, October 17, 1879.

10. CPP, *Moskovskii sbornik* (third edition, Moscow, 1896), 31-52, 142-46; CPP, *Uchenie i uchitel'. Pedagogicheskiia zametki* (second edition, Moscow, 1905), II, 49-50; CPP (translator), Edmond Demolins, *Novaia shkola* (Moscow, 1898), 70, 72, 81-82, 86-87, 96; Edmond Demolins, *L'Education nouvelle* (Paris, 1899), 86-87, 132-42; Demolins, *A quoi tient la supériorité des Anglo-Saxons* (Paris, 1899), 26-27; Herbert Spencer, *The Study of Sociology* (New York, 1893), 367-71; Ralph Waldo Emerson, *Society and Solitude* (Boston, 1898), 149-77; MDLL, CPP letters to Olga Novikov, October 26, 1877; February 11, 1891; April, 1899; April 24, 1901.

11. CPP, *Moskovskii sbornik* (fourth edition, Moscow, 1897), 83-92, 307; CPP (translator), George L. Calderon, *Pravda o gr. Leve Tolstome* (Moscow, 1901), 7, 24; George L. Calderon, "The Wrong Tolstoi," *The Monthly Review*, III (1901), 130, 141; William E. Gladstone, *The Impregnable Rock of Holy Scripture* (Philadelphia, 1896), 414-18.

12. Archbishop Savva of Tver, *Khronika moei zhizni* (Sergiev Posad, 1897–1911), VIII, 209; Dalton, *Lebenserinnerungen*, III, 154-55; Dalton, *On Religious Liberty in Russia* (Leipzig, 1890), 21-23, 27-36; MDLL, CPP letters to Olga Novikov, July 3, 1891; January 24, 1894.

13. CPP, *Moskovskii sbornik* (third edition, Moscow, 1896), 31-52; CPP, "Za-

pisnaia knizhka. Velikaia lozh' nashego vremeni," *Grazhdanin*, Number 4, January 22, 1884; Number 19, May 6, 1884; Number 24, June 10, 1884; Baron Alexander E. Nolde, "Obzor nauchnoi iuridicheskoi deiatel'nosti K. P. Pobedonostseva," *Zhurnal Ministerstva narodnago prosveshcheniia*, VIII (1907), 114; Max Nordau, *Die conventiollen Lügen der Kulturmenschheit* (sixth edition, Chicago, 1884), 142-57; Sergius Yakobson (editor), "Pis'ma K. P. Pobedonostseva k V. F. Putsykovichu," in Kruzhok liubitelei russkoi stariny, *Stat'i i materialy* (Berlin, 1932), 77.

14. CPP, *Prazdniki Gospodni*, 14; CPP (translator), *Fomy Kempiiskago o podrazhanii Khristu* (fifth edition, St. Petersburg, 1893), 276, 282, 287-89; Maurice Bompard, *Mon Ambassade en Russie, 1903–1908* (Paris, 1937), 257-58.

15. CPP, "Otvet russkago cheloveka Kropotkinu," *Moskovskiia Vedomosti*, October 15, October 16, 1901; CPP, "Russia and Popular Education. A Reply to Prince Kropotkin," *North American Review*, CLXXIII (1901), 349-54; Grand Prince Alexander Mikhailovich, *Vospominaniia* (Paris, 1933), 189; Jan Heidler (editor), *Příspěvky k listáři Dra. Frant. Lad. Riegra* (Prague, 1924–26), II, 61, 68; MDLL, CPP letter to Catherine Tiutchev, December 9, 1878.

16. CPP, *Pis'ma k Aleksandru III*, II, 38-41, 223-25; CPP, "Le Plè," *Russkoe obozrenie*, XXIII (1893), 14-15.

17. CPP, *Moskovskii sbornik* (third edition, Moscow, 1896), 267-76; (fourth edition, Moscow, 1897), 259-61; (fifth edition, Moscow, 1901), 327-30; MDLL, CPP letter to Catherine Tiutchev, June 12, 1874.

18. CPP, *Pis'ma k Aleksandru III*, I, 248-50; II, 3-5, 32-34, 275-76, 349, 358; CPP and Babst, *Pis'ma*, 85-87; MDLL, CPP letters to Anna Tiutchev, June 23, July 5, 1863.

19. CPP, *Moskovskii sbornik* (third edition, Moscow, 1896), 57-76, 92-99, 116-19, 126-30, 238, 275-76, 286-88; (fourth edition, Moscow, 1897), 259-60, 282-83, 296-98; (fifth edition, Moscow, 1901), 151-58, 327-29; CPP, "Kritika i bibliografiia. Svoboda, ravenstvo i bratstvo," *Grazhdanin*, Number 35, August 27, 1873, 958-60; Iurii F. Samarin and O. Dmitriev, *Revoliutsionnyi konservatizm* (Berlin, 1875), 10; Grossman, "Dostoevskii i pravitel'stvennye krugi," 126, 138; MDLL, CPP letter to Catherine Tiutchev, July 12, 1878.

20. CPP, *Moskovskii sbornik* (third edition, Moscow, 1896), 57-74, 92-98, 121-30, 181-85, 238; CPP, *Pis'ma k Aleksandru III*, I, 5-6, 38-40; II, 223-25; CPP, "La Lutte contre l'alcoolisme," 947-49; CPP, *Vsepoddanneishii otchët oberprokurora Sviateishago sinoda K. Pobedonostseva po vedomstvu Pravoslavnago Ispovedaniia za 1888–1889* (St. Petersburg, 1891), 77-79; "Perepiska Vitte i Pobedonostseva," 100; Markov, *K istorii raskola-staroobriadchestva*, 504-505, 521-22; Savva, *Khronika moei zhizni*, VIII, 589-92; MDLL, CPP letters to Anna Tiutchev, November 8, 1864; February 2, 1865; CPP letters to Catherine Tiutchev, February 12, February 28, October 18, 1868; October 24, 1869; November 22, 1870; March 13, October 12, October 31, 1874; November 17, 1875; December 30, 1876; January 18, September 16, 1877; February 23, 1878; June 8, 1879; January 2, 1881; January 8, February 15, 1882.

21. CPP, *Uchenie i uchitel'* (second edition, Moscow, 1905), II, 49-50.

22. CPP (translator), *Novaia shkola*, preface, 3-4, 25-30, 69-72, 95-102; CPP, "Ob universitetskom prepodavanii," *Moskovskiia Vedomosti*, June 26, 1899; CPP, *Uchenie i uchitel'* (fifth edition, Moscow, 1903), I, 31-38; (first edition, Moscow, 1904), II, 38-54; White, "A Statesman of Russia," 114.

23. CPP, *Moskovskii sbornik* (third edition, Moscow, 1896), 69; CPP and Babst, *Pis'ma*, 88-89; CPP, *Vechnaia pamiat'. Vospominaniia o pochivshikh* (Moscow, 1896), 9-20; CPP, *Uchenie i uchitel'* (fifth edition, Moscow, 1903), I, 27-44; (first edition, Moscow, 1904), II, 48-49, 54; Petrovskii (editor), "Pis'ma Pobedonostseva preosviashchennomu Illarionu," 363; Grossman, "Dostoevskii i pravitel'stvennye krugi," 138; Heinrich W. Thiersch, *On the Christian Commonwealth* (Edinburgh, 1877), 141; MDLL, CPP letter to Catherine Tiutchev, June 9, 1880.

24. CPP, *Uchenie i uchitel'* (fifth edition, Moscow, 1903), I, 3-61; (second edition, Moscow, 1905), II, 38-39.

25. CPP, *Kurs grazhdanskago prava* (third edition, St. Petersburg, 1890), II, 4, 128, 134, 632-35, 645; (fourth edition, St. Petersburg, 1896), II, 6-7, 15-17, 215-16; Friedrich Engels, *The Origin of the Family, Private Property, and the State* (Chicago, 1902), 9-26; Lewis Morgan, *Systems of Consanguinity and Affinity in the Human Family* (Washington, 1868).

26. CPP (translator), Frederick Le Play, *Osnovnaia konstitutsiia chelovecheskago roda* (Moscow, 1897); CPP (translator), *Khristianskiia nachala semeinoi zhizni* (first edition, Moscow, 1861); (second edition, Moscow, 1901); CPP, "Le Plè," 5-30; Louis Thomas, *Frédéric Le Play, 1806–1882* (Paris, 1943), 71-76, 114-24; Carle C. Zimmerman and Merle E. Frampton, *Family and Society. A Study of the Sociology of Reconstruction* (New York, 1935), 81-82, 96-97; William T. Stead (editor), *The M.P. for Russia. Reminiscences and Correspondence of Madame Olga Novikov* (London, 1909), II, 141-42, 224; Dalton, *Lebenserinnerungen*, I, 331; MDLL, CPP letter to Count Dmitrii A. Tolstoy, July 17, 1886; CPP letters to Olga Novikov, November 6, November 18, November 30, 1876; August 23, 1885.

27. CPP, *Kurs grazhdanskago prava* (second edition, St. Petersburg, 1875), II, 23-24, 45-54, 75-112, 146-68, 210, 644-66; CPP (translator), *Osnovnaia konstitutsiia chelovecheskago roda*, 66-69, 180-82; CPP (translator), *Khristianskiia nachala semeinoi zhizni, passim*, especially 7-20, 28-30, 122-45, 193-206; CPP, "Le Plè," 9-25.

28. CPP, *Pis'ma k Aleksandru III*, II, 147-48; CPP, *Kurs grazhdanskago prava* (second edition, St. Petersburg, 1875), II, 5-9, 99-101, 103-112, 149-55; CPP, *Uchenie i uchitel'* (first edition, Moscow, 1904), II, 11-12; CPP (translator), *Osnovnaia konstitutsiia chelovecheskago roda*, preface, 1-6, 82-87; CPP (translator), *Khristianskiia nachala semeinoi zhizni*, 11-30; CPP, "Le Plè," 10, 14-18; Thiersch, *On the Christian Commonwealth*, 15-29, 43, 63-81, 96-100, 129-48.

29. CPP, *Kurs grazhdanskago prava* (third edition, St. Petersburg, 1883), I,

504-558, especially 524-39; (fourth edition, St. Petersburg, 1896), I, 548; (second edition, St. Petersburg, 1875), II, 646-47; (fourth edition, St. Petersburg, 1896), II, 530-32; Vladimir Gsovski, *Soviet Civil Law* (Ann Arbor, Michigan, 1948–49), I, 671 fn.

30. CPP, *Kurs grazhdanskago prava* (third edition, St. Petersburg, 1883), I, 504-511; (fourth edition, St. Petersburg, 1896), I, 730-45; (second edition, St. Petersburg, 1875), II, 177, 333-34; CPP, "Semeinye uchastki," *Russkii vestnik*, CCIV (1889), 56-72.

31. CPP, *Kurs grazhdanskago prava* (third edition, St. Petersburg, 1883), I, 504-511; (fourth edition, St. Petersburg, 1896), I, 484, 532, 570, 730-35; (second edition, St. Petersburg, 1875), II, 333-34; (fourth edition, St. Petersburg, 1896), II, 11; CPP, "Semeinye uchastki," 71-72.

32. CPP, *Vsepoddanneishii otchët za 1888–1889*, 7-8.

33. CPP, *Moskovskii sbornik* (third edition, Moscow, 1896), 17-19, 23, 173, 219-22; CPP, *Istoriia pravoslavnoi tserkvi do nachala razdeleniia tserkvei* (second edition, St. Petersburg, 1892), 11, 122-30, 161-62; Fedor M. Dostoevsky, *Sobranie sochinenii* (Paris, 1945–46), IV, 384-85; Claude G. Bowers, *Beveridge and the Progressive Era* (Cambridge, Mass., 1932), 147-48; Emile J. Dillon, *The Eclipse of Russia* (New York, 1918), 83; Rose J. Birkbeck, *Life and Letters of W. J. Birkbeck* (London, 1922), 69-70; Eduard Winter, *Russland und die slawischen Völker in der Diplomatie des Vatikans, 1878–1903* (Berlin, 1950), 75; K. Istomin (editor), "Pis'mo g. ober-prokurora Sv. sinoda K. P. Pobedonostseva k Pateru V. Vannutelli," *Vera i razum*, I (1893), 355-56; Nicholas Riasanovsky, *Russia and the West in the Teaching of the Slavophiles* (Cambridge, Mass., 1952), 130-31; MDLL, CPP letter to Catherine Tiutchev, December 20, 1881.

34. CPP, *Moskovskii sbornik* (third edition, Moscow, 1896), 2-3, 20-22; CPP, *Pis'ma k Aleksandru III*, II, 297-99.

35. MDLL, CPP letters to Catherine Tiutchev, October 23, 1871; August 11, 1875.

36. CPP, *Moskovskii sbornik* (third edition, Moscow, 1896), 179, 192-93, 201, 204; CPP, *Pis'ma k Aleksandru III*, I, 404; CPP, "K voprosu o vozsoedinenei tserkvei," *Grazhdanin*, Number 33, August 13, 1873, 893-96; CPP, "Bor'ba gosudarstva s tserkoviu v Germanii," *Grazhdanin*, Number 34, August 20, 1873, 915-17; CPP, "Novaia vera i novye braki," *Grazhdanin*, Number 39, September 24, 1873, 1047-1048; Creighton, *Life and Letters of Mandell Creighton*, II, 250-51.

37. John S. Curtiss, *Church and State in Russia. The Last Years of the Empire, 1900–1917* (New York, 1940), 169-70; Creighton, *Life and Letters of Mandell Creighton*, II, 160-61; von Schweinitz, *Denkwürdigkeiten*, II, 384.

38. CPP, *Moskovskii sbornik* (third edition, Moscow, 1896), 3-9, 12-13, 20-23, 140-49, 154-56, 159-73, 186-88, 211-27, 271, 277-85; CPP, *Pis'ma k Aleksandru III*, II, 79-82, 102-104, 108-110, 191-92, 259-60, 308-309; CPP, *Novum Regnum,*

832-34, 921; CPP, *Vsepoddanneishii otchët za 1902* (St. Petersburg, 1905), I; CPP, "Iz chernovykh bumag K. P. Pobedonostseva," *KA*, XVIII (1926), 205; CPP and Babst, *Pis'ma*, 54-56; N. Nikol'skii, "K. P. Pobedonostsev," *Tserkovnyi vestnik*, XXXIII (1907), 382; von Schweinitz, *Denkwürdigkeiten*, II, 243-44, 275, 302, 388, 395-96; White, "A Statesman of Russia," 113-16; Dalton, *On Religious Liberty*, 47-50; Grossman, "Dostoevskii i pravitel'stvennye krugi," 137-38; MDLL, CPP letter to Catherine Tiutchev, August 8, 1879.

39. von Schweinitz, *Denkwürdigkeiten*, II, 223.

40. CPP, *Vechnaia pamiat'*, 74-94; Nicholas I. Ilminskii, *Pis'ma Nikolaia Ivanovicha Ilminskago k ober-prokuroru Sviateishago sinoda Konstantinu Petrovichu Pobedonostsevu* (Kazan, 1895), 1-414, *passim*; Sergei A. Rachinskii, *Sel'skaia shkola* (fifth edition, Moscow, 1902), i-xv; Father S. Tanaevskii, *Pamiati Sergeia Aleksandrovicha Rachinskago* (Kazan, 1904), 6-83, 140-78; Ivan D. Udal'tsov (editor), *Ocherki po istorii Moskovskago universiteta* (Moscow, 1940), I, 69-70; Evgenii N. Medynskii, *Istoriia russkoi pedagogiki do Velikoi Oktiabrskoi Sotsialisticheskoi Revoliutsii* (second edition, Moscow, 1938), 323-24, 350-56.

41. CPP, *Novum Regnum*, 494, 560; CPP, *Vechnaia pamiat'*; Iurii V. Gotie, "K. P. Pobedonostsev i naslednik Aleksandr Aleksandrovich, 1865–1881," *Publichnaia Biblioteka SSSR imeni V. I. Lenina. Sbornik*, II (1929), 126-27; MDLL, CPP letters to Anna Aksakov, February 2, March 12, 1867; CPP letters to Catherine Tiutchev, December 2, 1866; October 18, 1868; December 22, 1874; August 8, 1879; July 23, 1880; September 20, 1881.

42. MDLL, CPP letters to Catherine Tiutchev, February 25, November 4, 1877; May 20, 1880.

43. CPP, *Pis'ma k Aleksandru III*, I, 292.

44. Evgenii M. Feoktistov, *Vospominaniia. Za kulisami politiki i literatury, 1848–1896* (Leningrad, 1929), 219-21; E. J. Dillon (E. B. Lanin, *pseud.*), "Constantine Pobedonostseff," *Contemporary Review*, LXIII (1893), 584; A. Kaminka, "K. P. Pobedonostsev," *Pravo*, I (1907), 823-24; Alexander V. Amfiteatrov and Evgenii Anichkov, *Pobedonostsev* (St. Petersburg, 1907), 101; Dalton, *Lebenserinnerungen*, III, 88-91; Preobrazhenskii, *Pobedonostsev*, 17-18.

45. CPP, *Moskovskii sbornik* (third edition, Moscow, 1896), 242-52; (fourth edition, Moscow, 1897), 253-59; CPP, *Pis'ma k Aleksandru III*, I, 116-20; II, 38-40, 46-47, 144-45, 223-26; CPP, *Kurs grazhdanskago prava* (St. Petersburg, 1880), III, 78-82.

46. CPP, *Moskovskii sbornik* (third edition, Moscow, 1896), 268-74; CPP, *Pis'ma k Aleksandru III*, II, 271; CPP, *Prazdniki Gospodni*, 10-11, 16-20, 26-27, 31-32, 48-51, 55-58, 64; Catherine A. Pobedonostsev (translator), Minnie Mackay (Marie Corelli, *pseud.*), *Istoriia detskoi dushi* (Moscow, 1897); Minnie Mackay (Marie Corelli, *pseud.*), *The Mighty Atom* (Philadelphia, 1896).

47. CPP, *Pis'ma k Aleksandru III*, II, 4-5; CPP (translator), *Pobeda, pobedivshaia mir* (tenth edition, Moscow, 1905), 16-49, 57-92, 133-84; *The Confessions of St. Augustine* (New York, 1927), 1-40; William S. Lilly, *Chapters in European*

History (London, 1886), I, 48-87; CPP (translator), *Osnovnaia konstitutsiia chelovecheskago roda*, 117-20; "Kievskii sobor 1884 goda. Poslanie k vysokopreosviashchennomu Pavlu, eksarkhu Gruzii. Zapiski arkhiepiskopa Nikanora," *RA*, III (1908), 89.

48. CPP, *Moskovskii sbornik* (fifth edition, Moscow, 1901), 54-57; CPP, *Pis'ma k Aleksandru III*, I, 170-71; II, 3-4, 46-47, 145; CPP, *Novum Regnum*, 832-35, 1004-1006; CPP, "Gosudar' Imperator Aleksandr Aleksandrovich," *RA*, I (1906), 619-24; Egor A. Peretts, *Dnevnik E. A. Perettsa, 1880–1883* (Moscow-Leningrad, 1927), 38; *Byloe*, I (1906), 192-93. In one characteristic attack on parliamentary government, Pobedonostsev remarked that the political machine in a parliamentary system required perfect balance to work effectively. Representation, he wrote, must be mechanical, impersonal, and mathematically perfect. This, he said, was impossible. The mystical relationship between the *narod* and the state was to accomplish the feat possible only to a perfectly representative system. (*Moskovskii sbornik* [third edition, Moscow, 1896], 31-33.)

49. CPP, *Moskovskii sbornik* (third edition, Moscow, 1896), 25-52; CPP, "Kritika i bibliografiia. Svoboda, ravenstvo, i bratstvo," *Grazhdanin*, Number 35, August 27, 1873, 958-62; Number 37, September 10, 1873, 1807-1810; CPP, "Zapisnaia knizhka. Velikaia lozh' nashego vremeni," *Grazhdanin*, Number 24, June 10, 1884, 1-4; CPP (translator), *Osnovnaia konstitutsiia chelovecheskago roda*, appendix, 222; White, "A Statesman of Russia," 114.

50. CPP, *Moskovskii sbornik* (third edition, Moscow, 1896), 228-34, 259; CPP, *Pis'ma k Aleksandru III*, I, 49-53, 73-78, 111, 170-71, 193-96, 208-209, 215, 248-52, 259-60, 270, 338-39, 346-47; II, 3-5, 32-34, 46-47, 53, 144-45, 197-202, 215-19, 319-21; CPP, *Novum Regnum*, 1004-1005; CPP, *Istoricheskiia izsledovaniia i stat'i* (St. Petersburg, 1876), 14-15, 47-55, 116-85, especially 116-18, 156-59; CPP, "Graf V. N. Panin," *Golosa iz Rossii*, VII (1859), 3-10, 15-31, 37-39, 76-92; CPP, "Ispaniia," *Grazhdanin*, Number 37, September 10, 1873, 991-94; *Vsepoddanneishii otchët za 1883* (St. Petersburg, 1885), 1-3; CPP, "Privetstvie starago vospitatelia Velikomu Kniaziu v den ego sovershennoletia," *Starina i novizna*, XII (1907), 1-9; CPP and Babst, *Pis'ma*, 85-86; CPP (translator), *Osnovnaia konstitutsiia chelovecheskago roda*, 221; Gotie, "Pobedonostsev i naslednik," 116-26; MDLL, CPP letter to Anna Tiutchev, November 8, 1864; CPP letter to Olga Novikov, November 30, 1876.

51. CPP, *Moskovskii sbornik* (third edition, Moscow, 1896), 250-66; CPP, *Pis'ma k Aleksandru III*, I, 259-60, 267-69; II, 153; CPP, *Novum Regnum*, 856-67; CPP, *Kurs grazhdanskago prava* (second edition, St. Petersburg, 1873), I, 287-89; CPP and Babst, *Pis'ma*, 249-51, 338-40, 346; CPP (translator), *Osnovnaia konstitutsiia chelovecheskago roda*, 222; M. N. Knorring, *General Mikhail Dmitrievich Skobelev* (Paris, 1939–40), 192-96, 226-27; Markov, *K istorii raskola-staroobriadchestva*, 645-48; MDLL, CPP letters to Catherine Tiutchev, October 17, November 2, 1881.

52. CPP, *Pis'ma k Aleksandru III*, II, 46-47; CPP, *Novum Regnum*, 452-53,

521-22; George Yaney, "The Concept of the Stolypin Land Reform," *Slavic Review*, XXIII (1964), 280.

53. CPP, *Uchenie i uchitel'* (fifth edition, Moscow, 1903), I, 35; (first edition, Moscow, 1904), II, 15-19, 42-48; CPP, *Novum Regnum*, 865-66.

XII. *Philosophy of History*

1. CPP, "Gosudar' Imperator Aleksandr Aleksandrovich," *RA*, I (1906), 622.

2. CPP, *Moskovskii sbornik* (third edition, Moscow, 1896), 142-43; CPP, *Kurs grazhdanskago prava* (second edition, St. Petersburg, 1875), II, 332-34; CPP, "Russkoe grazhdanskoe sudoproizvodstvo v istoricheskom ego razvitii ot Ulozheniia 1649 goda do izdaniia Svoda Zakonov," *Arkhiv istoricheskikh i prakticheskikh svedenii otnosiashchikhsia do Rossii*, I, Part I (1859), 1-4.

3. Morris R. Cohen, *The Meaning of Human History* (La Salle, Illinois, 1947), 9; R. G. Collingwood, *The Idea of History* (Oxford, 1946), 1; Maurice Mandelbaum, "Can There Be a Philosophy of History?" *American Scholar*, IX (1939–40), 74-83. See also, Alexander von Schelting, *Russland und Europa im russischen Geschichtsdenken* (Bern, 1948).

4. Quoted by R. E. Saddler, "National Education and Social Ideals," in R. D. Roberts (editor), *Education in the Nineteenth Century* (Cambridge, England, 1901), 210-11.

5. CPP, *Kurs grazhdanskago prava* (third edition, St. Petersburg, 1883), I, 356-57; (second edition, St. Petersburg, 1875), II, 276; (first edition, St. Petersburg, 1880), III, 362, 564-65, 573-75; CPP, "O reformakh v grazhdanskom sudoproizvodstve," *Russkii vestnik*, XXI (1859), 546-48; CPP, "O zhalobakh na deistviia dolzhnostnykh lits administrativnago vedomstva," 1864, Manuscript Division, Saltykov-Shchedrin Library, Leningrad, 1-7; CPP, "Zapiska o grazhdanskom sudoproizvodstve," December, 1861, Manuscript Division, Saltykov-Shchedrin Library, 1, 6-7; Josef Jirásek, *Rusko a my* (Prague, 1945–46), IV, 50-51; Emile J. Dillon, *The Eclipse of Russia* (New York, 1918), 83; Andrew D. White, "A Statesman of Russia: Constantine Pobedonostzeff," *Century Magazine*, LVI (1898), 114.

6. CPP, *Istoriia pravoslavnoi tserkvi do nachala razdeleniia tserkvei* (second edition, St. Petersburg, 1892), 210-15, 217-24; Hermann Dalton, *On Religious Liberty in Russia* (Leipzig, 1890), 4-7, 13-19; Evangelical Alliance, *Rapport présenté aux branches de l'Alliance évangélique par le comité de Genève, sur des démarches faites au près de S. M. l'Empereur de Russie rélativement à la liberté religieuse dans l'empire russe* (Geneva, 1889), 3-20; Rose J. Birkbeck, *Life and Letters of W. J. Birkbeck* (London, 1922), 69-70, 110-16; MDLL, CPP letters to Catherine Tiutchev, November 23, 1871; August 11, 1875.

7. CPP, *Moskovskii sbornik* (third edition, Moscow, 1896), 55-56, 208-209; (fourth edition, Moscow, 1897), 50-54; (fifth edition, Moscow, 1901), 54-57; CPP, *Istoricheskiia izsledovaniia i stat'i* (St. Petersburg, 1876), 281-83; CPP, "Kritika

i bibliografiia. Svoboda, ravenstvo i bratstvo," *Grazhdanin*, Number 35, August 27, 1873, 958-62; Number 36, September 3, 1873, 976-79; Number 37, September 10, 1873, 1007-1010; CPP (translator), *Vseobshchaia podacha golosov (Suffrage Universel)* (St. Petersburg, 1896), 5-6, 34-37; Adophe Prins, *De l'esprit du gouvernement démocratique. Essai de science politique* (Brussels, 1905), 159-232; CPP, "O zhalobakh na deistviia dolzhnostnykh lits," 6-8; Baron Alexander E. Nolde, "Obzor nauchnoi iuridicheskoi deiatel'nosti K. P. Pobedonostseva," *Zhurnal Ministerstva narodnago prosveshcheniia*, VIII (1907), 115; MDLL, CPP letter to Olga Novikov, December 21, 1881.

8. *Istoricheskaia perepiska o sud'bakh pravoslavnoi tserkvi* (Moscow, 1912), 32-47.

9. CPP, *Pis'ma Pobedonostseva k Aleksandru III* (Moscow, 1925–26), II, 70-71; CPP, *Moskovskii sbornik* (fifth edition, Moscow, 1901), 158-60; CPP, *Kurs grazhdanskago prava* (third edition, St. Petersburg, 1883), I, 717-20; (second edition, St. Petersburg, 1875), II, 454-55, 533-34, 555-56; CPP, *Istoricheskiia izsledovaniia*, 124-25, 175-80, 279-81; CPP, "Gosudar' Imperator Aleksandr Aleksandrovich," 619-20; CPP and Ivan K. Babst, *Pis'ma o puteshestvii gosudaria naslednika tsesarevicha po Rossii ot Peterburga do Kryma* (Moscow, 1864), 434-35.

10. CPP, *K. P. Pobedonostsev i ego korrespondenty. Pis'ma i zapiski. Novum Regnum* (Moscow, 1923), 555-57, 590-93, 651-52, 661-63, 726-27, 1064; CPP, *Pis'ma k Aleksandru III*, I, 83-85; II, 218-21, 589, 651-52, 677-78; Count Richard von Pfeil und Klein-Ellguth, *Neun Jahre in russischen Diensten unter Kaiser Alexander III. Erinnerungen* (Leipzig, 1907), 183; General Hans von Schweinitz, *Denkwürdigkeiten des Botschafters General v. Schweinitz* (Berlin, 1927), II, 223; Leonid Grossman, "Dostoevskii i pravitel'stvennye krugi 1870-kh godov," *Literaturnoe nasledstvo*, Number 15 (1934), 139; Vladimir S. Markov, *K istorii raskola-staroobriadchestva vtoroi poloviny XIX stoletiia. Perepiska prof. N. I. Subbotina* (Moscow, 1915), 337-38; Cohen, *The Meaning of Human History*, 291; Evangelical Alliance, *Rapport*, 36; MDLL, CPP letter to Catherine Tiutchev, December 20, 1881.

11. CPP, *Pis'ma k Aleksandru III*, II, 211-14; CPP, *Kurs grazhdanskago prava* (third edition, St. Petersburg, 1883), I, 267-69; (second edition, St. Petersburg, 1875), II, 273-74; (first edition, St. Petersburg, 1880), III, 521; CPP, *Istoricheskiia izsledovaniia*, 14-15, 47-55, 116-85, especially 116-18, 124, 156-59; CPP, "Alexandre III," *Revue Anglo-Romaine*, I (1895), 40-44; CPP and Babst, *Pis'ma*, 5-6, 12-20, 526-30; Peter V. Pobedonostsev, "Zaslugi Kheraskova v otechestvennoi slovesnosti," *Trudy Obshchestva liubitelei rossiiskoi slovesnosti pri Imperatorskom Moskovskom universitete*, I (1812), 111-18.

12. CPP, *Istoricheskiia izsledovaniia*, 1-91, 118-19, 185-229, especially 1-2, 21-24, 42-50, 55-56, 118-19, 224.

13. CPP, *Kurs grazhdanskago prava* (second edition, St. Petersburg, 1873), I, 1-3, 20-30, 104-106; (third edition, St. Petersburg, 1883), I, 123-48, 174-80, 240-63, 293-308, 370-73, 386-89, 405-413, 465-503, 566-82, 620-21, 659-706; (first edition,

St. Petersburg, 1880), III, 75-76, 504-528; CPP, "Priobretenie sobstvennosti i pozemel'nyia knigi," *Russkii vestnik*, XXVIII (1860), 195-221; S. L. Evenchik, "Reaktsionnaia deiatel'nost' Pobedonostseva v 80-kh gg. XIX-go veka," a Moscow University Thesis for Candidate Degree in History in 1939, in its first chapter provides a complete misinterpretation of Pobedonostsev's views with regard to landholding.

14. CPP and Babst, *Pis'ma, passim*.

15. CPP, *Moskovskii sbornik* (third edition, Moscow, 1896), 131-34, 289-300; CPP (translator), Frederick Le Play, *Osnovnaia konstitutsiia chelovecheskago roda* (Moscow, 1897), 45-69; CPP, *Kurs grazhdanskago prava* (second edition, St. Petersburg, 1873), I, 9-13; (third edition, St. Petersburg, 1883), I, 123-25, 575-79; (second edition, St. Petersburg, 1875), II, 23-24, 73-74; (first edition, St. Petersburg, 1880), III, 78, 278-88, 362-67, 505-506, 523; CPP, "Veshchnyi kredit i zakladnoe pravo," *Russkii vestnik*, XXXIII (1861), 425-27, 443, 449-50; CPP, "O zhalobakh na deistviia dolzhnostnykh lits," 7-9; CPP and Babst, *Pis'ma*, 5-6, 573-74; Jan Heidler (editor), *Příspévky k listáři Dra. Frant. Lad. Riegra* (Prague, 1924–26), II, 61-68; Jirásek, *Rusko a my*, IV, 50-51.

16. CPP, *Moskovskii sbornik* (third edition, Moscow, 1896), 289-300; (fifth edition, Moscow, 1901), 30-37; CPP, *Kurs grazhdanskago prava* (third edition, St. Petersburg, 1883), I, 370-73, 380-87, 510; (first edition, St. Petersburg, 1880), III, 75-76, 504-505, 510, 521, 538-45, 550-51; CPP, "O iuridicheskoi dostovernosti telegraficheskikh izvestii," *Iuridicheskii vestnik*, I (1860), 39; CPP, "Veshchnyi kredit," 409-451, especially 444-45; CPP and Babst, *Pis'ma, passim*, especially 5-6, 144-45, 167-73.

17. CPP, *Moskovskii sbornik* (fifth edition, Moscow, 1901), 30-31; CPP, *Kurs grazhdanskago prava* (third edition, St. Petersburg, 1883), I, 536; (fourth edition, St. Petersburg, 1896), II, 418-19; CPP, *Uchenie i uchitel'. Pedagogicheskiia zametki* (fifth edition, Moscow, 1903), I, 20-21; (first edition, Moscow, 1904), II, 4; CPP, *Vsepoddanneishii otchët ober-prokurora Sviateishago sinoda K. Pobedonostseva po vedomstvu Pravoslavnago Ispovedaniia za 1896–1897* (St. Petersburg, 1899), 73-74; . . . *za 1902* (St. Petersburg, 1905), 122-24; CPP and Babst, *Pis'ma*, 7-20.

18. CPP, *Kurs grazhdanskago prava* (third edition, St. Petersburg, 1883), I, 525-40, 545; (fourth edition, St. Petersburg, 1896), I, 548, 730-45; (second edition, St. Petersburg, 1875), II, 9, 646-48; CPP, "Priobretenie sobstvennosti," 221-30.

19. CPP, *Pis'ma k Aleksandru III*, I, 122-23, 146, 171-72; CPP, *Kurs grazhdanskago prava* (first edition, St. Petersburg, 1880), III, 82, 521; CPP, "Mestnoe naselenie Rossii," *Russkii vestnik*, XL (1862), 5-34; CPP and Babst, *Pis'ma*, 5-6, 17-18, 157-58, 167-77, 325-27, 371-78, 530-31; A. N. Kulomzin (editor), *Istoricheskii obzor deiatel'nosti Komiteta Ministrov* (St. Petersburg, 1902–1903), IV, 390, 414-15; MDLL, Catherine Tiutchev letter to CPP, July 28, 1881.

20. CPP, *Pis'ma k Aleksandru III*, I, 179; CPP, *Novum Regnum*, 603-605, 1067-1068; CPP, *Kurs grazhdanskago prava* (second edition, St. Petersburg, 1873), I, 21-31; (first edition, St. Petersburg, 1880), III, 75-81, 245-46, 418-52,

589-600; (fourth edition, St. Petersburg, 1896), III, 431-33, 562-76; CPP, "O zhalobakh na deistviia dolzhnostnykh lits," 7-11; CPP, "Veshchnyi kredit," 427-40; CPP, "Mestnoe naselenie Rossii," 5-34, especially 26-27.

21. CPP, *Kurs grazhdanskago prava* (first edition, St. Petersburg, 1880), III, 393-413, 593-94; (fourth edition, St. Petersburg, 1896), III, 409-414, 538-40; CPP, *Uchenie i uchitel'* (fifth edition, Moscow, 1903), I, 20-21; CPP and Babst, *Pis'ma*, 7-20; Theodore H. von Laue, "Tsarist Labor Policy, 1895–1903," *Journal of Modern History*, XXXIV (1962), 138-39; von Laue, "Die Revolution von aussen als erste Phase der russischen Revolution von 1917," *Jahrbücher für Geschichte Osteuropas*, IV (1956), 149; Ivan Kh. Ozerov, *Politika po rabochemu voprosu v Rossii za poslednye gody* (Moscow, 1906), 146-53; MDLL, CPP letter to Catherine Tiutchev, January 23, 1876.

XIII. *Russia and the West*

1. Abel Mansuy, *Le Monde slav et les classiques français au XVIe–XVIIe siècles* (Paris, 1912), 1-2; Emile Haumant, *La Culture française en Russie, 1700–1900* (Paris, 1913), 11-68, 130-319; Renato Poggioli, *The Poets of Russia, 1890–1930* (Cambridge, Mass., 1960), 9-13; Mikhail Shtrange, *La Révolution française et la société russe* (Moscow, 1960), 47-48, 53, 66, 77-86, 183-85.

2. Wladimir Weidlé, *Russia: Absent and Present* (New York, 1952), 48-49; B. H. Sumner, *Peter the Great and the Emergence of Russia* (New York, 1962), 5, 84, 190; Sumner, *A Short History of Russia* (New York, 1943), 331.

3. Stepan S. Volk, "Dekabristy o burzhuaznom Zapade," *Izvestiia. Akademiia Nauk SSSR. Seriia istorii i filosofii*, VII (1951), 78-81; A. Molok, "Tsarskaia Rossiia i iiul'skaia revoliutsiia 1830 g.," *Literaturnoe nasledstvo*, Number 29-30 (1937), 734-40, 750-55; Sidney Monas, *The Third Section. Police and Society in Russia under Nicholas I* (Cambridge, Mass., 1961), 135-40, 190-96; Alexander von Schelting, *Russland und Europa im russischen Geschichtsdenken* (Bern, 1948), 25-26, 319; B. H. Sumner, "Russia and Europe," *Oxford Slavonic Papers*, II (1951), 4; Haumant, *La Culture française*, 69-118, 320-403; Poggioli, *The Poets of Russia*, 43-45.

4. Albert Gratieux, *A. S. Khomiakov et le mouvement slavophile* (Paris, 1939), I, 115-26; II, 33-34; William J. Birkbeck, *Russia and the English Church in the Last Fifty Years* (London, 1895), xxv; Serge Bolshakoff, *Russian Nonconformity* (Philadelphia, 1950), 8-18, 110-12.

5. Quoted by Nicholas Riasanovsky, *Russia and the West in the Teaching of the Slavophiles* (Cambridge, Mass., 1952), 108.

6. Kyra Sanine, *Les Annales de la patrie et la diffusion de la pensée française en Russie, 1868–1884* (Paris, 1955), 12, 45-46; Herbert Bowman, *Vissarion Belinski, 1811–1848* (Cambridge, Mass., 1954), 37-38, 141, 145-46; Vasilii V. Zenkovsky, *Russian Thinkers and Europe* (Ann Arbor, Michigan, 1953), 27-32; Iurii F. Samarin, *Sochineniia* (Moscow, 1911), I, 394; Pavel V. Annenkov, *Litera-*

turnye vospominaniia (Moscow, 1960), 291; Ivan S. Aksakov, *Biografiia Fedora Ivanovicha Tiutcheva* (Moscow, 1886), 240-45; Riasanovsky, *Russia and the West*, 29-33, 100-108; Weidlé, *Russia: Absent and Present*, 2, 56; Poggioli, *The Poets of Russia*, 33-35; Haumant, *La Culture française*, 417-32, 472-83.

7. Alexander Herzen, *Memoirs. My Past and Thoughts* (London, 1924–27), I, 50-54; Martin Malia, *Alexander Herzen and the Birth of Russian Socialism, 1812–1855* (Cambridge, Mass., 1961), 9-37.

8. Alexander Herzen, *Pis'ma iz Frantsii i Italii, 1847–1852* (Moscow-Leningrad, 1934), 284; Franco Venturi, *Roots of Revolution* (New York, 1960), 1-35; Sanine, *Les Annales de la patrie*, 28-30, 35-37, 100-102; Haumant, *La Culture française*, 359; Malia, *Herzen*, 99-133, 313-68; Zenkovsky, *Russian Thinkers and Europe*, 62-67.

9. Sergei Tatishchev (S. Nevedenskii, *pseud.*), *Katkov i ego vremia* (St. Petersburg, 1888), 323, 403; Marc Raeff, "A Reactionary Liberal: M. N. Katkov," *Russian Review*, XI (1952), 160-67; B. H. Sumner, *Russia and the Balkans, 1870–1880* (Oxford, 1937), 37-43; Aksakov, *Biografiia Tiutcheva*, 318.

10. Ernest J. Simmons, *Dostoevsky. The Making of a Novelist* (New York, 1962), 289-90, 319-32; Riasanovsky, *Russia and the West*, 206-207; Haumant, *La Culture française*, 437-39, 461-62, 489-90.

11. William L. Langer, *The Franco-Russian Alliance, 1890–1894* (Cambridge, Mass., 1929), 10, 90-92, 253-55, 270-71; Haumant, *La Culture française*, 422, 442; Zenkovsky, *Russian Thinkers and Europe*, 120, 126, 197.

12. CPP, *Pis'ma Pobedonostseva k Aleksandru III* (Moscow, 1925–26), I, 10, 18, 31-32, 36, 38, 196-97, 277-78, 403; II, 53; CPP, *K. P. Pobedonostsev i ego korrespondenty. Pis'ma i zapiski. Novum Regnum* (Moscow, 1923), 1014-1016; "Pis'ma K. P. Pobedonostseva k E. M. Feoktistovu," *Literaturnoe nasledstvo*, Number 22-24 (1935), 528, 542; Alexander A. Polovtsev, "Dnevnik," *KA*, III (1923), 94-96. Pobedonostsev's correspondence contains frequent references to his reading and to his travel.

13. CPP, *Pis'ma k Aleksandru III*, I, 249, 285-88, 354; II, 83-84, 112-17, 229-34, 240-51, 255-56; CPP (editor), "Pis'ma I. I. Lazhechnikova k S. P. i K. P. Pobedonostsevym," *Russkoe obozrenie*, XXXII (1895), 881; Sergei A. Petrovskii (editor), "Pis'ma K. P. Pobedonostseva preosviashchennomu Illarionu, arkhiepiskopu Poltavskomu," *RA*, LIV (1916), 131, 369-71; Vladimir S. Markov, *K istorii raskola-staroobriadchestva vtoroi poloviny XIX stoletiia. Perepiska prof. N. I. Subbotina* (Moscow, 1915), 188, 458, 461, 484; Vasilii V. Rozanov (editor), "Iz perepiski S. A. Rachinskago," *Russkii vestnik*, CCLXXXI (1902), 622-23; Rose J. Birkbeck, *Life and Letters of W. J. Birkbeck* (London, 1922), 29, 111-16; MDLL, CPP letters to Catherine Tiutchev, September 14, 1869; October 23, 1871; August 11, 1875.

14. CPP, *Moskovskii sbornik* (fifth edition, Moscow, 1901), 293-95; CPP, *Pis'ma k Aleksandru III*, I, 65-68; II, 292-94; CPP, *Uchenie i uchitel'. Pedagogicheskiia zametki* (Moscow, 1904), II, 40; General Hans von Schweinitz, *Denkwürdigkeiten des Botschafters General v. Schweinitz* (Berlin, 1927), II, 395;

Louise Creighton, *Life and Letters of Mandell Creighton* (London, 1904), II, 155; Claude G. Bowers, *Beveridge and the Progressive Era* (Cambridge, Mass., 1932), 147-48; France, Ministère des Affaires Etrangères, *Documents diplomatiques français, 1871–1914* (Paris, 1929–51), second series, I, 648; MDLL, CPP letters to Catherine Tiutchev, November 26, 1875; January 25, November 4, 1877; February 23, 1878; CPP letters to Olga Novikov, January 28, October 11, 1877; November 21, 1891; October 23, November 20, 1892.

15. CPP, *Moskovskii sbornik* (third edition, Moscow, 1896), 53-55, 111, 125, 159-63, 167-79, 188-94, 208; CPP, *Pis'ma k Aleksandru III*, I, 273-75; II, 292-94; CPP, *Kurs grazhdanskago prava* (third edition, St. Petersburg, 1883), I, 263, 723-27; (second edition, St. Petersburg, 1875), II, 12, 14, 85-87; *Kurs grazhdanskago prava. Ukazateli i prilozheniia* (St. Petersburg, 1896), 110; CPP, "Knizhnyia zagranichnyia vesti o Rossii," *RA*, IV (1866), 260-62; CPP, "Iz Londona," *Grazhdanin*, Number 27, July 2, 1873, 751-52; "Pis'ma Pobedonostseva k Feoktistovu," 531, 540; Viscount Eugène de Vogüé, *Les Routes* (Paris, 1910), 136; Alexander A. Polovtsev, *Dnevnik gosudarstvennago sekretaria A. A. Polovtsova* (Moscow, 1966), II, 102; Birkbeck, *Life and Letters*, 151-52, 169-70; Creighton, *Life and Letters*, II, 155, 250-51; MDLL, CPP letters to Catherine Tiutchev, November 30, 1868; November 20, 1875; November 4, November 25, 1877; February 23, November 30, 1880; March 4, 1882; CPP letters to Olga Novikov, December 3, December 25, 1876; September 6, 1882; June 24, July 20, 1885; January 11, November 26, 1889; July 3, October 15, 1891; October 23, 1892; June 24, 1894; November 3, 1896; September 3, 1898; March 30, 1900.

16. CPP, *Pis'ma k Aleksandru III*, I, 31-32; CPP, *Novum Regnum*, 975; CPP (translator), Ralph Waldo Emerson, "Dela i dni," in *Skladchina; literaturnyi sbornik* (St. Petersburg, 1874), 217; Jeremiah Curtin, *Memoirs* (Madison, Wis., 1940), 467-68, 486-87, 775-76, 781; Andrew D. White, "A Statesman of Russia: Constantine Pobedonostzeff," *Century Magazine*, LVI (1898), 114-15; MDLL, CPP letters to Catherine Tiutchev, December 5, 1870; March 11, 1874; June 22, 1876; September 30, 1877; CPP letters to Olga Novikov, March 2, 1877; November 21, 1891; February 13, November 20, 1892.

17. CPP, *Moskovskii sbornik* (third edition, Moscow, 1896), 176-78; CPP, *Kurs grazhdanskago prava* (third edition, St. Petersburg, 1883), I, 713-14, 721-30; (first edition, St. Petersburg, 1880), III, 121, 171, 580-82; Baron Alexander E. Nolde, *K. P. Pobedonostsev i sudebnaia reforma* (Petrograd, 1915), 13-14; Norman Douglas, *Looking Back. An Autobiographical Excursion* (New York, 1933), 62; MDLL, CPP letters to Anna Tiutchev, December 24, 1863; CPP letters to Catherine Tiutchev, September 5, 1875; September 6, September 20, September 27, 1876; CPP letters to Olga Novikov, April 21, 1894; March 30, 1900.

18. CPP, *Moskovskii sbornik* (fourth edition, Moscow, 1897), 260; CPP, *Pis'ma k Aleksandru III*, II, 510; CPP, *Kurs grazhdanskago prava* (third edition, St. Petersburg, 1883), I, 426, 714, 727-28; (second edition, St. Petersburg, 1875), II, 8; CPP, *Moskovskiia vospominaniia. V. P. Zubkov* (Moscow, 1904), 11-12;

"Pis'ma Pobedonostseva k Feoktistovu," 553; Polovtsov, *Dnevnik*, I, 349, 530; II, 271; MDLL, CPP letters to Catherine Tiutchev, December 11, 1875; March 15, May 25, 1876; June 15, 1878; October 4, 1879; CPP letters to Olga Novikov, January 11, 1889; December 23, 1893.

19. CPP, *Pis'ma k Aleksandru III*, I, 8-9, 16-17, 38, 403; CPP, "Iz Londona," 750-51; MDLL, CPP letters to Anna Tiutchev, November 8, 1864; October 20, 1868; CPP letters to Catherine Tiutchev, October 18, 1868; February 25, 1869; April 29, August 14, 1873.

20. CPP, *Pis'ma k Aleksandru III*, I, 29, 42-46; II, 83, 182, 188; CPP, *Novum Regnum*, 313-15, 824-28, 1084; "Pis'ma Pobedonostseva k Feoktistovu," 529; Hermann Dalton, *Lebenserinnerungen* (Berlin, 1906–1908), III, 154; MDLL, CPP letters to Catherine Tiutchev, June 12, 1874; August 11, September 5, September 21, 1875; June 22, July 6, 1876; CPP letters to Olga Novikov, August 4, 1897; June 14, 1900; May 3, 1902.

21. Institut de France. Académie des sciences morales et politiques, *Séances et travaux*, CXXXI (1889), 359-60; CIL (1898), 418, 703-705; Institut de France, *Annuaire pour 1889* (Paris, 1889), 89-90; Birkbeck, *Life and Letters*, 111; MDLL, CPP draft letter to Académie des sciences morales et politiques, 1892; Jules Simon letter to CPP, March 22, 1892.

22. CPP, *Pis'ma k Aleksandru III*, II, 316-17; Birkbeck, *Life and Letters*, 110-15; MDLL, CPP letter to Catherine Tiutchev, October 10, 1875; CPP letter to Olga Novikov, November 3, 1896.

23. CPP, "Vestminsterskoe abbatstvo," *Grazhdanin*, Number 32, August 6, 1873, 870-73; CPP, "Protivorechiia v anglikanskoi tserkvi," *Grazhdanin*, Number 34, August 20, 1873, 921-23; CPP, "Irvingity v Londone. Deisty i unitarii v Londone," *Grazhdanin*, Number 35, August 27, 1873, 949-51; CPP, "Vorovskii uzhin," *Grazhdanin*, Number 36, September 3, 1873, 974-76; CPP, "Iz Londona," 750-51; Leonid Grossman, "Dostoevskii i pravitel'stvennye krugi 1870-kh godov," *Literaturnoe nasledstvo*, Number 15 (1934), 124-25; Birkbeck, *Life and Letters*, 114; MDLL, CPP letters to Catherine Tiutchev, October 23, 1871; July 11, 1875.

24. Quoted by E. H. Carr, in " 'Russia and Europe' as a Theme of Russian History," in Richard Pares and A. J. P. Taylor (editors), *Essays Presented to Sir Lewis Namier* (London, 1956), 362.

25. Frederick C. Barghoorn, "Some Russian Images of the West," in Cyril E. Black (editor), *The Transformation of Russian Society* (Cambridge, Mass., 1960), 575-78; Riasanovsky, *Russia and the West*, 78-80; Sumner, "Russia and Europe," 1-3; Weidlé, *Russia: Absent and Present*, 2.

26. CPP, *Moskovskii sbornik* (third edition, Moscow, 1896), 55-56, 157-73; (fourth edition, Moscow, 1897), 50-54; (fifth edition, Moscow, 1901), 54-57; CPP, "K voprosu v vozsoedinenei tserkvei," *Grazhdanin*, Number 33, August 13, 1873, 893-96; CPP, "Kritika i bibliografiia. Svoboda, ravenstvo i bratstvo," *Grazhdanin*, Number 35, August 27, 1873, 958-62; Number 36, September 3, 1873, 976-79; Number 37, September 10, 1873, 1007-1010; CPP, "Lionskiia

grazhdanskiia pokhorony. V protestanskikh khramakh," *Grazhdanin,* Number 31, July 30, 1873, 848-49; CPP (translator), *Vseobshchaia podacha golosov (Suffrage Universel)* (St. Petersburg, 1906), especially 5-23, 34-37, 57-64; Adolphe Prins, *De l'esprit du gouvernement démocratique. Essai de science politique* (Brussels, 1905), 159-232; Nicholas I. Ilminskii, *Pis'ma Nikolaia Ivanovicha Ilminskago k ober-prokuroru Sviateishago sinoda Konstantinu Petrovichu Pobedonostsevu* (Kazan, 1895), 34-36; MDLL, CPP letter to Anna Tiutchev, November 8, 1864; CPP letters to Olga Novikov, December 3, 1876; December 21, 1881; October 10, October 28, 1891; CPP letters to Count Dmitrii A. Tolstoy, February 24, March 12, 1883; Sergei A. Rachinskii letter to CPP, January 13, 1894.

27. von Schelting, *Russland und Europa,* 14.

28. Venturi, *Roots of Revolution, passim.*

XIV. Fading Away

1. CPP, *K. P. Pobedonostsev i ego korrespondenty. Pis'ma i zapiski. Novum Regnum* (Moscow, 1923), 991; Boris B. Glinskii, "Konstantin Petrovich Pobedonostsev. Materialy dlia biografii," *Istoricheskii vestnik,* CVIII (1907), 247-54; Vladimir S. Markov, *K istorii raskola-staroobriadchestva vtoroi poloviny XIX stoletiia. Perepiska prof. N. I. Subbotina* (Moscow, 1915), 323, 492; Russia. Gosudarstvennyi sovet, *Gosudarstvennyi sovet, 1801–1901* (St. Petersburg, 1901), appendix, 6, 38; *Tserkovnyia Vedomosti,* January 9, 1888; *Illustrierte Zeitung,* March 28, 1907; MDLL, CPP letter to Olga Novikov, August 20, 1898.

2. Vladimir I. Lenin, *Sochineniia* (second edition, Moscow, 1927–32), II, 521; IV, 326; V, 160; IX, 62, 548; X, 60,78.

3. CPP, *Novum Regnum,* 977-78; S. Mel'gunov (editor), "K. P. Pobedonostsev v dni pervoi revoliutsii. Neizdannyia pis'ma k S. D. Voitu," *Na chuzhoi storone,* VIII (1924), 180, 184-85; P. Tverskoi, "Iz delovoi perepiski s K. P. Pobedonostsevym," *Vestnik Evropy,* XII (1907), 654; Alexander A. Polovtsev, "Dnevnik," *KA,* III (1923), 83-84; Alexandra V. Bogdanovich, *Dnevnik, 1880– 1912* (Moscow, 1924), 315-17; Boris Nicolaevsky, *Aseff* (London, 1934), 56-57; Markov, *K istorii raskola-staroobriadchestva,* 605, 625; MDLL, CPP letter to Sergei A. Petrovskii, June 22, 1893.

4. CPP, *Pis'ma Pobedonostseva k Aleksandru III* (Moscow, 1925–26), II, 332-34; CPP, "Russia and Popular Education. A Reply to Prince Kropotkin," *North American Review,* CLXXIII (1901), 352-54; "Perepiska Vitte i Pobedonostseva, 1895–1905," *KA,* XXX (1928), 89, 98; Archbishop Savva of Tver, *Khronika moei zhizni* (Sergiev Posad, 1897–1911), IX, 67; Count Vladimir N. Lamzdorf, *Dnevnik V. N. Lamzdorfa, 1886–1890* (Moscow, 1926), 26, 36; General Hans von Schweinitz, *Denkwürdigkeiten des Botschafters General v. Schweinitz* (Berlin, 1927), II, 301; Alexis Souvorine, *Journal intime de Alexis Souvorine* (Paris, 1927), 281; A. N. Kuropatkin, "Dnevnik A. N. Kuropatkina," *KA,* V (1924), 88; Princess Marie Radziwill, *Lettres de la princesse Radziwill*

au général de Robilant, 1889–1914 (Bologna, 1933–34), II, 7, 314-15; Russia. Gosudarstvennyi sovet, Opis' del arkhiva Gosudarstvennago soveta (St. Petersburg, 1908-1913), XVI, 199-200; William L. Langer, The Diplomacy of Imperialism, 1890–1902 (New York, 1935), I, 330-49; Arkadii S. Erusalimsky, Vneshnaia politika i diplomatiia germanskago imperializma v kontse XIX veka (second edition, Moscow, 1951), 168; Vladimir M. Khvostov, "Problemy zakhvata Bosfora v 90-kh godakh XIX veka," Istorik marksist, XX (1930), 117, 127-28; A. V. Zhirkevich, "Arkhiepiskop Ieronim. Opyt' kharakteristiki," Istoricheskii vestnik, CXIII (1908), 902-903; Charles E. Smith, "The Young Czar and His Advisers," North American Review, CLX (1895), 26-27; Mel'gunov, "Pobedonostsev v dni pervoi revoliutsii," 177-78; Tverskoi, "Iz delovoi perepiski," 654, 666-67.

5. CPP, Novum Regnum, 484, 560; I. V. Preobrazhenskii, Konstantin Petrovich Pobedonostsev, ego lichnost' i deiatel'nosti v predstavlenii sovremennikov ego konchiny (St. Petersburg, 1912), 20-21; Polovtsev, "Dnevnik," 86; Radziwill, Lettres au général de Robilant, II, 35.

6. CPP, Pis'ma k Aleksandru III, I, 114-15, 176, 179, 191; II, 178, 267-69; CPP (editor), "Pis'ma I. I. Lazhechnikova k S. P. i K. P. Pobedonostsevym," Russkoe obozrenie, XXXII (1895), 882; Sergei A. Petrovskii, "Pis'ma K. P. Pobedonostseva preosviashchennomu Illarionu, arkhiepiskopu Poltavskomu," RA, LIV (1916), 151, 361, 376; Peter I. Bartenev (editor), "Iz dnevnika K. P. Pobedonostseva," RA, I (1907), 636-37; Sergius Yakobson (editor), "Pis'ma K. P. Pobedonostseva k V. F. Putsykovichu," in Kruzhok liubitelei russkoi stariny, Stat'i i materialy (Berlin, 1932), 74; Nicholas I. Ilminskii, Pis'ma Nikolaia Ivanovicha Ilminskago k ober-prokuroru Sviateishago sinoda Konstantinu Petrovichu Pobedonostsevu (Kazan, 1895), 73; Leonid Grossman, "Dostoevskii i pravitel'stvennye krugi 1870-kh godov," Literaturnoe nasledstvo, Number 15 (1934), 134, 136; Savva, Khronika moei zhizni, VIII, 518; Markov, K istorii raskola-staroobriadchestva, 305-306, 310, 332, 360, 368, 371; MDLL, CPP letter to Anna Aksakov, March 21, 1867; CPP letters to Catherine Tiutchev, November 23, 1872; March 17, 1874; December 18, 1875; January 29, 1877; January 18, January 26, October 7, 1879; February 25, February 26, 1880; September 6, 1881; CPP letter to Olga Novikov, March 23, 1902; Catherine Tiutchev letters to CPP, November 29, 1875; February 5, 1880.

7. CPP, Pis'ma k Aleksandru III, II, 334; Petrovskii, "Pis'ma Pobedonostseva k Illarionu," 360, 369; "Perepiska Vitte i Pobedonostseva," 110-11; Mel'gunov, "Pobedonostsev v dni pervoi revoliutsii," 177-78, 185; Andrew D. White, Autobiography (New York, 1905), II, 270; Polovtsev, "Dnevnik," 78; Radziwill, Lettres au général de Robilant, II, 42; Markov, K istorii raskola-staroobriadchestva, 624-25, 629-30; MDLL, CPP letters to Olga Novikov, December 16, December 28, 1900.

8. CPP, Moskovskii sbornik (third edition, Moscow, 1896), 92-99; CPP (translator), Fomy Kempiiskago o podrazhanii Khristu (fifth edition, St. Petersburg, 1893), 302-305; Jeremiah Curtin, Memoirs (Madison, Wis., 1940), 780, 849; Sir Bernard Pares, My Russian Memoirs (London, 1931), 118-19; "Perepiska Vitte

i Pobedonostseva," 110-11; Mel'gunov, "Pobedonostsev v dni pervoi revoliutsii," 179; Petrovskii, "Pis'ma Pobedonostseva Illarionu," 360; Yakobson, "Pis'ma Pobedonostseva k Putsykovichu," 77-78; Polovtsev, "Dnevnik," 156; Bogdanovich, *Dnevnik*, 260; von Schweinitz, *Denkwürdigkeiten*, II, 429-30; Markov, *K istorii raskola-staroobriadchestva*, 624-25, 642-45, 653-54; MDLL, CPP letters to Catherine Tiutchev, November 12, December 10, December 27, 1881; CPP letters to Olga Novikov, December 16, December 28, 1900.

9. Mel'gunov, "Pobedonostsev v dni pervoi revoliutsii," 185-87; Bogdanovich, *Dnevnik*, 295-97, 302, 304, 307, 343.

10. "Iz chernovykh bumag K. P. Pobedonostseva," *KA*, XVIII (1926), 205-207; N. Chuloshnikov (editor), "K istorii manifesta 6 avgusta 1905 goda," *KA*, XIV (1926), 262-70; Sergei E. Kryzhanovskii, *Vospominaniia. Iz bumag S. E. Kryzhanovskago, poslednago gosudarstvennago sekretaria Rossiiskoi Imperii* (Berlin, 1938), 15-16, 25-26; B. V. Titlinov, *Tserkov' vo vremia revoliutsii* (Petrograd, 1924), 11-12; Varvara I. Iasevich-Borodaevskaia (editor), *Materialy k vysochaishemu ukazu 12 dekabria 1904 g.* (St. Petersburg, n.d.), II, *passim*; John S. Curtiss, *Church and State in Russia. The Last Years of the Empire, 1900–1917* (New York, 1940), 211.

11. *Istoricheskaia perepiska o sud'bakh pravoslavnoi tserkvi* (Moscow, 1912), 7-31; Count Sergei IU. Witte, *Vospominaniia* (Moscow, 1923), I, 296-98; S. IU. Kamenev, "S. IU. Vitte i K. P. Pobedonostsev o sovremennom polozhenii pravoslavnoi tserkvi," *Vestnik Evropy*, II (February, 1909), 651-57; Russia. Komitet ministrov, *Zhurnaly Komiteta ministrov po ispolneniiu ukaza 12 dekabria 1904 g.* (St. Petersburg, 1908), 185-248; "Perepiska Vitte i Pobedonostseva," 106-109, 111-16; Titlinov, *Tserkov' vo vremia revoliutsii*, 8-14.

12. "Iz chernovykh bumag Pobedonostseva," 203-205; Kamenev, "Vitte i Pobedonostsev," 668-77.

13. *Istoricheskaia perepiska o sud'bakh pravoslavnoi tserkvi*, 32-48; Witte, *Vospominaniia*, I, 297-98.

14. "Iz chernovykh bumag Pobedonostseva," 204-205; "Perepiska Vitte i Pobedonostseva," 109-111; *Istoricheskaia perepiska o sud'bakh pravoslavnoi tserkvi*, 49-63; Kamenev, "Vitte i Pobedonostsev," 677-85; Mel'gunov, "Pobedonostsev v dni pervoi revoliutsii," 187-88.

15. CPP, "O preobrazovanii tserkovnago upravleniia v Rossii na sobornom nachale," *Tserkovnyia Vedomosti*, November 5, 1905, 1898-99; *K tserkovnomu soboru. Sbornik* (St. Petersburg, 1906), 37-61; Witte, *Vospominaniia*, I, 290-98; Kamenev, "Vitte i Pobedonostsev," 688-90; Curtiss, *Church and State*, 213-14, 227-28.

16. Witte, *Vospominaniia*, II, 46-47, 355, 455; Glinskii, "Pobedonostsev. Materialy dlia biografii," 248-49, 254; Mel'gunov, "Pobedonostsev v dni pervoi revoliutsii," 179, 191; *London Times*, March 25, 1907.

17. Victor Obninski, *Poslednyi samoderzhets. Ocherk zhizni i tsarstvovaniia Imperatora Rossii Nikolaia II-go* (Berlin, 1912), 428; N. D. Tal'berg, *Muzh' vernosti i razuma. K 50-letniiu konchiny K. P. Pobedonostseva* (Jordanville,

New York, 1957), 42; Alexander V. Gavrilov, "Konstantin Petrovich Pobedonostsev v ego pismakh," *Tserkovnyia Vedomosti*, March 24, 1907, supplement, 541-44; Russia. Gosudarstvennyi sovet, *Stenograficheskie otchety ses. 1-13 (28 apr. 1906 g.–14 fevr. 1917 g.)* (St. Petersburg, 1906–1917), II, 140; II, index, 21; Mel'gunov, "Pobedonostsev v dni pervoi revoliutsii," 194-201; Bartenev, "Iz dnevnika Pobedonostseva," 652; Preobrazhenskii, *Pobedonostsev*, 6-124; *Tserkovnyia Vedomosti*, March 17, 1907, 512-14; *Novoe vremia*, March 21, 1907; *London Times*, April 8, 1907.

INDEX

The following abbreviations have been used in the index: CPP—Constantine P. Pobedonostsev, PVP—Peter V. Pobedonostsev, and SPP—Sergei P. Pobedonostsev.

Carlyle, Thomas—(*Cont.*)
  and reading of, 38, 49, 86, 250, 316, 318, 327, 346, 353; friend of Olga Novikov, 126; on Jews, 346; mentioned, 293
Carpathian Ruthenia: CPP interest in, 120, 211, 221; Uniates in, 218, 224; groups residing in, 221-22; annexed by Soviet Union, 224. *See also* Dobriansky, Naumovich
Catherine the Great: admired by PVP, 9, 11; CPP views on, 54, 323, 326; on Old Believers, 180; interest in Middle East, 225; mentioned, 12, 332, 351
Catherine Mikhailovna, Grand Duchess, 89, 214, 306, 307
Catholics: Dostoevsky on, 104, 341; CPP on, 102, 104, 122, 170, 173, 176, 190, 212, 303; Alexander II on, 95, 212-13; position in Russia, 192-94, 213. *See also* Poles and Poland
Caucasus, 195
Cavour, Count Camillo de, 114
Censorship: PVP as censor, 5, 9, 334; Fedor Tiutchev as censor, 84; CPP manipulates, 147, 248-64, 294, 361; used against Old Believers, 181; Ivan Aksakov on, 265; mentioned, 98, 116, 209. *See also* Feoktistov
Central Asia, 76, 170, 176, 196-201, 343
Central Chuvash School in Simbirsk, 201
Chaadaiev, Peter, 317, 336, 351
Chamberlain, Houston Stewart, 348
Chambord, Count Henry de, 102
Chancery court, 26, 67-68
Chekhov, Anton, 255
Cheremiss, 201-202
Cherkasskii, Prince Vladimir A., 192-94
Chernaiev, General Michael G., 115, 116, 136
Chernovitz, 223
Chernyshevsky, Nicholas G., 60
Chicago, 218
Chicherin, Professor Boris N.: as colleague and friend of CPP, 32, 40, 52, 92; as jurist and tutor of heir, 33, 42; ideas in 1881, 163; mentioned, 275, 342
China, 217
Church of England. *See* Anglicanism
Church songs, 19, 277-79, 286, 304, 316
Chuvash, 201, 202
Cicero, 8
The City of God, 310
Civil Law. *See* Kurs grazhdanskago prava
Clergy: salaries, 166, 178; number and

quality, 168-70, 176-78, 185, 294, 315, 366; role in parish schools, 277-81. *See also* CPP on religion and the Church
Columbus, Christopher, 234, 237
Commune, 355
Comte, Auguste, 42, 316, 317, 340
Congress of Berlin, 85, 105, 116, 118-19, 124, 129, 132, 139
Constantine Alexandrovich, Grand Duke, 99
Constantine Constantinovich, Grand Duke, 99
Constantine Nikolaevich, Grand Duke: quarrel over Volunteer Fleet, 135, 137, 141; supports Loris-Melikov, 148, 155, 160, 163; organizes Palestine Committee, 226
Die conventiollen Lügen der Kulturmenschheit, 290
"Cook's children decree," 247
Cooper, James Fenimore, 346
Copenhagen, 348
Copernicus, 18
Corelli, Marie. *See* Mackay, Minnie
Cossacks, 232
Council of Ministers: role in 1881, 154-58; CPP as member, 145-46, 168, 305, 327, 358, 363; mentioned, 140, 327
Council of State: function, 61-62, 77, 149; CPP service in, 77, 247, 327
Council of Twenty-Five, 208
Cracow, 221
Creighton, Bishop Mandell, of Peterborough and of London, 22, 49, 216
Crime and Punishment, 95
Crimean War: influence of, 46, 84-85, 113, 127, 225, 226, 332; and panslavs, 118; mentioned, 81, 82, 85, 124, 135, 149, 245, 338, 342
Czechs, 116, 121. *See also* Prague

Dalton, Reverend Hermann, 189-90, 191-92, 283
Damascus, 228, 230
Damskii zhurnal, 16
Danilevsky, Professor Nicholas J., 117-18, 318, 340
Dante, 347
Darwin, Charles, 316, 340, 346, 357
Darwinism, 101
Daudet, Alphonse, 253
Decembrists, 321
Delianov, Count Ivan D., 240, 244-45, 247, 252, 263-64